PRACTICAL ASPECTS OF MEMORY: CURRENT RESEARCH AND ISSUES

VOLUME 2

Clinical and Educational Implications

PRACTICAL ASPECTS OF MEMORY: CURRENT RESEARCH AND ISSUES

VOLUME 2

Clinical and Educational Implications

EDITED BY

M. M. Gruneberg
University College of Swansea

P. E. Morris
University of Lancaster

R. N. Sykes
University College of Swansea

JOHN WILEY & SONS
Chichester · New York · Brisbane · Toronto · Singapore

Proceedings of the 2nd International
Conference on Practical Aspects
of Memory held under the auspices
of the Welsh Branch of the British
Psychological Society, in Swansea
from August 2nd–8th 1987

Copyright © 1988 by John Wiley & Sons Ltd.

British Library Cataloguing in Publication Data available

ISBN 0 471 91867 9

Printed in Great Britain

CONTENTS

PREFACE

This volume (together with Volume 2) comprises an edited selection of papers presented at The Second International Conference on Practical Aspects of Memory, held under the auspices of The Welsh Branch of The British Psychological Society in Swansea, from the 2nd-8th August 1987. As with the first Conference on Practical Aspects of Memory, the conference sought to examine ways in which our theoretical understanding of memory could be applied to real life memory problems.

Interest in the application of memory research has undoubtedly advanced considerably since the first conference in 1978. Evidence for this is to be seen in the number of papers presented at this conference, approximately twice as many as nine years ago, and the large number of eminent psychologists who are now investigating useful and interesting everyday memory phenomena, and seeking to apply the fruits of their work. Many psychologists are no longer solely concerned with theoretical questions, and insist, as does Dr. Alan Baddeley in the Opening Address, in asking "What the hell is it for?". In the intervening period between the two conferences an academic journal - Applied Cognitive Psychology - has been founded to cater for the burgeoning activity in a field which Professor Neisser (Volume 2) describes as being barely at the margins of respectability only nine years ago.

It would, however, in our view, be mistaken to be complacent about the progress being made. It is important to realise that in many areas we are at the start of the enterprise and that effective application to the real world has still to begin. Again, as Professor Neisser points out, there are large gaps in important areas and the concern of some conference delegates that a gap between underlying theory and application could develop is one which must be taken seriously. Nevertheless it can reasonably be claimed that these are teething troubles in a rapidly developing field.

Because of the large number of papers that are being published, it has been necessary to divide the book into two volumes. Volume I deals with memory in everyday life and covers the following topics: Eyewitnessing, Child Witnesses, Face Recognition, Metamemory, Autobiographical Memory, Ecological Perspectives, Prospective Memory, Maintenance of Knowledge, Action Events, Memory for Broadcast Information, Memory in Everyday Life. Volume 2 deals with clinical and educational implications and covers: Neurological Memory Deficit, Memory and Aging, Drugs and Memory, Stress Illness and Memory, Miscellaneous Clinical Applications, Children's Memory, Reading, Dyslexia, Student Learning, Mnemonic Aids, Motoric Memory, Time of

Day, General Educational Implications. Papers presented in symposia at the conference have been supplemented by other papers where it seemed appropriate.

As with the last conference, we feel that the importance of these volumes lies as much in terms of the questions posed as of the answers given. However, for a variety of reasons, a number of the conference presentations could not be included.

We would like to thank the large number of people who contributed so much to the success of the conference. We especially wish to thank the following: Dr. Hugh Foot, Chair, and the committee of The Welsh Branch of The British Psychological Society for their support of the conference; Mrs. Maureen Rogers and Mrs. Jackie Davies, our secretaries, for their highly professional and good humoured labours; the symposium organisers for ensuring that so many eminent psychologists attended; the stewards for their considerable enthusiasm, hard work and courtesy; Dr. Alan Baddeley and Professor Ulric Neisser, not only for their stimulating Opening and Closing Addresses, but for the support they have given over the years to our aim of applying memory research. Finally we should like to thank all the delegates for providing the conference with such stimulating contributions.

Michael M. Gruneberg
Peter E. Morris
Robert N. Sykes

REFERENCE

Gruneberg, M.M., Morris, P.E., and Sykes, R.N. (Eds.) (1978). Practical Aspects of Memory, Academic Press, London.

NEUROLOGICAL MEMORY DEFICIT

WHAT FUNCTIONAL DEFICITS UNDERLIE ORGANIC AMNESIA?

A. R. Mayes

Department of Psychology, University of Manchester,
Manchester M13 9PL.

ABSTRACT
Identifying the functional deficit(s) that underlies amnesia has both theoretical and practical importance. Currently, an influential view is the context-memory deficit hypothesis which postulates that amnesics have a selective deficit in remembering the independent context of target material. This deficit secondarily causes their memory failure for target material itself. The present status and difficulties in testing this hypothesis are discussed, and then illustrated by reference to recent findings on amnesic forgetting rates, disproportionately severe problems with cross-modal recognition judgments and memory for the modality in which items are presented, excessive sensitivity to proactive interference in story recall, and the occurrence in normal subjects of context-dependent forgetting for priming.

SOME BASIC ISSUES

Organic amnesia is caused by lesions to midline diencephalic structures or to the limbic system structures of the medial temporal lobes. It is characterized by relative preservation of intelligence and short-term memory in the face of what may be profound anterograde and retrograde amnesias. Both these forms of amnesia involve poor recall and recognition of episodic and semantic information although retrograde amnesia does not seem to extend to massively overlearnt memories. Identification of the underlying functional deficit(s) is important for its theoretical implications about normal human memory and for its possible therapeutic significance. Successful identification depends on interpreting a detailed characterization of the pattern of memory performance shown by amnesics. It will also depend on whether damage to different brain regions causes qualitatively distinct forms of the syndrome or is responsible for separate components of the disorder. If amnesia is heterogeneous in one or both of these ways, then it will be necessary to identify more than one functional deficit although the different deficits may be closely related. In recent years, hypotheses about the functional deficit(s) causing amnesia have varied along three dimensions. First, some hypotheses postulate that amnesia is a unitary deficit whereas others postulate that it is a heterogeneous disorder. Second, some hypotheses postulate that there is an encoding deficit, others a storage deficit, yet others a retrieval deficit, and some postulate that all three memory stages are affected. Third, some hypotheses postulate that all aspects of episodic and semantic memory are impaired in the same way whereas others postulate that some aspects (for example, memory for contextual material) are primarily impaired, and that poor recognition of other aspects is secondary to this impairment (Mayes et al., 1985).

At present, there is no consensus about whether amnesia is a unitary or compound memory deficit, what deficit(s) underlies it, or even about the precise locations of the lesions that cause it. This lack of consensus arises mainly because of the difficulty in comparing normal and amnesic patterns of memory performance. The difficulty is well illustrated by attempts to test the predictions of the context-memory deficit hypothesis (CMDH), a currently influential view about the deficit underlying amnesia (see Mayes et al., 1985). The hypothesis states that amnesia is caused by a selective failure of memory for the independent context of target information which lies at the focus of attention. Independent context comprises background spatiotemporal features and the format in which targets are presented. Recall and recognition of target information is postulated to depend on the retrieval of independent context and is, therefore, extremely poor in amnesics, who cannot remember context. The hypothesis makes two important predictions. The first is that because amnesics store targets normally they should show preserved target memory if memory tests can be devised that do not depend on retrieving context. The second is that amnesics should be particularly poor at retrieving context or at memory tasks that depend on such retrieval. Assessment of these two predictions involves determining whether amnesics ever show normal memory for targets and whether they are disproportionally bad at context-dependent forms of memory. Such assessments face problems because many amnesics have damage to non-limbic-diencephalic regions where lesions cause incidental impairments unrelated to the core memory symptoms. They also face problems because the sensitivity of memory tests probably differs so that it needs to be shown that apparent preservation of a specific kind of memory is not an artefact arising from test insensitivity. Finally, they face problems because in order to prove that, for example, spatial memory is disproportionately poor in amnesics it is necessary to match amnesics and their controls on a reasonably high level of target recognition or recall, and then to see whether, under the same conditions, amnesics are still worse at spatial memory. Matching can also be achieved by either testing controls after a much longer delay, allowing them less chance to learn, or both.

It has proved very hard to overcome all these problems. Nevertheless, there is good evidence that amnesics do sometimes show normal memory both for targets that already have a representation in well-established memory and for novel targets (Schacter, in press). Schacter has argued that amnesics are impaired at explicit memory tasks, such as recall and recognition, where memory is directly indicated by pointing or a verbal statement, but normal at implicit memory tasks, where memory is indirectly indicated by changes in the way remembered information is processed or acted upon. As well as good conditioning and skill memory, amnesics show normal priming where priming can be defined as a change in the way in which an item is processed that results from having perceived it. Some tests of priming cannot be insensitive because performance on them declines to chance within two hours whereas recognition does not greatly change over this delay (see Schacter, in press). The CMDH must claim that normal priming for familiar and novel targets does not depend on the retrieval of contextual information (at least not in the same way that is deemed important for explicit memory). This claim is unproved, but would have some difficulty in explaining context-dependent forgetting of priming. It is also polemical whether priming of familiar, let alone novel, targets is always preserved in amnesics.

There have been few studies that have examined whether amnesics are disproportionately poor at remembering context where appropriate control procedures were used. Those using such procedures have found some evidence that certain amnesics are disproportionately bad at remembering items' temporal order and others are disproportionately bad at remembering the source of recalled factual information (see Mayes et al., 1985). It is, however, unsure that these disproportionate context memory deficits are found in all amnesics. Furthermore, in two studies, it was found that the severity of the impairment correlated with the extent to which performance on tests, sensitive to frontal lobe lesions was disrupted (for example, see Schacter et al., 1984). These findings suggest that the deficit may be a result of frontal lobe damage that is incidental to the core amnesia. This kind of explanation for disproportionate context memory deficits in amnesics can only be conclusively eliminated if, first, all or, at least, some amnesics without frontal lobe damage, show disproportionately poor contextual memory; second, there is either no correlation between patients' context memory and their performance on tests sensitive to frontal lobe lesions or there is a trivial explanation for the correlation (for example, larger lesions are more likely to affect adjacent brain regions); and third, frontal lobe lesions do not cause similar contextual memory deficits and also cause no detectable amnesia. These tests remain to be done.

STATUS OF THE CONTEXT-MEMORY DEFICIT HYPOTHESIS: SOME RECENT TESTS

Most hypotheses about amnesia are merely descriptive of which kinds of memory are impaired and which preserved. In contrast both the CMDH and the view of Warrington and Weiskrantz (1982) begin to explain why amnesics' recall and recognition are poor. Warrington and Weiskrantz argue that amnesics fail to store and/or retrieve those kinds of semantic information that require elaborative, planned and effortful encoding. Lacking the ability to retrieve such information amnesics show very poor explicit memory for all target information. This hypothesis predicts that amnesics should not benefit like normal people from effortfully encoding semantic information. Most evidence indicates that they do, however (see Mayes et al., 1985). As the evidence seems to be inconsistent with the Warrington and Weiskrantz view this section will focus on the CMDH because there is, at present, no published evidence that flagrantly contradicts it. The hypothesis will be regarded as postulating a deficit in context memory that applies to all memory stages. If refuted, it may be necessary to accept that all aspects of semantic and episodic memory are similarly affected in amnesics.

Before considering tests of the CMDH's main predictions it is important to acknowledge the possibility that amnesia may be heterogeneous as this would alter the hypothesis. For example, Mishkin (1982) has suggested that permanent, severe amnesia only occurs after lesions both to a part of the hippocampal circuit and part of the amygdala circuit. Mayes et al. (1985) have extended this suggestion to argue on the basis of Mishkin's findings with lesioned monkeys that hippocampal lesions impair spatial memory whereas amygdala lesions impair temporal memory and memory for cross-modal judgments. These lesions and lesions to other parts of the circuits may also impair memory for other, as yet unidentified, kinds of context. An alternative possibility arises from the claim that "temporal lobe" and "diencephalic" amnesias are functionally distinct. If so the kinds of context-memory deficit found in the two amnesias may differ. The claim is based on evidence that "temporal lobe" amnesics forget faster than "diencephalic" amnesics. A standard technique has been used to support this position. Recognition, after a short initial delay, is equated between amnesics and their controls by allowing patients much longer to encode and learn the study material. Recognition for material not shown at the short initial delay is then tested at longer intervals, such as a day and a week. Forgetting rate is the difference in recognition between the initial delay and a longer one. The technique has produced equivocal results although usually amnesics have all been found to forget at a normal rate (see Kopelman, 1985). It suffers however, from a major methodological fault. As the patients require longer exposures and timing of the delay begins after all items have been shown, the mean delay for the amnesics between item presentation and its recognition test is much longer than it is for their controls. If controls were tested after the same delay their recognition would probably be significantly worse. This means that the technique is likely to underestimate amnesic forgetting rates in a systematic way. The risk is particularly great for severe amnesics who need very long exposure to match their recognition to that of controls.

A modification of the standard technique may obviate this problem. All subjects learn the target items with the same item-to-item spacing. Whereas the whole interval will be devoted to learning an item for amnesics, controls will only see each item for perhaps one second and fill the remaining time until the next item is shown in performing an irrelevant task to prevent rehearsal. This modified technique allows amnesics and controls to be matched at a high level of recognition after the same mean item-to-test delay. In a preliminary study, Shankland and I have used the modified technique to compare the rate at which a group of Korsakoff patients and a group of matched control subjects forget pictures of faces. Six Korsakoff patients were matched to a group of control subjects on age, socioeconomic background and intelligence. All subjects inspected 40 face pictures with eight seconds between pictures. Most of the amnesics saw the picture for eight seconds whereas the controls saw them for two seconds, then performed a counting task for the remaining six seconds. Recognition of the two groups was closely matched at two minutes delay. The procedure was repeated with a new list, recognition being tested after a one hour delay. The Korsakoff patients' mean level of recognition between the two minutes and the one hour delay fell by 19.8% from 78.5% correct whereas that of the controls fell by 14.7% from 77.0% correct. This difference was significant (t = 2.57,df=10, p<0.05) although confirmation is needed with a much larger group. As Korsakoff patients are believed to be "diencephalic" amnesics it may be that all amnesics forget pathologically fast. Interestingly, one patient with an anterior communicating artery aneurysm that had been clipped, whom we also tested, showed a 28% decline in recognition between two minutes and one hour, greater than all the Korsakoff patients (her forgetting rate was, in fact, over two standard deviations greater than the Korsakoff mean forgetting rate). These kinds of aneurysm may cause a secondary disruption of the medial temporal lobes and may therefore lead to a form of "temporal lobe" amnesia. Our results therefore leave open the possibility that, even if all amnesics forget pathologically fast, "temporal lobe" amnesics forget faster than "diencephalic" amnesics. The CMDH may therefore have to explain not only why "temporal lobe" amnesics forget faster than "diencephalic" amnesics, but also why all amnesics forget abnormally fast. Few variables are known to affect rate of forgetting but degree of interference after learning may accelerate forgetting. It is interesting to note therefore that one prediction of the CMDH is that amnesics should be excessively sensitive to interference (see below).

The CMDH's main prediction is that performance on recall and recognition tasks that directly depend on contextual memory will be disproportionately bad in amnesics. Support for this prediction is still fragmentary and equivocal. Three recent findings from my laboratory illustrate this point. First, Bateman and I have found that when amnesics and controls were shown a series of objects and then tested under conditions that matched visual recognition of half the objects (by testing the controls at a much longer delay), the amnesics were still significantly worse at a tactual recognition task for the rest of the objects, that was given under the same conditions. The decline in recognition from the purely visual condition to the cross-modal condition was significantly greater in the amnesics (t = 2.6, df = 12, p<0.05). The result is interesting and consistent with the work of Mishkin (1982) but it needs to be shown that the disproportionate amnesic deficit with cross-modal memory judgments is related to context memory and central to amnesia rather than an incidental result of frontal lobe damage. Although the extent of the cross-modal judgement deficit did not correlate with degree of impairment on tests sensitive to frontal lobe lesions more work needs to be done before the possibility of the effect being incidental to amnesia can be excluded. Furthermore, although a disproportionate deficit in cross-modal recognition judgments in humans might be predicted from Murray and Mishkin's (1985) finding that amygdalectomy impairs such judgments in monkeys it is unclear to what extent the deficit can be regarded as one of contextual memory that causes a secondary problem with explicit memory for targets.

Some light may be thrown on the relationship between the disproportionate deficit in cross-modal recognition judgments and context-memory impairments by the second of our recent findings. Pickering, Fairbairn and I presented a mixed group of amnesics and their matched controls several lists of words. Half of the words

were presented visually and half auditorily, order being randomly
determined. Controls and patients were matched on forced choice
recognition of the words by using longer lists, tested at greater
delays, with the controls. Despite being matched on word
recognition, however, the amnesics were significantly worse at
identifying the sensory modality in which recognized words had been
presented (F = 30.8, df = 1, 24, p<0.001). Although they recognized
83% of the words the amnesics could only identify the sensory
modality of 60% of these words whereas their controls recognized 86%
of the words and correctly identified the modality of 75% of these
words. The results could not be explained by emerging differences in
test expectancies between the groups because the pattern was the same
with all the lists. In other words intention to encode the modality
in which items are presented does not improve memory for it, so
information about sensory modality may be automatically encoded.
This supports the view that amnesics are disproportionately poor at
remembering automatically encoded features, which may include
background context and sensory modality in particular. It could be,
therefore, that amnesics have a special problem with remembering
information relevant to the making of modality judgments and this
problem might also lead to their deficit in making cross-modal
judgments. The disproportionate deficit in memory for format context
(modality memory) may, however, be incidental to amnesics' memory
failure. The extent of the deficit correlated significantly with the
degree of impairment, shown by patients, on tests sensitive to
frontal lobe lesions. Nevertheless, this correlation may have a
trivial explanation because there was a stronger correlation between
the size of the memory deficit for format context and the degree of
impairment of patients' recognition for targets. The former
correlation may simply mean that larger lesions are more likely to
damage adjacent regions.

The difficulty of interpreting correlations also applies to
the third of our recent findings. If amnesics have special problems
with contextual memory then they should be disproportionately
sensitive to proactive interference because they will be unable to
distinguish from where targets are drawn even when they can recall
them. Although it is well established that Korsakoff patients make
excessive numbers of intrusion errors in recalling a series of short
stories amnesic recall is always impaired so the effect could be a
result of amnesia rather than indicative of its cause. To eliminate
this possibility, Ratcliffe and I presented four stories so that
recall of the first was matched in seven amnesics and their controls
(patients received more presentations and controls were tested after
a delay). The amnesics still made more intrusion errors from earlier
stories in stories two to four (F = 10.7, df = 1,15, p<0.01) and,
unlike the controls, showed a significant increase in intrusions
between stores two and four (t = 2.56, df = 6, p<0.05). There was
also a significant interaction between groups and story number with
recall (F = 3.34, df = 3,42 p<0.05), indicating that amnesic recall
declined relative to that of the controls across the stories as
intrusion errors increased in the patients. These results are
interesting but may be incidental to the patients' poor memory as
there was a nearly significant correlation between the number of
intrusions made by the amnesics and their degree of impairment on a

test sensitive to frontal lobe lesions. In contrast, there was no correlation between the severity of patients' amnesia and the number of inter-story intrusions they made. The correlational evidence is, however, weak. If excessive sensitivity to interference is caused by frontal lobe lesions then amnesics without such complications should show normal sensitivity to interference. This has not yet been demonstrated.

The case for the CMDH is still very shaky. The three results described above illustrate the problem. Although they broadly fit one of the predictions of the hypothesis it still needs to be proved that the effects found are not caused by frontal lobe lesions and incidental to the main memory deficit shown by amnesics. The matter will only be resolved by studies of memory for independent context that use large numbers of amnesics with lesions in both temporal lobe and diencephalic sites, and also examine, in the same way, patients with focal frontal lobe damage, who do not have amnesia. It will also be necessary to test systematically whether priming, as a form of target memory that is preserved in amnesics, does not depend on retrieving context. Recently, Hargreaves and I have found preliminary evidence that one form of priming that is preserved in amnesics is reduced in normal subjects if there is a change between presentation and test in either the format of item presentation or the background context. If both are changed the reduction in priming is proportionately greater. This study needs confirmation, but if context-dependent reductions in priming occur, it is almost certain that priming normally depends on the retrieval of the independent context of targets. Unless this contextual retrieval is radically different from that which underlies explicit memory the CMDH may have to be rejected.

REFERENCES

Kopelman, M.D. (1985). 'Rates of Forgetting in Alzheimer-Type Dementia and Korsakoff's Syndrome', Neuropsychologia, 23, 623-638.

Mayes, A.R., Meudell, P.R. and Pickering, A. (1985). 'Is Organic Amnesia Caused by a Selective Deficit in Remembering Contextual Information?', Cortex, 21, 167-202.

Mishkin, M. (1982). 'A Memory System in the Monkey', Philosophical Transactions of the Royal Society, B298, 85-95.

Murray, E.A. and Mishkin, M. (1985). 'Amygdalectomy Impairs Cross-Modal Associations in Monkeys', Science, 228, 604-606.

Schacter, D.L. (in press). 'Implicit Memory: History and Current Status', Journal of Experimental Psychology: Learning, Memory and Cognition.

Warrington, E.K. and Weiskrantz, L. (1982). 'Amnesia: A Disconnection Syndrome', Neuropsychologia, 20, 233-238.

PATTERN OF VERBAL MEMORY DEFICITS IN
PATIENTS WITH BIFRONTAL PATHOLOGY AND
PATIENTS WITH THIRD VENTRICLE LESIONS

Narinder Kapur
Wessex Neurological Centre, Southampton

ABSTRACT

A group of patients with third ventricle tumours (TV) was
compared with a group of patients with bifrontal tumours (BF)
on a short-term and a long-term verbal memory task. On the short-
term memory task, a marked impairment was shown by BF patients,
who performed at a lower level than the TV group. However, on
the long-term memory task, TV patients obtained the poorest
scores, and performed significantly lower than BF patients. The
findings suggest that significant long-term memory deficits are
a hall-mark of third ventricle rather than bifrontal pathology,
and that short-term memory deficits in some forms of amnesia
may be more closely related to frontal lobe than to third
ventricle pathology.

The association between third ventricle pathology and memory
disorders has been demonstrated   in a number of neurological
conditions - e.g. alcoholic Korsakoff patients, whose pathology
usually involves thalamic nuclei (Mair et al., 1979), patients
with thalamic infarction   (Graff-Radford et al., 1985),   and
patients with cerebral tumours (Williams and Pennybacker, 1954).
However, in some of these conditions,   especially   alcoholic
Korsakoff's syndrome, there is evidence that some of the memory
deficits displayed by patients may be more closely related to
direct/indirect frontal lobe pathology rather than lesions to
structures around the third ventricle. For example, patients
with evidence of specific frontal lobe pathology appear to show
semantic encoding deficits in their pattern of memory performance
similar to those shown by alcoholic Korsakoff patients (Zatorre
and McEntee, 1983), and alcoholic Korsakoff patients show impairments on memory tasks which   are   sensitive   to frontal lobe
dysfunction (Squire, 1982). While a considerable   amount   of
evidence has   been   gathered   on memory   deficits   displayed
by   patients with   frontal   lobe lesions   (e.g.   Milner, 1982),
no specific comparisons   have   been   made   between   patients
with third ventricle lesions and those with frontal lobe damage.
In addition, earlier studies of amnesia-related phenomena after
frontal   lobe   damage   have   usually not taken into account the

clinical pathology of the lesion. In the present investigation, we compared the verbal memory performance of a group of patients with third ventricle tumours with that of a group of patients with bifrontal tumours. One of the reasons for considering patients with bifrontal rather than unilateral frontal lesions is because of the likelihood that any frontal pathology in conditions such as alcoholic Korsakoff's syndrome is likely to affect both frontal regions, and therefore data from patients with bifrontal pathology would appear to be more appropriate from the neuropsychological point of view.

METHOD

Two groups of neurological patients were included, a group of five patients with bifrontal lesions (mean age = 57.6 years, range = 36-70 years) and a group of four patients with tumours in the area of the third ventricle (mean age = 53.5 years, range = 37-62 years). The bifrontal group included two patients with bifrontal gliomas, one bifrontal meningioma and two patients with gliomas originating in the anterior corpus callosum and invading both frontal regions. Three of the patients with third ventricle lesions had mass lesions in the region of the pineal gland, as indicated by CT scan features. None of these was directly amenable to removal, and so these tumours were histologically unverified. The fourth patient had a bithalamic glioma which was verified at post-mortem. The two groups were similar in terms of socio-economic status and educational level. All patients were tested prior to any shunt procedure to relieve hydrocephalus.

A group of control patients was also tested. These mainly comprised neurological patients with extra-cerebral disease, though a few relatives of neurological outpatients were also included. For the short-term memory task, eight control subjects were tested (mean age = 59.6 years), and for the long-term memory task, six subjects were assessed (mean age = 57.5 years). They were also matched to the bifrontal and third ventricle groups on educational level and socio-economic status.

Procedure.   Patients were administered a short-term verbal memory task, using a Brown-Peterson paradigm. The test used in this study was similar to that described in more detail elsewhere (Kapur, 1985). The test required recall of a triad of female Christian names after a 20 second period of counting backwards, with a total of eight triads and a maximum possible score of 24 items. This type of task was chosen in view of its sensitivity in detecting susceptibility to proactive interference. The two main scores of interest were the number of correct responses (maximum = 24) and the number of intrusions from previous trials, i.e. where the patient offered a response which was incorrect but selected from one of the triads presented in earlier trials. Extra-list intrusions, i.e. response items which were not amongst earlier items, were too few to merit separate analysis.

The long-term verbal memory task comprised a modified

version of the story recall task frequently used in neuropsychological assessment. These modifications permitted an assessment of long-term retention which was not contaminated by the effects of an initial recall from short-term memory, and allowed for an assessment of long-term memory under "incidental" instructions, which tend to more closely parallel everyday memory situations. A story similar to the first story from the logical memory subtest of the Wechsler Memory Scale (Wechsler, 1946) was extended to include 25 rather than 23 items. Prior to the patient hearing the story, he/she was given the following instructions: "I am going to read you a short story, and after I have read the story I want you to tell me whether or not it sounds realistic". Such instructions both maintain the attention of the patient and allow for some degree of "deep" processing which permit assessment of longer-term memory performance. Thirty minutes later, the patient was given an unexpected recall task for the story. Approximately 60-90 seconds were permitted for recall. Subjects were encouraged to recall as much as they could, with the recall trial being terminated after a 20 second period where no further items were offered for recall.

RESULTS

The scores of cerebral tumour and control patients on the two tests are shown in Figure 1.

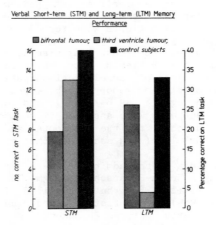

Verbal Short-term (STM) and Long-term (LTM) Memory Performance

Figure 1. Short-term and long-term memory performance of patients with bifrontal lesions, III ventricle lesions and control patients

A one-way analysis of variance was carried out for each of the two sets of short-term memory scores and for long-term memory performance. Significant group effects were found for performance on each task. Post-hoc comparisons were computed using the Tukey (hsd) test. On the short-term memory task, BF patients were significantly impaired relative to control subjects ($p < .05$), both for number of correct responses and number of prior-list intrusions, offering a mean of 10.2 intrusions compared to a mean of 2.0 given by control subjects.

No other differences were statistically significant. In the case of the long-term memory task, TV patients were significantly impaired (p< .01), and also performed at a lower level than BF patients (p< .05).

DISCUSSION

Patients with bifrontal pathology were impaired on a short-term verbal memory task, but performed better than the near-normal scores of patients with third ventricle tumours. By contrast, on a long-term verbal memory task, the latter patients were markedly impaired, performing much lower than the normal scores of patients with bifrontal lesions.

Our findings have some bearing on the possible role of frontal lobe pathology in the memory performance of amnesic patients. One of the sources of controversy in amnesia research has been the issue of whether amnesic patients have normal short-term memory. While most alcoholic Korsakoff patients have been found to display marked short-term memory deficits (Butters and Cermak, 1980), others have shown normal or near-normal scores (Mair et al., 1979; Kopelman, 1985), and some patients with amnesia resulting from other aetiologies, e.g. herpes encephalitis, have also been found to display normal short-term memory (Cermak, 1976). Some features of alcoholic Korsakoff's short-term memory performance has also been found in patients with evidence of focal frontal lobe pathology (e.g. Moskovitch, 1982). The latter source of evidence has been somewhat indirect, in that no formal comparisons were made with the test performance of amnesic patients with similar aetiologies. In the present investigation, where we compared groups of patients with similar clinical aetiologies, our observation that impaired short-term memory performance may be present in patients with bifrontal lesions, in the absence of significant long-term memory impairment, lends support to the view that the impaired short-term memory of alcoholic Korsakoff patients may indeed be related to frontal lobe pathology. The nature of such pathology remains to be elucidated - it may reflect direct cortical damage related to the effects of alcohol, or it may be related to the secondary effects of damage to thalamic nuclei which have anatomical connections to frontal lobe structures. Whatever may be the precise neural basis of such deficits, at the neuropsychological level it is clear that short-term memory deficits are not a prerequisite for long-term memory impairment. In this respect, our findings complement those from single case studies of patients with conduction dysphasia (Warrington and Shallice, 1969; Basso et al., 1982).

Our findings relating to the high level of prior-list intrusions in bifrontal patients support previous observations on the susceptibility of patients with frontal lobe pathology to interference effects on memory tasks. Stuss et al. (1982) pointed to significant interference effects in the short-term memory performance of patients who underwent frontal leucotomy, and Luria (1976) has also commented on increased interference as

being particularly common after frontal lobe pathology. The
precise mechanisms of such interference effects remain to be
determined. Although a lack of inhibition in the retrieval of
verbal responses may account in part for such interference
effects, this does not readily explain the similar intereference
effects shown by such patients in recurrent recognition
paradigms (Milner and Teuber, 1968).

The performance of our patients with third ventricle tumours
was in keeping with the proximity of their lesion to limbic
system structures. However, it should be borne in mind that all
patients suffered from a variable degree of obstructive
hydrocephalus, seondary to the presence of the tumour, and it is
possible that this may have contributed in part to their memory
deficit. It is also worth noting that some patients with large
frontal lobe tumours may show ventricular distortion/dilatation
resulting from effects of the tumour mass, and that in some
cases this may result in such patients displaying marked
cognitive impairment which includes both short-term and
long-term memory impairment. However, it is unlikely that such
ventricular dilatation played a critical role in the performance
of our patients with third ventricular pathology for two
reasons: firstly, the presence of a double-dissociation in our
patients (resulting from better short-term memory and worse
long-term memory compared to bifrontal patients) points to the
relatively discrete rather than generalized effects of such
ventricular dilatation. Secondly, a number of cases of third
ventricle pathology, without any associated ventricular
dilatation, have been found to show marked memory impairment
(e.g. Ziegler et al., 1977).

REFERENCES

Basso, A., Spinnler, H., Vallar, G. and Zanobia, M.E.
(1982).'Left-hemisphere damage and selective impairment of
auditory verbal short-term memory. A case study',
Neuropsychologia,20, 263-274.

Butters, N. and Cermak, L.S. (1980). Alcoholic Korsakoff's
Syndrome: An Information Processing Approach to Amnesia,
Academic Press, New York.

Cermak, L.S. (1976). 'The encoding capacity of a patient with
amnesia due to encephalitis', Neuropsychologia, 14, 311-326.

Graff-Radford, N.R., Damasio, H., Yamada, T., Eslinger, P.J. and
Damasio, A.R. (1985). 'Nonhaemorrhagic thalamic infarction:
clinical, neuropsychological and electro-physiological findings
in four anatomical groups defined by computerized tomograpy',
Brain, 108, 485-516.

Kapur, N. (1985). 'Double dissociation between perseveration in
memory and problem solving tasks', Cortex, 21, 461-465.

Kopelman, M.D. (1985). 'Rates of forgetting in Alzheimer-type dementia and Korsakoff's syndrome.', Neuropsychologia, 15, 527-541.

Luria, A.R. (1976). The Neuropsychology of Memory, Winston & Sons, Washington.

Mair, W.G., Warrington, E.K. and Weiskrantz, L. (1979). 'Memory disorder in Korsakoff's psychosis: a neuropathological and neuropsychological investigation of two cases', Brain, 102, 749-783.

Milner, B., Teuber, H.L. (1968). 'Alteration of perception and memory in man: reflections on methods', Analysis of Behavioural Change (Ed, L. Weiskrantz), pp. 268-375, Harper & Row, New York.

Milner, B. (1982). 'Some cognitive effects of frontal lobe lesions in man', in The Neuropsychology of Cognitive Function (Eds, D.E. Broadbent and L. Weiskrantz), pp. 211-226, The Royal Society, London.

Moskovitch, M. (1982). 'Multiple disssociations of function in amnesia', in Amnesia (Ed. L.S. Cermak), pp. 337-370, Lawrence Erlbaum Associates, Hillsdale, N.J.

Squire, L.R. (1982). 'Comparisons between forms of amnesia. Some deficits are unique to Korsakoff's Syndrome', Journal of Experimental Psychology: Learning, Memory and Cognition, 8, 560-571.

Stuss, D.T., Kaplan, E.F., Benson, D.F., Weir, W.S., Chuilli, S. and Sarazin, F.F. Evidence for the involvement of orbitofrontal cortex in memory functions: an intereference effect. Journal of Comparative and Physiological Psychology, 96, 913-925.

Warrington, E.K. and Shallice, T. (1969). 'The selective impairment of auditory verbal short-term memory', Brain, 92, 885-896.

Wechsler, D. (1945). 'A standardized memory scale for clinical use', Journal of Psychology, 19, 87-95.

Williams, M. and Pennybacker, J. (1954). 'Memory disturbances in third ventricle tumours', Journal of Neurology, Neurosurgery and Psychiatry, 17, 115-123.

Zatorre, R.J. and McEntee, W.J. (1983). 'Semantic encoding deficits in a case of traumatic amnesia', Brain and Cognition, 2, 331-345.

Ziegler, D.K., Kaufman, A. and Marshall, H.E. (1977). 'Abrupt memory loss associated with a thalamic tumour', Archives of Neurology, 34, 545-548.

AETIOLOGICAL VARIATION IN THE AMNESIC SYNDROME

Alan J. Parkin and Nicholas R.C. Leng
Laboratory of Experimental Psychology, University of Sussex,
Brighton, East Sussex, BN1 9QG, England.

ABSTRACT

This chapter summarizes evidence concerning aetiological differences in the amnesic syndrome. It is shown that diencephalic amnesics forget less rapidly than temporal lobe amnesics. Furthermore, diencephalic amnesics show consistently severe retrograde amnesia whereas temporal lobe cases show marked variation. Finally, diencephalic amnesics seem far more sensitive to interference manipulations. The theoretical and practical implications of these differences are considered.

The amnesic syndrome can arise from lesions in different parts of the brain. Korsakoff's Syndrome has a well established mid-line diencephalic pathology (e.g. Victor, Adams, & Collins, 1971; Mair, Warrington, & Weizkrantz, 1979). Damage to medial temporal lobe structures also produces amnesic deficits (e.g. Scoville & Milner, 1957) and there is growing agreement that hippocampal damage may be the critical lesion site (e.g. Zola-Morgan, Squire, & Amaral, 1986).

Despite these aetiological variations, amnesic patients present the same basic features. They perform normally on tests of immediate memory such as digit span thus indicating that short-term storage is intact. However, they demonstrate a severe anterograde amnesia which impairs the permanent retention of most kinds of new information. There may also be a substantial retrograde amnesia and, if present, this will be most noticeable for recent information - the "temporal gradient" of retrograde amnesia. Amnesic patients perform similarly to normal subjects on standardized measures of intelligence and are assumed free from intellectual impairment. Finally, amnesics show a considerable degree of residual learning capability (e.g. Parkin, 1982; Moscovitch, 1985).

These general similarities have led some to conclude that the amnesic syndrome is a unitary disorder. Such a view can be reinforced by stressing that the various structures implicated in the neuropathology of amnesia form part of the limbic system. However, this argument is weakened when one notes that damage to other limbic structures, notably the fornix, is not associated with amnesia (e.g. Horel, 1978; Parkin, 1984; Parkin & Leng, 1987). The alternative view, and the one that we will now examine further, is that the amnesic syndrome associated with midline diencephalic lesions differs significantly from the memory impairment associated with medial temporal lobe damage. Aside from their considerable theoretical importance, aetiological differences are of interest to those concerned with the design and implementation of memory rehabilitation. Clearly, if memory impairments have different characteristics they may well demand different therapeutic approaches and have differing chances of success.

EVIDENCE FOR MORE THAN ONE KIND OF AMNESIA

There is growing behavioural evidence for the existence of two distinct amnesic syndromes. Objectors to this view argue that all amnesics exhibit a common "core deficit" and that aetiological distinctions, where they occur, arise from differences superimposed on the amnesic state, or failures to match differing aetiological groups for the severity of their amnesia. LHermitte & Signoret (1972) were the first to propose aetiological differences in the nature of the amnesic syndrome. They compared Korsakoff patients with two patients who were amnesic following herpes simplex encephalitis - this disease causes necrosis centred on the medial temporal lobe. They found evidence of more rapid forgetting in the encephalitic patients even though these patients performed better than the Korsakoffs on problem solving tasks. More rapid forgetting in encephalitic amnesics compared to Korsakoffs has also been shown by Mattis, Kovner, & Goldmeier (1978) but one must note that this was only shown when the retention test did not require the use of specific contextual information for correct recognition - a fact that we will return to subsequently.

More recently Parkin and Leng (1987) compared forgetting rate in a group of Korsakoff patients with six medial temporal lobe cases (four encephalitis and two posterior cerebral artery occlusion). The task involved learning four pictures to criterion and then identifying them from within an array of sixteen pictures at different retention intervals. Although the groups did not differ in trials to criterion, the temporal lobe group forgot the pictures more rapidly. The authors also presented other findings consistent with more rapid forgetting in temporal lobe amnesia. Retrograde amnesia, as assessed by memory for famous faces and public events, also appears to differentiate the groups. Korsakoff's Syndrome seems associated with a consistently severe deficit with a marked temporal gradient (e.g. Albert, Butters, & Levin, 1979) whereas temporal lobe amnesia produces a retrograde amnesia that varies from mild to extremely severe (Parkin, 1984; Parkin & Leng, 1987).

Korsakoff patients are known to be abnormally sensitive to interference manipulations. They perform very poorly on the Brown-Peterson distractor task compared with temporal lobe cases (e.g. Butters & Cermak, 1980; Parkin & Leng, 1987). An exception is provided by Mair et al. (1979) whose two Korsakoffs perform normally on this task. Recent evidence suggests a possible resolution of this discrepancy. Parkin and Leng (1987) report that performance of their amnesic patients on the Brown-Peterson is correlated with estimates of frontal lobe dysfunction, as measured by the Wisconsin Card Sorting Test. They suggest that impaired Brown-Peterson performance may be a consequence of superimposed frontal pathology - a conclusion that is supported by reports of poor Brown-Peterson performance in patients with frontal lesions (Parkin, Leng, Stanhope, & Smith, 1987).

There is a widespread incidence of frontal lobe damage in

chronic alcoholics and, by implication, Korsakoffs. As well as
Brown-Peterson performance, there are other behavioural dimensions
of Korsakoff's Syndrome that most likely reflect a superimposed
frontal pathology. These deficits include, temporal discrimination,
abnormal source forgetting, release from proactive interference,
problem solving, and concept formation. In contrast to this temporal lobe amnesics are not commonly associated with frontal impairments even though, in the case of encephalitis, there may well be
some frontal involvement evident at the neuropathological level. It
might be argued that these deficits reflect part of the underlying
cause of amnesia in Korsakoff's Syndrome. However, Squire (1982)
and Parkin and Leng (1987) have demonstrated that the degree of
frontal impairment in Korsakoff's Syndrome seems unrelated to the
extent of anterograde amnesia. From a practical view, however, the
presence of frontal signs in Korsakoff's Syndrome must be considered
when devising remedial procedures.

A THEORETICAL INTERPRETATION
     Aside from the complication of frontal impairments, one is left
with two clear aetiological differences between Korsakoff's Syndrome
and temporal lobe amnesics. First, the latter appear to forget more
rapidly and, second, Korsakoff's Syndrome presents a consistently
severe retrograde amnesia whereas temporal lobe amnesia presents an
extremely variable retrograde impairment. Are these group differences consistent with a qualitative or quantitative differences in
the nature of the underlying deficit? Mattis et al. (1978) only
found less rapid forgetting in Korsakoffs when the memory assessment
did not require any utilization of contextual information. Parkin
(1987) has reviewed all the studies in which Korsakoff patients show
"normal" or near normal recognition performance compared with controls. In every case the retention procedure is yes/no recognition
and the distractor items have never been seen before. At an operational level, therefore, recollection the original learning context
is not required since the task can be performed effectively on the
basis of a familiar/unfamiliar discrimination. However, when contextual information becomes crucial Korsakoff performance falls off
dramatically. Huppert and Piercy (1978), for example, showed that
Korsakoff patients were quite good at recognizing previously exposed
pictures but almost totally unable to recall on which of two days
each picture had been seen (see also Parkin & Leng, 1987).
     These findings suggest that Korsakoffs Syndrome may represent a
deficit at the level of contextual encoding - i.e. the memory system
is capable of storing sufficient information for evaluating a
stimulus as familiar or unfamiliar, but unable to associate a new
stimulus with a defining context such as would be necessary for
effective free recall. An advantage of this interpretation is that
it can also be extended to deal with retrograde amnesia - the argument being that the deficit responsible for encoding new context
also affects the maintenance of exisiting contextual relations, thus
impairing the recall of premorbid memories. Temporal gradients can
be accounted for by assuming that the contextual elements associated
with older memories are more extensive and thus less vulnerable to
disruption.
     In temporal lobe amnesia the deficit may be one of

consolidation (e.g. Squire, Cohen, & Nadel, 1984). The rapid forgetting associated with these patients is consistent with such an interpretation, and their insensitivity to familarity, as shown by Parkin and Leng (1987) also supports this view. However, consolidation deficits cannot explain variations in retrograde amnesias and, in particular, cases showing retrograde deficits of twenty years or more (e.g. Butters & Cermak, 1980; Leng & Parkin, 1987). Here one must suggest that some aspect of temporal lobe damage has destroyed the storage sites of premorbid memory.

An alternative to this qualitative view is that aetiological differences are merely ones of severity, i.e. the more rapid forgetting of temporal lobe cases arises because their deficit is in some sense worse than that of Korsakoff patients (e.g. Weiskrantz, 1985). To support this argument one must first establish independent criteria for measuring severity but this is not easy because standardized tests may often give misleading impressions of impairment (e.g. Mayes, 1986). Second, if this were possible there is, as yet, no single proposed deficit that could easily account for the variations in performance observed. Finally, one would also have to explain why diencephalic pathology consistently produces a milder amnesia if all amnesia stems from the same basic deficit (Parkin, 1987).

IMPLICATIONS FOR THERAPY

In considering therapeutic implications one must first note that there is little indication of aetiological variation in residual learning capability (Parkin, 1982), although Kapur (1987) and Schacter and Graf (1986) both demonstrate that some amnesics may not show direct priming. However any remedial strategies based on residual learning, particularly skills, are unlikely to be influenced by aetiology. Mediational strategies, particularly imagery, have played a central role in memory rehabilitation (e.g. Wilson, 1987) and the question of how aetiology might affect this has been recently addressed by Leng and Parkin (1987). They showed that both Korsakoffs and temporal lobe amnesics show considerable benefits from instructions to use imagery during verbal learning. Furthermore, they suggest that failures to find such effects in other studies may be due to methodological differences although the possibility that some amnesics, notably severe temporal lobe cases, may fail to show mediational effects is not ruled out.

At a general level differences in forgetting rate will influence the likely effectiveness of any remedial strategy aimed at improving a patient's ability to acquire new declarative knowledge. Indeed confronted with a severe case of temporal lobe amnesia, a therapist may wish to consider whether any such therapy is worth pursuing. Potential interference effects (e.g. massing learning trials) would, on balance, be more likely to affect diencephalic than temporal lobe cases. A final point concerns metamemory and insight. It has often been claimed that Korsakoffs lack insight into their disorder whereas temporal lobe cases do not (Parkin, 1984). Where lack of insight occurs the therapist faces an uphill struggle because the patient fails to acknowledge that there is a problem to be solved. This issue was examined by Bell, Parkin, and Leng (in prep.) by means of a metamemory interview. Contrary to some earlier views, Korsakoffs had extremely good insight into their memory disorder. However, when questioned about the properties of human memory in general, there was some indication of an impairment in the Korsakoff group relative to temporal lobe cases and controls.

REFERENCES

Albert, M.S., Butters, N. and Levin, J. (1979). 'Temporal gradients in retrograde amnesia of patients with alcoholic Korsakoff's disease', Archives of Neurology, 36, 211-16.

Bell, W.P., Parkin, A.J. and Leng, N.R.C. (in preparation). 'Metamemory and the amnesic syndrome'.

Butters, N. and Cermak, L.S. (1980). Alcoholic Korsakoff's Syndrome. An Information Processing Approach to Amnesia, Academic Press, London.

Huppert, F.A. and Piercy, M. (1978). 'The role of trace strength in recency and frequency judgements by amnesic and control subjects', Quarterly Journal of Experimental Psychology, 30, 346-54.

Leng, N.R.C. and Parkin, A.J. (1987). 'Amnesics can benefit from instructions to use mental imagery: Evidence against the cognitive mediation hypothesis', - ms submitted for publication.

L'Hermitte, F. and Signoret, J.L. (1972). 'Analyse neuropsychologique et differenciation des syndromes amnesiques', Revue Neurologique, 126, 86-94.

Mair, W.G.P., Warrington, E.K. and Weiskrantz, L. (1979). 'Memory disorder in Korsakoff's Psychosis', Brain, 102, 749-83.

Mayes, A.R. (1986). 'Learning and memory disorders and their assessment', Neuropsychologia, 24, 25-40.

Parkin, A.J. (1982). 'Residual learning capability in organic amnesia', Cortex, 18, 417-40.

Parkin, A.J. (1984). 'Amnesic Syndrome: A lesion-specific disorder?', Cortex, 20, 497-508.

Parkin, A.J. (1987). Memory and Amnesia, Blackwells, Oxford.

Parkin, A.J. and Leng, N.R.C. (1987). 'Comparative studies of human amnesia: Methodological and theoretical issues', in Information Processing by the Brain (Ed. H.J. Markowitsch), Huber, Toronto.

Schacter, D.L. and Graf, P. (1986). 'Preserved learning in amnesic patients: Perspectives from research on direct priming', Journal of Experimental and Clinical Neuropsychology.

Scoville, W.B. and Milner, B. (1957). 'Loss of recent memory after bilateral hippocampal lesions', Journal of Neurology, Neurosurgery and Psychiatry, 20, 11-21.

Squire, L.R. (1982). 'Comparisons between forms of amnesia: Some deficits are unique to Korsakoff's Syndrome', Journal of Experimental Psychology:Learning, Memory and Cognition, 8, 560-71.

Squire, L.R., Cohen, N.J. and Nadel, L. (1984). 'The medial temporal region and memory consolidation: A new hypothesis', in Memory Consolidation, (Eds. H. Weingartner and E. Parker), pp. 635-4, Erlbaum, Hillsdale, NJ.

Victor, M., Adams, R.D. and Collins, G.H. (1971). The Wernicke-Korsakoff Syndrome, Davis, Philadelphia.

Weiskrantz, L. (1985). 'Issues and theories in the study of the amnesic syndrome', in Memory Systems of the Brain (Eds. N.M. Weinberger et al.), Guildford, New York.

COMPONENTS OF MEMORY AND AMNESIA

W. Hirst

Cornell University   Medical College
U.S.A.

ABSTRACT
         A components approach to memory and amnesia is reviewed and
the dissociation between what is variously called procedural and
declarative memories or explicit and implicit memories is discussed.
This dissociation has been called into question by recent experiments
that show that amnesic recognition is relatively preserved when
compared to amnesic recall. An alternative, stressing deficits in
the encoding process of amnesics rather in the components of memory,
is suggested.

         Recently a number of cognitive psychologists have used the
discovery of functional dissociations in amnesics to motivate and
support theories of normal memory. However, the path from the
discovery of a dissociation to the construction of a theory is rocky.
In a dissociation, the performance in one task is preserved with
brain damage whereas performance in another is disrupted. That is,
the dissociation is expressed in terms of task performance, but a
task is not the same thing as the mental components and processes
that the task calls upon. An amnesic may not be able to recall a
past event, but that does not mean that there is a memory component
responsible for recall. Recall probably involves more than one
component or process of memory. The theorist must go beyond a
dissociation, as described in terms of task, and pinpoint the
components and processes disrupted with amnesia. This theoretical
task is as difficult, or perhaps more difficult, than the discovery
of the dissociation.
         Generally, one can assume that neurological injury either
disrupts processing or damages components of the mental system.
Those theorists concentrating on process try to understand what
amnesics are doing when memorizing and remembering and try to specify
the normal processes disrupted in amnesics. By looking at the
consequences the disruption of these normal processes have on memory,
the relation between the successful performance of these processes
and the successful performance of a range of memory tasks can be
better understood.
         Those theorists who concentrate on components (or
structures) argue that different kinds of memories rather than
different kinds of mnemonic processes are disrupted with amnesia.
The distinction between process and structure should be clear. One
can talk about the different ways information can be transferred from
short-term memory into long-term memory, and any one of these
processes could be disrupted. On the other hand, one can concentrate
on short-term memory, as a structure, and long-term memory, as a

structure.   The structures themselves could be damaged.   Processing
might, as a consequence, also be disrupted, but the word consequence
is paramount.   Men may load grain into a storehouse accessible only
by a single bridge by dragging sacks or pushing wheelbarrows over the
bridge.   If the bridge burns down, the dragging and the pushing will
stop.   But this disruption in activity has a quite different cause
than one where the sacks are not delivered or the workers go on
strike.   Theorists adopting a components approach offer explanations
of the bridge-burning variety.   They specify that memory X is
disrupted with amnesia, but not memory Y.   They rarely say anything
about what the amnesic is doing while memorizing and remembering.
The reason is clear.   The assumption is that with disruption of the
component, any process that depends on that component will also be
disrupted.   Just as the workers can no longer load the storehouse
when the bridge burns down, so must encoding and retrieval breakdown
when the storehouse of memory is damaged.

THE COMPONENTS APPROACH

The components approach has lead to conceptual confusion in
the amnesic literature.   The study of amnesia came into its own with
Milner's work on patient H.M., who suffered a severe anterograde
amnesia following bilateral removal of the hippocampus.   This classic
work was used to support a components model of memory.   H.M. could
retain information for a short period without rehearsal, but would
quickly forget new information if distracted.   However, his memory
for information acquired before the onset of the amnesia was
relatively intact.   This pattern of results suggests a dissociation
between the consolidation of short-term memories and the
consolidation of long-term memories.   Although the emphasis on
consolidation could have lead to a process model of amnesia, the
dissociation was taken as support for a model of memory positing
separate short-term and long-term stores.

It became clear with additional research that this simple
dichotomy would not do. For instance, Cohen and Squire (1980)
reported that amnesics learned to read mirror-images of words at the
same rate as normals, even though amnesics might not remember
learning the task.   These researchers argued that amnesics can learn
to know how, but not to know that, or to use terminology from
Artificial Intelligence, amnesics' procedural memory was intact;
their declarative memory deficient. Long-term memory, it appeared,
had to be further subdivided into procedural and declarative memory.

For all of its intuitive appeal, the distinction between
procedural memory and declarative memory has also undergone revision.
It does not adequately account for the discovery of normal priming in
amnesics (see Schacter, 1987a, for a review).   If exposed to the word
GARBAGE and then later asked to say the first word that comes to mind
that completes the stem GAR, amnesics are as likely to say GARBAGE as
are normals.   However, if asked instead to complete GAR with a
studied word, amnesics are much less likely to say GARBAGE than are
normals.   Squire (1986) has argued that subjects set up a procedure
with the presentation of the word, but what kind of procedure is
unclear.   On the surface, the priming task does not seem to have any
relation to the perceptual-motor task that Cohen and Squire
investigated.

The distinction between declarative memory and procedural memory could be preserved if one subdivided declarative memory into episodic memory and semantic memory. Accordingly, the amnesic deficit would be said to be confined to episodic memory, with both semantic memory and procedural memory preserved. The memory system would be a three-tier hierarchy, with the memory system first divided into long-term memory and short-term memory, long-term memory then divided into declarative memory and procedural memory, and declarative memory finally divided into episodic memory and semantic memory. Yet even this complex hierarchy of memories cannot account for two recent findings.

First, amnesics demonstrate normal associative priming (see Schacter, 1987a). That is, when subjects study a paired associate TULIP-GARBAGE and are later asked to complete the stem GAR, they are more likely to complete it with GARBAGE if the stem is given in the same context in which it was learned (TULIP) than if given in a novel context. Inasmuch as the context is semantically unrelated to the target, the improved priming cannot be accounted for by simple spreading activation in semantic memory.

Schacter has explained normal associative priming by arguing that the amnesic deficit manifests itself only when memories are explicitly probed -- as in recognition and recall -- and not when they are implicitly probed -- as in a priming task or a procedural task. This description, however, cannot account for another finding. Johnson, Phelps, myself and others have been exploring amnesic recognition, in part because recognition is generally accepted as both an explicit memory task and a task that probes episodic memory. Some direct memory acts are easier for amnesics than are other memory acts. In particular, amnesics can respond to retrieval cues and can recognize information that they cannot recall. These observations may be uninteresting, however. Episodic or explicit memory may be disrupted uniformly, but not completely. One could think of the voltage being turned down without any change in the architecture. A memory trace, for instance, may be weakened, but still maintain its normal structure and function. In such circumstances, one would expect amnesic recognition to be better than amnesic recall because normal recognition is better than normal recall. That is, if F is the relation between normal recall and normal recognition (that is, $F(recog) = recall$), then we should be able to predict amnesics' recall given their recognition performance and F, i.e., $F(recogam) = recallam$.

Johnson, Phelp, myself and others checked this prediction by equating amnesics' and normals' recognition and then investigating whether their recall is also equated (Hirst, Johnson, Kim, Phelps, Risse, & Volpe, 1986). Amnesics were given 8 seconds of study whereas controls were given .5 seconds. Huppert and Piercy (1976) reported that amnesic and normal recognition could be equated under these conditions, and we corroborated their findings. We also found that when amnesic and normal recognition was equated, amnesic recall was from 200% to 1200% worse than normal recall. Amnesic recognition is clearly not predictive of amnesic recall.

In follow-up research, we found similar results when we equated amnesic and control recognition by extending the retention interval of controls. Both amnesics and controls studied the to-be-remembered words for 8 seconds. The amnesics were then given a minute after study, a free recall test followed by a forced-choice recognition test; controls received the memory tests a day later. Again, when amnesic and normal recognition were equated, amnesic recall remained depressed. Other studies showed that similar findings existed for yes-no recognition, and more importantly, that amnesic recall remained depressed even when amnesic recognition was raised to levels above that of normals. The pattern of relatively preserved recognition cannot be traced to the relative sensitivity of recognition and recall tests.

We are currently investigating whether amnesics' relatively preserved recognition is a direct result of their intact priming. One explanation for the priming effect is that entries in semantic memory are activated and thereby facilitate word completion. The same activation could account for the relatively preserved recognition of amnesics if recognition judgements are swayed by activation levels in semantic memory. Preliminary work suggests that this explanation is unsatisfactory. We varied exposure time for amnesics and normal controls so that two-item forced choice recognition was equated at short retention intervals. We also found a clear priming effect for stem completion at this short retention interval. The priming effect went away as the retention interval was extended. Yet despite the disappearance of the priming effect, amnesic recognition was still matched to the recognition performance of controls.

PROCESSING MODELS AS AN ALTERNATIVE?

None of the available component models of memory can account for relatively preserved recognition of amnesics. Nor is it clear how one would extend extant component models to accommodate the finding of relatively preserved recognition. This is not to say that differences between recognition and recall do not exist. The differences, however, are better stated in terms of processes rather than components. It is well-known, for instance, that elaborating and organizing materials as one memorizes will have a more pronounced effect on subsequent recall than on subsequent recognition. Similarly, the encoding of the spatio-temporal context of an event is more important for successful recall of the event than for successful recognition.

Consequently, the amnesic deficit may rest not with the disruption of a component of memory -- be it declarative memory, explicit memory, or episodic memory -- but with the failure to carry out mnemonic processes such as elaborating, organizing, and encoding context. These processes supply the glue that holds individual events together and creates the larger picture. Without this glue, memory would consist of a collection of individual traces of past events unconnecterd to one another. An amnesic might be able to obtain direct access to these memories if provided the appropriate probe, but would not be able to search through memory in a systematic fashion.

Several researchers have made similar proposals, falling by and large into two camps, those who stress a disruption in elaborating and organizing and those who stress a disruption in the encoding of context. Because of space limitation, I cannot adequately explore both models. Instead I will concentrate on those theories that claim that amnesics do not encode the environmental context in which to-be-remembered events occurred.

A context theory of amnesia. I want to be clear by what I mean by "environmental context". An event can be thought of as a core proposition (presumably, the focus of attention), attributes specifying its physical manifestation (or a mental equivalent of a physical manifestation), and the elaborational and organizational features that capture its relation to associated events and schemata. By environmental context, I am referring to some of the attributes specifying the physical manifestation of the event. One must distinguish between integral and separable attributes of the event. A word cannot be presented to a subject if it does not have a modality, and a word cannot be visually presented if it does not have a color. Attributes of an event necessary for the physical manifestation of the event will be called integral attributes. Other attributes -- which I will call separable attributes -- may give an event physical manifestation, but they are not necessary. Thus, if a word is written on a placard, its color and modality may be integral attributes, but the vase to the right of the placard is not. To put it another way, one could see the word without seeing the vase, but if one sees the word, one must "see" its modality and color.

The distinction between integral and separable attributes is not always clear. They may be end points on a continuum. Nevertheless, the encoding of integral attributes probably differs qualitatively from the encoding of separable attributes. Integral attributes may be encoded automatically.

According to the context theory, amnesics do not encode integral attributes, or to the extent that they do, the encoding is no longer automatic, but effortful. As already noted, such a deficit would account for the relatively preserved recognition observed in amnesics. But the theory's support does not rest on this finding alone. There is also a growing number of studies that show that integral features of events are remembered relatively poorly by amnesics when compared to their event recognition. Hirst and others (Hirst & Volpe, 1984) have reported that amnesic memory for the spatial location of objects is worse than that of normals, even when recognition of the objects themselves is comparable to normals. Schacter, Harbluck, & McLachaln (1984) reported that amnesics are less likely to report the source of a recognized fact than are normals, again, even when normal and amnesic recognition is equated. And Mayes (personal communication) has reported that amnesics' memory for the modality of a word is worse than controls even when word recognition is equated. To some extent these results have been clouded by the possible contribution of the frontal lobes (Schacter, 1987b). These context deficits do not, however, appear in patients with frontal lobe damage when a memory problem is not present.

Whether the context model in the end adequately characterizes amnesia is still a matter for future research. At present, it offers a viable alternative to the confusion arising from the component models. It should be clear that the context model is of a different kind than the various component models. It emphasizes the processes undertaken while memorizing and remembering and not the structures of memory. And in doing so, it offers the possibility of improving amnesics' memory by designing memory strategies that bypass the disrupted process. It treats memories as products of processes rather than passive deposits in a storehouse. The storehouses of memory may be biologically elusive, but the processes of pushing the wheelbarrow and pulling the sacks may be neurologically real and identifiable.

REFERENCES

Cohen, N.J. & Squire, L.R. (1980). 'Preserved learning and retention of pattern analyzing skills in amnesia: Dissociation of knowing how and knowing that', Science, 210, 207-210.

Hirst, W., Johnson, M.K., Kim, J.K., Phelps, E.A., Risse, G., & Volpe, B.T. (1986). 'Recognition and recall in amnesics', Journal of Experimental Psychology: Learning, Memory, and Cognition, 12, 445-451.

Hirst, W. & Volpe, B.T. (1984). 'Encoding of spatial relations with amnesia', Neuropsychologia, 22, 631-634.

Schacter, D.L. (1987a). 'Implicit memory: History and current status', Journal of Experimental Psychology: Learning, Memory, and Cognition, 13, in press.

Schacter, D.L. (1987b). 'Memory, amnesia, and frontal lobe dysfuntion', Psychobiology, 15, in press.

Schacter, D.L., Harbluck, J.A., & McLachlan, D.R. (1984). 'Retrieval without recollection: An experimental analysis of source amnesia', Journal of Verbal Learning and Verbal Behavior, 23, 593-611.

Squire, L.R. (1986). 'Mechanisms of memory', Science, 232, 1612-1619.

FACT MEMORY AND SOURCE AMNESIA

A. P. Shimamura
San Diego Veterans Administration Medical Center and
University of California, San Diego

ABSTRACT
   The ability to learn new facts and the ability to remember where and when facts were learned was assessed in amnesic patients and control subjects. On both intentional and incidental learning procedures, amnesic patients exhibited marked fact memory impairment. In addition, some amnesic patients exhibited source amnesia--that is, they recalled a few facts but then could not remember where or when those facts had been learned. Source amnesia appeared to be unrelated to fact memory impairment because the patients who exhibited source amnesia recalled as many facts as the patients who did not.

   Most conventional tests of new learning capacity assess memory for episodic information. In these tests, subjects are asked to determine whether a particular stimulus was presented at a particular time (e.g., "Can you remember the word that I just showed you?"; "Did you see this picture a few minutes ago?"). Subjects fail if they cannot remember the context or episode in which the stimulus was presented. Memory for episodic information can be contrasted with memory for semantic or factual information (e.g., "What is the name of the town through which Lady Godiva supposedly made her famous ride?" [Coventry]). Unlike tests of episodic memory, subjects need not remember when or where the information was learned; they are required only to remember the fact itself. Many everyday situations involve this kind of fact learning. Practically speaking, it is often important to remember what was said rather than when or where it was said.
   The distinction between memory for content and memory for context has been useful for understanding the organization of memory. Tulving (1983) has cogently argued for a distinction between semantic and episodic memory. Some have suggested that this distinction is prominently reflected in the organization of brain systems. One view is that amnesia reflects a selective or disproportionate deficit of episodic memory (see Schacter & Tulving, 1982). Another similar view is that amnesic patients have a disproportionate deficit in remembering contextual information (see Mayes, Meudell, & Pickering, 1985).
   The two experiments reported here test fact learning ability in amnesic patients, using either intentional learning instructions (Experiment 1) or incidental learning instructions (Experiment 2). In addition, these two experiments test source memory--that is,

memory for when and where information was learned (a detailed report of these experiments can be found in Shimamura & Squire, 1987). The experiments were based on a study by Schacter, Harbluk, & McLachlan (1984) in which memory-impaired patients could recall some facts but could not recall that they had been recently presented. That is, they exhibited source amnesia.

EXPERIMENT 1

Method

A group of 11 amnesic patients was tested: seven with alcoholic Korsakoff's syndrome, three with amnesia due to an anoxic or ischemic episode, and case N. A. These patients averaged 49.7 years of age and 12.5 years of education and had an average Wechsler Adult Intelligence Scale (WAIS) IQ score of 108.5. Their average Wechsler Memory Scale (WMS) score was 83.0. Neuropsychological screening and independent neurological examination indicated that memory impairment was the only remarkable deficit of higher cortical function. Detailed neuropsychological.assessment of these patients can be found in Squire & Shimamura (1986).

Two groups of alcoholic control subjects were tested. They averaged 51.4 years of age and 13.5 years of education. One group of seven alcoholic control subjects was tested after a 2-hr retention interval just as the amnesic patients. Another group of 10 alcoholic subjects was tested after a 7-day retention interval at a time when fact memory performance for this group matched that of the amnesic patients tested after a 2-hr delay.

Subjects were given the answers to general information questions and told to try to remember them. In order to ensure that the questions could not be recalled from prior knowledge, the study session began by asking subjects to answer each question (e.g., Where is Angels Falls located? [Venezuela]). If the answer to a question was known to a subject, then that question was discarded. If the answer to a question could not be correctly recalled, then the answer was read by the experimenter. This procedure continued until the answers to 20 previously nonrecalled questions had been presented. Following this initial input phase, the answers to the 20 questions were presented for study a second time.

After a 2-hr retention interval, subjects were given tests of fact recall, source recall, and 8-alternative, forced-choice recognition. During the test phase, no reference was made to the previous study phase--subjects were simply asked to answer some general information ("trivia") questions. If a subject correctly recalled a fact, we asked, "When was the last time you heard this information?" The experimenter recorded the time and place at which the fact was last heard. Source memory performance was scored by calculating the number of source errors out of the total number of study facts recalled. Fact and source memory was also tested for 10 new difficult facts and 10 new easy facts. These new facts were included so that the source of some remembered information would have originated outside the experimental situation.

Results

Amnesic patients exhibited impaired fact memory as measured by tests of both recall, t[16]= 4.3, p< .01 and recognition t[16]= 3.6, p< .01. Source memory was also impaired in amnesic patients (AMN) compared with alcoholic control subjects (ALC), and "delayed" alcoholic subjects who were tested after a 7-day delay (ALC-D) (see Table 1). That is, patients often failed to remember that a correctly recalled fact was one that was learned during the study session 2 hours before. Instead, they attributed the fact to some other source, such as a newspaper article or television show. Source memory impairment, however, was variable across amnesic patients. Four amnesic patients exhibited 100% errors, two patients made about 40% errors, one patient made 10% errors, and four patients did not make any source errors. The four patients who committed 100% source errors were three patients with Korsakoff's syndrome and one patient who became amnesic following a cardiac arrest.

Table 1: Fact Memory and Source Amnesia

Subjects	Fact Recall	Fact Recognition	Source Errors
ALC	74%	91%	3%
AMN	31%	56%	45%
ALC-D	34%	67%	14%

Interestingly, source memory impairment was not related to fact memory impairment. Alcoholic subjects tested after a 7-day retention interval exhibited the same level of fact recall and recognition memory as amnesic patients tested after a 2-hr delay. Yet, the delayed control subjects exhibited better source memory than amnesic patients. Furthermore, the four amnesic patients who made 100% source errors remembered about the same number of facts as the four patients with the best source memory (none of these patients made any source errors). Specifically, the four patients who made 100% source errors recalled 31% facts and recognized 46% facts, whereas the four patients who made 0% source errors recalled 25% and recognized 48% facts. Thus, the source memory impairment exhibited by some amnesic patients could not be explained as a consequence of poor or weak fact memory.

EXPERIMENT 2

In this experiment, incidental learning of factual information was assessed in amnesic patients. Much of the information that we learn in daily life is learned incidentally. Perhaps fact learning would be preserved in amnesia if information were learned incidentally. Source memory for correctly recalled facts was also tested.

Methods

Ten of the 11 patients described in Experiment 1 were tested; one patient with Korsakoff's syndrome was not available for testing. A new group of alcoholic subjects was also tested and they averaged 52.1 years of age and 12.2 years of education. One group of eight alcoholic subjects was tested after a 5-min delay, just as the amnesic patients. Another group of six subjects was tested after a 2-hr delay in order to assess source memory in subjects whose fact memory performance matched that of the amnesic patients.

In the study task, subjects were asked to read 15 general information facts, without any instructions to learn or remember them. Subjects were asked to read each fact and place it next to one of five category names--1) BOOKS & COMICS, 2) MOVIES & PLAYS, 3) HISTORY, 4) GEOGRAPHY, 5) SPORTS. After sorting all 15 facts, subjects sorted the facts a second time, reading the facts aloud and placing them in a category.

After a 5-min retention interval, tests of fact recall, source recall, and fact recognition were given for the 15 study facts. In addition, fact and source memory for 15 new facts was assessed. Source memory was assessed by asking subjects to report the last time a correctly recalled fact had been encountered. The test phase procedure was identical to the procedure used in Experiment 1.

Results

As in Experiment 1, amnesic patients exhibited impaired fact recall (t[16]= 2.15, p< .05) and recognition memory (t[16]= 3.28, p< .01) (see Table 2). Because of the incidental nature of the study task, the fact questions could not be screened for prior recall ability. Thus, for each subject baseline recall performance was assessed for 15 fact questions that had been used as study material for other subjects. Baseline performance was not significantly different across amnesic patients (AMN), alcoholic control subjects (ALC), and delayed alcoholic control subjects (ALC-D) (see Table 2). Thus, even when facts were presented incidentally, amnesic patients exhibited fact memory impairment.

Source memory was also impaired in amnesic patients (see Table 2). Amnesic patients committed an average of 69% source errors, somewhat more than the number of errors they committed in Experiment 1. One patient with Korsakoff's syndrome was excluded from this analysis because she did not correctly recall any facts and therefore did not have an opportunity to exhibit source errors. As in Experiment 1, source memory impairment was variable across amnesic patients. However, the four amnesic patients who committed 100% source errors also committed 100% errors in this experiment. One patient who had committed 0% source errors in Experiment 1 committed 100% source errors in this experiment, but that score was based on only one item. The other four amnesic patients, who averaged 23% source errors in Experiment 1, averaged 30% source errors in this experiment. Thus, even though source memory impairment was variable across patients, it was relatively consistent within patients in two separate experiments.

Table 2: Incidental Fact Memory and Source Amnesia[*]

Subjects	Fact Recall	Fact Recognition	Source Errors
ALC	44% (6%)	70% (40%)	3%
AMN	31% (14%)	54% (42%)	69%
ALC-D	30% (10%)	54% (36%)	0%

[*]Values in parentheses indicate baseline memory performance.

As in the previous experiment, source memory impairment was not related to poor fact memory ability. Alcoholic subjects tested after a 2-hr delay did not make any source errors, yet their fact memory performance matched that of amnesic patients. Moreover, the four patients who made 100% source errors in both this and in the previous experiment, exhibited about the same fact recall score as the four patients who made the fewest source errors. Specifically, the four patients who made the most source errors recalled 36% facts and recognized 58% facts, whereas the four patients who made the fewest source errors recalled 40% facts and recognized 54% facts. Thus, source memory impairment can be dissociated from the general fact memory impairment exhibited by amnesic patients.

DISCUSSION

All of the amnesic patients exhibited impairment in the ability to learn and remember recently acquired factual knowledge. Fact memory was impaired even when material was presented incidentally and then requested implicitly without making reference to the learning episode. These findings replicate the finding of Schacter et al. (1984). They also extend our understanding of source amnesia in several important ways. First, source amnesia was not restricted to those etiologies of memory impairment that produce relatively widespread cognitive impairment (e.g., Alzheimer's disease, head injury). Second, only some amnesic patients exhibited source amnesia. Nevertheless, the ones who exhibited the impairment did so consistently in two experiments. Third, source amnesia was unrelated to the severity of fact memory impairment. That is, patients who exhibited source amnesia recalled and recognized as many facts as the patients who did not.

Source amnesia appears to constitute a true dissociation between fact and context memory, or between semantic and episodic memory. That is, some but not all amnesic patients exhibited a disproportionate deficit in remembering the spatial-temporal context in which facts were presented. In other words, their impairment in episodic memory was greater than would have been expected, given their level of fact memory performance. Source amnesia--that is, a loss of spatial-temporal context--appears to represent a neurologically dissociable deficit that can occur in addition to a general impairment of recall and recognition memory. Source amnesia may be related to damage in brain areas other than the diencephalic and medial temporal areas that have been linked to amnesia (see Squire, 1987). One possibility is that damage to frontal lobes produces source amnesia because these brain areas are involved in processing or storing spatial-temporal information.

The findings from these experiments showed that fact memory was impaired in all amnesic patients. Thus, the findings create some difficulties for the view that amnesia causes a selective impairment in episodic memory. Yet, some but not all amnesic patients did exhibit a disproportionate impairment of source amnesia. Source amnesia in some patients may indicate a particular impairment in the encoding and memory of spatial-temporal information. Such specific impairment may be analogous to encoding and memory impairment seen as a result of discrete cortical damage--for example, the specific face and object recognition impairment seen in patients with prosopagnosia. By this view, additional impairment in a particular aspect of memory can occur in conjunction with a general impairment of declarative or explicit memory.

REFERENCES

Mayes, A. R., Meudell, P. R., and Pickering, A. (1985). Is organic amnesia caused by a selective deficit in remembering contextual information? Cortex, 21, 167-202.

Schacter, D. L., Harbluk, J. L., and McLachlan, D. R. (1984). Retrieval without recollection: An experimental analysis of source amnesia. Journal of Verbal Learning and Verbal Behavior, 23, 593-611.

Schacter, D. L., and Tulving, E. (1982). Memory, amnesia, and the episodic/semantic distinction. In R. L. Isaacson and N. E. Spear (Eds.), Expression of knowledge (33-65). New York: Plenum Press.

Shimamura, A. P., and Squire, L. R. (1987). A neuropsychological study of fact memory and source amnesia. Journal of Experimental Psychology: Learning, Memory, and Cognition, 13, 464-473.

Squire, L. R. (1987). Memory and Brain. New York: Oxford University Press.

Squire, L. R., and Shimamura, A. P. (1986). Characterizing amnesic patients for neurobehavioral study. Behavioral Neuroscience, 100, 866-877.

Tulving, E. (1983). Elements of episodic memory. Oxford: Clarendon Press.

ACKNOWLEDGEMENTS

    This research was supported by the Medical Research Service of the Veterans Administration, by a National Research Service Award (MH08992) from the National Institute of Mental Health to Arthur P. Shimamura, and by a grant (MH24600) from the National Institute of Mental Health to Larry R. Squire. I thank Joyce Zouzounis, Armand Bernheim, Patty Feldstein, Kim Rivero-Frink, and Deborah Rosenthal for research assistance and Larry R. Squire for support and guidance. Request for reprints should be sent to Arthur P. Shimamura, VA Medical Center (V116), 3350 La Jolla Village Drive, San Diego, California, 92161.

REVEALING THE CONCEALED:
MULTIPLE MEASURES OF MEMORY IN DEMENTIA

Felicia A. Huppert and Lynn Beardsall

Department of Psychiatry,
Cambridge University School of Clinical Medicine.

ABSTRACT

A simple memory test is described in which three measures of declarative memory and two measures of priming are obtained on the same set of material. Subjects with definite dementia show evidence of priming in the absence of declarative memory. Those whose dementia is minimal show some preservation of declarative memory, but are impaired in comparison with normals. The implications for memory management are discussed.

INTRODUCTION

Memory dysfunction plays a central role in dementia. Forgetfulness, loss of belongings, repetitiveness and other evidence of recent memory impairment are among the earliest symptoms. As the disease progresses, this impairment becomes increasingly widespread and disabling, and involves other aspects of memory, such as remote memory and recognition of names and faces. We argue that multiple measures of memory are required to determine the existence and extent of memory dysfunction for purposes of diagnosis and effective management, as well as basic research. Further, we believe the emphasis should be as much on ascertaining the individual's memory potential as on uncovering their failures.

We describe here a simple computer-based memory test which assesses memory in five ways, from the most effortful retrieval method, free recall, through cued recall, forced-choice recognition and initial letter priming, to a method requiring minimal effort - perceptual priming. Valid comparison between the effectiveness of these different methods requires (a) a within-subject design and (b) that the same material be tested by each method. These requirements have been incorporated into the test design.

One aim of the memory test is to determine whether demented patients resemble patients with organic amnesia in showing a normal priming effect despite impaired recall and recognition (e.g. Shimamura and Squire, 1984). The more diffuse pathology of Alzheimer's disease compared with amnesic syndromes may lead to the absence or reduction of priming effects. Any evidence that demented patients show priming and are thus able to benefit from prior experience, has implications for memory management. In the test described below, we examine the effectiveness of two different forms of priming and compare priming measures with performance on tests of free recall, cued recall and forced-choice recognition.

The test is only one of a range of memory tests which we are administering in a study whose aim is to differentiate the memory disorder of early or borderline dementia from 'normal' memory decline in the elderly. Our subjects come from a large sample of community residents aged 75+ from six group general practices in Cambridge, who have been screened for dementia as part of the Hughes Hall Project for Later Life. In addition to memory and other detailed cognitive tests, all subjects are given a standardized structured psychiatric interview and examination, the CAMDEX (Roth et al., 1987) to aid in the diagnosis of dementia. The CAMDEX incorporates a 20 min. mini-neuropsychological battery, the CAMCOG - Cambridge Cognitive Examination - as well as an interview with an informant. The CAMCOG yields a wide range of scores (maximum = 107) and avoids ceiling effects. A cut-off score of 79/80 has been found to differentiate normal subjects from those with mild dementia (Roth et al., 1986).

The range of memory measures which we use includes:

a)   **Clinical Assessment.** Thirteen of the 60 items of the CAMCOG are concerned with memory function. They cover the areas of recent memory, remote memory and new learning, of both incidental and intentional type, where the effect of method of retrieval is examined (recall versus recognition).

b)   **Behavioural assessment,** using the Rivermead Behavioural Memory Test of Wilson et al. (1985). This standardised assessment of real life memory performance includes recall of a name, a story, recognition of faces, retracing the path around a room, recalling where a personal belonging has been located, and remembering to make an appointment when a timer sounds (prospective memory).

c)   **Laboratory tests of memory.** These are mainly computer based and described in detail below. A test of procedural memory using a sentence anagram task (Beardsall and Huppert, 1987) and a quantitative test of prospective memory (Huppert, 1987) are given.

d)   **Self-report and informant report of memory function.** These subjective measures are part of the CAMDEX interview. Although self-report of memory function is known to be influenced by depressed mood (Kahn et al., 1975), it is included for comparison with objectively obtained data, along with information about depressive symptoms. In previous work (Roth et al., 1986), we have shown that in contrast to self-report, the informant's assessment of the patient's memory function is highly correlated with objective measures of memory performance.

Although the methods described above do not by any means encompass all areas of memory function, we believe they cover most of the important areas. For the remainder of this presentation, we will discuss the computerised laboratory tests of memory which we are employing. These tests take 15 minutes altogether.

METHOD

Subjects are required to read out and remember a list of 16 words, six or seven letters in length, presented one at a time for

two seconds in large letters on a monitor controlled by a BBC Master 128 microcomputer. The words are divided into four categories (animals, occupations, food, clothing) and begin with one of four initial letters (B, C, P, S). Each category contains only one word beginning with a given letter. Memory is tested after a brief delay in five ways:
1) free recall - one min. duration;
2) cued recall with category name provided - 30 sec. per category;
3) four-choice recognition where the distractors belong to the same category and are the same length, but begin with different initial letters to the targets. Each array is presented for eight seconds.
4) letter priming where subjects are asked to produce as many words as they can think of beginning with the target letters - 30 sec. is allocated for each letter.
5) perceptual priming where eight of the target words and eight new distractors of the same length, belonging to the target categories and beginning with the same initial letters are presented in a degraded form and subjects are required to identify them. The words are progressively built up on the screen in two second sweeps, each sweep followed by a two second stationary period. The screen is blank at the start, and by the end of the first sweep a random 10% of the word has appeared, composed of tiny white blocks on a black background. A further 10% of the remaining information is added by the end of each subsequent sweep. The number of sweeps required for the word to be identified is therefore a close approximation to the percentage of the total information which is available.

SUBJECTS

Most of our subjects come from a community sample. Cases are identified as cognitively impaired if they fall below the standard cut-off (23/24) on the Mini Mental State Examination (Folstein et al., 1975). They are further classified as low scoring normal (LSN) or as minimal dementia using the CAMDEX diagnostic interview. A group of normals scoring above the MMSE cut-off were also tested. A group of patients diagnosed on the CAMDEX as having mild or moderate dementia were recruited from a Day Centre at Fulbourn Hospital, Cambridge.

Subjects have been selected who are free from other conditions which might impair cognitive function. Exclusion criteria are: Parkinson's disease, insulin-dependent diabetes, severe sensory deficit, stroke interfering with physical function, (i.e., sight, speech or limb function), alcoholism, current depressive illness or other psychiatric illness. There were 11 normals (eight female, three male) with a mean age of 80.6 years and a mean CAMCOG score of 91.2 (range 86-101) and 30 low scoring subjects (18 female, 12 male), mean age of 83.4 years and mean CAMCOG score of 88.0 (range 73-100). There were ten minimally demented subjects (six female, four male), mean age 88.7 years and mean CAMCOG score 79.0 (range 64-95), and 10 mildly/moderately demented subjects (six female, four male), mean age 79.3 years and mean CAMCOG score 50.8 (range 15-73).

RESULTS

        Table 1 shows that free and cued recall, recognition and
initial letter priming are related to severity of dementia and that
on all but the priming measure, the LSN group performs midway
between the normal and minimal dementia groups. One-way analyses
of variance showed that the group differences were significant for
the two recall tests and the recognition tests (p<.001), but not
for initial letter priming. Post hoc Tukey tests (p<.05) revealed
that the mild/moderate dementia group performed significantly worse
than the normal and LSN groups in all conditions except initial
letter priming and significantly worse than the minimal dementia
group on the recognition task only.   On this task, the
mild/moderate dementia group, unlike the other groups, performed no
better than chance. The minimal dementia group differed
significantly from the normals on free and cued recall and
recognition and their performance was significantly worse than the
LSN group on free recall. The normals performed significantly
better than the LSN group only on category recall.

Table 1. **Mean and standard deviation of target words retrieved in
        four conditions.**

	Normal N=11	Low Scoring Normal N=30	Minimal Dementia N=10	Mild/Moderate Dementia N=10
Free Recall	4.8 (1.9)	3.6 (1.7)	1.9 (1.8)	0.3 (0.7)
Cued Recall	5.3 (2.0)	2.7 (1.7)	1.2 (1.5)	0.0 (0.0)
Recognition	14.1 (2.0)	11.7 (2.8)	9.8 (4.0)	4.9 (2.4)
Initial Letter Priming	2.5 (1.9)	2.2 (1.2)	2.2 (1.9)	1.3 (1.1)

        Contrary to expectation, the groups derived little benefit
from the cued recall condition. Table 1 shows that, for these
groups, the mean number of targets produced was slightly less than
for free recall. On the other hand, it can be seen in Table 2
that, while none of the mildly/moderately demented subjects
produced a single target word to the category cue, 81% of normals,
67% of the LSN and 40% of minimally demented subjects produced new
target words under the cued recall condition which they had not
recalled during free recall.
        In the initial letter priming task, the mean total number
of words produced in each of the four groups was: normals 27.9, LSN
24.4, minimal dementia 15.3 and mild/moderate dementia 12.6.
Despite the fact that the demented subjects produced only half as
many words as the normal and LSN group, the proportion of target
words was the same in the four groups. Both the demented groups
produced more target words in the initial letter priming condition
than in either of the recall conditions (Table 1) and this
difference was significant for the mild/moderate dementia group
(p<.03). This was not true for the two normal groups, despite the

fact that the target words had been presented for a second time in the recognition test. Nevertheless, Table 2 shows that a high percentage of subjects in all groups produced new target words in the priming condition which they had not produced in either of the recall tests. Each group contained subjects who produced no target words in initial letter priming: normals 18%, LSN 3%, minimal dementia 10%, mild/moderate dementia 30%.

Table 2. Percentage of subjects producing additional target words in successive conditions.

	Normal N=11	Low Scoring Normal N=30	Minimal Dementia N=10	Mild/Moderate Dementia N=10
Cued vs Free Recall	81	67	40	0
Initial Letter Priming vs Recall	64	93	70	70

Table 3 reveals that each of the four groups showed an advantage for the target words over the non-target words in the perceptual priming task. The significance of the priming effect within each group was calculated using Sign tests to compare the number of individuals showing the target word advantage with the number not showing the advantage. These indicated a significant effect in the normal and LSN group ($p<.01$), and the mild/moderate dementia group ($p<.05$), but not in the minimal dementia group. The percentage of subjects who failed to show a difference in the predicted direction was 9% for normals, 20% for LSNs, 40% for minimals and 30% for mild/moderate dementia. A Chi square test showed no significant difference between the groups in the percentage of subjects showing the perceptual priming effect.

Table 3. Percentage of total information required for the identification of words in the perceptual priming task.

	Normal N=11	Low Scoring Normal N=30	Minimal Dementia N=10	Mild/Moderate Dementia N=10
Target Words	27%	36%	38%	41%
Non-target words	31%	40%	40%	46%

DISCUSSION

This report indicates that much useful information about the relative effectiveness of different measures of memory can be obtained in a brief computer-based test. Using the same material to test memory in five different ways, we have found that a group of subjects with mild/moderate dementia shows no evidence of remembering a word list when tested by conventional free recall, cued recall and recognition methods, but shows clear priming effects on two different measures: initial letter priming and perceptual priming. A group of subjects diagnosed as having minimal dementia, performed at an intermediate level between the normal and mild/moderate dementia groups on all five measures.

It therefore appears that like patients with organic amnesia, demented subjects are able to benefit from prior experience. This finding has implications for memory management. It may be possible to elicit recent information or new behaviours by using non-declarative or 'automatic' retrieval techniques. However, for the 30 percent or so of mildly/moderately demented subjects who do not show evidence of priming, the use of external memory aids may be the only approach to memory management.

ACKNOWLEDGEMENT

We wish to thank Dr. N. Miller for his role in diagnosing and selecting the sample and the members of the Hughes Hall Project team, Drs. C.P. Brook, B. Reiss, D. O'Connor and P. Pollitt. We also wish to acknowledge Dr. A. Iserles for his innovative programming of the perceptual priming task. This research is funded by a grant from the Medical Research Council.

REFERENCES

Beardsall, L. and Huppert, F.A. (1987). Procedural memory in elderly normal and demented subjects. (In preparation).

Folstein, M.F., Folstein, S.E. and McHugh, P.R. (1975). Mini Mental State. A practical method for grading the cognitive state of patients for the clinician. Journal of Psychiatric Research, 12, 189-198.

Huppert, F.A. (1987). A new quantitative test of prospective memory: comparative performance in normal elderly, demented and depressed subjects. (To be submitted).

Kahn, R.L., Zarit, S.H., Hilbert, N.M. and Niederche, G.M. (1975). Memory complaint and impairment in the aged. Archives of General Psychiatry, 32, 1569-1573.

Roth, M., Tym, E., Mountjoy, C.Q., Huppert, F.A., Hendrie, H., Verma, S. and Goddard, R. (1986). CAMDEX: a standardised instrument for the diagnosis of mental disorder in the elderly with special reference to the early detection of dementia. British Journal of Psychiatry, 149, 698-709.

Roth, M., Huppert, F.A., Tym, E. and Mountjoy, C.Q. (1987). CAMDEX: The Cambridge Mental Disorders of the Elderly Examination. Cambridge University Press. (In press).

Shimamura, A.P. and Squire, L.R. (1984). Paired associate learning and priming effects in amnesia: a neuropsychological study. Journal of Experimental Psychology, 113, 556-570.

Wilson, B., Cockburn, J. and Baddeley, A. (1985). The Rivermead Behavioural Memory Test. Thames Valley Test Co., Reading.

RETROGRADE AMNESIA, ANTEROGRADE AMNESIA, AND CHOLINERGIC DEPLETION

M.D. Kopelman
Wellcome Lecturer in Psychiatry
Institute of Psychiatry, London SE5 8AF

ABSTRACT

There is evidence that retrograde amnesia (RA) and anterograde amnesia (AA) may be partially dissociable; that an extensive remote memory loss is only partially attributable to a progressive anterograde impairment; that accelerated forgetting (faulty storage) does not mediate AA; and that cholinergic depletion could produce an anterograde but not a retrograde deficit. Partially independent neuropathological/neurochemical systems may contribute to RA and AA in amnesic and dementing disorders.

INTRODUCTION

Several pieces of evidence point to the partial independence of retrograde and anterograde memory impairment in organic amnesia:
1. Severe anterograde memory loss can coexist with very variable degrees of retrograde loss, as Korsakoff himself noted. In head injury, for example, there may be a very brief or no retrograde loss in the presence of a lengthy period of post-traumatic amnesia.
2. By contrast, claims have been made that retrograde amnesia (RA) can exist in the absence of any anterograde impairment. Certainly, it seems to be the case that a disproportionately severe RA can occur in the presence of only a very mild anterograde amnesia (AA), although reports of an apparently 'pure' RA usually contain evidence of either some degree of AA or of the possible contribution of psychogenic factors.
3. At least one study has reported the absence of any correlation in amnesic patients between the overall severity of remote memory impairment and performance on various (anterograde) learning tests (Shimamura and Squire, 1986).
4. Of less direct relevance, theories postulating an 'acquisition' deficit in anterograde amnesia are incompatible with a unitary account of RA and AA; and, to the extent that there is evidence to support them, we need to look elsewhere for a psychological explanation of retrograde amnesia.

RETROGRADE AMNESIA

In his so-called law of regression, Ribot (1882) argued that "the progressive destruction of memory follows a logical order (beginning) with the most recent recollections which .... represent organisation in its feeblest form." Such a view implies that remote memory impairment involves a destruction of memory storage, an

accelerated forgetting of remote memories. By contrast, Sanders and
Warrington (1971), in the first modern study using objective
techniques, reported that there is a uniform loss of remote memories
across all earlier decades in both organic amnesia and normal aging.
On their 'famous faces' test, the curves of the amnesic and elderly
groups were shifted downwards but remained in parallel with those of
their respective comparison groups;   and Sanders and Warrington
interpreted this as resulting from a generalised retrieval deficit.
However, several subsequent studies have found a temporal gradient
in the remote memory loss of Korsakoff patients with relative
sparing of the most distant memories.   Consequently, Butters and
Albert (1982) have argued that an anterograde/acquisition impairment
occurs during the period of Korsakoff patients' heavy drinking,
resulting in a particularly severe loss of the most recent memories;
and Squire and colleagues (1984) have suggested that organic amnesia
produces a disruption of a 'long-term' consolidation process which
normally lasts as long as two years.
         There are difficulties with each of these arguments:
(i)   Ribot's view is inconsistent with the modern finding that, at
least in anterograde amnesia, the rate of forgetting is normal once
initial learning has been accomplished (see below).
(ii) Warrington's 'flat' remote memory curve has not been replicated
in studies of the amnesic syndrome, and it may have reflected a
'floor' effect or an artefact of her particular test material.
(iii) Butters and Albert do not provide a psychological explanation
for the generalised loss of remote memories in Korsakoff patients,
which they say is superimposed upon the anterograde component at the
time of the Wernicke encephalopathy.
(iv) Squire's notion of a prolonged consolidation process is purely
an inference from the common occurrence of a 2 to 3 year period of
RA; and there is no independent physiological evidence in support of
such a process.
         At the same time, there is some evidence that Alzheimer and
Huntington dementing patients may show a 'flat' remote memory loss
across all earlier time-periods (Wilson et al,1981; Butters and
Albert, 1982), although this has not been found in all studies
(Moscovitch, 1982) and clinical 'lore' suggests that there should be
some sparing of the most distant memories ('temporal gradient').   In
order to examine this issue more closely, the present author has
compared the performance of Alzheimer and Korsakoff patients on
various remote memory tasks: these included a semi-structured
autobiographical memory interview, developed jointly with Barbara
Wilson and Alan Baddeley, as well as more conventional tests of
memory for famous news events and personalities.   A preliminary
analysis of data from the first subjects tested indicated that on
recognition tests the Alzheimer and Korsakoff groups both showed a
'gentle' but statistically significant temporal gradient relative to
healthy controls.   On recall tests, the Korsakoff patients did
indeed show a significantly steeper 'gradient' than the Alzheimer
group, and this was particularly marked on the autobiographical
memory schedule, performance at which was much less confounded by
the subjects' estimated premorbid intelligence.
         These findings indicated some degree of gradient and, in
addition, a marked response to recognition testing in both the

Korsakoff and Alzheimer groups. Several factors may have contributed to this pattern of results: (i) an anterograde impairment
during the years immediately preceding the diagnosis (because of
heavy drinking or the early stages of dementia, respectively); (ii)
a superimposed retrieval deficit, producing the response to recognition testing; and (iii) the relative salience and over-rehearsal
of early memories may have provided a partial protection against
this retrieval deficit, thereby contributing to the gradient. The
correlates of differing gradients are now being studied.

ANTEROGRADE AMNESIA

The distinction between primary and secondary memory has
commonly been criticised, but remains a framework within which much
amnesia research is still conducted. Whereas a severe impairment
of secondary memory in amnesic disorders occurs by definition, the
extent of any involvement of primary or working memory remains a
controversial topic.

Most studies are agreed that there is a fairly severe
impairment of primary memory in dementing disorders whether assessed
by span tests, measures of short-term forgetting, or the recency
component of free recall (e.g. Kopelman, 1985; Morris, 1986). In
the Korsakoff and other specific amnesic syndromes, there is agreement that span is preserved, but measures of short-term forgetting,
such as the Brown-Peterson test, have produced conflicting results
(see Parkin 1987). Kopelman (1985) found only very mild impairment
in Korsakoff cases and severe impairment in Alzheimer patients; in
the former group, impairment was associated with the degree of
cortical atrophy on CT scan (computerised tomography), and in the
latter with low IQ and an early age of onset (younger Alzheimer
patients have the more severe and widespread neocortical pathology).
Parkin and Leng (this volume) have found that impairment on this
test is correlated with deficits on a test of 'frontal' function.
These results would appear consistent with the view that a deficit
of primary memory is not an integral part of the amnesic syndrome
but results from a superimposed 'cortical' dysfunction.

The severe impairment of secondary memory in the amnesic
syndrome appears to result from pathology within the diencephalon or
the medial aspects of the temporal lobes (Kopelman, 1987a; Parkin,
1987). In particular, it seems that two limbic circuits (the
hippocampal and amygdaloid) both have to be implicated for severe
amnesia to ensue (Mishkin, 1986). There have been claims that
diencephalic lesions may differ from medial temporal pathology in
that, whereas the former produces a severe 'acquisition' deficit but
a normal forgetting rate once learning has been accomplished, the
latter may produce both impaired learning and accelerated
forgetting. Evidence of a 'normal' forgetting rate in organic
amnesia has been obtained in four studies of the Korsakoff syndrome,
two studies of head injury (penetrating and non-penetrating), three
studies of Alzheimer-type dementia, and one study of Huntington's
disease (e.g. Huppert and Piercy, 1978; Kopelman, 1985; Becker et
al., 1987). Evidence in favour of accelerated forgetting in medial
temporal lesions comes from one study of HM (subsequently refuted),
a study of post-ECT confusional states (of dubious localising
significance), and a study of 'temporal lobe' and Korsakoff patients

(Leng and Parkin, reported by Parkin, 1987). The last study is of particular interest, but the 'faster forgetting' appears to have occurred entirely between the first and second test intervals. At the first test interval, 'temporal lobe' and Korsakoff patients both performed at 'ceiling', and beyond the second test interval their forgetting curves were in parallel: in short, the more severely impaired performance of 'temporal lobe' patients at the longer delays may simply have reflected the severity of their amnesia rather than accelerated forgetting.

Mayes (1986) has raised the possibility that an 'artefact' might account for normal forgetting in the above experiments, but his argument neglects (i) the potential importance of controlling for extra-test interference effects between the end of stimulus presentation and initial testing, and (ii) the above studies all show normal forgetting beyond the second test interval. Moreover, interpolation of the results of two of these studies suggests that modifying the design to Mayes's requirement would have had negligible effect on forgetting rates (Huppert and Piercy, 1978; Kopelman, 1985). If structural lesions do not produce accelerated forgetting, as the bulk of the above evidence suggests, then anterograde amnesia must, presumably, result from either an encoding deficit, an encoding-retrieval interaction, a 'pure' retrieval deficit, or an impairment of some physiological process of 'consolidation'. The arguments in favour or against these various hypotheses have been rehearsed many times elsewhere (e.g. Meudell and Mayes, 1982; Kopelman, 1987a); but, in brief, it appears that an impairment of (e.g. semantic) encoding is neither universal nor of sufficient severity to account for amnesia, and any deficit in retrieval appears to be explicable in terms of an initial 'acquisition' impairment and the 'weak' memory which results. Consequently, the somewhat paradoxical situation has arisen in which, failing to identify any irrefutable psychological explanation, various authors (e.g. Moscovitch; Meudell and Mayes) have opted for a presumed failure of physiological 'consolidation' as the basis of organic amnesia although, until recently, there was also very little positive evidence in favour of this view.

CHOLINERGIC DEPLETION

Evidence that cholinergic depletion may contribute to the severe memory impairment in Alzheimer and other dementing disorders comes from three sources, which have been reviewed in detail elsewhere (Kopelman, 1986): (i) neuropathological studies demonstrating reduction in cholinergic enzymes and synthesis; (ii) pharmacological studies demonstrating memory impairment following cholinergic 'blockade'; (iii) clinical trials indicating (weak) benefits after administering cholinergic agents to Alzheimer patients. The earlier studies of cholinergic 'blockade' employed only a limited range of tests; but the author has recently completed a detailed study of cholinergic 'blockade' in healthy subjects (as a model for cholinergic depletion) using tests closely similar to those employed in neuropsychological studies (Kopelman and Corn, in preparation; Kopelman, 1987b).

In brief, cholinergic 'blockade' produces only a mild impairment on tests of primary memory, marked impairment on tests requiring the new learning of either verbal or visuospatial material (whether tested by recall or recognition), a 'normal' forgetting rate on several measures (including the Huppert–Piercy test), and relatively intact performance on tests of 'implicit' memory. However, cholinergic 'blockade' does not appear to cause any deficit on remote memory tests, whether assessed by recall or recognition, or any loss of information learned before drug administration, i.e. it cannot account for retrograde amnesia.

This pattern of results is consistent with the hypothesis that cholinergic depletion might be the basis of a 'consolidation' failure in anterograde amnesia.   Consistent with this view, Mishkin (1986) has argued that cholinergic depletion within his hippocampal and amygdaloid circuits would produce amnesia; and Arendt et al. (1983) have produced evidence of a loss of cholinergic neurons in three Korsakoff patients at autopsy.   However, it should be noted that the cholinergic loss in the Arendt study was relatively mild and the authors lacked a detailed clinical or psychometric assessment of their cases.   Moreover, other drugs, such as the benzodiazepines, produce an amnesia which, to date, has proved indistinguishable from that which follows cholinergic blockade; and abnormalities in other neurotransmitter systems may well contribute to anterograde amnesia.   What is now required are careful studies in clinical groups of patients, seeking correlation between particular patterns of memory deficits and in vivo or autopsy measures of specific neurochemical changes.

CONCLUSION

In summary, it seems unlikely that we will find a unitary explanation of retrograde and anterograde amnesia, and we are still only groping towards an adequate psychological or physiological account.   The anterograde impairment in the amnesic syndrome probably results from lesions within Mishkin's limbic circuits, and its pattern is indeed consistent with that attributable to cholinergic depletion.   However, it is far from proved that there is a definite causal association with cholinergic abnormalities;   and it seems unlikely that cholinergic depletion would account for the full range of deficits (including primary and semantic memory) seen in Alzheimer–type dementia (Kopelman, 1986, 1987b).   The extensive retrograde impairment in the Korsakoff syndrome and Alzheimer–type dementia may result, in part, from a superimposed retrieval deficit; this cannot be attributed to cholinergic depletion, and we must look elsewhere (perhaps to a failure of 'frontal' retrieval processes) for an explanation.   Despite these cautious conclusions, the newly burgeoning techniques for studying brain neurochemistry, as well as the quest for effective pharmacotherapies, provide an important opportunity for the reconciliation of theoretical with 'practical' issues in the study of organic amnesia.

REFERENCES:
Arendt, T., Bigl, V., Arendt, A. & Tennstedt, A.   (1983)   'Loss of neurons in the nucleus basalis of Meynert in Alzheimer's diseases, Paralysis Agitans and Korsakoff's disease.'   Acta Neuropathologica (Berlin, 61, 101–108

Becker, J.T., Boller, F., Saxton, J. & McGonigle–Gibson, K.L. (1987)

'Normal rates of forgetting of verbal and non-verbal material in Alzheimer's disease.'   Cortex, 23, 59-72

Butters, N. & Albert, M.   (1982)   'Remote memory, retrograde amnesia and the neuropsychology of memory.'   In Human Memory and Amnesia (ed. L.S. Cermak)   Lawrence Erlbaum: Hillsdale, N.J.

Huppert, F.A. & Piercy, M.   (1978)   'Dissociation between learning and remembering in organic amnesia.'   Nature, 275, 317-318

Kopelman, M.D.   (1985)   'Rates of forgetting in Alzheimer-type dementia and Korsakoff's syndrome.' Neuropsychologia, 23, 623-638

Kopelman, M.D.   (1986)   'The cholinergic neurotransmitter system in human memory and dementia: a review.'   Quarterly Journal of Experimental Psychology, 38A, 535-573

Kopelman, M.D.   (1987a)   'Amnesia: Organic and Psychogenic.' British Journal of Psychiatry, 150, 428-442

Kopelman, M.D. (1987b)   'How far could cholinergic depletion account for the memory deficits of Alzheimer-type dementia or the alcoholic Korsakoff syndrome?'   In Cognitive Neurochemistry (Eds S. Stahl, S. Iverson & E. Goodman), pp 304-326, Oxford University Press: Oxford

Mayes, A.R.   (1986)   'Learning and memory disorders and their assessment.'   Neuropsychologia, 24, 25-40

Meudell, P.R. & Mayes, A.R. (1982)   'Normal and abnormal forgetting: some comments on the human amnesic syndrome.'   In Normality and Pathology in Cognitive Functions (Ed A.W. Ellis) pp 203-238. Academic Press: London

Mishkin, M.(1986) Paper presented at Merck, Sharp & Dohme Conference on Cognitive Neurochemistry, Terlings Park, Harlow, U.K.

Morris, R.G.   (1986)   'Short-term forgetting in senile dementia of the Alzheimer's type.'   Cognitive Neuropsychology, 3, 77-97

Moscovitch, M. (1982)   'A neuropsychological approach to perception and memory in normal and pathological aging.'   In Aging and Cognitive Processes (Eds F.I.M. Craik and S. Treub) Plenum N.Y.

Parkin, A.J. (1987)   Memory and Amnesia: an introduction.   Basil Blackwell Ltd.: Oxford

Ribot, T.   (1882)   Diseases of Memory. Appleton: New York

Sanders, H. & Warrington, E.   (1971)   'Memory for remote events in amnesic patients.'   Brain, 94, 661-668

Shimamura, A.P., Squire, L.R. (1986)   'Korsakoff's syndrome: a study of the relation between anterograde amnesia and remote memory impairment.'   Behavioral Neuroscience, 100, 165-170

Squire, L.R., Cohen, N.J. & Nadel, L.(1984)   'The medial temporal region and memory consolidation: a new hypothesis.'   In Memory Consolidation (Eds H. Weingartner & E. Parker). Erlbaum: Hillsdale, N.J.

Wilson, R.S., Kaszniak, A.W., & Fox, J.H.   (1981) 'Remote memory in senile dementia.'   Cortex, 17, 41-48

THE PRICES TEST: A SIMPLE TEST OF RETROGRADE AMNESIA

B. A. Wilson and J. Cockburn
University Rehabilitation Unit, Southampton General Hospital
and Rivermead Rehabilitation Centre, Oxford, England.

ABSTRACT

This paper describes a short test of retrograde amnesia. The Prices Test was developed because of limitations of other R.A. tests most of which are unsuitable for people younger than 40 years. One hundred control subjects estimated the cost of 25 common objects The 10 items showing least variability were selected for inclusion in the Prices Test which was then given to 200 brain injured people, including 20 severe amnesics. The results of 76 brain injured and 12 severe amnesics are reported here. All the amnesics gave estimates which were several years out of date. The advantages and disadvantages of the Prices Test are discussed.

Several procedures have been employed to assess retrograde amnesia. Squire and Cohen (1982), for example, used a test of famous events. Albert, Butters and Levin (1979) devised a test based on famous faces; a test by Stevens (1979) required the remembering of famous personalities; and a test by Muedell, Northen, Snowden and Neary (1980) used famous voices. All of these have one or more of the following disadvantages:-

(1) Contents on which the tests are based vary according to the amount of time they have been exposed to the testees over previous years.

(2) Overlearning will occur when certain faces, events or voices are so familiar through media exposure that they will be known long after the time period in which they were currently famous.

(3) People's knowledge of faces, events and voices will vary according to different levels of interest they have in those areas.

(4) Previous knowledge of earlier events and famous people may vary according to the respective ages of testees. The younger subjects might have been too young to notice certain media occasions or personalities.

(5) Such tests are likely to be insensitive to short periods of R.A. because the time intervals (usually decades) are too gross for some of the short R.A.'s occurring after severe head injury.

(6) Tests such as these are virtually impossible to update proportionally.

Although when work first began on the Prices Test there was

no conscious attempt made to avoid the deficiencies listed above, it became obvious as work progressed that the test did in fact overcome some of these design problems. In 1980 we tested a man with classic amnesic syndrome. Each time he was asked the name of the present Prime Minister he would reply, "Harold Wilson." We wondered if he would remember anything within the ten years that had elapsed since Harold Wilson's resignation. It would also be interesting to find out if the subject was 'locked in' the time period circumscribed by Harold Wilson's premiership. Answers to these questions would tell us whether the subject's period of retrograde amnesia was well defined and consistent.

We began by asking the subject how much he thought certain goods such as a pint of milk or a first class stamp would cost. His estimates were consistently inaccurate and out of date, some being more out of date than others. For example, he was in '1976 time' for some items but in '1968 time' for others. He believed the present year was 1972. His answers confirmed a diagnosis of an inconsistent period of R.A.

The second stage of what was the development of the Prices Test involved a more systematic approach to questioning. Initially, 25 items were selected for pricing on the basis of their familiarity with the general purchaser. The test was administered to 100 control subjects, most of them from the housewives' panel at the Applied Psychology Unit in Cambridge, and others from staff and relatives at Rivermead Rehabilitation Centre in Oxford.

The 10 items showing least variability were selected for the next version of the test, and the standard deviations of the 100 control subjects were used to establish the scoring procedure. The score for each item was obtained as follows:-

Step 1- Deduct the subject's estimated price from the actual price.

Step 2 - Divide by the Standard Deviation.

Step 3 - Score 0 if the result from Step 2 is equal to or less than one S.D.; if it is more than one but less than two S.D.'s score 1; if it is more than two but less than three S.D.'s score 2; if it is more than three S.D.'s but less than four score 3; if it is more than four score 4.

The range of scores is thus 0 to 4 and is similar to a Z score. Since then, a further 120 non brain-damaged controls have been assessed on the 10 item Prices Test (approximately 40 each year in 1983, 1984 and 1985). The standard deviations remain virtually identical to those obtained in the original sample of 100.

Table 1 illustrates the scoring of responses by a 42 year old patient with an amnesic syndrome following a ruptured aneurysm on the anterior communicating artery and a sub-arachnoid haemorrhage.

It can be seen from Table 1 that scores can be totalled to give an overall measure of severity. Over 200 brain injured and two futher groups of normal controls (young and old) have been tested since 1982. Results from a number of these are produced in Table 2.

From Table 2 we learn that certain patients overestimate the price of items. This is particularly true when frontal lobe or widespread brain damage is present. Thus, some of the post encephalitic patients overestimated grossly, and so did the Alzheimer and

Table 1

ITEM	ESTIMATED PRICE	ACTUAL PRICE	DIFFERENCE	S.D.	SCORE
Loaf of bread	20p	46p	26p	6p	-4
Pint of milk	15p	22p	7p	2p	-3
New 'mini' car	£700.00	£3098.00	£2398.00	£900.00	-2
20 'brand' cigarettes	60p	£1.25p	65p	13p	-4
A Guardian newspaper	20p	23p	3p	6p	0
Gallon of 4 star petrol	75p	£1.84	£1.09	17p	-4
1 lb. jar of jam	35p	35/46p	0	15p	0
Portion of fish & chips	£1.00	96p	4p	19p	0
First class stamp	15p	17p	2p	0.5p	-4
Cup of coffee British Rail	20p	32p	12p	8p	-1
				T =	-22

Examples of an amnesic patient's responses on the Prices Test (1984 prices)

Table 2

GROUP	N	UNDERESTIMATES		OVERESTIMATES	
		X̄	SD	X̄	SD
ELD CONTROLS	36	1.33	2.31	2.75	2.43
ALCOHOLICS	26	2.50	3.70	3.10	5.10
SEVERE H.I.	44	8.40	6.50	3.50	3.40
AMNESICS	12	15.66	6.80	1.16	1.53
POST-ENC.	4	12.25	10.87	8.75	12.35
ALZHEIMERS	9	17.20	6.50	5.70	3.50

100 control subjects under 65 years have a mean score of 0 as the test was standardised on this group.

Performance of groups on the Prices Test

litic patients overestimated grossly, and so did the Alzheimer and Frontal lobe syndrome patients. For such patients the Prices Test may be considered as similar to the Cognitive Estimates Test (Shallice, 1982). However, the Prices Test is more particularly suited to amnesic patients when attempting to assess the extent of their R.A. In order to plot this, Helen Kennerley and Janet Cockburn, working at Rivermead Rehabilitation Centre in Oxford, have charted the prices of the 10 items since 1974. Thus if we consider the data of the 42 year old amnesic patient presented in Table 1, we can plot these item-by-item in order to obtain a picture of how 'out of date' he is (Table 3).

Table 3

YEAR	Jam	Fish chip	Stamp	News paper	Coff-ee	Milk	Cigar ettes	Bread	Mini car	Petrol
pre-1974										*
1974									*	
1975										
1976								*		
1977										
1978							*			
1979					*	*				
1980										
1981				*						
1982			*							
1983										
1984	*	*								

Plotting the R.A. for each item

for a 42 year old amnesic patient

It is clear from Table 3 that the R.A. is not consistent. Obviously, prices change at different rates, and an explanation for discrepancies could be sought for here. However, further consideration will show that such an explanation cannot stand on its own. A new mini car and a cup of coffee, for example, increased by similar percentages from 1975 to 1984, yet the man's estimates for these were discrepant. Even wider differences can be seen in the estimates for jam and petrol, the two items which increased by similarly small percentages over the years. Variability in price increases does not therefore determine the extent of the R.A. In the unlikely event of inflation stopping completely we might have to abandon this test, although we would still pick up those with retrograde amnesia for some years to come.

An alternative way to score responses on the Prices Test is to determine the mean number of years the amnesic person is out of date. Thus, the patient in Table 3, with a severity score of −24, was, on average, 6.6 years out of date. Another patient, with a severity score of −30, was, on average, 11.15 years out of date.

It will be interesting to investigate the possibility that the Prices Test can be used to monitor recovery from Post Traumatic Amnesia following severe head injury. Certainly in the case of one young man who was tested on admission to a rehabilitation centre and again a month later, scores showed an improvement from −10 and +3 to −2 and +3.

The Prices Test appears to be a valid test of memory as the correlation between underestimates on the Prices Test and errors on the Rivermead Behavioural Memory Test (see Wilson, Baddeley and Cockburn, this volume) was 0.54 (N=42; p<.001). There was a low (0.12) and non-significant correlation between overestimates and errors on the RBMT, which is as we would expect.

The Prices Test is not only a valid test of memory but it also seems to be a valid test of remote memory. We have developed an autobiographical memory schedule with Michael Kopelman and Alan Baddeley (see Kopelman, this volume). Correlations were determined between scores on the Prices Test and scores on the Autobiographical Memory Schedule (AMS) for 20 amnesic subjects. There was a correlation of 0.72 (p<.01) between scores on the Prices Test and scores on the personal semantic section of the AMS (the section asking for details of childhood and early adulthood). There was a correlation of 0.52 (p<.05) between the scores on the Prices Test and the background information section of the AMS (that which asks for information about the subject's parents and siblings, and their own place and date of birth. Thus, people who had difficulty remembering their own past also had difficulty in estimating prices. As other tests of remote memory are developed we hope to get better validation of the Prices Test.

Like any test, the Prices Test has its weaknesses. It is, for instance, an unsuitable test for long term psychiatric patients, who will not have been in a position to buy goods on a regular basis over the years. Certain items are less precise than others: fish and chips cost less in the North of England than in the South; prices of items change at different rates, and some items (petrol is a good example) actually go up and down in price several times over the years; overall percentage increases can vary greatly, and petrol, which rose in percentage terms by only 0.6 between 1975 and 1984, contrasts with a pint of milk which increased by 340 per cent in the same period. For these reasons, individual items should be considered in isolation and testers should use the overall score.

We would not want to argue that the Prices Test is the only measure to use in investigations of remote memory. As an initial measure, however, it has advantages over many other tests of R.A. It reduces the effect of exposure/learning, it is easy to up-date, it is suitable for a wide range of age groups, and it is quick and easy to administer.

References

Albert, M.S., Butters, N. and Levin, J. (1979).'Memory for Events in Chronic Alcoholics and Korsakoff Patients', in Alcohol Intoxication and Withdrawal (Eds. H. Begleiter and B. Kissen) Plenum Press, New York.

Muedell, P.R., Northen, B., Snowden, J.S. and Neary, D. (1980) 'Long Term Memory for Famous Voices in Amnesic and Normal Subjects', Neuropsychologia, 18, 133–139.

Shallice,T. (1982) 'Specific Impairments of Planning', Philosophical Transactions of the Royal Society of London, B, 298, 199–209.

Squire, L.R., and Cohen, N.J. (1982) 'Remote Memory, Retrograde Amnesia and the Neuropsychology of Memory', in Human Memory and Amnesia (Ed. L. Cermak), pp. 275–303, Hillsdale, New Jersey.

Squire, L.R. and Slater, P.C. (1975) 'Forgetting in Very Long–Term Memory as Assessed by an Improved Questionnaire Taxonomy', Journal of Experimental Psychology: Human Learning and Memory, 104, 50–54.

Stevens, M. (1979) 'Famous Personalities Test: a Test for Measuring Remote Memory', Bulletin of the British Psychological Society, 32, 211.

Wilson, B.A. (1982) 'Success and Failure in Memory Training Following a Cerebral Vascular Accident', Cortex, 18, 581–594.

MEMORY FOR REPETITIONS AND WORD FRAGMENT COMPLETION IN NORMAL, DEPRESSED AND DEMENTED ELDERLY

John Joseph Downes,
Department of Experimental Psychology, University of Cambridge,
Downing Street, Cambridge CB2 3EB, England.

ABSTRACT

Frequency, temporal, and spatial information serve to define item information in terms of particular contextual attributes. The present study investigates the ability of normal, depressed, and demented elderly to remember frequency information under different test conditions. Despite being unable to discriminate between single and repeated words on a frequency estimation task, the performance of the dementia group on word fragment completion, an implicit memory task, showed a reliable increase in completions as a function of the number of repetitions.

INTRODUCTION

Numerous taxonomies characterising the diversity of memory operations and performance have been suggested. Two such systems are relevant to the present study: The proposed distinctions between automatic and effortful encoding (Hasher & Zacks, 1979), and between memory which can be evinced either implicitly or explicitly (Graf & Schacter, 1985).

Specifically, the experiments reported here focus on frequency of occurrence as a purported automatic attribute and on word fragment completion as a form of implicit memory. The dementia group were predicted to be particularly impaired on the frequency monitoring task and the rationale for also looking at implicit memory was to establish whether repetitions influenced performance on the word fragment completion task. This being the case, one can infer that despite the unavailability of frequency information, repetitions have some coded basis in the cognitive system of the memory-impaired, demented subject.

The results are of value for three reasons. First, there is considerable overlap between the Hasher and Zacks taxonomy and context theories of amnesia (Mayes, Meudell, & Pickering, 1985), and it follows that any work adopting the former as a framework will be of relevance to the latter. Secondly, the framework does seem to possess some ecological validity in that many of the reported complaints of early dementia involve loss of information about spatial, frequency, and recency attributes. Thirdly, results from the priming experiment should be of value for rehabilitation techniques. The vanishing cues technique described by Glinsky, Schacter, and Tulving (1986) is a good example of this approach, but less sophisticated studies require critical evaluation (Downes, 1987a).

METHOD

Subjects

Fourteen each of normal, depressed, and demented elderly people (mean ages 73.24, 75.78, 76.01 respectively) were tested on several occasions. The normal group were recruited from two day hospitals and most were attending for physiotherapy treatment of various arthritic complaints. None had a history of psychiatric illness. The majority of the depressed and demented groups were also community resident and attending daycare facilities on a regular basis. Subjects comprising these latter two groups had all been diagnosed by a consultant psychiatrist and had no other psychiatric or neurological complications.

All Subjects were screened with a selection of instruments to assess verbal IQ, verbal fluency, depression, and mental status, all of which were confirmatory for the appropriate diagnosis.

Procedure and Materials

Subjects were seen on several occasions for variable time periods depending on individual responses to the test procedures. On two of these test sessions subjects were given three lists, each containing words repeated either once, twice, or four times. Following list presentation one of three memory tests was given: An absolute frequency test, in which list words were given intermixed with new words and subjects were required to estimate how often each had been seen; a relative frequency test, in which all possible pairings of zero (i.e. new), one, two, and four frequency words were shown and subjects had to indicate which of the two had occurred more often; and thirdly, a forced choice recognition test. Instructions oriented the subject to the particuar task demands of the test being given. Words were printed on flash cards and stimulus presentation was paced at approximately three seconds per card during which time subjects were required to read aloud the word.

Word stimuli comprising the three lists were used for the word fragment completion test given towards the end of the session. Fragments were generated by the author deleting letters in a psuedo random fashion and this produced a final set containing 60% with initial letter stems, the more common stimulus type adopted in repetition priming studies. Equal numbers of list and test words were included to give a total of 24 at each session. The new words allowed the estimation of baseline completion levels. Instructions stressed that subjects should produce the first word that came to mind and no reference was given to the previous lists. As with the prior list words, fragments were shown on flash cards in the same style of print but with dashes substituting missing letters. Both accuracy and speed of response were recorded with a maximum permissable time of 10 seconds before subjects were shown the next test item.

RESULTS

Frequency Estimation

Figure 1 shows for each group the mean frequency estimates corresponding to actual frequencies of 0, 1, 2, and 4. An ANOVA applied to these data revealed a significant main effect for frequency, $F(3,114)=104.004$, $p<.0005$, and more importantly, a significant group by frequency interaction, $F(6,114)=8.597$, $p<.0005$. The lack of a significant group main effect reflects simply that there was no difference between groups when average estimates across all frequency levels were considered.

Simple main effects showed that for all three groups there was a significant frequency effect: Normal $F(3,114)=72.116$, $p<.0005$; depressed $F(3,114)=39.032$, $p<.0005$; demented $F(3,114)=10.050$, $p<.0005$, and polynomial trend contrasts revealed significant linear and quadratic components for each of the groups. Figure 1 shows that there is noticable group divergence after frequency 1 reflecting a differential ability to discriminate between single and repeated words. Further analysis revealed that for the dementia group mean estimates increased significantly only from 0 to 1. All comparisons were significant for the normal group and both the 0-1 and 1-2, but not the 2-4 comparisons for the depressed group.

Word Fragment Completion

Words in the frequency discrimination lists for the above experiment were shown either 1, 2, or 4 times. In addition, each was shown once more in the test phase and frequencies were adjusted accordingly to 2, 3, and 5. The frequency 1 words for the following analyses derive from the frequency judgement and recognition tests in which they served as new words. Evidence for a priming effect is based on an enhanced probability that a particular response is more readily produced over others. Evaluation of baseline completion rates is therefore critical when making between group comparisons. In terms of total completions (i.e. including both correct and alternative solutions across two tests) the following results were obtained: (the first mean value refers to new previously unseen words and the second to old, prior list words) normal 13.79, 18.07; depressed 11.07, 15.00; demented 9.08, 11.08. These estimates clearly suggest that prior exposure to a word affects subsequent completion performance, although baseline levels are clearly different. In addition, analysis of the number of correct and alternative completions comprising these totals established that the improvement was taken up entirely by correct completions. For new, previously unseen words and for old, prior list words mean values for correct completions as a proportion of the total were as follows: normal .600, .727; depressed .592, .728; demented .584, .752. Analysis of variance established that the only significant effect was for new/old words, $F(1,38)=19.58$ $p<.0005$. Thus, expressed as proportions, the increase in fragment completion due to prior exposure is equivalent across the three groups.

To examine whether repeating a word increases further the likelihood that fragments are completed correspondingly trend analyses were carried out on the following two related dependent variables: total number of completions per frequency cell and the number of completions as a proportion of baseline completion rate. Graphs of these two functions are shown in Figure 1. Of particular interest was whether the linear component relating completions to frequency of prior occurrence was significant for each of the three groups. Initial ANOVAs showed that for each dependent variable the

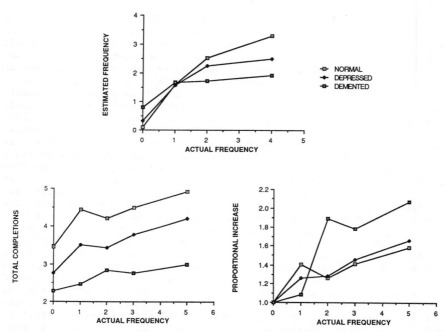

Figure 1 The top graph relates to the absolute frequency judgement experiment; the bottom two graphs to the word fragment completion experiment.

group by frequency interaction was not significant but the main effect of frequency was, F(4,148)=8.19 p<.0005 for total completions and F(4,148)=5.63 p<.0005 for the proportion score.

For the trend analyses, with total completions as the dependent variable, significant linear components were found for both the normal and the depressed groups (F(1,37)=8.963 p=.005, F(1,37)=9.926 p=.003 respectively) but for the demented group the effect was only significant using a more lenient error criterion F(1,37)=3.130 p=.085. In contrast, with the proportional score as dependent variable, the demented group, but not the other two groups, had a significant linear component: Normal F(1,37)=1.300, p=.262; depressed F(1,37)=2.141, p=.152; demented F(1,37)=6.432, p=.015.

DISCUSSION

The results from these two experiments are clearcut. First, both the depressed and demented groups are different from the normal group in their frequency estimations. Both the normal and depressed groups were able to discriminate between single and repeated words whereas the demented group could only discriminate between new and old words. This result shows that for the demented group, the information on which frequency estimations are based is unavailable and replicates the results of Strauss, Weingartner, and Thompson (1985). The present finding is also a more convincing demonstration because in the Strauss et al. study there was no evidence that their dementia patients could reliably distinguish between new and old items. This is important because there is a necessary dependence between item and attribute information, that is, attribute judgements are meaningful only if they are made in relation to items that are acknowledged as having been seen during the prior list exposure. For the depressed group, the mean estimates for frequencies 2 and 4 were not significantly different and in this respect they were different from the normal group. However, a separate experiment using relative frequency judgements showed that this divergence could be explained in terms of a response bias rendering them less likely to use extreme values (Downes, 1987b).

The second important finding is that repetition priming, as measured by word fragment completion in this experiment, is equivalent across all three groups. Thus, for none of the analyses did an interaction approach significance and group differences were absent when proportional measures were used. The present demonstration included baselines by which completion rates could be individually adjusted and it satisfied closely the criteria for implicit memory testing. Other studies which have examined stem completion ability in dementia (e.g. Miller, 1975; Diamond & Rozin, 1984) have reported a similar null effect, and Moscovitch, Winocur, and McLachlan (1986), using reading speed as an index of implicit memory, observed equivalent improvements for both normal and dementia groups. However, Shimamura, Salmon, Squire, and Butters, (1987) reported a deficit in word completion performance for their dementia group and it is possible that the presence of intact priming is a function of severity of the disorder. To check this, the dementia group was divided into two according to severity, the first of which showed no evidence of old/new discrimination (i.e. the curve for their mean requency estimates was essentially flat from 0 to 4) and the second which was clearly able to discriminate old from new, in terms of proportion correct completions, the groups were very similar with the more impaired group actually exhibiting the larger priming effect (first group: old .597, new .815; second group: old .573, new .698; an ANOVA revealed that the only significant effect was old/new).

The third important finding is that despite the failure of the dementia group to show any explicit appreciation of frequency of occurrence, repetitions did reliably enhance the probability that fragments would be completed. From this we can infer that frequency has some coded basis but the finding is also at odds with the view that implicit memory is context-free. The tendency to stress the differential effects of experimental manipulations on explicit and implicit forms of memory has been at the expense of some more obvious parallels between the two forms. However, the results provide little information concerning the source of these effects, that is, whether implicit memory is episodically based or due to a separate system or process. Conceivably, repetition could produce similar effects with each of these proposals. Finally, the finding suggests a further possible reason why normal-amnesic differences are sometimes found: Because there is some degree of cross-modal transfer to word fragment completion, then differences in covert rehearsal rates might lead to differences in completion rates.

REFERENCES

Diamond, R., & Rozin, P. (1984). Activation of existing memories in anterograde amnesia. Journal of Abnormal Psychology, 93, 98-105.

Downes, J.J. (1987a). Classroom reality orientation and the enhancement of orientation - A critical note. British Journal of Clinical Psychology, 26, 147-148.

Downes, J.J. (1987b). Memory for frequency of occurrence in old age depression and dementia. Manuscript in preparation.

Glinsky, E.L., Schacter, D.L., & Tulving, E. (1986). Learning and retention of computer related vocabulary in memory-impaired patients: Method of vanishing cues. Journal of Clinical and Experimental Neuropsychology, 8, 292-312.

Graf, P. & Schacter, D.L. (1985). Implicit and explicit memory for new associations in normal and amnesic subjects. Journal of Experimental Psychology: Learning, Memory and Cognition, 11, 501-518.

Hasher, L., & Zacks, R.T. (1979). Automatic and effortful processes in memory. Journal of Experimental Psychology: General, 83, 356-388.

Mayes, A.R., Meudell, P.R., & Pickering, A. (1985). Is organic amnesia caused by a selective deficit in remembering contextual information? Cortex, 21, 167-202.

Miller, E. (1975). Impaired recall and memory disturbance in presenile dementia. British Journal of Social and Clinical Psychology, 17, 143-148.

Moscovitch, M., Winocur, G., & McLachlan, D. (1986). Memory as assessed by recognition and reading time in normal and memory-impaired people with Alzheimer's disease and other neurological disorders. Journal of Experimental Psychology, 115, 331-347.

Shimamura, A.P., Salmon, D.P., Squire, L.R., & Butters, N. (1987). Memory dysfunction and word priming in dementia and amnesia. Behavioural Neuroscience, 101, 347-351.

Strauss, M.E., Weingartner, H., & Thompson, K. (1985). Remembering words and how often they occurred in memory impaired patients. Memory and Cognition, 13, 507-510.

Acknowledgements: The financial support of Liverpool University is gratefully acknowledged. The chapter was prepared while employed on a Major Award from the Wellcome Trust to Dr. Trevor W. Robbins.

PRIMING TASKS IN NORMAL SUBJECTS: WHAT DO THEY REVEAL ABOUT AMNESIA?

A. D. Pickering*, A. R. Mayes, and M. Shoqeirat
Department of Psychology, University of Manchester.
(*Now at Department of Psychology, Institute of Psychiatry, London.)

ABSTRACT

The effects of orienting tasks upon different kinds of priming memory were explored in two experiments. Related word-pair priming was shown to require a degree of intra-pair semantic elaboration whereas the amount of word-completion priming was no different after semantic or graphemic orienting tasks. The latter was, however, affected by a divided-attention manipulation, and thus must require some attentional effort. The implications for models of amnesic disorders, in which both kinds of priming may be normal, are briefly explored, stressing that the differences between preserved forms of priming could provide valuable insights.

Priming, and other forms of implicit memory, do not depend upon the conscious recollection of a prior event, but memory is demonstrated as a facilitation of task performance. Interest in these kinds of memory has been stimulated by recent demonstrations that they need not be affected in patients with severe memory disorders, and now several new investigations into the properties of priming have been conducted with normal subjects (see Schacter, in press, for a review). For example, Schacter (in press) reviews evidence that the degree of word-completion priming (Study: MOTEL; Cue: MOT---; Task: Complete cue to first word which comes to mind) is little different following graphemic or semantic orienting instructions during the study phase. This is in contrast to explicit memory performance (recall or recognition). Schacter also points out that the priming of idiomatic phrases (Study: SOUR GRAPES; Cue: SOUR; Task: Give first free-associate to cue which comes to mind) displays similar properties.

On the other hand, it has been demonstrated that word-completion priming is subject to associative influences. Graf and Schacter (1985) showed that after generating a sentence to link the words BALANCE and CHAIR, for example, the word-completion cue BALANCE-CHA--- produced more priming than the cue DETAIL-CHA--- (DETAIL had not been studied previously). Some amnesics showed this effect to a normal degree, but it was absent when BALANCE and CHAIR were studied under conditions which prevented their semantic elaboration (for example, comparing the number of vowels in the two words). Hence, it could be argued that some amnesic patients retain the ability to engage in a degree of semantic elaboration, even if they can only express the effects of this processing in an implicit memory task.

The current experiments also investigated priming in normal subjects. The first employed verbal paired-associates for which amnesics display normal priming when tested under free-association conditions (for example, see Mayes, Pickering, & Fairbairn, 1987). The effects of semantic and graphemic orienting tasks upon word-pair priming were studied and compared to the effects upon an explicit memory test (recognition). The second experiment derives from the view (for example, see Graf & Mandler, 1984) that word-completion priming is an automatic process, requiring little attentional capacity. The experiment explores the effects of a divided-attention orienting condition upon priming performance, in contrast with its effects on recall and recognition.

EXPERIMENT ONE

Subjects: 34 prospective psychology undergraduates, who were randomly assigned (17 per group) to the two orienting-task conditions (Semantic, denoted SEM; Non-Semantic, denoted NS).

Materials: A list of 26 moderately related paired-associates (e.g. ARMY-SOLDIER, denoted A-B) was chosen from a larger corpus of such pairs (see Mayes et al., 1987, for further details). These word-pairs formed the presentation list, shown to each subject in a fixed random order. The central 20 A-B pairs from the presentation list were used in subsequent memory tests. In the first of these, a free-association priming task, the A words from the critical pairs were presented, randomly interspersed with 20 similar, but not previously studied, A words (fillers) from the same corpus. This was followed by a two-alternative forced-choice (2AFC) recognition task involving the 20 A-B targets and 20 A-C distractors (e.g. ARMY-NAVY). A specially-programmed Apple II microcomputer controlled the experiment.

Procedure: The appropriate processing task, Semantic (classify relationship between pair members: SYNONYM/ANTONYM/OTHER) or Non-Semantic (comparing number of vowels in pair members), was explained to the subjects with examples. They were told to record responses via ticks on response sheets, and warned to expect a rapid presentation. The word-pairs were shown, one per 2.5 seconds. Immediately after this, subjects were introduced to a "second experiment" in which they would be shown a series of single words. They were told to write down the "very first word which is brought to mind" by each stimulus word. The importance of speed and compliance with these instructions was stressed. The 40 free-association stimuli were presented individually, in a fixed random order at a rapid, subject-paced rate (approximately four seconds per item). Finally, the subject-paced recognition test (20 items, individually presented) was given. Subjects indicated, in writing, the word-pair which they remembered studying earlier.

RESULTS AND DISCUSSION

The corrected priming measure (following Graf & Mandler, 1984) was the number of presented B words given as free-associates for the critical A words, minus the number of filler A words to which the 'correct' B word was given by chance. (SEM group mean: 5.8; NS group mean: 1.3.) The recognition measure was the number of

A-B word-pairs chosen, corrected in the standard fashion for a 2AFC test. (SEM: 15.9; NS: 6.6.)

A 2x2 mixed-design ANOVA revealed a significant interaction between the factors of 'Orienting Task' and 'Memory Test' ($F[1,32]= 8.7$, $p<0.01$), which arises because the free-association score is less affected by the orienting task manipulation than the recognition measure. With scaling differences, differential test sensitivities and possible floor effects, this interaction is of doubtful significance. However, what is absolutely clearcut is the large increase in priming in the SEM condition, compared with the near-floor performance of the NS group ($F[1,64]= 9.2$, $p<0.01$). This is in contrast to the result found for word-completion or idiomatic priming (see Schacter, in press), which might seem odd given the similarity between the idioms (e.g. SOUR-GRAPES) and the current material.

However, Graf and Schacter (1985) suggest that priming of words and idioms is not affected by the study conditions because these materials have 'highly integrated representations that are completely activated even when only some of their components are processed deliberately [p. 514].' Although moderately related word-pairs (e.g. ARMY-SOLDIER) do have preexisiting mental representations, they may well not be of this highly integrated, or unitized, kind. Hence, a degree of semantic elaboration of the pair members is needed for priming to occur. The present pattern of results resembles Graf and Schacter's (1985) findings concerning the influence of newly-established intra-pair associations on word-completion for one pair member. Interestingly, Graf and Schacter found comparable results for moderately related (e.g. RIPE-APPLE; Cue: RIPE-APP---), as well as previously unrelated, word-pairs. It is conceivable that more highly related pairs (e.g. TABLE-CHAIR) may have unitized representations, and priming of these pairs would be unaffected by study tasks. However, an independent measure of unitization is needed for this possibility to be tested.

One of us (MS) has recently replicated this experiment, with methodological refinements, in 40 further subjects. A different set of 20 word-pairs was used, with 40 fillers (cf. 20) in the free-association test, thus increasing the disguise of the study-test relationship. A different explicit memory test (cued recall) was also used. Finally, a more extensive debriefing was given, and subjects who gave indications that they had not fully complied with the free-association instructions were excluded from the analysis. The pattern of results was very similar: little or no priming occurred in the NS condition, and both priming and cued recall improved dramatically ($p<0.001$) in the SEM condition.

EXPERIMENT TWO

McDowall (1984) suggested that the recall deficits in amnesia may be caused by a reduction of processing capacity, and that this may be experimentally modelled with normal subjects in divided-attention (DA) conditions. If the model is valid, then the priming performance of DA normals should not be impaired relative to standard, single-task conditions, in the same way that amnesic priming is usually within normal limits. Moreover, no impairment in

DA conditions would give support to the view that priming of unitized entities (such as words) proceeds through the relatively automatic activation of their preexisting mental representations.
        The present experiment addressed these issues by looking at word-completion priming in three groups of subjects. The Non-Semantic group (NS) performed a vowel-counting task while the study-words were presented, whereas the semantic group (SEM) categorized them as living or non-living. The Divided-Attention (DA) group carried out the same semantic task, whilst simultaneously performing simple arithmetic (judging whether numbers were divisible by four).

METHOD

        Subjects: 108 undergraduates, who were randomly allocated (36 subjects per group) to the three conditions.
        Materials: Two lists of 20 common nouns were generated. Each word began with a different three-letter stem, each stem starting at least nine other common English words. One of these lists was studied by approximately half the subjects in each group, the remainder studying the other list. Subsequently, they were tested on a standard word-completion test (subjects were given the three-letter stems which they had to complete to give "the first word which came to mind"). The stems from the nonpresented list, along with 20 further three-letter stems, served as fillers in this test and were randomly interspersed amongst the critical items. Word-completion was followed by free recall and then by a 20-item 4AFC recognition test. Each item had three distractors: a word from the nonpresented list, a potential completion of one of the other twenty word-completion filler items, and one other word. The experiment was again automated (via Caramate projector).
        Procedure: The appropriate study-task was explained with examples. The DA group was informed that numbers would be presented under the words which they would be classifying. They were to put a second tick (in addition to the semantic judgement tick) if the number was divisible by four. It was stressed that both tasks were important but that they should try to allocate attention between the tasks roughly in the proportions 70 : 30 (Semantic : Arithmetic). They were forewarned of the rapid presentation rate (one item per three seconds). After study, there was a two-minute filled delay (writing 1 to 60 in three columns) followed by the instructions for the "second experiment" (word-completion). The importance of speed, and writing down the very first completion which came to mind, were strongly emphasized. Subjects, who on debriefing indicated non-compliance with these instructions, were excluded from the analysis. Following word-completion, two minutes was allowed for written free recall of words from the study list. Finally, the 4AFC recognition test was given, with guessing encouraged.

RESULTS AND DISCUSSION

        Firstly, the accuracy of the semantic processing task was assessed. For the SEM group, the mean number of correct classifications was 17.8 which was significantly reduced to 14.8 for the DA group ($t[70]= 3.35$, $p<0.001$). Furthermore, the arithmetic task, responsible for this reduction, was being performed at above-chance levels (DA group mean: 13.2 correct out of 20; chance= 10; t[35]= 5.8, p<0.0001).

The corrected priming measure was the number of presented words given as completions, minus the number of nonpresented words (from the other list) given as completions by chance. The recognition measure was the number of target words correctly identified, corrected in the standard fashion for a 4AFC test. The number of words correctly recalled was also scored. These data are summarised in Table 1.

Table 1: Mean corrected memory measures for the different orienting conditions.

Group	Memory Task		
	Word-Comp.	Recog.	Free Recall
NS	4.6	10.1	2.1
SEM	5.1	17.9	6.9
DA	3.7	15.4	4.4

A 3x3 mixed-design ANOVA revealed a highly significant interaction between 'Memory Test' and 'Orienting Task', which was further analysed by a priori one-tailed t-tests between pairs of means. Word-completion was not significantly different between the NS and SEM groups (t=0.76, p>0.2), whereas both recognition and free recall were vastly superior in the SEM group (t>7.3, p<0.0001 in both cases). This replicates earlier work (for example, Graf & Mandler, 1984). However, all memory measures were significantly reduced in the DA group compared with the SEM group (word-completion, t=2.1, p<0.02; free recall and recognition, t=3.8, p<0.001). Clearly, word-completion priming is not totally insensitive to the conditions under which the words were studied – it is reduced by divided-attention, relative to single task, conditions.

One might maintain that, relative to recall or recognition, word-completion priming is insensitive to attentional manipulations. This seems premature without independent evidence about the scaling properties and general sensitivities of all the memory measures concerned. Alternatively, one might argue that the DA subjects simply missed a (higher) number of the study words. This interpretation is vitiated by the near-zero correlations, in the DA group, between accuracy on the study-tasks and word-completion score (semantic/w-c: r= -0.09; arithmetic/w-c: r= +0.01), whilst the analogous correlations for recall were significant (r> +0.42 in both cases).

Finally, the results also provide evidence for the stochastic independence of priming and explicit forms of memory. In the SEM and DA groups, word-completion did not correlate with either recall or recognition (+0.02< r <+0.21). However, in the NS group, it correlated significantly with recall (r= +0.33, p=0.025) and even more strongly with recognition (r= +0.50, p<0.001). A tentative explanation for this pattern might be that in the NS condition there is no elaborated semantic information upon which explicit memory can draw, and so, particularly for recognition, it depends upon the activational processes which support word-completion. In the SEM and DA conditions, only explicit memory makes use of the elaborated semantic information, and so the stochastic dependence disappears.

GENERAL CONCLUSIONS

A divided-attention manipulation in normal subjects is not a good model of amnesia, for it does not leave word-completion priming intact. This result also suggests that such priming is not 'automatic', but depends on attentional processing. Nissen and Bullemer's (1987) findings, with a different type of implicit memory, support these conclusions. They showed that normals in a dual-task condition did not demonstrate any implicit mnemonic benefit from a repeating sequence in one task (choice RT), unlike normals or Korsakoff amnesics performing choice RT alone.

Finally, this work further emphasizes that priming is not a unitary phenomenon. The first experiment, using moderately related word-pairs, showed that a certain amount of intra-pair semantic elaboration is needed if priming is to occur. (As word-pair priming is normal in amnesics, this implies that these patients can accomplish such processing.) By contrast, the second study, confirming previous research, indicated that semantic elaboration has little effect on the priming of single words. By delineating the differences between forms of priming in this way, one may reveal a common denominator which could explain why these forms are preserved in amnesia.

REFERENCES

Graf, P., & Mandler, G. (1984). Activation makes words more accessible, but not necessarily more retrievable. Journal of Verbal Learning and Verbal Behavior, 23, 553-568.

Graf, P., & Schacter, D. L. (1985). Implicit and explicit memory for new associations in normal and amnesic subjects. Journal of Experimental Psychology: Learning, Memory and Cognition, 11, 501-518.

McDowall, J. (1984). Processing capacity and recall in amnesic and control subjects. In L. R. Squire & N. Butters (Eds.), The neuropsychology of memory (pp. 63-66). New York: Guilford Press.

Mayes, A. R., Pickering, A., & Fairbairn, A. (1987). Amnesic sensitivity to proactive interference: Its relationship to priming and the causes of amnesia. Neuropsychologia, 25, 211-220.

Nissen, M. J., & Bullemer, P. (1987). Attentional requirements of learning: Evidence from performance measures. Cognitive Psychology, 19, 1-32.

Schacter, D. L. (in press). Implicit memory: History and current status. Journal of Experimental Psychology: Learning, Memory and Cognition.

COGNITIVE PROCESSES INVOLVED IN TEMPORAL CONTEXTUAL MEMORY

H.J. Sagar
Department of Neurology, Royal Hallamshire Hospital,
Sheffield, U.K.

E.V. Sullivan
Ashton Graybiel Spatial Orientation Laboratory,
Waltham, Massachusetts, U.S.A.

ABSTRACT

Previous studies of normal subjects and amnesic patients have suggested that temporal context of past events is processed in memory independently from event content. We have investigated remote memory, recency discrimination and sequencing of nonmnemonic material in Parkinson's disease, Alzheimer's disease and the amnesic patient, H.M. The results showed dissociations between temporal context and content in recent memory and remote memory for personal and public events. Impaired temporal contextual memory in Parkinson's disease was associated with defective nonmnemonic sequencing. We propose a role for a frontally based mediational system, superordinate to memory, in the processing of temporal context.

INTRODUCTION

Many theories of memory embrace the concept that temporal context of past events is linked to particular subprocesses of memory although the nature of these processes differs among theories. The episodic/semantic theory of memory processing, for example, identifies episodic memory with autobiographical events defined by specific temporal and spatial context, whereas semantic memory is concerned with rules, language and world knowledge poorly defined by time and place (Tulving, 1972; Kinsbourne and Wood, 1975). Broader theories of contextual memory distinguish processing of temporal or temporospatial context from memory for event content but do not stress any obligatory relationship to autobiographical events (Huppert and Piercy, 1976; Hasher and Zacks, 1979; Hirst and Volpe, 1982). The role of temporal contextual processes in the handling of nonmnemonic material is rarely addressed.

Our studies of Parkinson's disease (PD), Alzheimer's disease (AD) and global amnesia (Sagar, 1987; Sagar et al., 1984; 1985a, b, and in submission; Sullivan et al., 1985, and in submission) provide converging evidence to suggest that temporal context is served by neural systems distinct from event or content processing. The relevant cognitive mechanisms may involve nonmnemonic as well as mnemonic material. The pattern of cognitive impairment in PD supports the notion that temporal judgements in memory are served by a higher order process for the manipulation, discrimination and comparison of facets of perceptual or stored information, such as the frontally-based cognitive mediational system (Warrington, 1985; Warrington and Weiskrantz, 1982). Our studies embrace remote memory for personal and public events, recency discrimination and sequencing of nonmnemonic material and are summarised in the following sections.

Remote Memory

For personal events, subjects received a modified version of Crovitz's test (Crovitz and Schiffman, 1974) in which they related personally experienced events that occurred at a specific time and place and were examined for consistency 24 hr later. Subjects estimated the dates of specific, consistent episodes. Recall tests of the list of cue words were given three times: after recall of episodes on day 1, and before and after recall of episodes on day 2. Patients with AD were impaired on all measures ($p < 0.01$). Patients with PD were inconsistent in dating; this deficit occurred even in patients who achieved normal scores on minimental state examination for dementia and who showed normal recall of the cue words as well as the episodes ($p < 0.001$).

The same subjects were required to recall and recognise the content and date of past public events from news photographs. Compared with the normal control group, the AD and PD groups showed a gradient of deficit in the recall of event-related information whereby remote events were relatively spared (for PD, $p < 0.02$; for AD, $p < 0.05$). Neither group, however, showed a gradient in the recall of date of the same event (Fig. 1). Thus, whatever the origin of the temporal gradient, the qualitatively different retention functions for event and date, both equally temporally-specific, show that event recall and dating capacity are dissociable processes. Content/scenario information is not temporally specific, and shows no gradient of deficit. In recognition, AD patients were impaired on all measures ($p < 0.001$); PD patients, regardless of severity of dementia, were however disproportionately impaired in recognition of date such that their content-dating difference scores were higher than those of the normal control ($p < 0.02$) or the AD ($p < 0.05$) groups. This result suggests that the pathology of PD may selectively disrupt remote memory processes serving dating capacity.

Recency Discrimination

The results of the remote memory experiments suggested that temporal contextual information is processed in memory independently from event content and may be selectively disrupted by disease. In a second experiment, we examined whether these conclusions applied also to memory for newly acquired information. The study participants were patients with PD, patients with AD and the amnesic patient H.M. (Scoville and Milner, 1957).

Subjects were presented with a series of words and were given item (content) recognition or recency discrimination tasks of stimuli presented 1 to 150 items earlier in the series. Two main

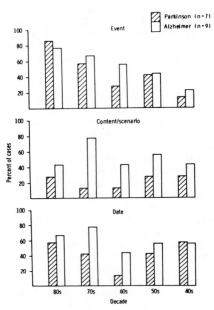

Figure 1
　　　Percentage of subjects in each patient group with scores below
the normal range in the Famous Scenes Recall Test.   Results
represented by decade for different classes of information.

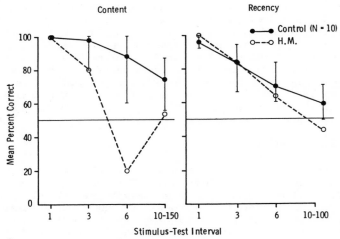

Figure 2
　　　Scores (mean % correct) of HM and control subjects related to
stimulus-test interval on the Verbal Temporal Ordering Test.
Vertical bars denote range of control scores.

results emerged: firstly, AD patients were impaired in making
content and recency judgements (p<0.002), whereas PD patients, like
patients with frontal-lobe lesions (Milner and Petrides, 1984),
were selectively impaired in recency discrimination (p<0.02; Group
x Task interaction, p<0.05); secondly, H.M.'s ability to make
recency judgements was normal while his recognition of content was
impaired (Fig. 2).

    These results suggest that judgements of temporal order
require neural mechanisms distinct from those serving memory for
content information, whether of recent or remote events. Temporal
contextual processing is selectively disrupted in PD but spared in
patient H.M.

Sequencing of nonmnemonic material

    In order to test whether the temporal ordering deficits
observed in PD patients occurred only in tasks requiring
manipulation of remembered items, we administered the Picture
Arrangement subtest of the WAIS-R, a sequencing task with minimal
mnemonic demands, to patients with PD or AD and to patient H.M. As
control measures, subjects received the Vocabulary subtest of the
WAIS-R, a test of overall intelligence, and the Blessed Dementia
Scale (BDS), a test of general cognitive impairment. The
Vocabulary-Picture Arrangement difference scores of the PD group,
regardless of severity of dementia, were greater than those of the
normal control group (p<0.02), the AD group (p<0.05) (Fig. 3) or
H.M., who achieved a score of 9 on both subtests. Furthermore, the
sequencing deficit of the PD group was not due entirely to an
inability to shift set: PD patients with normal BDS scores showed
no set-shifting deficit yet were impaired in sequencing (p<0.001)
whereas PD patients with abnormal BDS scores were impaired on both
measures (p<0.002).

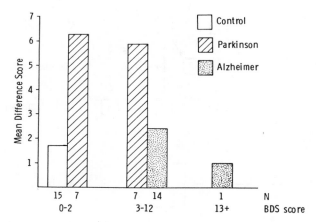

Figure 3
    Mean difference between Vocabulary and Picture Arrangement
scaled scores related to severity of dementia (BDS score; normal 0-
2).

These results show that PD patients, who show particular difficulty in judgements of temporal order, are also selectively impaired in a nonmnemonic sequencing task.

Model of temporal contextual processing

Our results show that dating capacity follows qualitatively different retention functions from event recall in remote memory and probably involves separate processes. The findings in H.M. indicate that recency discrimination is dissociable from item recognition in recent memory. In PD, the selective disruption of Picture Arrangement as well as recency discrimination and dating capacity suggests that poor ordering in PD involves nonmnemonic as well as mnemonic material. Many of the defective functions in PD are traditionally those associated with frontal-lobe function. Taken together, these observations suggest that deficits in a single frontally-based ordering system, superordinate to memory, may explain the majority of our experimental findings in PD.

Within the realm of memory, we propose that a declarative trace normally serves recall or recognition of single events. Some information of past events is, however, simultaneously encoded in parallel in a system that is independent of medial temporal structures but which is available to a frontally-based cognitive mediational system, similar to that proposed by Warrington and Weiskrantz (1982) and Warrington (1985). This system organises and structures <u>multiple</u> memoranda along functionally coherent lines, but is not operative in recall or recognition of <u>single</u> traces (Fig. 4). We propose that the system also serves nonmnemonic as well as mnemonic domains and may be involved in many of the cognitive and motor deficits of PD.

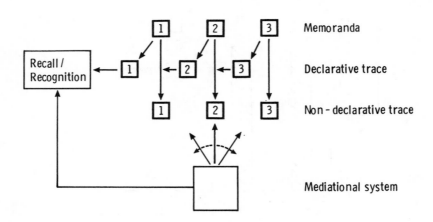

Figure 4

Cognitive mediational model of temporal judgement and sequencing of nonmnemonic material.

REFERENCES

Crovitz, H.F. and Schiffman, H. (1974) 'Frequency of episodic memories as a function of their age', Bulletin of the Psychonomics Society, 4, 517-518.

Hasher, L. and Zacks, R.Y. (1979) 'Automatic and effortful processes in memory', Journal of Experimental Psychology: General, 83, 356-388.

Hirst, W. and Volpe, B.T. (1982) 'Temporal order judgements with amnesia', Brain and Cognition, 1, 294-306.

Huppert, F.A. and Piercy, M. (1976) 'Recognition memory in amnesic patients: effect of temporal context and familiarity of material', Cortex, 12, 3-20.

Kinsbourne, M. and Wood, F. (1975) 'Short-term memory processes and the amnesic syndrome', in Short-term memory (Eds. D. Deutsch and J.A. Deutsch), pp. 258-291, New York, Academic Press.

Milner, B. and Petrides, M. (1984) 'Behavioural effects of frontal-lobe lesions in man', Trends in Neuroscience, 7, 403-407.

Sagar, H.J., Cohen, N.J., Corkin, S. and Growdon, J.H. (1985a) 'Dissociations among processes in remote memory', in Memory dysfunctions: an integration of animal and human research from preclinical and clinical perspectives. Annals of the New York Academy of Sciences (Eds. D.S.Olton, E. Gamzu, S. Corkin), 444, pp. 533-535.

Sagar, H.J., Gabrieli, J.D.E., Sullivan, E.V. and Corkin, S. (1984) 'Temporal contextual memory in amnesia', Society for Neuroscience Abstracts, 10, 384.

Sagar, H.J., Sullivan, E.V., Cohen, N.J., Gabrieli, J.D.E., Corkin, S. and Growdon, J.H. (1985b) 'Specific cognitive deficits in Parkinson's disease', Journal of Clinical and Experimental Neuropsychology, 7, 158.

Sagar, H.J. (1987) 'Clinical similarities and differences between Alzheimer's disease and Parkinson's disease', Journal of Neural Transmission (in press).

Scoville, W.B. and Milner, B. (1957) 'Loss of recent memory after bilateral hippocampal lesions', Journal of Neurology, Neurosurgery and Psychiatry, 20, 11-21.

Sullivan, E.V., Sagar, H.J., Gabrieli, J.D.E., Corkin, S. and Growdon, J.H. (1985) 'Sequencing deficits in Parkinson's disease', Journal of Clinical and Experimental Neuropsychology, 7, 160.

Tulving, E. (1972) 'Episodic and semantic memory', in Organization of memory (Eds. E. Tulving and W. Donaldson), New York, Academic Press.

Warrington, E.K. (1985) 'A disconnection analysis of amnesia', Annals of the New York Academy of Sciences, 444, 72-77.

Warrington, E.K. and Weiskrantz, L. (1982) 'Amnesia: a disconnection syndrome?', Neuropsychologia, 20, 233-248.

SUBJECTIVE MEMORY AFTER SUBARACHNOID HAEMORRHAGE

Christer Larsson/1+2, Jerker Ronnberg/6, Lars-Goran Nilsson/1
Ake Forssell/3, Margareta Lindberg/2+4 and Harald Fodstad/5
Departments of Psychology/1, Physical Medicine and
Rehabilitation/2, Neuroradiology/3, Surgery/4 and Neurosurgery/5
University of Umea and Department of Education
and Psychology/6, Linkoping University, Sweden

ABSTRACT

A subjective memory questionnaire (SMQ) and a set of verbal memory tests were administered to 224 patients who had suffered from subarachnoid haemorrhage (SAH). No difference between the total SMQ scores for the SAH population and a control group was obtained. Patients with aneurysms of the middle cerebral arteries, but not patients with other loci had lowered SMQ ratings. This result was not related to the number of patients with a verbal memory deficit. It appears that for correct metamemory judgments to occur the function of the frontal/prefrontal cortex must remain intact. Finally, suggestions for improving the SMQ are made.

INTRODUCTION

One of the emerging trends in the psychology of memory is the focus on subjective reports (Herrmann, 1983). In spite of problems related to the validity of subjective memory questionnaires (Morris, 1983), some studies have dealt with the possibility that questionnaire data might represent an important key for the understanding of various kinds of brain injury. Temporal lobectomized patients rated themselves as having poorer memory (Bennett-Levy, Polkey and Powell, 1980), while patients with severe head injuries did not report higher frequencies of memory failures than normal controls (Sunderland, Harris and Baddeley, 1983).

The results seem somewhat inconclusive with respect to the sensitivity of subjective questionnaires' potential for reflecting brain injury. To elucidate this problem, the present study was conducted on a population of patients with subarachnoid haemorrhage (SAH). The following main issues were addressed: First, is it possible to distinguish the SAH population from a control group on the basis of subjective ratings only? Second, are certain items in the questionnaire more sensitive than other items, and can they be classified into relevant categories? Third, can subgroups in the SAH population be identified in terms of subjective ratings? The last question was approached by analysing the effect of different loci of the ruptured aneurysms. Finally, performance on a set of verbal memory tests was used to identify patients with a verbal memory deficit.

METHOD
Subjects

Between 1969-80, 578 patients with SAH were treated at the

Department of Neurosurgery, Umea University Hospital. In 1983, a follow-up study revealed that 314 were still alive. Patients with dementia or brain damage not caused by SAH, severe aphasia, or with difficulties in understanding Swedish were excluded from memory testing. As one part of the follow-up study, verbal memory tests and a subjective memory questionnaire were administered to 224 patients, 92 men and 132 women. The average age of the patients at the time of testing was 56 years, (range 18-80), and the time elapsed since SAH varied from 2-14 years. A total of 192 patients had verified ruptured intracranial aneurysms, while 32 had an SAH of unknown origin.

The SMQ scores of the SAH population were compared to the scores of a control group (n=36) matched for age and education. Another control group (n=12) was used for the verbal memory tests, matched to the SAH patients younger than 50 years old for age and education.

Material

Memory questionnaire: A Swedish version of the Subjective Memory Questionnaire (SMQ) was used (Bennett-Levy and Powell, 1980). The questions were in two formats: (1) How good is your memory for, e.g., faces, names of people, everyday times? (items 1-36) and (2) Do you often, e.g., forget a particular word in mid-sentence? (items 37-43). The responses were given on a five-point scale, from very bad to very good for items 1-36, and from very rarely to very often for items 37-43.

Verbal memory tests: The tasks used were free recall and cued recall of words. Eight lists with twelve words each were presented. Each list consisted of four words from three semantic categories. After the presentation of each list the subjects were to recall immediately, in any order, as many words as possible. A final free recall test of all lists was carried out after ten minutes. Finally, after another ten minutes, a final cued recall test was administered. The 24 semantic categories to which the presented words belonged were then presented as retrieval cues.

RESULTS

The mean total SMQ score for the control group was 142.0, whereas the Bennett-Levy and Power (1980) control group score was 145.9. Restricting the control group age range to that of Bennett-Levy and Powell (1980) produced an even closer score, 145.0. Thus, there were encouragingly small or nonexisting cultural differences between the two studies. Also, age was not a potent factor in either the control group or the SAH population, (cf. Martin, 1986). The age variable was therefore excluded from further analyses.

There was no overall difference between the control group and the SAH population, 142.0 vs 135.6. Neither Time since SAH nor Sex affected the SMQ scores significantly (p>.05). However, it was revealed that the SAH patients rated themselves as having worse memory than the controls on five items, (n. 7) appointments, (n.18) facts about people, (n.37) set off to do something, then can't remember what, (n.38) forget what you were going to say in mid-sentence and (n.39) forget a particular word in mid-sentence. Four of these items (ns. 7, 37, 38 and 39) may be con-

sidered as "remembering to remember' tasks which require a high level
of self-initiated activity (cf. Craik, 1983). Three of those items
(ns. 37, 38, 39) particularly emphasize the importance of carrying
out an action based on the patient's own intention without being
triggered by external events. Only one of the five items concerns
fact learning (n.18). This may thus be seen as an a posteriori
categorization of the items not based on a memory systems view.
Episodic-semantic categories (Tulving, 1983), produced a priori by
ten professional memory psychologists, did not reveal any main effect
of type of category or interaction with the group factor (p>.05).

        Since amnesia is most frequently reported and studied in
patients with ruptured aneurysms of the anterior communicating artery
(ACoA) (e.g. Corkin, Cohen, Sullivan, Clegg, Rosen and Ackerman,
1985), the SAH population was divided into one subgroup consisting of
such patients as well as into subgroups with other loci (See Table
1). The rationale for this was to explore whether the memory
dysfunction after ruptured aneurysm of the ACoA could be captured by
the SMQ, and also, if other loci produce a memory disorder with
qualities that could be tapped by the SMQ. As there were no
significant differences between left and right hemisphere aneurysms,
the basic data summarized in Table 1 are collapsed over this
variable. Since age had an effect on performance on the verbal
memory tests but not on the SMQ, an age correction was made for Table
1 (prevalence of verbal memory deficit) in order to reveal deficits
caused by the SAH itself.

TABLE 1

SMQ total score and prevalence of verbal memory deficit* in terms
of the location of the ruptured aneurysm

Location	SMQ total score	t-value	Prevalence of verbal memory deficit
Anterior Communicating Artery	135.8	1.45	.62
Middle Cerebral Arteries	132.4	2.55**	.51
Internal Carotid Arteries	136.3	1.41	.44
Other	136.0	1.27	.46
SAH, unknown origin	137.5	0.99	.50
Total	135.6	1.79	.51

* Deficit defined as one out of three tests (immediate free, final
free or final cued recall of words) below the cut-off score of 1.25
SD from the mean for the control group (cf. Corkin et al., 1985).
**Significantly lower than the control group, p<.05, two-tailed.

        Somewhat surprisingly only patients with ruptured aneurysms
of the middle cerebral arteries (MCA) produced significantly lower
SMQ scores than the controls. This result, however, is not
proportional to the number of patients with an objective memory
deficit on the verbal memory tests (see Table 1). Patients with
ruptured aneurysms of the ACoA were afflicted by the largest
quantitative deficit, but this was not sufficient to affect the SMQ

scores.
          Closer analysis of the data for the patients with aneurysms
of the MCA revealed that those items which were given significantly
lower ratings overall also constituted critical items in this
subgroup.   In addition to these five items another three, (n.5)
shopping lists, (n.12) number of a house/flat and (n.21) when you've
borrowed something, giving it back, were included in their lowered
ratings. Of these three, item 21, could be included in the category
of "remembering to remember" items.

TABLE 2

SMQ total score in terms of the location of the ruptured   aneurysm
             and presence of verbal memory deficit.

Location		SMQ total score	t-value
Anterior Communicating	Deficit	134.4	1.54
Artery	No Deficit	138.1	0.78
Middle Cerebral	Deficit	131.1	2.48*
arteries	No Deficit	133.8	1.81
Internal Carotid	Deficit	134.2	1.75
Arteries	No Deficit	138.2	0.81
Other	Deficit	124.6	3.05*
	No Deficit	145.7	0.69
SAH, unknown origin	Deficit	130.2	2.13
	No Deficit	144.8	0.58
Total	Deficit	131.8	2.70*
	No Deficit	138.7	0.93

* significantly lower than the control group, p<.05, two-tailed.

          In our final analysis of subgroups, the objective beha-
vioural criterion based on the verbal memory tests was used.   Table 2
shows a main effect of verbal memory deficit implying that verbal
memory capability has a rather substantial effect on everyday memory
ratings.   With respect to loci and verbal memory deficit, patients
with ruptured aneurysms of ACoA and internal carotid arteries (ICA)
did not report any significant subjective memory problem.   On the
other hand, all the other patients with a verbal memory deficit
including those with SAH of unknown origin, believed that their
memory was failing.

CONCLUSIONS AND IMPLICATIONS
          In order to interpret the results it is necessary to
realize that the rupture of ACoA aneurysms may affect the blood
supply of the medial and part of the lateral frontal lobe (greater
part of the frontal/prefrontal cortex), while the rupture of MCA
aneurysms may affect the lateral temporal lobe and part of the

lateral frontal lobe. The ICA gives off a number of small arteries, in addition to the MCA and anterior cerebral artery, that irrigate subcortical structures, e.g. the hypothalamus (Kolb and Whishaw, 1985).

The SAH population as such cannot be identified by means of the SMQ instrument. However, on a localization-of-the-aneurysm basis, it is possible to obtain positive identification of patients with ruptured aneurysms of the MCA, but not of patients with aneurysms of the ACoA and ICA. This result suggests that the frontal/prefrontal cortex must be preserved in order to render a correct metamemory judgment possible. A host of independent evidence (e.g. Ingvar, 1985) suggests that the frontal/prefrontal regions of the brain are responsible for the production and storage of behavioural programmes and plans for guidance for future behaviour. It appears likely also that the information handled by other regions of the brain is perceived relative to these action plans. No other region is capable of this supervisory function (Ingvar, 1985). Patients with ACoA aneurysms do not perceive their memory failures because the feedback between existing behavioural plans and the actual behaviour is possibly disrupted. Therefore, their SMQ ratings are not lowered. Why then do patients with ICA aneurysms not give lower SMQ ratings? One may speculate that it depends on the fact that the rupture of ICA aneurysms disrupt the blood supply of subcortical structures. These structures also project to the cortical regions, for example the frontal/prefrontal cortex. Damage may therefore disturb the "flow" of information to and from these regions with a poor subjective memory as a consequence.

For task analysis purposes it is important to note that it is principally the "remembering to remember" items that are, both on a general level and for the patients with MCA aneurysms, responsible for the subjectively perceived deficit. These items are considered to be very personally relevant for social and emotional reasons. For example, if you do not remember what to say when giving a lecture (cf. item 38), or if you do not find the proper words (cf. item 39) this would be very embarrassing. Socially it is very important to keep appointments (cf. item 7) and if you forget to give things back that you have borrowed, for example money, (cf. item 21) the number of friends you have will probably decrease.

To improve questionnaires, it is therefore suggested that items should be used that are: a) personally relevant in the sense discussed above; b) oriented towards task requirements of the "remembering to remember" type; and c) more clear cut with respect to temporal reference, that is, the patients must be aware of whether the questions refer to pre- or postmorbid events. This source of confounding may have been decisive as we discussed the a priori classification into episodic and semantic memory systems.

In sum, the SMQ seems to have some validity since it has been possible to claim sensitivity for patients with ruptured MCA aneurysms as well as for temporal lobectomized patients (Bennett-Levy et al., 1980). As a proposal for further research, real-life "tests" compatible with a questionnaire based on the three suggestions mentioned above, would probably boost the validity of the questionnaire as well as the ecological validity of the behavioural tests.

ACKNOWLEDGEMENTS

This research was supported by grants from the Swedish Council for Research in the Humanities and the Social Sciences and from the Karl Oskar Hansson Fund. We are indebted to the other members of the "SAH-group", Umea University Hospital: K.A. Angquist, A. Fogelsjoo, A.R. Fugl-Meyer and K. Fugl-Meyer.

REFERENCES

Bennett-Levy, J., Polkey, C.E. and Powell, G.E. (1980). 'Self-report of memory skills after temporal lobectomy: The effect of clinical variables', Cortex, 16, 543-557.

Bennett-Levy, J. and Powell, G.E. (1980). 'The Subjective Memory Questionnaire (SMQ). An investigation into the self-reporting of "real-life" memory skills', British Journal of Social and Clinical Psychology, 19, 177-188.

Corkin, S., Cohen, N.J., Sullivan, E.V., Clegg, R.A., Rosen, T.J. and Ackerman, R.H. (1985). 'Analyses of global memory impairments of different etiologies', in Memory dysfunctions: An integration of animal and human research. From clinical and preclinical perspective (Eds D.S. Elton, E. Gamzu and S. Corkin), Annals of New York Academy of Sciences, 444.

Craik, F.I.M. (1983).'On the transfer of information from temporary to permanent memory', Philosophical Transactions of the Royal Society, London B, 302, 341-359.

Herrmann, D.J. (1983). 'Questionnaires for memory', in Everyday memory, actions and absentmindedness (Eds. J. Harris and P.E. Morris), Academic Press, London.

Ingvar, D.H. (1985). 'Memory of the future: an essay on the temporal organization of conscious awareness', Human Neurobiology, 4, 127-136.

Kolb, B. and Whishaw, I.Q. (1985). Fundamentals of human neuropsychology (2nd ed.), Freeman, New York.

Martin, M. (1986). 'Aging and patterns of change in everyday memory and cognition', Human Learning, 5, 63-74.

Morris, P.E. (1983). 'The validity of subjective reports on memory', in Everyday memory, actions and absentmindedness (Eds. J. Harris and P.E. Morris), Academic Press, London.

Sunderland, A., Harris, J.E. and Baddeley, A.D. (1983). 'Do laboratory tests predict everyday memory? A neuropsychological study', Journal of Verbal Learning and Verbal Behavior, 22, 341-357.

Tulving, E. (1983). Elements of episodic memory. Oxford University Press, London.

MEMORY
AND AGING

MEMORY AND AGING: TOWARD AN EXPLANATION

Gillian Cohen
The Open University, Milton Keynes, U.K.

ABSTRACT

Research on the effects of aging on memory is currently a growth industry, and the practical importance and theoretical interest of this area is reflected in the number, range and variety of the studies reported here. Although united in the common enterprise of seeking to explain how and why memory is affected by normal aging, it is apparent that very different routes towards this goal are chosen. This chapter attempts to analyse some of the approaches exemplified in this symposium, and to indicate how they differ in aims and scope; and, finally, to show how some of the findings might fit together to form a more global account of memory and aging.

EXPERIENCE OR EXPERIMENT?

One important distinction echoes the methodological issues that are a major concern of this conference. This is the distinction between age effects in everyday memory and age effects in laboratory experiments on memory.

Several of the studies reported here focus on age differences in performance for activities or experiences that occur naturally in everyday life. Burke responded to a challenge issued by her subjects to explain why elderly people subjectively experience increasing difficulty in retrieving proper names. McEvoy and Moon developed and evaluated training procedures designed to improve memory in everyday situations that involve remembering faces, routes, or appointments, or remembering to perform routine tasks such as taking medicine or watering plants. Abson and Rabbitt studied age differences in subjective estimates of everyday memory ability, and in self ratings of the frequency of everyday memory lapses such as losing objects. Kemper analysed age differences in the syntactic complexity of the spontaneous, naturally occurring language of written diaries.

Traditional laboratory experiments are represented by other studies such as Belmont, Freeseman and Mitchell's examination of age differences in the strategies people use to remember digit lists, or Light's series of experiments on priming effects.

Although both approaches are examining the effects of aging on memory there is surprisingly little common ground between them. They usually have different goals. Where the aim of the research is primarily pragmatic, as in the development of remedial training procedures, or the design of appropriate environments, or the assessment of an individual's competence to cope with the demands of everyday life, it is obviously more appropriate to focus on naturally occurring situations. Both Herrman, Rea and Andrzejewski, and McEvoy and Moon have noted that training in the kind of general memory strategies developed in laboratory research, such as the method of loci, the use of imagery or categorization, yield only small and transient improvements in specific everyday tasks. The absence of significant correlations between performance on laboratory memory tasks and self ratings of everyday memory ability (Abson and Rabbitt) also underlines the difficulty of using measures derived from one sphere to predict or explain performance in the other.

Several of the studies reported here suggest that, in everyday life, age-related impairment of cognitive components such as speed of processing, or working memory span, can be offset, masked or neutralized by the use of external aids, or by retreating to a life style which is cognitively less demanding. Elderly people may also maintain their performance at a high level in particular domains such as chess, or bridge (Charness, 1985) by accumulating a rich and highly specialized knowledge base which enables them to continue operating efficiently within that domain. It has also been suggested that age-related changes in cognitive function may sometimes be exacerbated by social and emotional factors such as depression, stress or low self-esteem, and, while opting out of demanding activities may preserve the illusion of competence, it could also initiate a downward spiral of progressive disuse of abilities and lowering of demands. Because of all these factors, age effects that are apparent in laboratory experiments may not be reflected in everyday life.

When the aim of the research is theoretical rather than practical, traditional laboratory experiments, with better opportunities to control and to measure performance, have obvious advantages. By manipulating the variables of interest, the researcher can reveal patterns of impairment and preservation, and may be able to localize the age deficit in a particular task component or operation, and formulate an explanation of age effects in terms of these patterns.

Is it the case, then, that everyday memory research and laboratory experiments are destined to proceed on two parallel lines that fail to meet? Ideally, the two approaches ought to be mutually beneficial and complementary. One way to achieve this might be to design studies tht combine both approaches. Studies of memory in everyday life, such as Burke's, which produced a rich harvest of observations about the nature and incidence of tip-of-the-tongue experiences, are descriptive rather than explanatory, but may serve as a preliminary exploratory phase before a more formal investigation. The observations gathered in a natural setting may suggest explanatory hypotheses whch can then be tested in controlled laboratory experiments.

Another way to reconcile experience and experiment is to study natural tasks, but use experimental methods. Hartley and Hartley's study of age differences in the acquisition of expertise in computer text editing is an example of this kind, which manages to incorporate many of the advantages of both naturalistic and experimental approaches. The task has the relevance, coherence and motivating properties of a real world problem, but with the advantage that all the subjects started from the same knowledge base-line, and information acquisition could be precisely monitored and measured.

EXPLAINING AGE EFFECTS
Looking for a Single Factor

Some approaches to the effects of aging on memory presuppose a unitary model of memory in which a single general factor governs memory efficiency across a wide range of tasks. Others presuppose a model of memory with more or less modular subsystems, some of which may be impaired by aging while others are not.

Rabbitt and his colleagues have tested the predictions of a unitary, single factor model and found little support for it. Neither a measure of general intelligence (overall scores on the AH4 test) which has a high loading on speed, nor task specific measures of speed of processing were able to account for more than a relatively small proportion of the variance in memory tasks (Goward). Rabbitt concluded that "information processing speed is not the sole, nor necessarily the most significant component of performance". In general, IQ proved a better predictor of performance than age. The effects of normal aging were slight when separated from the effects of intelligence which were relatively greater. Where age effects could be identified, these seemed to be highly specific ones such as failure to complete a theme which had been initiated in recounting an autobiographical episode (Winthorpe and Rabbitt), or a decline in confidence in recognizing famous names (Stuart-Hamilton, Perfect and Rabbitt).

The low intercorrelations between different kinds of memory tasks that were noted both by Rabbitt and by Herrman et al. are further evidence against a unitary, single factor model. Self-ratings of memory abilities also show no sign of the across-the-board deficits that would be expected if aging affects a single factor which pervades a unitary system, and the specificity of training effects also suggests that modular subsystems are independently affected by aging.

Looking for Patterns

If, instead of being a unitary system, memory consists of a set of specific subsystems controlled, or fuelled, by general resources, questions arise about the nature of the distinctions between the subsystems and about the locus of age effects. A common research strategy is to look for patterns of age effects whereby some tasks, processes or conditions are age sensitive while others are age resistant. The researcher characterizes the age deficit in terms of the nature of the pattern that is discerned. Some of the researchers here distinguish between memory subsystems on the basis of types of knowledge. Subjective reports of memory problems identify deficits for highly specific knowledge domains such as names or routes. However, the types of knowledge that are age-impaired or age-resistant are more often characterized at a higher level. Distinctions of this kind include (in the order impaired/preserved) episodic versus semantic; procedural versus

declarative; fluid versus crystallized; unfamiliar versus familiar.
These distinctions are difficult to draw since knowledge cannot
always be clearly classified. Episodic knowledge may be converted
to semantic knowledge over time; unfamiliar facts become familiar,
and declarative knowledge can be transformed into procedural
representations. Also, exceptions to the predicted patterns of age
impairment continue to be found. Hartley and Hartley found that
there were no age differences in the acquisition of either
declarative or procedural knowledge of computer text editing in
spite of the unfamiliarity of this domain, and Burke's results
revealed an age deficit in episodic memory for names of
acquaintances.

Another way to distinguish between memory sub-systems and
identify the locus of age effects is in terms of types of process.
Many of these distinctions turn out to co-occur and overlap and
include (again in the order impaired/preserved) explicit versus
implicit processes (Light and Burke, in press); effortful versus
automatic processes (Hasher and Zacks, 1979); concept-driven versus
data-driven processes (Rabbitt, 1979). In Light's study old people
demonstrated impaired performance on explicit recall and
recognition of word lists while the implicit memory processes that
underlie repetition priming were preserved.   This was true for
semantic, concept-drive priming as well as physical, data-driven
priming, so that, in this case, the dissociation of
explicit/implicit cuts across the distinction between data-driven
and concept-driven processes. The explicit/implicit distinction
does not necessarily apply only at the retrieval stage. In Light's
study, tasks were labelled as implicit because, although list
encoding was apparently intentional and explicit, overt retrieval
was not required.   However, in studies of frequency judgements
(e.g. Hasher and Zacks, 1979) the encoding stage is automatic and
implicit, but retrieval is overt and explicit. Generally speaking,
there is a danger that distinctions may be applied post hoc to
characterize the patterns that appear in data, and thus become
self-validating.

A further distinction may also be made between optional and
mandatory processes. Age effects may be attributed to defective
optional strategies, or to limitations in resources. All memory
subsystems draw, to a greater or lesser extent, on a common pool of
processing resources and memory processes that are intentional may
also invoke optional strategies. Strategies and resources are not
independent factors, however, since a shortfall of resources may
constrain the selection of strategy, and judicious choice of
strategy may compensate for a decline in resources. For example,
Salthouse (1984) has demonstrated that skilled older typists may
preserve their performance level, in spite of general slowing, by
shifting to a more time saving strategy.

Several of the studies in this symposium investigated the
hypothesis that age effects can be traced to differences in
strategies. However, Hartley and Hartley's fine-grain, move by
move analysis of text editing revealed that skilled and less
skilled individuals used different strategies, but age groups did
not differ. Selecting optimal strategies appears to require
expertise.   Dixon and Backman sought evidence that older adults

compensate for a deterioration in the component processes involved
in prose recall by shifting to a thematic or metaphoric style of
processing. Although a group of unselected older adults failed to
demonstrate a compensatory shift of this kind, Dixon and Backman
are currently invesigating whether expert elderly language users
can compensate more effectively.

Belmont et al.'s study of memory for digit lists indicated that
age group differences in span could be attributed to differences in
developing and utilizing effective chunking strategies. Those
elderly subjects who did use an optimal strategy performed like the
young subjects, but fewer elderly people chunked effectively. As
Belmont pointed out, we cannot make crude generalizations
identifying aging effects with defective strategies because elderly
individuals differ in the strategies they select.

In real life people set themselves goals for the level of
performance they want to achieve. When performance begins to
decline, they can either find a way to prop up their performance
and arrest deterioration, or lower the standards they are aiming
at. Elderly people may scale down their expectations. Kemper's
aging diary writers adopted a less complex literary style consonant
with their diminished resources. Hartley and Hartley's elderly
subjects tackled a smaller proportion of the tasks than the young
group and, in the Belmont et al. study, elderly subjects did not
attempt the longer length digit lists.

Aging research is handicapped by the lack of a cognitive model
which specifies exactly the scope and role of processing resources,
but has tended to select some aspect such as working memory
capacity and examine correlations between resource and performance.
So, for example, measures of working memory were found to correlate
significantly with the amount of specific detail in recounted
autobiographical episodes (Winthorpe and Rabbitt); acquisition of
text editing knowledge (Hartley and Hartley); and the 'depth' of
written sentences (Kemper).

Competence and Performance

When an age-related decline in resources is found, we might
expect to find that age differences in performance can be explained
in terms of the interaction of this decreased capacity and the task
demands. In fact, however, age effects turn out to be much more
complex. Why is this the case? To understand why, we need to
invoke a form of competence-performance distinction. The effects
of age on competence will not necessarily emerge in performance for
a variety of reasons. Some tasks make only minimal demands on
processing resources (e.g. those that operate automatically or
implicitly). Some tasks make demands that are still within the
diminished capacity of the aging person. Some individuals start
with an initially higher endowment of resources so that, even if
these are diminished by aging, they are still above average. Some
individuals offset a reduction in processing resources by finding
more economical, cost-effective ways to perform the task. Some
individuals avoid doing tasks which they know, or fear, they may
not be able to do well. Distinguishing between competence factors
and performance factors helps to unify and reconcile some of the
separate, and sometimes disparate, findings that have accumulated.

Aging and Cognitive Architecture

In so far as different approaches converge, they produce a complex account of multiple interacting factors, operating at different levels in the system, which may either enhance or obscure the effects of aging on memory. There are many gaps, ambiguities and poorly specified elements in this account. Some of these problems are not peculiar to aging research, but reflect the lack of a satisfactory model of the cognitive system. Current research on aging has been slow to explore the possibilities of examining age effects within the framework of some more recent models of cognitive architecture such as a production systems architecture like ACT*, or parallel distributed processing models, which might provide new insights and fresh impetus. It is difficult to see how aging research can advance much further without some new or better cognitive models to guide it.

REFERENCES

Charness, N. (1985). 'Aging and Problem-Solving Performance', in Aging and Human Performance (Ed. N.Charness), Wiley, Chichester.

Hasher, L. and Zacks, R.T. (1979). 'Automatic and Effortful Processes in Memory', Journal of Experimental Psychology: General, 108, 356-388.

Light, L.L. and Burke, D.M. (1988) 'Patterns of Language and Memory in Old Age', in (Eds. D.M. Burke and L.L. Light) in press, Cambridge University Press, New York.

Rabbitt, P.M.A. (1979) 'Some Experiments and a Model for Changes in Attentional Selectivity with Old Age', in Baye-Symposium VII: Brain Function in Old Age, Springer-Verlag, Berlin.

Salthouse, T.A. (1984) 'Effects of Age and Skill in Typing', Journal of Experimental Psychology: General, 113, 345-371.

MEMORY AS PROBLEM SOLVING:
THE CASES OF YOUNG AND ELDERLY ADULTS

John M. Belmont, Laura J. Freeseman and D. Wayne Mitchell
Department of Pediatrics and R.L. Smith Research Center
University of Kansas Medical Center
Kansas City, Kansas, U.S.A.

ABSTRACT

Young adults perform better than elderly on some memory tasks because, it is thought, they are abler problem solvers, and hence adopt more effective memory strategies. Here we tested these ideas using digit span. The general hypothesis was supported on a group basis, but there were wide individual differences in strategy use, and young and elderly who adopted the same strategies for similar problems executed them similarly.

INTRODUCTION

Martin and Fernberger (1929) showed that extended practice can yield changes in chunking strategies that lead to large increases in digit span. From this we conclude that young adults can usefully treat the laboratory task as a problem—can deliberately invent strategies for memorizing cumbersome materials. The strategy-invention idea was importantly formalized by Miller, Galanter and Pribram (1960), and has since been used repeatedly to explain changes in voluntary memory during child and adult development (Flavell, 1976; Reese, 1976; Poon, 1985). Yet, notwithstanding the popularity of problem solving in developmental memory theory, the child and aging literatures contain precious few demonstrations of deliberate changes in strategy that would signify adaptation. Indeed, in aging studies it is rare to arrange even for the observation of memory strategies, much less to try to distinguish among strategies so as to account for variability in recall accuracy either between or within age groups; and no aging study has yet documented dynamic **changes** in strategies over the course of experience with a memory problem. Such changes could serve to separate active strategy invention from automatic strategy use, and hence would permit comparison of young and elderly adults' inventive efforts. Our aims here were: (a) To observe young and elderly adults' memory strategies as a function of practice; (b) To establish a basis for inferring common process-product linkages by showing that strategy measures correlate with recall accuracy **within each age group separately**; and then, (c) To test the theoretical literature by determining how differences in recall accuracy **across** age groups are related to differences in strategy use.

TASK ANALYSIS

The task was digit span, which requires immediate recall of random digit strings that increase in length over trials. The span is the longest string of digits recalled in perfect order. MacGregor (1987) notes that organization of such materials can be done by chunking in groups of three or four, and such organization is more efficient than unorganized memory if lists exceed four items.

Martin and Fernberger (1929) noted that young adults shift from unorganized to chunked memory as digit strings get longer. Moreover, practicing for many sessions, subjects lengthen their chunks to five digits to achieve spans of 15. As our study involved only a single session with maximum list length 12, we expected that memory activity would be restricted to the three- or four-item chunking suggested by MacGregor, and would begin to appear on lists of five digits, with increasing consistency on progressively longer lists.

PROBLEM SOLVING AND STRATEGY MEASUREMENT

Problem solving is here defined as changes in cognitive processes intended to improve performance. To document such an event requires direct measures of task-relevant processes, and a suitable opportunity for subjects to assess their performance and adjust accordingly (Belmont, 1983). We therefore gave subjects two open-ended digit-span tasks with instructions to solve them as problems. In both tasks they memorized as many lists as they wished and selected ad lib the number of digits presented on each list. The two tasks were identical except that the first was computer-paced, while the second was self-paced. In the self-paced task, evidence of chunking (and hence also of problem solving) was obtained from the subjects' patterns of pause times (Belmont, Ferretti & Mitchell, 1982).

SUBJECTS

There were 30 introductory psychology students (ages 18-23 yr, mean 19.0), and 30 retired professors and university professional staff (ages 64-81 yr, mean 71.2). Most of the elderly had advanced academic degrees (including 8 B.A.s, 7 M.A.s and 10 Ph.D.s), and they continued to attend scheduled events on campus, were active members of the retired staff club, and had volunteered for a multi-project study only part of one component of which will be reported here. They thus stand as a biased sample, but one which seems to meet Labouvie-Vief's (1985) call for matching the two age groups on study-related attitudes and motivations. The elderly also appear to have remained intellectually active enough to stand as appropriate subjects for the cognitive laboratory (Murrell & Humphries, 1978).

MATERIALS AND APPARATUS

There were 40 unique 12-digit lists, 20 per task. Digits were presented simultaneously to the eye and ear. For auditory presentation, tape-recorded lists were controlled by a TRS-80 Model 100 microcomputer. For visual presentation, the subject viewed a second Model 100 on whose LCD screen digits were displayed as 3.5 x 6.0 mm characters synchronized (±0.1 sec) with the corresponding auditory presentations. To begin each list the subject announced his choice of list length (up to 12 digits), which the examiner keyed into her computer. For Task 1 the subject then pressed a button once and received all the digits in the list at 1-sec intervals. For Task 2 the subject pressed the button separately to receive each digit, and every resulting offset-onset pause was automatically timed/recorded to 0.01 sec.

PROCEDURES

Task 1's digit-presentation and serial-recall requirements were demonstrated on two 3-digit lists. The challenge was then issued: Discover how to memorize the digits perfectly at non-trivial list lengths. Definitions were left vague. The examiner never suggested any particular memory strategy, but she did explain that the subject could select any list length on any trial, that lists of different length might present different problems, and that the subject should work until satisfied that he had confronted truly challenging list lengths and could bring nothing new to the problem. Throughout the task the examiner conducted a running open-ended intertrial interview concerning the subject's current memory strategies, with occasional prompts such as, "Is there anything else you could do to make it easier?" Immediately after Task 1 the examiner introduced Task 2 as having the same requirements as Task 1, except that digit presentation would now be self-paced, "so you can take as much time as you want between the digits." The self pacing was practiced on two 3-digit lists, and the subject was then freed to attack the problem under the problem-solving instructions given previously.

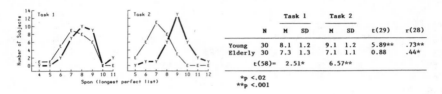

Figure 1. Young (Y) and elderly (E) digit spans under Task 1's automatic vs. Task 2's self-paced digit presentation.

RESULTS

Figure 1 shows the two age-groups' spans. An Age x Task ANOVA yielded reliable main effects plus the interaction (all p's <.011). The simple-effects t-tests (Fig. 1, right) confirm that the young's spans were longer than the elderly's on both tasks, and going from automatic to self-paced presentation the elderly's spans were unchanged even as the young's increased. The question now is, are these effects related either to problem solving or to on-line chunking?

Analysis of Pause-Time Patterns

'Know the method your subject is using to perform the experimental task....Never average over methods' (Newell, 1973, pp. 294-295). We classified all subjects' Task-2 pause-time patterns, then grouped the patterns by type and looked for age-group differences. We assumed the following model: As the subject chunks a list of digits, the pause following the last digit in a chunk will be longer than for the digit before or the one after (which will be included in the next chunk). Thus, an initial 3-digit chunk will show a pause at serial position 3 (SP 3) that is longer than those at SP 2 or SP 4. We call this rise-fall pattern a "peak". The first such peak in the list signifies the size of the first chunk, and that first chunk's size stands as our qualitative measure of strategy.

For any given list length (LL), there are one less pauses than LL (LL—1). The first and last cannot be peaks, so there are LL—3 SPs where peaks **can** occur. The first question was, did the subjects agree as to where their first peaks **should** occur (strategy concordance)? For each LL every subject's pause times for their last list at that LL

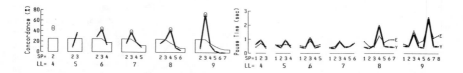

Figure 2. Most-common strategies (left), with corresponding average pause-time patterns (right) for young (Y) vs. elderly (E) subjects.

were classified by the SP of the first peak (if any). Random pause times would peak at each SP about 25% of the time (.50 for the rise x .50 for the subsequent fall). However, since we classified only the first peak, chance for any particular SP = $(SP-1)x.5^{SP}$. For SPs 2-7 these chance probabilities = .250, .250, .188, .125, .078, and .047.

Figure 2 (left) shows these chances (enclosed areas) along with with the proportion of subjects (all ages) who had first peaks at each SP for LLs 4-9. At all LLs binomial tests (all p's <.03) showed significant concordances excepting at LL 5, whose peak at SP 3 was not significant (p =.061). Beyond LL 4, the common first peaks were at SP 3 excepting for LL 8, whose common first peak was at SP 4. There were thus three different chunking strategies (circled in Fig. 2, left): At SP 2 for LL 4; at SP 3 for LLs 6, 7 and 9; and at SP 4 for LL 8.

Age-group differences in the uses of the common strategies were assessed as follows: For each LL separately we took all the pause patterns that had contributed to the common peak, grouped them by age, and computed the group-median pause time for each SP. The resulting group-median patterns (Fig. 2, right) obviously show the common peaks for which they were selected. They also show that for both age groups at LL 9, the common peak at SP 3 (about 1.5 sec) was followed by a longer second peak at SP 6 (about 2.4 sec). Separate Age x SP ANOVA's for each LL all showed significant (built-in) SP effects; at no LL, however, was either Age or Age x SP significant (all p's >.27). It seems that at each LL, the young and elderly who used the common strategy did so quite similarly, both in quality and in the amount of time devoted to its execution. We can therefore now ask, are the common chunking strategies related to recall accuracy?

Recall Accuracy vs. Chunking

We begin by examining within-group strategy-accuracy relations at the LLs where variability in accuracy was maximal: LL 8 for the elderly; LL 9 for the young. There were 16 elderly who failed their first try at LL 8 but tried again. Of these, seven ultimately solved and nine did not. The young were analyzed similarly at LL 9 (12 solvers vs. 5 non-solvers). Figure 3 shows these groups' median pause patterns for the subjects' single best-accuracy trials following initial failure. In both groups the solvers used the common strategy (5/7 elderly solvers and 11/12 young solvers did so vs. only 3/9 elderly nonsolvers and 2/5 young nonsolvers). Moreover, as Figure 3 shows, the solvers in both age groups had longer pause times.

Concerning the all-important **changes** in strategy (problem solving): There were 19 elderly who had a trial at LL 7 followed by one at LL 8. Nine of these subjects ultimately solved at LL 8 or better, while 10 did not. The 10 nonsolvers showed no significant SP

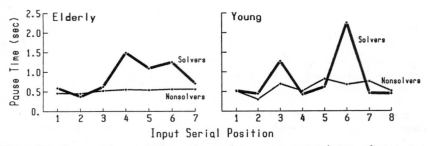

Figure 3. Pause-time patterns for solvers vs. nonsolvers, by age.

effects on their last LL-7 trial or on the immediately following LL-8
trial. By contrast, the solvers showed peaks at SP 3 for LL 7 and SP 4
for LL 8 (ps <.05). This shift from one common strategy to another is
exactly what would be expected of people who ultimately solve both
problems. A similar look at N=10 young solvers vs. 5 young nonsolvers
at the transition from LL 8 to LL 9 showed that both groups had significant peaks at SP 4 for LL 8, but only the solvers reliably shifted
to peaks at SPs 3 and 6 for LL 9. Thus, at both ages, appropriate
trial-by-trial changes in strategy across changing tasks did occur,
but the shifting patterns were reliable only for the problem solvers.

        Given the within-group process-product links, we tested for
between-group differences in the proportions of subjects who showed
consistent chunking across LLs and consistent chunking over trials
within LLs. For these analyses we excluded LL 5 (no common strategy)
and LLs 9-12 (too few elderly subjects). At each of LLs 4,6,7 and 8
we classified each subject's last trial as having or not having a peak
(any SP would do). The proportions of young and elderly who had peaks
on at least 75% of their LLs were 28/30 vs. 18/30 respectively,
χ^2=9.32, p <.005. Thus, the young showed overall more consistent
chunking than the elderly across different LLs.

        For each LL separately, subjects who had more than one trial
were classified as to whether or not their last two trials had first
peaks at the same SP (two-trial strategy consistency). The chance
value for any particular LL is the sum of the squared probabilities
shown above for the individual SPs. Thus, for LLs 4, 6, 7 and 8
chances are .06, .18, .23 and .28. Binomial tests showed that neither
group had a significant proportion of consistent subjects at LL 4. At
LLs 6-8 the proportions of consistent young and elderly were .46, .63,
.71 and .18, .33, .84, with respective binomial probabilities of .01,
.00, .00 and .55, .15, .00. Thus, at each LL from 6 to 8 there were
significant numbers of strategically consistent young. By contrast,
as a group, the elderly were consistent only on the longest lists.

CONCLUSIONS

        Many young and elderly adults respond to the digit span prob-
lem with spontaneous chunking strategies, the most common forms of
which are quantitatively similar across the age groups. These common
strategies are used by nearly all of those young and elderly who
manage to perform long lists perfectly, and not by those who do imper-
fectly. The young on the average show considerably longer spans than
the elderly; the young are also consistently strategic at most list
lengths whereas the elderly are consistent only on very long lists.

In as much as young adults who achieved long spans were strategic even on relatively short lists, we conclude that the age-group difference in strategic thinking does underlie at least some of the observed group differences in digit span. Whatever the group tendencies, however, the fact that many of the elderly were successfully strategic argues strongly against gross generalizations concerning this population. Indeed, to the contrary, it argues that related research or remediative pursuits may well benefit from careful analysis of individual differences in strategy use among the elderly.

ACKNOWLEDGMENTS

We thank Profs. W. Crockett, S. Kemper, and G. Kellas (University of Kansas, Lawrence) for recruiting the subjects, providing the laboratory, and discussing the plans for this work, which was supported in part by USPHS grants HD15854 and HD02528. Also, many thanks to the editors of this volume for their crucial statistical insights.

REFERENCES

Belmont, J.M. (1983). 'Concerning Hunt's New Ways of Assessing Intelligence', Intelligence, 7, 1-7.

Belmont, J.M., Ferretti, R.P., and Mitchell, D.W. (1982). 'Memorizing: A test of Untrained Mildly Retarded Children's Problem Solving', American Journal of Mental Deficiency, 87, 197-210.

Flavell, J.H. (1976). 'Metacognitive Aspects of Problem Solving', in The Nature of Intelligence (Ed. L.B. Resnick), pp. 231-235, Erlbaum, Hillsdale, New Jersey.

Labouvie-Vief, G. (1985). 'Intelligence and Cognition', in Handbook of the Psychology of Aging (2nd edition) (Eds. J.E. Birren and K.W. Schaie), pp. 500-530, Van Nostrand, New York.

MacGregor, J.N. (1987). 'Short-Term Memory Capacity: Limitation or Optimization?', Psychological Review, 94, 107-108.

Martin, P.R. and Fernberger, S.W. (1929). 'Improvement in Digit Span', American Journal of Psychology, 41, 91-94.

Miller, G., Galanter, E., and Pribram, K. (1960). Plans and the Structure of Behavior, H. Holt, New York.

Murrell, H. and Humphries, S. (1978). 'Age, Experience, and Short-Term Memory', in Practical Aspects of Memory (Eds. M.M. Gruneberg, P.E. Morris, and R.N. Sykes), pp. 363-365, Academic, New York.

Newell, A. (1973). 'You Can't Play 20 Questions with Nature and Win: Projective Comments on the Papers of this Symposium', in Visual Information Processing (Ed. W. Chase), pp. 283-308, Academic, New York.

Poon, L.W. (1985). 'Differences in Human Memory with Aging: Nature, Causes, and Clinical Implications', in Handbook of the Psychology of Aging (2nd edition) (Eds. J.E. Birren and K.W. Schaie), pp. 427-462, Van Nostrand, New York.

Reese, H.W. (1976). 'The Development of Memory: Life-Span Perspectives', in Advances in Child Development and Behavior, Vol. 11 (Ed. H.W. Reese), pp. 189-212, Academic, New York.

PRESERVED IMPLICIT MEMORY IN OLD AGE

Leah L. Light
Department of Psychology, Pitzer College, Claremont, CA, USA

ABSTRACT
        Relative to young adults, older adults demonstrate memory
impairment in traditional tests of explicit memory, such as free
recall, cued recall, and recognition, which require deliberate acts
of recollection. However, there do not appear to be age-related
decrements on implicit memory tasks, such as repetition priming, in
which the subject is not asked to remember but rather simply to
perform a task in which the effects of prior experience may be
manifested. These results are similar to those obtained with
amnesics and suggest that older adults are impaired on tasks which
require a conscious effort to remember an event but that memory
without awareness is unaffected by age.

        Older adults complain about memory problems and there is
ample evidence from laboratory studies to confirm the existence of
an age-related decline in memory (Burke & Light, 1981). This
chapter addresses two issues in the study of memory and aging. The
first is whether age-related deficits in memory are to be found in
all memory tasks or whether some aspects of memory are unaffected by
aging. The second issue is whether the nature of the memory
impairment in old age is unique or whether it shares functional
similarities with deficits shown by other memory impaired
populations, such as anterograde amnesics. Such commonalities might
be expected given that the physiological basis of the memory
deficits in normal older adults may be similar to that involved in
anterograde amnesia (Squire, 1987).
        In this chapter, we present evidence that in normal aging,
as in amnesia, there is a dissociation between explicit and implicit
memory and consider some practical implications of preserved
implicit memory. Although amnesics show little evidence of learning
when asked to deliberately recall or recognize new information,
their performance is normal when they are simply requested to
perform a task in which the effect of prior experience may be
manifested without either the intention to remember or conscious
awareness of the relevant prior experience. For instance,
Warrington and Weiskrantz (e.g., 1970) found that patients with
severe anterograde amnesia showed low levels of recall or
recognition of word lists, but performed normally when presented
with either fragmented words or the first three letters of
previously seen words as cues and asked to complete them with the
first word that came to mind. Tasks such as these are said to tap

implicit memory rather than explicit memory (Graf & Schacter, 1985) and are thought to rely largely on relatively automatic processes.

The class of implicit memory tasks we have investigated is that of repetition priming. In each of the studies described below, measures of both implicit and explicit memory were obtained for samples of young and older adults. Several repetition priming tasks were used: word completion, identification of degraded words, and generation of category exemplars. In each task, the magnitude of repetition priming was assessed by comparing the likelihood of producing previously seen words to the likelihood of producing these same words when they were not recently seen.

WORD COMPLETION

Light, Singh, and Capps (1986) tested young (mean age = 23.4 years) and older (mean age = 69.4 years) adults. As in all the studies described here, subjects were healthy, well-educated, community dwelling adults. Subjects were presented with a list of 80 words and were tested both immediately and seven days later for yes/no recognition and for ability to complete fragments such as _E_D_L_M, with words, some of which had been studied previously and some of which were new. The fragment completion task was not described as a memory test and people were encouraged to respond to all word fragments. Younger adults scored higher on recognition than older adults on the delayed test though performance on the immediate recognition test did not vary reliably with age. However, there were no age differences in repetition priming. The mean proportion of correct fragment completions for previously seen words was .58 for the young and .53 for the old; the baselines (proportions of new words correctly completed) were .45 and .43, for young and old respectively. The priming effects (old – new) were thus .13 and .10 for the two age groups. In contrast to the recognition results, there was no evidence of an interaction between age and retention interval for repetition priming in fragment completion.

Using a slightly different paradigm, Light and Singh (in press, Experiment 2) examined repetition priming in a word stem completion task. Young (mean age = 23.1 years) and older (mean age = 68.3 years) adults made pleasantness judgments for a list of 20 words. No mention was made of a forthcoming memory test. Immediately after list presentation, half of the subjects in each age group were given a word completion test and half were given a cued recall test. The cues were the same in both cases--the first three letters of the studied words randomly mixed with an equal number of stems for words which had not been studied. Each word stem could be completed by at least four English words and the target was never the most common of these. The word completion instructions requested subjects to give the first English word that came to mind; hence this task constitutes a measure of implicit memory. Finally, all subjects were given a yes/no recognition test.

The outcome of this study was identical to that of the previous one. Young adults scored higher than older adults on both measures of explicit memory. In cued recall, the young had a mean proportion correct of .63 as compared to .36 for the older adults, with baselines (number of new stems completed with words that

matched items seen by other subjects) of .08 and .09. In word
completion, the mean proportions correct were .36 for the young
adults and .27 for the older adults against baselines of .08 and
.07. Two aspects of these results are notable. First, older adults
again demonstrated preserved implicit memory and impaired explicit
memory. Second, the cued recall scores of older adults were not
much different from their scores on word completion whereas those of
young adults were much higher. We return to this point later.

IDENTIFICATION OF DEGRADED WORDS
        A number of studies have found that identification of words
under poor viewing conditions (rapid presentation or visual
degradation) is improved by a single presentation in both amnesic
(e.g., Warrington & Weiskrantz, 1970) and normal (Hashtroudi,
Parker, DeLisi, Wyatt, & Mutter, 1984; Jacoby & Dallas, 1981)
populations. Light and Singh (in press, Experiment 3) compared the
performance of young (mean age = 21.3 years) and older (mean age =
69.1 years) adults on perceptual identification of degraded words,
free recall, and yes/no recognition. In the perceptual
identification task, previously studied words were presented
together with an equal number of new words. Words were degraded by
filters which covered 50%, 65%, or 80% of their areas. Each word
was presented first in its most degraded (80% obscured) form, with
less degraded forms presented if identification was unsuccessful.
        Subjects engaged in one of two encoding tasks as they
studied a list of intact words. In one condition, subjects
indicated whether successive words shared any vowels. In the second
condition, designed to induce semantic encoding, subjects rated the
pleasantness of each word on a 7-point scale. Both recall and
recognition are known to benefit from semantic encoding whereas
repetition priming does not (Graf & Mandler, 1984; Jacoby & Dallas,
1981). Further, age differences in recall and recognition may be
greater following semantic encoding (Burke & Light, 1981).
        Consistent with prior work, both free recall and recognition
were better following semantic encoding. In addition, the
difference in performance between young and older adults on these
explicit memory tasks was magnified by semantic encoding. However,
there were no effects of age or encoding condition on the amount of
repetition priming observed in perceptual identification and there
was no interaction between these two variables. In the most
degraded condition, young adults correctly identified .27 of the old
words while older adults got .17 correct. The baselines (number of
new words correctly identified) were .14 for the young and .07 for
the old. Thus the magnitude of the repetition priming effect
(targets - baseline) was .13 for the young and .10 for the older
adults. Once again, young adults scored higher than older adults on
explicit but not implicit measures of memory.

GENERATION OF CATEGORY EXEMPLARS
        Word completion and perceptual identification tasks may
involve data driven processes. That is, successful performance on
these tasks may depend on the physical similarity between the
materials studied and the test items (Jacoby & Dallas, 1981). It is
possible that age differences in implicit memory are smaller for

data driven memory tests than for those requiring use of conceptual information and that this is why we have not observed age-related differences in repetition priming in our previous research. Graf, Shimamura, and Squire (1985) found that amnesics performed normally on a conceptually driven test of implicit memory although their free recall was at floor. Their task involved asking people to produce members of several taxonomic categories, some of which had appeared on a study list. Because this task does not solicit deliberate remembering, it constitutes a measure of implicit memory. Because the test cues are conceptually rather than physically similar to the target items and are not mentioned in the study list, it is a conceptually driven task. Shirley Albertson and I have adapted this technique to determine whether there are age differences in conceptually driven implicit memory tasks.

Young (mean age = 21.7 years) and older (mean age = 69.7 years) adults rated a list of 50 words for pleasantness. Among these were 18 critical words, 3 members of 6 taxonomic categories. The category members chosen were not among the most frequent responses to the category names in published category norms. The pleasantness rating task and the subsequent tests of implicit and explicit memory were imbedded in a long series of unrelated tasks. In the exemplar generation task, subjects were asked to produce 8 instances for each of the categories on the study list and an equal number of new categories. Finally, the names of the 6 studied categories were presented again for cued recall.

Young and older adults did not differ in the magnitude of priming. The mean proportions of studied category members generated by young and older adults were .30 and .26, respectively; the baseline proportions were .12 and .13. As in our earlier studies, however, young adults were much better than older adults on cued recall, with proportions correct of .40 for the young and .20 for the old. Thus, the constancy of priming across age does not depend on the physical similarity of originally experienced and test materials. As in the word stem completion task the difference between cued recall and free association was much smaller for older than for younger adults. Here older adults' scores were actually somewhat higher on the priming task.

SUMMARY AND IMPLICATIONS

We are now in a position to answer the two questions posed initially. First, older adults are not impaired in all memory tasks. Although age-related decrements were found on all explicit measures used in the four studies described here, there were no reliable effects of age on the three types of repetition priming investigated. It is true that in each of the four studies there were very small age differences in repetition priming which favored the young, but the size of these effects was much smaller than those found in explicit memory.

Second, the pattern of impaired and preserved memory abilities in old age bears a strong resemblance to that found in anterograde amnesics. We should, however, be careful not to overgeneralize from these results. The magnitude of the decline in explicit memory tasks is much smaller in old age than in amnesia. In addition, amnesics generally have no awareness of having participated in a previous learning situation; this is certainly not the case for the normal older adults we have tested. Finally, it is claimed that the memory impairment observed in amnesia can exist in the absence of other forms of cognitive deficit. However, Squire (1987) has pointed out that older adults, but not amnesics, have problems in word retrieval and object naming. It is not clear whether problems in memory and in language coexist in the same elderly people or whether there are people who exhibit memory problems without language impairment. Advances in the study of amnesia have come in part from careful case studies of individual patients. A similar approach might prove fruitful in the study of cognitive aging.

Does preserved repetition priming have implications for everyday memory or is the dissociation between explicit and implicit memory in old age of theoretical interest only? This question has received little, if any, attention, and we offer the following as speculation. Our starting point is the observation that in the two studies in which we used the same cues for explicit and implicit memory tasks (word stem completion and generation of category exemplars), older adults did not benefit as much from explicit instructions to remember as did young adults. It has been argued that implicit memory, at least in repetition priming tasks, depends on relatively automatic activation processes but that successful explicit memory requires retrieval of information about the context in which information was originally experienced (Graf & Mandler, 1984). The pattern of impaired and spared memory abilities in old age suggests that automatic processes are intact whereas context retrieval is deficient. Given that older adults appear to benefit less from explicit instructions to recall than young adults and that any memory protocol probably reflects contributions of both types of processes, it is possible that their explicit memory performance contains a larger share of information recovered by the mechanisms underlying implicit memory.

If this were true, we might expect to find that older adults are more likely than young adults to produce information that is correct, but that they are uncertain about, because they cannot identify the circumstances in which that information was acquired. Craik and McIntyre (1986) have performed a study that bears on this issue. They found that older adults were more likely to display source amnesia than young adults. In other words, older adults were more likely to remember information without being able to correctly report how they came to know that information. This finding is consistent with the analysis given above.

Similar processes may account for older adults' tendency to use plausibility judgments in deciding whether they have experienced particular events (Reder, Wible, & Martin, 1986). If older adults cannot explicitly remember new information, they may rely on automatically activated schemata and respond in accordance with estimates of plausibility based on general world knowledge. To the extent that the world is regular and predictable, this is an entirely reasonable strategy. It will not work when something out of the ordinary has been experienced. Thus, the main problem with relying too heavily on the mechanisms that support implicit memory is that they may lead us astray in novel circumstances. One suggestion that emerges from this work is that older adults might be encouraged to trust their memory even when they cannot identify the source of their knowledge.

REFERENCES

Burke, D.M. and Light, L.L. (1981). 'Memory and Aging: The Role of Retrieval Processes', Psychological Bulletin, 90, 513-546.

Craik, F.I.M. and McIntyre, J.S. (1986). 'Age Differences in Memory for Facts and Their Source', Paper presented at the Annual Meeting of the Psychonomic Society.

Graf, P. and Mandler, G. (1984). 'Activation Makes Words More Accessible, But Not Necessarily More Retrievable', Journal of Verbal Learning and Verbal Behavior, 23, 553-568.

Graf, P. and Schacter, D.L. (1985). 'Implicit and Explicit Memory for New Associations in Normal and Amnesic Subjects', Journal of Experimental Psychology: Learning, Memory, and Cognition, 11, 501-518.

Graf, P., Shimamura, A.P. and Squire, L.R. (1985). 'Priming Across Modalities and Priming Across Category Levels: Extending the Domain of Preserved Function in Amnesia', Journal of Experimental Psychology: Learning, Memory, and Cognition, 11, 386-396.

Hashtroudi, S., Parker, E.S., DeLisi, L.E., Wyatt, R.J. and Mutter, S.A. (1984). 'Intact Retention in Acute Alcohol Amnesia', Journal of Experimental Psychology: Learning, Memory, and Cognition, 10, 156-163.

Jacoby, L.L. and Dallas, M. (1981). 'On the Relationship Between Autobiographical Memory and Perceptual Learning', Journal of Experimental Psychology: General, 110, 306-340.

Light, L.L. and Singh, A. (in press). 'Implicit and Explicit Memory in Young and Older Adults', Journal of Experimental Psychology: Learning, Memory, and Cognition.

Light, L.L., Singh, A. and Capps, J.L. (1986). 'The Dissociation of Memory and Awareness in Young and Older Adults', Journal of Clinical and Experimental Neuropsychology, 8, 62-74.

Reder, L.M., Wible, C. and Martin, J. (1986). 'Differential Memory Changes With Age: Exact Retrieval Versus Plausible Inference', Journal of Experimental Psychology: Learning, Memory, and Cognition, 12, 72-81.

Squire, L.R. (1987). Memory and Brain, Oxford University Press, New York.

Warrington, E.K. and Weiskrantz, L. (1970). 'Amnesic Syndrome: Consolidation or Retrieval?', Nature, 228, 628-630.

MEMORY FOR DETAILS IN AGING AND DEMENTIA

Herman Buschke

Albert Einstein College of Medicine
Bronx, New York U.S.A.

ABSTRACT
          Cued recall of details and target items by young, middle-aged, and aged adults, and by aged nursing home residents with and without dementia, was compared. The normal aged recalled nearly as many targets and fewer details, but their learning progressed through stages similar to those of younger adults, with increasing recall of details and targets as units. Aged with dementia recalled fewer targets and essentially no details or units. All groups recalled additional targets when details were presented after cuing failed.

          Memory for details is of interest because the aged are believed to have difficulty remembering details (Kral, 1978), and impaired memory for details might help to identify 'age-associated memory impairment' (Crook, Bartus, Ferris, Whitehouse, Cohen and Gershon, 1986). Analysis of memory for details as well as target items also may reveal stages of learning in the elaboration of memory traces and may be used to investigate the encoding and retrieval of information in memory traces (Buschke, in press). This study used a search procedure to control learning for effective cued recall (Buschke, 1984) in order to identify genuine memory deficits that are not due to impaired attention, reduced processing capacity, use of inefficient strategies, or impairment of other cognitive processes that may limit learning and memory (Buschke and Grober, 1986; Grober and Buschke, 1987).

METHOD
          Each subject was tested individually. Each of the target items was printed together with a descriptive adjective (wet grapes) in sets of two on cards that were placed in front of the subject, one at a time. The subject was asked to search for and identify each target item on the card when given its cue (fruit), and was asked to report the entire phrase specified by that cue (wet grapes). The card was removed and the subject was asked for immediate cued recall of each phrase, including both the target and the detail (wet grapes) when given the cue (fruit). After recall of each phrase the subject was given each target item (grapes) to elicit recall of the detail with the target as an entire phrase (wet grapes). If the subject failed to recall either a target or its detail in immediate recall, the search and immediate recall for that detail and target were repeated until both the target and the detail were recalled together. Then the other items were studied by the same controlled learning

procedure.

    After all of the targets and details were studied by this procedure, there were four trials of cued recall, each preceded by 30 seconds of interference by counting backwards. Cued recall was tested on each trial by presenting the same cues used in the search, one at a time, to elicit cued recall of each target item with its detail. If the subject recalled a target but not its detail, the detail was immediately presented with the target. If the subject could not recall the target, then its detail was presented (together with the cue) in a further attempt to elicit recall of that target by reinstating its context. If this also failed to elicit recall of the target, then the subject was reminded of both that target and detail before testing cued recall of the next target.

    After completing the four trials of cued recall, recognition of targets, details, and the association of details and targets was tested. Recognition of targets was tested by presenting each target together with a new item from the same category used as a cue for that target (grapes/peaches). Related foils were used to avoid recognition based on category information alone. Forced-choice recognition was used to avoid apparent false alarms due to recognition of category information when using foils from the same category, and to avoid the effects of differences in response criteria.

    Recognition of details was tested by presenting each detail together with a new but similar detail (wet/dry).

    Recognition of the association of details and targets was tested by presenting each target with its own detail and another compatible detail that was associated with some other target in the list (wet/cheap:grapes).

Materials: Two different lists were used, each consisting of 16 target items from the Battig and Montague (1969) category norms, selected from the less frequent responses to minimize any effects of guessing in cued recall. Category labels were used as cues. The details to be remembered were easily associated adjectives that should not require mediators, such as 'wet' for 'grapes'. The results obtained from both lists were combined because anovas including list as a between subjects factor did not show a significant list effect.

Subjects: Memory for details and targets by 12 normal community dwelling aged (73.0 years, s.d.=6.4) from the Aging in America senior citizens center in Bronx, N.Y. was compared with memory by 12 young (29.2, s.d.=6.4) and 12 middle-aged (50.6,s.d.=6.2) adults employed at Albert Einstein College of Medicine in Bronx, N.Y. Verbal IQ estimated by vocabulary, similarities, and information subtests of the WAIS was not significantly different for these young (109.3), middle-aged (116.5), and aged (116.4) subjects. The aged had significantly less education (11.1 years) than the young (15.6), p<.0001 by Scheffe test, or the middle-aged (14.3), p<.0001 by Scheffe test, but the young and middle-aged did not differ in years of education. All of the young and middle-aged and seven of the aged were women.

    Memory for details and targets by 8 aged with dementia

(83.9 years, s.d.=6.5) was compared with memory by 12 aged without dementia (80.6 years, s.d.=8.4), all of whom were residents of Morningside House Nursing Home in Bronx, N.Y. Those with dementia did not differ significantly in age or years of education (8.5) from those without dementia (10.3). The IQ of those with dementia (97.8) was significantly less than the IQ of those without dementia (113.8), $F(1,18)=9.0$, p=.007. Those with dementia made more errors on the Blessed mental status test (16.0) then those without dementia (2.0), $F(1,18=62.2$, p<.0001, and had lower scores on the Mattis Dementia Rating Scale (115.1) than those without dementia (133.0), $F(1,18)=23.6$, p=.0001. All of those with dementia and 10 of those without dementia were women.

RESULTS
        In addition to counting the total number of target items or details recalled on each trial, it is possible to describe stages of learning of targets and details by analyzing the components of recall on each trial. Some target items are recalled together with their details as a single phrase ("wet grapes") that suggests recall of a single unit. Other targets are recalled first, followed, after a pause, by recall of the associated detail ('grapes'....'wet'), suggesting recall of separate but associated memory traces. Still other target items are recalled alone, without recall of their detail. And finally, some targets are recalled only when their detail is presented. In reverse order, these different kinds of recall of details and targets may indicate successive stages of learning. Analysis of the composition of recall may reveal qualitative differences of learning and memory in age-associated memory impairment and dementia.
        Memory for Details and Targets in Aging is shown in Figure 1. Analysis of variance showed significant differences in recall of targets, $F(2,33)=8.2$, p=.001, details, $F(2,33)=6.9$, p=.003, and units, $F(2,33)=6.5$, p=.004. Scheffe tests showed no significant differences in recall by young and middle-aged adults, but did show that the aged recalled fewer targets, p<.02, fewer details, p<.02, and fewer units, p<.02, than the young or middle-aged. The aged recognized targets (16.0), details (15.9), and the association of details and targets (15.8) as well as young or middle-aged did.
        Figure 1 shows that while the aged recalled nearly as many targets (14.6) as the young (15.6) and the middle-aged (15.8), the aged clearly recalled fewer details 10.8) than the young (14.0) and middle-aged (14.4), and fewer units (9.2) than the young (13.2) and the middle-aged (13.4). However, recall by the aged appears

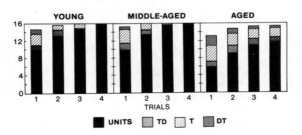

qualitatively similar to recall by younger adults. The aged do recall details and units, and their recall of details and units increases over trials as recall of targets alone and targets elicited by presentation of details decrease. The aged can learn details and can encode details and targets as units, and it appears that their progress through the stages of learning shown by these different kinds of recall of details and targets is similar to that of younger adults. Examination of transition matrices suggests that recall of details and targets as units indicates that they have been encoded as units, because once recalled as a unit the probability of recall as a unit on the next trial was .98 for the young, .97 for the middle-aged, and .94 for the aged.

Memory for Details and Targets by the aged nursing home residents with and without dementia is compared in Figure 2. Those without dementia were older (80.6 years) than the previous group of community dwelling aged (73.0 years), $F(1,22)=6.1$, $p=.02$, but their IQ, years of education, Blessed score, and their recall and recognition of targets, details, or units did not differ significantly from those of the community dwelling aged.

Those with dementia recalled far fewer targets, $F(1,18)=204.0$, $p<.0001$, details, $F(1,18)=99.0$, $p<.0001$, and units, $F(1,18)=36.1$, $p<.0001$. They recognized fewer targets (12.5 vs 15.5), $F(1,18)=14.6$, $p=.001$, details (9.0 vs 15.8), $F(1,18)=295.0$, $p<.0001$, and the association of details and targets (9.6 vs 15.5), $F(1,18)=130.0$, $p<.0001$.

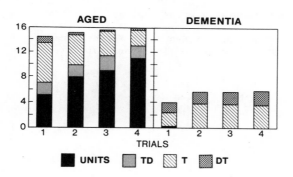

Figure 2. Cued recall of targets and details by aged nursing home residents with and without dementia. Target recall on each trial consists (from bottom to top) of units (UNITS) + targets followed by details (TD) + targets alone (T) + targets elicited by presentation of details (DT). Detail recall on each trial consists of UNITS + TD.

These preliminary findings show how learning details as well as targets may provide a more detailed and complete analysis of learning and memory in aging and dementia, and might be used to investigate stages of learning and the elaboration of memory traces.

ACKNOWLEDGMENTS: This research was supported by U.S. Public Health Service Grants AG 04623, AG 03949, NS 19234 and HD 01799. I thank the residents, staff and administration of Moringside House Nursing Home, the members, staff and administration of Aging in America, and Miriam Aronson, Shereen Bang, Ellen Grober, and Nina Silverman for making this study possible.

REFERENCES

Buschke, H. (1984). 'Cued recall in amnesia', Journal of Clinical and Experimental Neuropsychology, 6, 433-440.

Buschke, H. (in press). 'Criteria for Identification of Memory Deficits', in Learning and Memory (Eds. D. Gorfein and R. Hoffman), Lawrence Erlbaum Associates, Hillsdale, New Jersey.

Buschke, H. and Grober, E. (1986). 'Genuine memory deficits in age-associated memory impairment', Developmental Neuropsychology, 2, 287-307.

Crook, T., Bartus, R.T., Ferris, S.H., Whitehouse, P., Cohen, G.D. and Gershon, S. (1986). 'Age-associated memory impairment: Proposed diagnostic criteria and measures of clinical change - report of a National Institute of Mental Health work group', Developmental Neuropsychology, 2, 261-276.

Grober, E. and Buschke, H. (1987). 'Genuine memory deficits in dementia', Developmental Neuropsychology, 3, 13-36.

Kral, V.A. (1978). 'Benign Senescent Forgetfulness', in Alzheimer's Disease (Eds. R. Katzman, R.D. Terry and K.L. Bick), pp47-51, Raven, New York.

TEXT RECALL AND AGING:
TOWARD RESEARCH ON EXPERTISE AND COMPENSATION

Roger A. Dixon and Lars Backman

University of Victoria, Canada
and
University of Umea, Sweden.

ABSTRACT
        After reviewing briefly selected trends in text recall and
aging research, we introduce a model of one mode through which
maintenance of overall recall performance level throughout adulthood
could occur. This model of compensation via substitution   of
alternative supportive skills (or components thereof) is tested for
the generality of its application in the area of text processing in
adulthood. Initial results suggest that if such compensation occurs,
it probably does so only for highly skilled and well-practiced
language experts.

        In this paper we discuss three successive issues.   First,
we briefly review some trends in research on text processing and
recall in adulthood. Second, we elaborate our view that some of the
most interesting issues in this area of research are those that
reflect a developing dynamic between expertise (e.g., maintained
skills or components thereof) and compensation (e.g., the use of
substitutable skills or components thereof to maintain overall
performance level) (Backman and Dixon, 1986). Third, we outline how
research pertaining to compensation in text processing in adulthood
may proceed. In so doing, we summarize our recent effort to
investigate whether an hypothesized naturally occurring expertise of
late adulthood (viz., metaphoric skill) can compensate for   a
naturally occurring decline in text processing and recall (for texts
involving the use of metaphoric skill).

SOME TRENDS IN TEXT RECALL AND AGING RESEARCH
        Although there is indisputable evidence for decline in, for
example, psychometric test performance or secondary   memory
performance, it has been suggested by a number of researchers that
there may be aspects of cognition that exhibit stabilization or even
progression, given a variety of "appropriate" testing methods or
supportive performance conditions (Baltes, Dittmann-Kohli and Dixon,
1984; Denney, 1982; Dixon and Baltes, 1986; Labouvie-Vief, 1985).
Overall, this argument may be summarized by three interrelated
principles of cognitive development throughout adulthood: (a) there
is, of course, age-related decline in the components of cognitive
functioning, especially in the very late years, but there may be some
stabilization, and perhaps even advancement, in some contextually
supported, well-practiced, skilled, and practical dimensions; (b)
under normal (and, especially, optimal) conditions there is often
sufficient reserve capacity or expertise so as to nurture an (at

least temporary) increase in performance, especially if appreciable interest, effort, practice, or social support are present; and (c) there seems to be a concomitant adaptive – sometimes selective and sometimes automatic – compensatory feature of mental functioning that allows for some inevitable decrements to be less debilitating and less generalized than might be otherwise expected.

These principles have led to the generation of a number of global and specific research questions. In the present context we concentrate on the following two: (a) Given a particular process of cognition (e.g., memory) and a particular domain of that process (e.g., text processing and memory), what are some conditions under which old adults develop or maintain skilled levels of performance?; and (b) Can objective deficits in some molecular components of comprehension and memory for text be compensated through the acquisition and use of substitutable components or skills, such that a "normal" level of proficiency is attained or maintained?

Skilled Text Recall

With regard to the first research question, the evidence regarding skilled performance in adulthood is not as complete or empirically sound as for such domains as chess and typing (see Charness, in press; Hoyer, 1985). There are, of course, some legendary exceptional performances stemming from the Oral Tradition of former times and the oral tradition in contemporary pre-literate societies (e.g., Yates, 1966).

In another review (Dixon and Backman, in press), we have summarized some examples of studies on expertise, broadly defined, in prose recall in adulthood (e.g., Stratton, 1982; Wilding and Valentine, 1985). Although none of this work is developmental, these studies are illustrative in at least two ways. First, this work has demonstrated that the notion of highly skilled cognitive performances is in a global way applicable to prose processing. Unusual and exceptional performances have been documented. Second, in some of the cases middle-aged and older adults have been found to be able to produce at highly skilled levels (although the age documentation has not been carefully done).

In those few studies examining prose processing skill and adult age, "expertise" has been conceived of within a normal range of functioning and usually as a variable with which to compare and differentiate within and across adult age groups. For example, old and young adult age groups might be divided into roughly equivalent high and low skill subgroups and compared on free recall of texts. There are at least three typical categories of skills related to text recall and aging. Specifically, age differences may be attenuated: (a) When pertinent prior knowledge, schemata, or practice are available to older adults (e.g. Hultsch and Dixon, 1983; Light and Anderson, 1983); (b) When language experience or verbal skill is maximized or invoked (e.g., Dixon, Hultsch, Simon and von Eye, 1984; Meyer and Rice, 1983); and (c) Given the presence of the hypothesized, naturally occurring developmental shift in processing style, verbal materials and critical tasks tapping such "metaphoric" or "thematic" styles are used in aging research (e.g., Adams, Dorosz, Holmes, Bass, Gossiaux and Labouvie-Vief, 1985).

All three categories of skills could conceivably act as

cognitive support systems for skilled memory for text in adulthood. A testable implication is that older adults who are "experts" or skilled in one of these areas may be able to compensate for general decline in the mechanics (or components) or reading fluency and text recall and maintain performance (for selected texts) at relatively high levels.

Some evidence pertaining to this testable implication, with respect to each of the three categories, has appeared. For example, Hultsch and Dixon (1983) found that old adults were able to recall information from stories about famous entertainment figures from their generation (about whom they had prior knowledge) at the same rate as young adults. With respect to the second category of skills, Dixon, Hultsch, Simon and von Eye (1984) found that for well-structured stories high verbal old adults were as capable as high verbal young adults in identifying and remembering the main ideas of well-organized texts, even though they recall less of the story, and that this example of attenuated age differences does not hold for low verbal old and young adults.

A number of qualifications and potential explanations apply to both of these examples (see the original articles). One potential explanation for the latter finding – that highly skilled verbal old adults are able to identify and remember the theme of a text – is related to the third category of skills. Specifically, there may be a generalized, naturally occurring shift in style of processing, interpretation or recall throughout adulthood, such that older adults may tend to process discourse thematically or metaphorically. In the remainder of this paper we will summarize the major conceptual and methodological issues involved, as well as a recent experiment designed to test this hypothesis.

COMPENSATION THROUGH AGING-SPECIFIC SKILLS

Can aging-specific skills related to processing, interpreting and remembering discourse serve to compensate for aging-related decline in skills and components normally associated with high levels of performance in this domain? To address this question, we summarize the main conceptual and methodological issues, as well as a recent experiment designed to reflect them (see Dixon and Backman, in press, for a more complete treatment).

The general conceptual issues may be summarized as follows. In reading some texts, (1) do older adults transform them into gist or interpretive units of meaning; (b) do they process them more thematically, metaphorically, wisely, or in terms of social meaning or morals; (c) do they thereby produce a qualitatively different form of response or recall from that produced by young adults; (d) if so, do these qualitatively different forms of recall serve functional or compensatory processes?

The most general methodological issue is the following: This hypothesized different form of response and recall might be overlooked with many irrelevant stimulus materials (e.g., many typical texts), inappropriate instructions, or insensitive scoring procedures (e.g., verbatim or even standard gist recall).

Thus, there are two general research questions, one of which we refer to as a "bold", and the other as a "modest", version. First, the "bold, naturally occurring version": Can unselected older adults compensate for decrements in the molecular components of prose reading and recall through the use of maintained skill in metaphor interpretation, thus performing at a level equivalent to that of young adults in the free recall of texts? Second, the "modest, expertise version": Can highly selected language experts compensate for such decrements and perform at levels equivalent to those of young adult experts or novices?

A logical pattern of age-related results is required before an initial inference of compensation can be proffered. A basic feature of this pattern is that an age-related deficit in the components of the skill (e.g., lexical decision) and the molar skill itself (e.g., free recall of typical texts) is counterbalanced by age-related equivalence or reverse superiority on a substitutable component (e.g., metaphor interpretation) such that equivalent performances on a selected molar skill is observed (free recall of metaphoric texts). The definition and model of compensation implied is elaborated elsewhere (Backman and Dixon, 1986; Salthouse, 1984). Supplemental experimental approaches - involving, for example, manipulation of the observed compensatory mechanism (Dixon and Backman, in press) or the use of alternative models of compensation in reading (e.g., Stanovich, 1984) - are also possible.

In the remainder of this paper we summarize our effort to pursue the "bold version" of the general research question. Thus, based on conceptions of cognitive aging which suggests that successful functioning may be associated a generalized development of an experience-based emphasis on thematic or metaphoric processing of discourse (e.g., Labouvie-Vief, Schell and Weaverdyck, 1980), we sought to investigate whether such a relationship could be demonstrated in normal, community-dwelling adults.

Summary of Procedures and Results

Details of the procedures are available elsewhere (e.g., Dixon and Backman, in press). Materials pertaining to each of the logical steps and associated predictions were collected and administered to young (n = 70; M age = 25.64) and old (n = 66; M age = 68.83) normal adults. Four stories were developed, each with an equivalent number of propositions, but designed to vary along two dimensions. There were two typical stories (non-metaphoric, expository texts) and two metaphoric stories. The hypothesized compensatory mechanism - metaphor interpretation - was measured via the task described in Boswell (1979). In her study, there was evidence that older adults were as skilled as younger adults in interpreting metaphors. There has also been some tentative evidence presented that this skill may influence the performance of older adults on some discourse processing tasks (e.g., Adams, Dorosz, Holmes, Bass, Gossiaux and Labouvie-Vief, 1985).

The pattern of results matches very closely the predicted pattern. First, there were significant component-molar task correlations (range: .1 to .6) and young adults performed reliably better than old adults in all cases (there were four component tasks). Second, there was evidence that old adults performed as well as young adults in the hypothesized compensatory mechanism of metaphor interpretation. Third, as expected young adults (M = 13.5) performed better than old adults (M = 7.9) on the free recall of propositions from typical texts. Thus, the stage is set for the evaluation of the fourth prediction: Is there indeed evidence in an unselected sample of adults for this form of compensation in text processing? For the free recall (and other response measures of metaphoric stories young adults (M = 12.0) still performed better than old adults (M = 5.0).

CONCLUSION

One issue with which we are concerned is the conditions under which old adults might maintain reading and memory for text skills. We introduced a model of one mode through which such maintenance could occur, namely, compensation via substitution of alternative, cognitively supportive skills (or components thereof). Our first effort was to investigate whether there was evidence supporting the boldest hypothesis. The present data do not support unequivocally the presence of a generalized, age-related compensation for deficits in basic cognitive capabilities through the utilization of a preserved metaphoric skill.

The present results, however, do not speak to the modest, or expertise, version of the hypothesis. In our present research we are investigating whether highly selected older adults (e.g., retired professors of linguistics and literature) may show evidence of this kind of developing dynamic between expertise and compensation.

REFERENCES

Adams, C., Dorosz, M., Holmes, C., Bass, S., Gossiaux, D. and Labouvie-Vief, G. (November 1985). 'Qualitative age differences in story recall', paper presented at the Annual Meeting of the Gerontological Society of America, New Orleans.

Backman, L. and Dixon, R.A. (1986). Compensation, unpublished manuscript, University of Umea, Sweden.

Baltes, P.B., Dittmann-Kohli, F. and Dixon, R.A. (1984). 'New perspectives on the development of intelligence in adulthood: Toward a dual-process conception and a model of selective optimization with compensation', in Life-span Development and Behavior (Vol. 6) (Eds. P.B. Baltes and O.G. Brim, Jr.), Academic Press, New York.

Boswell, D.A. (1979). 'Metaphoric processing in the mature years', Human Development, 22, 373-384.

Charness, N. (in press). 'Age and expertise: Responding to Talland's challenge', in Everyday Cognition in Adulthood and Late Life' (Eds. L.W. Poon, D.C. Rubin and B.A. Wilson), Cambridge University Press, New York.

Denney, N.W. (1982). 'Aging and cognitive changes', in Handbook of Developmental Psychology (Ed. B.B. Wolman), Prentice Hall, Englewood Cliffs, NJ.

Dixon, R.A. and Backman, L. (in press). 'Reading and memory for prose in adulthood: Issues of expertise and compensation', in

Reading Across the Lifespan (Eds. S.R. Yussen and M.C. Smith), Springer-Verlag, New York.

Dixon, R.A. and Baltes, P.B. (1986). 'Toward life-span research on the functions and pragmatics of intelligence', in Practical Intelligence: Nature and Origins of Competence in the Everyday World (Eds. R.J. Sternberg and R.K. Wagner), Cambridge University Press, New York.

Dixon, R.A., Hultsch, D.F., Simon, E.W. and von Eye, A. (1984). 'Verbal ability and text structure effects on adult age differences in test recall', Journal of Verbal Learning and Verbal Behavior, 23, 569-578.

Hoyer, W.J. (1985). 'Aging and the development of expert cognition', in New Directions in Cognitive Science (Eds. T.M. Schlecter and M.P. Toglia), Ablex, Norwood, NJ.

Hultsch, D.F. and Dixon, R.A. (1983). 'The role of pre-experimental knowledge in text processing in adulthood', Experimental Aging Research, 9, 17-22.

Labouvie-Vief, G. (1985). 'Intelligence and cognition', in Handbook of the Psychology of Aging (2nd ed.) (Eds. J.E. Birren and K.W. Schaie), Van Nostrand Reinhold, New York.

Labouvie-Vief, G., Schell,D.A. and Weaverdyck, S.E. (November 1980). 'Recall deficit in the aged: A fable recalled', paper presented at the Annual Meeting of the Gerontological Society of America, San Diego, CA.

Light, L.L. and Anderson, P.A. (1983). 'Memory for scripts in young and older adults', Memory and Cognition, 11, 435-444.

Meyer, B.J.F. and Rice, G.E. (1983). 'Learning and memory from text across the adult life span', in Developmental Studies in Discourse (Eds. J. Fine and R.O. Freedle), Ablex, Norwood, NJ.

Salthouse, T.A. (1984). 'Effects of age and skill in typing', Journal of Experimental Psychology: General, 113, 345-371.

Stanovich, K.E. (1984). 'The interactive-compensatory model of reading: A confluence of developmental, experimental, and educational psychology', Remedial and Special Education, 5, 11-19.

Stratton, G.M. (1982). 'The mnemonic feat of the "Shass Pollak"', in Memory Observed: Remembering in Natural Contexts (Ed. U. Neisser), pp. 311-314, W.H. Freeman, San Francisco.

Wilding, J. and Valentine, E. (1985). 'One man's memory for prose, faces and names', British Journal of Psychology, 76, 215-219.

Yates, F.A. (1966). The Art of Memory, Routledge and Kegan Paul, London.

SPEECH AND WRITING ACROSS THE LIFE-SPAN

Susan Kemper and Shannon J. Rash
University of Kansas
Lawrence, KS U.S.A.

ABSTRACT

Several studies of adults' language are reviewed including a cross-sectional analysis of oral language from adults ages 50 to 90 years and a longitudinal analysis of written language from diaries kept by adults for seven or more decades. The review focuses on syntactic changes that minimize the demands placed on working memory during sentence production. Yngve's model of sentence planning processes is reviewed in light of the observed syntactic changes. Finally, implications of these analyses for the preparation of written materials for elderly adults are discussed.

INTRODUCTION

Adults' language is commonly assumed to "crystallize" during adolescence and remain invariant across the life-span. This assumption is not warranted; rather, language development appears to be a life-long process such that adults' language undergoes a continual process of change in response to other changes in adult cognition. In particular, it appears that adults' production of complex syntactic constructions is affected by age-related performance limitations that reduce their use of complex syntactic constructions such as subordinate and embedded clauses.

Age-related decrements in adults' production of complex syntactic constructions are evident in the data reported in Table 1, taken from Kemper (1986). Language samples were taken from spontaneous oral narratives produced by adults 50 - 59, 60 - 69, 70 - 79, and 80 - 89 years. In this analysis, each sentence was parsed into main, subordinate, and embedded clauses. Then, the mean number of clauses per sentence was computed for each sample. Finally, the mean number of subject-embedded, right-branching clauses and the mean number of object-embedded, left-branching clauses was determined. Right-branching clauses include sentence-final subordinate clauses, relative clauses modifying the direct object, and infinitive or other verb phrase complements. Left-branching clauses include sentence-initial subordinate clauses, relative clauses modifying the sentential subject, and gerunds or that-clauses used as sentential subjects.

As the table indicates, there is a reduction in the mean number of clauses per sentence across this age-range, indicating that the overall complexity of the adults' speech declines. Further, there are reductions in both the incidence of right-branching or subject-embedded clauses and the incidence of left-branching or object-embedded clauses across this age range. Although right-branching clauses are more numerous than left-branching clauses, the decline for left-branching clauses (75%) is greater than that for right-branching clauses (12%).

Table 1
Results of the analysis of adults' speech.

	Age Group			
	50 - 59	60 - 69	70 - 79	80 - 89
Clauses/sentence	2.8	2.3	1.9	1.7
Right-branch #	1.6	1.6	1.5	1.4
Left-branch #	1.2	.7	.3	.3

A similar loss of syntactic complexity is evident in adults' written language. The data in Table 2 are from Kemper's (1987a) analysis of diaries adults kept for seven or more decades. The adults were born between 1856 and 1876 and died between 1943 and 1967. From each set of diaries, only the two longest, analyzable entries from each half-decade were analyzed. The analysis involved classifying each clause as main, subordinate, or embedded and determining the mean number of clauses per sentence and the incidence of left-branching and right-branching clauses. Not only is there a net reduction in the mean number of clauses per sentence across this age range, but the number of subject-embedded, right-branching clauses and the number of object-embedded, left-branching clauses show age-related declines. Further, the decline for left-branching clauses (83%) is somewhat more precipitous than that for right-branching clauses (41%).

Table 2
Results of the analysis of adults' written diaries.

	Decade						
	20s	30s	40s	50s	60s	70s	80s
Clauses/sentence	7.40	6.73	5.49	4.75	3.21	2.76	3.21
Right-branch #	4.69	5.10	4.06	3.57	2.51	2.37	2.76
Left-branch #	2.71	1.63	1.43	1.18	.76	.39	.45

Although the comparison of these two language samples suggests that written language is somewhat more complex than oral language, a similar pattern of age-related changes to syntactic complexity emerges in both samples. It appears that there is an overall decline in the complexity of adults' language, whether written or oral. Further, this loss of syntactic complexity is primarily due to a loss of subject-embedded, left-branching constructions. These changes do not appear to result from functional changes in topic or discourse genre (Kemper, 1987b) but to reflect underlying changes in basic psycholinguistic processes.

The asymmetry in the production and decline of left- and right-branching clauses suggests a possible explanation for the reduction in the complexity of adults' oral and written language. Left-branching constructions have been assumed to be more difficult to comprehend than right-branching constructions because they impose greater demands on working memory during comprehension (see Kemper, 1987a). Working memory limitations, thus, may affect adults' production of complex syntactic constructions if a similar argument holds for sentence production.

SENTENCE PRODUCTION PROCESSES

An asymmetry in the production of left- and right-branching sentences is commonly assumed in recent models of sentence production processes, yet the most extensive examination of the role of syntactic structure during sentence production remains that of Yngve (1960). Yngve assumed that sentences are produced from the top down and from left to right and that a temporary storage buffer, perhaps limited to 7 ± 2 nodes, is required to hold "unrealized" constituent nodes during sentence production. Yngve proposed a "depth" metric in order to compute the memory requirements of different sentences. For example, the sentence "When very clearly projected pictures appeared, they applauded" has a depth = 5 while the sentence "John mumbled, Mary giggled, Bill laughed, and Tom went home" has a depth = 2. The left-branching sentence has greater depth because the unrealized subject and predicate nodes must be held in memory while the subordinate clause is being produced; the coordinate sentence is shallow because each subject-predicate pair is produced serially.

Because Yngve's model of sentence production processes allows for the precise measurement of memory requirements, it was applied to samples of adults' spontaneous oral speech. Samples of adults' speech were selected from the data reported in Kemper (in press-a). The mean depth of each sample was computed by following Yngve's rules, assuming a generalized phrase-structure approach to the analysis of English syntax. These depth measures are reported in Table 3. Average WAIS digit spans for these adults are also reported from Kemper (1986).

Table 3
Adults' mean Yngve depth and digit span.

	Age Group			
	50 - 59	60 - 69	70 - 79	80 - 89
Yngve Depth	5.9	5.4	4.1	3.2
Digit span	6.3	5.9	5.4	5.3

Clearly, both the Yngve depth and the mean number of clauses per sentence decline with the age of the speaker and with their digit spans. Indeed, mean Yngve depth correlates $r(60) = .76$ with the adults' digit span. This finding is consistent with the hypothesis that a reduction in working memory capacity restricts elderly adults' ability to produce complex syntactic structures.

IMPLICATIONS

This research on adults' production of complex syntactic constructions has clear implications for the preparation of prose materials for use with elderly adults. The research indicates that elderly adults have difficulty producing complex sentences involving embedded and subordinate clauses. Conversely, they may have difficulty processing prose materials containing complex sentences.

To explore this possibility, several passages used in studies of adults' prose recall were analyzed. These passages were: the "Monkey" passage used by Mandel and Johnson (1984), the "Farmer," "Parakeet," and "Circle Island" passages used by Zelinski, Light, and Gilewski, (1984), and the "Tulip" and "Emma" texts used by Spilich (1985).

TABLE 4
Summary measures of syntactic complexity and recall.

	Monkey	Farmer	Parakeet	Circle Island	Tulip & Emma
Right-branch %	34%	34%	15%	42%	42%
Left-branch %	2%	11%	8%	3%	13%
Main clause %	64%	54%	77%	55%	45%
Clauses/sentence	1.56	1.94	1.50	1.83	2.38
Recall$_{young}$	26.8[a]	69%[b]	30%[b]	47%[b]	31.1[c]
Recall$_{elderly}$	24.2[a]	58%[b]	25%[b]	30%[b]	13.8[c]
Recall$_{e/y}$	93%	84%	83%	64%	45%

[a]Nodes.   [b]Idea units.   [c]Propositions.

In the analysis, each main, subordinate, and embedded clause was identified and classified according to branching direction; the mean number of clauses per sentence and the proportion of each type of clause were computed. These measures were correlated with the measures of young and elderly adults' recall given in the original reports and with the elderly adults' recall expressed as a percentage of the young adults' recall. The results are summarized in Tables 4 and 5.

While neither the young nor elderly adults' recall is correlated with any of these measures of syntactic complexity, there is a significant correlation between syntactic complexity and the elderly adults' recall expressed as a percentage of the young adults' recall. In other words, syntactic complexity, as measured by the mean number of clauses per sentence, correlates with the elderly adults' *decrement* in recall. Consider the extremes: the "Monkey" passage is written in relatively simple syntax averaging only 1.56 clauses per sentence and the elderly adults' recall was equivalent to that of the young adults; in contrast, the "Tulip" and "Emma" texts are written with relatively complex syntax averaging 2.58 clauses per sentence and the elderly adults' recall was only 45% of that of the young adults'. The other texts fall within these extremes.

TABLE 5

Correlations between syntactic complexity and recall measures.

	$Recall_{young}$	$Recall_{elderly}$	$Recall_{e/y}$
Right-branch %	+.22	-.04	-.60
Left-branch %	-.37	-.18	-.30
Main clause %	-.31	-.04	+.71
Clauses/sentence	+.21	-.09	-.84*

*$p < .05$

Although based on a small sample, these findings may partially explain the wide variety of results found in studies of adults' prose comprehension and recall. Other factors, such as differences in educational level, intelligence, or text genre, may also determine whether or not quantitative and qualitative differences are found in comparisons of young and elderly adults' prose recall. These results, however, suggest a simple explanation for the variety of research findings: young and elderly adults may have equivalent recall of syntactically simple prose but elderly adults' recall of syntactically complex prose may be quantitatively and qualitatively different from that of young adults' due to working memory limitations that reduce elderly adults' syntactic processing abilities.

Indeed, such appears to be the case. Kemper (in press) conducted a study of adults' prose recall that explicitly compared middle-aged and elderly adults' recall of syntactically simple and complex sentences. Short paragraphs were created that included left- and right-branching sentences. Recall was scored in terms of propositions, broken down by the syntactic form of the original sentence expressing each proposition. Overall, middle-aged adults in their 40s and 50s recalled 65% of the propositions regardless of the syntactic form in which they were expressed. The elderly adults in their 70s and 80s recalled 60% of the propositions from the right-branching clauses but only 22% of the propositions from the left-branching clauses. Thus, the middle-aged and elderly adults had nearly equivalent recall of the right-branching sentences but the elderly adults had significantly worse recall of the more complex left-branching sentences.

CONCLUSIONS

Our argument is a simple one: working memory limitations appear to affect elderly adults' production and comprehension of complex syntactic structures and, consequently, may affect their performance on other psycholinguistic processing tasks including tests of prose comprehension and recall. This review of

S. KEMPER AND S.J. RASH

longitudinal and cross-sectional changes in adults' oral and written language has examined the processing demands imposed by complex syntactic structures. The loss of sentence embeddings, hence a reduction in the mean number of clauses per sentence, appears to result from a decline of working memory capacity, although other explanations, such as changes in syntactic processing strategies or an alteration in the speed of syntactic processing operations, are consistent with these findings. A practical aspect of this line of research is that it has clear implications for the development of prose materials to optimize adults' comprehension and recall by minimizing memory demands during sentence processing.

ACKNOWLEDGEMENT
          This research was supported by University of Kansas Biomedical Research Support Grant RR0737 and by grant AG06319 from the National Institute on Aging.

REFERENCES

Kemper, S. (1986, November). 'Capacity limits and syntactic complexity in adults'. Paper presented at the Psychonomics Society, New Orleans.

Kemper, S. (1987a, July). 'Adults' diaries: Changes to written language across the life-span'. Paper presented at the Conference on Social Psychology and Language, Bristol.

Kemper, S. (1987b). 'LIfe-span changes in syntactic complexity', Journal of Gerontology, 42, 323-328.

Kemper, S. (in press). 'Syntactic complexity and the recall of prose by middle-aged and elderly adults', Experimental Aging Research.

Mandel, R.G. and Johnson, N.S. (1984). 'A developmental analysis of story recall and comprehension in adulthood', Journal of Verbal Learning and Verbal Behavior, 23, 643-659.

Spilich, G. J. (1983). 'Life-span components of text processing: Structural and procedural differences', Journal of Verbal Learning and Verbal Behavior, 22, 231-244.

Yngve, V. H. (1960). 'A model and a hypothesis for language structure', Proceedings of the American Philosophical Society, 104, 444-466.

Zelinski, E., Light, L.L. and Gilewski, M.J. (1984). 'Adult age differences in memory for prose: The question of sensitivity to passage structure', Developmental Psychology, 20, 1181-1192.

I'LL NEVER FORGET WHAT'S-HER-NAME:
AGING AND TIP OF THE TONGUE EXPERIENCES IN EVERYDAY LIFE

Deborah Burke, Joanna Worthley and Jennifer Martin
Department of Psychology, Pomona College
Claremont, CA 91711, U.S.A.

ABSTRACT
          We examined young and older adults' spontaneous tip of the
tongue   experience (TOTs) using structured diaries   to   record
information about each lapse. Older adults had more frequent   TOT
experiences and knew less about the sound of TOT words than   young
adults.   Most TOTs were for proper names but there were   age
differences in the types of words involved in other TOTs. While most
TOT's were resolved, the method of resolution was also age dependent.
The results suggest that aging affects automatic retrieval processes,
in contrast to the popular view emerging from laboratory   research
that aging affects only effortful processes.

          Cognitive   psychology has seen a substantial increase over
the last ten years in research concerned with the nature of cognitive
change in old age. The methodology and theory for   much of this
research is guided by general principles derived from young adults'
behaviour in the laboratory. This approach to research has been
criticized by Neisser and others (Neisser, 1978; 1985; Bruce, 1985)
who   have   suggested   that   studies   should   be   motivated by
characteristics of ordinary human experience, not just by general
theories of memory. This suggestion is particularly apt in the study
of aging.   Older adults' performance in the laboratory appears to
bear little relation to their everyday memory problems (e.g.,
Sunderland, Watts, Baddeley and Harris, 1986).   Thus, processes
involved in age differences in laboratory tasks may be irrelevant for
memory problems which are of primary concern to older adults.
          Indeed, one of the most frequent memory problems in
everyday life according to self reports of older adults is the   TOT
experience (Sunderland et al., 1986). Yet there has been only one
published study of TOTs in old age (Cohen and Faulkner, 1986).
Further, if TOTs do increase with age, this phenomenon would seem to
be incompatible with theoretical principles motivating current aging
research, namely that memory and language impairment in old age are a
consequence of attentional deficits.
          The present study examines the nature of spontaneous TOT
experiences and their relation to aging. Our rationale for this
study includes an interest in basic memory principles and their
relevance to age-related memory declines. We are, however, also
interested in the practical problem of helping older adults cope with
TOT experiences. Indeed, our study was motivated in part by our wish
to respond to the older participants in our laboratory research who
commented, "If you want to study something really important, find out
why I can't remember the name of my friend of 20 years when I go to

introduce her."

THE TOT EXPERIENCE
Occasionally the flow of fluent speech is interrupted because a desired word does not come to mind even though we are certain we 'know' it. The cognitive failure and emotional discomfort associated with this TOT state was well described by William James (1890) as '... a gap that is intensely active.' (p.243) Since then, there have been a few studies of TOTs induced in the laboratory (e.g., Brown and McNeill, 1966) and of spontaneous TOTs (Reason and Lucas, 1983) which suggest certain processes involved in TOTs and their resolution.

First, TOT states appear to be the result of a temporary and partial inaccessibility of phonological and orthographic information in the lexicon. People usually know the correct initial letter and number of syllables of the target word (e.g., Brown and McNeill, 1966). Often a familiar word related to the target semantically and phonemically comes to mind and refuses to leave (Reason and Lucas, 1983). Subjects use more retrieval strategies when such 'blockers' occur, but it is not known if blockers impair resolution. Subjects described a variety of retrieval strategies such as the use of an internal cue, e.g., alphabetical search through memory, and the use of an external cue, e.g., a dictionary. TOTs are also resolved by the target word popping into mind spontaneously at a time when attention is not being directed to the search. Finally, the feeling of knowing (FOK) for an inaccessible word is a good indicator of the likelihood of recall (Gruneberg and Sykes, 1978).

THE PRESENT STUDY
We report here findings from subjects who kept a structured diary of all TOTs occurring during a four week interval. For each TOT they answered a set of 11 questions in the diary including questions about the type of word involved, FOK, familiarity of the word, features of the word, retrieval strategies, blockers, and method of resolution if resolved.

Our subjects were 30 young adults (mean age=19.7 years) and 30 older adults (mean age=70.5 years) who were part of a larger study of TOT experiences during the life span (Burke, Worthley and Martin, 1987). Older adults were well educated (mean years of education=15.7) and had significantly higher WAIS vocabulary scores than young adults (means=72.0 and 68.5, respectively). All young adults were undergraduates.

As can be seen in Table 1, older adults had more TOTs over the four week interval (p<.005). Most TOTs were resolved in both age groups. Only 5 out of 183 TOTs were unresolved for older adults and 10 out of 117 for young adults. Consistent with these high resolution rates, FOK was high for both young and older adults (means=6.3 and 6.6, respectively on a 1-7 scale). Certainty of recall was also high but was significantly higher for older adults (means=5.3 and 6.1 for young and older adults respectively, on a 1-7 scale).

TABLE 1

Mean TOTs Per Month, Percent Resolved and Percent Blocked

	TOTs	Resolved	Blocked
Young adults	3.9 range=1-7	91.5%	70.1%
Old adults	6.1 range=1-17	97.3%	47.3%

Although young and older adults had equivalent success in resolving their TOTs, they did so in different ways. Subjects indicated one of the three methods of resolution shown in Table 2 for each resolved TOT. There was a signfiicant interaction of resolution method with age group, $F(2,110)=5.23$, $p<.01$. Older adults had relatively fewer resolutions through memory search or external consultation, and relatively more resolutions through "pop ups" in which the word came to mind without conscious effort to retrieve it. Young adults also used significantly more different retrieval strategies while in the TOT state than did older adults. The mean number of strategies for each TOT was 2.1 for young adults and 1.5 for older adults, $p<.01$. However the effectiveness of any strategy was about the same across age. Given that a strategy was used, the probability of success in terms of target retrieval was .26 for young adults and .28 for older adults. Thus the age differences in method of resolution seem to reflect younger adults' greater utilization of strategies. That is, younger adults might have had more "pop ups" if they had used fewer strategies.

TABLE 2

Percent of Resolved TOTs by Method of Resolution

	Memory Search Strategy	Consulted Book/Person	Popped Up
Young Adults	22.4%	36.5%	41.2%
Older Adults	15.2%	27.0%	57.8%

Blockers occurred significantly more frequently for young than older adults ($p<.01$), as can be seen in Table 1. Thus the increase in frequency of TOTs in old age seems unrelated to the occurrence of blockers. It also seems unlikely that blocking affected the probability of resolution as almost all TOT's were resolved. Blocked TOTs did not seem more difficult to resolve as there was no difference between blocked and unblocked TOTs in FOK or certainty of recall. Further, the method of resolution was also unaffected by blocking. The frequency of occurrence of blockers for young adults is almost identical to that found by Reason and Lucas (1983) for a similar age group. We did not, however, replicate their finding that blocked TOTs are more likely to involve external strategies for resolution.

Not only did young adults have more blockers come to mind while in the TOT state, they also knew more features of the TOT word than older adults. The mean number of features reported for each TOT was 2.17 and 1.51 for young and older adults respectively, p<.01. Features involving the sound of the word were reported most frequently for both age groups. Thus, we are inclined to agree with Cohen and Faulkner (1986) that 'blockers' may be associated with increased access to information about the TOT word.

Finally, there was an interesting age difference in the types of words involved in the TOTs. In Table 3 TOTs are grouped into three categories: proper names, common names of objects and a third category of non-object nouns (e.g., "carbonation"), adjectives and verbs. The category construction was based on patterns in the data. Older adults' TOTs were almost exclusively proper names or common names of objects. Young adults had slightly over half of their TOTs for proper names and the rest for the more abstract words in the third category, with almost no TOTs for object names. Within the proper name category, both age groups and more TOTs for names of acquaintances than names of famous people, 24.5% and 13.0%, respectively for young and 29.1% and 16.4% respectively for older adults.

TABLE 3

Type of Word in TOTs

	Name of Person/ Place/Movie	Name of Object	Non-object Noun, Adj., Verb
Young adults	55.9%	4.0%	39.7%
Older adults	68.2%	22.0%	9.0%

Examples

Young	"Jessica"	"steer"	"idiomatic"
Old	"Casablanca"	"tagamet"	"exude"

CONCLUSIONS

Older adults are indeed correct in their perception that TOT experiences are an increasing problem in old age. The usually effortless process of word retrieval becomes more susceptible to temporary disruption with age. Further, older adults have available less information of any kind about the lexical code, including "blockers", a finding consistent with Cohen and Faulkner (1986). Young adults have relatively more TOTs for a category of words that includes procedures (e.g., "amniocentesis"), abstract nouns (e.g., "typicality") and adjectives and verbs (e.g., "ambitious"; "alienate"). We think this type of word effect arises, in part, because our young subjects were in college. We have some evidence that most of the TOTs in this category occurred when they were writing papers or speaking in class.

Older adults were less likely to engage in strategies to retrieve target words, relying instead on spontaneous retrievals ("pop-ups) for resolution. And this was in fact a quite reliable method of resolution. Indeed, older adults had greater confidence that they would recall the TOT word. This may reflect years of experience with TOTs and their habit of eventually popping into mind.

Our findings lead us to the conclusion that lexical retrieval processes, which usually seem to require little attention, are disrupted in old age. Of course, these naturalistic data may be subject to reporting biases (e.g., if one age group had greater accuracy in reporting), so confirmation of our findings with TOTs induced in the laboratory is necessary. Nonetheless, our results demonstrate the importance of the investigation of spontaneous behaviour for the development of empirical and theoretical principles of cognition.

REFERENCES

Brown, R. and McNeill, D. (1966). 'The "Tip-of-the-Tongue" Phenomenon', Journal of Verbal Learning and Verbal Behavior, 5, 325-337.

Bruce, D. (1985). 'The how and why of ecological memory', Journal of Experimental Psychology: General, 114, 78-90.

Burke, D.M., Worthley, J. and Martin, J. (1987). 'Aging and the Tip-of-the-Tongue Phenomenon through the adult life span', Unpublished manuscript, Pomona College, Claremont, CA.

Cohen. G. and Faulkner, D. (1986). 'Memory for proper names: Age differences in retrieval', British Journal of Developmental Psychology, 4, 187-197.

Gruneberg, M.M. and Sykes, R.N. (1978). 'Knowledge and Retention: The feeling of knowing and reminiscence', in Practical Aspects of Memory (Eds. M.M. Gruneberg, P.E. Morris and R.N. Sykes), pp.189-196, Academic Press, New York.

James, W. (1890/1981). The Principles of Psychology, Vol. 1, Harvard University Press, Cambridge, MA.

Neisser, U. (1978). 'Memory: What are the important questions?'. In Practical Aspects of Memory (Eds. M.M. Gruneberg, P.E. Morris and R.N. Sykes), pp.189-196, Academic Press, London.

Neisser, U. (1985). 'The role of theory in the ecological study of memory', Journal of Experimental Psychology: General, 114, 272-276.

Reason, J.T. and Lucas, D. (1983). 'Using cognitive diaries to investigate naturally occurring memory blocks'. In Everyday Memory, Actions and Absent-Mindedness (Eds. J.E. Harris and P.E. Morris), pp.53-70, Academic Press, London.

Sunderland,   A., Watts, K., Baddeley, A.D. and Harris,   J.E.   (1986).
'Subjective   memory assessment and test performance in the   elderly',
Journal of Gerontology, 41, 376-384.

PROSPECTIVE MEMORY AND AGING

Robin L. West

Department of Psychology,
University of Florida at Gainesville, U.S.A.

ABSTRACT

In the first of two studies, adolescents, young adults, and old adults had to make a phone call and mail a postcard including a message describing their strategies. All groups performed the basic task on time, but the older adults were most likely to forget the strategy message. External aids were reported more often by the younger groups. Participants in a second study had to deliver messages on cue during an interview. The young remembered more message details and were more accurate than the old. Variations in external cue type had more impact on the older adults. These data do not support the notion, based on earlier research, that greater use of external aids allows the old to perform prospective memory tasks as well as the young. Instead, cue effectiveness is determined by cue context.

Prospective memory stands alone as a type of memory in which remembering, per se, is not enough. Prospective memory is remembering to carry out an activity or task. An individual may recall the need to make a doctor's appointment six or seven times (this would be called retrospective remembering in that the person remembers an item of information) but in terms of prospective memory, no "credit" is given until the appointment is actually made. It is easy for prospective memory to fail between the retrospective recall and the completion of the required action (Harris, 1984; Poon & Schaffer, 1982; Wilkins & Baddeley, 1978). In Meacham's terms, the memory itself is a means to a goal (Meacham, 1982), and the assessment of performance looks at goal accomplishment as an indication of memory success.

Prospective memory is important to study, not only because its characteristics are different from retrospective memory (Baddeley & Wilkins, 1984; Meacham, 1982). It also deserves special consideration because prospective memory is not correlated with secondary memory (e.g., Wilkins & Baddeley, 1978) and because it represents a common memory activity (Cavanaugh et al., 1983; Harris, 1980; West, 1984). Studies of prospective memory have also resulted in no age differences in performance (Moscovitch, 1982; Poon & Schaffer, 1982; Sinnott, 1986). (Sinnott's tasks do not fit the usual definition of prospective memory and will not be reviewed here.)

Poon and Schaffer (1982) asked younger and older adults to call a phone number 25 times in three weeks. The calls were made at a prearranged time designated by the experimenter or the subject and

monetary incentives were varied. Older adults remembered more calls
and were more accurate than the younger adults. Older adults were
more accurate with higher payments, whereas the young generally were
late, regardless of payment. The performance of the young, but not
the older adults, deteriorated during the three week study.

Moscovitch (1982) asked older and younger adults to call a
telephone answering service. When subjects picked one time to call
every day for two weeks, older adults were less likely to forget
calls than the young. When experimenters selected two call times at
random over a two-week period, age differences were smaller but the
older adults still remembered more calls. These results appeared to
be due to a reliance on internal strategies by the young and external
aids by the old -- when experimenters strongly discouraged external
mnemonics, they obtained comparable performance by the two age groups
(Moscovitch, 1982).

The present research examined age-related differences in
the use of external aids, a strategy particularly appropriate for
prospective memory (Harris, 1984). Existing self-report data has
shown that older adults use external aids at least as often as
younger adults (Cavanaugh et al., 1983; Moscovitch, 1982; West,
1984), but there are no studies examining age-related differences in
prospective memory strategies. This research was also designed to
avoid lifestyle variations that may have affected earlier
investigations of this type. Moscovitch (1982) did not think that
lifestyle was critical, arguing that both age groups consisted of
busy, active people, but Poon and Schaffer (1982) found that younger
subjects performed better when call times were self-selected, to fit
personal schedules.

INVESTIGATION I
In this study, adults from three age groups were asked to
perform two prospective memory tasks and to report on their
strategies. The frequency of internal and external strategies was
recorded. To avoid the influence of lifestyle, the prospective tasks
were very flexible. Subjects had to respond only on a particular
day, rather than at a particular time.

Methods
Adolescents, group A (14-18 yrs, M = 16.3, N = 23), younger
adults, group Y (25-40 yrs, M = 32.4, N = 24) and older adults, group
O (60-81 yrs, M = 73.9, N = 24) participated. All individuals were
healthy and residing in the community.

The prospective memory task instructions were administered
at the end of an hour-long interview in which a number of everyday
memory tasks were completed. Participants were asked to leave a
message on a telephone answering machine before retiring for the
night and to mail a postcard two days after the interview. They were
also instructed to give a strategy message explaining how they
remembered each prospective task.

Results and Discussion
Of the 73 participants, 19% failed to make the phone call,
11% failed to mail the card, and only 36% completed both tasks on the
correct day, as instructed. The best strategy for the subjects who

remembered to make the phone call was to write a note. Among those who used a note, 95% completed the call correctly. Note writing was used more often by the younger groups: 41% A, 36% Y, 23% O. Strategy data were not available for the subjects who forgot to call. Chi-square analysis was used to examine errors. Although it appeared that older adults were most likely to forget the strategy message (13% A, 29% Y, 38% O) and that the younger groups were more likely to forget the call completely (26% A, 21% Y, 12% O), there were no significant group differences in error types.

For the postcard task, the most effective strategies (used more by the younger groups) were to leave the card in a prominent place or write a note: 35% A, 38% Y, 19% O. Error types varied with age group, X (4,N=41) = 5.9, p < .05 - older adults were most likely to send in the postcard without strategy message (21% A, 42% Y, 61% O); adolescents were most likely to forget to mail the card (23% A, 8% Y, 4% O).

These results failed to confirm the notion that older adults use external cues more often than young people. However, the data are confounded by the fact that many subjects forgot to describe their strategies, and they were often the older subjects. Anecdotally, there was an indication that the older adults probably used external cues because they remembered to mail the postcard (likely to be remembered with an external cue as described above) and failed to include the required strategy message (probably "rehearsed" internally if at all). More controlled studies of cue usage are needed to explore this issue further.

INVESTIGATION II

In this study a prospective task was embedded in an interview and participants had to perform the task on cue. The critical variable was the type of cue -- verbal + situational or verbal + visual. In previous research, no age deficit in prospective memory was observed in timing accuracy or basic task completion. In all previous studies, the external cues were subject-generated, in the home. To test the generality of previous findings, the cues in this study were provided by and controlled by the experimenter in a testing situation. Nevertheless, they were still external cues and their presence should have eliminated age-related performance differences if the use of external cues is the critical factor explaining the lack of age differences in the past. In this study, two different types of external cues were compared.

Methods

There were 26 older adult volunteers (63-83 yrs, M = 72.0) and 26 students participating for course credit (19-23 yrs, M = 19.8). None of the older adults were institutionalized and individuals with dementia or cardiovascular problems were excluded.

Participants were asked to deliver messages during two everyday memory interviews (EMI-I and EMI-II). Each interview lasted one hour. In EMI-I, subjects were told to remind the interviewer to make a phone call, and to describe one activity planned for the next day. They were also told that the interviewer would say, "the interview is over now" to notify them that the appointed message time had come. Interview closing procedures also provided the subjects with a situational cue. Many activities occurred at the end of the interview. The interviewer put away the materials, a debriefing form was signed, and closing social comments were made. Any one of these could have served as a cue. Together, they provided a rich situational cue for remembering the two messages. The interviewer gave the prospective task instructions 30 minutes before the end of the interview (range = 18-43 min, M = 30.3 min). The average time delay between the task instructions and the verbal cue was significantly longer for the old, $F(1,50) = 17.3$, p < .001. There was no relationship between performance and time interval (young r = -.03, old r = .04).

In EMI-II, individuals were asked to remind the interviewer to check her tape recorder and to get a pen out of a folder. Subjects were also told that the interviewer would say, "that is the end of the passage recall test" to notify them that the appointed message time had come. Also, the folder was visible on the table throughout the entire interview as a visual cue. The interviewer gave the instructions 35 minutes before the end of the passage recall test (range = 21-47 min, M = 34.6 min). The average time delay between instructions and verbal cue was significantly longer for the told, $F(1,50) = 9.34$, p < .005. There was no relationship between performance and time interval (young r = .09, old r = -.14).

Results and Discussion

For EMI-I and EMI-II, one point was given if the subject recalled that there was a message to give but forgot its contents. Additional points were given for correct recall of the contents of each message. The analysis examined the number of points using a 2 (Age) X 2 (Interview version) mixed analysis of variance. A second analysis examined timing accuracy. Individuals were categorized as "accurate" only if they completed the prospective task within two minutes of the verbal cue.

There was a significant main effect for age in recall points, with the younger adults (M = 2.6) remembering more message details than the older adults (M = 1.7). There was no interaction of age and interview version. Cue type did not affect recall, but it did affect timing accuracy. Among the young, 85% in EMI-I and 81% in EMI-II were accurate. Older adults, on the other hand, were accurate significantly less often in EMI-II (31%) than EMI-I (50%). Age accounted for 13% of the variance in EMI-I and 25% of the variance in timing accuracy in EMI-II. The impact of cue type was confirmed in a loglinear analysis (saturated model) examining the interaction of age and interview version. The dependent variable was accuracy. There was no interaction of age and accuracy in EMI-I, but there was a significant interaction in EMI-II, $z = 2.8$, p<.05.

GENERAL DISCUSSION

This research confirmed that there are no age differences in making phone calls or mailing postcards from home. At the same time, the second investigation indicated that previous research results based on in-home prospective memory tasks are not generalizable to all kinds of prospective memory. When messages had to be delivered during ongoing memory testing in the laboratory, older adults did not perform as well as younger adults. This finding cannot be explained by the lack of available external cues for the older adults because two external cues were present in both interview versions. Age-related lifestyle differences that could affect timing accuracy are not a problem in this research.

There are a number of potential explanations for the discrepant results of these two investigations. One possibility focuses on the source of the cue. In earlier studies, participants were expected to develop meaningful cues for themselves. In this study, the cues were provided by the experimenter and may have been less effective for that reason. This seems an unlikely explanation because older adults do no better with self-generated cues than with experimenter-generated cues for recall (e.g., Rabinowitz & Ackerman, 1982). Another rejected explanation focuses on motivation (cf. Poon & Schaffer, 1982; Sinnott, 1986). There is no reason to believe that a prospective task assigned in the laboratory (to be completed at home) should carry with it higher motivational consequences than a prospective task assigned and carried out in the laboratory. If anything, motivation ought to be higher in the latter case because the experimenter is present and could chastise an individual for failure to perform a prospective assignment.

An alternative explanation focuses on the time frames of the two studies. Perhaps older adults are more mindful of long-term obligations, set up as appointments or responsibilities, than they are of short-term obligations to deliver messages. Perhaps external cues that are available for long periods are more likely to be heeded than those available for short periods because of greater opportunity for review. This explanation is now under investigation. It should be noted, however, that this explanation cannot account for the interaction of age and cue type in Investigation II.

A better interpretation focuses on context. Unlike previous studies in which prospective tasks were done in the home, the messages in Investigation II had to be delivered in the laboratory, as part of ongoing memory testing. It may be that the cues present in the laboratory context were less salient than the external cues subjects developed in the home in other studies. Sinnott (1986) suggested that older adults compensate with 'focusing of skills on salient context-embedded events' (p.111). An at-home reminder to telephone a university as part of a research project is likely to stand out in its context whereas a folder on a desk and statements about the completion of tests are not likely to stand out in the context of an interview including many tests and many materials.

Context differences could also explain the greater effectiveness of the situational + verbal cue for the older adults. The folder was present as a visual cue throughout the interview. The verbal statements also were not unique in that context. However, the situational cue (the end of the interview) was a distinctive event in the testing sequence. Successful cues for older adults may need to possess high "attention-grabbing" qualities. This notion is supported by evidence that older adults performed quite well on a prospective task in the laboratory when direct cues were given (Sunderland et al., 1986). Harris (1978) emphasized the importance of cues that are specific, active, available, easy to use, and well-timed. For older adults, in this case, "distinctive" should be added to the list. For example, a note on white paper in the middle of a bulletin board of notes is not as likely to succeed as a single blue note in a location where notes are seldom found.

REFERENCES

Baddeley, A.D. and Wilkins, A.J. (1984). 'Taking Memory Out of the Laboratory', in Everyday Memory, Actions and Absent-mindedness (Eds. J.E. Harris and P.E. Morris), pp. 1-17, Academic Press, London.

Cavanaugh, J.C., Grady, J.G., and Perlmutter, M. (1983). 'Forgetting and Use of Memory Aids in 20- to 70-Year Olds' Everyday Life', International Journal of Aging and Human Development, 17, 113-122.

Harris, J.E. (1980). 'Memory Aids People Use: Two Interview Studies', Memory and Cognition, 8, 31-38.

Harris, J.E. (1984). 'Remembering to Do things: A Forgotten Topic', in Everyday Memory, Actions and Absent-mindedness (Eds. J.E. Harris and P.E. Morris), pp. 71-92, Academic Press, London.

Meacham, J.A. (1982). 'A Note on Remembering to Execute Planned Actions', Journal of Applied Developmental Psychology, 3, 121-133.

Moscovitch, M. (1982). 'A Neuropsychological Approach to Memory and Perception in Normal and Pathological Aging', in Aging and Cognitive Processes (Eds. F.I.M. Craik and S. Trehub), pp. 55-78, Plenum Press, New York.

Poon, L.W. and Schaffer, G. (1982, August). 'Prospective Memory in Young and Elderly Adults', Paper presented at the meeting of the American Psychological Association, Washington, D.C.

Rabinowitz, J.C. and Ackerman, B.P. (1982). 'General Encoding of Episodic Events by Elderly Adults', in Aging and Cognitive Processes (Eds. F.I.M. Craik and S. Trehub), pp. 145-154, Plenum Press, New York.

Sinnott, J.D. (1986). 'Prospective/Intentional and Incidental Everyday Memory: Effects of Age and Passage of Time', Psychology and Aging, 1, 110-116.

Sunderland, A., Watts, K., Baddeley, A.D., and Harris, J.E. (1986). 'Subjective Memory Assessment and Test Performance in Elderly Adults', Journal of Gerontology, 41, 376-384.

West, R.L. (1984, August). 'An Analysis of Prospective Everyday Memory', Paper presented at the meeting of the American Psychological Association, Toronto.

Wilkins, A. and Baddeley, A. (1978). 'Remembering to Recall in Everyday Life: An Approach to Absent-mindedness', in *Practical Aspects of Memory* (Eds. M.M. Gruneberg, P.E. Morris and R.N. Sykes), pp. 27-34, Academic Press, London.

RECOGNITION MEMORY IN THE NORMAL AGED:
THE ROLE OF SEMANTIC ELABORATION

Donald H. Sykes, Peter Colqhoun and Ruth Leitch
Department of Psychology
The Queen's University of Belfast

ABSTRACT

The impairment in memory following semantic analyses in the normal aged raises questions as to the locus and nature of the failure. Using an indirect measure of individual semantic complexity, the failure is located at later stages of information processing which are involuntary and automatic. The possibility of rectifying the inertia in these stages in the aged by bringing them under voluntary control is discussed.

A useful distinction can be drawn between voluntary and involuntary memory (Smirnov, 1973). Voluntary (intentional) memory refers to memory which is the goal of the cognitive activity engaged in by the individual. Memory, in other words, which results from some mnemonic activity. Involuntary memory is memory which is a consequence of some cognitive activity, the goal of which activity is other than the memorization of the material.

It takes but a moment's reflection to realize, firstly that since the majority of our everyday cognitive activities do not have a mnemonic goal, but rather are concerned with the processing of information leading to comprehension and possible action, that it is probably that the greater part of the contents of memory are the product of involuntary memorization processes. Secondly, it is highly likely that the different non-mnemonic cognitive activities routinely engaged in do not have equivalent mnemonic consequences. The inference to be drawn from this is that the study of memory necessitates an analysis of the cognitive activities routinely engaged in by individuals as they act upon their environment.

The environment in which we act is a largely, if not wholly symbolic one, in that it is largely understood by us in terms of its significative functions. The majority of our cognitive acts are concerned with some form of analysis of meaning (semantics). What is interesting is that semantic processing has been implicated as a factor in the decline in memory performance in the normal aged (Eysenck, 1977; Craik and Simon, 1980). Memory following a semantic task is poorer in older as compared to younger subjects.

The obvious question facing the researcher is where and why this failure occurs. Does it reflect a failure to perform the semantic orienting task effectively? Or does the failure occur at later stages of processing, concerned with the elaboration of stimuli? We do not have an instrument that would permit the direct observation of covert cognitive processes. However, there is a means for the indirect observation of at least some of these processes. In a task testing memory for words, cognitive analyses are presumably concerned with the extraction and elaboration of meaning. The nature of the analysis should be determined, at least in part, by the complexity of the semantic network or knowledge base in which the words are embedded. An objective measure of the complexity of the semantic network is the Vocabulary subscale of the Wechsler Adult Intelligence Scale (W.A.I.S.). Items in this subscale are scored along the dimension concrete-abstract, which would correspond to lesser-greater complexity of knowledge. Variations between subjects in terms of their scaled Vocabulary scores should provide, therefore, an indirect measure of the potential complexity of semantic analyses available to subjects. Vocabulary scaled score can be used, therefore, as a predictor variable.

EXPERIMENT 1
Levels of Processing and Recognition Memory in the Elderly
The purpose of the first experiment was to replicate the finding that memory is relatively more impaired in older subjects following semantic analyses. If replicated, the second and main purpose of the study was to locate the locus of the failure, using direct and indirect measures of variations between individuals in terms of their semantic complexity.

Sixty men and women (37 females and 23 males), aged between 60 and 96 years, were tested. Each subject was administered the W.A.I.S. Vocabulary subscale, this being the measure of semantic complexity brought to the task by each subject. Forty words were presented sequentially to the subject. There were three experimental conditions, namely the Structural (check for presence of letter A), the Semantic (provide a verbal definition), and the Intentional (instructions to learn). Twenty subjects were assigned to each of the three conditions. Following the orienting activities, a recognition memory test was carried out.

The step-wise multiple regression of the independent variables (Age, Semantic Complexity, and the three Orienting Activities) on the criterion (recognition memory, A') produced a R=0.74 (F(4,55)=17.102, p<.005), with a substantial 55% of the variance in recognition memory determined. The three experimental conditions accounted for 36% of the variance, which reflects the effectiveness of a semantic analysis for later memory (A' Semantic Condition = 0.92, Intentional Condition = 0.83, Structural Condition = 0.75). This result was expected, and conforms to similar findings with younger subjects.

Of more interest are the findings relating to Semantic Complexity and Age within the three experimental conditions. Within all three experimental conditions, Structural, Intentional and Semantic, Semantic Complexity regresses on the criterion (18%, 40% and 23% variance respectively), indicating that semantic complexity leads to better memory. The enhancing effect on memory of high Semantic Complexity appears to have its greatest effect in the younger subjects in the age range, with the effect reducing as individuals become older. Thus, if the subjects in the three experimental conditions are split into younger and older age groups (i.e., 60-75 years versus 76-96 years), and the magnitude of the zero-order correlations between Semantic Complexity and A' are examined, whereas with the younger age groups in the three experimental conditions, Structural, Semantic and Intentional, the variance shared between the two variables is 30%, 42% and 53% respectively, it is only 6%, 16% and 32% for the older subjects.

The Age effect, which is found only in the Semantic Condition, indicates that older people tend to have poorer recognition memory. The contributions of Age and Semantic Complexity to the determined variance in the criterion are quite independent of each other, since the two variables are not related (correlation between Age and Semantic Complexity = 0.012, df=18, ns).

Discussion

The presence of an age effect in the Semantic condition, but not in the Structural condition, replicates earlier findings by other investigators that with ageing, memory becomes relatively more impaired following semantic analyses.

The relatively poorer memory performance of the older as compared to the younger subjects following the semantic orienting task, implies that the semantic analyses carried out on the stimuli by the older subjects are not as complex as those engaged in by the younger subjects. This is the argument put forward by investigators such as Eysenck (1977) and Craik (1977). But the findings of the present study are unequivocal in indicating that it is not at the initial stages of semantic analysis that older subjects fail. Taking the scaled Vocabulary score as an indicator of the integrity of the semantic memory network, there is no evidence that this network, which is presumably the source for semantic analyses, is in any way impaired in the old. Age was not correlated with scaled Vocabulary score. More importantly, in the Semantic Condition the quality of the definitions provided for the stimuli was as good in the older subjects as in the younger. The source of the failure in the older subjects would therefore appear to occur at a later stage in stimulus processing.

The conclusion that one is drawn to is that, following the initial, conscious and voluntary analysis of the word, there is a further unconscious, involuntary and automatic elaboration of the stimulus. To use the terminology of Collins and Loftus (1975), following the initial, voluntary analysis, there is an involuntary 'spread of activation' within semantic memory, the nature and extent of the spread reflecting the complexity and structure of the semantic network. An element activated within a complex semantic network would result in a greater spread of activation, which would then facilitate later recognition of the element. The reduction in this facilitating effect in the older subjects, despite initial complex analyses of the stimuli, suggests a developing inertia in the aged, an inertia in the semantic memory network that inhibits the spread of activation. The locus of the failure in the aged for memory following a semantic analysis occurs, we suggest, at later stages in stimulus processing, stages concerned with the automatic, and unconscious elaboration of stimuli via the excitation of semantic networks.

Since the main finding of the study is based on a relatively small sample of subjects, an obvious question is concerned with the replicability of the finding. This the second study attempts to do. If the finding is replicated, this will provide extra support for locating the problem in the aged at the post-initial, involuntary, unconscious and automatic stages of stimulus processing and elaboration. That being so, can a forced, voluntary, conscious elaboration of the stimuli overcome the apparent inertia of the covert processes? That question constitutes the second purpose of the second study.

EXPERIMENT 2
Stimulus Elaboration and Recognition Memory in the Elderly

Forty-eight subjects (24 men and 24 women), aged between 62 and 94 years, were selected from a city different from that of the first study There were two experimental conditions, namely the Semantic (identical to that in the first study), and the Semantic Elaboration. As with the Semantic condition, here subjects were required to provide a verbal definition for each of the stimuli. But in addition, following the verbal definition, the subject was required to provide both a synonym and an antonym for the word. The logic here is that such an activity, involving as it does the basic cognitive acts of generalization (synonym) and discrimination (antonym), is fundamental to any cognitive elaboration of a stimulus. This task was designed therefore to examine whether an enforced elaboration of the stimulus would recompense the older subjects for the reduced memory facilitation following high Semantic Complexity.

The step-wise multiple regression of the independent variables (Age and Semantic Complexity) on the criterion measure of A', for the Semantic Condition, produced a multiple correlation of 0.72 ($F(2,21)=11.579$, $p<.001$) with 52% of the variance determined by the predictors. The results are similar to those achieved in Study 1, with Age determining 36% of the variance, and Semantic Complexity 16%. Thus, with increasing age there is a decline in recognition memory, but high semantic complexity facilitates memory.

Does the facilitating effect of Semantic Complexity hold across the age range? The 24 subjects were split into younger/older groups. For the 11 subjects comprising the younger group the correlation between Semantic Complexity and memory was 0.69 ($df=9$, $P<.05$), with 48% of the variance shared. With the younger subjects, therefore, the facilitating effect of semantic complexity is again present. For the 13 older subjects the relationship was substantially less, the correlation being 0.53 ($df=11$, $.05<p<.10$), with only 28% of the variance in common. The facilitating effect is thus considerably reduced in the older group. As with the first study, there is no relationship between Age and Semantic Complexity ($r = -0.114$, $df=22$, ns). It can be concluded that the findings of the first study in regard to the differential effect of Semantic Complexity in facilitating memory in younger and older subjects have been replicated.

The next question concerns the effect of enforced stimulus elaboration on memory. In the case of the younger subjects, there is no change in memory between the Semantic condition ($M = .945$) and the Semantic Elaboration condition ($M = .951$)($t = 0.417$, $df = 21$, ns). However, it is evident that a ceiling effect is present, and therefore it cannot be concluded from the data that enforced stimulus elaboration has no effect on the memory of the younger subjects. But the more important question concerns its effect on the older subjects, and here it produces a substantial improvement in memory, raising memory from a mean value of 0.86 in the Semantic condition to 0.94 in the Semantic Elaboration condition ($t = 2.29$, $df = 23$, $p < .05$).

Conclusion

In the development (or, in adults, the acquisition) of many cognitive and perceptual motor skills, there is a general transition from overt, conscious control, to covert, unconscious control, known as the automatization of skilled behaviour. This transition is important, since it frees processing capacity, which capacity can now be devoted to new elements in the task situation, leading to more effective problem solving.

Observation of the young child set a task, the solution to which requires the implementation of several skilled behaviours, clearly demonstrates that the whole of the limited processing capacity of the child is required for the successful implementation of the component skills. There is little spare capacity left over for additional analyses. With practice, the component activities become skilled, they no longer require the child to deploy conscious attention to their activation and control. They have become, in this sense, involuntary. The sequence for children, then, is from voluntary control to involuntary control. We suggest that, with the aged this sequence may have to be reversed.

The conscious, voluntary stages of analysis of tasks in this study were performed as efficiently and as effectively by the older subjects as by the younger subjects. What determined the quality of the initial, voluntary stages of stimulus analysis was not the age of the subject, but rather the level of skill of the relevant cognitive processes brought to the task by the subject. The problem appears to reside at the level of the covert, involuntary processes, which in the younger subjects would appear to be activated automatically, but which seem to be subject to inertia in the very old.

Clearly, if involuntary cognitive processes are subject to an inertial effect with increasing age, but cognitive processes under the voluntary control of the individual are not, then a possible way forward would be to bring the involuntary processes under voluntary control. And this, the Semantic Elaboration condition, in a modest way, attempted to do, with some degree of success. Thus, in the aged the 'development' of cognitive skills may require the reverse of that seen in the child, with previously involuntary, unconscious skills being externalized, and brought under voluntary, conscious control.

REFERENCES

Collins, A.M. and Loftus, E.F. (1975). 'A spreading activation theory of semantic processing', Psychological Review, 82, 407-428.

Craik, F.I.M. (1977). 'Age differences in human memory'. In J.E. Birren and K.W. Schaie (Eds), Handbook of the Psychology of Aging, Von Nostrand: New York.

Craik, F.I.M. and Simon, E. (1980). 'Age differences in memory: The roles of attention and depth of processing'. In L.W. Poon, J.L. Fozard, L.S. Cermak, D. Arenberg and L.W. Thompson (Eds.), New Directions in Memory and Aging, Erlbaum: Hillsdale, N.J.

Eysenck, M.W. (1977). Human Memory, Theory, Research and Individual Differences, Pergamon: Oxford.

Smirnov, A.A. (1973). Problems of the Psychology of Memory, Plenum: New York.

EFFECTS OF AGE AND INTELLIGENCE ON EVERYDAY MEMORY TASKS

Janet Cockburn and Philip T. Smith

Rivermead Rehabilitation Centre, Oxford
and University of Reading, U.K.

ABSTRACT

A test, designed to identify everyday memory problems, was given to 38 independent-living elderly subjects to investigate the effects of ageing on everyday memory. Subjects also completed Raven's Matrices and Heim's AH4 tests of intelligence. Two memory items, both measuring prospective memory, showed a systematic decline with age but no association with the measures of intelligence. Other items were dependent on intelligence irrespective of age, although not necessarily on all measures. It is argued that test items simulating real-life memory skills may be better predictors of functional ability in the elderly than are short tests of intelligence.

It is widely accepted that the ability to learn, retain and use new information changes with age. However, the decrement that appears part of normal ageing and is rarely perceived as a serious hindrance to everyday life (Sunderland, Watts, Baddeley and Harris, 1986) is in start contrast to the devastating memory loss that accompanies degenerative illnesses. It is important to be able to discriminate between the modest loss that is a correlate of normal ageing and the loss that is a precursor of dementia. In order to do this there must be a baseline of 'normal' memory performance among an elderly population.
Many studies have sought to quantify memory loss by comparing old and young on laboratory-based material (e.g. Craik, 1977) and have found measurable differences. Such studies, however, tend to be biased in favour of the young whose formal education is more recent and whose everyday lives are more attuned to reacting under pressure. Rabbitt (1984) has suggested that the poorer performance of the old relative to the young on some memory tasks may be an artefact of subject selection criteria. It is common practice to match subject groups on age-scaled IQ scores. Since these are normed to take into account expected decrement with increasing age, the elderly will have a lower absolute level of current function than the young subjects. This factor may, in itself, contribute significantly to their apparently poorer performance. Rabbitt claims that chronological age in itself is not the major determinant of diminution of abilities such as learning new associations, but that it is subordinate to level of performance IQ.
The recent development of an ecologically valid, standardised, objective assessment of everyday memory (The Rivermead Behavioural Memory Test - RBMT; Wilson, Cockburn and Baddeley, 1985) has provided material that is appropriate for investigating memory skills in elderly subjects and for comparing the relative influences

of age and current cognitive status on tasks that are modelled on common everyday activities. The test covers a range of memory functions, such as remembering a name, a route and an appointment, tapping verbal and visuo-spatial skills in immediate and delayed situations. It also provides measures of prospective memory, which is rarely tested formally but which plays an essential part in successful independent living.

This paper reports on the performance on the RBMT, other standardised tests of memory and measures of intelligence by 38 subjects, aged between 52 and 90 years, (mean 70.05 years, S.D. 9.01), 28 of whom were women. They were all living independently in Oxford or one of the surrounding villages and had volunteered to help provide normative data for the RBMT. Half of them had been or were currently in manual occupations and 21% were classified as being of professional or managerial status.

All subjects were tested on version A of the RBMT; a test of new skill learning (Wilson, Cockburn and Baddeley, 1987); Digit Span (Wechsler, 1945); a paired associate learning task (Randt, Brown and Osborne, 1980) and Raven's Standard Progressive Matrices (Raven, 1958). This was administered as a manual version of the tailored form devised by Watts, Baddeley and Williams (1982). Testing took about one hour and items were always presented in the same order.

Analysis of the results showed the range of RBMT screening scores to be 6-12, with a mean of 9.58, S.D. 1.70, compared with a score of 10.78, S.D. 1.45 for 72 adults under 50 years. This is significantly different at the 0.1% level. However, six of the items proved sufficiently easy to be performed at ceiling level by this elderly group and have not been considered further here. Thus the differences between subjects arose from only half the test items. Scores from these six items:- remembering a belonging, an appointment, a route immediately following demonstration and after a 20 minute delay; remembering to deliver a message; recalling a prose passage, together with scores from the other memory tests, were analysed to investigate the relative influence of age and measured intelligence.

Those items that could meaningfully be classified only on a pass-fail basis - remembering an appointment, a belonging, a message, immediate and delayed route, and also the new skill learning - were analysed by logistic regression, treating age and Matrices scores as continuous variables and estimating their contribution to predicting the probability of passing any test. Items that could be treated as continuous variables - prose recall, digit span and paired associate learning - were analysed by multiple regression. In what follows, all effects described as significant are significant at the five per cent level or better.

Logistic regression identified remembering an appointment and remembering to deliver a message as being dependent on Age but not on Matrices score. Remembering a hidden belonging and learning a new skill were significantly dependent on Matrices score but not Age. Multiple regression showed no effect of Age or Matrices score on prose recall or forward or backward digit span, but Matrices score proved a good predictor of performance on the paired associate learning task. Figure 1 gives plots of performance against Age and Matrices score for those results that reached significance.

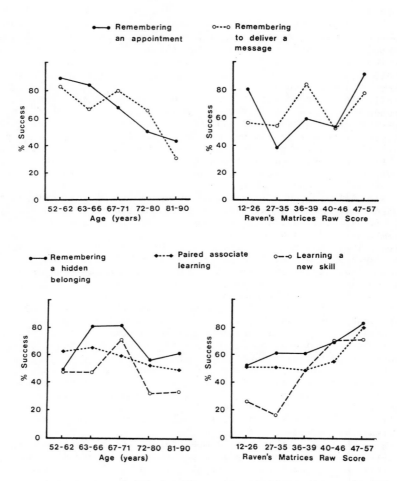

The effect of other potentially influential variables, such as occupational status, sight, hearing, marital status and current medication was also investigated. Only occupational status (essentially manual v. non-manual) had any influence, slightly diluting the effect of Matrices for remembering a hidden belonging and proving an excellent predictor of digit span.

As scores on Heim's (1970) AH4 test of intelligence were available for 25 of the subjects it was decided to renalyse the data using parts 1 and 2 separately as measures of intelligence. AH4 Part 1 consists mainly of vocabulary and arithmetic items, Part 2 contains more visual items. Correlations between these two parts and the Matrices score were not high (r = 0.41, p < 0.05 for Part 1 and r = 0.63, p < 0.001 for Part 2) raising the possibility that our conclusions might be affected by the measure of intelligence used. Effects of Matrices scores were also reanalysed for this 25 subject subgroup, showing very similar results to those obtained from the whole sample.

The pure Age effect found on the larger sample remained evident whichever measure of intelligence was used. Taking success on appointment and message tasks combined, logistic regression gives a significant effect of Age even when all three measures of intelligence are partialled out. The pattern is far less uniform for other tasks. Remembering a hidden belonging seems dependent on intelligence, whichever measure is used, but learning a new skill is dependent only on Matrices score and forward digit span only on AH4 part 1. Paired associate learning and prose recall are predicted by two measures but not the third. The following results were obtained:

1. Significant effect of age but not intelligence: (a) remembering an appointment, (b) remembering to deliver a message.

2. Significant effect of intelligence but not age: (a) remembering a hidden belonging, (b) learning a new skill (Raven's Matrices only), (c) paired associate learning (Matrices and AH4 Part 2 only), (d) remembering prose (immediate or delayed AH4 only), (e) digit span forward (AH4 Part 1 only).

3. No significant effects: (a) remembering a route, immediate or delayed, (b) digit span backward.

In general, performance of this group of subjects on these tests is in line with Rabbitt's (1984) view that much of the decline in old age can be attributed to decline in some aspect of cognitive functioning. However, two of the items, both measuring prospective memory, show no association with intelligence as measured here but do show a systematic decline with age. It has been suggested, (Craik and Rabinowitz, 1984), that prospective memory tasks require spontaneous initiation of cognitive operations, which proves especially difficult for the elderly, although they have no difficulty with the actual task when reminded to do it. This apparent relationship between prospective memory items and age is worth studying further with a larger sample. Few standard tests of memory look at prospective measures and yet they play an essential part in successful independent living. It would be premature to suggest that such skills as remembering to collect one's pension or take medication as directed are independent of intelligence per se but they may be independent of intelligence as measured by some tests. What is perhaps surprising is that remembering a hidden belonging, which, subjectively, appears to measure prospective memory, shows a different pattern of results from the other two prospective items. One possible explanation for this is that there is more incentive to remember the belonging, which is a personal possession, but this again needs to be explored with a larger sample.

Another point that merits further study is the question of the most appropriate measure of intelligence to use when assessing elderly people. Both the AH4 and Matrices tests appear to be good predictors of performance on some of the memory test items but not always for the same ones. Since the AH4 is a speeded test it may underestimate old peoples' capabilities, as one recognised effect of ageing is a general slowing down. They may not have been able to complete all they knew in the time allowed. On the other hand, the Matrices scores indicate that our subject population is of above average intelligence (mean age corrected IQ = 120, S.D. 13) and this may have reduced the sensitivity of the test for some memory items. It may be that there is no one short test of intelligence that will be a satisfactory predictor for all types of memory task and that the best way to find out about real life memory skills is to model test items closely on such skills.

REFERENCES

Craik, F.I.M. (1977). 'Age Differences in Human Memory', in Handbook Of The Psychology Of Aging (Eds. J.E. Birren and K.W. Schaie), Van Nostrand Reinhold, New York.

Craik, F.I.M. and Rabinowitz, J. (1984). 'Age Differences in the Acquisition and Use of Verbal Information', in Attention And Performance X (Eds. H. Bouma and D. Bouwhuis), Lawrence Erlbaum Associates, Hillsdale, New Jersey.

Heim, A. (1970). AH4 Group Test Of General Intelligence: Manual. N.F.E.R., Windsor.

Rabbitt, P. (1984). 'How Old People Prepare Themselves for Events Which They Expect', in Attention And Performance X (Eds. H. Bouma and D. Bouwhuis), Lawrence Erlbaum Associates, Hillsdale, New Jersey.

Randt, C.T., Brown, E.R. and Osborne, D.P. Jr. (1980) 'A Memory Test for Longitudinal Measurement of Mild to Moderate Deficits', Clinical Neuropsychology, 2, 184-194.

Raven, J.C. (1958). Standard Progressive Matrices, H.K. Lewis & Son Ltd., London.

Sunderland, A., Watts, K., Baddeley, A.D. and Harris, J. (1986). 'Subjective Memory Assessment and Test Performance in Elderly Adults', Journal of Gerontology, 41, 376-384.

Watts, K., Baddeley, A.D. and Williams, M. (1982). 'Automated Tailored Testing Using Raven's Matrices and the Mill Hill Vocabulary Tests: A Comparison with Manual Administration', International Journal of Man-Machine Studies, 17, 331-344.

Wechsler, D. (1945). 'A Standardised Memory Scale for Clinical Use', Journal of Psychology, 19, 87-95.

Wilson, B., Cockburn, J. and Baddeley, A.D. (1985). The Rivermead Behavioural Memory Test, Thames Valley Test Co., Reading.

Wilson, B., Cockburn, J. and Baddeley, A.D. (1987). 'Assessment of Everyday Memory Functioning Following Severe Head Injury', in Neurotrauma: Treatment, Rehabilitation and Related Issues (Eds. M.E. Miner and K.A. Wagner), Butterworth, Stoneham, MA. (In press).

DO MEMORY AIDS AID THE ELDERLY IN THEIR DAY TO DAY REMEMBERING?

J.L. Jackson, H. Bogers & J. Kerstholt
Institute of Experimental Psychology, University of Groningen,
The Netherlands.

ABSTRACT

A self-rating questionnaire showed a group of older Ss to be reporting fewer memory lapses than the younger group. Compensatory behaviour, in the form of an increase in the number of memory aids used by the elderly, was not found when judgments were made on a standard list of memory aids. With specific situations and free report, however, the two age groups were found to differ in the type of aids they used: older Ss relied more on external aids in future situations but used external and internal aids equally in past situations; younger Ss relied more on internal aids in both types of situation. Differences between these findings and others in the literature are discussed in relation to normal memory operations.

A robust finding from the aging literature is that memory deficits increase with age (e.g. Birren & Schaie, 1977). However, such results have been mainly derived from laboratory tasks and may not therefore be entirely relevant for the type and degree of memory failures that are experienced by the elderly in their daily functioning. For example, such a conclusion makes no concession to the possible role of compensatory behaviour in everyday life. Moreover, while memory complaints such as forgetting names, missing appointments and misplacing objects are frequently reported by the elderly as evidence of their increasing forgetfulness, Cavanaugh, Grady & Perlmutter (1983) have suggested that such memory failures may well be fairly common in all age groups. The question therefore still remains, how frequently do the elderly experience memory problems in their daily lives and how do they cope with them?

One way researchers have set out to explore the aspects of memory involved in day to day living has been to devise questionnaires which examine the frequency of everyday memory problems (e.g. Harris, 1980). One such questionnaire (Perlmutter, 1978) explicitly set out to explore age differences in everyday memory lapses. Results from this study suggest that older subjects (Ss) do in fact report more memory problems than do younger Ss. Baddeley (1983) on the other hand suggests that, despite objective evidence that memory performance declines with age, older people often report fewer memory lapses than do younger people.

The answer to this seeming contradiction probably lies in

the highly subjective nature of self-rating questionnaires. Perlmutter (1980) as well as Cavanaugh et al. (1983) have argued that
the increases in self-reported frequency of memory failures with
age found in their studies may reflect a response bias in the
elderly caused by their greater sensitivity to memory failures and
their tendency to conform to negative stereotypes about aging. On
the other hand, in order to be able to report accurately the
frequency of one's forgetting, one must first remember that something has been forgotten! Sunderland, Harris & Baddeley (1983)
conclude from their study that even when memory is within the
normal range, more forgetful Ss may report a smaller proportion of
their memory errors than will Ss with better memories. It follows
that if older Ss tend to belong to a more forgetful group, this
would in turn lead to the lower frequency of memory lapses suggested by Baddeley.

In section one of the present questionnaire age differences
in memory lapses are explored further. A group of young and active
older adults are asked to rate their everyday memory performance by
completing a self-rating questionnaire similar to that described by
Baddeley (1983). Results from a pilot study carried out with a
similar population had suggested that the older Ss might indeed
rate their memory failures at a lower level of frequency than would
the younger Ss. If this result were to be replicated in the larger
study, it need not, however, imply that the older Ss have not
remembered what they have forgotten! Instead, such a result could
be seen as evidence of a more highly organised and structured
lifestyle in which fewer demands were placed on their memory, and
hence fewer opportunities would exist for making errors. Or,
alternatively, a lower level of memory failure might result from
the use of compensatory behaviour, namely more reliance on memory
aids. Section two of this study was devised to explore these ideas
further. More specifically, the question which is addressed asks
whether older adults use more, less or different memory aids in
their everyday life than do younger adults.

Memory aids can be defined as strategies or devices for
organising and/or encoding information to be remembered such that
learning and later recall is enhanced. Many such aids (e.g. peg-
word mnemonics, method of loci and story mnemonics) have been
explored in laboratory studies and have been shown to be very
effective in producing high levels of recall (Bellezza, 1981). In
general, however, dependence on such devices is not spontaneous:
their use requires explicit training, practice, time and effort.
It is therefore not surprising that in his study of the memory aids
that people use in the context of their everyday lives, Harris
(1980) found that his Ss reported at best, a very infrequent use of
such mnemonic devices. He classified memory aids into two general
types: internal and external aids. Internal aids were described as
involving internal manipulation of information and included encoding mnemonics such as described above as well as mnemonic
techniques that were purely retrieval strategies such as mental
retracing and alphabetic searching. Of the internal aids his Ss did
report using, the majority were of this latter type. External aids
were viewed as involving external manipulation of the environment
and included strategies such as writing notes in diaries and
calendars, making shopping lists and asking others for the required

information. Such external aids were reported by his Ss to be used more frequently than were the internal aids.

Intons-Peterson and Fournier (1986) not only explored how often students reported using external and internal memory aids in everyday life, but also when such aids would be used. These authors used a number of explicit situations similar to those described by Herrmann and Neisser (1978) and found that, although external memory aids were used more frequently for future remembering, remembering past situations produced a higher frequency of internal memory aids. In a pilot study which used similar specific situations to those described by Intons-Peterson and Fournier, our young Ss behaved in a similar fashion but the older group showed a tendency to use external aids for the past as well as future remembering. For example, in a situation which states 'You are in a grocery store to pick up a few things you noticed you needed when looking in your cupboards earlier. Now you can't remember them all. How do you remember?', younger Ss would report using internal strategies such as mental retracing and visual imagery. Older Ss, on the other hand, would report using an external aid, namely checking the shopping list that they made when looking in their cupboards. Such possible age differences in the use of memory aids in specific situations are tested in this study.

Although in both the Harris (1980) and Intons-Peterson and Fournier (1986) studies Ss were presented with a standard list of memory aids plus descriptions, both sets of authors reported the difficulty of distinguishing between internal aids and normal memory operations. In our pilot study, we encountered a similar difficulty. For example, in response to the question about the grocery store mentioned earlier, several of the younger Ss stated that their strategy would be to walk around the various shelves until they recognised the articles they needed. To reduce the demand characteristics inherent in presenting a list of memory aids and to encourage reports that could include more natural memory operations, a list of situations will be presented and Ss are simply asked 'how they would set about remembering'.

The next part of the study presents a list of 20 memory aids similar to those used by Intons-Peterson and Fournier (1986) but with one extra aid, visual imagery, and requires Ss to report how frequently, in general, they make use of each of these aids. The final part of the questionnaire once again presents specific situations, but now requires Ss to select the aids they would use in these situations from the presented list.

METHOD
Subjects: 114 young (mean=20.5 yrs, range=18-30 yrs) and 39 older Ss (mean=62.5 yrs, range=51-78 yrs) participated in the study. The young Ss were following an introductory psychology course. The older Ss were recruited from two sources: an extra-mural course on political science and an adult education course in psychology.
Materials: Material consisted of a booklet containing, in order, a memory lapses questionnaire with a 7-point scale; a set of open-ended questions asking how one would try to remember in six specific situations (3 future, 3 past); a memory aids frequency questionnaire with a 7-point scale and finally, a second set of six specific situations. The 12 situations were adapted from those

devised by Herrmann & Neisser (1978) and had two parallel forms, past and future. The situations were randomised and balanced across Ss and experimental order.
Procedure: Questionnaires were administered to the young Ss in one large group and to the older Ss in small groups or individually.

RESULTS
Total scores for the memory lapses questionnaire were calculated. The proportion of Ss falling within each of three ranges of score, high (72-124), medium (53-71) and low (29-52) is shown in Table 1.

Table 1. Proportion of Ss with low, medium and high forget scores

| | Forget Scores | | |
Age	Low	Medium	High
Young	.18	.35	.47
Old	.74	.23	.03

The relative proportion of Ss falling within each level of forget score differs significantly, X^2 (2,N=153)=38.42, p<0.0001, with the largest proportion of older Ss rating themselves as having a low-forget score. An example of this difference in subjective rating is illustrated in Figure 1. In response to question 1, 'How often do you forget where you have put something or lose things around the house', half of the older Ss report doing this about 1-2

Figure 1. Frequency of subjective ratings on Question 1.

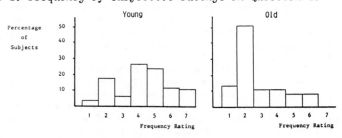

times in the last six months (rating 2), while half of the younger Ss report doing this either 1-2 times in the last month (rating 4) or 1-2 times in the last week (rating 5).
General Use of Memory Aids: The standard list contained 13 internal and 7 external aids. The young Ss reported using an average of 16 of the possible 20 memory aids at some level of frequency (81% of the external and 77% of the internal), while the older Ss used only an average of 11 (69% of the external and 51% of the internal). Frequency scores showed both groups to be using external aids more frequently than internal aids. Wilcoxon, Z=4.47, p<.0001 and Z=3.84, p<.001 for young and old Ss respectively.
Aids in Specific Situations: The open-ended responses to the specific questions were categorised using the standard list of

memory aids. This list proved to be too limited to enable coding of

Table 2. Extra Memory Aids.

Type		Memory Aid Description
Recognition		in correct context, items spring out
Assimilation		activate appropriate schema, learning by comprehension
Concentration	(a)	look or listen very carefully
	(b)	think (search?) very carefully
Chunking		organise into simpler or more meaningful units
Rhythm		organise by sound or rhythm
Association		organise by making associations

all responses. Several extra aids (shown in Table 2) were added. Inter-rater reliability was high (98%).

Since analyses showed Ss, in spite of differing instructions, to be performing identically in the first and second set of situations further analyses were carried out on the combined data. Young Ss were found to use significantly more internal aids in both the past and future situations, Wilcoxon $Z=8.3$, $p<.0001$ and $Z=6.7$, $p<.0001$ respectively. With the older group no difference was found between use of external/internal aids in the past situations, but significantly more external aids were used in the future situations, $Z=4.4$, $p<.0001$.

DISCUSSION

Unlike Perlmutter's older Ss, the elderly in this study did not show a negative but in fact a positive response bias. Whether this resulted from forgetting, the particular sample of active Ss tested, or to the elderly making what they considered to be most socially desirable responses (see Morris, 1983) remains unclear. Nor was the hypothesis that the elderly would use more memory aids to compensate for memory failures confirmed when judgments were made on a standard list of aids: indeed, older Ss reported using fewer aids. In response to this list, both young and old reported using external aids more frequently than internal aids. When specific situations were presented, however, and Ss simply asked 'how they would set about remembering' age differences were found. Intons-Peterson & Fournier (1986) found that although external aids were used more frequently for future remembering, remembering past situations produced a higher proportion of internal aids. The older Ss in this study also made use of significantly more external aids for future situations, but for past situations there was no difference between use of internal and external. They reported using recognition and mental retracing but, as in the pilot study, they also frequently reported that they would have written the information down and would only have to look it up at time of recall. Such results lend support to the notion that older Ss may rely less on their own memory systems and organise their lives by using external aids whenever possible.

The younger Ss, on the other hand, did use more internal aids in the past situations thereby replicating Intons-Peterson and Fournier's results, but in contrast they also used significantly more internal aids in the future situation. This result can be explained by the difference between our internal aids and those of the previous authors. The free report situation forced us to make new strategies (those described in Table 2). Examination of this list shows these strategies to fall, in the main, more within the realm of normal memory operations than mnemonic strategies as studied in the laboratory. The fact that young Ss report using these in free report situations, but the older Ss seldom, adds extra support to the contention that older Ss do indeed try to compensate for deficits in normal memory functioning by increasing their reliance on external memory aids.

REFERENCES

Baddeley, A.D.(1983) Your Memory: A User's Guide, Pelican Books, Middlesex.

Bellezza, F.S. (1981). 'Mnemonic Devices:Classification, Character-istics, and Criteria', Review of Educational Research, 51, 247-275.

Birren, J.E. and Schaie, K.W.(1977). Handbook of the Psychology of Aging, Van Nostrand Reingold, New York.

Cavanaugh, J.C., Grady, J.G. and Perlmutter, M.(1983). 'Forgetting and Use of Memory Aids in 20 to 70 Year Olds Everyday Life', International Journal of Aging and Human Development, 17, 113-122.

Harris, J.E. (1980). 'Memory Aids People Use: Two Interview Stu-dies', Memory & Cognition, 8, 31-38.

Herrmann, D.J. and Neisser, U.(1978). 'An Inventory of Everyday Memory Experiences', in Practical Aspects of Memory (Eds. M.M. Gruneberg, P.E.Morris and R.N. Sykes), pp. 35-51, Academic Press, London.

Intons-Peterson, M.J. and Fournier, J.(1986). 'External and In-ternal Memory Aids: When and How Often Do We Use Them?', Journal of Experimental Psychology: General, 3, 267-280.

Morris, P.E. (1983). 'The Validity of Subjective Reports on Memo-ry', in Everday Memory (Eds. J.E. Harris and P.E. Morris), pp. 153-172, Academic Press, London.

Perlmutter, M.(1978). 'What is Memory Aging the Aging Of?', Devel-opmental Psychology, 14, 330-345.

Sunderland, A., Harris, J.E. and Baddeley, A.D.(1983). 'Do Labora-tory Tests Predict Everyday Memory? A Neuropsychological Study', Journal of Verbal Learning and Verbal Behavior, 22, 341-357.

AGE-RELATED MEMORY IMPAIRMENTS IN RATS:
POTENTIAL PARADIGMS FOR PHARMACOLOGICAL MODULATION

M. Soffie and C. Giurgea

Centre Albert Michotte - Biologie du Comportement
University of Louvain - Belgium

ABSTRACT
        The behaviour of aged and adult rats was investigated using
three comparative experiments. Age-related impairments can be seen
in the three experimental situations. In Experiment I (three-path
maze) a STM impairment with a relative preservation of immediate
memory was evidenced. In Experiment II (PA) the long term
deterioration of the avoidance response seemed to be directly related
to an encoding deficit during acquisition. Finally in Experiment III
(visual reversal), increased behavioural rigidity appeared only in
the food motivated conditioning, i.e. when the first discrimination
was slowly learned. A parallelism with aged human disorders and the
interpretation in terms of cognitive processes are discussed.

INTRODUCTION
        There is abundant evidence showing a decrease with age in
performance of memory tasks. The major problem consists however in
distinguishing whether the impairment observed is directly related to
specific cognitive disorders or to non-specific factors such as
sensory or motor deficits, emotivity enhancement, vigilance
reduction, or motivational changes. Equally, a lack of cognitive
effort rather than an incapacity to learn is often proposed to
explain the poor performances obtained by old people in complex
knowledge and memory tasks (review in Birren and Schaie, 1977;
Giurgea et al., 1981). However, the conceptual difference existing in
the response itself has to be underlined in the rational development
of a reliable animal model. In man, the performances are generally
evaluated by language or by symbolic representation, while in rodents
the response is mostly estimated by motor performances. Moreover, it
has often been postulated that spatial orientation is guided by
environmental stimuli (see Olton et al., 1979). Motor and sensory
impairments would therefore interfere in rodent responses more than
in human ones. Despite these differences, the use of aged rats in
comparative and appropriate paradigms provides some rational
similarities with human subjects about memory disturbances occurring
during ageing. By the comparison of different experiments, this
paper will attempt to determine and to discuss whether the
behavioural impairments observed in old rats can be generalized to
different tasks involving a specific cognitive function.
        Our experimental approach consisted of an analysis of short
term memory by comparing two experimental designs (Exp.I). The
forgetting curve was verified in two acquisition conditions (Exp.II).

Finally, the behavioural rigidity was studied in positive and
negative conditioning (Exp.III).

EXPERIMENT I: SHORT-TERM MEMORY
         Short-term memory (STM) deficit is often mentioned as a
common ageing process. In animals, STM is usually analysed in
spatial memory paradigms requiring the intervention of working memory
as defined by Honig (1978). For example, working memory consists of
remembering which paths of a maze have been previously visited. This
memory is considered as transient, having no consequences for
subsequent sessions.

Three-Path Maze
         The purpose of this test was to examine whether STM of the
working memory type was altered in old rats. Aged (27 months) and
adult (7 months) male naive Sprague Dawley rats were used.

Procedure. The test was based on an elimination principle, i.e. the
animal had to learn to visit each arm of the three-path maze only
once in each session. The apparatus and the procedure were inspired
by Lachman (1969). The maze consisted of three diverging pathways
radiating from a starting area. The food reinforcement was placed at
the end of each path. After each choice, the rat was put back in the
starting area until the next trial. A session consisted of the total
number of trials necessary to obtain the three reinforcements, with a
minimum of three and a maximum of 10 trials per session. Each animal
was submitted to one session per day. Each age-group was divided
into two subgroups: one subgroup was submitted to 20 sessions with an
ITI of 30sec followed by 10 sessions with an ITI of 4min; the other
subgroup had an ITI of 4min for the first 20 sessions and of 30sec
for the last 10.

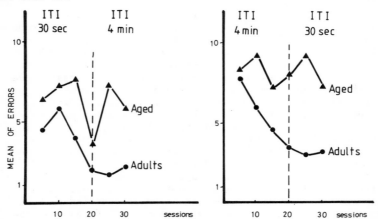

Fig.1. Mean number of errors per block of five sessions as a function
of age and ITI (n=9 in each of the 4 groups). For sessions 1-20 and
20-30: ANOVA age effect p<.001; for sessions 15-20: ANOVA age effect
p<.01 and ITI effect p<.01. Performance drop for aged animals when
ITI switched from 30sec to 4min: t-test p<.01.

Results and Discussion. The performance drop (Fig.1) observed when ITI is lengthened suggests a memory component and validates the interpretation in terms of STM deficit in the aged rat, with a relative preservation of immediate memory. A sensory or motivational deficit often described in old animals (Goodrick, 1968; Kametani et al., 1984) could indeed not explain the difference found between the two ITI conditions.

EXPERIMENT II: LONG-TERM MEMORY
        Long-term memory (LTM) is also affected during ageing. Recall memory seems to be more impaired than recognition memory. Many studies conducted with humans have reported that old people do not organize their material storage during encoding as well as younger adults.
        The importance of equalizing acquisition before inferring a LTM defect was also underlined in animal studies (Goodrick, 1968; Kubanis et al., 1981). LTM deterioration is often detected in rodents by measuring the passive avoidance (PA) response. Although the practical advantage of the one-trial PA test is obvious, the interpretation of this paradigm is questionable. The acquisition is not controlled and the cognitive character of the response is not clear. We consider as speculative an interpretation in terms of mnemonic deficit, as there is actually a lack of maintenance of the response. A PA deficit is indeed often reported with a latency during retention test markedly superior to that of training. Nevertheless we have used this test because we thought it interesting to compare the PA performances in two training and testing conditions.

Passive Avoidance Test
        The aim of this experiment was to control the relative importance of acquisition strength and of the duration of the PA response in order to decide whether the encoding or the maintenance of the response was affected during ageing. 28 months old and 8 months old male SD rats were used. All rats had been previously submitted to an appetitive discriminative task (three-path maze or Y-maze).

Procedure. A classical one-trial step-through PA test was used. The shock (1mA) was given in the dark compartment for 3sec, either immediately after entrance (1), or after a 30sec delay (2). The PA response was measured after 24 hours and again 29 days after training. The maximum latencies during the retention tests were either 180sec (1) or 360sec (2).

Results and Discussion. As can be seen in Fig.2, an impairment with age only appears in the shock delay condition, i.e. with a weaker strength of acquisition (Xavier and Bueno, 1984). It appears therefore that old animals required a higher level of training to maintain a good performance after a long time. The significant difference only appears after 29 days. Thus we cannot rule out an acceleration of the forgetting curve. An explanation in terms of extinction could also be proposed since the latency of old rats was already low after 24 hours. It follows that most of them had

experienced the non-reinforcement during the first retention test.
The absence of deficit in old rats in favourable training conditions
(shock without delay) contrasts with previous results (Bartus et al.,
1980 and Lippa et al., 1980) but could be explained by the effect of
handling and of previous learning. It is well known that old animals
are more emotional and that their performances are improved by
handling and environment (Doty, 1972). The mere fact that an animal
enters the dark compartment in a PA task does not indicate by itself
a forgetting of the electrical shock, since it can also be ascribed
to an escape behaviour reaction due to a high emotional state.

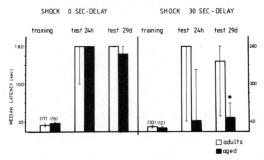

Fig.2. Long-term modulation of the PA response as a function of age
and test condition (*p<.05 significant difference between aged and
adult rats, Mann Whitney U test). Numbers in parentheses indicate
the number of animals in each group. The vertical lines indicate the
I.Q.R.

EXPERIMENT III: BEHAVIOURAL RIGIDITY

Resistance to change is often reported in aged people.
Although this phenomenon is directly related to behavioural
inhibition, the capacity for changing the reactivity as a function of
previous stimulation, i.e. the CNS-plasticity (Konorski, 1967), is
also related to the ability to form a new memory ruling out the
previously fixed events. Behavioural rigidity is generally measured
in animals by the capacity to learn a reverse task. Age-related
impairments have in particular been reported in monkeys (Bartus et
al., 1979) and in rats (Zornetzer et al., 1982).

In our experiment, behavioural rigidity was compared in two
paradigms. Naive male SD rats (27 and 7 months old) were used.

Visual Reversal Learning

The aim of this experiment was to control whether the
behavioural rigidity of aged rats is comparable in two distinct
paradigms differing only in the reinforcement (food or shock) used.

Procedure. The visual reversal learning was studied in two Y-mazes:
one positively reinforced (peanuts) and one negatively reinforced
(electrical shock). The task consisted first in going to the bright
arm (light discrimination) and afterwards in going to the dim arm
(reversal). The position of the illuminated arm was random. Ten
daily trials were made and the acquisition criterion was 9/10 correct
choices for both discriminations.

Results   and   Discussion.   As shown in Fig. 3, aged   rats   were   only
impaired in appetitive learning. This suggests that the   age—related
impairment is directly linked to motivation: when highly   motivated,
as in the shock-escape, aged rats were not impaired. The   impairment
could,   however, also be related to difficulty in learning the   first
discrimination.   Both   adult   and old rats were slower to   learn   the
light   discrimination   in   the   positively   than   in   the   negatively
reinforced task. The fact that in one situation the food was at   the
end   of   the   arm   while in   the other one the   shock   stopped   at   the
entrance   of   the   arm,   may   also   be   important.   Therefore,   the
association   between unconditioned and conditioned stimuli would   not
be the same in both situations.

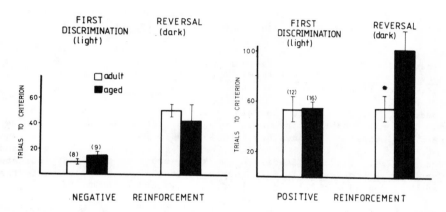

Fig.3.   Effect   of   age on two   independent   visual   discriminations
(*p<.05 significant difference between adult and aged rats, t-test).
Mean values + SEM are shown.

FINAL COMMENTS

          In   this   paper we attempted to stress   the   importance   of
comparative   analyses before interpreting any behavioural   impairment
in   aged   animals.   It appears that most of   the   time,   age-related
disorders   were   more specific to a particular task   and/or   paradigm
than to a precise cognitive function. The three experiments reported
here have revealed that old rats' performances were impaired in   only
one   of the two experimental conditions successively   compared.   The
fact that our animals were all living in groups and were   intensively
handled before each task could have reduced the interference   between
emotivity   and   cognitive processes and could therefore   explain   the
relatively   good   performance of old   animals   in   our   experimental
approach.   These   animals may therefore be   more   representative   of
normal   ageing disorders than of pathological ones. Drugs acting   on
attentional   processes or enhancing the impact of relevant stimuli   —
and therefore their association with unconditioned stimuli — could be
predicted to have beneficial effects.

Acknowledgements: This   research   has been   supported   by   IRSIA-UCB
Grants No 4294 and No 4805.

REFERENCES

Bartus, R.T., Dean, R.L. and Fleming, D.L. (1979). 'Aging in the Rhesus Monkey: effects on visual discrimination learning and reversal learning', Journal of Gerontology, 34(2), 209-219.

Bartus, R.T., Dean, R.L., Goas, J.A. and Lippa, A.S. (1980). 'Age-related changes in passive avoidance retention: modulation with dietary Choline', Science, 209, 30-303.

Birren, J.E. and Schaie, K.W. (1977). Handbook of the Psychology of Aging, 787p. Van Nostrand Reinhold, New York.

Doty, B.A. (1972). 'The effects of cage environment upon avoidance responding of aged rats', Journal of Gerontology, 27(3), 358-360.

Giurgea, C., Greindl, M.G. and Preat, S. (1981). 'Experimental behavioral pharmacology of gerontopsychopharmacological agents', in Handbook of Experimental Pharmacology, (Ed. Hoffmeister, Stille), vol.55, ch.11, pp.461-492, Springer, Berlin.

Goodrick, C.L. (1968). 'Learning, retention, and extinction of a complex maze habit for mature-young and senescent Wistar albino rats', Journal of Gerontology, 23, 298-304.

Honig, W.K. (1978). 'Studies of working memory in the pigeon', in Cognitive Processes in Animal Behaviour, (Eds. S.H. Hulse, H. Fowler and W.K. Honig), pp.221-248, Hillsdale, Lawrence Erlbaum, NJ.

Kametani, H. Osada, H. and Inoue, K. (1984). 'Increased novelty-induced grooming in aged rats: a preliminary observation', Behavioral and Neural Biology, 42, 73-80.

Konorski, J. (1967). Integrative Activity of the Brain, 530p, University of Chicago Press, Chicago.

Kubanis, P., Gobbel, G. and Zornetzer, S.F. (1981). 'Age-related memory deficits in swiss mice', Behavioral and Neural Biology, 32, 241-247.

Lachman, S.J. (1969). 'Behavior in a three-path multiple-choice elimination problem under conditions of overtraining', Journal of Psychology, 73, 101-109.

Xavier, G.F. and Bueno, O.F.A. (1984). 'On delay-of-punishment and preexposure time: effects on passive avoidance behavior in rats', Brazilian Journal of Medical and Biological Research, 17, 55-64.

Zornetzer, S.F., Thompson, R. and Rogers, J. (1982). 'Rapid forgetting in aged rats', Behavioral and Neural Biology, 36, 49-60.

ACQUISITION AND APPLICATION OF EXPERTISE AT COMPUTER TEXT EDITING BY YOUNGER AND OLDER ADULTS

Joellen T. Hartley
Department of Psychology
California State University
Long Beach, CA

Alan A. Hartley
Department of Psychology
Scripps College
Claremont, CA

ABSTRACT

Groups of younger and older adults learned to use a computer text editor. Measures of both knowledge and performance were collected at regular intervals. Better recall of material learned was correlated with better performance; there were no age group differences in recalled knowledge or in performance. Models of more skilled individuals showed richer knowledge representations and more sophisticated performance rules than models of less skilled individuals. Age accounted for very little of the variation in skilled performance.

INTRODUCTION

There are clear differences between older and younger adults in learning as it is studied in the psychological laboratory. It is an open question whether the same phenomena appear in learning that more closely represents that which occurs in everyday life. Intentional learning in everyday life is frequently done not for the purpose of being tested, but, rather, so that problems can be solved. An individual masters a body of knowledge so that the acquired expertise can be applied to achieve some necessary or desired ends. To explore learning-for-problem-solving, younger and older adults were taught to use a microcomputer for word processing in a program of computer-assisted instruction. A computer-based skill was selected for two reasons. First, computerization of society has been both rapid and extensive. Mastery of computer-use skills will soon be essential to adults of all ages both in and out of the workplace. Second, although late middle age and elderly adults have been characterized as slow to adopt and master innovations, there is little empirical evidence to validate this claim. Text editing was selected because it is a paradigmatic example of human computer interaction (Card, Moran, & Newell, 1983). Text editors are probably the most widely used computer application, they are representative of a broad range of applications, and they become a tool that can be an unconscious extension of the skilled user.

METHOD

Participants were 12 older and 12 younger adults (aged 65-75 and 18-30 years, respectively) who had no prior experience with computer use. They learned to use a word processing program (called EDITOR) that surreptitiously recorded the user's actions and the time taken to select and execute them. EDITOR is a "line-oriented" text editor, that is, one in which line numbers are displayed next to each line of text and the user issues a single-letter command and specifies to which line it is to be applied. The principal commands allow the user to print a line (P), delete an existing line (D), insert a new line (I), replace an existing line (R), find a specified string of characters in the text (F), change a specified character string, replacing it with another (C), or request help with any command (H). The general format for a line command is Command+Line Specification: P200 or D100. The general format for a string command is Command/String Specification/Line Specification: F/string/320 or C/remove string/insert string/165. A command can operate over several lines if line range is specified.

Eight computer-assisted lessons took place over six separate sessions. The lessons included presentation of text editing concepts, commands and functions, examples, simple practice exercises on new concepts, and more complex exercises that drew on all the material covered to that point. At the beginning and end of every session, learners were asked to provide a written recall of what they had learned to that point. This was done to prompt rehearsal and consolidation of the material, and to provide evidence about the current state of declarative knowledge. Evidence of procedural knowledge was obtained from the time-stamped protocols of EDITOR use.

The major findings from the study concerning recall and performance were summarized by Hartley, Hartley, and Johnson (1984): At the end of training, there were no significant differences between younger and older adults either when overall recall was considered or when the material was separated into concepts, names, functions, and procedures. It is interesting to note that subsequent research on individuals from the populations studied here (many of whom also participated in this study) has found that recall of both word lists and connected prose is significantly lower for older than for younger adults (Hartley, 1986). These results are consistent with other findings of age differences in laboratory memory tasks, and they reduce the likelihood that the absence of age differences in recall of information about EDITOR is due to subject selection artifacts. The younger and older adults also did not differ in the correctness or efficiency with which editing operations were carried out. The older adults, however, worked more slowly, completing fewer tasks in the time allotted.

The present report is concerned with the relations between memory and performance. First, "macro" measures of each will be described and relations among them reported. Next, more fine grained, "micro" analyses of knowledge and of performance will be presented. Finally, possible relations at the micro level will be explored.

RELATIONS BETWEEN RECALL AND PERFORMANCE

The measures of recall selected for analysis were written protocols taken at the end of the last session of instruction (R1) and at the end of the next session, which was devoted entirely to editing problems with no additional instruction (R2). The measures of performance were taken from the final problem session: the proportion of the tasks that were attempted in the limited time (ATT), the proportion of tasks attempted that were completed correctly (COR), and the average efficiency (EFF), defined as the optimal number of operations per task divided by the actual number of operations. Several individual difference measures were also collected in order to assess the general level of cognitive functioning of the participants: (a) the reading span measure described by Daneman and Carpenter (1980) which provides an index of working memory capacity (RS), (b) a measure of vocabulary (VOC), (c) a measure of abstract reasoning (ABS), and (d) a measure of reading comprehension (COM).

Table 1.   Correlations Between Measures of Memory, Performance, and Individual Differences

	R1	R2	EFF	ATT	COR	VOC	COM	RS
R2	.81							
EFF	.54	.26						
ATT	.61	.64	.21					
COR	.44	.33	.28	.49				
VOC	.58	.51	.40	.50	.13			
COM	.47	.30	.61	.53	.43	.57		
RS	.38	.36	.35	.49	.09	.47	.60	
ABS	.17	.08	.17	.43	-.13	.06	.22	.58

(Coefficients greater than .36 are significant at $p<.05$)

The only significant difference between older and younger adults for recall and performance measures was in the proportion of editing tasks that were attempted.   For the individual difference measures, however, older adults scored lower on the reading span and abstract reasoning measures and higher on the vocabulary measure. Because of this pattern of age differences, correlations between the three sets of measures (recall, performance, and individual differences) were determined with the effect of age controlled. Table 1 shows the partial correlation coefficients among the measures.   The memory measure that was most predictive of performance was the amount of declarative knowledge at the end of the last lesson: All three measures of performance were related to the amount recalled at this point.   In the set of individual difference measures, reading comprehension was the best predictor of performance, but both vocabulary and reading span showed substantial correlations with the efficiency and tasks-attempted measures. The same individual difference measures were related to the memory measures as well. Within the performance measures, the only significant correlation was between the tasks-attempted and tasks correctly accomplished measures. The pattern of relationships suggests that general level of verbal competence and working memory resources may determine both the acquisition of information about a text editor and the performance of problem-solving tasks with the

text editor. Further, declarative knowledge was a good predictor of
procedural knowledge in both older and younger adults.

MICROANALYSIS OF RECALL

To examine the form of declarative knowledge, a subset of the
research participants was selected for finer-grained analysis.
Three older and three younger adults who were judged to be high
skill individuals, and an equivalent number who were judged to be
low skill individuals, were selected for this analysis.   The
selection was based on a combination of recall and performance
measures, with the teaching assistant's judgment of overall
competence used as an additional criterion. Declarative knowledge
representations based on recall protocols were constructed for each
of these participants. The sequence of information from each of
seven recall periods during learning and one following the final
editing problems session was coded to show the connections between
concepts. Concepts were defined as being connected in a network if
they appeared adjacent to each other on two or more occasions. A
summary of the information obtained from these representations is
shown in Table 2, and includes the total number of concepts that
appeared at least once on a recall protocol, the average number of
connections that each concept had associated with it, the number of
concepts that were part of the knowledge network (defined above),
and the percent of those concepts recalled that were included in the
network.   The numbers reported in Table 2 are averaged over the
three participants in each of the age/skill groups.

Table 2. Characteristics of Knowledge Networks

Measure	High Skill		Low Skill	
	Young	Old	Young	Old
Concepts Recalled	42.7	42.3	31.7	34.7
Connections	11.1	9.2	5.0	4.1
Concepts in Network	34.0	34.7	17.3	15.3
% Concepts in Network	79.5	77.6	52.4	44.6

Because of the small number of cases examined, statistical
analyses of these data were not appropriate. However, it is
apparent that the networks of younger and older learners were quite
similar. The primary distinction between the ability groups was in
the connectedness of the networks: The high skill individuals had
twice as many links between concepts, twice as many concepts in the
networks, and a greater percentage of the recalled concepts were
included in the networks.

MICROANALYSIS OF PERFORMANCE

A generic Goals-Operators-Methods-Selection (GOMS) model of text
editing, similar to that proposed by Card, Moran, and Newell (1983),
was constructed (Figure 1) and editing performance for the subsets
of participants was examined.   GOALS derive mostly from analysis of

```
GOAL:   EDIT_MANUSCRIPT
   .    GOAL:   ACQUIRE_TEXT
   .    GOAL:   EDIT_UNIT_TASK until no more or out of time
   .   .  GOAL:   ACQUIRE_UNIT_TASK
   .   .  GOAL:   EXECUTE_UNIT_TASK
   .   .   .select  USE_DELETE_METHOD
                       if all of a line to be removed
                    USE_INSERT_METHOD
                       if a new line to be added
                    USE_DELETE/INSERT_METHOD
                       if more than 40 characters to
                       be removed or if a line of fewer
                       than 20 characters to be completed
                       or if...
                    USE_REPLACE_METHOD
                       if more than 40 characters to be
                       removed or if a line of fewer than
                       20 characters to be completed
                       or if...
                    USE_CHANGE_METHOD if . . .
                     . ISSUE_CHANGE_COMMAND
                     . SPECIFY_DELIMITER
                     . GOAL:   SPECIFY_OLDSTRING
                     .  .select  WORD_METHOD
                                 LETTER_METHOD
                                 MINIMAL_STRING_METHOD
                                 TARGET_WORD_METHOD
                     . REPEAT_DELIMITER
                     . SPECIFY_NEWSTRING
                     . REPEAT_DELIMITER
                     . SPECIFY_LINE
                    USE_MULTILINE-CHANGE_METHOD if . . .
   .   .   .GOAL:   VERIFY_UNIT_TASK
   .   .   .   .  GOAL:   RECTIFY_ERROR until no error
   .   .   .   .  .EXECUTE_UNIT_TASK
```

*Fig. 1. Generic Goal-Operator-Method-Select (GOMS) model for
editing performance*

the task, and were consistent across individuals. Individual
differences were reflected in the METHODS that were selected and
when they were used; those in which there were substantial
differences are indicated by an incomplete conditional (*if...*). The
selection rules inferred from the protocols of skilled individuals
were strikingly different from those of less skilled, but age
differences were minimal. Skilled individuals used the change
command (CHANGE_METHOD) except when the change involved more than
about 15-20 characters. Less skilled individuals either replaced
whole lines or shifted unsystematically between replacing and
changing, making frequent errors when using the change command.
There were consistent individual differences in whether a
replacement was done by deleting the old line and inserting a new
one (DELETE/INSERT_METHOD) or by specifying the replace command
(REPLACE_METHOD), but the differences were not related to skill
level. Skilled individuals were more likely to make multiline
changes (MULTILINE-CHANGE_METHOD), though this was somewhat more

likely in younger than in older adults. When skilled individuals used the change command to make a correction, they were most likely to specify the smallest string logically possible or one a few letters longer (average length was four characters); less skilled individuals specified one or more surrounding words. When an entire word was to be replaced, all users tended to specify the target word.

The principal difference between skilled and less skilled individuals was in the use of the powerful but syntactically complex change command. During learning, skilled individuals may have achieved sufficient mastery that the syntax could be handled automatically and attention could be directed to locating strings that would specify changes efficiently. Nonetheless, few skilled individuals escaped syntax errors in using the change command. An alternative is that less skilled individuals brought lower levels of cognitive resources to bear on the task, so both the syntax and string specification imposed significant burdens. Support for this alternative was found in two observations. First, skilled individuals were more likely to scan the manuscript to locate repeated changes, consistent with the interpretation that they had more resources available. Second, correlation of the measure of working memory capacity with both recall and performance measures suggests that limitations in processing resources are important in both declarative and procedural knowledge acquisition.

ACKNOWLEDGEMENTS

This research was supported by a grant from the Spencer Foundation, and by the Scholarly and Creative Activities Committee of California State University at Long Beach.

REFERENCES

Card, S.K., Moran, T.P., and Newell, A. (1983). The Psychology of Human -Computer Interaction, Erlbaum, Hillsdale, New Jersey.

Daneman, M., and Carpenter, P.A. (1980). 'Individual Differences in Working Memory and Reading', Journal of Verbal Learning and Verbal Behavior, 19, 450-466.

Hartley, A.A., Hartley, J.T., and Johnson, S.A. (1984). 'The Older Adult as Computer User', in Aging and Technological Advances (Eds. P.K. Robinson, J. Livingston, and J.E. Birren), pp. 347-348, Plenum Press, New York.

Hartley, J. T. (1986). 'Reader and Text Variables as Determinants of Discourse Memory in Adulthood', Psychology and Aging, 150-158.

ASSESSMENT AND TREATMENT OF EVERYDAY MEMORY PROBLEMS IN THE ELDERLY

Cathy L. McEvoy and James R. Moon
Department of Aging and Mental Health
Florida Mental Health Institute, University of South Florida

ABSTRACT

A common complaint of many elderly adults is that their memory "isn't as good as it used to be." A program of research was designed to determine whether everyday memory problems can be effectively treated by utilizing principles from basic memory research and applying them to problems of everyday remembering. The results are reported below.

Elderly adults frequently complain of memory problems, and generally report that the problems have increased with age (Lowenthal et al., 1967). Several recent studies have noted discrepancies between subjective complaints and actual memory performance, leading some authors to propose that the complaints reflect age stereotypes or depression (e.g., Kahn et al., 1975). While there is ample evidence that depression is frequently associated with memory complaints, self reports of memory problems in everyday living by non-depressed elders may still be valid.

One reason for the discrepancy between memory complaints and memory performance may be a discrepancy between the skills addressed by the two types of measures. Subjective complaint scales generally ask about memory problems in everyday situations (e.g., misplacing one's glasses or forgetting to keep a doctor's appointment). In contrast, memory performance is frequently measured by laboratory tests such as digit span, paired-associate learning, free recall, etc. Memory problems among healthy elders may be reflected more in everyday remembering situations than in laboratory tests. Furthermore, when the self-report measure involves an in-depth report of problems, effort expended, and memory aids used in daily living, self-report and laboratory test measures are correlated for older adults (Zelinski et al., 1980).

The discrepancy between memory complaints and memory performance is also evident in the literature on memory skills training. In general, research on memory training programs for older adults indicates that the training produces improvement in memory performance, but little or no change in memory complaints (Scogin et al., 1985; Zarit et al., 1981). These findings may result from the skills taught in the training programs, including the method of loci, categorization, and interacting imagery. The performance measures used in these programs, including digit span, free recall, and name-face recall, are known to be improved by the skills taught. However, the everyday problems reported in the memory complaints assessments may be less affected by those skills. Although these well-established mnemonic devices **can** be applied to everyday problems, the application is not obvious to most people and requires considerable practice to be useful in non-laboratory settings (e.g., Cermak, 1976). Thus, the lack of relationship between memory training and changes in memory complaints may reflect difficulty in applying the skills beyond the training setting. In addition, these studies rarely address stereotypes of aging and memory that may contribute to the elders' complaints.

The present research was motivated by the presumed discrepancy between skills usually taught in memory-training programs and skills normally used in everyday remembering. We developed a training program that addressed the older adults' memory complaints directly, teaching techniques that could be used with only a minimum of practice and that had obvious applicability to everyday settings. We attempted to base the techniques on findings from the research literature on human memory.

Subjects   The subjects were recruited from the local community for participation in a memory-skills training workshop for older adults. Two workshops were held, approximately four months apart. The first was five sessions of one hour each, over five consecutive weeks. The second was three sessions of two hours each over three consecutive weeks. All participants were over age 50, living independently in the community, and reported their health to be average or better. All had Beck Depression Inventory scores below a significantly impaired range. Thirty four subjects were included in the study, 17 from each workshop. Eight males and 26 females participated, with a mean age of 68.0 (range 52 to 81).

Memory-skills training program   The training program was designed to teach skills that could be used to improve memory in everyday situations. The skills included established mnemonic techniques, use of external memory aids, and skills that incorporated basic research findings in human memory. Each workshop began with a discussion of memory and the effects of aging, medications, depression and anxiety on memory. Simple relaxation techniques and self-instructional exercises intended to dispel stereotypes of aging and memory were also included. After the introduction, six areas of memory problems were addressed:

Names and Faces: Subjects learned the use of imagery mnemonics; associating the person's name with that of someone already known (i.e., assimilation to existing knowledge); the importance of repeating the name in conversation after longer and longer time periods (distributed practice); etc. They were also taught to review the names of people that they knew but saw infrequently right before meeting with them (priming). Subjects then practiced by learning the names of some participants.

Appointments: Subjects learned the effective use of external aids for remembering non-routine appointments. The importance of reviewing appointments prior to their occurrence (increasing practice trials) was also emphasized.

Routine Tasks: This section dealt with remembering to complete routine tasks, such as watering plants, taking medications, etc.   Again, both external and internal memory aids were included.   Check lists were taught for remembering when a task was to be done, and for recording that it had been completed. Subjects were also taught to associate the routine tasks with appropriate environmental events occurring at the same time, (increasing cue specificity), such as watering plants immediately after watching the weekly T.V. show on gardening.

Spatial Orientation: This section covered common problems in spatial orientation, including remembering where the car is in the parking lot, what door was used to enter the department store, etc.   Subjects were taught to both verbally and visually code landmarks and other location information (cue redundancy); and to look behind them to see their return route from the returning perspective, rather than from the incoming perspective (increasing cue-target compatibility).   Subjects were also taught to analyze a new environment before navigating in it, using maps and general knowledge about the layout of buildings, towns, etc. (establishing knowledge structures for assimilating new information).   Practice included a walking tour of the building complex, with each participant attempting to use the skills taught in the section.

Locating Objects: Remembering where items have been placed, either for long-term storage or misplaced by accident, was covered in this section.   Skills included storing objects in function-related rather than unlikely locations (Winograd & Soloway, 1986); marking frequently-misplaced objects with easily seen colors, etc. (increasing salience); and using a central temporary placement location for objects that must be put down for a short time and then used again.

Concentration: The last section included maintaining concentration on stories being read, viewed, or listened to. Participants were taught to review the material as it was encountered, and relate it to existing schema.   They were also told to try to predict upcoming events in order to maintain concentration on the material and prevent attention from being diverted to other environmental stimuli.

Memory Questionnaire   The memory questionnaire was used to measure the frequency of occurrence of specific problems of everyday remembering.   The questions covered 10 different areas of everyday forgetting.   Six of the areas were those outlined above as the components of the training program.   Four additional areas were assessed but not taught.   These areas served as a control to determine whether changes in memory complaints reflected the training provided or resulted from unintentional causes, such as demand characteristics, etc.   The 10 areas and a sample question from each are listed below:

Areas Taught in the Training Program:

Names and Faces: About how often do you forget the names of people that you have just met?

Appointments: About how often do you forget to keep appointments?

Routine Tasks: About how often do you forget to do routine things, like taking your medicine or watering your plants?

Spatial Orientation: About how often do you get lost or turned around when you are in a new place that you have been to only one or two times?

Locating Objects: About how often do you forget where you have placed things, such as your glasses or wallet?

Concentration: When you are reading, about how often do you forget what you have just read and have to go back and re-read it?
Areas Not Taught in the Training Program:

Conversations: About how often do you start saying something, then forget what it was you wanted to say?

New Learning: About how often do you have trouble learning a new game or skill, like a new card game or craft?

Recalling Multiple Things: When you have several things to do, about how often do you forget to do one or more of the things?

Recalling Old Information: About how often do you forget the names of common objects, or have trouble finding the word you want?

Each question was followed by six boxes labeled with the following frequencies of occurrence:

Never	I have never had this problem.
Seldom	I seldom have this problem – it happens less than once a month.
Monthly	I have this problem about 1-3 times per month.
Weekly	I have this problem about 1-4 times per week.
Daily	I have this problem about once per day.
Often	I have this problem 2 times per day or even more often.

Responses were scored by allocating the values 0-5 to the above six frequencies of occurrence. Thus the higher the score, the more frequent is the reported occurrence of the problem. The questionnaire also included several questions intended to check whether the frequency scales were being used appropriately. These questions asked about the frequency of occurrence of events that normally happen on a set time schedule, such as "About how often does the mail come?" and "About how often do you eat a meal?"

Design   Each subject completed the Memory Questionnaire twice, once at the beginning of the first session and once after the completion of the entire training program. The post-test questionnaires were mailed to the participants' homes approximately two weeks after the last session. Questionnaires were scored by computing the total frequency of occurrence for each of the ten memory problem areas. These values were computed separately for the subject's pre- and post-tests. We also included the two groups as a between-subject variable, in case there were differences in effectiveness for the 5-week vs. 3-week format. Thus the data conformed to a 2 (groups) X 2 (pre- vs. post-test) X 10 (memory problem area) analysis of variance.

Results   The ANOVA indicated that there was a main effect of groups, with the first workshop subjects reporting a greater frequency of occurrence of memory problems, $F(1,32) = 8.91$. However, groups did not interact with memory problem area, pre- vs. post-test, or the interaction of those two variables, so the data for the two groups were combined and are reported together. The ANOVA also indicated a main effect of problem area, $F(9,288) = 9.88$. Problems with concentration and remembering names were reported most frequently, remembering appointments and spatial orientation were reported least frequently, and the other problems fell between these two extremes. The pre- and post-test means for each problem area, and the amount and direction of change from pre- to post-test are displayed below. Higher scores indicate more frequent problems.

	Pre-test	Post-test	Difference
Areas Taught in Training Program:			
Names and Faces	2.64	2.07	.57 —
Appointments	1.32	1.02	.30 —
Routine Tasks	1.79	1.55	.24 —
Spatial Orientation	1.43	1.28	.15 —
Locating Objects	1.86	1.79	.07
Concentration	2.21	2.37	-.16
Areas Not Taught in Training Program			
Conversations	1.97	1.98	-.01
New Learning	1.56	1.66	-.10
Recalling Multiple Things	1.75	1.76	-.01
Recalling Old Knowledge	1.81	1.76	.05

Pre- vs. Post-test was not a significant variable in this analysis, but the interaction of that factor with problem areas was significant, $F(9,288) = 2.38$. Fisher's Least Significant Difference (LSD) for comparisons between pre- and post-test means for each problem area is 0.15. As can be seen in the table, four of the six problem areas taught in the program showed significant positive change from pre- to post-test, one showed no change, and one (Concentration) showed a significant negative change. In comparison, none of the four areas not taught in the program showed significant change from pre- to post-test.

Discussion   The primary purpose of this study was to determine whether a memory-skills training program for the elderly directed at everyday problems would result in a decrease in self-reported occurrence of those problems. Results of this study indicate that although the magnitude of change in memory complaints is somewhat small and varies according to the problem area being addressed, training people in skills directed at everyday memory problems does reduce complaints for many of those areas. Four of the six memory problem areas addressed in the program showed significant decreases in reported problems, while no change was reported for the control areas not taught in the program. These results suggest that subjects were experiencing changes in everyday remembering in the areas taught in the program, and that they were not simply responding to demand characteristics or other sources of bias.

Although the training program appeared to be effective, two of the areas taught in the program did not show significant decreases in memory complaints. The Locating Objects section showed a nonsignificant decrease in complaints, and the Concentration section showed a significant increase in reported problems. One explanation for these findings is that the skills taught in these sections were more difficult to learn, and that a temporary deterioration in performance may precede competent use of the skill (as in converting from years of hunt-and-peck typing to touch typing). This explanation may be particularly applicable to the Concentration section, which was taught on the last day of the program and thus had the least time to benefit from practice before the post-test was administered.

One other thing that is noticeable in the above data is the low frequency of reported memory problems for these subjects. This level of occurrence is consistent with the fact that the subjects were all living independently in the community and had no diagnosed severe memory impairment. The fact that these individuals volunteered for a memory-skills workshop is consistent with findings that elderly adults are worried about their memory problems disproportionately more than their performance would justify. Although these individuals reported fewer problems than was anticipated, their enthusiastic participation in the workshops and the finding of small but significant improvements in four of the six areas taught in the program suggest that memory-skills training for everyday problems should receive further study.

References

Cermak, L.S. (1976). Improving your memory. Norton, New York.

Kahn, R.L., Zarit, S.H., Hilbert, N.M. & Niederehe, G.A. (1975). Memory complaint and impairment in the aged: The effect of depression and altered brain function. Archives of General Psychiatry, 32, 1560-1573.

Lowenthal, M.F., Berkman, P.L., Buehler, J.A., Pierce, R.C., Robinson, B.C. & Trier, M.L. (1967). Aging and mental disorder in San Francisco. Jossey Bass, San Francisco.

Scogin, F., Storandt, M. & Lott, L. (1985). Memory-skills training, memory complaints, and depression in older adults. Journal of Gerontology, 40, 562-568.

Winograd, E. & Soloway, R.M. (1986). On forgetting the locations of things stored in special places. Journal of Experimental Psychology: General, 115, 366-372.

Zarit, S.H., Cole, K.D. & Guider, R.L. (1981). Memory training strategies and subjective complaints of memory in the aged. The Gerontologist, 21, 158-164.

Zelinski, E.M., Gilewski, M.J. & Thompson, L.W. (1980). Do laboratory tests relate to self-assessment of memory ability in the young and old? In L.W. Poon, et al. (Eds.) New directions in memory and aging. L. Erlbaum Associates, Hillsdale, New Jersey.

DOES FAST LAST? IS SPEED A BASIC FACTOR
DETERMINING INDIVIDUAL DIFFERENCES IN MEMORY?

Patrick Rabbitt
Age and Cognitive Performance Research Centre
University of Manchester
MANCHESTER M13 9PL

ABSTRACT
        Recent studies have suggested that individual differences
in memory competence with age and IQ are best described in terms
of loadings on a single factor, identified with information processing
rate. Recent experiments suggest that such descriptions are simplistic and distract attention from more interesting functional models.
There are also grounds for concluding that models for memory
are inadequate if they do not take environmental and social factors
into account

        Changes in memory efficiency do occur in old age. The
only question is how they are best to be understood and precisely
what changes they imply for the ways in which older people carry
on their everyday lives. Current theories of age changes have
been formulated within three distinct descriptive frameworks:
        Psychometric models, began as 'bottom up' data driven
models, i.e. as **post hoc** speculations as to which factor structures
best describe inter-individual variance in the accuracy and speed
of solution of problems selected on pragmatic, rather than theoretical grounds. Limiting cases of factor structures are assumptions
that a single factor is common to nearly all cognitive tasks
(e.g. Spearman's 'g') and elaborate descriptions in terms of clusters
of special abilities (e.g. Guildford, 1980). It has been difficult
to relate any of these models to the functional models of cognitive
processes developed by neuropsychologists or cognitive psychologists.
While cognitive psychologists and neuropsychologists have intensively
studied particular **tasks** in order to describe the functional processes
necessary to carry them out, psychometricians have, until recently,
tried to derive structures from data across wide ranges of disparate
tasks without trying to describe the functional processes which
may mediate performance in any one of them.
        Cognitive models are (at least ostensibly) proposed as
'top down', theory-driven descriptions of hypothetical information
processing systems which are (at least purportedly) tested, **post
hoc,** by experimental paradigms especially designed for that purpose.
Such paradigms have been carefully designed to eliminate the effects
of all but one or two variables. These can then be manipulated
to demonstrate (allegedly) 'pure' effects within a closed, determinate
sub-system. This tradition of tightly controlled experiments has
led to the ingenious exclusion of variance due to individual
differences. Consequently, cognitive psychologists have typically

modelled hypothetically independent and 'modular' (Fodor, 1984)
cognitive sub-systems which can only perform very limited, and
sometimes artificial tasks.   It is a reasonable criticism that
failures in cognitive psychology occur when it becomes the psychology
of tasks rather than of cognition.

       Neuropsychological models have classically been driven by
the hope of discovering tightly specifiable performance deficits
in patients suffering from tightly localised brain damage.   Thus
it has been natural for neuropsychologists to treat memory in
terms of 'modular' independent sub-systems and to borrow for this
purpose the models, and associated paradigms, developed by cognitive
psychologists. Because focal lesions are rarely found, and because
few focal lesions result in very clear-cut changes in performance,
there has been little interest in individual differences.   This
is unfortunate for gerontology because the diffuse brain changes
accompanying normal ageing have been of little interest to neuropsychologists.   Gross diffuse changes such as those in Alzheimer's
disease, have been intensively studied, but in this condition
overall performance is reduced to such low levels that particular,
characteristic, performance decrements cannot easily be isolated.

Attempts to integrate levels of description.
       Two different kinds of attempts have been made to integrate
psychometric and cognitive descriptions in order to provide functional
rather than merely factor analytic models for individual differences.
Very many studies (ably reviewed by Cooper and Regan, 1982; Hunt,
1985; Kail and Pelligrino, 1985; and Daneman, 1984 among others)
have tried to describe differences in attainment at special abilities,
such as verbal or spatial skills, in terms of characteristic
differences in functional processes. Elaborate task analyses purportedly allow us to 'decompose'   overall performance indices from
tasks into 'sub-indices' yielding estimates of relative efficiency
of hypothetical functional sub-processes.   The tacit concept is
again that of a 'modular mind' in which independent sub-systems
may attain different levels of efficiency.   These descriptions
leave open the question whether the relative efficiency of modules
is determined by individual differences in neuropsychological function, or whether individuals may 'educate' particular modules to
different levels of efficiency by extensive practice on different
tasks so as to build up elaborate, and independent, 'domain specific'
sub-systems.

       If individual differences are described in terms of the
relative efficiency of independent 'modular' processes, the basic
questions about age changes are whether or not changes in some
modules begin earlier and proceed faster than in others; whether
extensive practice may maintain the 'knowledge basis' on which
the efficiency of particular modules depend, or whether loss of
competence is due to underlying biological changes which cannot
be mitigated by training.

       A contrary premise is that individual variations in compe-
tence on all cognitive skills can be described in terms of differences
in a single common factor, such as Spearman's 'g'. Recent studies
have tried to reify this factor in terms of overall 'information
processing rate' with the corollary that 'information processing

efficiency' must directly reflect 'general' CNS efficiency (Brand and Dearie, 1982; Eysenck, 1986; Hendricksen, 1982; Jensen 1982a; 1982b; 1985, among many others). On these assumptions it is natural to suppose that, in normal old age, when both the number and the connectivity of cortical neurons decline, information processing efficiency is also correspondingly reduced and scores on psychometric tests heavily loaded for 'g' correspondingly decline. Salthouse (1985) has based a detailed theory of cognitive change in old age on the premise that changes in all cognitive systems, including, and especially, memory are secondary to changes in information processing rate and so, inferentially, in global neural efficiency. Can we choose between 'modular' and 'single factor' descriptions of changes in memory efficiency in normal old age?

Predictions from the single-factor framework.
        The single factor model makes some strong predictions.
        (a)   Performance on **all** cognitive tasks, including all memory tasks, must correlate with performance on IQ tests which are highly loaded for 'g'.
        (ai)   The corollary for age-differences is that, on all cognitive tasks, differences between age groups simply reflect the decline of 'g' as age advances. Thus when chronological age and current scores on tasks yielding good estimates of 'g' are compared as predictors for any performance index, variance due to age should be completely comprised in variance due to differences in 'g'. In other words age should cease to be a significant predictor when effects of 'g' have been taken into consideration.
        (b)   A neglected consequence of prediction (a) is that all information processing tasks, including memory tasks, should correlate with each other. It is an important proviso that this association should be entirely explained by common correlations with IQ tests measuring 'g' or with simple tasks which give direct measures of information processing speed.
        (c)   If a single paradigm yields separate performance indices, including an independent index of information processing rate, we should find that information processing rate emerges as a 'master index' predicting levels of all other indices and underlying associations between them. In the strongest form of the single factor hypothesis, predictions by IQ test scores of efficiency in cognitive tasks should also be solely mediated by information processing rate.
        Empirical data to test some of these predictions have recently become available.

Age, IQ test score, choice reaction time and performance on laboratory memory tests.
        284 volunteers aged from 50 to 79 years were each given five different memory tests (digit span for visually presented material, span for auditorily presented digits and for the voices (randomly male or female for individual digits in each list) in which they were read, free-recall of a list of 30 words, recognition memory for a set of 40 line drawings presented among distractors and a cumulative recall test [total number of words

correctly reported cumulated over four successive presentations and recalls of the same list of 15 words]). Each volunteer took the AH4 intelligence test and received 2000 trials on a self-paced four choice serial CRT task. (Mean correct RTs were derived from the last 500 trials.) Table One gives correlations between chronological age and all task performance indices.

TABLE ONE
Matrix of Correlations Between Age and Tasks

	Age	AH4	CRT	Pictures	Learning	Free Recall	Digit Span	Digits/ Voices
Age	-.229	.189	-.165	-.022	-.264	-.132	-.027	
AH4		-.439	.371	.47	.386	.569	.534	
CRT			-.179	-.359	-.227	-.272	-.134	
Pictures				.371	.282	.235	.301	
Learning					.49	.361	.331	
Free Recall						.312	.289	
Digit Span							.519	

Correlations between performance on apparently very similar tasks are surprisingly low. The highest, between scores on 'digit span' and 'span for digit and voices', apparently almost identical tasks, is an unimpressive 0.519 (i.e. 27% of variance between individuals). Free-recall and cumulative learning (again very similar tasks), correlate at 0.49 (24% of variance). This suggests that even small differences in the functional demands made by simple tasks allow scope for considerable differences in the efficiency with which individuals carry them out, a direct demonstration of the striking 'domain specificity' of memory skills discussed by Herrmann, Rea and Andrezejewski in this symposium. In this context it is impressive that correlations between memory task performance and AH4 total scores are as high as between the memory tasks themselves; the highest, for digit span, is 0.569 (32% of variance) and the lowest, for picture recognition, 0.371 (14% of variance). A point in favour of a 'single factor' model of age changes is that all correlations between chronological age and task performance lapse into non-significance when effects of differences in IQ test score are partialled out.

Do predictions of performance on each memory task from other memory tasks, and predictions of performance on memory tasks from AH4 total scores occur because all tasks, and the AH4, pick up common variance in a single factor, such as 'g'? Or is the variance which different memory tasks have in common with each other different, and separate to, the variance picked up by the AH4? To test this a series of multiple regression analyses compared AH4 raw scores, and scores on each memory task as joint predictors for scores on each other memory task. The analyses were run so as to obtain the residual prediction from each of the two predictors after variance attributable to the other had been partialled out. Memory tasks were found to cluster. Each of the two digit-span tasks predicted a significant amount of individual variance in the performance of the other which was independent of, and additional to, the variance predicted by AH4. The same was true of the two verbal recall tasks. Thus AH4 picks up variance which is separate from, and additional to, that shared by similar tasks. Picture recognition was an exception. Predictions of picture recognition performance from digit span and verbal recall tasks were barely significant on their own, and entirely absent when variance predicted by AH4 scores was partialled out.

In terms of the strong version of the Eysenck/Jensen/Salthouse single factor theories the successful prediction by the AH4 of performance across a wide range of cognitive tasks must occur because all have common loadings on a single factor 'g'. In all these theories 'g' is reified as an index of 'information processing efficiency'. The AH4 is a paced task, in which scores on each of two parts represents the total number of questions correctly attempted in 10 minutes. It thus tests information processing speed, among other aspects of performance. A further question was whether a different, independent measure of individual differences in processing speed, CRT, picked up variance in memory task performance in addition to that picked up by the AH4 (and vice versa). Multiple regression analyses were run, as before, to compare AH4 total raw scores and mean correct CRT as predictors for each memory task in turn. For cumulative learning, free-recall, and picture recognition tasks, both CRT and AH4 scores predicted significant, independent and roughly equal proportions of variance. But CRT gave no residual prediction for the digit span and digit and voice span tasks after the significant proportion of variance predicted by AH4 had been partialled out.

Evidently clear-cut answers to these questions require factor analyses of much larger volumes of data. These are currently in progress. Meanwhile it seems that if we use the psychometric laboratory tasks, individual differences in memory task performance are not best explained in terms of a single factor of information processing efficiency directly associated with individual differences in decision speed. Associations between tasks seem to be well explained by a common sense model of their 'clustering' in terms of the particular and distinct functional demands which they make. Do detailed functional analyses of particular memory tasks clarify this impression?

Functional analyses of age, AH4 test scores and information processing speed as predictors of performance in memory tasks.

Goward and Rabbitt (this symposium) found that recognition memory accuracy for word-lists is predicted by either of two task internal measures of information processing rate, the speed with which words are initially classified, and the speed with which individual words are subsequently recognised. However, AH4 test scores pick up variance in performance which is separate and additional to that picked up by decision speed. A complete description of individual differences in recognition memory evidently cannot be articulated in terms of information processing speed alone.

Goward's second experiment makes a stronger point. Both AH4 test scores and individual differences in information processing rates (word recognition latencies) predicted overall success at delayed recognition of words, but neither predicted the rate at which words were lost from memory as a function of elapsed time and interference. In terms of slightly old-fashioned functional models of memory, such as those which Kriaciunas (1967) and Talland (1967) used to discuss similar findings in age comparisons, information processing rate, or psychometric 'g' may partly determine individual differences in the efficiency with which words are encoded and retrieved from memory, but they do not seem to determine rates of forgetting.

The most tightly specified current functional description of immediate memory is Baddeley's (1986) 'working memory' model. This predicts a direct relationship between information processing rate (articulation rate and reading rate) and immediate memory span, and thus offers a functional explanation for relationships between immediate memory efficiency and information processing rate. However, Goward finds that while articulation rate, reading rate and span are all predicted by AH4 test scores, **working memory efficiency,** assessed as the rate at which information is lost if items are not continuously re-cycled around the articulatory loop, is invariant with IQ test score, with articulation rate and with reading rate alike.

For recognition of items held for many years in long term memory, Stuart-Hamilton, Perfect and Rabbitt (this symposium) found that chronological age predicts individual variance in recognition memory sensitivity which is **additional and separate** to that predicted by IQ test scores. Moreover, recognition confidence is predicted by age but not by AH4 test score. As in the immediate recognition tasks investigated by Goward and Rabbitt, AH4 test scores predict variance in individual recognition scores which is independent of, and additional to, the variance predicted by a task internal measure of information processing rate (item recognition latency).

DISCUSSION

Most paradigms in experimental cognitive psychology can be adapted to give measures of information processing speed. It follows that models to describe data obtained with these paradigms can also be adapted to include descriptions of rate-governed processes. But it is simplistic to regard these rate-governed processes as more 'fundamental' to the functional efficiency of the sub-systems in which they occur than any of the numerous other, non-rate-governed processes which the same models specify. This error would lead us gravely to underestimate the power of the functional descriptions given by cognitive models. If we use this explanatory power we can produce much better descriptions of individual differences.

It is important to remember that the AH4, like any other IQ test, is in effect only a collection of separate tasks deliberately selected for complexity and for diversity. A 'good' IQ test is one in which the functional processes used to solve at least some problems overlap with those involved in a very wide range of complex everyday activities. On this common-sense view it is inevitable that some functional processes should be common between most IQ tests and most paradigms in cognitive psychology. We should therefore expect to find weak but significant correlations between gross IQ test scores and most performance indices, which is what we get. In this simple framework our data show that 'information processing speed' is not the sole, nor necessarily the most significant component of performance which a particular IQ test shares with each of several different memory paradigms. They also make the stronger point that individual variability in particular performance indices, such as rate of loss of information in immediate memory, articulatory loop capacity, and confidence level in recognition of names held in long term memory, are not picked up by a paced IQ test nor by task-internal indices of information processing rate.

If we look at things in this way, the trouble with 'single factor' models for individual differences in IQ or age is not that they are 'wrong' but that they are inadequate and distracting. Their enthusiastic proponents are bound to find evidence for them everywhere in terms of pervasive, weak associations. This wastes time better spent on articulating the cognitive psychology of age differences in terms of better functional models which can, eventually, be meaningfully mapped on to neuropsychology.

Social and experiential factors in age changes in memory.

The studies in this symposium suggest that the oppositions which we have been discussing, i.e. 'psychometric' vs. 'cognitive' levels of description and 'single factor' vs. 'multi-factor' models provide only weak and superficial insights into the ways in which people adapt to changes in their memory efficiency to cope with their daily lives. For example, Stuart-Hamilton, Perfect and Rabbitt find that people's confidence in the reliability of their long term recognition memory for 'once famous names' may change as they grow older, **independently** of changes in the objective accuracy of these judgements. Abson and Rabbitt find that people's subjective impressions of their memory competence in everyday life is affected by depression and poor self-regard, but much more subtly and pervasively by their interplay with the environments which they choose for themselves; the ecological niches to which they adapt. Younger people, performing well in demanding lifestyles, may have worse opinions of their own competence than older, and objectively much less efficient, people who have moved into much less demanding 'niches'. 'Metamemory', in the sense of the way one feels about one's memory and everyday competence, is evidently based on information 'negotiated' in terms of social and environmental demands.

REFERENCES

Baddeley, A.D. (1986). Working Memory, OUP, Oxford.

Brand, C.R. and Deary, I.Z. (1982). 'Intelligence and "Inspection Time"' in A Model for Intelligence (Ed. H.J. Eysenck), Springer, New York.

Cooper, L.A. and Regan, D.T. (1982). 'Attention, perception and intelligence' in Handbook of Human Intelligence (Ed. R.J. Sternberg), CUP, Cambridge.

Daneman, (1984). 'Why some people are better readers than others; a process and storage account' in Advances in the Psychology of Human Intelligence Vol II (Ed. R.J. Sternberg), Lawrence Earlbaum, New Jersey.

Eysenck, H.J. (1986). 'Intelligence and cognition' in Advances in the Psychology of Human Intelligence Vol III (Ed. R.J. Sternberg), Lawrence Earlbaum, New Jersey.

Fodor, J. (1984). The Modularity of Mind, MIT Press, Cambridge, Mass.

Guildford, J.P. (1980). 'Components versus Factors', Behavioural and Brain Sciences, 3, 591-592.

Hendricksen, A.E. (1982). 'The biological basis of intelligence, Part I, Theory' in A Model for Intelligence (Ed. H.J. Eysenck), Springer, New York.

Hunt, E. (1985) 'Verbal ability' in Human Abilities, an Information Processing Approach (Ed. R.J. Sternberg), W.H. Freeman, New York.

Kail, R. and Pelligrino, J.W. (1985). Human Intelligence; Perspectives and prospects, W. H. Freeman, New York.

Jensen, A.R. (1982a). 'Reaction Time and Psychometric 'g'' in A Model for Intelligence (Ed. H.J. Eysenck), Springer, New York.

Jensen, A.R. (1982b). 'The chronometry of intelligence' in Advances in the Psychology of Human Intelligence Vol I (Ed. R.J. Sternberg), Lawrence Erlbaum, New Jersey.

Jensen, A.R. (1985). 'The nature of the black-white difference on various psychometric tests; Spearman's hypothesis', The Behavioural and Brain Sciences, 8, 193-219.

Salthouse, T.A. (1985). A Theory of Cognitive Aging, N Holland, Amsterdam.

Spearman, C. (1904). ''General intelligence' objectively determined and measured', American Journal of Psychology, 15, 201-293.

REMEMBERING WHO WAS WHO

Ian Stuart-Hamilton   Tim Perfect
Patrick Rabbitt
Age and Cognitive Performance Research Centre
University of Manchester
MANCHESTER M13 9PL

ABSTRACT

Stevens' (1979) 'Famous Names Test' investigates recognition of relatively recent and remote public figures. For 924 volunteers aged from 50 to 80 years, age and AH4 IQ test score predicted recognition sensitivity, but only age affected recognition confidence. The FNT was computerised to obtain item recognition latencies from 106 volunteers aged from 18 to 36 and 50 to 82 years. IQ test scores predicted individual differences in recognition memory which were not predicted by age or by recognition speed.

INTRODUCTION

Recall and recognition of remote events worsens in old age (Craik, 1977), but it is not clear whether memory for distant events becomes poorer than memory for recent events, or whether the reduced performance of the elderly may be due as much to their increasing subjective doubts of their own memory efficiency as to any objective change. It is also not clear whether age changes in long term memory efficiency are related to, or separate from, the decline in general cognitive function which IQ tests pick up.

The Stevens' (1979) 'Famous Names Test' (FNT) requires the identification of names of real people, briefly famous at different times since the 1920s, embedded among 'dummy' names. It offers a means of testing; (i) whether names from the same period (e.g. 30 years ago) are best remembered by individuals now in their 50s, 60s or 70s, thus allowing probabilities of recognition to be compared after the same long time interval between individuals of different ages; (ii) whether or not recognition 'sensitivity' (measured by indices such as d' or non-parametric equivalents), or recognition caution, or criterion (measured by Beta or equivalent indices) change with age; (iii) whether sensitivity or caution vary with current IQ and (iv) whether all age changes in recognition memory efficiency are picked up by concomitant changes in IQ test scores, or whether changes in memory efficiency in old age are additional to, and to some extent independent of, the broader changes in cognitive efficiency picked up by IQ tests.

EXPERIMENT ONE

924 volunteer members of the ACPRC research panel, aged

between 50 and 86 years, completed the pencil and paper version of the FNT. They took as long as they wished to complete the test. All had previously completed the AH4 intelligence test.

The FNT comprises a printed list of 80 names which have to be identified as 'real', or by exclusion, as 'dummies'. There are 30 dummies. The 50 names of real public figures are classified by Stevens' (1978) standardisation of 5 sets of 10. One set is of 'very famous' names recognised by all members of Stevens' sample. Ten names were recognised only by members of her sample aged over 50, and other sets of ten by members of her sample who were over 40, 30 and 20 in 1978. Thus '50s', '40s', '30s' and '20s' provides a rough guide to temporal remoteness of the periods when the names in the test were well known. Both parallel forms of Stevens' test were administered, equally often and at random, to the present volunteer sample.

Scoring

For the AH4 test the combined scores on general performance and spatial reasoning sub-tests were computed for each volunteer. These raw scores were used to classify volunteers into 'high, 'medium' and 'low' scoring groups. Orthogonal to this classification volunteers were divided into groups aged 50 to 59, 60 to 69 and 70 and above. The FNT was scored for 'hits' (correct identifications), 'omissions' (failures to identify names) and 'false positives' (acceptance of dummy lures). Numbers of hits were separately computed for the categories '50s' through '20s'.

Results

The mean number of hits achieved by each age and IQ group are given in Table One. A 3-way Within-Between-Between ANOVA gave significant main terms for age ($F=21.87$, df 2:16, $p<0.01$), for IQ test score ($F=26.93$, df 2:16, $p<0.01$) and for temporal remoteness of name ($F=943.6$, df 4:16, $p<0.01$). Name type interacted significantly with age ($F=38.91$, df 8:16, $p<0.01$) and with IQ test score ($F=12.97$, df 8:16, $p<0.01$). Table One shows that older groups identified more names in total then younger groups because they could identify more remote names. Consistent with Stevens' original standardisation, volunteers in their 50s identified more recent and fewer remote names than volunteers in their 60s and 70s. Higher AH4 score volunteers recognised more names. Table One shows that the IQ/name-remoteness interaction occurred because the difference between high and low test scorers was greater for remote than for recent names.

Since false positives cannot, of course, be attributed within remoteness categories, differences in sensitivity and criterion could only be compared across age and IQ groups over the test as a whole. Because many volunteers had zero false-positive scores a conventional signal detection analysis was not appropriate. Instead a non-parametric signal detection index giving indices SI equivalent to d' and RI equivalent to Beta was computed (Grier, 1971 and Frey & Colliver, 1973). A multiple regression analysis tested predictions from unbanded age and test score for SI and RI. Regression equations were computed to assess the residual variance accounted for by each predictor after all variance accounted

for by the other had been taken into account. Both age (T=12.8
p<0.0005) and test scores (T=8.08 p<0.0005) predicted sensitivity,
SI, when the other had been taken into account. But age alone
predicted RI (T=2.85 p<0.05) when effects of test score had
been taken into account.

Table One : Mean scores on Famous Names Test divided by age, IQ band and name type

Group	n	Name Type 50	40	30	20	VF	False +ve
50 Low	34	4.97 ±2.63	6.03 ±2.58	7.82 ±1.87	9.18 ±1.19	9.85 ±0.56	2.53 ±4.22
50 Med	98	5.02 ±2.36	7.05 ±2.17	8.46 ±1.77	9.41 ±1.14	9.98 ±0.20	1.13 ±1.46
50 High	121	5.50 ±2.15	7.87 ±1.93	8.90 ±1.57	9.68 ±0.76	9.93 ±0.34	1.20 ±1.96
60 Low	108	6.29 ±2.56	7.46 ±2.17	8.34 ±1.96	9.13 ±1.35	9.86 ±0.55	1.69 ±2.53
60 Med	186	6.80 ±1.99	8.34 ±1.55	9.13 ±1.41	9.58 ±0.90	9.94 ±0.54	1.12 ±1.88
60 High	149	7.16 ±1.78	8.66 ±1.34	9.38 ±1.04	9.58 ±0.90	9.96 ±0.20	1.15 ±1.75
70 Low	101	6.43 ±2.22	7.20 ±2.28	8.17 ±1.95	8.78 ±1.73	9.88 ±0.64	1.64 ±2.89
70 Med	104	7.43 ±1.85	8.15 ±1.85	8.89 ±1.54	9.26 ±1.13	9.81 ±0.76	1.40 ±2.46
70 High	27	7.67 ±1.84	8.85 ±1.51	9.19 ±1.00	9.37 ±1.28	9.93 ±0.38	1.30 ±1.44

Discussion

These results to some extent confirm, on a much larger
sample, Stevens' original standardisation of her test; older volunteers identify more names than younger volunteers because they
identify more temporally remote names. To this we add the finding
that high test scorers identify more names in total than low
test scorers, and that this advantage is particularly marked
for remote names. The triple interaction between age, test
score and remoteness was not significant, so this effect is
general across age groups, and not simply due to better remote
recall by high IQ volunteers over 70.

It might be tempting to conclude that high test scorers
forget familiar names less rapidly than low test scorers, but
this cannot be proved with Stevens' test or with any other test
probing autobiographical memory for public events. 'Famous names'

and 'events' do not abruptly drop out of currency; rather their frequency of occurrence gradually reduces.   High test scorers show an advantage for recent, as well as for more remote names. This is probably due as much to their more active interest in the media and in public events as to differences in rates of forgetting.   In general, as the period of maximum notoriety of a public figure becomes increasingly remote, his or her name will appear with decreasing frequency in the media (unless, like Adolph Hitler, such a level of notoriety has been attained that a report-frequency plateau remains constant over many decades). It follows that, apart from possible differences in rate of forgetting, high test scorers may have a marked advantage over low test scorers in their greater probability of detections of rare media recapitulations of remote public figures and events. Equally, the fact that older volunteers identify fewer recent names than younger volunteers may as much reflect decreasing interest in the media as poorer memory for recent events.

The main facts about changes in memory efficiency with advancing age which we can derive from this experiment are that both age and IQ test score, **independently** predict recognition sensitivity.   In other words, there is a change in long term recognition memory sensitivity with age, and some, **but not all** of this change is picked up by an IQ test as part of a 'packaged' general decline in cognitive skills which occurs with age.   In contrast, differences in IQ test scores do not predict individual differences in confidence of recognition.   But, as age advances, independently of the general decline in cognitive abilities assessed by an IQ test, there is growing decline in the confidence with which recognition judgements are made.

Why are IQ tests such good predictors of performance across a wide variety of tasks?   A recent hypothesis is that IQ tests have a high loading on a single common factor **'g'**, and that this may be identified with speed and efficiency of information processing; (Eysenck, 1986; Jensen, 1983; 1985). Similarly a recent 'Cognitive Theory of Aging' suggests that a key common factor underlying most age changes in performance is a reduction in information processing rate (Salthouse, 1985). According to these theories variance in recognition efficiency between individuals associated with IQ test scores or with age should be subsumed under variance due to individual differences in information processing rate.   To test this directly Stevens' tests were computerised so that latencies for responses to each item could be timed, giving a measure of individual differences in the speed of information processing from within the task itself.

Experiment Two

The computerised 'Famous Names' test was taken by 52 young (mean age 25.71 sd 5.66) and 54 older people (mean age 62.52 sd 11.34), students at Manchester Adult Education College. All also completed the AH4.

It is important to note that the young group had encountered all except the most recent names only as 'historical figures'. Thus 'recognition' meant something different for the two groups. This, and the fact that volunteers in both groups made almost no false positives, made separate computations of 'sensitivity' and 'caution' inappropriate for these data. Accordingly all analyses were based on total numbers of names correctly recognised.

Results

The younger group knew relatively few of the names of public figures who had been famous before they were born, but they did recognise some, averaging 2.6 hits in each decade category. Because the older volunteers, who were also slower, tended to recognise more names in total than did the fast young, the only valid comparison of the predictive power of IQ test scores and recognition latencies was on the category of most recent names, on which the younger and older groups did not differ in accuracy. It followed that for this sub-set of names a multiple regression analysis found age to be a non-significant predictor. More surprisingly, recognition latency also gave no significant independent prediction ($T= -1.01$). AH4 part one raw scores alone predicted recognition accuracy when the effect of the other two variables had been partialled out; ($T=2.95$ $p<0.01$).

GENERAL DISCUSSION

Stevens' FNT is certainly a useful index of general efficiency of recognition memory but cannot tell us much about the rate of loss of information over time. This is because 'famous names' are often revived in the media after their period of maximum exposure so that dates of 'last encounters' cannot be assumed. This point is illustrated by the fact that, in Experiment Two, volunteers in their 20s showed considerable knowledge of people famous before they were born. Bearing this in mind it is unsurprising that older people should recognise more distant figures than the young. They may also keep their memories vivid by recent, spontaneous, reminiscence or sensitivity to media recurrences of names of people associated with their own youth. It is also not surprising that, in Experiment One, recognition accuracy should have been predicted by scores on a simple pencil and paper IQ test. People with high IQ test scores might be expected to be better educated, to show greater attention to the media and to take a greater interest in public events both early and late in their lives, making them more sensitive both to the original appearances of public figures, and to retrospective accounts of them which occur after their disappearance from the public scene.

However, these uncertainties do not affect the use of the FNT as an index of general efficiency of long-term recognition memory. In this context Experiment One makes the new point that, even when effects of individual differences in IQ test score have been taken into account, the caution with which names are recognised increases with age. More importantly, not all age changes are picked up by changes in scores on a single IQ test.

Experiment Two tested whether individual differences in recognition accuracy were better predicted by IQ test scores or by information processing rate (recognition speed). Age effects were uninteresting because they related to differences between experience of names as part of a personal past and as merely historical figures. It is inevitable that the speed with which individual names are recognised should correlate highly with the total number of names recognised. The new finding is that AH4 test scores predict variance **additional and independent** to that predicted by recognition speed. The Eysenck/Jensen/Salthouse 'single factor' models for individual differences due to age and intelligence are currently inadequate to discuss these findings. It seems that at least one IQ test does predict efficiency of acquisition, retention and updating of general knowledge, because it picks up sources of individual differences different to, and in addition to, those associated with individual differences in information transmission efficiency.

REFERENCES

Craik, F.I. (1977). 'Age differences in human memory', in Handbook of the Psychology of Aging (Eds. J.E. Birren and K.W. Schaie), pp 384-420, Van Nostrand Reinhold, New York.

Eysenck, H.J. (1986). 'The Theory of Intelligence and the Psychophysiology of Cognition' in Advances in Psychology of Human Intelligence Vol III, (Ed. R.J. Sternberg), Lawrence Erlbaum, New Jersey.

Frey, P.W. and Colliver, J.A. (1973). 'Sensitivity and responsivity measures for discrimination learning', Learning and Motivation, 4, 327-342.

Grier, J.B. (1971). 'Nonparametric indexes for sensitivity and bias: computing formulas', Psychological Bulletin, 75, 424-429.

Jensen, A.R. (1983) 'The chronometry of Intelligence' in Advances in Psychology of Human Intelligence, Vol II, (Ed. R.J. Sternberg), Lawrence Erlbaum, New Jersey.

Jensen, A.R. (1985). 'The nature of the black-white difference on various psychometric tests: Spearman's hypothesis', The Brain and Behavioural Sciences, 8, 193-263.

Salthouse, T. (1985). A Cognitive Theory of Aging, Springer, Berlin.

Stevens, M. (1979). 'Famous personality test. A test for measuring remote memory', Bulletin of the British Psychological Society, 32, 211.

WORKING MEMORY CAPACITY, IQ, AGE AND THE ABILITY
TO RECOUNT AUTOBIOGRAPHICAL EVENTS

Carol Winthorpe   **Patrick Rabbitt**
Age and Cognitive Performance Research Centre
University of Manchester
MANCHESTER M13 9PL

ABSTRACT
        Spontaneous recall of autobiographical memories was evaluated in relation to independent estimates of working memory capacity, efficiency of recall and probed recognition of text, age (60 to 79) and IQ test score, in a group of 33 volunteers. The number and kinds of errors made in structuring recall were predicted by IQ test score but not by age. The ability to recall specific details of described events was found to correlate with estimates of working memory capacity and current IQ test score, but not with age alone. These results are discussed in the context of processing resource deficits.

        Older people begin to have problems organising discourse; they wander from the point of an anecdote, forget what they have just said and fail to specify referents for pronouns (Hutchinson and Jensen, 1980). These difficulties may reflect loss of working memory capacity (Kausler, 1982; Baddeley and Hitch, 1974). Loss of working memory capacity with age may be expected to affect comprehension, storage and recall of discourse (Light and Anderson, 1985). Does this contribute to the errors which older people make in giving an account of an event which they once experienced? Is efficiency at organising an account of an event mediated by general intelligence ('g'), or are there effects of age on working memory capacity and on discourse management which are not picked up by IQ tests?
        A different approach is to ask whether the types of errors which older people make in recounting events which they have themselves experienced are similar to those which occur when they try to recall text presented in laboratory experiments. Spilich (1983) probed recognition of single sentences extracted from a previously presented passage of continuous text. Target sentences were presented for identification, embedded in sets of three distractor sentences. One distractor sentence had the same meaning as the correct target, but was syntactically altered (semantic identity, surface structure difference). A second was syntactically similar but altered in meaning, (surface identity, semantic difference). The third was a sentence which bore some relation to information presented in the text, and was consistent with general 'knowledge of the world' but had not actually occurred in the presented text (related distractor). Young adults were better than the elderly at correctly identifying target sentences. Memory

impaired elderly volunteers most often accepted 'related distractors'. These results illustrate the general point made by Rabinowitz,
Craik and Ackerman (1982) that older people may encode text,
or everyday events in terms of their general knowledge of the
world rather than in terms of specific details and an unique
context.   Young adults attempting to recall past events appear
first to recall the general context and then to 'home in' on
specific details.   Do the diminished processing resources of the
elderly allow them only to access the general gist of an incident
in their past but not to go on to access specific details?
        These possibilities reduce to three empirical questions:
first, whether the efficiency with which people organise their
reports of past events is predicted more strongly by their current
age or by their current IQ test scores; second, whether efficiency
of recall of events correlates with independent estimates of current
working memory capacity (such as those assessed by Daneman and
Carpenter's (1980) 'sentence span' technique); third, whether difficulties in organising reports of past life events correlates with
difficulties in recognition of sentences from previously presented
text, (such as those assessed by Spilich's (1983) probe technique).

Method
        33 volunteers from the ACPRC Manchester panel were divided
into four groups in terms of age and IQ test score; i.e. 10
high test score volunteers (35+ on AH4, mean 44.3, sd 5.7) aged
60 to 69 (mean 65.7, sd 2.0), eight low test score volunteers
(28- on AH4, mean 23.25, sd 5.33) aged from 60 to 69 years (mean
65.7, sd 1.93), six high test score volunteers (mean AH4 44.67,
sd 5.7) aged 70 to 79 (mean 73.0, sd 2.31), and nine low test
score volunteers (mean AH4 20.33, sd 5.31) aged 70 to 79 (mean
74.0, sd 2.05).
        All volunteers were assessed for sentence span using Daneman
and Carpenter's (1980) technique.   They were given sentences of
13 to 16 words to read aloud and were asked to remember the
last word of each, beginning with a 'span' of two sentences and
increasing this span until one or more words began to be forgotten.
The highest number of sentences at which no errors were made
over three consecutive trials was taken as the effective 'span'.
        During a 30 to 45 minute interview, all were asked to
recall and describe specific incidents from their past lives for
the experimenter.   It was stressed that they should try to recall
very specific incidents rather than vague generalisations or a
verbal life history.   To aid recall they were, if necessary,
given time period cues, e.g. 'can you describe an incident from
the time you were at school, first started work, retired etc.'.
Their reports were recorded, transcribed and scored for (i) specificity of autobiographical incidents recalled (ii) incidence of three
categories of errors, i.e. (a) total failure to complete an introduced
theme or idea (b) temporary failure to complete a theme or idea
(c) failure of anaphor (missing referent for a pronoun).   On
a later day volunteers were invited back and given a set of
four to six requests for more specific information prepared from
their transcripts.   Answers were scored on a four point scale
as 1. highly specific, 2. medium or low specificity, 3. non specific,

4. failure to recall any appropriate detail.

All were tested on recall and recognition of the 440 word 'tulip' text adapted from Spilich (1983). The text was set out in large print. Volunteers were told that they would have to remember it after a single, careful reading. They were then asked to recall as much of the text as possible, and their responses were tape recorded. They were then given Spilich's sentence probe identification task. Recall protocols· were scored separately for (i) number of propositions correctly recalled and (ii) number of irrelevant additions in recall. Probe recognitions were scored separately for types of distractors wrongly accepted.

RESULTS
Recall of life events.

Specificity of recall: A two way ANOVA on rated specificity of original recall showed a significant main effect of IQ test score (F=10.593, F crit=7.56, df 1,29 p<0.01) but no effect of age, and no interaction.

Sentence span predicted specificity of recall of life events (r=-.734). But AH4 test score also predicted both specificity of recall (r=-.612) and sentence span (.613). When partial correlation coefficients were calculated to separate out the effects of differences in AH4 scores the correlation coefficient between sentence span and specificity of recall remained significant at r=-.574 (r crit=.463).

The correlation between rated specificity of recall on the first interview and specificity of answers to questions on the second interview was r=.438 which falls just short of significance (r crit=.468 for df 16).

The correlation between specificity of recall of life events and number of propositions correctly recalled from text was not significant (r=-.161).

There was no significant correlations between specificity of recall of life events and incidence of type a, b, c or d errors in probed recognition of sentences from text.

Errors in organisation of recall of life events:
(a) Complete failure to finish a theme. These errors were predicted by IQ test scores, (r=-.354, r crit.339, p<0.5) but not by age. Nevertheless high IQ 70 year olds made more of these errors than high IQ 60 year olds; this trend might well reach significance in a larger sample.
(b) Temporary failure to complete a theme. Neither IQ nor age predicted these errors.
(c) Frequency of failure of anaphoric reference. This was predicted by IQ test score (r=-.423, r crit=.339, p<0.05) but not by age.
Recall and probed recognition of text.

Number of propositions correctly recalled: A two way ANOVA showed a significant effect of IQ test score (F=8.0, F crit=7.56, df 1,29, p<0.01) but no main effect of age. However, there was a significant age x IQ test score interaction (F=6.16, F crit=4.49, df 1,29, p<0.05). The low IQ 70 year old volunteers remembered fewer propositions than any other group.

Erroneous additions in recall: There was a main effect

of IQ. High test score volunteers made fewer such errors (F=6.16, F crit=4.49, df 1,29, p<0.05). There was no main effect of age and no interaction.
Probed sentence recognition:
(a) Correct recognition. High test score subjects recognised significantly more correct sentences (F=9.3, F crit=7.56, df 1,29, p<0.01). There was no age effect and no interaction.
(b) False recognition of syntactically changed sentences. There was no significant effect of age or intelligence.
(c) False recognition of semantically changed sentences. High test score volunteers made fewer of these errors (F=9.59, F crit=7.56, df 1,29, p<0.01). There was no main effect of age, and no interaction.
(d) False recognition of thematically related distractors. No effects of age or test score, and no interaction.

DISCUSSION

Errors made by volunteers in organisation of their recall of autobiographical events are well predicted by their IQ test scores but, on the whole, poorly predicted by their age. An exception is failure to continue with an idea or theme. Incidence of these errors was predicted by IQ test score, but also by age; the high test score 70 year olds made more of these errors than the high score 60 year olds. It seems that, irrespective of their IQ test scores, our oldest volunteers were becoming vulnerable to this kind of lapse.

Errors in failing to specify anaphoric reference were well predicted by IQ test score, but also, independently, by sentence span. This again suggests that IQ test scores do not pick up all individual differences in working memory capacity which affect competence in this task.

In all other respects, efficiency at organising recall and reports of memories of life events is predicted by IQ test scores and not by chronological age alone, i.e. groups of younger and older people who are matched for IQ test score show equal competence in organising their recollections and their discourse. This does not, of course, mean that 'age does not matter', but rather that change with age in ability to organise recall of life events is, very efficiently, picked up by a single, simple IQ test. The methodological implications of this for ageing studies are obvious.

IQ test scores also predict the degree of specificity of detail which people provide in their recollections of life events. An obvious question is whether this relationship reflects a difference in the styles of anecdote adopted by high and low IQ volunteers, or whether loss of specificity of recall reflects a basic difference in cognitive resources. People who provided few specific details on initial recall were also unable to provide them when specifically interrogated during a second testing session. This non-significant trend might have emerged more strongly with larger groups of volunteers. It seems probable that people who do not provide specific details of life events on unstructured recall cannot do so because this information is not available to them.

The suggestion by Rabinowitz, Craik and Ackerman (1982)

that older people may encode new information in terms of their general knowledge of the world rather than in terms of specific context was examined by comparing incidence of irrelevant additions to recall of text between age and IQ groups. There was no effect of age, but IQ test scores did predict incidence of these errors.

The difficulties encountered by older people in successfully organising anecdotes of their lives must very considerably affect the ease and pleasantness, and so eventually the frequency and quality, of their daily social interactions. This study shows that these difficulties probably do not represent isolated failures of learning of appropriate social skills, but rather basic difference in available cognitive resources. However, there are hints from the data that, in older age groups, current levels of cognitive resources are much better predicted by current IQ test score than by current age. Age changes in working memory capacity may antedate the other cognitive changes which IQ tests so efficiently detect, and critically influence the quality of presentation of self in everyday life.

REFERENCES

Baddeley, A.D. and Hitch, G. (1974). 'Working Memory', in The Psychology of Learning and Motivation (vol. 8), (Ed. G.H. Bower), Academic Press, New York.

Daneman, M. and Carpenter, P.A. (1980). 'Individual differences in working memory and reading', Journal of Verbal Learning and Verbal Behavior, 19, 450-466.

Hutchinson, J.M. and Jensen, M. (1980). 'Pragmatic evaluation of discourse communication in normal and senile elderly in a nursing home', in Language and Communication in the Elderly (Eds. L.K. Obler and M.L. Albert).

Light, L.L. and Anderson, P.A. (1985). 'Working memory capacity, age and memory for discourse', Journal of Gerontology, 40, (6), 737-747.

Rabinowitz, J.C., Craik, F.I.M. and Ackerman, B.P. (1982). 'A processing resource account of age differences in recall', Canadian Journal of Psychology, 36 (2), 325-344.

Reiser, B.J., Black, J.B. and Abelson, R.P. (1985). 'Knowledge structures in the organisation and retrieval of autobiographical memories', Cognitive Psychology, 17, 89-131.

Spilich, G.J. (1983). 'Life span components of text processing: Structural and procedural differences', Journal of Verbal Learning and Verbal Behavior, 22, 231-244.

WHAT INTELLIGENCE TESTS DON'T MEASURE

Louise Goward   **Patrick Rabbitt**
Age and Cognitive Performance Research Centre
University of Manchester
MANCHESTER   M13 9PL

ABSTRACT
        Claims that scores on simple pencil-and-paper IQ tests predict performance on a variety of psychomotor tasks have been used to support the idea that Spearman's single intellectual factor 'g', may be reified in terms of information processing efficiency (Eysenck, 1986; Jensen, 1980, 1982, 1985). Reduced information processing rate has also been proposed as a common factor underlying all cognitive changes in old age (Salthouse, 1982). A review of three recent experiments shows that neither IQ test scores, nor information processing rate, completely account for individual differences in recognition memory, rate of loss of information in short term memory or differences in immediate memory span. The logic, and the evidence, for 'single factor' models of individual differences are found inadequate.

Introduction

        Significant negative correlations are sometimes found between people's scores on pencil-and-paper IQ tests and their choice reaction times (CRTs), eg Jensen (1982, 1985). These are typically very modest ($r=-0.2$ to -0.4, accounting for between four and 16% of the variance). There are also significant positive correlations between RTs and chronological age, but these are also modest. An unpublished study by Rabbitt and Fleming found $r=0.45$ between CRT and age across a group of 200 volunteers aged 50 to 78 years. Nevertheless, these relationships have been taken as evidence that individual differences in competence at problem solving and psychomotor tasks alike may be assessed in terms of a single factor, Spearman's (1904) 'g' which can be identified with information processing speed. Also a 'cognitive theory of ageing' has been premised on the idea that changes in information processing rate underlie age changes in competence at all other cognitive tasks, including those involving access to information in long and short term memory (Salthouse, 1982).

        These attempts to bridge the gap between psychometric and cognitive models of human performance beg unresolved questions. First, whether all psychometric tests which provide consistent and useful indices of individual differences in cognitive skills do, indeed, have high loadings on a single common factor. Second, whether age-changes in all cognitive skills are best expressed in terms of changes in the loading of this single factor. But for cognitive psychologists the most severe conceptual problem is that existing cognitive models of human performance are, typically, models of small, putatively independent, cognitive sub-systems, eg models for 'memory scanning', 'working memory' or 'reaction times'. Each of these models is based on a different subset of experimental paradigms. Some models do, to some extent, involve assumptions about the way in which information is processed over time. But when these cognitive psychological models are adapted to describe individual differences in competence, or the cognitive changes that occur as people grow old, 'information processing rate' neither appears consistently, nor as the sole construct in any model. It is not even a common index able to be derived from the many and diverse experimental paradigms on which these models have been based.

Cognitive models of memory, in particular, are highly articulated, and are based on experimental paradigms which can produce a variety of independent performance indices. This allows us to ask the questions posed by Eysenck, Jensen and Salthouse in a new way. When we examine individual differences in performance on memory paradigms which yield two or more separate indices of competence, does variance on indices of information processing rate subsume variance in all other indices? Further, do individual differences in scores on pencil-and-paper IQ tests predict individual differences in all other performance indices only by virtue of their predictions of individual differences in information processing rate? Or do IQ test scores predict individual differences on other performance indices even when variance attributable to individual differences in information processing rate has been directly partialled out?

Three experiments to investigate these questions are briefly described; encompassing the areas of recognition memory, the rate of forgetting of information, and the relationship between articulation speed and immediate memory span. Populations of volunteers aged 50 to 81 were selected according to their age decade and their score on a standard pencil-and-paper IQ test (part one of the Alice Heim 4 Test, a very general test of logical, numerical and verbal reasoning ability).

EXPERIMENT ONE
Method

This study used a recognition memory paradigm based on Craik and Lockhart's (1972) 'levels of processing' model. Two groups of 72 and 79 volunteers classified each of two lists of nouns. One was a semantic classification, eg 'living or not'; the other concerned the surface features of the word, ie presence or absence of a particular vowel. After categorising each list, subjects were given a recognition list with the original words embedded amongst distractors. Words were presented one at a time on a computer screen, and accuracy and response times were measured.

Results and Discussion

Three way analyses of variance between age and AH4 groups and within depth of processing, on initial classification time,

recognition time and recognition accuracy, revealed no main effects
of age groups, but all produced main effects of test score group
and depth of processing.   Words processed to a semantic level
took longer to classify but were more accurately and rapidly
remembered.   High scorers were faster at both classification
and recognition, and also recognised more targets.   However,
if classification speed is regarded as a measure of information
processing rate, a multiple regression analysis can directly compare
processing speed and AH4 score as predictors of recognition memory
performance.

Within both groups of subjects, regression analyses over
all groups produced large significant predictions (t<3.8, p<.001)
of recognition accuracy by AH4 score, and only in the surface
condition of one experimental group did speed of processing manage
to make an additional prediction at a much reduced significance
level (t=2.32, p<.05).   The amounts of variance in recognition
accuracy accounted for by these two factors varied from 18 to
51%, leaving a large amount still unexplained.   This residual
variance increased when the test score groups were examined separately, with few predictions reaching significance, and the amount
of explained variance in recognition accuracy reducing to between
9 and 20%.   However, in six out of eight cases the partial
correlation coefficient was higher for test score (when differences
in processing speed were allowed for) than for processing speed
(when differences in test score were allowed for).

It would appear that although test score predicts differences
in speed of performance, information processing rate does not
explain the ability of test score to predict recognition accuracy.
Also, even if test score and processing speed are taken together,
at least half the variance in performance accuracy still remains
unexplained.

EXPERIMENT TWO
Method

An experiment by Shepard and Teghsoonian (1961) provided
an alternative method to the Brown-Peterson paradigm of studying
the decay of information in short-term memory.   By providing
a continuous list of to-be-remembered items, certain target item
pairs can be made to recur with varying numbers of items intervening.
Characteristically, recognition accuracy reduces the further apart
the two items are in the list.   In a 200 word list, 95 words
recurred either one, four, nine, 19 or 49 items later.   Each
of 77 volunteers was required to press one of two computer keys
to each stimulus, to indicate whether they had seen the word
before or not.   Response times and accuracy were recorded.

Results and Discussion

When the data were analysed, as for Experiment One, there
was no significant prediction from age after test score had
been considered.   Analyses of variance showed main effects of
test score group and number of intervening items on both response
times and accuracy.   The effect of intervening items was as
expected; immediately recurring words were more quickly and accurate-

ly recognised than words which recurred at longer intervals. As in Experiment One, high test scorers made faster and more accurate recognitions, but speed differences were largely due to the slowness of the 70 year old low scorers. The other groups did not differ significantly.

Importantly though, there was no interaction between test score group and number of intervening items, indicating that although the high scoring group were remembering more than the low group, there were no differences between the test score groups in the **rate** of loss of information across intervening items. The lack of a difference also between age groups supports several studies, eg Kriauciunas (1968), Talland (1967), who found that elderly subjects lose information at a similar rate to the young. Thus, here is an index which is independent of age, IQ test score, and information processing rate alike.

EXPERIMENT THREE
Method
This study was based on the model of the articulatory rehearsal loop (Baddeley and Hitch, 1974) in working memory. Baddeley, Thomson and Buchanan (1975) argue that individual differences in rates of articulation determine individual differences in memory span (measured in syllables), with the slope of the regression between these measures indicating the capacity of the articulatory loop. Reading rate, articulation rate and memory span, on word lengths of one, two, three, four and five syllables, were measured for each of 72 volunteers.

Results and Discussion
Analyses of variance again showed no significant main effects of age decade, but main effects of test score group and number of syllables on reading rate, articulation rate and memory span were significant. Longer word lengths induced slower articulation and lower span estimates. Overall the high test scoring group read faster and had longer memory spans. To investigate differences in capacity, regressions of articulation and reading rate upon memory span were computed, but the slopes of these functions were the same for all age and test score groups.

These results replicate Baddeley et al's (1975) data, and are consistent with the idea that differences in memory span can be accounted for by differences in articulation speed. Although the high scoring groups have better memory spans and faster reading and articulation rates, the regression analyses produce similar relationships between memory span and articulation measures for both high and low scorers. Thus, in Baddeley et al's terminology, the **capacity** of the articulatory rehearsal loop is invariant between individuals with very different levels of measured intelligence, and different infomation processing speeds.

General Discussion
The common finding in all three experiments was that IQ test scores predict differences in speed of processing and access to information. However, information processing speed

does not predict some important performance differences, eg recognition accuracy in Experiment One, rate of forgetting in Experiment Two, and articulatory rehearsal loop capacity in Experiment Three.

On the other hand, test scores proved to be better predictors of performance than information processing rate for recognition accuracy in Experiment One and in Experiment Two. Also, any age differences are completely preempted when test scores are taken into account. However the rate of forgetting, and articulatory rehearsal loop capacity remain invariant with test score as well as with differences in information processing rate, providing rare examples of performance indices which are unaffected by individual differences in intellectual ability or processing speed.

Conclusion

Models for individual differences in performance which are premised on the existence of a 'single factor' of information processing rate do not do justice to the complexity, and success, of cognitive psychological models and of the paradigms which support them. One pencil-and-paper test, the AH4, was a good predictor of individual differences on a variety of distinct indices generated by these paradigms. But in spite of this, there are cognitive qualities which remain invariant with test score. Further, even using test scores and information processing rate as joint predictors, up to 50% of the variance remains unaccounted for. It is still intriguing as to why simple IQ tests give low levels of prediction over such a wide range of tasks. However, these experiments weaken the case that they do so only because they pick up common loadings on a single factor associated with information processing rate.

REFERENCES

Baddeley, A.D. and Hitch, G.J. (1974). 'Working Memory' in The Psychology of Learning & Motivation : Advances in Research & Theory (Vol. 8) (Ed. G.H. Bower), pp. 47-90, Academic Press, New York.

Baddeley, A.D., Thomson, N. and Buchanan, M. (1975). 'Word length & the structure of short term memory', Journal of Verbal Learning & Verbal Behaviour, 14, 575-589.

Craik, F.I.M. and Lockhart, R.S. (1972). 'Levels of processing : A framework for memory research', Journal of Verbal Learning & Verbal Behaviour, 11, 671-684.

Eysenck, H.J. (1986). 'The theory of intelligence and the psychophysiology of cognition' in Advances in the Psychology of Human Intelligence (Vol. 3) (Ed. R.J. Sternberg), Erlbaum, Hillsdale, NJ.

Jensen, A.R. (1980). Bias in Mental Testing, Methuen, London.

Jensen, A.R. (1982). 'Reaction time & psychometric g' in A

Model for Intelligence (Ed. H.J. Eysenck), pp. 93-132, Springer--Verlag, Berlin.

Jensen, A.R. (1985).   'The nature of the black-white difference on various psychometric tests : Spearman's hypothesis', The Behavioural and Brain Sciences, 8, 193-263.

Kriauciunas, R. (1968).   'The relationship of age & retention interval activity in short term memory', Journal of Gerontology, 23, 169-173.

Salthouse, T.A. (1982). Adult Cognition : An Experimental Psychology of Human Ageing, Springer-Verlag, New York.

Shepard, R.N. and Teghtsoonian, M. (1961). 'Retention of information under conditions approaching a steady state', Journal of Experimental Psychology, 62, 302-309.

Spearman, C. (1904). 'General intelligence, objectively determined and measured', American Journal of Psychology, 15, 201-293.

Talland, G. (1967). 'Age & the immediate memory span', Gerontologist, 7, 4-9.

WHAT DO SELF RATING QUESTIONNAIRES TELL US ABOUT CHANGES IN
COMPETENCE IN OLD AGE?

Vicki Abson
North East Age Research, University of Newcastle upon Tyne
Patrick Rabbitt
Age and Cognitive Performance Research Centre
University of Manchester
MANCHESTER M13 9PL

ABSTRACT
            The Harris and Sunderland Memory Questionnaire (MQ), the
Broadbent Cognitive Failure Questionnaire (CFQ) and a questionnaire
probing frequency of loss of possessions (LF), were administered
to three large (476-900) groups of people aged from 50 to 85
years, for whom scores on verbal and non-verbal IQ tests, laboratory
memory tasks and the Beck Depression Inventory were also obtained.
All questionnaires correlated modestly with each other.   None
correlated with any objective test of competence.   The CFQ alone
correlated with the Beck.   The LF showed a negative correlation
with age.   It seems that answers to memory questionnaires reflect
the adaptation of the elderly to changing environments, and sometimes
their self esteem, but not changes in their competence.

            It would be convenient if we could reliably discover
how memory changes in old age simply by asking older people to
tell us. This might not only reveal changes in everyday efficiency
but also whether 'metamemory' skills (the knowledge of the way
information is organised in memory, knowledge of how to use memory
and the appreciation of ones own memory efficiency; Flavell and
Wellman, 1977), change in old age. Unfortunately, recent surveys
suggest that while young adults' scores on self rating memory
questionnaires correlate with each other at modest levels, there
is as yet no evidence that self rating scores predict performance
on objective laboratory memory tests (Herrmann, 1982).
            This is not surprising nor, on its own, an indication
that self rating questionnaires can tell us nothing about objective
competence. Questionnaires probe a wide range of everyday scenarios
while laboratory tests are deliberately designed to assess very
specific skills and so, typically, correlate only modestly even
with each other. They are very brief, and are deliberately administered in quiet, unstressed conditions in which distraction is
minimised. Most everyday tasks are far more complicated, involving
continuous flexible updating, selection and transformation of information which may simultaneously arrive from disparate sources in
a rapidly changing context. Most lapses occur because of distraction,
loss of efficiency under stress and poor maintenance of vigilance
(Reason, 1979).   They may also represent vulnerability to time
of day effects (Broadbent, 1987) which are deliberately controlled
out of laboratory memory experiments. Finally, laboratory memory

tasks do not simply fail to predict self ratings of competence. They have been found to correlate very weakly (Zeaman and House, 1967), or not at all (Woodrow, 1940), with scores on IQ tests which, for all their notorious weaknesses, remain the best predictor of everyday competence yet developed. Thus a better question is 'how do self ratings of competence correlate with IQ test scores?'.

Study One

        Between 1978 and 1980 Rabbitt, Fleming, Vyas and Wright gathered data on 900 volunteers aged from 50 to 78 years during a longitudinal ageing study. All completed the Harris and Sunderland Memory Questionnaire (MQ), (Harris, 1980) and the Broadbent Cognitive Failure Questionnaire (CFQ), (Broadbent et al., 1982), a battery of six laboratory memory tests, a test of general intelligence (the AH4 parts one and two) and a vocabulary test (Mill Hill parts A and B). The MQ and CFQ correlated at a modest level (r=0.36, or 13% of common variance). Since these questionnaires were administered eight months apart, apparently they both pick up common subjective impressions which remain stable over some time. As expected (Herrmann, 1982), neither questionnaire correlated with any laboratory memory test. AH4 test scores correlated negatively with chronological age (r=-0.42 or 17.64% of the variance), again illustrating the decline of IQ in older populations. AH4 scores weakly predicted performance on laboratory memory tasks (r=0.29 to r=0.46). Performance on laboratory memory tests correlated negatively with age (r=-0.26 to r=-0.46). Self ratings on neither questionnaire correlated with AH4 or Mill Hill scores. Since IQ test scores are the best available indices of general intellectual competence this is surprising. It is also very surprising that MQ and CFQ scores did not vary with age because, as people grow older, loss of memory efficiency is one of their most frequent complaints.

        In brief, all the objective tests of intellectual efficiency correlated positively with each other and negatively with age. Self ratings also correlated with each other, but not with tests of objective competence or with age. Why?

        One possible reason is that self rating questionnaires implicitly ask people to rate their own competence in some absolute sense. Competence can probably only be rated relatively, i.e. by comparing one's own efficiency in meeting everyday life demands against that of one's colleagues, family and acquaintances, or against publicly available norms. If we ask people to make relative rather than absolute judgements, will their self ratings better reflect their true abilities?

Study Two

        Rabbitt, Fleming and Vyas adapted instructions on the MQ, asking 564 new volunteers aged 50 to 79 years to estimate how much their performance in the particular scenario probed by each question, had changed over the last 30 years (i.e. since age 20 to 29 for those currently aged 50 to 59 and so on). Volunteers also took all other tests administered in Study One. Self ratings of cognitive change on the MQ correlated with self ratings of current competence on the CFQ (r=0.32), but, once again, not with current AH4 or Mill Hill scores, nor with performance on any laboratory memory test. All volunteers felt that their memory efficiency had changed for the worse over the last 30 years, formally confirming the commonplace complaint of loss of memory efficiency with advancing age. But, surprisingly, groups of all ages indicated the same **amounts** of perceived change over the last 30 years.

It is possible that cognitive efficiency truly declines linearly between ages 20 and 70, but it is worthwhile considering at least three other explanations before accepting this dubious hypothesis. First, re-defining the MQ as a **relative** comparison between past and present performance does not solve the problem that people must judge their efficiency in terms of their ability to cope with current life demands. Although people's 'absolute' cognitive efficiency may change with age, so do the life styles they adopt. An impression of roughly constant success at coping with the environment may thus remain valid over many years. A different, theoretical, point is that self rating questionnaires have been developed on the tacit assumption that there exist 'general factors' which account for competence across all everyday scenarios in which memory is used. It is increasingly questioned whether such general factors actually exist (Keile, 1984), and whether memory competence may not rather be intensely 'domain specific' to particular task demands (Herrmann, Rabbitt and Hitch, 1987, paper submitted). In other words, specific practice rather than general capacity may be responsible for most of the variation between individuals in terms of their special skills at remembering faces, names, appointments or telephone numbers. In this case we would not necessarily expect scores on self rating tests to have factor loadings on the factor of 'general intelligence' ('g') picked up by IQ tests and vocabulary tests. Further, because memory questionnaires probe a wide range of everyday scenarios, but competence in any one scenario does not necessarily reflect competence in any other, individuals of different ages might quite validly achieve the same total scores on any given questionnaire summed ratings across quite different **patterns** of scenarios, repres-enting their personal adaptations to quite different lifestyles. A final point is that self ratings of competence may be affected by depression and poor self regard as much as by actual levels of efficiency in everyday life.

Study Three

To test these possibilities, Rabbitt and Abson (in prepara-tion), adapted a questionnaire designed by Tenney (1984) which focussed on only a single type of memory lapse, mislaying one's objects. Tenney had found no difference in the ways in which people mislaid and recovered objects reported with increasing age. Rabbitt and Abson considered the possibility that age differences might have been confounded by poor recall in the elderly who may 'forget that they forget', thus failing to report losses. To mitigate this Rabbitt and Abson used cued recognition rather than recall, providing a check list of 32 items, each of which was rated for loss on a scale from one (never) to five (very often). Volunteers also indicated which items in the list they actually possessed. After cued recognition they were asked to recall as many items as possible, not mentioned on the list, which they had recently mislaid, and to rate each for frequency of loss. This 'Lost and Found Questionnaire' (LF) was administered to 476 volunteers aged 50 to 85 years, who had all previously completed all tests used in Study Two. In addition most had completed the Beck Depression Inventory within 3 months of completing the LF, the CFQ and the adapted MQ. Correlations are based on the 446 out of 476 volunteers who, besides completing the LF, had also been scored on all other indices.

Scores on the CFQ, the adapted MQ, the LF and the Beck did not correlate with scores on IQ or vocabulary tests or any laboratory memory test. As expected, scores on the two general questionnaires, the CFQ and the adapted MQ, again correlated with each other (r=0.328), and with the specific questionnaire, the LF. The correlation between the CFQ and the LF (r=0.425) was, indeed, significantly higher than the correlation between the MQ and the LF (r=0.238) or that between the CFQ and the MQ (r=0.328).

One empirical question was whether self ratings on questionnaires reflect depression and poor self image as much as actual competence. The CFQ did, indeed, correlate significantly with the Beck (r=0.329) but the adapted MQ (r=0.133) and the LF (r=0.174) did not.

The new finding was that while, as in Studies One and Two, scores on the CFQ and the MQ did not correlate with chronological age, there was a significant negative correlation between chronological age and the LF (r=-0.243). A one way ANOVA showed that this occurred because volunteers aged from 50 to 59 years recognised and recalled more instances of losses than members of the other decade samples. The possibility that this difference occurred because younger volunteers actually owned more possessions mentioned on the list was checked by a one way analysis of variance. There was no significant difference between groups.

Discussion

In all three studies, scores on self rating questionnaires correlated modestly with each other. Clearly they all tap common subjective impressions of everyday competence. Because, in each study, the various questionnaires were administered over periods of four to twelve months, the subjective impressions of everyday competence which they commonly reflect apparently can remain stable over periods as long as a year. Correlations were no higher between questionnaires which probed performance across a wide range of scenarios (the CFQ and the MQ) than between each of these and a check list which only probed losses of possessions (the LF). But while all losses of items represent one result of cognitive failure, they may occur in very different scenarios and have very diverse origins, e.g. distraction and inability to schedule two concurrent activities, failure to update working memory, lapses of attention or concentration, failure to correctly follow a learned routine etc. Thus these data do not yet challenge the view that we may be mistaken to seek for 'general factors of memory' and that individuals may rather show very diverse

competence across a wide range or learned, 'domain specific' skills.
If memory test questionnaires all correlated inversely with IQ
test scores we might make a case that people can successfully
rate themselves in terms of the factor 'g' which is also common
to most intelligence tests and which determines everyday competence.
But this was not found.

A different possibility is that self ratings correlate
across tests because they all pick up subjective feelings of
depression or poor self regard. The data do not bear this out.
Only the CFQ correlated withthe Beck Depression Inventory; (r=0.329),
and correlations between the CFQ on the one hand, and the MQ
and the LF on the other, remained significant when variance due
to common loadings on the Beck was taken out by computing partial
correlations (in Study Three for CFQ and MQ partial correlation
r=.304 and for CFQ and LF partial r=0.395).

On the adapted MQ all volunteers made it clear that
they felt that their memory efficiency had markedly declined with
age. Their rated assessments of this decline correlated with
their estimates of their current cognitive efficiency both on
the CFQ in Study Two and on the CFQ and LF in Study Three.
But, paradoxically, their related assessments of subjectively experienced cognitive decline over the last 30 years did not correlate
with their current ages; (adapted MQ in Studies Two and Three).
So, although most of our volunteers strongly felt that they had
lost cognitive competence as they aged, and although we know
that they were probably right, on none of three large samples
did ratings of frequencies of current lapses increase with current
age. Indeed, on the LF, people aged 50 to 59 reported significantly
more lapses than their seniors.

This latter, counter intuitive, finding offers an explanation for these paradoxical results. People cannot rate their
own cognitive efficiency in any absolute terms because they can
only estimate their competence by comparing their performance with
that of others, or in relation to their success in coping with
daily demands. As they grow older both the company they keep
and the environmental demands which they face change markedly.
People in their 50s still have active, even pressurised, lives
in which demands made upon them may make lapses inevitable. They
may be surrounded by young colleagues. Moreover, since they
are becoming increasingly more conscious about their own ageing,
trivial lapses which might have been laughed off at age 30 or
40 may now be remembered as ominous symptoms of impending decline.
People in their 60s and 70s have usually retired, and may have
attained more control over their environments than they ever had
before. They may have begun to worry less about their own ageing.
In sum, answers to self rating questionnaires can only, possibly,
reflect people's assessments of their own ability to meet very
complex, very disparate, and very rapidly changing social demands.
People with high and low IQs and younger and older people have
to attempt to cope with very different worlds. Their identical
perceptions of their competence may thus reflect very different
absolute levels of ability. Self rating questionnaires may give
us some insights into the social relativities of ageing, but
they are probably not the best instruments for such studies.

Their value as objective measures of everyday competence is increasingly obscure.

REFERENCES

Broadbent, D.E., Cooper, P.E., Fitzgerald, P. and Parkes, K.R. (1982). 'The Cognitive Failure Questionnaire (CFQ) and its Correlates', British Journal of Clinical Psychology, 21, 1-16.

Flavel, J.H. and Wellman, H.M. (1977). 'Metamemory', in Perspectives on the Development of Memory and Cognition (Eds. R.V. Kail Jnr. and J.W. Hagen), Lawrence Earlbaum, Hillsdale NJ.

Harris, J.E. (1980). 'Memory Aids People Use: Two Interview Studies', Memory and Cognition, 8, 31-38.

Herrmann, D.J. (1982). 'Know They Memory; the Use of Questionnaires to Assess and Study Memory', Psychological Bulletin, 92, 434-452.

Herrmann, D.J., Rabbitt, P.M. and Hitch, G. (1987). 'The Generality of Memory Training' submitted to Psychological Bulletin, January 1987.

Keile, F.C. (1984). 'Mechanisms in Cognitive Development and the Structure of Knowledge', in Mechanisms of Cognitive Development, (Ed. R.J. Sternberg), W.H. Freeman, New York.

Reason, J. (1979). 'Actions not as planned: The Price of Automatization', in Aspects of Consciousness, (Eds. G. Underwood and R. Stevens), Academic Press, London.

Tenney, J.R. (1984). 'Aging and the Misplacing of Objects', British Journal of Developmental Psychology, 2, 43-50.

Woodrow, H. (1940). 'Interrelations of Measures of Learning', Journal of Psychology, 10, 49-73.

Zeaman, D. and House, B.J. (1967). 'The relation of IQ and Learning', in Learning and Individual Differences, (Ed. R.M. Gagne), Merril, Columbus, Ohio.

DRUGS AND MEMORY

THE EFFECTS OF DRUGS ON HUMAN MEMORY

C. Idzikowski
Clinical Pharmacology Unit,
Janssen Pharmaceutical Ltd.,
Grove, Wantage, Oxon., U.K. OX12 0DQ.

ABSTRACT

This review of the drug and human memory literature attempted to associate the effects of drugs with particular components of human memory. Before considering a drug a number of pharmacological and psychological entry criteria were defined. Virtually no drugs were found to satisfy all the criteria. By ignoring weaknesses in methodology it appeared that benzodiazepines inhibited acquisition of episodic memory whilst sparing semantic memory whereas drugs reducing cholinergic transmission reduced access to semantic memory. All other drug classes examined -- neuropeptides, catecholamines, nootropics, corticosteroids and opioids -- did not show consistent effects on memory.

INTRODUCTION

For the years 1966 to 1st quarter 1987 591 papers dealing with the effects of drugs on human memory were retrieved from the Medline database. The number of papers published each year on this topic is still rising (figure 1 below).

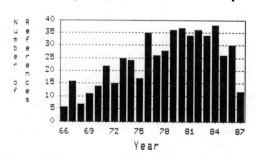

Drugs and Human Memory

In order to produce a short review of the field, it was necessary to reduce the number of papers to manageable proportions. The intention was to tabulate drug effects with specific components of human memory. A number of pharmacological, psychological and experimental criteria were set up to determine whether a drug would enter the classification table. It was noted

that many papers failed to report the pharmacokinetic properties
of drugs, such as the time to reach peak plasma levels, the peak
plasma levels achievable in the experiment and the half-life of the
drug. Without knowing these properties it was difficult to assess
whether the design of the experiment was sensible. These were the
criteria:

1. Pharmacological
    1. The pharmacokinetics of the drug.
    2. Dose-response curves.

2. Psychological
    1. General tests of performance.
    2. Measures of motivation and mood.
    3. Repeated experiments with alternative measures.

3. Experimental
    1. Positive control
    2. Adequate design
    3. Circadian effects

No single series of experiments satisfied entirely the
criteria! The literature does not provide the answer to the
following type of question "Given drug X, what are its specific
effects on human memory?" . This is partly because human memory
systems are still ill-defined and the methods used to measure
the hypothesized systems are invariably affected by the drugs used
to explore those systems. Less ambitious questions framed in
operational terms dealing with the day-to-day (clinical) use of drugs
can be answered.

This paper will 1) expand on the criteria, so as to provide
guidelines for future experiments and 2) ignoring methodological
problems describe what appears to be the relationship between
drug classes and human memory.

PHARMACOLOGICAL CRITERIA
It is vital to have an appreciation of the kinetics of the
drug. Generally, with novel compounds the only information
available deals with the plasma levels. It may be argued that
plasma levels may not be adequate indicators of how a drug or its
metabolites are distributed in the body but as a rough guide in a
preliminary experiment they are very useful.

It is also necessary to know the consequences of varying
the route of adminstration (oral, intravenous, subcutaneous,
intramuscular, nasal, etc.). Metabolism may differ if the drug is
given intravenously instead of orally.

The half-life of a drug provides an indication of the length
of time a drug may exert its effect. Neuropeptides have very short
half-lives (i.e. they are broken down very rapidly to non-active
metabolites in several minutes) and consequently a crossover
experiment could be run rapidly but on the other hand it may be
difficult to exert an effect on memory processes that last a long
time. In contrast some benzodiazepines and especially their
initial metabolites (e.g. diazepam, flurazepam, nitrazepam) have

half-lives   of several   hours   or   days   which   can   lead   to   very
extended crossover experiments or incomplete elimination of the drug.

Generally,   a   drug   experiment   attempts   to   show   some
relationship   between   a   drug   and   its effect.   It is good practice
to   demonstrate   a   dose-response   relationship. Invariably   drugs
affect   many different systems.   Using the lowest effective dose   may
minimize   effects   that   interfere with   the   desired response,   e.g.
sedation   may   occur   at   high doses   along   with   memory   changes,
whereas   low   doses   may affect only memory.

Comparison   of acute versus repeated adminstration   of   drugs
can   shed   light on their action apart from elevating   concentrations
if the half-life is short.

PSYCHOLOGICAL CRITERIA

More   often   than   not   drugs   have   many   effects   and
currently   there   are   no   drugs   that are claimed to affect   memory
alone.   As memory tests could be considered a   subset of   performance
tests   it   is possible that drugs which affect memory are   likely   to
affect other   aspects   of   performance. It   is   essential   that   any
experiment examining a drug and human   memory   should   also   examine
other   aspects   of performance that   could   be   affected.   If   it
seems that an important variable such as arousal or attention or mood
are   being   affected   then   the   interpretation of the results of that
experiment   need to be qualified.   Benzodiazepines are a drug   class
which   always   produce   some degree of sedation, making it difficult
to   assess precisely   what   their   "pure" effects   are   on   memory.
It   has   been   argued   that   all benzodiazepine anterograde   effects
on   memory   are   actually retrograde effects of sleep (Roth et   al.,
1984).

Unfortunately   negative   results   of   other   performance
variables   may   still lead to difficulties in interpretation as   the
sensitivity of most tests can usually be questioned.

Often   in   a non-drug laboratory   the   assumption   is   made
that   a   subject's motivation or mood remains constant throughout the
experiment.   This assumption cannot   be   made   in   drug   experiments
because   many   drugs have been shown to affect   mood   and   motivation
(occasionally with placebo).

Given   that   most   memory   tests rely   on   other   aspects   of
performance,   and given that few if any drugs currently have a   pure
effect   on   memory,   an   attempt   at   separating   out effects   could
be   made   by   repeating   experiments using different measures.   So
if   a   drug   appears   to affect   semantic   memory   retrieval   in   one
experiment,   the experiment should be repeated using   an   alternative
measure   and   preferably   one that relies on a   different   response
mechanism (e.g. reaction times versus errors).

EXPERIMENTAL CRITERIA

It   is   useful   to   run at least   two   controls   in   drug
experiments: a   placebo control and a positive control   (a   drug
which   exerts   known   effects).   The   latter   is   used   to check
whether   the test battery and subjects are responding   as   expected.
The   positive   control   is   in   effect   a   partial   replication   of   a
previous experiment.

Experiments need to be designed so that measurement of drug effects is occurring at the optimal time. Millar(1983) has suggested that within-subject drug and memory experiments are particularly sensitive to the effects of asymmetric transfer. Unfortunately the effects of drugs on memory tend to be very small (often less than 5%) and the variability of the responses very high. If the appropriate statistical power calculations are made this soon leads to the number of subjects in each condition becoming very large, subject numbers of at least 30 being not uncommon.

Circadian effects should if possible be checked. Both short-term memory (Baddeley et al. ,1970) varies throughout the day and sleep also exerts an effect (Idzikowski, 1984). The absorption and metabolism of drugs also varies diurnally (Reinberg, 1969).

REVIEW

Table 1 lists the number of references dealing with the effects of drugs on human memory since the last Practical Aspects of Memory Conference (Gruneberg, Morris and Sykes, 1978). The drugs are grouped roughly into the classes benzodiazepines, cholinergic drugs, neuropeptides, anticonvulsants, nootropics, solvents, beta-blockers and miscellaneous.

Previous authors have already reviewed the literature and the consensus agreement at the moment seems to be that there are no drugs that have been shown to affect only memory (Wolkowitz, 1985a). The suggestion has been made that the cholinergic system is most intimately involved with memory, affecting the intrinsic system (Squire and Davis, 1981), consolidation and access to semantic memory; if the problems with sedation are ignored the benzodiazepines inhibit acquisition of episodic memory whilst sparing semantic memory; whilst all other classes appear to affect so many other aspects of performance to make it impossible to tease out in a meaningful manner their effects on memory.

DISCUSSION

Despite the work conducted on the effects of drugs on memory a consistent story is yet to emerge. There are a number of reasons why this is the case. Some experiments are designed to check whether chemicals such as solvents have any toxic effects on performance, and memory is part of the battery of tests used. Other experiments use drugs as models of pathological conditions such as dementia, Korsakoff's syndrome and various organic amnesias.

Nevertheless it is disappointing that clearer relationships have not yet been found. There are four possible reasons for this: 1) Animal memory experiments tend to rely on models derived from the Behaviourist tradition and these are not translated easily into tests that can be performed with people. 2) The gap between the explanations used in the neurobiology and the cognitive psychology of memory is so vast that it is difficult to formulate links. Drug action is usually described at the neuronal level in terms of changes of synaptic conductivity terms whereas the current description of human memory in cognitive psychology terms involves a working memory system linked

Table 1. Number of publications, from 1978, dealing with the effects of drugs on memory.

23	Diazepam	20	Vasopressin
13	Lorazepam	10	ACTH
4	Chlordiazepoxide	2	Oxytocin
5	Nitrazepam	11	Scopolamine
5	Flunitrazepam	12	Physostygmine
4	Triazolam	4	Choline
3	Midazolam	5	Lecithin
1	Temazepam	2	Atropine
1	Lormetazepam	1	Benzhexol
1	Tofisopam	1	Benztropine
1	Clobazam	1	THA
1	Oxazepam	10	Lithium
1	Flurazepam	15	Alcohol
3	Nicotine	4	Fentanyl
4	Zopiclone	4	Naloxone
1	Amobarbital	1	Codeine
4	Amphetamine	1	Morphine
4	Methylphenidate	8	Marijuana
3	Secobarbital	1	Alprazolam
1	Amobarbital	1	Mianserin
1	Thiopental	1	Vinpocetine
2	Methyldopa	1	Chlovoxamine
4	Amitryptiline	1	Mercury
1	Desipramine	1	Iron
1	Zimelidine	1	Pyridoxine
1	Trihexyphenodyl	1	Toluene
1	Fluvoximine	1	Nitrous Oxide
1	Hydrocortisone	1	Reserpine
1	Vitamin C	1	PCB
1	Beta endorphin	1	PBB
1	Oxiracitam	1	P-xylene
1	Ritalin	1	Theophylline
1	Ethimizol	1	Atenolol
1	Phenytoin	1	Propranolol
1	Carbamazepine	1	Oxprenolol
1	Valproate	1	Clonidine
1	Heroin	1	Maprotiline
1	CO2		

to a long-term memory system composed of distinct procedural, semantic and episodic components. 3) Existing drugs are still not sufficiently specific to affect specific memory systems, or those systems are still themselves classified incorrectly. 4) Finally, the method drugs are normally applied in human experiments makes it virtually impossible virtually to assess the physiology of the system. An analogy: if the mechanism of car movement is being studied and petrol is poured over the car (oral or i.v. administration) instead of into the petrol tank (normal metabolic route for a neurotransmitter) then the act of turning the ignition key may still result in the car, or parts of the car moving even though the mechanisms are not the same !

CONCLUSION
        Considerable work must still be conducted before a
taxonomy of drugs and their effect on human memory can be
composed.

REFERENCES

Baddeley, A.D., Hatter, J.E., Scott, D.   and Snashall, A.   (1970)
'Memory and time of day', Quarterly Journal of Experimental
Psychology, 22, 605-609.

Gruneberg, M.M., Morris, P.E. and Sykes, R.N. (Eds.) (1978) _Practical
Aspects of Memory_. London: Academic.

Idzikowski, C.   (1984) 'Sleep and memory', British Journal of
Psychology, 75, 439-449.

Millar, K. (1983) 'Asymmetrical transfer: an inherent
weakness of repeated-measure drug experiments', British Journal
of Psychiatry, 143, 480-6.

Reinberg, A. (1969) 'Perspectives en chronopharmacologie,
chronotoxicologie et chronotherapeutique', European Journal of
Toxicology 6, 319-320.

Roth, T., Roehrs, T., Wittig, R., and Zorick, F. (1984)
'Benzodiazepines and memory', British Journal of Clinical
Pharmacology, 18, 45S-49S.

Squire, L.R. and Davis, H.P. (1981) 'The pharmacology of memory:
a neurobiological perspective', Annual Review of Pharmacology and
Toxicology, 21, 323-356.

Wolkowitz, O.M.   (1985a) 'A psychopharmacological perspective of
cognitive functions, I, Theoretical overview and
methodological considerations', Neuropsychobiology, 14, 88-96.

Wolkowitz, O.M.   (1985b) 'A psychopharmacological perspective of
cognitive functions, II, Specific pharmacologic agents',
Neuropsychobiology, 14, 133-156.

MEMORY DRUGS AND READING

C. R. Wilsher
Department of Psychology, University College of North Wales,
Bangor, Wales and UCB (Pharma) Ltd., England.

ABSTRACT
     The first of the nootropic drugs, piracetam, has been the
subject of several double-blind trials of its effectiveness in
children with specific reading difficulties. An American, 36-week,
double-blind, placebo-controlled, multi-centred study of 3.3 grams
of piracetam daily in 225 dyslexic children, aged seven and a half
to 13, is reported (see Wilsher et al., 1987). The results of this
study show significant drug-related increases in reading ability
(Gray Oral Reading Test) and comprehension (Gilmore Oral Reading
Test). The results are interpreted as showing that the fluent
retrieval of previously learned words from long-term memory, and
the understanding of these words in context, are enhanced.

     In the last decade considerable interest has been focussed
upon the use of nootropic drugs to promote memory and learning.
The first of this class of drugs, piracetam (2-oxo-1 pyrrolidine
acetamide, trade names Nootropil, Nootropyl, Nootrop, Noostan,
Barcan), has been the subject of investigation in many patient
populations with memory and learning problems. Recently there
have been several double-blind trials to test the effectiveness of
this drug in children with specific reading difficulties
(developmental dyslexia).
     Many studies have shown that dyslexic children have a
deficit in certain verbal memory skills. Vellutino et al.(1975)
found dyslexics to be poor at paired associate verbal learning and
this was confirmed by Thomson and Wilsher (1978). Dyslexics have
also been shown to have poor verbal short term memory and coding
ability (Corkin, 1974; Jorm, 1983) and to have deficient naming
abilities (Denkla & Rudel, 1976). The practical outcome of such
memory difficulties for these children is severely reduced reading
ability and concomitant failure at school.
     The neurological aetiology underlying these cognitive
differences is only now being partially understood. In 1979
Galaburda and Kemper completed the first microscopic examination
of slices of brain from a developmental dyslexic. This
neuroanatomical study revealed no gross abnormalities, but did
find 'ectopias' of cells from different layers in the cortex
protruding into other cell layers. These differences were mainly
in the left hemisphere and were consistent with a developmental
failure of cell migration during gestation. This brain also

showed a deviation from the standard pattern of cerebral assymetry, characterised by symmetry of the planum temporale. Subsequently, the same group (Galaburda et al., 1985) published findings on four consecutive dyslexic brains. They concluded that "all brains showed developmental anomalies of the cerebral cortex....consisting of neuronal ectopias and architectonic dysplasias located mainly in perisylvian regions and affecting predominantly the left hemisphere."

Piracetam is a psychoactive compound structurally similar to GABA (gamma-aminobutyric acid), and is reported to facilitate memory (see Giurgea and Salama, 1977, for a review). Several studies of piracetam have shown improvements in memory in dyslexic children. Wilsher et al.(1979) used a double-blind crossover design to test the memory of young adult developmental dyslexics in a rote verbal learning paradigm. Sixteen dyslexics (aged 16 to 21 yrs.) and 14 control subjects (university students) were given 4.8 grams of piracetam per day (or a matching placebo) for three weeks. The task was to learn ten nonsense syllables upon a number cue. At baseline the dyslexics took almost twice as long to learn the syllables as the controls ($p < 0.001$) and made three times as many 'forgetting mistakes' (occasions when a syllable was learned on one trial and then forgotten on the next) ($p < 0.001$). The results of the study showed that piracetam-treated dyslexics improved their verbal learning by 15%, and their forgetting score was almost halved when compared to the placebo conditon.

Rudel and Helfgott (1984) showed that dyslexic children (aged eight to 13 yrs.), treated double-blind with 3.3 grams of piracetam for 12 weeks, improved their recall on the Neimark Memorisation Task. In addition, these children did not suffer as much loss of recall when a delay was introduced as did the placebo-treated children. In a recent paper Helfgott et al.(1986) report that these children also improved their naming ability on the Rapid Automised Naming Test. DiIanni et al.(1985) reported a large-scale double-blind study of 257 dyslexic boys treated with 3.3 grams of piracetam for 12 weeks. This study showed increased reading fluency in the treated group and increased short term memory (Digit Span from the WISC-R) in those children with poor digit span scores at baseline.

Levi and Sechi (1986) conducted a double-blind study of 127 learning disabled children, aged seven and a half to twelve and a half, treated with 3.2 grams of piracetam per day for 20 weeks. All of the children were of average IQ, had no psychiatric or medical problems and were at least two years behind in one of the following reading sub-tests: silent reading comprehension, oral reading accuracy, oral reading speed, and writing accuracy. The results of the study showed a complete lack of action of piracetam on tests of spatial ability or tests of concentration (attention). This would seem to confirm that piracetam is unlike a stimulant such as methylphenidate (ritalin) which has the opposite effect (Gittelman et al.,1976; 1983). In addition, a sensory-motor evoked potential study by Chiarenza (1986) showed piracetam to have no effect on behavioural motor responses nor on sensory processing systems (again unlike a stimulant). However, in the

Levi and Sechi study, piracetam did significantly improve the recall of an oral story; the ability to solve anagrams; and prose reading accuracy on a standardised reading test. In a special subgroup (n=38) of children with very poor written language ability, piracetam significantly improved reading accuracy and writing accuracy. Although silent reading comprehension was more significantly improved in the piracetam group, there was no significant difference between treatment groups.

A large-scale, long-term study of piracetam in dyslexia was undertaken at five universities in the USA. The investigative teams were led by Dr. C. K. Conners (Washington, D.C.), Dr. L. Feagans (North Carolina), Dr. L. Hanvik (Minneapolis), Dr. R. Rudel (New York) and Dr. P. Tallal (San Diego). Two hundred and twenty-five dyslexic children were recruited in a 36-week double-blind trial of 3.3 grams of piracetam per day. Children of below average intelligence, or with abnormal findings on audiologic, ophthalmologic, neurologic, psychiatric and physical examinations, were excluded from the trial. The children were of average IQ (Full-scale IQ, WISC-R = 104.3) and an average of 3.4 school grades behind expectancy (range 1.1 to 7.6) on the Gray Oral Reading Test. Two hundred children completed the 36-week study, conducted during the 1983-84 school year. Primary efficacy measures were the Gray Oral Reading Test (Gray, 1963), the Gilmore Oral Reading Test (Gilmore and Gilmore, 1968), and the Wide Range Achievement Test - Revised (WRAT-R) Reading sub-test (Jastak and Wilkinson, 1984).

Analysis of baseline scores revealed that although the demographic profile of the piracetam treatment group was similar to that of the placebo group, the reading test scores were slightly lower. One site had significant differences between treatment groups at baseline, and the removal of that site's data eliminated all significant baseline differences for the whole group. Covariance analyses, covarying change scores by baseline scores, were reported both with and without the discrepant site. Significant effects common to both analyses were found on the Gray Oral Total Passage score and the Gilmore Oral Comprehension score. There were also significant effects found in the more homogeneous sample (the sample with equal baselines) on the Gray Oral Comprehension score and the WRAT-R Reading score (details of these results are reported in Wilsher et al.,1987). Summaries of the consistent and significant effects reported are contained in the histograms Figs. 1, 2 and 3.

These show the percentage change on the Gray and the Gilmore tests both with and without one site. As can be seen, the significant effect of piracetam on the Gray Oral Reading score and the Gilmore Oral Comprehension score is enhanced when the more homogeneous sample (with equal baselines) is considered. It would appear from this comprehensive study that the fluent retrieval of words from long-term memory and the understanding of these words in context was enhanced by piracetam. The Gray Oral Reading Test Total Passage score is a combination of reading accuracy and speed in connected prose. If errors increase or the speed of reading is reduced then the total passage score decreases.

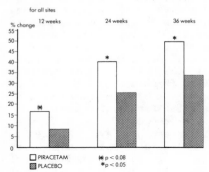

FIG. 1   GRAY ORAL TOTAL PASSAGE SCORE - PERCENTAGE CHANGE
(n = 203 - 197)

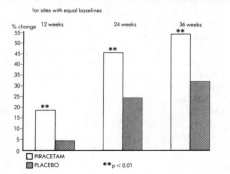

FIG. 2   GRAY ORAL TOTAL PASSAGE SCORE - PERCENTAGE CHANGE (n = 160 - 158)

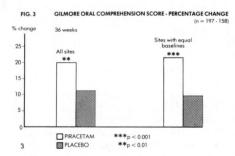

FIG. 3   GILMORE ORAL COMPREHENSION SCORE - PERCENTAGE CHANGE
(n = 197 - 158)

3

A treatment-related increase in this score indicates that the piracetam-treated group must have been able to learn more material initially and access that material more fluently.

Comprehension of that which is read is a vital outcome of the process of reading. The Comprehension score of the Gilmore Oral Reading Test reflects the ability to recall the salient features of a story that has just been read and to understand the questions asked about it, and in this study of piracetam in dyslexic children, comprehension was significantly enhanced. It cannot be determined from the present evidence whether this improvement was due to an increase in understanding per se or to an improvement in recall of salient features of the text. One can speculate from the previous research on piracetam, however, that the latter is the more probable explanation.

There has been one attempt to determine if such enhanced performance is retained. Following the Wilsher et al.(1985) study, a small group of children were followed up after eight weeks of normal schooling only. This was not a random design because only those children living locally and interested in participation returned for reassessment. The study was blind, however, because the children were not informed of their previous treatment. Fourteen children returned for follow-up (seven previously treated with piracetam and seven with placebo) and were tested on the Neale Analysis of Reading Ability (Neale, 1966). Fig. 4 shows the results at baseline, after eight weeks' treatment, and then after eight weeks' follow-up. Significant results were seen for the piracetam group in fluency of reading during treatment, i.e. baseline to end of treatment (Wilcoxon T = 0, p = 0.02, two-tailed); and in accuracy of reading from baseline to the end of follow-up (Wilcoxon T = 0, p = 0.02, two-tailed).

Fig. 4   Follow-up study of reading: Changes in reading ages (n = 14)

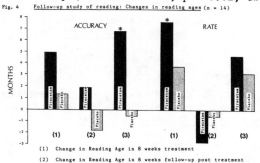

(1)   Change in Reading Age in 8 weeks treatment

(2)   Change in Reading Age in 8 weeks follow-up post treatment

(3)   Combined amount of change in Reading Age over 16 weeks,
i.e. (1) + (2)

*   Wilcoxon T = 0, p = 0.02 two-tailed

Due to the small numbers involved and the non-random design, it is very difficult to draw any conclusions. However, the results do suggest an increase in fluency of retrieval of words learned during treatment, and a consolidation in terms of accuracy of recall in the long term, so that it is possible to speculate that piracetam not only increases the fluency of initial learning but also aids retention of this material. In this study comprehension was not measured, so it is impossible to determine if the improved fluency and accuracy led to improved comprehension in the long term. However, the total length of this small study was 16 weeks (eight weeks' treatment + eight weeks' follow-up), and if we examine the 36-week study for evidence of long-term effects, we see the most significant findings were in the area of reading comprehension.

Throughout the trials described, treatment with piracetam has been remarkable for its lack of serious adverse effects (DiIanni et al.,1985; Wilsher et al.,1987).

ACKNOWLEDGEMENTS
Mrs. J. Taylor in the preparation of this paper; and UCB Pharmaceutical Sector, Belgium.

REFERENCES
Corkin, S. Serial ordering deficits in inferior readers. Neuropsychologia, 1974, 12, 347-354.

Denckla, M.B. and Rudel, R.G. Rapid automized naming

(R.A.N.)dyslexia differentiated from other learning disabilities. Neuropsychologia, 1976, 14, 471-479.

DiIanni M., Wilsher C.R., Blank M.S., Conners C.K., Chase C.H.,Funkenstein H.H., Helfgott E., Holmes J.M., Lougee L.,Maletta G.J., Milewski J., Pirozzolo F.J., Rudel R.G.,and Tallal P. The effects of piracetam in children with dyslexia. Journal of Clinical Psychopharmacology, 1985, 5, 5, 272-278.

Galaburda, A.M. and Kemper, T.L. Cytoarchitectonic abnormalities in developmental dyslexia: A case study. Annals of Neurology, 1979, 6, 2, 94-100.

Galaburda, A.M.,Sherman,G.F., Rosen G.D.,Aboitiz, F. and Geschwind, N. Developmental dyslexia: Four consecutive patients with cortical anomalies. Annals of Neurology 1985, 18, 2,222-233.

Giurgea, C. and Salama, M. Nootropic drugs. Prog. Neuro-psychopharmacol., 1977, 1, 235-247.

Helfgott, E.,Rudel, R.G., and Kairam, R. The effects of piracetam on short and long term verbal retrieval in dyslexic boys. International Journal of Psychophysiology, 1986, 4, 1, 53-61.

Jorm, F.A. Specific reading retardation and working memory:A review. British Journal of Psychology, 1983, 74, 311-342.

Levi, G. and Sechi, E. Clinical experience with piracetam in learning disorders. Results of a study. Symposium on "Current concepts in the diagnosis and treatment of developmental dyslexia",IARLD, Venice, Italy, April 1986.

Rudel, R.G. and Helfgott, E. Effect of piracetam on verbal memory of dyslexic boys. Journal of American Academy of Child Psychiatry, 1984, 23, 695-699

Thomson,M.E. and Wilsher,C.R. Some aspects of memory in dyslexics and controls. In M.M. Gruneberg, P.E. Morris and R.N.Sykes (eds.) Practical aspects of memory. London:Academic Press, 1978.

Vellutino, F.R., Steger, J.A., Harding, C. and Phillips, F. Verbal and non verbal paired associates learning in poor and normal readers. Neuropsychologia, 1975, 13, 75-82.

Wilsher, C.R., Atkins, G. and Manfield, P. Piracetam as an aid to learning in dyslexia: Preliminary report. Psychopharmacology, 1979, 65, 107-109.

Wilsher, C.R., Bennett, D., Chase, C.H., Conners, C.K., DiIanni,M., Feagans, L., Hanvik, L.J., Helfgott, E., Koplewicz,H., Overby, P., Reader, M.J., Rudel, R.G. and Tallal, P. Piracetam and dyslexia: Effects on reading tests. Journal of Clinical Psychopharmacology, 1987.

VASOPRESSIN AND HUMAN MEMORY

Keith Millar
Behavioural Sciences Group, University of Glasgow
Faculty of Medicine, Glasgow G12 8QQ.

ABSTRACT

Methodological   and conceptual issues may underlie   the
inconsistent effects of vasopressin upon human memory.   Crossover
designs confound the treatment effects of vasopressin with those of
treatment presentation order. The variable effects of the vasopressin analogues administered, and variable pathology in amnesic
patients selected for study, make negative results difficult to
interpret.   The conceptual issue concerns the hypothesis that
vasopressin may not affect memory directly but as a secondary
consequence of cognitive facilitation due to the behaviourally
arousing influence of its pressor activity. However, a small group
of studies indicate that the vasopressin analogue DDAVP reliably
enhances initial acquisition processes unconfounded with an arousal
effect.   Conclusions are drawn for the direction of   further
research.

Animal studies have indicated a role in memory function for
the peptide hormone vasopressin and its synthetic analogues.   Rats
deficient in endogenous vasopressin following hypophysectomy show
learning impairments which can be corrected by exogenous treatment
with the hormone.   Exogenous treatment has also been reported to
enhance the learning of intact rats. (See Jolles 1983).   However,
despite many studies of the influence of vasopressin upon human
memory, the precise effect of the peptide remains uncertain.   The
intention in this paper is to describe the common difficulties which
arise in interpreting the diverse and often contradictory results,
and to identify a small number of studies which may provide some
limited insight.

Three main methodological shortcomings make it difficult to
interpret both positive and negative effects of vasopressin on
memory.   These failings involve small sample sizes, crossover designs and general methodological confounding. A second problem,
which is more conceptual than methodological, concerns the issue of
whether the supposed effects of vasopressin upon memory are, in fact,
secondary manifestations of a general facilitation of cognitive
performance due to the arousing action of vasopressin which derives
from its pressor activity.

The use of small samples of patients in vasopressin studies
probably reflects clinical conditions where relatively few patients
are available for testing. However, small samples carry the penalty
of reduced statistical power so that negative effects of vasopressin

require very careful evaluation. Authors never report power calculations and it is likely that many studies have had little chance of detecting true differences between vasopressin and placebo conditions.

The problem of small sample size is usually associated with the use of a crossover design where each subject receives vasopressin and placebo in a balanced order. However, the crossover design is well-known to mask or distort treatment effects when the latter interact and become confounded with the factor of treatment-order presentation (Armitage & Hills, 1982; Millar, 1983). The common effect is to reduce differences between treatments, such that the reliability of results of crossover studies of vasopressin which show no significant effect may be questionable.

Millar et al. (1987) have shown that few researchers report analyses for order effects in crossover studies of vasopressin. Of four groups of researchers who did make such analyses (Beckwith et al., 1983; Eisenberg et al., 1984; Jennekens-Schinkel et al., 1985; Nebes et al., 1984), two found that the effect of vasopressin was dependent upon its position in the treatment sequence (Beckwith et al. and Eisenberg et al.). Beckwith et al. (1983) found that vasopressin improved memory only when volunteers had first experienced a placebo session. Often, such asymmetries can be of such magnitude as to give an overall, and misleading, main effect of treatment. The implication then is that failure to analyse for treatment-order effects must render the reliability of results uncertain, regardless of whether positive or negative effects are found.

Further difficulties which are related to within-subject designs are found in the studies of Laczi et al. (1982, 1983a). Superficially, the results seem to demonstrate an improvement in memory due to the peptide analogues lysine vasopressin (LVP), desamino-8-D-arginine vasopressin (DDAVP) and desglycinamide-arginine-8-vasopressin (DGAVP) in auditory, visual and spatial memory of normal and memory-impaired subjects. However, the supposed beneficial effect of vasopressin is completely confounded with improvement due to practice because vasopressin was always presented after placebo in the unbalanced design. In a subsequent separate-groups study, Laczi et al. (1983b) found no effect of DGAVP upon amnesic patients. Jenkins et al. (1982) employed similar tasks to those of Laczi et al. (1982, 1983a) and found no effect of DDAVP on separate groups of normal subjects.

A final potential problem for crossover trials of vasopressin lies in the fact that the behavioural effects of LVP and DGAVP can be detected long after their administration. This implies that placebo performance would be particularly vulnerable to incomplete inter-treatment washout (Jolles 1983).

While the difficulties of the crossover design are avoided by use of a separate-groups design, the latter is not without its own problems. Beckwith et al. (1982) reported a facilitative effect of DDAVP upon concept learning in a separate-groups study of normal subjects. However, the authors took no pre-treatment baseline measures and therefore left uncertain whether the vasopressin-treated group was simply better regardless of treatment.

A final methodological consideration concerns the administration of vasopressin to memory-impaired patients where there is often poor control of the nature and degree of impairment. Jolles (1983) has reviewed evidence to suggest that the peptide may only be beneficial in cases of relatively mild memory impairment, where organic deterioration is limited. This implies that studies which average the effects of vasopressin across heterogeneous samples of patients, both within and across different disease states, are unlikely to find reliable effects. Studies of memory-impaired patients also carry the difficulty that attendant pathologies of mood and behaviour may mask any positive effect of vasopressin. Mood states have further relevance to the hypothesis that vasopressin does not influence memory directly but via general cognitive facilitation due to pressor effects. Sahgal (1984) has provided an excellent critique of the "vasopressin-memory hypothesis" and suggests that the central role of vasopressin may be to modulate the level of arousal. The administration of vasopressin is associated with physiological signs of arousal, and clinical studies show that enhancement of mood, motivation and reaction time may follow treatment. It would then seem entirely plausible that memory performance might be only one of a number of cognitive processes that would benefit as a secondary consequence of enhanced motivation and heightened mood.

If vasopressin does exert an alerting influence, then it should benefit performance on long, monotonous vigilance tasks. Sahgal et al. (1986) employed DDAVP in such a study and, somewhat ironically, found no support for the arousal hypothesis: performance with DDAVP was no different from placebo across the one-hour session. (The sensitivity of the task to drug effects was not in doubt; performance was significantly impaired by ethanol).

Sahgal et al. (1986) acknowledge that the result creates difficulties for the arousal hypothesis but they suggest that DDAVP may have been an inappropriate vasopressin analogue with which to test the hypothesis because it lacks cardiovascular potency. The behavioural effects of vasopressin may be determined by its cardiovascular action.

While the negative results of Sahgal et al. (1986) leave the status of the arousal hypothesis uncertain, they do have implications for memory researchers. First, memory studies should include a task of simple cognitive performance - for instance, reaction time - to check for non-specific improvement in performance due to vasopressin. Secondly, they might profitably employ a vasopressin analogue such as DDAVP which may be less likely to provoke general behavioural arousal. The fact that the vasopressin analogues vary in their behavioural effects is a further confounding factor to be added to the list of methodological problems.

Despite the difficulties described above, it does seem possible to assemble a group of reasonably reliable studies of vasopressin and memory. The 'reliability' is ascribed simply on the basis that the studies largely avoid the difficulties above and does not imply that the studies are without flaw; indeed, the use of small sample size is common to them all. Three of the studies employed crossover designs, but two of these included an analysis which indicated that order effects were absent (Jennekens-Schinkel et al., 1985; Nebes et al., 1984). The data presentation of Weingartner et al. (1981) also showed that asymmetries due to order were not pronounced. Recent criticism of this study by Millar et al. (1987) on the grounds of order effects is probably not justified.

Considering first the positive results, Legros et al. reported improvement in memory span, attention and general learning ability in a placebo-controlled study of normal subjects treated with LVP. While enhancement of attention may imply an arousing effect of LVP, such interpretation seems implausible in a further study of normal subjects by Millar et al. (1987) who found short-term recall of twelve-word lists to be significantly improved by DDAVP. The study included a test of simple reaction time to detect any general facilitation of performance due to vasopressin. No significant effect was found, perhaps strengthening the conclusion that the result reflects a true influence of vasopressin upon memory. Weingartner et al. (1981) also reported improvement in serial learning, prompted free recall and recall of semantically-related words in normal subjects treated with DDAVP. Nebes et al. (1984) found that DDAVP improved Sternberg task performance but the difficulties in interpreting performance of this task in terms of specific memory processes are well known.

However, none of the three studies above found any effect of DDAVP upon retrieval of information from long-term memory which had been learned prior to treatment with vasopressin. When these positive and negative effects are contrasted, one might conclude that vasopressin exerts its effects upon the acquisition of information, but this conclusion must be viewed in the light of other negative results from studies of short-term recall. Fehm-Wolfsdorf et al. (1985) found no effect of LVP upon normal short-term recall of word lists and Peabody et al. (1986) found no effect of DDAVP upon Alzheimer patients' short-term memory. Similarly, Jennekens-Schinkel et al. (1985) and Laczi et al. (1983) found no effect of DGAVP upon memory span, word-list learning, maze learning or paired-associate learning of Korsakoff patients.

From the above one might conclude that the negative effects upon short-term memory are found primarily with amnesic patients whose organic pathologies might mask, or inhibit, any improvement due to vasopressin (Jolles, 1983). In contrast, positive results are found primarily with normal individuals. Furthermore, note that DDAVP is associated with consistent improvement in short-term memory processes in three studies of normal individuals (Millar et al., 1987; Nebes et al., 1984; Weingartner et al., 1981). Given evidence above that the effects of DDAVP may be less easily ascribed to behavioural arousal, then one might conclude that a relatively 'pure' effect upon memory is present.

From the above review one can abstract the elements of a long-overdue, systematic study of vasopressin and human memory. First, the possible differential effects of the various vasopressin analogues need careful examination because they may differ in the extent to which they induce behavioural arousal. One needs to distinguish between effects which are due to a general facilitation of cognitive processes, and effects solely upon memory processes (Sahgal, 1984, 1986). The evidence suggests that DDAVP might seem a useful choice for memory research.

Secondly, a systematic analysis of the influence of vasopressin upon the separate components of working (short-term) memory is required. The fact that normal subjects treated with DDAVP recall more material on a task of learning twelve-word lists is relatively uninformative (Millar et al., 1987).

Thirdly, studies of vasopressin in amnesic patients would benefit from more homogenous patient samples. Even within a diagnostic category, there may be different underlying cortical dysfunction such that patients may show considerable variation in memory deficits, and hence in response to vasopressin. By averaging performance, one may mask positive effects of vasopressin upon individual patients.

Finally, in studies of normal volunteers, one should consider whether evidence of a facilitated memory process necessarily implies an overall enhancement of memory. Millar et al. (1987) have described how facilitation of a particular process, for instance consolidation, might have negative effects upon subsequent learning due to proactive interference. In other words, facilitation by vasopressin of a specific process may be completely outweighed by its consequent disturbance of other processes.

REFERENCES

Armitage, P. and Hills, M. (1982). 'The two-period crossover trial', The Statistician, 31, 119-131.

Beckwith, B.E., Couk, D.I. and Till, T.S. (1983). 'Vasopressin analog influences the performance of males on a reaction time task', Peptides, 4, 707-709.

Beckwith, B.E., Petros, T., Kanaan-Beckwith, S., Couk, D.I. and Haug, R.J. (1982). 'Vasopressin analog (DDAVP) facilitates concept learning in human males', Peptides, 3, 627-630.

Eisenberg, J., Chazan-Gologorsky, S., Hattab. J. and Belmaker, R.H. (1984). 'A controlled trial of vasopressin treatment of childhood learning disorder', Biological Psychiatry, 19, 1137-1141.

Fehm-Wolfsdorf, G., Born, J., Elbert, T., Voigt, K-H, and Fehm, H.L. (1985). 'Vasopressin does not enhance human memory: a study in human twins', Peptides, 6, 297-300.

Jenkins, J.S., Mather,H.M. and Coughlan, A.K. (1982). 'Effect of desmopressin on normal and impaired memory', Journal of Neurology, Neurosurgery and Psychiatry, 45, 830-831.

Jennekens-Schinkel, A., Wintzen, A.R. and Lanser, B.K. (1985). 'A clinical trial with desglycinamide arginine vasopressin for the treatment of memory disorders in man', Progess in Neuro-Psychopharmacology and Biological Psychiatry, 9, 273-284.

Jolles, J. (1983). Vasopressin-like peptides and the treatment of memory disorders in man. In The Neurohypophysis: Structure, Function and Control, Progress in Brian Research (Eds. B.A. Cross and G. Leng), 60, 169-182. Elsevier: Amsterdam.

Laczi, F., Valkusz, Zs., Laszlo, F.A., Wagner, A., Jardanhazy, T., Szasz, A., Szilard, J. and Telegdy, G. (1982). 'Effects of lysine-vasopressin and 1-deamino-8-D-arginine vasopressin on memory in healthy individuals and diabetes insipidus patients', Psychoneuroendocrinology, 7, 185-193.

Laczi, F., Van Ree, J.M., Wagner, L., Valkusz, Zs., Jardanhazy, T., Kovacs, G.L., Telegdy, G., Szilard, J., Laszlo, F.A. and De Wied, D. (1983a). 'Effects of desglycinamide-arginine-vasopressin (DGAVP) on memory in diabetes insipidus patients and non-diabetic subjects', Acta Endocrinologica, 102, 205-212.

Laczi, F., Van Ree, J.M., Balogh, L., Szasz, A., Jardanhazy, T., Wagner, A., Gaspar, L., Valkusz, Z., Dobranovics, I., Szilard, J., Laszlo, F.A. and De Weid, D. (1983b). 'Lack of effect of desglycinamide-arginine-vasopressin (DGAVP) on memory in patients with Korsakoff's syndrome', Acta Endocrinologica, 104, 177-182.

Legros, J.J., Gilot, P., Seron, X., Claessens, J., Adam, A., Moeglen, J.M., Audibert, A. and Berchier, P. (1978). 'Influence of vasopressin on learning and memory', Lancet, i, 41-42.

Millar, K. (1983). 'Clinical trial design: the neglected problem of asymmetrical transfer in crossover trials', Psychological Medicine, 13, 867-873.

Millar, K., Jeffcoate, W.J. and Walder, C.P. (1987). 'Vasopressin and memory: improvement in short-term recall and reduction of alcohol-induced amnesia', Psychological Medicine, 17, 335-341.

Nebes, R.D., Reynolds III, C.F. and Horn, L.C. (1984). 'The effect of vasopressin on memory in the healthy elderly', Psychiatry Research, 11, 49-59.

Sahgal, A. (1984). 'A critique of the vasopressin-memory hypothesis', Psychopharmacology, 83, 215-228.

Sahgal, A., Wright, C. and Ferrier, I.N. (1986). 'Desamino-D-arg8-vasopressin (DDAVP), unlike ethanol, has no effect on a boring visual vigilance task in humans', Psychopharmacology, 90, 58-63.

Weingartner, H., Gold, P., Ballenger, J.C., Smallberg, S.A., Summers, R., Rubinow, D.R., Post, R.M. and Goodwin, F.K. (1981). 'Effects of vasopressin on human memory functions', Science, 211, 601-603.

EFFECTS OF R 58 735 ON LEARNING AND MEMORY FUNCTIONS

G.H.C. Clincke & L. Tritsmans
Departments of Neuropharmacology and Clinical Research,
Janssen Pharmaceutica, Beerse, Belgium.

ABSTRACT

In several animal studies, R 58 735 enhanced learning and memory. In two double-blind, placebo-controlled experiments, the effect of chronic treatment (10 mg b.i.d.) was studied in groups of volunteers (median ages 45 and 59 years). Serial learning of non-sense syllables was better under R 58 735. Free recall and re-learning of the same material were superior as compared to the same tasks with material originally learned under placebo. Proactive inhibition induced by consecutive presentation of word lists was attenuated by R 58 735. In poor performers, a significant improvement of consistent long-term retrieval was seen with Buschke's Selective Reminding Procedure. These results and others indicate positive effects on encoding, consolidation and retrieval in verbal declarative-memory tasks.

INTRODUCTION

R 58 735 (4-[(2-benzothiazolyl)methylaminol-α-[(4-fluorophe-noxy) methyl]-1-piperidine ethanol) is a potent protector against several types of cerebral hypoxia (Wauquier et al., 1986). In one of these experiments, hypoxia induced functional deficits could be antagonized and the results suggested that the compound might have some impact on learning and memory functions. By using a combined active and passive avoidance task first described by Carew (1970), Clincke and Sahgal (1986) found that post-training injection with R 58 735 resulted in more efficient coping with an aversive situation as a result of improved retention of context specific information. Based on these favourable effects on animal cognition, a series of double-blind studies on memory functions in healthy elderly volunteers was undertaken. This population was chosen because memory functions tend to decline mildly as a consequence of aging.

The present paper is intended to give an overview of experimental work in both animals and humans.

ANIMAL EXPERIMENT 1

Groups of 10 male guinea-pigs (body weight 250 ± 10 g) were pretreated p.o. with either solvent or a dose of R 58 735 (range 1.25 to 40 mg/kg) one hour before the onset of a single training session in a two-way avoidance task. A training session consisted of 50 trials, each lasting 30 seconds. At the onset of a trial, a 500-Hz tone was presented for 10 seconds as conditioned stimulus (CS). Avoiding shock (1.5 mA) by shuttle behaviour during the CS was scored as a correct avoidance response (detailed description in Clincke & Wauquier, 1984).

Pretreatment with R 58 735 dose-relatedly enhanced correct responding in the two-way avoidance task (Fig. 1). The lowest dose which significantly enhanced avoidance responding was 2.5 mg/kg. A maximal four-fold increase was observed at 40 mg/kg. This increase in shuttle-box avoidance was not due to an aspecific effect on locomotor activity since the same doses did not increase locomotion.

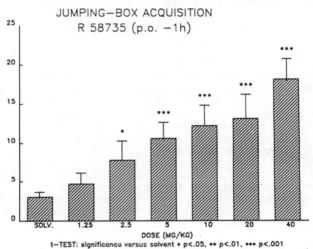

JUMPING—BOX ACQUISITION
R 58735 (p.o. −1h)

DOSE (MG/KG)

t—TEST: significance versus solvent • p<.05, •• p<.01, ••• p<.001

Figure 1: Mean number of avoidance (± S.E.M.) in a single, two-way avoidance training session. N = 10 guinea-pigs at each dose level.

ANIMAL EXPERIMENT 2

The previous results were obtained in a representative sample of an animal population with normally distributed learning and memory capacities. This raised the question of whether the positive effects were dependent upon base-line learning and memory capacity. In order to investigate if the drug could initiate learning in animals with extremely low learning ability, we screened a large number (> 200) of guinea-pigs by training them daily for one week in the two-way avoidance task described above. Ten animals achieved less than 1 % correct responses over the whole training week and were considered as having poor learning ability. These animals were further trained for three consecutive weeks. During that period, four were treated p.o. with solvent one hour before the daily training (50 trials), four received 20 mg/kg of R 58 735 and the two remaining animals received 2.5 mg/kg in the first, 10 mg/kg in the second and 40 mg/kg in the third treatment week. All the drug-treated animals (6/6) reached the learning criterion of at least 80 % correct responses by the end of the third treatment week. In the solvent group, only one of the four animals reached this level. The remaining animals did not learn at all despite the pro-longed training and achieved less than 1 % correct responses during the treatment period. These results illustrated that the drug could effectively enhance learning in animals with very low ability.

HUMAN EXPERIMENT 1

Twelve volunteers (median age 59 years) were included in this four-week-long experiment. During the first week the subjects received either R 58 735 (5 mg b.i.d. for the first two days, 10 mg b.i.d. for the remainder of the week) or placebo with a treatment cross-over in the third week. In the second week they all received placebo and in the fourth week no treatment was given. Learning tasks were given at the end of the first and third week, whereas relearning and recall were tested at the end of the other weeks (Clincke et al., 1987).

One of the tests was a classical Ebbinghaus serial learning task with 12 nonsense syllables (NSS). In Fig. 2 the mean number of correctly predicted NSS per trial is depicted for the learning and the relearning session. It is obvious that the learning of NSS was better under R 58 735 than under placebo. This was confirmed by a significant main treatment effect (df = 1,10; F = 11.8; p < .01) in the ANOVA. In addition, relearning of NSS initially learned under R 58 735 was significantly better (df = 1,10; F = 21.0; p = .001), as can be seen in Fig. 2. Furthermore, free recall one week after termination of treatment was significantly better for R 58 735 (df = 1,10; F = 15.4; p < .01).

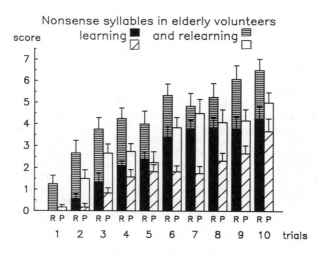

Figure 2: Mean number (± S.E.M.) of correctly predicted NSS per trial for R 58 735 (R) and placebo (P) in both learning and relearning session.

Another test consisted of the consecutive presentation of four equivalent word lists of ten words each. After each list, 30 seconds was given for free recall, but the use of short-term memory had been prevented by an arithmetic task. The total recall was significantly better under R 58 735, as illustrated by the main treatment effect (df = 1,10; F = 5.5; p < .05), but was dependent upon the level of induced interference. The proactive inhibition was thus maximally attenuated in the fourth list, as shown by the significantly higher recall (df = 1,10; F = 11.2; p < .01 see Fig. 3). The free recall one week after termination of the treatment fell short of statistical significance (df = 1,10; F = 4.0; p = .07).

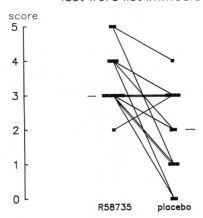

Figure 3: Number of words recalled from the last list (individual scores) under R 58 735 and placebo.

HUMAN EXPERIMENT 2

Twenty volunteers (median age 45 years) were included in a second double-blind parallel experiment (Tritsmans et al., 1987). The same dosage schedule of R 58 735 was used as in the first experiment. The volunteers were subjected to a Selective Reminding Procedure (Buschke & Fuld, 1974) at the beginning (baseline) and end of the treatment week. Two lists of 20 unrelated words were used, instead of the original 10 words from a single category. Testing was discontinued after 15 trials or whenever all 20 words had been recalled three times in a row without reminders. Poor performers were defined as those having a baseline consistent long-term retrieval (cLTR) of 50 % or less.

A significant trials x treatment interaction was found for the cLTR (df = 14,252; F = 3.7; p = .0001) in the general ANOVA. The separate analysis for the poor performers revealed a significant treatment effect of R 58 735 (df = 1,10; F = 8.5; p = .02) together with a trials x treatment interaction (df = 14,140; F = 5.9; p = .0001). For the good performers, no such significant effects were found. The analysis of the maximal cLTR showed a significant difference between R 58 735 and placebo in the poor-performance group (Fisher's exact test, p = .02). Consequently, it may be concluded that list learning improved under R 58 735 specifically in those subjects who were least efficient during baseline testing.

In an additional single-blind study with the same population as described in the first human experiment (median age 59 years), R 58 735 again improved cLTR in the poor performers.

DISCUSSION

So far, the effects on human memory of drugs that modulate animal memory and learning have been disappointing. Animals have rather limited "cognitive" capacities, which can only be evaluated by interpreting behavioural performance. This limits the predictability of the effects of drugs on the complex human cognitive abilities in which verbal skills play a major role. Response latency in avoidance tasks is by far the most often used parameter (Heise, 1984), though a non-negligible body of evidence has cast upon its reliability as a measure of memory (Carew, 1970; Saghal & Wright, 1984, Sahgal & Mason, 1985).

Like many other compounds, R 58 735 increased re-entry latency in passive avoidance (Clincke & Sahgal, 1986). In addition, however, it probably increased the level and depth of information processing, since contextspecific cues were appropriately used for initiating active avoidance responses in the same task. This suggestion was confirmed in the experiments described above. Both naive animals and animals with poor learning abilities reached unexpected levels of performance under R 58 735. Most importantly, these results were obtained in two different species and were not related to secondary effects on motor functions.

In a clinical context, efforts with other medications have been focused mainly on treating failing memories in patients with dementia. The progressive and complex nature of the disease renders straightforward evaluation of drug effects difficult. Therefore, it does not seem to be a suitable initial target population for profiling a new compound in the complex field of memory functions. On the other hand, elderly volunteers not suffering from dementia do appear to be a suitable population for such profiling, since memory is known to decline with increasing age (Zornetzer, 1986). In two consecutive studies, R 58 735 influenced several aspects of memory function. In the first study, learning of NSS significantly improved under R 58 735. This effect was maintained, as one week after the end of treatment, free recall and relearning of the same material were still better compared to recall and relearning of material originally learned under placebo treatment. Such an effect indicates improved encoding and storage. It is noteworthy that this result was consistent with the hypothesis suggested by the findings of the animal experiments. The attenuated proactive inhibition is yet another indication to this effect. The second experiment demonstrated that retrieval functions could also be influenced positively.

In the human experiments, only verbal tasks assessing declarative memory were used. Other tests will be required to obtain a full picture of the activity profile of this new drug. So far, the results are encouraging since it were the slightly deficient subjects who benefitted most from treatment with R 58 735. A logical next step would be to treat patients with more pronounced memory problems.

REFERENCES

Buschke, H. and Fuld, P.A. (1974). "Evaluating storage, retention, and retrieval in disordered memory and learning", Neurology, 24, 1019-1025.

Carew, T.J. (1970). "Do passive-avoidance tests permit assessment of retrograde amnesia in rats?", Journal of Comparative Physiology and Psychology, 72, 267-271.

Clincke, G. and Sahgal, A. (1986). "R 58 735, a novel antihypoxic drug improves memory in rats", Drug Development Research, 8, 381-385.

Clincke, G.H.C., Tritsmans, L., Idzikowski, C., Amery, W.K. and Janssen, P.A.J. (1987). "The effect of R 58 735 on memory functions in healthy elderly volunteers", Psychopharmacology, in press.

Clincke, G.H.C. and Wauquier, A. (1984). "The effect of hypoxia on the acquisition of a two-way avoidance task in the guinea-pig", Behavioural Brain Research, 14, 131-137.

Heise, G.A. (1984). "Behavioral methods for measuring effects of drugs on learning and memory in animals", Medicinal Research Reviews, 4, 535-558.

Sahgal, A. and Mason, J. (1985). "Drug effects on memory: Assessment of a combined active and passive avoidance task", Behavioural Brain Research, 17, 252-255.

Sahgal, A. and Wright, C. (1984). "Choice, as opposed to latency, measures in avoidance suggest that vasopressin and oxytocin do not affect memory in rats", Neuroscience Letters, 48, 299-304.

Tritsmans, L., Clincke, G.H.C. and Amery, W.K. (1987). "The effect of R 58 735 on memory retrieval functions in volunteers", Psychopharmacology, submitted.

Wauquier, A., Clincke, G., Ashton, D., De Ryck, M., Fransen, J. and Van Clemen, G. (1986). "R 58 735: A new antihypoxic drug with anticonvulant properties and possible effects on cognitive functions", Drug Development Research, 8, 373-380.

Zornetzer, S.F. (1986). "Applied aspects of memory research: Aging", in Learning and Memory: A Biological View (Eds. J.L. Martinez and R.P. Kesner), pp. 203-233, Academic Press, London.

ACKNOWLEDGEMENT
        Part of this study was supported by a grant from the I.W.O.N.L.

STATE-DEPENDENT RETRIEVAL EFFECTS WITH SOCIAL DRUGS

Geoff Lowe
Department of Psychology, University of Hull
Hull   HU6 7RX, U.K.

ABSTRACT
        The interactions between alcohol and social stimulants
(e.g. caffeine and nicotine) are generally regarded as complex, with
antagonistic, synergistic, and mixed effects being reported. These
social drugs are frequently ingested in close temporal proximity, yet
relatively little is known about the cognitive effects of such drug
combinations. Several experiments are reported in which moderate
doses of alcohol, caffeine and nicotine were administered to groups
of subjects in a state-dependent learning design. The results
demonstrate the dissociative effects of alcohol-caffeine and alcohol-
nicotine combinations on learning and recall. Hence a significant
proportion of everyday forgetting could be due to state-dependent
learning effects, particularly since drug combinations offer an
increased range of dissociation possibilities.

        Drug-induced state-dependent learning (SDL) is now a well-
established phenomenon (Overton, 1978). The term is used to describe
the finding that behaviour learned in one drug state is better
remembered when retention is tested in the same drug state. This
refers to an ability to access information under the same or a
different set of retrieval cues and might indeed, be more accurately
described as state-dependent retrieval.
        In studies with human subjects, alcohol (Lowe, 1981),
marijuana (Darley et al., 1974) barbiturate and amphetamine
(Bustamente et al., 1970), and nicotine (Peters and McGee, 1982)
have all been shown to produce SDL effects. In some cases, the
effect was asymmetrical. That is, recall tended to be poorest when
the acquisition stage is under a drug (D) state but the retrieval
stage is drug-free (ND). With drug-free acquisition and drug-state
retrieval (ND-D), recall is also poor but less so than under D-ND
conditions. However, in studies reporting asymmetrical effects, it
is worth noting that there were slight drug-induced deficits in Day 1
learning, compared with drug-free learning. When equivalence of
original learning between D and ND states is obtained, symmetrical
SDL effects have been observed, at least in the case of alcohol
(Lowe,1981).
        The combined use of alcohol and cigarettes, and
subsequently caffeine, is a common occurrence,and concern has been
shown for the disproportionate increase in susceptibility to disease
in populations where the incidence of joint consumption is high (e.g.
Keller,1977; Walton,1972). However, few researchers have examined

the psychopharmacological interactions of alcohol, nicotine and caffeine particularly in relation to SDL.

The interaction between alcohol and stimulant drugs is generally regarded as complex, with antagonistic (e.g. Knott and Venables,1979); synergistic (e.g. Lee and Lowe,1980; Leigh,1982); and negligible or mixed (e.g. Tong et al.,1974) effects being reported. Since both alcohol and nicotine have separately been shown to produce SDL in humans,it is reasonable to expect that the A+N combination should produce similar state-dependent effects. Although caffeine has not yet been shown to produce SDL in man, cognitively disruptive effects of alcohol-caffeine combinations have been observed (Lee and Lowe,1980), and thus SDL effects would also be expected from the A+C combination. However, in terms of the possible antagonistic/synergistic interaction, of particular interest is the recall performance of those subjects given a single drug on Day 2 after previously undergoing the acquisition phase under the influence of an alcohol-nicotine/caffeine combination. Recall decrements (or otherwise) on Day 2, when either alcohol or nicotine/caffeine is absent, should shed more light on the nature of these drug combination interactions, at least in relation to the phenomenon of SDL.

EXPERIMENT 1:   ALCOHOL AND NICOTINE
Method

Twenty four undergraduate students, aged between 18 and 28 years, volunteered as subjects. There were 12 females and 12 males, and all were smokers who regularly combined both alcohol and cigarettes. Their smoking histories ranged from 8 months to 7.5 years (mean length 2.84 years). The mean consumption of nicotine was 9.2 cigarettes per day; and of alcohol was 24.5 units per week.

The alcoholic beverage consisted of vodka (37.5% alcohol per vol.) in mix with an equal volume of "Schweppes Russchian" aromatic tonic water. 4.4ml of this mixture was given for every kg of subject's bodyweight, so the alcohol dose was moderate (at 0.66g per kg), and designed to produce a blood alcohol concentration (BAC) of around 80 mg/100ml (the U.K. legal limit for driving). In the placebo drink, the vodka was replaced by an equivalent amount of water, and the rim of the drinking glass was smeared with vodka to give an identical initial olfactory cue. Nicotine was administered by subjects smoking two "Benson & Hedges Pure Gold" middle tar cigarettes within a 12 minute period. These cigarettes have a rated average nicotine delivery of 1.4 mg. In the placebo condition, two "Honeyrose" herbal cigarettes (nicotine-free) were given. Although 'puff' frequency was monitored, no direct measure of inhalation was possible.

Design and Procedure

On Day 1 (learning), all subjects received the same drug treatment (A+N) immediately prior to the acquisition stage. On Day 2 (retrieval) male and female subjects were randomly allocated to one of four conditions to receive either (i) both drugs (A+N); (ii) nicotine plus placebo (O+N); (iii) alcohol plus placebo (A+O); or (iv) no drugs (O+O). There were three males and three females in each subgroup.

Prior to the experiment, subjects were asked to refrain from smoking, and from consuming caffeinated beverages for at least three hours before each daily session. They were also required to consume no alcohol for at least 18 hours before the experiment. Upon arrival in the laboratory, each subject was weighed and required to complete a questionnaire concerned with smoking and drinking history. They were then breathalysed with an Alcolmeter AE-D1 (Lion Laboratories) in order to check that subjects were 'alcohol-free' and to familiarize them with this instrument.

Pairs of subjects consumed their alcoholic beverages and smoked two cigarettes within a 20-min period. Approximately 40 min after starting drinking, subjects were breathalysed again before undertaking the learning task which consisted of a simplified geographical map, visually displayed together with an aurally presented 19-item set of instructions regarding a particular route (Lowe, 1981). An arbitrary criterion of at least 14 items correct was adopted as a learning measure. If, after four learning trials, the subject had not attained this level, then the highest number correct in any of the four trials was taken as the learning performance score. This learning session lasted approximately five mins, and preceded another breathalyser reading. Day 1 ended with this final breath-alcohol concentration (BAC) reading, approximately 50 mins after commencing the drinking session.

The procedure for Day 2 (recall) was the same as that for Day 1 (learning) except for the different drug conditions of the sub-groups and the fact that there was only one recall trial. The number of correctly recalled items from the Day 1 presentation of the route map was recorded as the recall performance score.

Results and Discussion:

Table I
Alcohol and Nicotine

Condition (on Day 2)	No. of correct items Day 1 (Learning)	Day 2 (Recall)	Mean recall decrements (D1-D2)	Mean BAC Day 1	Day 2
A + N	12.25	12.75	-0.5 (ns)	69.5	80.1
A + O	12.75	8.00	4.75 (p 0.01)	87.4	73.0
O + N	15.00	6.67	8.33 (p 0.01)	74.2	-
O + O	12.00	4.00	8.0 (p 0.01)	81.4	-

Table 1 shows the mean number of items correct from the route map for learning (day 1) and recall (day 2) sessions, and for each condition. Mean BACs during route map performance are also shown. A one-way analysis of variance on the learning scores of Day 1 revealed no significant difference amongst the four subgroups [F(3,20 = 1.053,p 0.05]. Table 1 shows the mean decrements between learning and recall for each condition. Apart from the slightly increased Day 2 recall performance in the A+N conditions, all other conditions resulted in significant recall decrements as determined by dependent 't' tests.

The lack of recall decrement when subjects ingested both alcohol and nicotine on Day 2 supports the notion of SDL induced by an alcohol-nicotine combination. Both the double placebo (0+0) and nicotine only (0+N) conditions resulted in the largest dissociation decrements from the (A+N) learning state. There was just as much dissociation when nicotine was ingested on Day 2 as with no drugs. This suggests that the major SDL effect was due to alcohol. However, it seems likely that nicotine had some influence, since when nicotine was absent during the alcohol session on Day 2 (A+0), the dissociation decrement was about half-way between that of the combination (A+N) and nicotine only (0+N) conditions. In other words, the alcohol alone state was insufficient to prevent a recall decrement on Day 2; the absence of nicotine led to a partial dissociation from the Day 1 (A+N) learning state.

If, as Leigh (1982) suggests, the combination of alcohol and nicotine can result in a synergistic interaction, it seems likely that the nicotine alone state is discriminatively different from the combination. It seems to be much more so than the alcohol alone state, in spite of the fact that the nicotine-free cigarettes were possibly distinctly unpleasant to smokers and thus not an ideal placebo.

EXPERIMENT 2:   ALCOHOL AND CAFFEINE
Method

Sixteen different undergraduate students, aged between 18 and 28 years, volunteered for this experiment. There were 8 males and 8 females and all were regular alcohol and coffee drinkers.

The experimental design and general procedure were identical to those of Experiment 1 except that the nicotine conditions were replaced by caffeine conditions. Caffeine was administered by subjects drinking two cups of Gold Blend (Nescafe) coffee each containing 1.5 5ml teaspoons, approximating a total dose of 300-375 mg caffeine. This was consumed within a 10 min period subsequent to the alcohol/placebo drinking period. In the placebo condition, Gold Blend de-caffeinated coffee was administered at the same concentration.

On Day 1 all subjects received the same drug treatment (A + C) immediately prior to the acquisition stage. On Day 2 (retrieval) subjects were randomly allocated to one of four conditions to receive either (i) both drugs (A + C); (ii) caffeine plus placebo (0 + C); (iii) alcohol plus placebo (A + 0); or (iv) no drugs (0 + 0).

Table 2
Alcohol and Caffeine

Condition (on Day 2)	No. of correct items Day 1 (Learning)	Day 2 (Recall)	Mean recall decrements (D1-D2)		Mean BAC Day 1	Day 2
A + C	14.25	14.00	0.25	(ns)	78	84
A + 0	14.25	10.75	3.55	(p 0.01)	79.5	81
0 + C	14.75	13.75	1.0	(ns)	79	-
0 + 0	13.75	8.25	5.5	(p 0.01)	80.5	-

Results and Discussion

A one-way analysis of variance on the learning scores of Day 1 revealed no significant differences amongst the four sub-groups $F(3,12) = 0.196$, p 0.05. Dependent 't' tests (comparing Day 1 with Day 2) were computed upon performance scores for each condition. In the caffeine conditions (A + C; O + C) there were no significant differences. But whenever caffeine was absent on Day 2 (A + O; O + O), significant recall decrements were observed.

The lack of recall decrement when subjects ingested both alcohol and caffeine on Day 2 supports the notion that SDL was induced by an alcohol + caffeine combination. Both the double placebo (O + O) and alcohol only (A + O) conditions resulted in the largest dissociation decrements from the (A + C) learning state. There was almost as little dissociation when caffeine only was ingested on Day 2 as with both drugs. This suggests that the major SDL effect was due to caffeine although the relatively high dose used could be the major determinant. The alcohol alone state was insufficient to prevent a recall decrement on Day 2: the absence of caffeine led to a partial but significant dissociation from the Day 2 (A + N) learning state.

If, as Waldeck (1974) suggests, the combination of alcohol and caffeine can result in a synergistic interaction, it appears that the caffeine alone state is not discriminatively different from the combination, whereas the alcohol alone state does seem to be. This contrasts somewhat with the results of Experiment 1 employing alcohol-nicotine combinations, which showed alcohol to be the dominant drug.

GENERAL DISCUSSION

These studies offer some initial insights, and confirm the complex nature of social drug combinations, in an area of cognitive behaviour (SDL) in which these particular drug combinations have not previously been applied. SDL can occur not only in carefully designed animal laboratory experiments but also under more naturalistic conditions of moderate social drinking, smoking and caffeine use. Hence a significant proportion of everyday forgetting could be due to SDL effects, particularly since drug combinations offer an increased range of dissociation possibilities. It would thus be helpful if people became more aware of the conditions capable of limiting the potential range of retrieval cues available when recall of information is required.

REFERENCES

Bustamente, J.A., Jordan, A., Vila, M., Gonzalez, A., and Insua, A. (1970). 'State-dependent learning in humans', Physiology and Behavior, 5, 793-796.

Darley, C.F., Tinklenberg, J.R., Roth, W.T. and Atkinson, R.C. (1974). 'The nature of storage deficits and state-dependent retrieval under marijuana', Psychopharmacologia, 37, 139-149.

Keller, A.Z. (1977). 'Alcohol, tobacco and age factors in the relative frequency of cancer among males with and without liver cirrhosis', American Journal of Epidemiology, 106, 194-202.

Knott, V.J., and Venables, P.H. (1977). 'EEG alpha correlates of non-smokers, smokers smoking and smoking deprivation', Psychophysiology, 14, 150-156.

Lee, D.J., and Lowe, G. (1980). 'Interaction of alcohol and caffeine in a perceptual-motor task', IRCS Medical Science, 8, 420.

Leigh, G. (1982). 'The combined effects of alcohol comsumption and cigarette smoking on critical flicker frequency', Addictive Behaviors, 7, 251-259.

Lowe, G. (1981). 'State-dependent recall decrements with moderate doses of alcohol', Current Psychological Research, 1, 3-8.

Overton, D.A. (1978). 'Major theories of state dependent learning', in Drug discrimination and state dependent learning, (Eds. B.T. Ho, D.W. Richards and D.L. Chute), Academic Press, New York.

Peters, R. and McGee, R. (1982). 'Cigarette smoking and state dependent memory', Psychopharmacology, 76, 232-235.

Tong, J.E., Knott, V.J., McGraw, D.J. and Leigh, G. (1974). 'Alcohol, visual discrimination and heart rate; effects of dose, activation and tobacco', Quarterly Journal of Studies on Alcohol, 35, 1003-1022.

Waldeck, B. (1974). 'Ethanol and caffeine: a complex interaction with respect to locomotor activity and central catecholamines', Psychopharmacologia, 36, 209-220.

Walton, R.B. (1972). 'Smoking and alcoholism; a brief report', American Journal of Psychiatry, 128, 1455-1456.

STRESS, ILLNESS
AND MEMORY

COMBINED EFFECTS OF NOISE AND NIGHTWORK ON RUNNING MEMORY

C. Miles
Department of Applied Psychology
University of Wales Institute of Science and Technology
Cardiff, U.K.

A.P. Smith
MRC Perceptual and Cognitive Performance Unit
University of Sussex, Brighton, U.K.

ABSTRACT

A study of the combined effects of noise and nightwork on a running memory task led to the following conclusions. Recent items were recalled better during the night than the day, but the opposite was found for items further back in the list. Noise had no effect on the number of items recalled nor did it modify the interaction between day/night and serial position. The difference between day and night did not reflect a change in recall strategy, but noise did influence the order of recall. Overall, these results confirm that the effects of noise and nightwork are largely independent.

INTRODUCTION

Both well being and safety at work may be influenced by environmental noise level and nightwork. Their identification as major occupational health hazards signals the importance of research aimed at specifying their influence on performance. Most research has studied these factors in isolation, which is unrepresentative of the real-life situation where the person is usually exposed to a combination of factors. The main aim of the present study was to provide preliminary data on the combined effects of nightwork and noise on human function.

Studies of these stressors in isolation have shown that their effects depend on the type of task being performed. For instance, Colquhoun et al. (1968) demonstrated impaired perceptual-motor task performance at night, but tasks with a memory component may be performed better at night (see Monk and Folkard, 1985). In contrast, the effects of moderate intensity noise (up to levels of 90dB) oppose those of nightwork, with tasks involving short-term memory being impaired (Jones et al., 1979) and perceptual-motor tasks being unaffected (Broadbent, 1979).

Precise effects of both noise and nightwork upon memory may vary according to the memory task employed. This can be illustrated by considering data we have already reported from the noise and nightwork study. Noise decreased accuracy on a memory loaded search task and a cognitive vigilance task, but had no effect on working memory tasks or a semantic processing task. In contrast, the semantic processing task was performed more slowly in the latter part of the night session, but none of the other memory tasks was impaired at night.

A simple, but parsimonious model of the effects of noise and nightwork posits 'arousal' level as its mediating function; arousal level is lowered at night, but increased by noise, thus an interaction between the two is predicted. However, the above data clearly contradict such a prediction, and are most suitably accommodated by the suggestion of the existence of independent mechanisms responsible for the observed effects. In order to clarify our understanding of the mechanisms(s) underlying the effects of noise and nightwork, the present study investigated the joint action of these factors upon a running memory task.

Previous studies examining the influence of noise upon running memory, and, therefore, of direct relevance to the present study, implicate an advantage for recall of recent items in noise, with impaired recall of those items further back in the list (Hamilton et al., 1977; Smith, 1983a). An attractive interpretation of this finding suggests that noise acts by altering the balance struck between the overview of present task demands and the effects of events in the immediate past, on current behaviour. Thus, in noise, the listener 'attaches' to present events at the expense of those events in the recent past, and, in effect, the throughput of information is facilitated. Such an explanation is characterised by the 'knock-down' store metaphor, wherein the acquisition strength of new items reflects negatively upon items held.

The findings for studies involving lowered arousal are different. Partially sleep deprived individuals tend to perform better on an auditory running memory task which requires them to recall the fourth digit back from that point at which the sequence stopped (Hamilton et al., 1972). These authors suggest that the lowered arousal affects both the processing rate of material and the decay rate of a buffer store, although direction of causality is not specified. In essence, their model suggests that presented items are available in the buffer store for longer when arousal is low, thereby accounting for the superior recall of an item presented four items back in the list.

In summary, Hamilton et al. (1977) suggest that noise facilitates the throughput of information, such that recently presented items are swiftly replaced by new items. Hamilton et al. (1972) suggest that when the level of arousal is lowered, the throughput of information is slowed. One would, therefore, expect an interaction between noise and nightwork. However, if the action of each is shown to be independent, then this suggests that noise and nightwork influence different mechanisms or processes.

METHOD
Subjects

24 students (12 male and 12 female) from the University of Sussex. They were paid #36 for participation.

Design

Subjects attended for a single day session (9.00 - 17.00) and a single night session (22.00 - 6.00). Each performed several batteries of tests during each session, and details are available in Smith and Miles (1985), along with details of meals, coffee breaks, etc. The order of day/night sessions was counterbalanced across subjects, and the two sessions were approximately one week apart. Two groups (each of six subjects) were tested in noise, and two further groups in quiet. Subjects attended a practice session (in quiet) from 17.00 - 21.00 in the week prior to the first experimental session. The times of testing for the running memory test were Day: 10.30 and 15.00; Night: 23.30 and 04.00.

Continuous free field noise was used. Sound level in the noise condition was 75dBA and in the quiet 40dBA.

The Running Memory Task

The visually presented running memory task comprised digits presented at the rate of 1 per 2 seconds, appearing in the centre of a television monitor. Each list length ranged from 21 to 36 digits. Upon the termination of the list '*****' appeared on the screen, and subjects were required to recall the last eight items presented. Although subjects had to write down each digit in its correct serial position, they could recall the digits in any order they chose, i.e. they could start from the most recent item and work backwards, or start from the first item and work forwards. Each subject was instructed to recall eight items (even if this involved guessing). Subjects indicated order of recall by placing a 1 under the digit recalled first, a 2 under the second, etc.

In total, subjects received 12 lists of digits at each time of testing.

RESULTS

Ratings of Alertness

Before considering the effects of noise and nightwork on running memory, their effects on subjective ratings of alertness will be described. Alertness was rated using a 100mm visual analogue scale with DROWSY at the left end and ALERT at the right. The mean alertness rating was significantly higher for subjects in noise (mean = 50.9) than those in quiet (mean = 43.0). Alertness was significantly higher in the day (mean = 51.9) than at night (mean = 42.0) but noise did not modify this day/night difference.

Number Correctly Recalled

An item was scored as correct only when recalled in the correct serial position. A five-factor (2x2x2x2x8) Analysis of Variance distinguishing the factors of Noise vs Quiet; Order of sessions (day/night vs night/day); Day/Night session; first/second test in a session and serial position, with the first two factors as between subjects and the last three as within subjects, was performed upon these data. Main effects of serial position ($F(7,140) = 165.8$ $p<.0001$) and first/second tests in a session ($F(1,20) = 18.24$, $p<.0005$) were observed, showing the traditional serial position effects and superior recall on the second test compared to the first, respectively. The interaction between order of sessions and day/night ($F(1,20) = 14.27$, $p<.005$) reflects a practice effect.

Main effects of both noise and nightwork failed to achieve significance (F's<1), and, contrary to predictions the interaction of noise and serial position was non-significant ($F<1$). However, the interaction of nightwork and serial position (see Figure 1) reached significance ($F(7,140) = 3.84$, $p<.001$). Clearly, the recall of those items most recently presented was facilitated at night, whereas for

items further back in the list, recall in the day   proved   superior.
There were no further main effects or interactions.

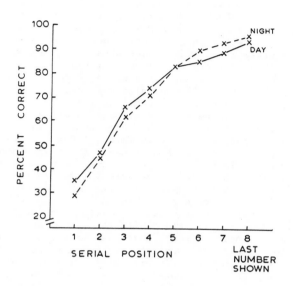

Order of Recall
         Comparison   of   the   tau   correlations   obtained   between
presentation order and recall order indicate a difference in the
recall methods adopted in the noise and quiet conditions. In quiet,
subjects tended to recall in reverse order, producing large negative
correlations (Test 1 in the day: -0.71; Test 2 in the day: -0.79;
Test 1 at night: -0.86; Test 2 at night: -0.71). In contrast, the
corresponding correlations in noise were considerably smaller (Test 1
in the day: -0.21; Test 2 in the day: -0.21; Test 1 at night: -0.21;
Test 2 at night: -0.29). The individual subjects' correlations were
subjected to a two-factor ANOVA (Noise/Quiet vs Night/Daywork), which
showed a significant difference between the correlations produced in
noise ($F(1,20)$ = 4.57, $p<0.05$).   All   other   main   effects   and
interactions were non-significant.

DISCUSSION
         Two positive findings of interest emerge: the first relates
to the improved recall of recently presented items at night, and
second to the differences in recall order adopted between noise and
quiet subjects. On the negative side, the expected noise by serial
position interaction was not observed and noise and nightwork failed
to interact. Each of these points will be discussed in turn.
         Nightwork facilitated recall of recently presented items
and impaired recall of earlier items. This result can be interpreted
within the account proffered by Hamilton et al. (1972), which
suggests that lowered arousal improves passive recall but impairs the

active processes necessary for recall of items presented earlier.

Moderate intensity noise did not act as earlier work (Hamilton et al., 1977) would predict. Their study employed a variety of item presentation rates (ranging from .56 to 3.3 items per sec.), and the interaction occurred at all rates, and always at approximately 5-items back in the list. It appears, therefore, to be a robust finding and it is uinlikely that rate of item presentation can account for the differing results. There were, however, further methodological differences between the present study and Hamilton et al. (1977), such as differences in noise intensity (75dBA vs 90dBA) and exposure duration. It should be noted, however, that the level of noise used here did influence alertness and a number of other performance measures (see Smith and Miles, 1985).

Noise did, however, demonstrate an effect upon strategy rather than efficiency of performance and this is consistent with a number of other recent results (see Smith, 1983b). This is clearly demonstrated by the correlations obtained between presentation order and recall order. In quiet, subjects recalled the most recently presented items first and worked backwards, in noise there tended to be a U-shaped relationship between presentation and recall order.

Finally, the effects of noise and nightwork failed to interact, which is consistent with the findings outlined in the Introduction. This result, taken with the accumulated findings of other studies, strongly suggests that the effects of noise and time of day are independent. The present data suggest that nightwork acts by affecting the relative efficiency of passive and active recall processes. In contrast, noise influences which strategy an individual adopts to perform the task. In the present study noise influenced the recall strategy (as in the study of Smith et al., 1981). If one assumes that noise can also influence whether passive or active methods of remembering are used, then one can account for the results of Hamilton et al. (1977) and Smith (1983a). What is now required are further studies to determine how and why noise influences strategy selection. Similarly, further experiments are required to investigate whether the nightwork effect reported here is produced by arousal changes or is due to some other factor.

CONCLUSION

Recent items were recalled better at night than during the day, but the opposite was found for items further back in the list. This may reflect an effect of nightwork on passive and active methods of recall. Noise had no effect on the number of items recalled, nor did it modify the interaction between day/night and serial position. However, noise did influence the method of recall, which agrees with results from other studies.

REFERENCES

Broadbent, D.E. (1979). 'Human performance and noise', in Handbook of Noise Control (Ed. C.M. Harris), pp. 1-20, McGraw-Hill, New York.

Colquhoun, W.P., Blake, M.J.F. and Edwards, R.S. (1968). 'Experimental studies of shiftwork II: Stabilized 8-hour shift system', Ergonomics, 11, 527-546.

Hamilton, P., Hockey, G.R.J. and Rejman, M. (1977). 'The place of the concept of activation in human information processing: An integrative approach', in Attention and Performance VI (Ed. S. Dornic), pp. 463-486, Erlbaum, Hillsdale, New Jersey.

Hamilton, P., Wilkinson, R.T. and Edwards, R.S. (1972). 'A study of four days partial sleep deprivation', in Aspects of Human Efficiency: Diurnal Rhythm and Loss of Sleep, (Ed. W.P. Colquhoun), pp. 101-114, English University Press.

Jones, D.M., Smith, A.P. and Broadbent, D.E. (1979). 'Effects of moderate intensity noise on the Bakan vigilance task', Journal of Applied Psychology, 64, 627-634.

Monk, T.H. and Folkard, S. (1985). 'Shiftwork and performance', in Hours of Work - Temporal Factors in Work Scheduling, pp. 239-252, Wiley, Chichester.

Smith, A.P. (1983a). 'The effects of noise and memory load on a running memory task', British Journal of Psychology, 74, 439-445.

Smith, A.P. (1983b). 'The effects of noise on strategies of human performance', in Proceedings of the Fourth International Congress on Noise as a Public Health Problem, (Ed. G. Rossi), pp. 797-808, Centro Richerche e studi Amplifon, Milan.

Smith, A.P., Jones, D.M. and Broadbent, D.E. (1981). 'The effects of noise on recall of categorized lists', British Journal of Psychology, 72, 299-316.

Smith, A.P. and Miles, C. (1985). 'The combined effects of noise and nightwork on human function', in Contemporary Ergonomics '85 (Ed. D. Oborne), pp. 33-41, Taylor and Francis, London.

MEMORY DURING ANAESTHESIA

Keith Millar
Behavioural Sciences Group, University of Glasgow
Faculty of Medicine, Glasgow G12 8QQ.

ABSTRACT
        Memory for anaesthesia is a real phenomenon whose detection
is principally determined by the sensitivity of the memory tasks
employed.   There is some advantage in drawing analogies between the
surgical patient who may have retained a memory for anaesthesia and
the organic amnesic patient: both have defective retrieval which can
be aided by subtle cueing techniques. Experimental studies indicate
that verbal information 'heard' during anaesthesia can exert a
subconscious influence upon subsequent behaviour. Memory tasks might
be used in conjunction with cortical evoked responses to define
precisely those anaesthetic conditions that are likely to permit
registration of events during surgery.

        Memory for anaesthesia is associated with "balanced" an-
aesthetic techniques where anaesthesia is maintained by combination
of an agent such as nitrous oxide with oxygen.   Patients derive
clinical benefit from this technique but risk entering a light plane
of anaesthesia with attendant "awareness" and consequent memory for
intra-operative events.   Awareness can be difficult to detect
because clinical signs of consciousness are eliminated by muscle
relaxants and premedicative drugs which are administered prior to
surgery.
        The present concern is with memory for anaesthesia but the
concept of awareness is relevant.   Jones and Koniezko (1986) and
Millar (1987a) have described how awareness, and hence memory, is
effectively blocked by anaesthetic concentrations which depress the
cortical component of the auditory evoked response.   Many studies
fail to account for the depth of anaesthesia in their studies of
memory, and therefore make difficult the interpretation of their
negative results.
        If learning does occur under anaesthesia, then the regis-
tration of input may be faint and the subsequent storage may be
fragile.   The sensitivity of the memory test is then crucial.   In
this regard it is useful to consider evidence concerning the similarity between the amnesic state induced by certain drugs in normal
subjects, and the memory deficit in organic amnesia (Brown et al.
1982).   One might then draw an analogy between the patient who
retains information from anaesthesia and the organic amnesic patient;
both patients may have grossly defective retrieval if asked to give
spontaneous recall of past events.   However, subtle cueing
techniques often retrieve information from the memory of amnesic

patients that would otherwise remain inaccessible. The surgical
patient may also show receptivity to more subtle assessment, but few
studies have pursued such an approach.

   Studies of memory for anaesthesia have tended to follow a
standard routine whereby auditory stimuli are presented during anaesthesia, sometimes with a concurrent attempt to detect periods of
consciousness. On recovery, the patient is required to recall any
events that occurred during anaesthesia. Most studies have found
either that patients have no recall or that very faint recall is
present in only a few patients (Eisele et al., 1976; McIntyre 1966;
Brice et al., 1970; Terrell et al., 1969).

   Millar and Watkinson (1983) and Millar (1983, 1987a,b,c) have
shown that the free-recall routine probably underestimates the
presence of material in memory. If one pursues the analogy between
the fragile retrieval state of amnesic patients and that of
anaesthetised patients who have been exposed to information while
unconscious, then tasks of cued recall and recognition may be more
sensitive in detecting memory for anaesthesia.

   Dubovsky and Trustman (1976) employed a recognition task to
examine memory in anaesthetised obstetric patients. Patients were
presented with letter-word pairs and their ability to recognise the
original pairings was tested when recovered. Patients who had been
presented with the original pairings did not differ from a control
group in their chance ability to choose the correct pairs. However,
the negative result is uncertain for two reasons. First, there was
no assessment of awareness during word presentation: the depth of
anaesthesia may simply have prevented any information from being
registered. Secondly, recognition performance was expressed only as
the number of correct responses: no analysis was made of the "false-
alarm rate". Experimental and control groups might score similar
correct detections but differ in their false alarms, the latter
perhaps implying a difference in the propensity to guess or, more
importantly, in discriminability. The correct detection and false-
alarm rates could be transformed by Signal Detection Theory to derive
d' and beta which represent the patient's ability to discriminate
between presented and non-presented words, and their degree of
caution, respectively.

   Millar and Watkinson (1983) extended Dubovsky and Trustman's
(1976) research by applying a signal detection analysis to
recognition performance in obstetric patients. Experimental
patients were presented with lists of 10 words while anaesthetised;
control patients heard a tape of radio static. Awareness was
assessed by the "isolated forearm technique" (IFT) which involves
inflating a blood pressure cuff to spare the patient's forearm from
paralysis by the muscle relaxant. The hand is then free to signal
awareness (Tunstall 1977). Millar and Watkinson found no evidence
of awareness in their control or experimental groups and no patient
had any spontaneous recall of intraoperative events. Analysis of
correct recognition performance revealed no significant difference
between the groups when asked to select the 10 target words from a
long list of distractors. However, when the data were transformed
to the values of d' and beta, the experimental group scored significantly higher in discriminating between presented and non-
presented words.

These results confirm that spontaneous recall from memory is not a reliable indicator of whether information has been retained from the anaesthetic period. Secondly, a recognition test requires close analysis involving all performance parameters if a sensitive assessment is to be made. A recent negative finding reported by Eich et al. (1985) when employing a recognition technique may be due to failure to make such an analysis. The authors also failed to assess awareness or to give sufficient details of the depth of anaesthesia which may have been such as to preclude any storage of events (see Bennett and Boyle, 1986).

Finally, given that some degree of arousal is necessary for information to be stored in memory during anaesthesia, Millar and Watkinson's (1983) results imply that the IFT may be insensitive to some states of arousal. However, their patients did produce more arm movements during intubation and at the first incision. This would suggest some sensitivity to noxious stimulation which in turn implies some awareness of events.

While such experimental studies of memory for anaesthesia help to determine the reality of the phenomenon and to define the tasks that are most likely to detect it, they have little real-life or "ecological" validity. There is then perhaps practical merit in establishing whether intra-operative events have a subconscious or conscious consequence for later waking thoughts and behaviour. This approach has been taken by Bennett et al. (1985) who presented their 11 anaesthetised experimental patients with the tape-recorded suggestion that, in a post-operative interview, they would pull their ear to indicate that they had heard the intra-operative message. Subsequently, no patient had any conscious recall of intra-operative events, but the experimental patients were reported to be significantly more likely to touch their ear during the post-operative interview, and to spend a longer time ear-pulling than did 23 control patients. While Bennett et al. claim that the result indicates a subconscious influence of information heard during surgery, and their results have gained widespread credibility, Millar (1987b) has shown a number of difficulties with the study.

The primary difficulty concerns the omission of a baseline assessment of 'ear-pulling' frequency. Without this, one cannot determine whether the post-surgical difference between the groups is due to the intra-anaesthetic suggestion or to chance allocation of patients to groups. With such small sample sizes, and the biased allocation of patients to groups, the latter probability is high.

Secondly, close inspection of the data reveals that the difference between experimental and control groups is due to the extreme reactions of two patients. If they are removed from the analysis, the difference between groups is not remotely significant. The statistical analysis of Bennett et al. is also incorrect.

An alternative approach to examining the more practical aspects of memory for anaesthesia, and its possible consequences for subsequent behaviour, is to consider changes in the dynamics of the memory system which can be assessed objectively, and which are predictable on the basis of established memory theory.

Following this approach, Millar (1987a) has described a study to influence semantic retrieval following presentation of verbal material during anaesthesia. Six tape-recorded lists of eight words were prepared such that each list defined a distinct semantic category within which the words were all moderately common category instances. Patients were allocated at random to one of the lists which was repeated during anaesthesia. It was hypothesised that presentation of the words during anaesthesia might prime their later retrieval when conscious. Following recovery, patients were required to generate examples of each of the six category names. (No patient had any recall of the intra-operative events). Words in the lists presented during anaesthesia were significantly more likely to be generated earlier in the retrieval sequence than were the 'control' words in the non-presented lists, suggesting that intra-anaesthetic exposure to the words raised their priority, or semantic "dominance", for retrieval.

The result illustrates a subconscious influence of intra-anaesthetic information upon subsequent verbal behaviour. The dynamics of the semantic memory system have been altered so as to bias patients towards retrieval of a particular class of information. One might suggest that other neutral, or emotionally-coloured, auditory information heard during anaesthesia may have a similar effect. Indeed, studies of retrieval under hypnosis provide quite strong influence for the impact of emotional material. Cheek (1959) describes a series of case histories illustrating hypnotic retrieval of traumatic events during surgery which were inaccessible to conscious recall by patients. Levinson (1965) has also demonstrated subconscious storage and hypnotic retrieval of traumatic events during surgery in a series of highly unethical experiments. Levinson fabricated anaesthetic crises and read out dire diagnosis within 'earshot' of anaesthetised patients. Subsequent behaviour of the patients implied subconscious, and traumatic, effects of the events during anaesthesia.

However, the reliability of hypnosis as an aid to retrieval of anaesthetic memories must be regarded cautiously (Millar, 1987a). One would propose that experimentation will benefit from the use of retrieval tasks derived from well-established findings of experimental psychology. Such tasks have the potential to provide an unambiguous measure of retrieval and the sensitivity to probe within memory for faintly-registered material that would remain inaccessible to spontaneous recall.

One also needs to consider the practical value of demonstrating retrieval by these measures. As a retrospective measure of awareness, it clearly has no value to the patient or anaesthetist as an indicator of possible consciousness at the moment it occurs during surgery (Millar, 1983). Moreover, there is little purpose in further studies to confirm that memory for awareness occurs and that it affects consequent behaviour: that fact is no longer controversial. Rather, the importance of such research probably will lie in conjunction with other tests of awareness in defining the levels of anaesthesia that will preclude any storage of experience. Monitoring of cortical evoked responses indicates the extent to which external events impinge upon the cortex. The parallel use of tests of memory indicates the degree to which such events, registered by the cortex, are likely to be stored in the long-term. It may be that one will then be able to determine a relationship between the physical magnitude of the evoked sensory event permitted by a

specified anaesthetic concentration, and the probability of
retrieval. Ultimately, as Jones and Koniezko (1986) have suggested,
such research may provide the anaesthetist with the ability to
maintain anaesthesia at a concentration which apparently pre-empts
memory, making the issue of awareness and memory for anaesthesia one
of purely historical interest.

REFERENCES

Bennett, H.L. and Boyle, W.A. (1986). 'Selective remembering: anesthesia and memory', Anesthesia and Analgesia, 65, 988-989.

Bennett, H.L., Davis, H.S. and Giannini, J.A. (1985). 'Non-verbal
response to intraoperative conversation', British Journal of Anaesthesia, 57, 174-179.

Brice, D.D., Hetherington, R.R. and Uting, J.E. (1970). 'A simple
study of awareness during anaesthesia', British Journal of Anaesthesia, 42, 535-542.

Brown, J., Lewis, V., Brown, M., Horn, G. and Bowes, J.B. (1982).
'A comparison between transient amnesias induced by two drugs
(diazepam and lorazepam) and amnesia of organic origin', Neuropsychologia, 20, 55-70.

Cheek, D.B. (1959). 'Unconscious perception of meaningful sounds
during surgical anesthesia as revealed under hypnosis', American
Journal of Clinical Hypnosis, 1, 101-113.

Dubovsky, S.L. and Trustman, R. (1976). 'Absence of recall after
general anesthesia', Anesthesia and Analgesia, 55, 513-518.

Eich, E., Reeves, J.L. and Katz, R.L. (1985). 'Anesthesia, awareness, and the memory/awareness distinction', Anesthesia and Analgesia, 64, 1143-1148.

Eisele, V., Weinreich, A. and Bartle, S. (1976). 'Perioperative
awareness and recall', Anesthesia and Analgesia, 55, 513-518.

Jones, J.G. and Koniezko, K. (1986). 'Hearing and memory in
anaesthetised patients', British Medical Journal, 292, 1291-1293.

Levinson, B.W. (1965). 'States of awareness during general anaesthesia', British Journal of Anaesthesia, 37, 544-550.

McIntyre, J.W.R. (1966). 'Awareness during general anaesthesia:
preliminary observations', Canadian Anaesthetists' Society Journal,
13, 495-499.

Millar, K. (1983). 'Awareness during anaesthesia', Annals of the
Royal College of Surgeons of England, 65, 350-351.

Millar, K. (1987a). 'Assessment of memory for anaesthesia' in _Aspects of Recovery from Anaesthesia_ (Ed. I Hindmarch), John Wiley, in press.

Millar, K. (1987b). 'Non-verbal response to intraoperative conversation - an artifact?', British Journal of Anaesthesia, in press.

Millar, K. (1987c). 'Memory and anaesthesia', Lancet, i, 688.

Millar, K. and Watkinson, N. (1983). 'Recognition of words presented during general anaesthesia', Ergonomics, 26, 585-594.

Terrell, R.K., Sweet, W.D., Gladfelter, J.H. and Stephen, C.R. (1969). 'Study of recall during anesthesia', Anesthesia and Analgesia, 48, 86-90.

Tunstall, M.E. (1977). 'Detecting wakefulness during general anaesthesia for Caesarean section', British Medical Journal, i, 1321.

CAN SCOPOLAMINE PRODUCE A MODEL OF THE MEMORY DEFICITS
SEEN IN AGING AND DEMENTIA?

K. A. Wesnes and P. M. Simpson,
Cognitive Drug Research,
Opus House, South Street, Reading RG1 4HW, U.K.

ABSTRACT
        The cognitive impairments produced by scopolamine and the
evidence of cholinergic involvement in the memory deficits seen in
dementia, suggest that   scopolamine   can   produce a psychopharmacological model of   aging. Work   from   our   laboratory
demonstrates that the pattern of memory failures with scopolamine
resembles that seen in studies of Alzheimer's patients (Beatty et
al.,1986). In another experiment using the selective reminding
task, scopolamine increased the relative dependence on primary over
secondary memory, paralleling findings with   this task when
Alzheimer's patients were compared to controls (Ober et al.,1985).
It is concluded that scopolamine does produce an adequate cognitive
model of dementia which can be used to screen potential nootropic
agents.

AGING, MEMORY AND THE CHOLINERGIC SYSTEM
        The everyday observation of increased forgetfulness in
elderly people is well supported by scientific study (see e.g.
Poon, 1985). The accumulating evidence, from human and animal
studies, of an important cholinergic role in age-related memory
disturbances (see, e.g. Coyle et al., 1983) has lead to the
cholinergic hypothesis of geriatric memory loss (Bartus et al.,
1986), which asserts that:
        a. significant, functional disturbances in cholinergic
activity occur in the brains of aged and especially demented
subjects;
        b. these disturbances play an important role in the memory
loss and related cognitive problems associated with old age and
dementia; and
        c. proper enhancement or restoration of cholinergic
function may significantly reduce the severity of cognitive loss.
        Support for the last assertion has come from work in which
physostigmine has been demonstrated to produce improvements in
memory performance in Alzheimer's patients (Davis and Mohs, 1982),
and also from a recent study, in which tetrahydroaminoacridine, a
cholinergic agonist, was found to be effective in the clinical
treatment of such patients (Summers et al., 1986).

THE SCOPOLAMINE MODEL OF AGING AND DEMENTIA
        There is considerable evidence that in healthy volunteers
scopolamine produces marked losses in secondary memory (for review,

see Kopelman, 1986). Since the primary neurochemical action of scopolamine is to attenuate transmission in muscarinic cholinergic pathways, these scopolamine-induced memory deficits together with the evidence of cholinergic dysfunction in age-associated memory impairment, imply that the drug can produce a psychopharmacological model of aging. However, the potential value of a scopolamine-model of aging and dementia lies not so much in its ability to help understand the mechanisms involved, but in its ability to provide a test situation in which drugs designed to counteract or prevent age-related cognitive impairment can be rapidly evaluated for potential efficiency prior to their use in long and costly trials in elderly populations.

Validity of the Scopolamine Model: Patterns of Memory Errors
        The validity of the model will lie primarily in its ability to produce cognitive impairments which mimic those seen in aging and dementia. Certainly a superficial comparison of the memory loss induced by scopolamine to that exhibited by the elderly shows good overall agreement. As mentioned earlier, the administration of scopolamine to healthy volunteers produces impairments in secondary (recent or long-term) memory, and it is just such losses which are seen in the aged (Crook et al.,1986). However, on the basis of experimental findings, Beatty et al.(1986) have cast doubt on the ability of scopolamine to adequately mimic the full range of memory impairments seen in dementia. In this study the memory effects of scopolamine 0.5 mg i.m. in six healthy volunteers were contrasted to the pattern of memory failure seen in patients with Alzheimer's disease (AD). In line with previous findings, scopolamine significantly decreased recall on a free-recall task and also on the Brown-Peterson task. The AD patients also showed decreased recall on these tasks when compared to age and education matched controls. However, despite these comparable losses in secondary memory, a different pattern of errors on the memory tasks was observed between the volunteers and the patients. On a recognition task, the volunteers did not show a significant increase in errors of omission or commission with scopolamine, nor an increase in perseverative responses (a summation of prior-list intrusions and words not on the original lists) on the Brown-Peterson task, whereas compared to controls the AD patients made significantly more of each type of error. This anomaly is used by Beatty et al.(1986) to support their arguments that scopolamine does not produce a valid model of the memory impairments in dementia.
        Evidence from our laboratory (Wesnes and Simpson, 1987a) contradicts these findings. Eighteen volunteers were given scopolamine 0.6 mg s.c. on one occasion and placebo on another. On each occasion, prior to injection, and 60, 90, 150 and 240 minutes later, a computerized battery of cognitive tasks (Wesnes, 1985) was performed. Of interest here were the patterns of errors on a verbal recall and recognition task. In this task the volunteers were presented with a list of 15 words and were immediately given 60 seconds to write down, in any order, as many of the words as possible. Twenty minutes later they were again given 60 seconds to

recall the list. Following this they were presented with the original words together with 15 new words in a recognition task. Each word appeared singly on a computer screen and the subjects signalled whether or not they recognized the word using response buttons. As in both the Beatty et al. study and previous work, the number of words recalled was significantly decreased in the immediate recall condition ($p<0.001$) and in the delayed condition ($p<0.001$). However, scopolamine also increased the number of prior-list intrusions and the number of words 'recalled' which were not on the original list. For prior-list intrusions, this increase only occurred in delayed recall ($p<0.001$), whereas for words not on the original lists, this occurred for both immediate ($p<0.05$) and delayed recall ($p<0.01$). Further, in recognition testing, scopolamine increased both errors of omission ($p<0.01$) and commission ($p<0.05$). Thus, we found scopolamine to produce precisely the sorts of errors that Beatty et al. failed to detect. The most likely explanation of this discrepancy was the sample size, Beatty et al. used only 6 volunteers compared to the 18 in our study. It should also be noted that Beatty et al. found no effects of scopolamine on a verbal fluency task and a symbol-digit association task, whereas the AD patients performed less efficiently on these tasks than did controls. However, negative results in such small samples should not be used to confirm the null hypothesis, and it will remain for future research to determine whether or not scopolamine affects performance on these tasks. Overall, this study provides evidence that the administration of scopolamine results in patterns of impairments of verbal recall and recognition memory which are directly comparable to those seen in AD patients, demonstrating that the drug can produce an adequate model of dementia for these aspects of memory.

Validity of the Scopolamine Model: Primary and Secondary Memory

The selective reminding task (Buschke and Fuld, 1974) permits the simultaneous evaluation of several aspects of memory. Of relevance here is the ability to separately quantify primary and secondary memory using this technique. In early stage AD patients, cholinergic therapy with physostigmine and lecithin produces improvements in secondary memory on the task (Thal et al., 1983). Further, in another study, it has been shown that AD patients depend more on primary memory and less on secondary memory when performing the test than do age and education matched controls (Ober et al., 1985). On the basis of this finding, if scopolamine were to produce a cognitive model of dementia, then it should increase the relative dependence on primary memory on the task. Evidence consistent with this comes from a second study from our laboratory in which 26 volunteers received scopolamine 0.7 mg s.c. on seven successive weeks (Wesnes et al., 1987a). Prior to and 60 minutes after injection the volunteers performed a battery of tests including the selective reminding task. In the latter task a list of 14 words was aurally presented for recall. Any words not recalled were then prompted and the subjects were again required to recall the entire list. This procedure was repeated four further times, giving a total of six recall trials per session. Primary memory was measured by recording those items which were recalled immediately following presentation. Secondary memory was measured by scoring the number of occasions on which items were recalled without prompting. The average scores over the seven sessions are presented below:

	Pre-Scopolamine		Post-Scopolamine	
	mean	s.e.	mean	s.e.
Primary Memory	24.13	0.69	24.23	0.65
Secondary memory	35.54	2.31	12.54	1.49

The decrement in secondary memory following scopolamine was large and highly significant ($F(1,25)= 298.8$, $p<0.0001$), while, as can be seen from the Table, there was no change in primary memory. Thus it is clear that on the selective reminding task, scopolamine increases the relative dependence of young volunteers to primary memory, and consequently mimics the difference found by Ober et al. (1985) between AD patients and controls.

METHODOLOGY AND USE OF THE MODEL TO STUDY NOOTROPICS

Having established the usefulness of the model in terms of the similarity of the induced memory failures to those seen in aging and particularly AD, it is now appropriate to consider its usefulness as an experimental tool to study nootropics. Previous work with the model has shown that the cognitive deficits produced by orally administered scopolamine can be antagonized by the cholinergic agonist, nicotine (Wesnes and Revell, 1984). However, recent work from our laboratory indicates that injected scopolamine produces more widespread and consistent cognitive decrements than does oral administration (Wesnes et al., 1987c), particularly when used with computerized assessment techniques (Wesnes, 1985) that have also proven sensitive to nootropic administration in the elderly (Wesnes et al., 1987b). Further, these effects persist for many hours (Wesnes and Simpson, 1987a) and permit drugs with slower absorption rates than nicotine to be tested for nootropic activity. Other important aspects of methodology which contribute to the sensitivity of the model include the use of within-subject designs, the establishment of pre-drug performance baselines and the evaluation of the cognitive effects of scopolamine prior to nootropic administration (Wesnes and Simpson, 1987b). The usefulness of the model, when the appropriate tasks and methodology are employed, is demonstrated by findings that various pyrrolidinone derivatives can antagonize the scopolamine-induced cognitive decrements (Wesnes et al., 1986a,b).

CONCLUSIONS AND IMPLICATIONS FOR FUTURE RESEARCH

Overall, the scopolamine model of aging and dementia stands scrutiny for the degree to which it mimics the patterns of memory deficits seen in clinical conditions. However, it has recently been demonstrated that scopolamine impairs information

processing, as well as the ability to retain and recall information
(Wesnes et al.,1987c), and it is yet to be determined whether the
memory deficits are related to or independent of the processing
deficits. A similar quandary exists for the basis of the memory
deficits seen in aging and dementia. Thus a secondary use of the
scopolamine model in future research could be to investigate the
role of the cholinergic system in the various stages of human
cognition. Nonetheless, the major similarities between the
cognitive effects of scopolamine and the mental deterioration in AD
provide a sound basis for use of the scopolamine model to evaluate
potential nootropic agents, providing the appropriate methodology
and cognitive tests are used.

REFERENCES

Bartus, R.T. Dean, R,L. and Fisher, S.K. (1986). 'Cholinergic
Treatment for Age-Related Memory Disturbances', in Treatment
Development Strategies for Alzheimer's Disease (Eds. T. Crook, R.
Bartus, S. Ferris and S. Gershon), pp. 421-450, Mark Powley
Associates, Connecticut.

Beatty, W.W., Butters, N. and Janowsky, D.S. (1986). 'Patterns of
Memory Failure after Scopolamine Treatment: Implications for
Cholinergic Hypotheses of Dementia', Behavioral and Neural Biology,
45, 196-211.

Buschke, H., and Fuld, P.A. (1974). 'Evaluating Storage, Retention
and Retrieval in Disordered Memory and Learning', Neurology, 27,
1087-1092.

Coyle, J.T., Price, D.L. and DeLong, M.R. (1983). 'Alzheimer's
Disease: A Disorder of Cortical Cholinergic Innervation', Science,
219, 1184-1190.

Crook, T. Bartus, R. Ferris S., Whitehouse, P., Cohen, G.D. and
Gershon, S. (1986). 'Age-Associated Memory Impairment: Proposed
Diagnostic Criteria and Measures of Clinical Change - Report of a
National Institute of Mental Health Work Group', Developmental
Neuropsychology, 2, 261-276.

Davis, K.L. and Mohs, R.C. (1982). 'Enhancement of Memory Processes
in Alzheimer's Disease with Multiple-Dose Intravenous
Physostigmine', American Journal of Psychiatry, 139, 1421-1424.

Kopelman M.D. (1986). 'The Cholinergic Neurotransmitter System in
Human Memory and Dementia: A Review', The Quarterly Journal of
Experimental Psychology, 38, 535-573.

Ober, B.A., Koss, E., Friedland, R.P., and Delis, D.C. (1985)
'Processes of Verbal Memory Failure in Alzheimer-Type Dementia',
Brain and Cognition, 4, 90-103.

Poon, L.W. (1985). 'Differences in Human Memory with Aging: Nature, Causes, and Clinical Implications', in Handbook of the Psychology of Aging (Eds. J.E. Birren and K.W. Schaie), pp. 427-462, Van Nostrand Reinhold, New York.

Summers, W.K., Majouski, L., Marsh, G.N., Tachiki, K. and Kling, A. (1986). 'Oral Tetrahydroaminoacridine in Long-Term Treatment of Dementia, Alzheimer Type', New England Journal of Medicine, 315, 1241-1245.

Thal, L.J., Fuld, P.A., Masur, D.M. and Sharpless, N.S. (1983). 'Oral Physostigmine and Lecithin Improve Memory in Alzheimer's Disease', Annals of Neurology, 13, 491-496.

Wesnes, K. (1985). 'A Fully Automated Psychometric Test Battery for Human Psychopharmacology', in Abstracts of IVth World Congress of Biological Psychiatry, Philadelphia, September 1985, p. 153.

Wesnes, K., Anand, R., Simpson, P. and Christmas, L. (1987a). 'The Effects of Scopolamine 0.7 mg s.c. on Cognitive Efficiency', in preparation.

Wesnes, K. and Revell, A. (1984). 'The Separate and Combined Effects of Scopolamine and Nicotine on Human Information Processing', Psychopharmacology, 84, 5-11.

Wesnes, K, Simmons, D., Rook, M. and Simpson, P.M. (1987b). 'A Double-Blind Placebo Controlled Trial of Tanakan in the Treatment of Idiopathic Cognitive Impairment in the Elderly', Human Psychopharmacology, in press.

Wesnes, K. and Simpson, P.M. (1987a). 'The Time Course of the Cognitive Effects of Scopolamine in Man', in preparation.

Wesnes, K. and Simpson, P.M. (1987b). 'The Scopolamine Model of Dementia: A Comparison of Different Methodologies, in preparation.

Wesnes, K., Simpson, P.M. and Christmas, L. (1986a). 'The Effects of Two Doses of CAS 997 on Mental Efficiency under Normal Conditions and Following the Administration Subcutaneously of 0.6 mg Scopolamine', report to Cassella AG, Frankfurt.

Wesnes, K., Simpson, P.M. and Christmas, L. (1986b). 'The Effects of Aniracetam on the Cognitive Decrements Induced by Scopolamine in Healthy Young Volunteers', report to F.Hoffmann-La Roche, Basle.

Wesnes, K., Simpson, P.M. and Kidd, A. (1987c). 'The Effects of Scopolamine on Human Cognition', submitted to Psychopharmacology.

NEUROTOXIC EXPOSURE AND MEMORY FUNCTION

B T Stollery
Department of Occupational Health
Stopford Building, University of Manchester
Manchester M13 9PT, England

ABSTRACT
        Psychological techniques are increasingly being used to
detect central nervous system dysfunction in workers exposed to
industrial toxins. The evidence accumulating from field studies
is that workers without clinical signs of toxicity may be impaired
on tests of sensory-motor speed, memory and attention. The nature
of the memory impairment has yet to be systematically explored and
the detailed analysis of subclinical effects using cognitive
models is urged. As this work develops, it is likely to form a
substantive link between neuropsychological investigations
involving frank pathology and theoretically orientated studies of
normal cognition.

INTRODUCTION

        The toxic nature of certain industrial chemicals is well
documented and statutory limits regulate their permissible levels
in the working environment. During the last thirty years, the
biomedical investigation and diagnosis of occupational disease has
led to improved hygiene standards and it is now rare for workers
to present with clinical signs of toxicity. This decline in the
incidence of clinical poisoning has been accompanied by increased
interest in detecting the early, and hopefully reversible, stages
of a toxic response. As the central nervous system is a known
target organ for many toxins, the quantitative assessment of
mental functioning is seen as forming an essential component in
the overall analysis of neurotoxicity and has posed a unique
challenge for applied psychological research.

BEHAVIOURAL TOXICOLOGY

        The evaluation of central nervous system functions in
workers exposed to industrial chemicals has only recently
coalesced into a well-defined area of psychological research
(Weiss, 1983), but recognition of the importance of this work has
grown rapidly. The historical development of behavioural
toxicology has been admirably charted by Hanninen (1985) and her
early studies of solvent poisoned workers were instrumental in
consolidating the role of psychological testing in occupational
health studies. As workers with suspected industrial poisoning
were seen at outpatient clinics, it was natural for psychologists

to employ the test methods of clinical neuropsychology since these methods had historically played an important role in the assessment of organic brain damage.

Currently, investigations are principally concerned with the study of clinically healthy workers who have been occupationally exposed to low-levels of a toxin for many years. In addition to psychological evaluations, studies include biochemical and pharmokinetic investigations of the toxin and its metabolites, and physiological examinations of the peripheral and central nervous systems. Evidence for exposure-response relations has been sought in epidemiological studies, normally using cross-sectional designs. The transient effects of organic solvent exposure have been studied both in the laboratory by using exposure chambers, and in the field by examining the acute effects occurring during a work shift (see Gamberale, 1985). The psychological test methods employed in these studies have been broadly similar to those used with industrially poisoned workers but, due to the time constraints placed on field studies by production activities, it has been necessary to devise short sensitive batteries of tests.

Psychological test batteries are usually constructed by combining a selected, but variable, number of items from the standard clinical repertoire. The proliferation of broadly similar test batteries has resulted in a recent attempt by the World Health Organisation to establish a standard "core" battery (WHO, 1985). This comprises the vocabulary, similarities, digit symbol and block design tests from the Wechsler Adult Intelligence Scale (WAIS), the digit span, associative learning and visual recognition tests from the Wechsler Memory Scale (WMS), and tests of simple reaction time, manual dexterity (Santa Ana) and a Profile of Mood States questionnaire (POMS).

Feldman, Ricks & Baker (1980) have reviewed the neuropsychological effects of several industrial toxins, including lead and mercury, and the neurotoxicity of organic solvents has been the subject of several recent reviews and editorials (Baker & Fine, 1986; Baker, Smith & Landrigan, 1985; Cavanagh, 1985; Waldron, 1986): these papers should be consulted for access to this large and expanding literature. In general terms, asymptomatic workers have impaired performance on tests of sensory-motor speed and manual dexterity. The evidence for impaired memory is less consistent and it will become apparent that the detection of early memory impairment is likely to require more precisely targeted tests than those currently advocated.

INDUSTRIAL TOXINS AND MEMORY

Evidence is accumulating that short-term memory may be impaired by a toxin at levels below its regulatory limit and two recent papers have tabulated the evidence with respect to lead (Baker et al., 1985) and organic solvents (Baker & Fine, 1985). The most common method of evaluating immediate memory for verbal material has been the digit span test and, while there are exceptions, impaired digit span is often reported for both lead and solvent workers. It is common, however, for investigators to combine forward and backward span into a single score. While this may be standard scoring practice, it is unfortunate that both measures have not been more commonly reported because there is evidence that backward span is more sensitive to lead exposure.

Workers exposed to lead and organic solvents are also reported to have poor scores on verbal paired-associate tasks. The most widely used task is from the Wechsler Memory Scale (WMS). Again, most investigators have adopted the standard scoring technique of reporting a single score (e.g., number correct after a fixed number of trials) and details of task performance are rarely provided. This makes it difficult to determine whether low scores derive from slower learning rates or a higher incidence of certain error types. Some studies do provide more detail. Williamson & Teo (1986) report that lead workers recalled fewer associates on the first trial and took more trials to reach the criterion of all correct. Baker at al. (1985) report that lead workers show greater difficulty with the low frequency associates from the WMS.

While the overall impression is that some aspects of short-term memory are impaired in asymptomatic workers, the details of performance reported do not allow a rigorous analysis of memory dysfunction to be undertaken. Much of this difficulty is a consequence of the relatively atheoretical approach adopted, which itself probably reflects the reliance on clinical tests. The choice of memory paradigm, together with relevant measures of performance, is necessarily undertaken within the context of a model of memory. It is worth emphasising that many of the practical limitations encountered when studying cognitive dysfunction in patients with brain damage will not apply when industrial toxins are studied because the workers are clinically healthy. Indeed, Stollery (1985) has argued that the characterisation of early cognitive impairment due to neurotoxic exposure is best approached from the background of normal, rather than abnormal, functioning.

The paradigms of cognitive psychology have been applied to the study of neurotoxic effects only recently. The study of lead workers by Williamson & Teo (1986), for example, examines retrieval from short-term memory using a Sternberg memory scanning task: the subject memorises a short set of digits and decides whether a probe digit, shown immediately after, is in the memory set. Those authors found, in more exposed workers, a steeper slope relating correct reaction time and memory load both for true and false decisions.

A study of the sequelae of an accidental solvent intoxication (Stollery & Flindt, 1986), found impaired recall on three auditory-verbal memory tasks: paired-associate learning of unrelated words, immediate free recall of 15 words (serial position task), and a short-term forgetting task based on the Brown-Peterson paradigm. The intoxicated workers were still symptomatic at the time of the first examination, two months after the accident, and their poorer performance in the paired-associate test reflected failure to produce responses rather than incorrect pairings of cue with response. However, that group's learning curve across acquisition trials was parallel to that of two reference groups. The intoxicated group also recalled fewer words in the serial position task, a finding not specific to the primacy, asymptote or recency component of recall. Their performance in the Brown-Peterson task, however, showed a substantially greater loss of information after only 5 seconds of rehearsal prevention (backward counting). Yet, the rate of loss after this time (maximum 30 seconds) was identical to the other groups. In summary, the memory sequelae of the intoxication was reflected to a small extent in a paired-associate and an immediate free recall task, but to a large extent in a task where memory was tested following rehearsal prevention. Furthermore, backward counting showed only an initially disruptive effect on recall rather than a continuous one.

The finding that some aspects of memory function may be impaired, while others are spared, is not surprising given the broad range of mental activities underlying performance in memory tasks. There may, of course, be several theoretical models available for understanding performance in a particular short-term memory task. One of the most successful recent models is that of working memory (e.g., Hitch, 1984) and, given the wide range of tasks to which it has been addressed, it is instructive to consider the available evidence for memory dysfunction following neurotoxic exposure within this framework.

Working memory comprises an alliance of specialised short-term storage systems and a "central executive" attentional system. Within this model, the ability to repeat an auditorily presented sequence of digits in serial order depends upon subvocal rehearsal within an articulatory loop system. With backward span, it seems likely that additional demands are made on the central processor. On this basis, the greater sensitivity of backward span to neurotoxins would indicate the involvement of the central processor, although impaired processing within the articulatory loop cannot be discounted. Several techniques exist for exploring the role of these subsystems in the impaired memory span of exposed workers (e.g., variation of word length, phonemic similarity and articulatory suppression).

The data on the memory sequelae of the solvent intoxication described above would be consistent with the involvement of the central executive attentional system. Forgetting in the Brown-Peterson task, for example, does not occur merely by prevention of subvocal rehearsal during the interval (e.g., the articulatory suppression task of repeating a single word), whereas rapid forgetting occurs when the processing demands of the interval task are increased. The allocation of processing resources to both tasks seems crucial in producing this initial forgetting. For the intoxicated group, the differential effects of backward counting were restricted to the first few seconds and this indicates difficulties in initial resource-allocation: once resources have been allocated forgetting occurs at a normal rate. Furthermore, there was some evidence that long-term exposure in asymptomatic workers was also associated with higher initial forgetting rates. The Brown-Peterson paradigm, therefore, would appear to be a useful one within which to explore the memory impairment reported in organic solvent workers and procedural variations should also allow further specification of subclinical memory impairment (e.g., varying the processing difficulty of the articulatory suppression task).

FUTURE ISSUES IN BEHAVIOURAL TOXICOLOGY

Although the adoption of a standard test battery (WHO, 1985) will certainly enable studies of neurotoxic effects to be compared, given the current failure to provide a convincing account of memory impairment, it seems necessary for test methodologies to develop. Indeed, it seems essential to the future development of behavioural toxicology that closer links are forged with the theories and paradigms of normal cognition. The use of cognitive models and theories as frameworks for describing early neurotoxic effects offers important advantages for both disciplines. Not only will it help to advance our understanding of early impairment through the process of hypothesis testing, it has the potential of shaping our models of normal cognition through the process of problem solving. As yet, however, behavioural toxicology does not enjoy the same degree of attention that is given to neuropsychology.

Additional work is clearly required to distinguish between the different neurotoxins. For example, lead provides the classic picture of a heavy metal poisoning: anaemia, peripheral neuropathy and, ultimately, a toxic encephalopathy. By contrast, organic solvents cross the blood-brain barrier, have short-term narcotic effects, penetrate nerve cells and sheaths, and have heterogeneous toxicity. Given the distinct effects of these toxins, it seems unlikely that they will affect cognitive functioning in the same way. A more rigorous analysis of the "impairment profile" may provide the much needed information to distinguish the toxins, but it is also likely that exposed workers attempt to compensate for early effects. As psychological functions have a collective organisation, and act cooperatively in the production of behaviour, changes in task strategy may be among the first changes associated with exposure.

Behavioural toxicology is a multidisciplinary field of research and the characterization of early effects is still at an exploratory stage. The theoretical debates within psychology should not detract from the utility of using cognitive models to explore early impairment because, as with the study of neuropsychology, the exchange of information will give breadth to the new models which develop. The study of neurotoxic effects is likely to help unify the study of normal cognition with that of neuropsychology by establishing substantial links with both.

REFERENCES

Baker, E.L., Fine, L.J. (1986). 'Solvent neurotoxicity: the current evidence.' Journal of Occupational Medicine,28,126-129.

Baker, E.L., Smith, T.J. and Landrigan, P.J. (1985). 'The neurotoxicity of industrial solvents: A review of the literature.' American Journal of Industrial Medicine,8,207-218.

Baker, E.L., White, R.F., Pothier, L.J., Berkey, C.S., Dinse, G.E., Travers, P.H., Harley, P.J., Feldman, R.G. (1985). 'Occupational lead neurotoxicity: improvement in behavioural effects after reduction of exposure.' British Journal of Industrial Medicine,42,507-516.

Cavanagh, J.B. (1985). 'Solvent neurotoxicity' British Journal of Industrial Medicine,42,433-434.

Feldman, R.G., Ricks, N.L., Baker, E.L. (1980). 'Neuropsychological effects of industrial toxins: a review.' American Journal of Industrial Medicine,1,211-227.

Gamberale. F. (1985). 'Use of behavioural performance tests in the assessment of solvent toxicity.' Scandinavian Journal of Work, Environment & Health,11,65-75 (supplement 1).

Hanninen, H. (1985). 'Twenty-five years of behavioural toxicology within occupational medicine: a personal account.' American Journal of Industrial Medicine,7,19-30.

Hitch, G.J. (1984). 'Working memory.' Psychological Medicine, 14,265-271.

Stollery, B.T. (1985). 'Psychological toxicology: new methods for detecting sub-clinical effects.' In Environmental Health 3: Neurobehavioural methods in occupational and environmental health, pp.81-85,World Health Organisation, Copenhagen.

Stollery, B.T., Flindt, M.L.H. (1986). 'Effects of acute solvent exposure on memory function.' Unpublished manuscript, Department of Occupational Health, University of Manchester, England.

Waldron, H.A. (1986). 'Solvents and the brain.' British Journal of Industrial Medicine,43,73-74.

Weiss, B. (1985). 'Behavioural toxicology and environmental health science: Opportunity and challenge for psychology.' American Psychologist,38,1174-1187.

Williamson, A.M., Teo, R.K.C. (1986). 'Neurobehavioural effects of occupational exposure to lead.' British Journal of Industrial Medicine,43,374-380.

World Health Organisation (1985). Environmental Health 5: Organic solvents and the central nervous system. World Health Organisation,Copenhagen.

MISCELLANEOUS CLINICAL APPLICATIONS

TRIALS, TRIBULATIONS AND TRIUMPHS IN THE DEVELOPMENT OF A TEST OF EVERYDAY MEMORY

B.A. Wilson, A.D. Baddeley and J. Cockburn
University Rehabilitation Unit, Southampton General Hospital,
Applied Psychology Unit, Cambridge, and
Rivermead Rehabilitation Centre, Oxford.

ABSTRACT

In recent years there has been an increase in the development of ecologically valid assessment procedures. While it is true to say that conventional tests that have been available within the field of memory assessment answer certain questions effectively, it is also recognised that they fail to answer other questions, particularly those relating to the effects of memory impairment on everyday life. This paper reports some of the difficulties and successes encountered in an attempt to produce a test that would answer some of the questions connected with everyday memory performance. The paper discusses the authors' reasons for embarking upon such a project, criteria for selection of test items, major obstacles that had to be overcome and how they were tackled, outcomes, and possible future developments.

INTRODUCTION

Conventional tests of memory serve many purposes. They may be used in a search for answers to theoretical questions, they can indicate how the scores of one individual compare with those of a general population, they can specify a particular memory deficit (whether, for example, a person has a problem with verbal or visual memory), and they can differentiate between organic memory impairment and disability caused by anxiety or depression. Unfortunately – and not least for the memory impaired person – these tests have not been designed to elicit answers which shed much light on ways an individual's daily life is affected by memory impairment: they tell us little about the nature or extent of everyday memory problems. Questionnaires, rating scales and checklists have not been able to probe, with any degree of accuracy, the daily world of the memory impaired, mainly because such instruments call for responses which are themselves dependent upon accurate remembering. Relying upon accounts given by relatives of the memory impaired person is speculative because relatives are not always available to observe memory failures, and such observations as they are able make may be distorted through anecdote. While it is likely that direct observation by a properly trained tester would produce an accurate record of everyday memory failure, such a procedure is highly impractical given the time and cost that would be involved.

Given this background, we looked for an alternative way of testing that would enable us to predict which people would be likely to experience everyday memory failures. We wanted to produce a test which would also recognise that memory problems are not necessarily static: a test that could tell us something about ways memory problems change with the passage of time. Such a test, we believed, would be welcomed by therapists as an instrument that could help them decide which of their patients' memory problems required treatment that might lead to some degree of alleviation in daily life.

When assessing the memory of a patient a clinical psychologist is likely to report information about that patient's immediate memory span, verbal and visual memory and learning ability. However, therapists are not necessarily informed by the data that illuminate such areas. They are likely to remain unimpressed by a patient's inability to remember the Rey Osterreith Figure or failure to manage paired – associate learning tasks. This is because therapists are looking for answers that can inform programmes of treatment that may eventually lead to improvements in the quality of the lives of their patients. They may ask questions such as, "What do those figures mean in terms of daily living? Can the patient return home? Can the patient go back to work?"

We knew that any test we designed would have to provide information that would help therapists to find answers to such questions. We also appreciated that any test we developed would require face validity for the patients themselves. In our previous experience, patients rarely saw conventional tests as instruments that were relevant to their needs. We had heard them ask, "What's this in aid of?" or complain, "We don't need that!" In the light of these messages we were receiving from patients, their relatives, and therapists we began designing the Rivermead Behavioural Memory Test (RBMT).

TRIALS AND TRIBULATIONS

Items to be included in the RBMT were selected partly on the basis of observations of patients' everyday memory failures over a period of several months at the Rivermead Rehabilitation Centre in Oxford, and partly on the basis of studies conducted at Cambridge by Sunderland, Harris and Baddeley (1984). Our guiding principle was to include only those items which matched tasks encountered in real life. In fact some of the trials and tribulations we were to suffer sprang from our adherence to this principle. The tasks we devised also had to comply with the demands of standardised administration and scoring; and, furthermore, they had to be adaptable to a wide variety of environmental settings. Initially, for example, we based the remembering of a new short route on pathways that led round the unit but this produced some discomfort and frustration among a number of the patients – particularly if it began raining! We also realised that our pathways contained certain unique features which rendered them unadaptable to other environments. Thus we had to modify the new route by bringing it indoors and setting it within typical features likely to occur in most buildings.

We had included learning a new skill in our earliest design

and were pleased with its inclusion because it could be undertaken by the majority of patients. It consisted of programming an electronic memory aid. Six steps were involved and four versions of the task developed for the four parallel versions of the RBMT. However, our satisfaction with this subtest was short lived owing to various disagreements with the company who manufactured the product. We were discouraged by the expense of the aid, and perturbed by the constant changes in design it was subjected to by the manufacturers. We were also concerned by the manufacturer's misgivings about the interest we were showing in their product. At first, they suspected us of being spies for a rival company, and when this suspicion was allayed they continued to show a lack of interest in our venture because we were dealing in comparatively low numbers that would be reflected in equally low sales and a subsequent lack of profitability. It was at this stage that we decided to abandon the item!

The final version of the test includes the following twelve items:-

1. Remembering a new name – first name.
2. Remembering a new name – second name.
3. Remembering a belonging.
4. Remembering an appointment.
5. Picture recognition.
6. Newspaper story – immediate and delayed recall.
7. Face recognition.
8. Remembering a new route – immediate recall.
9. Remembering a new route – delayed recall.
10. Remembering to deliver a message.
11. Orientation.
12. Date.

In order to avoid practice effects that follow repeated assessmemts, we have produced four parallel versions of the RBMT.

Validation was even more difficult than selecting tasks because it placed therapists in the demanding role of observers of patients for a period of two weeks while recording everyday memory failures. Numbers of reported memory failures were correlated with patients' RBMT scores. Initially we had hoped to include a hundred patients in the validation study but we had made insufficient allowance for the fact that therapists are extremely busy people who cannot always stop work they are doing in order to record information required by researchers and designers of tests. A happy compromise was reached eventually, enabling therapists to complete specially designed forms at the end of each rehabilitation session. Despite this arrangement, and the regular sessions of feedback and morale-boosting which were organised, the strains felt by all those taking part were so great that we settled for a figure of 80 rather than 100 patients. We were nevertheless pleased with our efforts, which produced between 30 and 55 hours of observation for each of the 80 patients, and a highly significant correlation of 0.75 between their memory lapses and their RBMT scores.

At the outset we had not anticipated how difficult it would be to gain the services of control subjects with below average ability. When searching for them it was amazing how few we could

find. It hardly seemed right to ask people if they were below
average ability before we tested them and our researchers were fear-
ful of receiving above average physical reactions had they attempted
to do so! Eventually we were able to test 118 control subjects
with a Mean I.Q. of 106 (range 68 - 136). We also tested 176 brain
damaged patients.

SUBJECTS

The patients were attending Rivermead Rehabilitation Centre
in Oxford. There were 113 men and 63 women, aged between 14 and 69
years. The sample comprised 60 head injured patients, 34 patients
who had sustained a left sided cerebral vascular accident, 42 who
had sustained a right CVA, 13 who had sub-arachnoid haemorrhage, and
27 others. The last group included patients who had cerebral
tumours removed, patients surviving carbon monoxide poisoning and
others with multiple sclerosis.

The scores of the control group were used to establish the
limits of normal performance on the test which, in turn, allowed us
to determine cut off points from individual components of the test.
Two scores were produced for each subtest, a simple pass/fail or
screening score and a standardised profile score, ranging in each
case from 0 to 2.

RELIABILITY

Inter-rater reliability was established by having 40
subjects scored separately but simultaneously by two raters. The
range of screening scores was 0 to 12 (standardised profile scores 0
to 24), indicating a range from severely impaired to normal
performance. Ten different raters, all of whom were psychologists or
students of psychology, took part in the inter-rater reliability
study. There was 100 per cent agreement between the raters for both
scoring procedures.

Parallel-form reliability was determined by giving two
versions of the test to 118 patients. All completed version A of
the test, approximately one third also completed version B, another
third completed version C, and the final third completed version D.
The order of presentation was randomised. Approximately half the
patients began with version A and the rest with the alternative
version. Correlations between performance on version A and on
version B, C and D on the Screening Score was 0.84, 0.80 and 0.67
respectively. On the standardised Profile Score the relevant
correlations were 0.86, 0.83 and 0.88 respectively. The change in
the apparent reliability of version D when scored in the 2 different
ways suggests a number of patients were narrowly failing to pass
items, leading to a somewhat lower screening score. This further
suggests that the finer grained Profile Score may give a somewhat
more reliable estimate of the patients memory capacities.
Considering data from all 118 patients who were tested twice, the
correlation between the two scores was 0.78 for the Screening Score
and 0.85 for the Profile Score.

WITHIN GROUP DIFFERENCES

The patient group was not, of course, homogenous: the
patients differed in age, sex, intelligence and aetiology. These

factors were confounded since the head injured patients tended to be predominantly young males while the stroke cases were typically older and showed a more balanced sex ratio. In the case of control subjects, however, we found no effect of age on RBMT performance across the age range of 16 to 70 years. A preliminary pilot study suggests that the test might be appropriate for children as young as 10 years. At the other end of the age range, subjects over the age of 70 years are increasingly likely to show decrement on the test, although some continue to score normally. The test contains 3 measures of prospective memory and these items appear to discriminate between 'young' elderly (up to 70 years) and 'old' elderly (71 to 90 years).

Neither patients nor controls showed any significant difference in performance as a function of sex, either for overall score or for performance on any of the subtests.

A total of 53 control subjects completed the Ravens Standard Progressive Matrices (Raven, 1960), and 68 completed the National Adult Reading Test (Nelson, 1982). The correlations between the RBMT and the Ravens Matrices was 0.21, and for the NART it was 0.27. This slight correlation accounts for about 10 per cent of the variance, primarily through the orientation and newspaper story recall components of the test.

In the case of patients, correlations with intelligence are higher (0.38 between RBMT and Ravens Matrices). This is to be expected in the patient sample since impairment in both intelligence and memory performance is likely to be greater the larger the lesion. Nevertheless, with a group of pure amnesics no significant correlations were found between the RBMT and intelligence (Wilson, 1987).

As far as aetiology was concerned there was a tendency for head injured patients to be more severely impaired and more variable than stroke patients. However, all the head injured patients had sustained particularly severe head injuries, and all had been in coma for at least 48 hours.

TRIUMPHS

Although the term 'triumph' may have some alliterative relevance in our title, we recognise of course that such a description has, in the case of a test, to be earned over a long period of time. Nevertheless, as far as our study is concerned, the RBMT has stood up to tests of reliability and validity; it also has the merit of being quick and easy to administer and interpret; it is acceptable to patients because of its good face-validity; and it is applicable to a wide range of settings. Norms for the elderly are currently being established, and we are about to embark upon a modified version for use with children. The RBMT is also being used in a number of research projects including studies of Alzheimer patients, people with epilepsy, patients undergoing heart sugery, patients with AIDS and the HIV virus, elderly stroke patients, patients with Parkinson's Disease and with Multiple Sclerosis.

REFERENCES

Nelson H.E. (1982) The National Adult Reading Test, NFER-Nelson, Windsor.

Raven J.C. (1960) Guide to the Standard Progressive Matrices Lewis and Co. London.

Sunderland, A., Haris, J.E. and Baddeley, A.D. (1984) 'Assessing Everyday Memory after Severe Head Injury', in Everyday Memory, Actions and Absentmindedness, (Eds. J.E. Harris and P. Morris). Academic Press, London.

Wilson, B.A., Cockburn, J. and Baddeley, A.D. (1985) The Rivermead Behavioural Memory Test Manual Thames Valley Test Co., 22 Bulmershe Rd., Reading, Berkshire.Berkshire.

Wilson B.A. (1987) Rehabilitation of Memory, Guilford Press, New York.

MEMORY DEFICIT IN DEPRESSION: THE ROLE OF RESPONSE STYLE

Fraser N. Watts
MRC Applied Psychology Unit,
Cambridge.

ABSTRACT

It has repeatedly been shown that depression is associated with poor memory performance, and it has been argued that this is due to cautious response strategies. However, a study of recognition memory is reported here that shows that performance on 'hits' is not explicable in terms of response criteria; on a signal detection analysis depression affects d' rather than β. A related explanation of depressives' poor free recall performance is in terms of poverty of verbal output. However, against this, evidence is presented here that reducing the amount of output required in a recall test does not affect the relative memory deficit of depressed patients.

There is now an accumulation of evidence that depression is associated with poor performance on tests of memory. However, it has been suggested that this is the result of response style, and does not represent a cognitive deficit. This paper will argue against such an interpretation.

The evidence that depressed patients perform poorly on tests of free recall will be summarised only briefly, as it is relatively uncontroversial and has been reviewed elsewhere (MacAlaistair, 1981; Johnson and Magaro, 1987). Within a sample of depressed patients, those who are most severely depressed perform least well on memory tests. There is also evidence from two kinds of controlled studies. Depressed patients perform less well on memory tests than non-depressed control subjects who are matched on intelligence or educational level. (Such matching is of course essential if group differences are to be attributed to depression). Also, depressed patients perform less well when ill than the same patients do when recovered. Such studies, though controlled, are only "quasi-experimental" as there is no direct manipulation of levels of depression. However, there is also evidence that depressed mood induced by direct experimental manipulation also results in poorer memory performance (e.g. Leight and Ellis, 1981; Ellis et al., 1984).

The view that the effects of depression on memory performance may be mediated, at least in part, by response style has been formulated recently by Johnson and Magaro (1987): '...Response bias has been demonstrated in depression such that a conservative

response bias may modulate performance and account for the apparent
memory deficit...It appears that depressed patients may have the
correct answer stored in memory but, because of an overly cautious
response strategy, may be unwilling to tell it to the experimenter.
This is not a thought disorder or deficient memory structure but
simply a decision to respond at a particular level of confidence.
The choice to respond conservatively may be due to the pathology
itself, that is, not wishing to display the confusion inherent in
the pathology' (p.32).

The argument to be presented here will be that, though
depressed patients sometimes respond conservatively in memory tests,
they do not invariably do so, and that their poor performance on
memory tests cannot be adequately explained in such terms. Evidence
suggesting that depression is often associated with a conservative
response style has come from studies both of recall and recognition,
and these will be considered in turn.

RECALL

Two studies of recall performance (Henry et al., 1973;
Whitehead, 1973) have shown that the errors associated with
depression are often those of omission. Thus, Whitehead found, in a
serial learning task, that depression was associated with an
increased rate of omission errors but a reduced rate of
transposition errors. This might be interpreted as showing that the
effects of depression on performance in recall tasks is due to
patients' poverty of output. Output might be limited because of
either poor motivation or lack of confidence.

Though it is probably correct that depressives tend to
produce less material in recall tests than is potentially accessible
to them, there is other evidence which indicates that their apparent
memory deficit cannot be explained in these terms. Leight and Ellis
(1981) used a 'forced recall' paradigm to clarify this point. Even
when subjects were **required** to respond, thus eliminating possible
differences between groups in the amount of output, depression was
still found to be associated with poorer recall performance.

Another way of investigating this follows from the
prediction that if the memory deficit in depression is due to
poverty of output the relative deficit should be greater with forms
of recall test that require relatively extensive verbal output.
Watts and Sharrock (1987) investigated this using a series of
different memory tests following a prose passage presented to
depressed patients and matched control subjects. Each subject
received two successive tests: a test of unaided free recall and a
cued recall test in which subjects were asked questions that could
generally be answered in one word or at most a short phrase. The
prediction was that, if verbal output was the basis of the apparent
memory deficit in depression, then the relative deficit would be
greater for free recall (which requires extensive output) than for
the cued recall test (which requires only restricted output.) In
fact, the cued recall test was found to differentiate groups very
slightly **better** than the free recall test, thus casting doubt on the
supposition that poverty of output is crucial to poor recall
performance in depression.

RECOGNITION

In studies of recognition, the hypothesised conservative response style of depressives would be expected to lead to reduced rates of both hits and false alarms, and to an effect on β on rather than d' when a signal detection analysis is performed. The two most satisfactory studies indicating that depressives show cautious response criteria are those of Miller and Lewis (1977) and Dunbar and Lishman (1984). (The Dunbar and Lishman study included both neutral and hedonically toned words, but it is the former that are of concern for the time being.) Both of these studies found that depression was associated with lower levels of both hits and false alarms. When signal detection analyses were carried out, both studies found that depressed subjects differed from controls in β but not d'. (The failure to find an effect of depression on d' in the Dunbar and Lishman study has to be interpreted cautiously as the controls did little better than chance, so the failure to find a difference between groups may have been due to a floor effect.) In contrast, another study (Silberman et al., 1983) found that depression affected hits but not false alarms. However, this must also be treated with caution, as there was no check that the depressed and control groups were matched on intelligence or educational level, so the group differences obtained may not have been due to depression at all. One further study (Larner, 1977) deserves mention because it is quoted by Johnson and Magaro (1987) as providing at least non-significant support for depression being associated with cautious response criteria. However, this appears to represent a misinterpretation of the study. In fact, the depressed subjects were more cautious than a group of dements, but showed no differences from controls (physically ill patients) on either discriminability or bias.

The two studies which have looked at the effects of depression on response criteria in the recognition of hedonically toned words have found somewhat conflicting results. Zuroff et al. (1983) found that depressive were less cautious with negative words but did not differ with positive words. Dunbar and Lishman (1984) found that depressives were more cautious with positive words but did not differ for negative words. One might reconcile these results by saying that depressives show a tendency to be relatively less cautious for negative than for positive words. However, this would be too easy a reconciliation, as Zuroff et al. did not carry out a test of the interaction between valence and groups and, as Martin and Clarke (1986) have argued, the fact that they also found a non-significant trend for depressives to be less cautious for positive words makes it highly unlikely that such an interaction term would have been significant.

My own recent work on recognition memory in depression (Watts, Morris & MacLeod, in press) indicates that whether depression is associated with reduced false alarms as well as reduced hits, and thus affects response bias in a signal detection analysis, may depend on the encoding procedure used. Studies of recognition memory in depression can easily find themselves short of statistical power for addressing satisfactorily the relevant questions. To guard against this, we used a relatively substantial (n = 36) group of quite severely depressed patients and compared them with normal controls matched on vocabulary scores. We also used three consecutive lists, each consisting of 20 concrete nouns, with recognition memory for each being tested before the next was presented. Two methods of presentation were used. Some subjects simply received visual presentations of words; others were required to vocalise the word as they saw it. We included the vocalisation condition partly to check that any memory deficit in depression held up even with a procedure that ensured at least a minimal level of attention to the word.

In both conditions, depressed subjects showed fewer hits than control subjects. (In the vocalisation condition the means for depressed and control groups were 43.8 and 48.1 respectively; in the silent condition they were 39.2 and 49.1 respectively.) In the silent condition we found that depression was also associated with reduced false alarms. (The means were 4.9 and 8.5 for depressed and control groups respectively). However, intriguingly, in the vocalisation condition, depression had the reverse effect on false alarms, with the depressed group now showing more (9.6 cf. 4.5). The analysis of the false alarms data showed a significant interaction between conditions and groups. When a signal detection analysis was applied to the data, d' showed a main effect of depression with no other terms approaching significance. In the analysis of β no terms at all approached significance.

In the light of this unexpected effect of presentation procedure on response bias, we went back to the earlier literature. Most studies such as Miller and Lewis (1977) and Dunbar and Lishman (1984) have not required any response from subjects at presentation. Our findings under the 'silent' condition parallelled theirs in that we found that depression was associated with a reduced rate of both hits and false alarms. However, hints can be found in other studies that requiring a response from subjects at presentation modifies this effect of depression on false alarms. Silberman et al. (1983) had required subjects to rate the emotionality of words, and found that depression reduced hits, but not false alarms. Zuroff et al. (1983) had used a self-description task at presentation, and found that depression was associated with increased false alarms (significantly for negative words, non-significantly for positive words).

One might suggest tentatively that the main effect of vocalisation in depressed subjects is on confidence. When depressives have vocalised words at presentation, they approach the recognition task with more confidence, using less conservative response criteria, and therefore show more false alarms. However, the effect of vocalisation in controls may be primarily on discriminability, with vocalisation simply reducing mistakes in the recognition task. Needless to say, this post-hoc interpretation of an unpredicted effect must be treated cautiously.

The important fact is that there are conditions under which depression is associated with a reduced level of hits without reduced false alarms. It would therefore be a mistaken to interpret the effect of depression on hits as being attributable in general to cautious response criteria. If reduced hits in depression were the result of cautious response criteria, it would be found   only where reduced false alarms were also found. In the overall analysis of the data from this study, depression had a highly significant effect on d' but no effect on β.

THE NATURE OF THE DEPRESSIVE MEMORY DEFICIT

In their review of the effects of mood on memory, Johnson and Magaro (1987) make another suggestion with which I am wholly in agreement, that depression is associated with reduced effort at encoding.   However, I am not altogether happy with their classification of this as a "non cognitive factor". It remains an open question whether reduced effort at encoding is the result of reduced cognitive capacity, motivational deficit, or whatever else.

An important aspect of this encoding deficit relates to the ability to impose structure and organisation on materials at presentation. There have been several studies (e.g. Weingartner et al., 1981) which have shown that depressives cluster words into categories at recall less than controls, which is interpretable as the consequence of a failure to structure material at encoding. However, it may be more fruitful to examine this hypothesised failure to structure materials at encoding in connection with prose. The well documented tendency for normal subjects to show selective good recall for the important units of a prose passage can be interpreted as the product of structuring the passage at encoding in such a way that it is apparent which are the important units.   My recent unpublished work on memory for prose shows that in depression this bias towards recall of important units does not occur.

We do not yet know how pervasive this phenomenon is in everyday life.   However, if depressives do not show the normal tendency to selectively recall important things, their memory deficit must be a much greater handicap to them in everyday life than might be thought from simply considering the shortfall in the amount of material that they recall.

Though depressives tend not to engage in effortful encoding as much as normals, they seem able to remedy this to some extent when trained to do so.   Watts, MacLeod & Morris (in press) found that requiring depressed patients to form visual images while encoding a passage of prose substantially improved their recall performance. It seems that imagery formation may be as helpful in depressives as it is in controls, but that depressed patients engage in it spontaneously less than controls do.

REFERENCES
Dunbar, G.C. and Lishman, W.A. (1984).   'Depression, recognition-memory and hedonic tone: A signal detection analysis', British Journal of Psychiatry, 114, 376-382.

Ellis, H., Thomas, R.L. and Rodrigez, I.A. (1984).   'Emotional mood states and memory: Elaborative encoding, semantic processing and cognitive effort', Journal of Experimental Psychology: Learning, Memory and Cognition, 10, 470-482.

Henry, G., Weingartner, H. & Murphy, D. (1973). 'Influence of affective states and psychoactive drugs on verbal learning and memory', American Journal of Psychiatry, 130, 966-971.

Johnson, M.H. and Magaro, P.A. (1987). 'Effects of mood and severity on memory processes in depression and mania', Psychological Bulletin, 101, 28-40.

Larner, S. (1977). 'Encoding in senile dementia and elderly depressives: A preliminary study', British Journal of Social and Clinical Psychology, 16, 379-390.

Leight, K.A. and Ellis, H.C. (1981). 'Emotional mood states, strategies and state-dependency in memory', Journal of Verbal Learning and Verbal Behavior, 20, 251-266.

Martin, M. and Clark, D.M. (1986). 'On the response bias explanation of selective memory effects in depression', Cognitive Therapy and Research, 10, 267-270.

McAllister, T.W. (1981). 'Cognitive functioning in the affective disorders', Comprehensive Psychiatry, 22, 572-586.

Miller, E. and Lewis, P. (1977). 'Recognition memory in elderly patients with depression and dementia', Journal of Abnormal Psychology, 86, 84-86.

Silberman, E.K., Weingartner, H., Laraia, M., Byrnes, S. and Post, R.M. (1983). 'Processing of emotional properties of stimuli by depressed and normal subjects', Journal of Nervous and Mental Diseases, 171, 10-14.

Watts, F.N., MacLeod, A.K. and Morris, L. (in press). 'A remedial strategy for memory and concentration problems in depressed patients, Cognitive Therapy and Research, in press.

Watts, F.N., Morris, L. and MacLeod, A.K. (in press). 'Recognition memory in depression', Journal of Abnormal Psychology, in press.

Watts, F.N. and Sharrock, R. (1987). 'Cued recall in depression', British Journal of Clinical Psychology, 26, in press.

Weingartner, H., Cohen, R.M., Murphy, D.L., Martello, J. and Gerdt, C. (1981). 'Cognitive processes in depression', Archives of General Psychiatry, 38, 42-47.

Whitehead, A. (1973). 'Verbal learning and memory in elderly depressives', British Journal of Psychiatry, 123, 203-208.

Zuroff, D.C., Colussy, S.A. and Wieglus, M.S. (1983). 'Selective memory and depression: A cautionary note concerning response bias', Cognitive Therapy and Research, 7, 223-232.

STROOP INTERFERENCE IN DEAF ADULTS AND CHILDREN USING SIGNED AND PRINTED STIMULI

Marc Marschark

University of North Carolina at Greensboro
Greensboro, North Carolina 27412, USA

ABSTRACT
        This study investigated the effects of Stroop interference in deaf individuals, using signed and printed stimuli. Experiment 1 involved color words and signs; Experiment 2 involved digits, number words, and number signs. Incongruent signed and printed stimuli consistently led to interference in reporting colors and quantities of stimulus elements; words created significantly more interference than signed stimuli. These problematic results suggest a novel interpretation of Stroop effects.

        For investigators interested in language and thought, deaf and hearing individuals who use sign language are an intriguing population. The extent to which they perform differently from hearing people and deaf people who use speech and lipreading (i.e., "oral" deaf) in cognitive and psycholinguistic tasks may clarify the role of language in cognitive processing. In an attempt to further understand the influence of sign language in cognitive processing of the deaf, the present study employed signed and printed versions of the Stroop task.
        "Stroop effects" refer to the interference in color naming created when the color is presented as the ink color of another color word (e.g., red ink that spells "BLUE"). Because Stroop effects reflect automaticity in semantic processing, the task has been useful in studying memory development (e.g., Rosinski et al., 1975) and bilingualism in the hearing (e.g., Chen & Ho, 1986; Magiste, 1984; Preston & Lambert, 1969) , and reading in the deaf (Allen, 1971; Leybaert et al., 1982, 1983).
        Allen (1971) examined Stroop effects in oral deaf children, finding that they showed less interference than hearing peers. She concluded that the deaf did not automatically process the "verbalness" of printed materials. Using alternative versions of the Stroop task to eliminate the need for verbal responding, however, Leybaert et al. (1982, 1983) found comparable interference effects in hearing and oral deaf children. Leybaert et al. (1983) further demonstrated that the magnitude of Stroop interference, in the standard paradigm, was directly related to the speaking abilities of her deaf subjects.
        The finding of automatic word recognition in oral deaf children may be encouraging, but many if not most deaf people rely on sign language rather than speech. In order to determine whether manually oriented deaf people also display automatic word and sign recognition abilities, sign language versions of the Stroop task were

developed for use with deaf children and adults.

EXPERIMENT 1

For the average deaf person, the usual Stroop paradigm would be an inter-lingual task, with ink colors of printed words being named in sign. An intra-lingual task for the deaf also was created here by presenting color-signs with hands painted in either congruent or incongruent colors. On the basis of previous findings with bilinguals (e.g., Fang et al., 1981), greater interference was expected with intra-language (sign-sign) than inter-language (print-sign) stimuli.

Method

Subjects. The subjects were 12 deaf adults and a 7-year-old deaf girl who insisted on being tested when the experimenter tested her mother. Although we intended to discard her data, they were retained because she performed perfectly on the task, and analyses showed that her inclusion did not change any of the results. All of the subjects were native-signers who were prelingually deaf and used sign language as their primary means of communication.

Materials and Procedure. The test colors were red, green, blue, yellow, black, brown, orange, and purple. Print stimuli were created using a 6.4 cm Gothic stencil to draw black outlines that were then colored in appropriately and photographed. Signed stimuli were created by painting the experimenter's hands with acrylic paints. For each color, she was photographed making each of the 8 test color signs, yielding 1 congruent and 7 incongruent stimulus pairings for each.

Each subject received 12 trial blocks: 4 baseline, 4 test, and 4 more baseline. The baseline tasks required signing (a) the identity of a color sign made bare-handed, (b) the color of a neutral "5-hand" (c) the identity of an uncolored color word, and (d) the color of a string of 5 filled X's. Each test block contained equal numbers of congruent (e.g., YELLOW made with a yellow hand) and incongruent (e.g., YELLOW made with a red hand) trials. Separate blocks required naming of either (a) signs, (b) hand colors, (c) words, or (d) word colors.

Subjects were tested individually by a fluent signer who used speech and sign in all interactions. Following practice trials, stimulus slides were projected onto a screen so that both the stimuli and subjects' signed responses could be recorded via a video camera, with a time generator superimposing elapsed time.

Results and Discussion

Response times were determined from the videotape. Mean response times across colors were calculated for each test block; baseline response times were the means of the pre- and post-test blocks of each type. Interference scores for each test type were obtained by subtracting the appropriate baseline mean from each test mean. The resulting scores were then analyzed using a 2 x 4 analysis of variance (the alpha level was set at .05 and response times below are noted in seconds).

Importantly, baseline response times to signs and words did not differ significantly, by a Wilcoxon signed-ranks test (.93 vs .84

respectively), suggesting that the subjects processed the two stimulus forms equally quickly. Nonetheless, interference from incongruent words (.50) was significantly larger than from incongruent signs (.37), leading to a main effect of congruence, $F(1,12)=7.53$, $MSe=.12$, and a congruence by dimension interaction, $F(3,36)=5.35$. (Similar results had been obtained in a pilot study using "live" presentations.)

Consistent with the Leybaert et al. (1982) findings with oral deaf children, the present results suggest that manual deaf individuals have relatively automatic access to the meanings of printed color words as well as to color signs. However, larger interference effects were obtained with inter-language (printed) than intra-language (signed) stimulus materials. This finding is interesting because it suggests that deaf, sign-English bilinguals may function differently from bilinguals with two vocal languages, but it is surprising because it suggests that signs may not be processed as automatically as words even when sign language is the primary mode of communication.

EXPERIMENT 2

This experiment extended the previous one in two ways. First, it included a younger age group. Rosinski et al. (1975) and Chen and Ho (1986) demonstrated that Stroop interference from words decreases with age, occurring in hearing children as early as second grade. Eleven- to 12-year-old deaf students were involved here, as they were the youngest deaf group available that could read well enough (at a second to third grade level) for this task. Second, this experiment involved number rather than color stimuli. Shor (1971) and Windes (1968) have demonstrated interference effects in reporting the numbers of digits or digit words in arrays when they conflict with stimulus identities. Greater interference with printed than signed stimuli here would rule out the possibility that the results of Experiment 1 were due to some peculiarity of color stimuli. This paradigm also provided the opportunity to examine Stroop interference with stimuli that are familiar but not language specific (i.e., digits).

Method

Subjects. Sixteen subjects were drawn from two residential schools for the deaf, both using bimodal language training. A younger group included 9 students ranging in age from 11;4 to 12;5 (mean=11;7). The older age group included 7 students from 14;5 to 16;4 (mean=15;4). Two of the subjects had moderate-to-severe hearing losses and the rest severe-to-profound losses. The ages at which hearing losses occurred were not known (but reported as "early") for 3 subjects; all others were prelingually deaf except for a single subject who became deaf at age 2.

Materials and Procedure. The stimulus slides included the numbers 1, 2, 3, and 4 presented as numerals, lowercase printed words, or signs (e.g., 3 "three"'s, 2 4-hands, or 4 "2"'s). Arrays of number signs (#, ##, ###, and ####) were constructed to serve as baseline trials in numerosity judgments. Arrays of signs were prepared by photocopying line drawings of 1-, 2-, 3-, and 4-hands. The other arrays were prepared using rub-on letters.

Procedure. The procedure was the same as in Experiment 1, except that subjects were asked to identify either "what number" was shown on a slide, ignoring how many there were, or to identify "how many" were shown on a slide, ignoring what they were.

Results and Discussion

Mean test trial, baseline, and interference times were calculated as before, using mean responses to pound sign arrays as the baseline scores for numerosity trials and responses to single stimulus arrays (e.g., one "3" or one 4-hand) as the baseline scores for identity-naming trials. Baseline response times to signs, printed words, and digits did not differ, by Wilcoxon signed-ranks tests. Signs produced slightly longer response times than digits, however, suggesting that subjects were not simply subitizing (i.e., recognizing small quantities without counting) fingers in the signs, but were processing them as symbolic stimuli.

The interference times for the complete design were analyzed using a 2 (age) x 2 (congruence) x 6 (response dimension) analysis of variance. Overall, the 11-year-olds showed more interference than the 16-year-olds (.60 vs .18), $F(1,14)=8.95$, MSe=.91, incongruent pairings created more interference than congruent ones (.61 vs .20), $F(1,14)=8.33$, MSe=1.13, and interference varied with response dimension for both age groups, $F(5,70)=2.24$, MSe=.72. Both printed (incongruent) digit words (.85) and number signs (.75) created significantly more interference in numerosity reports than did digits (.25), whereas the difference between word and sign interference was marginally significant ($p<.07$).

As with color stimuli in Experiment 1, the results here indicate that printed and signed number names are relatively automatically processed in deaf individuals and can interfere with ongoing judgments of numerosity. Number signs (like color signs) created less interference than number (or color) words for deaf children, while digits created little interference. Consistent with the Rosinski et al. (1975) and Chen and Ho (1986) studies, interference effects here declined significantly with age and did not interact with material type.

SUMMARY AND CONCLUSIONS

The present experiments demonstrate Stroop-like interference with deaf individuals, using both color stimuli and number stimuli. Perhaps most importantly, significantly greater interference was observed with printed than with signed stimuli. Because the response mode was the same in both cases, interpretations of this finding based on response stage effects are ruled out. Thus, the interpretation of these findings demanded by traditional accounts of Stroop interference would be that deaf individuals find it harder to ignore printed words than signs (cf. Leybaert et al., 1983).

There is, however, another possible explanation consistent with all of the present results. Suppose that both words and signs automatically activate their meanings in memory, and that signs do so faster than words. Faster "decoding" (Preston & Lambert, 1969) of signs than words, as indicated by the fact that baseline response times to signs were as fast or faster than to words, would create larger interference effects to print than sign, as evidenced here.

From this view, the small interference effects created by digits in Experiment 2 would then be interpretable as due to their extremely rapid decoding. Otherwise, one would have to conclude that digits are not automatically processed. Given the highly overlearned nature of digits and the interference effects demonstrated by Shor (1971) and Windes (1968), this latter conclusion seems dubious.

Clearly, this alternative explanation of relative differences in Stroop interference effects remains to be explicitly tested. At the very least, however, the present results demonstrate both some interesting differences between deaf and hearing individuals and some intriguing consequences of examining the language and cognitive abilities of deaf individuals.

ACKNOWLEDGEMENTS

This research was supported by grant RO1-NS20064 from the National Institute for Neurological and Communication Disorders and Stroke and a grant from the Research Council of UNC-Greensboro. Special thanks are due to Trish Dempsey for conducting this research, Tom Trabasso for suggesting the hand-painting methodology, and, most importantly, the students and administrations of the Central North Carolina School for the Deaf (Greensboro) and the North Carolina School for the Deaf (Morganton).

REFERENCES

Allen, D.V. (1971). 'Color-word interference in deaf and hearing children', Psychonomic Science, 24, 295-296.

Chen, H.-C. and Ho, C. (1986). 'Development of Stroop interference in Chinese-English bilinguals', Journal of Experimental Psychology: Learning, Memory, and Cognition, 12, 397-401.

Fang, S.-P., Tzeng, O.J.L. and Alva, L. (1981). 'Intralanguage and interlanguage Stroop effects in two types of writing systems', Memory and Cognition, 9, 609-617.

Leybaert, J., Alegria, J. and Morais, J. (1982). 'On automatic reading processes in the deaf', Cahiers de Psychologie Cognitive, 2, 185-192.

Leybaert, J., Alegria, J. and Fonck, E. (1983). 'Automaticity in word recognition and in word naming by the deaf', Cahiers de Psychologie Cognitive, 3, 255-272.

Magiste, E. (1984). 'Stroop tasks and dichotic translation: The development of interference patterns in bilinguals', Journal of Experimental Psychology: Learning, Memory, and Cognition, 10, 304-315.

Preston, M.S. and Lambert, W. E. (1969). 'Interlingual interference in a bilingual version of the Stroop color-word task', Journal of Verbal Learning and Verbal Behavior, 8, 295-301.

Rosinski, R.R., Golinkoff, R.M. and Kukish, K.S. (1975). 'Automatic semantic processing in a picture-word interference task', Child Development, 46, 247-253.

Shor, R. E. (1971). 'Symbol processing speed differences and symbol interference effects in a variety of concept domains', The Journal of General Psychology, 85, 187-205.

Windes, J. D. (1968). 'Reaction time for numerical coding and naming of numerals', Journal of Experimental Psychology, 78, 318-322.

MEMORY IN MENTALLY RETARDED 'IDIOTS SAVANTS'

Michael J. A. Howe
Department of Psychology,
University of Exeter, England

ABSTRACT

Mentally handicapped 'idiots savants' are sometimes remarkably successful at remembering: most of their feats make heavy demands on memory. However, their memory systems are not fundamentally extraordinary. Their feats are caused by largely the same factors as the ones responsible for good memory performance in normal people. Idiots savants' memory achievements are related to the particular interests and needs of each individual. In some circumstances, information is more likely to be recalled by a mentally retarded person than by someone of normal intelligence.

INTRODUCTION

Most of the reported feats of the mentally handicapped individuals who by virtue of their ability to perform certain tasks with an exceptionally high level of expertise have been called 'idiots savants', make heavy demands on memory. Some of the feats are essentially ones of memory as such. The different kinds of information which idiots savants have taken it upon themselves to remember are numerous and diverse: they include telephone numbers, licence numbers, zip codes, area codes, engine numbers, birthdays, timetables, addresses, many types of population statistics, road maps, menus, weather reports, news items, astronomical information, film scripts, street sequences, word-by-word records of conversations, station names on railway routes, and many other things besides. The information may be highly specific and apparently unrelated to any of the individual's other interests. For example, there exists a report of an autistic child who knew the names in English and Latin of 18 varieties of deer, but could recognize none of these animals and had no knowledge at all of Latin as a language.

Extraordinary accomplishments of remembering are also involved in the majority of those idiot savant feats that are not, strictly speaking, ones of memory as such. For instance, feats of mental arithmetic depend heavily on an ability to recall data, as do the calendar date skills which have been described in a substantial number of reports (see, e.g., Hill, 1978; Smith and Howe, 1985).

The memory feats of mentally retarded idiots savants raise a number of interesting questions. Some of them are particularly relevant to the issue of how it is that individuals who are so lacking in ability in other areas are able to perform very

impressively at certain particular mental skills. Others are more
relevant to broader questions about the nature and explanation of
extraordinary feats of human memory.

ARE THERE FUNDAMENTAL DIFFERENCES IN REMEMBERING?

The first question I shall look into is that of whether or
not those idiots savants who display remarkable feats of memory
possess memory systems that are in some fundamental way special.
Afterwards, I shall look at some more detailed questions and
suggestions about the causes of exceptional remembering in these
individuals.

With the possible exception of a few rare cases, the memory
skills of mentally retarded savants appear to operate along
principles that are not very different from the ones underlying
memory skills in people of normal intelligence. When the memory
abilities of retarded savants have been measured by standard mental
tests, scores have tended to be somewhat higher than those on items
assessing other abilities, but not greatly so, and lower than the
scores of normally intelligent individuals. Fairly typical is the
case of a seven-year-old mentally retarded boy described by Goodman
(1972) who could give the name and the closest neighbour of most
American states and many foreign countries, and could also recite
large numbers of telephone numbers, addresses, and various lists of
detailed information. His IQ was 37, his mental age two-and-a-half
years, and his memory test performance that of an average four-year-
old.

But there are a few reported cases of individuals who seem
to have been able to reproduce large bodies of data to which they
have been only briefly exposed. Typically, these individuals have
been described as being autistic or psychotic. For instance, a six-
year-old girl described by Cain (1969) was autistic, would never
look at other people, lacked language, was passive and apparently
aimless, but would repeat verbatim lengthy conversations or radio
or television dialogues, even ones heard years before, and could
read and correct other people's misspellings of long words that she
had seen only once and were beyond her understanding. A case like
this one lends some support to the view that a very few remarkable
individuals possess what we might call 'photographic' memory
capacities, possibly having something in common with the less rare
capacity for some children to experience 'eidetic' memory images.
But too much of the evidence is anecdotal and second-hand. For
example, one author (Viscott, 1970) gives a fascinating account of a
woman who, after her father had read her the first three pages of
the Boston telephone directory could give any number from these
pages on request, over a period of several years. The account may
well be true, but we ought to be aware that all we have to go on is
the author's description of an account by the woman's elderly father
of events that are said to have occurred more than thirty years
before they were written down.

The levels-of-processing literature and a large body of
evidence about remembering in children and adults have alerted us to
the fact that a person's lack of awareness about memory tasks
demands need not seriously restrict what is actually recalled.

Consequently, many ordinary people can remember lots of popular songs, or information about soap-opera characters or football teams, without ever deliberately 'studying' these topics. What is vital is that the attention of an individual is engaged, and in retarded savants it sometimes is for hours at a stretch. The interests of these people are often very different from those or ordinary individuals. For instance, a person who does calendar calculations may be preoccupied with calendar dates for much of his waking time. Certainly, because the interests of retarded savants are so very different from those of other people, savants are often extraordinary in the kinds of information they remember. But that is different from being unusual in the way in which they remember things.

Having said this, I should point out that it is not true that retarded savants never study things or never make a deliberate effort to remember. Sometimes they do. My point is simply that these actions are not essential. A person who is unable to engage in them is not rendered unable to remember.

THE IMPORTANCE OF INDIVIDUALS' INTERESTS

Like everyone else, mentally retarded savants are especially good at recalling information from an area of knowledge that is already highly familiar. Accordingly, memory feats usually occur within a person's areas of particular interest. One reason why retarded savants sometimes recall items that other people rarely remember is that savants can be extremely interested in things that others find boring.

The likelihood of you or I finding something sufficiently interesting to keep our attention largely depends upon whether or not we have the opportunity to turn our minds to matters that seem more interesting. Because of this, we do not choose shops or theatres as places to study in: there are too many interesting distractions. And an intelligent individual who starts to think about a topic as narrow as, say, calendar dates will probably begin to make associations that direct his thoughts to more interesting matters. Consequently, so far as attending to details is concerned, having a sparsely furnished mind may have some real advantages.

REMEMBERING AS AN AVOIDANCE DEVICE

Another reason for giving prolonged attention to events and information that most people would find boring is that concentrating on inanimate things can be a way to avoid painful situations or frightening thoughts. Someone who finds it difficult to get on with other people may find that the private nature of the mental activities that lead to details being memorized may provide a welcome relief from stress.

Memory tasks can usually be done in complete isolation. Most retarded savants are essentially self-taught: even the limited amount of social contact that is necessary for a skill to be taught to a retarded person can form a barrier to progress. The memory-dependent skills of calendar calculating and arithmetic ("lightning") calculating are both ones that that substantial numbers of retarded savants have learned with little or no assistance from other people.

As it happens, most of the non-retarded people who have been
highly successful at mental calculating have also taught themselves.
It has been suggested that arithmetic is "the most independent and
self-sufficient of all the sciences" (Brill, 1940). To a
considerable extent you can do it on your own, without instruments
or apparatus, or face-to-face tuition. In this respect it contrasts
with language skills, especially reading. I sometimes read
biographical accounts of people's early lives. When I am trying to
get an idea of the reliability of a particular biographical
account, something which always makes me smell a rat is the
statement "She taught herself to read". No-one can teach herself to
read. Think about it. Learning to read depends to a marked degree on
having both the opportunity and the willingness to interact.

For a small number of retarded savants, a reason for
specializing in memory tasks is that concentrating one's energies in
the direction of a particular narrow interest can serve to keep
threatening thoughts and anxieties out of mind. By directing all
one's attention to calendar dates, for example, a person may be able
to block out certain unbearable ideas.   Special abilities
sometimes seem to originate in what one author has called "desperate
need states" in children (Cain, 1969). For example, one child who
eventually gained remarkable calendar calculating skills was first
observed to be poring through calendars at a time when he had just
been separated from his mother. Another individual's interest in
dates and arithmetic began at a time when his therapist's absence on
holiday led to preoccupation with the time of return, and in his
geographical location while on holiday.

THE REWARDS FOR HAVING MEMORY SKILLS

Despite the fact that retarded savants often dislike the
kinds of activities that involve mixing with other people, savants
often seem to welcome the approval which their special skills gain
for them. The feats can bring social rewards without incurring the
social costs involved in working with others. Having a special
talent may be as a safe way to maintain social relationships with
significant other people.

One reason why some retarded savants devote enormous amounts
of time and attention to seemingly boring tasks may be that success
at the tasks and the encouragement they receive may be particularly
rewarding for them. Rewards which would not satisfy most people may
have a very powerful effect on a mentally handicapped individual.
And having a special competence may give a person a way to express
individuality and get recognition. In common with others, mentally
handicapped people enjoy succeeding at something, yet there are
limits on the kinds of success they can achieve. Specializing can
make sense for someone whose abilities are very limited, maximizing
the likelihood of one's gaining a degree of competence at something,
and enjoying the consequences.

CAN MEMORY SKILLS CONTRIBUTE TO RETARDATION?

For one reason or another mentally retarded individuals may become more "channelled" or "canalized" in their interests than normal people. One possibility is that is that a young child's development may be affected by certain reactions of other people to the extent that the child is pressed towards repetitive or stereotyped behaviours, benefitting some specialized abilities to the detriment of other needed competences. It can be hard to sort out cause and effect, as for instance in the case of a patient who, as Forrest (1969) reported, tried to structure his environment and avoid his sensations of loosing control by gathering 16 clocks around himself and spending virtually all his time typing.

CAN MEMORY FEATS BE EASIER FOR MENTALLY RETARDED PEOPLE?

I have already mentioned that in some circumstances individuals who are mentally handicapped my be spared some of the distractions that might prevent an intelligent person from concentrating on a very narrow task. A person's absence of symbolic skills may facilitate concentration of surface features and physical attributes. An intelligent person would be less likely to recall these details, because attention would be directed to meanings of things. It follows that people of low ability are especially likely to recall certain kinds of information. Moreover, in some tasks the possession of certain kinds of knowledge can impede performance in one way or another (e.g., Ceci & Howe, 1978), giving an advantage to learners who are young or ill-informed.

Of course, normal people also can gain some relief from competing thoughts and ideas by deliberately shutting themselves off from information that competes. It is said that the well-known early jazz musician "Blind Lemon" attributed his talent to his blindness and that the New York street musician "Moon Dog" blinded himself to escape from being distracted by visual things. (Lindsley, 1965). How strange are the ways of our species!

In conclusion, there is nothing miraculous about the fact that some mentally handicapped individuals are successful at tasks that depend upon the retention of large amounts of information. For each individual, what is remembered is largely determined by the person's knowledge, interests, and mental activities.

REFERENCES

Brill, A.A. (1940). 'Some peculiar manifestations of memory with special reference to lightning calculators', Journal of Nervous and Mental Diseases, 92, 709-726.

Cain, A.C. (1969). 'Special "isolated" abilities in severely psychotic young children', Psychiatry, 32, 137-147.

Ceci, S.J. and Howe, M.J.A. (1978). 'Semantic knowledge as a determinant of developmental differences in recall', Jorunal of Experimental Child Psychology, 26, 230-235.

Forrest, D.V. (1969). 'New words and neologisms: with a thesaurus of coinages by a schizophrenic savant', Psychiatry, 32, 44-73.

Goodman, J. (1982). 'A case study of an "autistic-savant": mental function in the psychotic child with markedly discrepant abilities', Journal of Child Psychology and Psychiatry, 13, 267-278.

Hill, A.L. (1978). Savants: mentally retarded individuals with special skills', in International Review of Research in Mental Retardation, Volume Nine (Ed. N.R. Ellis), pp. 277-298, Academic Press, New York.

Lindsley, O.R. (1965). 'Can deficiency produce specific superiority - the challenge of the idiot savant', Exceptional Children, 31, 225-232.

Smith, J. and Howe, M.J.A. (1985). 'An investigation of calendar-calculating skills in an "idiot savant"', International Journal of Rehabilitation Research, 8, 77-79.

CHILDREN'S MEMORY

PEER TUTORING AND CHILDREN'S MEMORY

H.C.Foot, R.H.Shute and M.J.Morgan.
Department of Applied Psychology, University of Wales
Institute of Science and Technology, Cardiff, Wales.

ABSTRACT
        Children's memory was explored in peer tutoring dyads.
Tutee participation during tutoring was predicted to influence
memory : specifically,   active participation would   promote
efficiency in a task involving the application of remembered
principles but   not memory for specific items.   An animal
classification task was used in which age of children and amount of
tutor-tutee participation were varied in same- and cross-age
tutoring pairs. Results from a series of memory tests confirm
active participation as a crucial variable, but no differences
attributable to participation were found between memory for items
and the application of remembered principles.

        The need to distinguish between memorizing specific items
of information and developing principles to be applied in other
learning tasks has been recognized in the practical training
literature.   Downs   and   Perry (1986),   for   example,   have
distinguished between ways of memorizing material which must be
recalled without distortion and ways of learning that lead to
understanding of a concept or principle which can be generalized to
other situations.   According to Downs and Perry aids to memory
involve association, rehearsal, forming mnemonics and self-testing;
aids to understanding involve comparing, contrasting and problem
solving.
        This   precise   distinction   between   memorization and
understanding has not been highlighted in the literature on
children's memory, although considerable attention has been paid to
developmental changes in metamemory which involves children's
understanding of the appropriate uses of particular memory
strategies for different situations (Flavell and Wellman, 1977;
Kail, 1979).
        The study (see Footnote) to be reported examines memory for
items of information and memory for principles to be generalized in
the context of a peer tutoring situation.   Peer tutoring has
received increasing attention as a means of enhancing children's
learning efficiency on the part of both the tutor and tutee (Allen,
1976, Cohen, Kulik & Kulik, 1982). One of the acclaimed reasons
for its success is the developmental similarity between teacher and
learner : the child enacting the role of teacher is better able
than an adult or older child to adopt the perspective of the
learner and is therefore more likely to appreciate the difficulties
that the learner may experience (cf. Allen, 1976). However this

argument has not been supported by findings that children tutored by adults perform better than those tutored by other children of the same or similar age (Ellis & Rogoff, 1982; Shute, Foot & Morgan, 1988). A crucial factor seems to be the extent to which the tutee participates in the task, the more efficient learners being those who participate most. Involving the tutee actively in the learning task appears to be the hallmark of the adult tutor's teaching style.

From the results of Shute, Foot and Morgan, however, there is some suggestion that the effectiveness of tutee participation is dependent upon the type of task. Whether with an adult or child tutor, tutees who participate most are relatively more efficient in a task involving the application of remembered principles than in a task involving memory of specific items. Indeed the data suggest that, with adult or older child tutors, greater tutee participation has a deleterious effect on memory for specific items.

The present study was designed to examine the learning efficiency of children in same- and cross-age tutoring dyads, when the amount of tutor and tutee participation in the learning task was manipulated. Specifically it was hypothesized that tutees in passive tutor dyads (i.e. where the tutees themselves participate more in the learning task) would be more efficient in applying remembered principles to new material, whilst tutees in active tutor dyads (i.e. where the tutees themselves participate less in the learning task) would be more efficient in memorizing specific pieces of information. These hypotheses are based upon the premise that understanding and applying principles require more active learning strategies and more 'cognitive work' on the part of the tutee than memory for specific pieces of information. Same- and cross-age dyads were used to explore developmental differences because, as mentioned, previous research had suggested that older child tutors elicited poorer memory for specific pieces of information.

In addition to the memory tests for information and for generalizing principles a third test was included which tapped children's use of resources over and above their ability to generalize what they had learned. Tutees who are more actively involved in using available resources during tutoring might be expected to use these resources more efficiently when tested.

METHOD

Subjects

Eighty-four boys and girls were selected at random and with parental permission from four classes in a Cardiff Junior School : there were forty-two ten-year-olds (mean age: 10.9, range : 10.3 - 11.2) and forty-two eight-year-olds (mean age : 8.8, range 8.3 - 9.2).

Design

Children were assigned at random to forty-two tutoring pairs in a 3 (age pairings) x 2 (tutor role) factorial design. The three age pairings were : ten-year-old tutor with ten-year-old tutee, ten-year-old tutor with eight-year-old tutee, and eight-year-old tutor with eight-year-old tutee. Tutor roles were 'active' or 'passive'. 'Active' was defined by the tutor demonstrating and performing the task while the tutee watched; 'passive' was defined by the tutor explaining the requirements of the task, leaving the tutee to perform it. Reciprocally therefore, active tutors had passive tutees and passive tutors had active tutees.

Task

The task involved the sorting of four items of information about each of six pictured animals which then had to be classified by reference to a chart. The six animals were : mouse, seal (mammals), kiwi (bird), cobra (reptile), newt (amphibian) and moray (fish). An extra mammal was used to avoid a simple elimination process operating in the categorization of the last animal. The items of information about each animal concerned skin-type, breathing, (air or water), blood (warm or cold) and milk production. These items were presented on cards to be placed in a 2 x 2 grid within each of six boards, one for each animal. The classification of the animals was achieved by scrutinizing the items of information in conjunction with a chart which related these animals to the five animal categories : thus, a seal must be a mammal because it breathes air, is warm-blooded, is covered with fur and feeds its young on milk. Decisions about each animal's classification were to be written on a slip of paper provided.

Procedure

The tutoring sessions took place in a laboratory (specially equipped caravan) towed to the school. The laboratory consisted of a children's playroom and a recording room fitted with video-equipment.

The children were familiarized with the laboratory through initial visits in small groups. All volunteered to return for the tutoring sessions which were video-taped.

Initial training of the tutors was conducted individually and each tutor was instructed how the cards were to be laid out one by one on the board, grouped by animal, and how the chart was to be used. This training by the Experimenter (RS) was undertaken with three of the six animals by sorting twenty-four cards into their appropriate positions on the board. Tutors in the group allocated to the active role were instructed to manipulate cards themselves and demonstrate the whole task to the tutee; tutors in the group allocated to the passive role were instructed to allow the tutees to manipulate the cards and place them on the boards themselves.

After tutoring both tutors and tutees had a series of three tests to perform involving memory of the material already seen; generalization of principles learned to new material and use of the chart.

Test 1 (memory). The children were tested for memory of the materials which they had already seen. Eighteen questions, three per animal, tapped their retention of specific information items and the classification of each animal.

Test 2 (generalization). The children were then given pictures of eighteen animals not seen before and were asked to classify each on the basis of a single piece of information: for example, an armadillo has warm blood: is it a mammal, reptile, amphibian or fish? (four choices in each case).

Test 3 (generalization plus chart use). Test 2 was repeated and children were encouraged to use the chart to assist their decisions.

All tests were scored out of eighteen.

Coding of Video-tapes

It was clear from the video-tapes that the tutors had not necessarily followed the Experimenter's instructions concerning their tutoring role: some tutors given active roles relinquished the cards to their tutees to sort, and some given passive roles kept the cards to sort themselves.

Two pairs of coders assessed the degree of tutor participation by noting the frequency with which tutors referred to the chart and the frequency with which tutors decided where to place each card. An integrated 'participation' rate was devised by averaging the percentages of chart use and decision-making by each tutor relative to his or her tutee. Previous research (Shute, Foot & Morgan, 1988) has established chart use and decision making as intercorrelated and as indicative of participation in this kind of classification task. Within each age group a median split was undertaken such that the tutors above the median (with high participation rates) were redesignated as active and those below the median (with low participation rates) were redesignated as passive. Overall tutor participation rates were 71.5% in the active role and 39.9% in the passive role.

RESULTS

Tutors' and tutees' test scores were analyzed separately.

Tutees' Test Scores

A three-way ANOVA was conducted on the tutees' test results: age pairings (3), tutor role (2) and test (3). All three main effects were significant. Ten-year-old tutees scored significantly higher across all three tests (M = 14.4, sd = 3.0) than the eight-year-olds tutored by ten-year-olds (M = 10.8, sd = 3.7) or than the eight-year-olds tutored by eight-year-olds (M = 10.2, sd = 3.3) (F= 12.64; df = 2,36; p<.001). The latter two groups did not differ significantly from each other indicating that the age of the tutor did not affect the performance of the eight-year-old tutees.

Tutor role also had a significant impact upon the overall test performance of the tutees, passive tutors eliciting higher scores from active tutees (M = 12.6 sd = 3.3) than active tutors from passive tutees (M = 10.9, sd = 3.4) (F = 4.89; df = 1,36; p<.05).

Test scores differed significantly (F = 16.71; df = 2,72; p<.001), generalization to the new material (Test 2 : M = 10.2, sd = 3.6) being lower than either the memory test (Test 1: M = 12.8 sd = 1.5) or the generalization test with chart use (Test 3 : M = 12.4, sd = 4.2). None of the interactions was significant.

Tutors' Test Scores

A similar analysis was undertaken of the tutors' test scores. There were no significant differences between different aged tutors, the eight-year-old tutors performing almost as well (M

= 11.8, sd = 4.2) as the ten-year-old tutors with eight-year-old
tutees (M = 12.9, sd = 3.6) or with ten-year-old tutees (M = 12.7,
sd = 3.30). Active tutors (M = 12.3, sd = 3.7) scored no more
highly than passive tutors (M = 12.6, sd = 3.8). Tests discriminated
significantly, the generalization test (Test 2) proved more
difficult (M = 10.8, sd = 4.0) than either the memory test (Test 1:
M = 13.5, sd = 2.9) or the generalization test with chart use (Test
3: M = 13.1, sd = 3.6) (F = 17.08, df = 2,72; p<.001). The age x
test interaction was significant (F = 2.77; df = 4,72; p<.05),
indicating mainly that, whereas the ten-year-old tutors made
considerable use of the chart in Test 3 to improve their scores,
the eight-year-old tutors did not. (see Table 1).

Table 1 : Tutor Mean scores : Table for Age of Tutor x Tests

Interaction

Age	1		2		3	
(Ttr) (Tte)	mean	sd	mean	sd	mean	sd
Ten-Ten	14.4	2.9	10.4	3.9	13.5	3.2
Ten-Eight	13.7	1.9	10.8	4.5	14.3	3.1
Eight-Eight	12.6	3.5	11.4	4.5	11.5	5.1

DISCUSSION
        Focussing upon tutee performance an expected developmental
difference emerged across all tests indicating that ten-year-old
tutees performed better than eight-year-old tutees whether tutored
by ten- or eight-year-olds. Similarly a clear difference in test
difficulty emerged across age groups with the generalization test
(Test 2) proving considerably more difficult than either the memory
test (Test 1) or generalization test with chart use (Test 3). This
pattern was reflected at each age level of tutoring pairs as
evidenced by the absence of any age x test interaction effect.
        Tutor role had a significant impact upon tutees' scores
lending support to the overall assumption that tutees' efficiency
is influenced by the extent to which they participate in the
learning task. Of course there is always a possibility that the
more able tutors were the more active participators and that tutee
performance was therefore dependent upon tutor ability. However,
from data collected elsewhere (c.f. Shute, Foot and Morgan, 1988),
children's ability, as measured by scholastic achievement in
English and Maths, is not related to participation rates in a
similar animal classification task (r=.02, ns). It is possible
that participation rates reflect more enduring personality
characteristics of dominance.
        Contrary to expectation tutor role did not interact
significantly with tests; therefore there was no evidence that
tutees who showed high participation during tutoring were any more
efficient at the generalization test (Test 2), or at using the
chart (Test 3), than at the memory test. The effects of tutee
participation were not influenced by same-age or cross-age
pairings.
        There is no reason to suppose that the predicted effects of
participation for the tutors would be any different from those for

the tutees. There were no significant age effects on tutor test performance although the eight-year-old tutors scored marginally lower than the ten-year-old tutors. Neither did tutor role affect scores across the three tests. Possibly tutor participation did not have the same impact upon tutors' performance as upon tutees' performance because tutors were still required to explain the task to their tutees and therefore had to be somewhat 'active' even in the passive role. In contrast tutees in the tutor active condition could be completely passive.

Tutors' scores differed significantly over tests and showed a similar trend to those of the tutees, Test 2 proving more difficult than Tests 1 and 3. Again tutor role did not interact with tests. A significant interaction was obtained, however, for age x tests (see Table 1). Two factors contributed to this interaction : firstly, the better performance of the eight-year-old tutors on the most difficult test (Test 2) relative to the ten-year-old tutors and in contrast with their much poorer performance on Tests 1 & 3 relative to the ten-year-old tutors; secondly, the eight-year-old tutors made no effective use of the chart as an additional resource to assist their performance on Test 3, whereas the ten-year-old tutors did. This is difficult to explain except as a cognitive maturational effect : perhaps the eight-year-old tutors did not appreciate the significance of the chart as a resource for helping their performance; possibly they thought that reference to it was in some sense cheating or an admission of their failure as tutors. (It is worth noting that the eight-year-old tutees made more efficient use of the chart to improve their performance on Test 3). It is also possible that their better score on Test 2 may reflect an increased effort to commit the principles to memory thus dispensing with the need to use the chart on Test 3.

Presumably the older tutors were more aware of the potential use of the chart and relied more heavily upon it, which explains their relatively poorer performance on Test 2 and their much improved performance on Test 3.

In conclusion, the amount of participation in the learning task was found to influence memory test scores of tutees but the expected differences on type of memory task did not occur. Participation was equally effective for facilitating memory of specific items of information and for applying learned principles.

Footnote : This research was conducted as part of a programme of work on children's understanding of misunderstanding, sponsored by the ESRC (Grant Ref : C00232235)

REFERENCES

Allen, V.L. (Ed). (1976). Children as Teachers : Theory and Research on Tutoring, Academic Press, New York.

Cohen, P.A., Kulik, J.A. and Kulik C.C. (1982). 'Educational outcomes of tutoring : a meta analysis of findings'. American Educational Research Journal, 19, 237-248.

Downs, S., and Perry, P. (1986). Can trainers learn to take a back seat ? Personnel Management, 42-45, (March).

Ellis, S. and Rogoff, B. (1982). The strategies and efficacy of child versus adult teachers. Child Development, 53, 730-735.

Flavell, J.H. and Wellman, H.M. (1977). Metamemory, in Perspectives on the Development of Memory and Cognition (Eds. R.V. Kail and J.W. Hagen), Lawerence Erlbaum, New Jersey.

Kail, R. (1979). The Development of Memory in Children. Freeman, San Francisco.

Shute, R., Foot, H and Morgan, M. (1988). 'Tutoring styles of adults, eleven- and nine-year-olds with nine-year-old tutees'. Submitted for publication.

CROSS-MODAL INTEGRATION IN CHILDREN'S MEMORY

S. Murray
Applied Psychology, University of Wales Institute of
Science and Technology, Cardiff, Wales.

ABSTRACT

What do children remember when they are presented with an illustrated story? Do they retain separate, modality-specific memories of the text and the pictures, or do they pool information from both sources to construct an amodal memory of the event as a whole? An experiment is reported which probes children's memory for an illustrated story immediately after its presentation, three days later or seven days later. The results suggest that children retain both modality-specific and amodal memories but as time passes they rely increasingly on the more general, amodal memories.

INTRODUCTION

Many of the texts children encounter during their pre-school and primary-school years are lavishly illustrated yet we know little about how children remember such material. Do they rely on separate, modality-specific memories or do they pool information from both sources within an integrated amodal memory? Preliminary investigations (Murray, 1986) revealed that whilst children did sometimes make use of integrated memories they were not wholly dependent on such memories. Accurate memory for the original verbal or pictorial material was particularly likely if the test was introduced immediately after presentation of the story.

On the basis of these earlier studies it was hypothesized that children's memory may comprise both detailed, modality-specific memories and more general, amodal memories; the latter being given priority in long term memory. Thus the current study set out to examine the effect of delay on children's memory for an illustrated text.

The following rationale was used to distinguish between the modality-specific and amodal options: if memory is modality-specific, input in one modality should have no effect on children's memory for input in the other. If, on the other hand, children are relying on integrated, amodal memories then clearly what happens in one modality should influence children's memory for the alternate modality. Thus we can investigate children's memory by looking at whether the content of the illustrations influences children's memory for the associated text and vice-versa. If amodal memories gradually come to the fore in children's memory we would expect cross-modal interference to increase with delay.

The current experiment involved a number of target sentence-picture pairs presented within the context of an

illustrated   story.   Two versions of each target item   were
constructed: a general version which made reference to a general
category   (e.g. man or woman) and a specific version in which   a
specific instance of that category was mentioned (e.g. policeman or
nurse).

        The crux of the experiment was to pair general   information
in   one modality (e.g. the sentence "There was a woman waiting   at
the bus-stop".) with specific information in the other (e.g.   a
picture   of   a nurse standing at a bus-stop).   A   subsequent
recognition   test probed whether the specific information   had
infiltrated   children's memory for the original, general item   as
would be predicted if input from both modalities interacts within
an amodal memory. In the recognition test subjects would be forced
to   choose between   the   original   general   item and a   foil
incorporating the specific information (i.e. in the above   example
children would choose between the following sentences "There was a
woman   waiting at the bus-stop" and "There was a nurse waiting   at
the   bus-stop").

        In order to ensure that any difficulty these children
might   experience in identifying the original sentence was due   to
interference from the pictorial material their performance was
contrasted   with that   of Control subjects who had read the   same
sentence but were shown a general rather than specific   illustration
(in this case a picture of a woman not in uniform).

        Thus the experiment compares subjects who have received
identical verbal input but slightly different pictorial input.   Any
differences   in their memory for the text can, therefore, be
attributed to the influence of the illustrations.

        The materials were such that it was possible to run   a
mirror-image version of this, in which all subjects saw identical
pictorial material (the general illustrations) but whilst   Controls
read the corresponding general sentence Experimental subjects were
given   the specific sentence. In a subsequent recognition   test
these children chose between the original general picture (of a
woman)   and a foil incorporating the specific information   (the
aforementioned   picture   of a nurse).   Any differences   between
Experimental   and Control subjects in their ability to identify the
original picture must be due to the influence of the text.

METHOD
        Subjects - a total of   288   primary-school children
participated   in the study, 144 from Primary 3 classes (mean age   7
years 5 months) and 144 from Primary 7 classes (mean age 11 years 4
months).   Approximately equal numbers of boys and girls   were
recruited at each age.

        Materials and Design - all subjects were   presented with
an   illustrated story containing 6 target sentence-picture   pairs.
For Experimental subjects one member of each pair referred to a
general category noun (e.g. man) whilst the other member of   the
pair referred to a specific instance of that category (e.g.
policeman).   Thus, half of the Experimental subjects   received
general sentences paired with specific pictures while for   the
remainder specific sentences were paired with general   pictures.
The subsequent recognition test took place in the modality in which

subjects   had   originally   been   presented   with   the   general
information.   In   the   test,   subjects   had   to   choose between   each
general   item   and   an   integrated   foil   incorporating   the   specific
information.

Control subjects were presented with general information
in   both   modalities.   Half of them were   subsequently   asked   to
identify   the   sentences   they   had   read,   the   rest were tested   for
picture   recognition.   These   recognition tests were the   same   as
those given to Experimental subjects.

A delay variable was included in the design: equal   numbers
of   children   in   each   condition   were   presented with the   forced-choice
test   immediately   after   presentation   (zero delay),   three days   later,
or seven days' later.

This   produced   a   2(age: 7/11   years)   x 2   (treatment:
Experimental vs. Control)   x   2(type   of   test: sentence
recognition vs. picture   recognition) x 3 (delay: 0/3/7 days)   design
in   which   all   variables   were   between-subject.   Twelve   subjects
participated in each condition.

Procedure - the   story was   presented via a   series   of
slides.   Both the text and the illustrations were presented in this
way.   Text and illustration slides alternated so that each   target
illustration   followed the slide   in   which   its associated   sentence
had   appeared. Each slide was presented for 10 seconds,   with   the
Experimenter   reading the   content   of   the text slides aloud   whilst
they were being shown.

The recognition test was introduced without warning.   Each
pair   of items (the original general item and the specific foil)   was
presented   on a single slide.   Subjects had to select the item   they
had   seen   or read before. Each test comprised six pairs of   items
and   subjects were awarded   one   point   for   each   general item   they
correctly identified.

SUMMARY OF RESULTS

Mean scores for the sentence and picture recognition   tests
are shown in Tables 1 and 2 respectively.

Table 1   Mean score for sentence recognition (maximum = 6)

	Experimental			Control		
	0	3 days	7 days	0	3 days	7 days
7yrs	3.00	2.92	2.00	5.25	5.17	5.75
11yrs	4.83	2.58	2.58	6.00	5.92	5.38

Table 2   Mean score for picture recognition (maximum = 6)

	Experimental			Control		
	0	3 days	7 days	0	3 days	7 days
7yrs	4.92	3.50	2.75	5.67	5.67	5.33
11yrs	5.42	4.67	3.50	5.83	5.58	5.67

The scores were analyzed initially using a 2 (age) x 2 (Experimental/Control) x 2 (sentence/picture recognition test) x 3 (delay) ANOVA where all variables were between subject. Only one main effect was not qualified by a significant interaction – overall older children were more accurate than the younger subjects (F=17.05; df=1,264; p<.0001).

A simple main effects analysis of the interaction between the Experimental/Control variable and delay (F=15.64; df=2,264; p<.0001) revealed the following pattern of results. Experimental subjects were less accurate than Controls at all three delays (at zero delay F=25.43; df=1,264; p<.0001, at three days F=90.91; df=1,264; p<.0001, and at seven days F=167.11; df=1,264; p<.0001). Whilst the performance of Experimental subjects deteriorated as the delay between presentation and test was increased (F=33.11; df=2,264; p<.0001) no such deterioration was apparent in the performance of Control subjects (F=0.11; df=2,264; p>.10).

A simple main effects analysis of the interaction between the Experimental/Control variable and type of test (F=19.13; df=1,264; p<.0001) revealed that Experimental subjects performed less accurately than Controls in both picture recognition (F=65.36; df=1,264; p<.0001) and sentence recognition (F=206.58; df=1,264; p<.0001). Whilst Control subjects performed equally well on picture and sentence recognition (F=0.02, df=1,264; p>.10), Experimental subjects were significantly worse at identifying sentences compared with pictures (F=37.68, df=1,264, p<.0001).

DISCUSSION

Comparisons between Experimental and Control subjects show that pictorial input influenced memory for verbal material (Table 1) and that verbal input influenced memory for pictorial material (Table 2). This two-way interference between text and illustrations is just what would be expected if children were relying on an integrated, amodal memory.

The effect of delay was to increase the incidence of this cross-modal interference, witness the increasing divergence between Experimental and Control subjects. Immediately after presentation children were relatively good at identifying the actual sentences they read or pictures they saw, but as time passed they seemed to rely increasingly on memories which preserve the overall meaning of an episode. In this respect they seem to be similar to adults whose memory for passages of text and for picture stories becomes increasingly schematic with time (Baggett, 1975, 1979; Singer, 1982).

This pattern of results would seem to be most readily explained by the kind of hierarchical model originally proposed by Dooling and Christiaansen (1977) in which detailed, item-specific memories give way, over time, to more general memories which combine elements from a variety of sources.

The delay effect would certainly seem to indicate that the more detailed, modality-specific memories have been irrevocably lost from the system but the possibility remains that this information is permanently stored in memory although, for some reason, not retrieved. Further experiments using a variety of retrieval techniques are obviously needed.

The experiment contrasted the performance of seven and eleven-year-old children. The results indicate that, across the board, the older children were more adept at recognizing the original material. The absence of any age x treatment interaction, however, suggests that both groups had access to integrated memories. If this is the case, how are we to explain the 'superior' performance of older children? It could be that they devote more effort to the finer details of the input during encoding or perhaps they respond differently during the test phase — recognizing the need to retrieve the most detailed memory available to effect a match. Again further studies are required to ascertain the source of this effect.

It is worth noting that the lack of any discernible age effect in the existence of integrated amodal memories is at odds with other studies which have probed cross-modal integration in children's memory (Pezdek, 1980; Pezdek and Miceli, 1982). These studies reported an age-related increase in the incidence of integration when subjects (8 and 11 year olds) were presented with a series of apparently unrelated items though the effect disappeared when presentation time was increased from 8 to 15 seconds per item. The most likely explanation for the apparent discrepancy between Pezdek's work and the results of the current study would seem to lie with the nature of the tasks. Whilst Pezdek's task focussed on memory for an isolated set of items, subjects in the current study were faced with a complex meaningful event. Young children, in particular, are likely to benefit from the contextual support provided by the story framework.

The final result to consider is the difference in performance between sentence and picture recognition. Illustrations were consistently better remembered (i.e. less susceptible to interference). This is probably due in part to the relatively greater memorability of the physical characteristics of pictures compared with verbal material (Nelson, Reed & Walling, 1976), but may also reflect problems in the design of recognition foils. Children may on occasion have retained an amodal memory (e.g. the idea of a policeman) but rejected the appropriate foil (of a man in policeman's uniform) because it is at odds with their idea of what the item should look like (e.g. they may think of policemen as having peaked caps rather than helmets).

SUMMARY

To summarise the results of this investigation. There was evidence of cross-modal integration in both seven and eleven year olds' memory for an illustrated story. Reliance on this amodal memory appeared to increase systematically with the delay between presentation and test, suggesting that children's memory gives priority to fairly general, schematic memories.

REFERENCES

Baggett, P. (1975). 'Memory for explicit and implicit information in picture stories', Journal of Verbal Learning and Verbal Behavior, 14, 538-548.

Baggett, P. (1979). 'Structurally equivalent stories in movie and text recall and the effect of medium on recall', Journal of Verbal Learning and Verbal Behavior, 18, 333-356.

Dooling, D.J. and Christiaansen, R.E. (1977). Levels of encoding and retention of prose. In G.H. Bower (Ed.), The Psychology of Learning and Motivation, Vol. 11.

Murray, S.L. (1986). 'Cross-modal semantic integration in children's memory for illustrated texts', Unpublished PhD dissertation, Aberdeen University, Scotland.

Nelson, D.L., Reed, V.S. and Walling, J.R. (1976). 'Pictorial superiority effect', Journal of Experimental Psychology: Human Learning and Memory, 2, 523-528.

Pezdek, K. (1980). 'Life-span differences in semantic integration of pictures and sentences in memory', Child Development, 51, 720-729.

Pezdek, K. and Miceli, L. (1982). 'Life-span differences in memory integration as a function of processing time', Developmental Psychology, 18, 485-490.

Singer, M. (1982). ' Comparing memory for natural and laboratory reading', Journal of Experimental Psychology: General, 11, 331-347.

UNDERSTANDING INEFFICIENT LEARNING: ATTRIBUTIONAL BELIEFS AND
THE TRAINING OF MEMORY AND COMPREHENSION STRATEGIES

John G. Borkowski
University of Notre Dame

ABSTRACT

A model of metacognition, which features attributional
beliefs as a by-product of strategy use and transfer, is used
to generate a series of training studies with hyperactive,
learning disabled, and underachieving students. The general
conclusion drawn from this research is that attributional
retraining, in the context of strategy training, promotes the
generalization of memory and comprehension strategies.

INTRODUCTION

Research on the assessment, explanation, and remediation
of learning disabilities (LD) has generally focused on
developmental inconsistencies, performance inadequacies, and
information processing deficits (Ceci, 1987; Houck, 1984).   LD
children have been found to be inactive, less planful,
disorganized, and lacking the skills and strategies necessary
to prosper in classroom environments (Torgesen, 1977, 1982;
Borkowski, Johnston, & Reid, 1987).   More recent findings
suggest that learning impaired children often develop
motivational and personal problems as a consequence of their
learning difficulties, including low self-esteem, inaccurate
perception of their talents, and a tendency to attribute
failure to diminished abilities (Borkowski et al., 1987;
Butkowsky & Willows, 1980; Johnson, 1981; Licht, 1983).   These
motivational-personality problems are eventually reflected in a
debilitating condition commonly referred to as learned
helplessness (Torgesen & Licht, 1983).

The present series of studies attempted to address
commonplace learning impairments in memory and in reading
comprehension from an interactive perspective, involving
motivational and cognitive variables (Borkowski et al., 1987;
Pressley, Borkowski, & Schneider, in press).   In our model,
metacognitive processes and attributional beliefs are
intimately related and, in combination, are used to explain the
emergence and use of a wide range of strategies across

settings.   We hypothesize that the acquisition of strategic
skills inevitably involves changes in motivational (e.g.,
self-attributions) and personality (e.g., self-esteem) states.
In turn, reshaped attributional beliefs serve to energize the
transfer of newly acquired strategies, especially on difficult
tasks.   In general, beliefs that attribute success to the
effort needed to be strategic and failure to insufficient
effort are likely to promote strategy generalization.

A positive attributional belief system is all the more
important for students with learning problems. For instance,
mentally retarded and learning disabled children often
encounter repeated learning failures, which may decrease their
expectancy of success and, therefore, their motivation to
succeed (Licht, 1983).   Three recent studies with inefficient
learners support the contention that attributional beliefs are
intimately involved in the acquisition and transfer of learning
skills.

Metacognition,   Attributional   Retraining,   and
Performance in Hyperactive Children.

Learning disabled and hyperactive children may not
understand the connection between effortful, strategic behavior
and successful performance and, as a consequence, fail on
transfer   tests.   Thus,   theoretically-based
interventions—designed to improve metacognitive-motivational
states—may be needed to enhance strategy transfer in learning
disabled children.   According to our model, interventions
should focus on specific strategies, general executive
strategies, metacognitive awareness, and motivational states.
The motivational component contains stable antecendent causal
beliefs as well as more malleable, program-specific
attributions.

To test the construct validity of the attributional
components in the metacognitive model, Reid and Borkowski (in
press) conducted a study comparing the effectiveness of three
training conditions: an Executive condition, an Executive plus
Attributional condition, and a Control condition.   The
Executive condition emphasized general self-control as well as
specific strategy training appropriate for paired associate and
sort recall tasks.   In the Executive condition, the instructor
modeled self-verbalization procedures for the child (e.g.,
"look to see how the problem might be solved"; "stop and think
before responding").   These self-control procedures, adapted
from a popular self-control program designed by Padawer, Zupan,
and Kendall (1980), were taught in the context of specific
strategy   training   which   focused   on   the   use   of
interrogative-associative mediators appropriate for the paired
associate task and a clustering-rehearsal strategy for use on
the sort-recall readiness task.   Self-control and strategy

training took place during four sessions.

Hyperactive and learning disabled children in the Executive plus Attribution condition were presented with all of the instructions that defined Executive training and were also given training designed to enhance both antecedent and program-generated attributions. Antecedent attributional training included three aspects: (a) discussion regarding beliefs about the causes of failure; (b) the opportunity to successfully perform a previously failed item using the self-control steps; and (c) reflection on long-standing beliefs about the causes of success. Program-specific attributions were trained by providing feedback to the child about the reasons for correct and incorrect performance on several learning tasks. Children in the control condition represented a "conservative" test of the hypothesis in that these children received the most effective strategy instructions available but were not given self-control or attributional instructions.

Tests of strategy generalization at a 3-week posttest showed striking changes in learning performances, especially for children in the Executive plus Attribution condition. Strategy scores on a transfer task were significantly higher for children receiving the Executive plus Attribution package than for children in the other two groups. For instance, on the sort recall and paired-associates tasks, strategy use was between 75% and 90% superior in the complex condition. Attributional responses, reflecting beliefs about the reasons for success and failure on the transfer tests, as well as more enduring beliefs about the causes of past performance on academic tasks, were altered in the Executive plus Attribution condition as was impulsivity. It should be noted that self-control training, without a focus on attributional beliefs, produce minimal changes in attributional beliefs, similar to those found in the control condition which received only strategy instructions. Additional results showed that changes in attributional beliefs persisted over a 10-month period following training. The group receiving attributional training scored significantly higher in general strategic knowledge and were more mature in their attributional judgments about the causes of learning successes and failures. In this sense, program-specific attributional beliefs had been "permanently" altered by the training routine. These findings highlight the importance of including attributional retraining in programs that focus on strategy use and self-control, especially when teaching educationally handicapped children who have a history of academic failures.

Reshaping Program-Specific Attributions and Retraining Reading Strategies

A second study, with learning disabled children,

assessed the impact of retrained attributional beliefs about specific strategies on the subsequent use of newly acquired comprehension strategies (Borkowski, Weyhing, & Carr, in press). Four conditions were formed: a Reading Strategies plus Complex Attribution group received attributional retraining on two learning tasks (paired-associates and sort recall readiness), instructions on the use of a paragraph summarization strategy (i.e., searching for the topic sentence), attributional statements about its efficacy, and posttests that assessed reading skills and general antecedent attributional beliefs. Another experimental group (Reading Strategy plus Attribution) received the identical package but without prior attributional retraining on the learning tasks; students in this condition, however, received attributional statements during summarization training. One of the control groups received only strategy training; the other control group received neither strategy nor attributional instructions. Attributional training consisted of the experimenter modeling appropriate attributional statements and then overtly ascribing the child's successes and improvements to the effort expended in deploying strategies. The instructor also made a series of intentional errors. After each error, an attributional dialogue, designed to strengthen antecedent attributions about effort, was introduced. First, the instructor noted the error and engaged the student in a discussion about the reasons for failure on school tasks. The importance of not attributing failure to non-controllable factors was stressed. Second, the instructor stated positive self-attributions, "You decided to use the strategy and it worked," following successful strategy deployment on the part of the student.

The results of this study were mixed, but generally encouraging. Students in the combined Reading Strategies plus Attribution conditions performed significantly better on paragraph summaries at the end of training than the two control conditions. The gain in the attribution conditions was 95% from pretest to posttest, versus a 30% gain in the control conditions. In addition, two weeks following training, summarization scores for the control groups declined, whereas the performance of the Reading Strategies plus Complex Attribution group rose slightly. The beneficial effects of the attributional conditions did not, however, generalize to the Stanford Diagnostic Reading Test, (except for questions about main ideas) nor did they alter long-standing, antecedent attributional beliefs. The improvements found by Borkowski, Weyhing and Carr (in press) on paragraph summarization, when combined with results from the Reid and Borkowski (in press) study on memory processes, suggest that commonly observed performance difficulties need to be approached simultaneously as a motivational problem and a deficit in strategic skills.

The Importance of Attributional Retraining for Underachievers

Since attributional and strategy training in combination was shown to promote strategy generalization in hyperactive and learning impaired students, even larger effects might be expected with underachieving students, whose talents are often hidden by motivational problems (Carr & Borkowski, 1987). Underachievers were selected using a two-step process: third, fourth, and fifth grade teachers were asked to nominate children currently receiving C and D grades, yet who appeared capable of working at a higher-level of performance; next, these children were given two tests of ability -- Slossen IQ and Peabody pictures vocabulary tests. Distributions of IQ scores and grades in reading were transformed to z distributions. The z-scores for each child's reading grade was then subtracted from his or her z-score for IQ. Children with difference scores of .5 or above were considered underachievers. Forty-four underachieving children were subsequently chosen and given the following tests: an attributional measure to assess beliefs about the causes of success and failure; a self esteem measure; a test of action control; a measure of reading awareness; a measure of strategic reading behavior; and tests of comprehension accuracy.

Underachievers were then divided into three treatment groups: Strategy-plus-Attribution, Strategy-only, and control conditions. Children in each condition were given six sessions of strategy training involving three comprehension strategies: topic sentence, summarization, and questioning strategies. The combined Strategy-plus-Attributions condition focused on training comprehension strategies for the main idea and included attributional instructions embedded in the steps of the strategy. Children were not only trained to use extra effort but were also taught how and why it might improve performance, especially when expended in deploying a strategy. At each step of the strategy, the need to use effort was reinforced. For example, following a reading of the to-be-learned paragraph the instructor asked the children if they had read the paragraph and understood each sentence. The instructor then suggested that reading and searching for meaning requires considerable effort but that this extra effort is necessary for successful recall. In the Strategy-only condition, comprehension strategies (but not attributions) were taught. The control condition exposed the children to the materials but involved no training. Two weeks following the last training session, children were given a posttest, using the same measures as at pretest. Fourth quarter grades were obtained from the schools.

The Strategy-plus-Attribution group was found to perform significantly better than the Strategy-only and control groups on three measures of reading: strategic behavior at posttest, recall at posttest, and fourth quarter grades. These findings suggest that the addition of attributional training to a standard comprehension training routine promoted the application and generalization of summarization strategies, such as the transfer of "searching for the main idea" to the classroom setting. Although the three groups did not differ at pretest on a reading awareness measure, both the Strategy-plus-Attributions group and the Strategy-only group had significantly higher reading awareness scores at posttest than the control group. These two groups, however, did not significantly differ from one another. It appeared that training strategies in isolation, and in tandem with attributions, facilitated the acquisition of metacognitive knowledge about reading. Finally, changes in attributional beliefs from the pretest to the posttest were analyzed in an effort to understand the role of self-efficacy in producing good reading performance. The data suggested that the combined Strategy-plus-Attribution condition significantly increased attributions about the importance of effort in strategy deployment.

CONCLUSIONS AND IMPLICATIONS

The data from the present studies suggest that teaching memory or reading strategies alone, or emphasizing the role of effort in isolation, will prove insufficient in educating LD or hyperactive students. Attributions linked to specific subject matters should be systematically manipulated in order to enhance the acquisition and generalization of domain-specific skills. Intensive, prolonged instructional programs—centering on attributional retraining across multiple domains—may eventually reshape more general, long-standing, self-defeating attributional beliefs of students with learning impairments, freeing them to become more active, strategic learners in many situations. In this way, instruction and remediation based on a multi-componential approach to cognitive development might reverse the negative motivational cycle, based on failure experiences, that is so common to children and adolescents who are inefficient learners. In turn, the processes that underlie strategy acquisition and transfer might be facilitated.

REFERENCES

Borkowski, J. G., Johnston, M. B., & Reid, M. K. (1987). 'Metacognition, motivation, and the transfer of control processes', in Handbook of cognitive, social, and neurological aspects of learning disabilities (Ed. S. J. Ceci), Erlbaum, Hillsdale, New Jersey .

Borkowski, J. G., Weyhing, R. S., & Carr, M.   (in press).
'Effects of attributional retraining on strategy-based reading
comprehension in learning disabled students',   Journal of
Educational Psychology.

Butkowsky, I. S., & Willows, D. M.   (1980).   'Cognitive
motivational characteristics of children varying in reading
ability: Evidence for learned helplessness in poor readers',
Journal   of   Educational   Psychology,   72,   408-422.

Carr, M., & Borkowski, J. G.   (1987, April).   Underachievement:
The   importance   of   attributional   retraining   for   the
generalization of comprehension strategies.   Paper presented at
the annual meetings of AERA, Washington, D.C.

Ceci, S. J.   (1987).   Handbook of cognition, social, and
neurological aspects of learning disabilities,   Vol 2, Erlbaum,
Hillsdale, New Jersey.

Licht, B. G.   (1983).   'Cognitive-motivational factors that
contribute to the achievement of learning disabled children',
Journal of Learning Disabilities, 16, 483-490.

Padawer, W. J., Zupan, B. A., & Kendall, P. C.   (1980).
Developing of self-control in children: A manual of
cognitive-behavioral strategies,   University of Minnesota
Press, Minneapolis.

Pressley, M., Borkowski, J. G., & Schneider, W.   (in press).
'Cognitive strategies: Good strategy users coordinate
metacogntion and knowledge', in   Annals of Child Development
Vol. 4   (Eds. R. Vasta and G. Whitehurst), JAI Press,
Greenwich, CN .

Reid, M. K., & Borkowski, J. G. (in press).   'Causal
attributions of hyperactive children: Implications for
training strategies and self-control', Journal of Educational
Psychology.

Torgesen, J. K.   (1977).   'Memorization processes in reading
disabled children',   Journal of Educational Psychology, 69,
571-578.

Torgesen, J. K.   (1982).   'The study of short term memory in
learning disabled children: Goals, methods, conclusions', in
Advances in learning and behavioral disabilities (Eds. K. D.
Gadow and I. Bialer), JAI Press, Greenwich, CT.

ATTENTION AND SHORT TERM MEMORY AMONG
ATTENTION DECIFIT DISORDER CHILDREN

Rita Agrawal

Department of Psychology,
Guru Nanak Dev University,
Amritsar, India.

ABSTRACT
This investigation attempted to isolate weak/absent attentional skills among school going ADD children. Three experiments on acquisition, selective attention and maintenance were conducted on 10 ADD male, school age children aged 6-12 years and a matched control group of non ADD children. The results show deficits in acquisition of information by the ADD and poorer functioning of selective attention processes. Group differences were also obtained in maintenance of information over time and ability to rehearse. In all three experiments, introduction of red stimulus arrays facilitated information processing. The results are interpreted in the light of memory and attention models. Implications for reduction of attentional problems are also discussed.

INTRODUCTION
Despite the diversity of explanations offered, the first essential feature of attention deficit disorder (ADD) children is that of attention deficit (Minde, 1983). This in turn produces other behavioural, cognitive and academic problems. The empirical results (reviewed by Routh, 1983), however, often fail to corroborate the clear clinical picture. Criticism has been focussed mainly on three aspects: (i) the lack of adequate specification of the ADD Syndrome (Rubenstein and Brown, 1984); (ii) the use of attention as an 'umbrella' term (Berlyne, 1970); (iii) the lack of integration of findings on ADD with current research and theory on normal attentional processes (Matlin, 1983).

The present investigation was an attempt to isolate weak or absent attentional skills among the ADD, keeping in view the issues raised above. To adequately define the population, ADD was specified across three commonly confused categories: hyperactivity, aggression and learning disability. The children finally chosen were exclusively ADD.

The term 'attention' was also explicitly delimited. Three separate but interacting neural systems controlling three distinct attentional systems (arousal, activation and effort) have generally been proposed (Pribram and McGuiness, 1975). Posner (1975) has also empirically identified three principal, psychobiologically independent components of attention. These are: alertness, or general receptivity to input information; selection, i.e. selection of some stimulus aspect for special handling; and conscious processing, concerned with the degree of conscious effort expended by

the person.
        An experiment by Agrawal (1985) on ADD children derived
information-processing indices for each of the above and deficit
performance of the ADD was noted. It was, however, felt that the
addition of certain methodological innovations would produce more
reliable results. Though in principle, the effects had been
statistically separated, the lack of encoding specificity was there.
The present investigation was therefore designed with three
independent experiments. These would be more tenable to
interpretation. Simultaneously, the number of trials per condition
could be increased for greater reliability, and separate instructions
for each condition would create 'encoding specificity'.

EXPERIMENT I

        Alertness to information is determined by various stimulus
variables. Colour is one such dimension, as found by Brydon (1968)
with normal children and with ADD children by Agrawal (1985). Since
most studies had used bi-coloured arrays, a need was felt for the
comparison of alertness to (and consequent acquisition of) arrays of
single colours. Thus, three types of arrays were used: all red, all
black and red-black (mixed) arrays.

Method

        Subjects: ten male ADD, and an equal number of non-problem
children were selected from a school catering to the lower middle
income group (Mean age, Experimental group = 8.8 yrs. S.D. = 1.6;
Mean age, Control group = 8.4 yrs. S.D. = 1.1). Using an iterative
process, subjects were chosen through teacher ratings on two factor-
analytically derived scales: the hyperactivity scale (Lahey,
Stempniak, Robinson and Tyroler, 1978) and a shortened version of the
aggression scale (Buss and Durkee, 1957). The teachers confirmed
that none of the children were learning disabled, suffering from
emotional disorder, or on drug treatment. The control group (CG)
were matched on age, sex, grade, and intelligence, and were non-ADD,
non-aggressive, non-learning disabled.
        Stimulus material: alphabetic arrays, consisting of two
rows of four randomly chosen consonants of the English alphabet, were
printed in the centre of 3" x 5" white cards. Ten all-red cards, 10
all-black cards and 10 mixed cards were prepared. The latter
consisted of an equal number of red and black items in each row, with
their positions being randomly determined.
        Experimental design: a within-subjects, groups x treatment
design, with 2 groups and three levels of the treatment variable
(stimulus colour) was used.
        Procedure: the experiment was conducted individually.
After appropriately instructing the subject, the 'ready' signal was
given, followed by tachistoscopic exposure of the stimulus. A fall
door tachistoscope with a fixed exposure of 200 msec. was used.
Thereafter oral recall was taken. Each ADD subject and his matched
control group pair were administered a different randomly arranged
sequence of 30 trials (10 for each colour modality). Three practice
trials preceded the experimental trials.

RESULTS
        The ADD had lower recall scores (RS) than the control group
(ADD RS = 85, 75, 96; CG RS = 133, 125, 122 for red, black and mixed
arrays respectively). A groups x treatment, repeated measures ANOVA,
however,   showed that all main and interaction effects   were
nonsignificant.   Calculated t-values for ADD-CG differences at each
treatment level were significant only for the black arrays (t = 2.46,
df = 18, p < .05).
        The   results therefore suggest the   possibility   that
alertness deficits in the ADD are colour specific and not due to any
structural deficit. In terms of the arousal model of ADD, the red
and mixed arrays may sufficiently stimulate the underaroused ADD, and
so facilitate acquisition. The more mundane black fails to stimulate
them causing significant performance decrements. The same had been
obtained earlier with bicoloured alphanumeric arrays (Agrawal, 1985).

EXPERIMENT II
        The most popular procedure to assess selective attention
has been the central-incidental paradigm (Hagen, 1967). Results on
ADD children have been unequivocal. This may be due to the nature of
the incidental material used. Rather than being detrimental, they
tended to enhance performance by optimising the under-aroused child
(Bremer and Stern, 1976). Failure to equate saliency values of both
central and incidental material for the ADD and control groups may
have also led to contradictory findings. In the present experiment
saliency across groups and the central-incidental dimension were
equated   by   using bi-coloured alphabetic arrays.   To   study
facilitative effects (if any) of the extraneous stimuli, each
stimulus aspect functioned as the central information in   one
condition and incidental in the second. The Sperling type partial-
whole paradigm with pre-cueing was used only as a powerful technique
for presenting incidental information within the stimulus array.

Method
        Experimental   design: a within-subjects, 2 groups x 2
treatment levels design was used with 15 trials for each level.
        Procedure: the experiment was conducted individually on
the Ss of Experiment I, under two conditions (i) red items as central
information and (ii) black items as central information, with
specific instructions being given before the start of each condition.
Thirty mixed arrays were used. The 'ready' signal was followed by
tachistoscopic   exposure of the array with oral recall taken
immediately after. Half the subjects of each group were administered
condition (i) first while the other half were given condition (ii)
first.

RESULTS
        Even after equating saliency values, higher RS scores were
obtained by the control group and for red items by both groups (ADD =
150, 134 and CG = 180, 145 for red and black respectively).   The
repeated measures, groups x treatment ANOVA indicated significant
main effects of groups (p < .05) and treatment (p < .01) but a non-
significant interaction effect.   Analysis or errors in terms of
omission, commission and irrelevant errors indicated that the ADD

made more errors of commission (an index of incidental recall) than the CG, and that more were made in the black than the red condition. That is, the subjects faced greater intrusion from red items.

The findings therefore verify that the ADD are deficient on selective attention due to continuous processing of task irrelevant material with the relevant. As with alertness, this attentional dimension appears to be colour-bound, with red being the more effective stimulus selection channel. Unlike alertness, changing stimulus colour to red fails to bring ADD scores to normal levels.

EXPERIMENT III

This experiment focussed on conscious processing. Specifically, maintenance of information in the STM was studied under three conditions: no rehearsal, spontaneous rehearsal and cued rehearsal. Since research findings show that deficit populations (e.g. the mentally retarded and those with learning deficits) can be trained in the effective use of memory strategies (Pressley, Heisel, McCormick and Nakamura, 1982), it was of interest to see whether the ADD could also benefit from such training.

Method

Experimental design: a within-subjects, groups x treatments design with two groups and two repeated treatment variables (5 levels of retention interval, RI, i.e. 5, 10, 15, 20 and 30 seconds; and 3 levels of rehearsal: no rehearsal, spontaneous rehearsal and cued rehearsal), with 5 trials per treatment combination (5 x 3 x 5 trials per subject) was used.

Procedure: the experiment was conducted individually using 75 red arrays. It consisted of three blocks of 25 trials each in the following order: no rehearsal, spontaneous rehearsal and cued rehearsal. No rehearsal condition: the Brown-Peterson paradigm was followed. The secondary task was forward counting by twos. Spontaneous rehearsal condition: the procedure was the same except that the RIs were unfilled. For the cued rehearsal condition, the subjects were given explicit instructions to repeat the items of the array during the RI. For each condition the RI was followed by oral unordered recall. Independent trial sequences were prepared for each ADD and his matched control group pair.

RESULTS

The ANOVA showed that all main and interaction effects were significant (p < .01). The ADD scored lower in all conditions. Performance tended to increase with cued rehearsal, but the amount of facilitation varied for the two groups. The characteristic decrement seen with length of RI also varied with group and rehearsal condition. In the no rehearsal condition the decrement with RI was in line with that generally obtained with the Brown-Peterson paradigm. (ADD RS = 35, 18, 12, 16, 9 CG RS = 41, 31, 22, 17, 10 at 5, 10, 15, 20, 30 seconds). However, between-group differences became negligible after 30 seconds. This may be interpreted in terms of Kahneman's model of resource allocation. Lack of flexibility of allocation of attentional resources and/or over-exertion of attention effort on the secondary task may have caused the ADD to show larger decrements than the CG over short RIs. For longer RIs, there was probably total utilization of resources by the secondary task for both groups, creating equal performance.

In the spontaneous rehearsal condition, between group differences increased over time, (ADD RS = 41, 22, 22, 14, 5 CG RS = 47, 36, 35, 31, 23 at 5, 10, 15, 20 and 30 seconds) with the performance of the ADD showing a sharper gradient (75% lost after 30 seconds as against only 50% for the control group). As found in Experiment I, alertness (or arousal) in the ADD was higher for the red arrays. Since this experiment had used red arrays, it could be argued that the ADD were characterized by higher arousal throughout the experiment. While such high arousal causes improvement in selective attention (as also obtained in Experiment II), it decreases divided attention (Wood, 1983). There is failure in the allocation policy and a narrowing of attention (Kahneman, 1973). This may explain the higher rate of decrement. In the cued rehearsal condition surprizingly parallel trends were noticed for both groups (ADD RS = 38, 36, 40, 36, 38 CG RS = 67, 65, 70, 64, 65 after 5, 10, 15, 20 and 30 seconds). There was no decrement even after 30 seconds, showing the efficacy of rehearsal in maintenance. More significantly, the ADD too, were capable of efficient rehearsal.

It may therefore be concluded that the ADD show deficient performance on all three attentional aspects. Rather than being structural deficients, they are apparently mediated by stimulus colour and explicitness of instructions. The results also provide tentative guidelines for reduction of attentional problems. (i) Change in stimulus colour would facilitate attentional process functioning; (ii) specific instructions regarding encoding and strategy usage are also necessary; (iii) the differential role of arousal on selective and divided attention tasks should be kept in mind.

REFERENCES

Agrawal, R. (1985). 'STM and Hyperactivity', Psychological Studies, 30, 9-15.

Berlyne, D.F. (1970). 'Attention as a Problem in Behavioral Theory', in Contemporary Theory and Analysis. Appleton-Century-Crofts, New York.

Bremer, D.A. and Stern, J.A. (1976). 'Attention and Distractibility During Reading in Hyperactive Boys', Journal of Abnormal Child Psychology, 4, 381-387.

Bryden, M.P., Dick, A.O. and Mewhort, D.J.K. (1968). 'Tachistoscopic Recognition of Number Sequences', Canadian Journal of Psychology, 22, 52-59.

Buss, A.H. and Durkee, A. (1957). 'An Inventory for Assessing Different Kinds of Hostility', Journal of Consulting Psychology, 21, 343-348.

Hagen, J.W. (1967). 'The Effect of Distraction on Selective Attention', Child Development, 38, 685-694.

Kahneman, D. (1973). Attention and Effort, Prentice-Hall, New Jersey.

Lahey, B., Stempniak, M., Robinson, E. and Turoler, M. (1978). 'Hyperactivity and Learning Disabilities as Independent Dimensions of Child Behavior Problems', Journal of Abnormal Psychology, 87, 333-340.

Matlin, M. (1983). Cognition, Holt-Rinehart, New York.

Minde, K. (1983). 'Disorders of Attention', in Psychological Problems of the Child in the Family (Eds. P.D. Steinhauer and Q. Rae-Grant), Basic Books, New York.

Posner, M.I. (1975). 'Psychology of Attention', in Handbook of Psychobiology (Eds. M.S. Gazzaniga and C. Blackmore), Academic Press, New York.

Pressley, M., Heisel, B.E., McCormick, C.B. and Nakamura, G.V. (1982). 'Memory Strategy Instruction with Children', in Verbal Processes in Children (Eds. C.J. Brainerd and M. Pressley), Springer-Verlag, New York.

Pribram, K.H. and McGuiness, D. (1975). 'Arousal, Activation and Effort in the Control of Attention', Psychological Review, 82, 116-149.

Routh, D.K. (1983). 'Attention Deficit Disorder: Its Relationship with Activity, Aggression and Achievement', Advances in Developmental and Behavioral Pediatrics, 4, 125-163.

Rubenstein, R. and Brown, R.T. (1984). 'An Evaluation of the Validity of the Diagnostic Category of Attention Deficit Disorders', American Journal of Orthopsychiatry, 54, 398-414.

Wood, G. (1983). Cognitive Psychology: A Skills Approach, Brooks-Cole, California.

READING

INDIVIDUAL DIFFERENCES IN READING SKILL AND LEXICAL MEMORY: THE CASE OF THE CROSSWORD PUZZLE EXPERT

Geoffrey Underwood, Joy MacKeith, and John Everatt
Department of Psychology
University of Nottingham
Nottingham NG7 2RD, England

ABSTRACT

Two experiments investigated the relationship between the single-word priming effect in a lexical decision task, and individual lexical knowledge as measured by a Mill Hill vocabulary test. Experiment 1 also investigated other predictors of single-word priming, including crossword puzzle skill. Crossword puzzlers were not found to show different performances on the laboratory tasks, in comparison with a group matched for their Mill Hill scores. These tasks included the timed generation of synonyms and antonyms and a word association task. Both experiments found an association between vocabulary score and the size of the single-word priming effect. With short prime-target intervals this was a negative correlation (better vocabulary associated with reduced priming), and with longer prime-target intervals it was a positive correlation.

Reading would not be possible without memory, but there is no single memory system which mediates this intellectual activity - the successful reader remembers story events, uses working memory to integrate the words within a sentence, and calls upon a lexical memory to interpret each word within the sentence. It is this finest level of analysis the meanings of individual words must be recognised, in a process in which the printed symbols must address the reader's lexical memory. It is this level of analysis which is the subject of our discussion, and in particular we pose the question of what predicts an individual's lexical fluency.

The measure of fluency which we focused on was the extent to which contextual information could be used during the recognition of a single word. Context effects have been found to predict reading ability, with young poor readers making greater use of context than good readers (West and Stanovich, 1978). Responses to single words can be more easily facilitated by appropriate contexts, and more easily inhibited by inappropriate contexts, for poor readers in comparison with good readers. This suggests that poor readers are less efficient at extracting the printed information from the page, and tend to use a hypothesis-driven reading strategy. Indeed, the prediction from the Posner and Snyder (1976) model of context effects is good here, for the readers showing the greatest effects of context are those who are recognising words most slowly, and it is this slow recognition process which allows time for the contexts to have their influence. The model allows only facilitation effects (with congruous contexts) if little time is allowed for context to be influential, and inhibition effects in addition to facilitation, if the reader has enough time to generate conscious expectancies. The Posner and Snyder model does not turn out to provide the best fit to the data however, with Becker (1982) finding a patern of inhibition dominance for category priming, and Briggs, Austin and Underwood (1984) found facilitation effects only for poor readers and a pattern of inhibition-without-facilitation for good readers.

The present experiments tested the hypothesis that single-word contextual priming effects are related to an individual's verbal ability, and that individuals who practice solving cryptic crosswords would have particularly rich lexical networks and therefore would show the greatest effects of contextual primes. The first experiment compared crossword solvers and non-solvers on a primed lexical decision task, together with a number of other laboratory tasks of lexical ability.

EXPERIMENT 1: Crossword Puzzle Experts
Subjects
Twelve crossword-puzzle aficionados were recruited from the local community through newspaper and radio announcements. The criteria for acceptance into this elite group was that candidates should be able to complete a cryptic crossword(e.g. 'The Times' crossword) within thirty minutes. Each non-puzzler was matched to one of the puzzlers on a modified Mill Hill vocabulary test. The vocabulary test used a multichoice format requiring subjects to select a synonym for each target word. Low frequency synonyms were used.

Design, Apparatus and Procedure
Three tasks were presented to each subject. **Task A** was a word association test, in which associates of a target word were to be generated within thirty seconds. Twelve words were presented, and subjects given 30 seconds to generate as many associates as possible. Words were medium to low frequency (Kucera and Francis, 1967), for example 'bramble', 'dogma', and 'oyster', and written responses were made to spoken targets.

Task B was a lexical decision task (manual yes/no response according to whether a letter-string was a word or not) employing six priming conditions, with 12 trials within each condition. There were also 72 non-word trials, and 24 practice trials. Words were matched across conditions for number of syllables, number of letters, and word frequency (Kucera and Francis, 1967). The six priming conditions were as follows: **(i) a strongly associated prime** (the associate with the highest production frequency in the Postman and Keppel (1970) norms of word association), e.g. "work" priming "office"; **(ii) a weakly associated prime** (the tenth most frequent associate in the Postman and Keppel norms), e.g. "ink" priming "paper"; **(iii) two associated primes** (using the first two most frequent associates from the Postman and Keppel norms), e.g., "ash" and "fire" priming "cinder"; **(iv) an indirect**

associate e.g. "strawberry" priming "traffic" indirectly through the unpresented word "jam"; **(v) a non-associated prime** (other words taken from the Postman and Keppel list), e.g. "file" priming "garden"; (vi) **a non-word prime** e.g. "refunt" priming "grammar". The last two conditions were included as controls for the associated primes. The lexical decision task required an oscilloscope controlled by an LSI 11/23 laboratory computer. The prime were shown for 150 msec, followed by a blank screen for 250 msec, and then the target, which remained on the screen until the subject responded. The priming field always contained two stimuli, and these appeared directly above and directly below the fixation cross.

Task C involved the generation of antonyms and synonyms, with 12 instances of each. For each target word, a stopwatch was started as the word was read aloud, and stopped when the subject finished articulating the response.

Results and Discussion

Two dependent measures were taken from the word association task: average number of associates generated within thirty seconds, and average normality of association. The measure of normality was calculated for each subject by taking the first three associates generated for each target, and comparing them against the associates listed in Postman and Keppel (1970). A score of ten was given if the associate was the most frequently produced associate in the norms, and a score of one if it was the tenth most frequently produced associate. The total normality score was then the sum of these individual word scores for that subject. Non-puzzlers generated an average of 71.9 words in this task (average normality score of 108.8), in comparison with an average of 62.5 for the puzzlers (average normality of 100.5). The data were carried forward to a correlation analysis.

The measures taken in the synonym and antonym generation tasks were response time and accuracy, with accuracy being assessed subjectively. Four independent judges rated each synonym and each antonym produced by each subject on a scale from zero to ten, where zero indicated that the target and response words had no relationship, and where a score of ten indicated that they were exact synonyms or exact antonyms. These scores were averaged, and for the non-puzzlers the average response latencies were 6.8 sec (synonyms) and 5.9 sec (antonyms), and for the puzzlers the latencies were 5.1 sec (synonyms) and 5.0 sec (antonyms). Judged accuracy for the non-puzzlers was 5.85 out of 10 (synonyms) and 5.83 (antonyms), and for the puzzlers was 5.98 (synonyms) and 6.13 (antonyms). These data were also entered into the correlation analysis.

The data from the lexical decision task were first inspected with an analysis of variance (Table 1). There was no effect of crossword-puzzling [F<1] and no interaction [F<1]. There was an effect upon reaction time due to the priming condition [F=7.03, df=5,110, p<0.001]. Pairwise comparisons were used to inspect the effects of priming. Non-words did not differ from unrelated word primes [p>0.1], and these controls differed only from the strongly related associate [p<0.05] and from the indirect associate [p<0.001]. Whereas a strong associate provides an average facilitation effect of 27 msec relative to the control, the indirect associate provides an average inhibition effect of 42 msec. It is not only the size of this effect of an indirect associate which comes as a surprise, but also its direction. The differences between crossword puzzlers and non-puzzlers were examined with an analysis of simple main effects at each of the six priming levels. No differences were found [all p>0.1].

    A correlation analysis was performed with 11 factors, including those described above. The full set of 11 factors was : (i) size of the priming effect - mean lexical decision time for unrelated word primes minus the LDT for related word primes; (ii) size of the inhibition effect caused by indirect associates; (iii) synonym score; (iv) antonym score; (v) synonym RT; (vi) antonym RT; (vii) number of associates generated in the word association task; (viii) normality of associates in the word association task; (ix) expertise with crossword puzzles (experts were assigned a score of 1, and non-puzzlers a score of 0); (x) laughing during the lexical decision experiment (some subjects occasionally laughed aloud upon seeing the pairs of primes and targets, and were assigned a score of 1 here, whereas non-laughers were given a score of 0); (xi) modified Mill Hill vocabulary score.

Table 1: Lexical Decision Task (LDT)
Mean response latencies from Experiment 1, in which subjects made timed (msec) decisions to target words and non-words which were preceded by primes. Only the data from the word trials were analysed, and standard deviations are in brackets.

	Crossword Puzzlers		Non-Puzzlers	
	RT	Errors	RT	Errors
Strong associate	608 (105)	12	593 (103)	12
Weak associate	618 (106)	10	595 (39)	7
Two associates	631 (85)	3	606 (96)	2
Indirect associate	680 (138)	2	658 (107)	5
Unrelated prime	623 (99)	2	624 (84)	5
Non-word prime	642 (88)	0	631 (82)	1

    The simple correlations which attained a significant level were those between the size of the strong associative priming effect and the size of the indirect associative inhibition effect [r= +0.61, df=22, p<0.01], between the size of the priming effect and the modified Mill Hill vocabulary score [r= -0.53, df=22, p<0.02], between the vocabulary score and the normality of associates generated in the word association task [r= -0.52, df=22, p<0.02], between the normality of associates and the antonym score [r= +0.47, df=22, p<0.05], and between the synonym generation RT and the antonym generation RT [r= +0.43, df=22, p<0.05]. The strongest correlation involving crossword puzzle expertise was that with the incidence of laughter during the experiment, possibly due to the enjoyment which puzzlers derive from recognising the ambiguities in words.

The factor of size of associate priming was entered as the dependent variable in a multiple regression analysis, and the two predictors of Mill Hill vocabulary score plus size of the indirect inhibition effect provided the best fit, accounting for 51% of the variance [F=10.7, df=2,23, p<0.001]. The next best fit included antonym response time [52% of the variance now accounted for], but the two models did not differ [F<1] and this suggests that the two variable model is adequate.

Our expectancies were not confirmed by this experiment. It was not crossword solving ability which was associated with single-word context effects, but Mill Hill vocabulary scores. Furthermore, the size of the associative context effect was negatively correlated with the vocabulary score: our highest scorers on the vocabulary test were those who showed the smallest facilitation from primes which were associated to the targets. Discussion of this provocative result will be postpones until Experiment 2 has been described.

EXPERIMENT 2: Associative Priming in Lexical Decisions

The purpose of Experiment 2 was to attempt to confirm the relationship between Mill Hill scores and the size of the associative priming effect, in an experiment with different stimulus onset asynchronies (SOAs) between prime and target. Posner and Snyder's (1975) two-process model predicts a pattern of facilitation-dominance at short prime-to-target intervals, and this is what was observed in Experiment 1. When there is only time for the automatic activation process to operate, then facilitation from related primes is observed, but no inhibition from unrelated words. As SOAs are increased there is time for the conscious attentional process to operate, and this gives the opportunity for unrelated primes to lead to incorrect anticipations, and with them, inhibition effects. Experiment 2 used longer SOAs to observe this relationship between inhibition and facilitation, as a function of vocabulary size. Thirty adults from the University community participated in this experiment.

Design, Apparatus and Procedure

The only laboratory task performed by the subjects in this experiment was a primed lexical decision task with three priming conditions. There were 12 item-pairs in each of the three conditions, a further 36 trials in which the target was a non-word, and 12 practice trials. The three conditions were as follows: **(i) an associated prime** selected from the same source as in the previous experiment, e.g. "heavy" priming "light"; **(ii) a non-associated prime** (a word with the same number of syllable, frequency, and number of letters as the associated prime for that target), e.g. "visit" priming "light"; **(iii) a neutral prime** (a row of crosses).

The apparatus was the same us that used previously, and the sequence of events for each trial was as follows: a fixation cross appeared in the centre of the screen for 1000 msec, followed by the priming item for 1500 msec, followed by a blank screen for 500 msec, and then the target, which remained on the screen until the subject responded. The subjects also completed a modified version of the Mill Hill vocabulary test.

Results and Discussion

The mean response latencies from the lexical decision task are as follows: associated prime 520 msec (SD=81; 6 errors overall); non-associated prime 560 msec (SD=89; 16 errors); neutral prime 562 msec (SD=89; 11 errors). These data were submitted to a one-way analysis of variance which indicated a main effect of priming conditions [F=11.29, df=2,58, p<0.001]. Pairwise comparisons indicated that the associated priming condition differed from both the non-associated prime and neutral prime conditions [both p<0.01], which in turn did not differ from each other. So, even with long SOAs the inhibition from unrelated primes did not appear, in contrast with the predictions from Posner and Snyder's two-process theory.

The size of the associative priming effect was taken for each subject, and a Pearson product-moment correlation calculated between priming and Mill Hill scores. The correlation proved reliable [r= +0.37, df=28, p<0.05], but in the opposite direction to that observed previously. With long SOAs higher vocabulary scores were associated with larger associative priming effects.

GENERAL DISCUSSION

When lexical knowledge is taken into account, by matching subjects on a Mill Hill vocabulary test, there are no apparent differences attributable to crossword puzzling ability on a range of laboratory tests which require responses to single words. The responses tested in Experiment 1 included word associate generation, synonym and antonym generation, and primed lexical decisions. A possible explanation for the failure of the crossword puzzlers to perform best in the priming task is that their skills are as much bound up in the cryptic puzzle codes as they are in lexical fluency. Crossword puzzlers certainly have some of the verbal gymnastics sought in Experiment 1, in that they are familiar with 'double definition' clues such as "State train" (7 letters), answer "express". Many crossword clues are a verbal code, however, and it is difficult to see how the priming task might tap the same processes which lead to the solution of a number of cryptic clues. For instance "The heights of experimental psychology" (4 letters) is not, as a psychologist might suggest, "mind" or "myth" or even "icon", but is "alps" (last two and first two letters of the last words). This 'part-word' clue is indicated by the possessive preposition. Similarly, "My Rome is ruined by reminiscence" (6 letters) is, appropriately enough for this volume, answered by "memory". In this case the anagram of the first two words is indicated by the code word "ruined".

Experiment 1 found that the facilitation effect attributed to the prior presentation of an association of the target in a lexical decision task - the associative priming effect - decreased in magnitude as the vocabulary knowledge of the individual increased. Experiment 2 found the converse: as vocabulary knowledge increased, so did the priming effect. The Posner and Snyder model fails to account for the pattern of facilitation (from related words) in the absence of inhibition (from unrelated words) when a long SOA was used in Experiment 2, but Becker (1982) may provide an alternative account. Becker's two-strategy account allows a pattern of facilitation dominance when targets are well predicted by their primes, as was the case in our experiments. Facilitation arises when a small 'semantic set' is generated in anticipation of the target, and no inhibition is observed because there are relatively little costs incurred in searching a small set of candidates. This much agrees with our data, but the problem now is to account for the different patterns of association with vocabulary when different SOAs are used.

Let us first assume that individuals with high vocabulary scores will be able to generate more candidates for the semantic set whenever they are expecting a target. In addition, we found that the high vocabulary scorers also generated free associates which were less conventional than the low scorers, and so their semantic sets might be expected to be less useful if very predictable targets are actually presented. Now, at short SOAs the semantic set will be small for all subjects because there is little time to compile it, in comparison with prime-target pairs with long SOAs. This accounts for reduced facilitation for high vocabulary scorers because the small semantic set will contain more unusual candidates and therefore fewer correct candidates. At the longer SOAs more candidates will be included in the semantic set for all subjects. The correct item is therefore more likely to be present, and facilitation more likely to result. The model has trouble accounting for the difference between high and low vocabulary scorers unless we can assume that the high scorers can generate larger sets in the available time. If they can, then they are more likely to anticipate the target, but this should also result in longer search times. Alternatively, we are left to conclude that the increased time prior to target presentation can be used better by the high scorers than the low scorers in the isolation of a probable target.Perhaps the high scorers appear to be more effective in correctly anticipating the target because they search the semantic set in a more organised way.

A more general implication of the association found here is that any gains for word recognition, which accrue from lexical priming, might be expected to depend upon the individual's size of vocabulary. High scoring on this vocabulary test is a good predictor of reading comprehension (Baddeley, Logie, Nimmo-Smith and Brereton, 1985), and so we might expect our high scorers to be good readers who show facilitated word recognition from single-word contexts. This conclusion is not entirely consistent with that drawn from studies of children, in which it was the poor readers who showed the greatest effects of context.

REFERENCES

Baddeley, A., Logie, R., Nimmo-Smith, I. and Brereton, N. (1985). 'Components of fluent reading', Journal of Memory and Language, 24, 119-131.

Becker, C.A. (1982). 'The development of semantic context effects; two processes or two strategies?', Reading Research Quarterly, 17, 482-502.

Briggs, P., Austin, S. and Underwood, G. (1984). 'The effects of sentence context in good and poor readers; a test of Stanovich's interactive compensatory model', Reading Research Quarterly, 20, 54-61.

Kucera, H. and Francis, W.N. (1967). Computational Analysis of Present-day American English, Brown University Press, Providence.

Posner, M.I. and Snyder, C.R.R. (1975). 'Facilitation and inhibition in the processing of signals', in Attention and Performance V (Eds. P.M.A. Rabbitt and S. Dornic), Academic Press, New York.

West, R.F. and Stanovich, K.E. (1978). 'Automatic contextual facilitation in readers of three ages', Child Development, 49, 211-219.

KNOWLEDGE REPRESENTATIONS DURING READING DEPEND ON READING SKILL AND READING STRATEGY

D. J. Townsend   and   T. G. Bever
Montclair State College   University of Rochester

ABSTRACT

In a clause-by-clause reading task, conceptual predictability reduced reading time for passive sentences for both skilled and average readers. In word-by-word reading, predictable contexts reduced only the reading time for active sentences for skilled readers, and actually increased reading time for passive sentences by average readers. We interpret these results to mean that superficial representations of context are more likely to occur when the reading format forces a word-by-word reading strategy. How context affects reading processes depends on how the reader represents the context.

Many behaviors require integrating different levels of representation of knowledge. For example, the spatial relationship between two cities can be represented in terms of a map of their locations in a larger context. It can also be represented in a more superficial way, in terms of directions that specify how to travel from one city to the other. This simple example reveals a general difference between different representations of knowledge (for a review, see Anderson, 1986). A conceptual level is configurational but unordered: it specifies the relationship between cities in terms of geo-spatial coordinates without any indication of particular operations. A superficial level presents operations that are local, and strictly ordered. When we travel from one city to another, we integrate these representations to some degree. How are distinct knowledge representations formed and integrated during ongoing behavior?

It is relatively easy to investigate these questions by studying reading comprehension because language contains well-defined, separate levels of representation. Consider the contrast between conceptual and superficial representations of a sentence. The conceptual representation is an integrated network of propositions that specifies agent, object, and patient roles of sentences. Superficial representations encode information about words and their linear order within sentences. The goal of language comprehension is to develop a conceptual representation that integrates superficial representations with prior knowledge. Accordingly, superficial details of a sentence are relatively inaccessible once the sentence is over (e.g., Sachs, 1967). If the sentence is in a context that allows for inferences based on conceptual knowledge, readers often interpolate that knowledge as part of their representation of the text (e.g., Bransford et al., 1971).

There are individual differences in knowledge representations. It is frequently claimed, for example, that skilled reading involves efficiently integrating conceptual representations during reading (e.g., Daneman & Carpenter, 1983). Supporting this claim, Townsend et al. (in press) found that skilled readers retain the conceptual content of text better than average readers do. They also found that although skilled readers are more sensitive to linear order in probes of the immediate representation of a sentence, average readers.are superior in recognizing the linear order of words over longer intervals.

Superficial representations do persist under certain conditions (e.g., Kintsch & Bates, 1977), and they play an extended role in comprehension. For example, Townsend (1983) found that the lexical form of an adversative clause ('though...') influences reading time for words in the next clause; in contrast, the semantic content of a causal clause ('if...') has a larger effect than its lexical content. This suggests that superficial representations are not merely transient way-stations to conceptual representations.

The relationship between different levels of representation during comprehension has been controversial. A crucial question is whether conceptual representations can influence the formation of superficial representations (e.g., Forster, 1979; Townsend & Bever, 1982; Tyler & Marslen-Wilson, 1977). A prima facie demonstration that they can is the fact that sentences are read faster in conceptually supportive text (Bower et al., 1979). Such findings demonstrate that conceptual information may reduce processing time, but they do not indicate the level at which the facilitation occurs -- conceptual, superficial, or both. For example, reading times might be reduced simply because a conceptual representation is determined more efficiently. The problem with any straightforward measure of comprehension complexity is that the formation of both superficial and conceptual representations can affect it.

We can, however, compare reading paradigms which emphasize conceptual or superficial representations. In this study, skilled and average readers read text either one clause at a time or one word at a time. We varied how strongly the preceding text supported the conceptual interpretation of active or passive target sentences, and measured reading times for the targets.

We expected the whole-clause task to encourage the formation of conceptual representations so that the conceptually predictive contexts would decrease reading time, especially for the more complex passive construction: by hypothesis, the conceptual representation 'primes' the subject, verb, and object concepts in the target, but in an unordered conceptual representation. Hence, subjects can use the conceptual representation of a predicted event to neutralize the fact that its passive expression is not in the simpler syntactic order.

But subjects who read word-by-word are under a different kind of pressure. Since the words disappear as they read through the sentence, they must assign a structure to each word in sequence and build up an ordered representation. We therefore expected less facilitation from conceptually predictive contexts. Furthermore, if word-by-word presentation favors a superficial representation of an anticipated event, we anticipate interactions between context and sentence structure of a rather different kind from above. Recall that information at the superficial level is ordered; in the case of a transitive proposition in English, the normal order is 'agent, patient'. In this case, we anticipate that the stronger the priming the faster actives will be read, since they correspond to the canonical order. Passives, however, will be read SLOWER in predictive contexts because of the stronger mismatch between the ordered prediction and the actual form of the sentence.

METHOD

Subjects read eight stories either clause-by-clause or word-by-word on a computer screen. Their task was to construct a title for each story. When the subject finished reading a segment of text, s/he pressed a key that recorded the time spent on the segment, removed it from the screen, and displayed the next one. Subjects read experimental instructions in similar fashion.

Target sentences appeared as the third through sixth sentence in eight pairs of stories. The story pairs described routine sequences of activities such as eating breakfast vs. watching television. They were designed so that a particular event (e.g., 'Johnny took out the cereal') would be nearly essential to the situation described by one member of a pair, but only possible in the other. Pretest ratings confirmed that target events were more essential in one member of the story pairs than in the other, $F (1,157) = 66.4$, $p < .01$.

Target sentences contained an inanimate logical object and a verb that required an animate logical subject. The target sentences were introduced by 'when.' Each subject received one story with each combination of syntactic form (active vs. passive) and predictability (predictive vs. neutral). Across lists, the eight target events appeared with each combination of form and predictability. Each list contained four filler stories.

The subjects were 64 right-handed Montclair State College and Columbia University undergraduates. Thirty-two skilled readers had Verbal Scholastic Aptitude Test (VSAT) scores of 540 or greater (mean = 645, s.d. = 76); thirty-two average readers had VSAT scores of 520 or lower (mean = 440, s.d. = 59).

RESULTS

We converted reading times into mean reading times per word for target sentences. We replaced 3.1% of the response times that were greater than 900 msec/word in the clause format with a value of 900, and 5.2% that were greater than 1100 msec/word in the word format with a value of 1100. The mean response times were 342 msec/word in the clause format, and 470 msec/word in the word format, $F_1 (1, 60) = 16.6$, $p < .01$, $F_2 (1, 7) = 15.6$, $p < .01$. Subjects read target sentences more quickly in active form than in passive form, $F_1 (1, 60) = 10.3$, $p < .01$, $F_2 (1,7) = 6.5$, p $<$ .05, and more quickly in predictive contexts than in neutral contexts, F_1 (1, 60) = 6.8, p $<$ .05, F_2 (1, 7) = 23.8, p $<$ .01.

Table 1
Mean Reading Times per Word (msec) in Target Sentences

	Clause Format		Word Format	
	Active	Passive	Active	Passive
Neutral Context	322	436	465	477
Predictable Context	294	316	439	497
Facilitation Score	28	120	26	−20

The predicted effects occurred (see Table 1). For the clause format, predictable contexts facilitated reading times more for passives than for actives, F_1 (1,60) = 9.8, p $<$ .01, F_2 (1,7) = 6.2, p $<$ .05. For the word format, predictable contexts facilitated reading times more for actives than for passives, F_1 (1,60) = 4.9, p $<$ .05, F_2 (1,7) = 3.1, p $>$ .10. In fact, the numerical effect of predictable contexts on passives in the word format was to INCREASE reading time.

Predictable contexts increased reading time throughout passive sentences in the word format. The slowing effect was 63 msec/word in the initial noun phrase, F_1 (1,60) = 14.5, p $<$ .01, F_2 (1,7) = 5.8, p $<$ .05, and 39 msec/word in the final noun phrase, F_1 (1,60) = 6.4, p $<$ .01, F_2 (1,7) = 3.6, p $<$ .10. In contrast, the only effect of predictability on reading active sentences was a 53 msec/word facilitation in the final noun phrase, F_1 (1,60) = 7.5, p $<$ .01, F_2 (1,7) = 4.9, p $<$ .10.

Table 2
Facilitation Scores for Skilled and Average Readers
(Neutral − Predictive, in msec/word)

	Clause Format		Word Format	
	Active	Passive	Active	Passive
Skilled Readers	40	168	59	24
Average Readers	17	72	−7	−63

Table 2 shows that predictive contexts reduced reading time more for skilled readers than for average readers, F_1 = 16.9, p $<$ .01, F_2 (1, 7) = 14.4, p $<$ .01. The interaction[1] between syntactic form, predictability and format was virtually identical for both groups of subjects. This had the surprising consequence that in the word format, average readers read passives more slowly in predictive contexts than in neutral contexts.

DISCUSSION

Discourse predictability interacts in different ways with sentence reading as a function of the size of the imposed reading unit. When subjects are allowed to read whole clauses at a time,

predictability has the usually expected effect: it facilitates
reading all sentences, especially those that are otherwise
structurally complex. But when subjects are constrained to read
one word at a time, predictability facilitates only active
sentences; most striking about this condition is that
predictability can actually slow down the processing of sentences
with non-canonical word order, especially for subjects who
normally focus more on superficial representations. We take this
to reflect a strategy of processing text at a superficial level of
representation when forced to read each word separately: since the
superficial level in English specifies word order, information
about predictability must be ordered at that level. Accordingly,
the reading time for a sentence in the unexpected order is
inhibited; since this inhibition is strongest for the first noun
phrase, it cannot be due to the passive form of the sentence, but
rather must be due to the unexpected order in which the phrases
appear.

     Our results confirm previous findings that conceptually
predictive contexts can prime information that is available to
both conceptual and superficial levels of representation. But our
results also show that priming information is available at the
superficial level only in an ordered form, which may actually
impede superficial processing.

     These results have two important implications. First, the
style of presentation affects the apparent nature of the
interaction between knowledge representations during
comprehension. One might argue that our results simply show that
"unnatural" tasks force subjects to focus on superficial
representations. However, Townsend et al. (in press) found that
subjects were actually better at answering conceptual questions
about unnatural speeded speech than they were for questions about
normal speech, but that speech rate had no effect on memory for
linear order. Second, skilled and average readers can give
results that are qualitatively different. Since current
controversies in reading often ignore reading skill and
interchange text presentation techniques (e.g., Clifton & Frazier,
1986; Crain & Fodor, 1985), we must interpret these controversies
with caution.

ACKNOWLEDGEMENT

     This research was supported by NSF grant BNS-8120463 to
Montclair State College, Upper Montclair, New Jersey, USA.

REFERENCES

Anderson, J. (1986). Cognitive Psychology and Its Implications,
Freeman, New York.

Bower, G., Black, J., and Turner, T. (1979). 'Scripts in Memory
for Text', Cognitive Psychology, 11, 177-220.

Bransford, J., Barclay, J., and Franks, J. (1972). 'Contextual
Prerequisites for Understanding: Some Investigations of
Comprehension and Recall', Journal of Verbal Learning and Verbal

Behavior, 11, 717-726.

Clifton, C. and Frazier, L. (1986). 'The Use of Syntactic Information in Filling Gaps', Journal of Psycholinguistic Research, 15, 209-224.

Crain, S. and Fodor, J. (1985). 'How can grammars help parsers?', in Natural Language Parsing (Eds. D. Dowty, L. Kartunnen, and A. Zwicky), Cambridge University Press, Cambridge.

Daneman, M. and Carpenter, P. (1983). 'Individual Differences in Integrating Information Between and Within Sentences', Journal of Experimental Psychology: Learning, Memory, and Cognition, 9, 561-584.

Forster, K. (1979). 'Levels of Processing and the Structure of the Language Processor', in Sentence Processing (Eds. W. Cooper and E. Walker), Erlbaum, Hillsdale, N.J.

Kintsch, W. and Bates, E. (1977). 'Recognition Memory for Statements from a Classroom Lecture', Journal of Experimental Psychology: Human Learning and Memory, 3, 150-159.

Sachs, J. (1967). 'Recognition Memory for Syntactic and Semantic Aspects of Connected Discourse', Perception and Psychophysics, 2, 437-442.

Townsend, D. (1983). 'Thematic Processing in Sentences and Texts', Cognition, 13, 223-261.

Townsend, D. and Bever, T. (1982). 'Natural Units of Representation Interact during Sentence Comprehension', Journal of Verbal Learning and Verbal Behavior, 21, 688-703.

Townsend, D., Carrithers, C., and Bever, T. (in press). 'Listening and Reading Processes in College- and Middle School-Age Readers', in Comprehending Oral and Written Language (Eds. R. Horowitz and J. Samuels), Academic Press, Orlando, Fla.

Tyler, L. and Marslen-Wilson, W. (1977). 'The On-Line Effects of Semantic Context on Syntactic Processing', Journal of Verbal Learning and Verbal Behavior, 16, 683-692.

MEMORY AND INFERENCE IN SKILLED AND LESS-SKILLED COMPREHENDERS

Jane Oakhill
MRC Perceptual and Cognitive Performance Unit, Laboratory of
Experimental Psychology, University of Sussex, Brighton, BN1 9QG.

Nicola Yuill and Alan Parkin
Laboratory of Experimental Psychology, University of Sussex,
Brighton, BN1 9QG.

ABSTRACT
          This chapter reports five experiments that explored aspects
of memory and text comprehension in skilled and less-skilled comprehenders. The first three experiments showed that the less-skilled
comprehenders' problem cannot be attributed to any general memory
deficit but, rather, to their failure to integrate and make inferences from information in text. The final two experiments suggest
that this failure is related to the less-skilled comprehenders'
poorer working memory skills.

INTRODUCTION
          This research addresses a reading problem that has received
little attention - that of children whose word recognition is normal,
but whose text comprehension is below the level expected from their
recognition ability and chronological age. We have compared the
reading skills of such 'less-skilled comprehenders' with those of
children of the same age who have similar word identification skills,
but whose comprehension is normal.
          All the children were selected from classes of 7-8 year-
olds, using the Neale Analysis of Reading Ability (Neale, 1966)
and the Gates-MacGinitie Vocabulary Test (Gates and MacGinitie,
1965). The Neale test provides measures both of children's ability
to read aloud words in context, and of their comprehension of short
passages. Groups of skilled and less-skilled comprehenders were
selected so that they were matched on reading aloud skill (Neale
Accuracy score) and on skill at comprehending isolated printed words
(Gates-MacGinitie score); they differed in ability to comprehend
text (Neale comprehension score). The characteristics of subjects
who participated in Experiment 1 are shown in Table 1.

TABLE 1: Characteristics of skilled and less-skilled comprehenders

	Chronol. age/yrs	Accuracy age/yrs	Compre. age/yrs	Gates-MacGinitie (score/48)
Less skilled	7.9	8.4	7.3	38.0
Skilled	7.9	8.4	9.1	38.3

Many measures of text comprehension impose memory demands on the
subject. For instance, the Neale test prevents children from looking back to the text to answer questions. The assumption behind
this mode of testing is that poorly understood material is not well
remembered. However, although there is evidence that understanding

and memory are highly correlated (e.g. Bransford and Johnson, 1972; Dooling and Lachman, 1971) this need not always be the case.

EXPERIMENT 1

To investigate the relation between comprehension skill and ability to remember text, Oakhill (1984) explored children's ability to answer questions both from memory, and when they were allowed to refer back to the text. The experiment also examined whether the groups differed in their ability to answer literal and inferential questions about short stories. In the experiment, 12 skilled and 12 less-skilled comprehenders each read four passages. Following each passage, they were asked four literal and four inferential questions about it, which they had to answer from memory. They were then allowed to look at the story and the questions were repeated. The skilled comprehenders were better able to answer both literal and inferential questions when they could not see the passages. When the text was made available, the less-skilled group remained poor at answering questions that required an inference, but their performance on literal questions was the same as that of the skilled group. Thus, the poorer question-answering ability of the less-skilled group cannot be explained in terms of poor verbatim memory. These results are consistent with the idea that skilled comprehenders undertake more inferential and constructive processing, which helps not only their understanding but also their memory for the text.

EXPERIMENT 2

Further support for this hypothesis was provided in another experiment by Oakhill (1982; see, also, Oakhill, Yuill and Parkin, 1986). In this experiment, groups of skilled and less-skilled comprehenders listened to and tried to remember a series of short stories. Following the stories, they were presented with a recognition test, and were asked whether or not each sentence in the test had appeared in the stories. The recognition test comprised original sentences and two types of foil: valid inference foils, which contained information that could be inferred from the story, and invalid inference foils which contained information that did not necessarily follow from the story, or that was inconsistent with it.

The number of errors on the original sentences was similar for the two groups, and both groups wrongly identified as 'old' more valid than invalid inference foils. However, the skilled comprehenders falsely identified more valid inference foils than did the less-skilled comprehenders, whilst the reverse pattern was found for the invalid inference foils. Thus, the skilled comprehenders were more likely to give false positive responses only to the foils that were valid inferences from the story. This pattern of results was interpreted as showing that the skilled comprehenders were more involved in the active construction of meaning than were the less-skilled group.

The less-skilled comprehenders' problem cannot, therefore, be attributed to any straightforward memory deficit. It seems, rather, that skilled comprehenders appear more readily to integrate the ideas in the text to derive the overall meaning. Oakhill (1981; experiment 6) provided additional evidence for such processing differences between the groups. Skilled and less-skilled comprehenders'

memory for sentences was similar when a verbatim criterion was used
to assess recall.   However, when scoring was relaxed to include
gist recall, the skilled comprehenders' performance was significantly better than that of the less-skilled group.   The greater
gist recall by the skilled group suggests that they made a more
active attempt to understand the sentences, rather than simply trying to retain the wording.
          The question naturally arises as to why skilled readers
are able to make more inferences, and to recall the meaning of the
text.   Recent research has shown that good comprehension depends
on having an efficient working memory.   A number of experiments
have shown that various aspects of skilled reading are related to
performance on a verbal test of working memory span (Daneman and
Carpenter, 1980, 1983; Baddeley, Logie, Nimmo-Smith and Brereton,
1985).   In particular, the articulatory loop component of working
memory may play an important part in reading.   In order to enter
the articulatory process,   or its associated phonological store
(Salame and Baddeley, 1982), visually-presented material must be
recoded to a phonological form.   Phonological coding may play an
important part in comprehension because it provides a more durable
medium than visual coding for storing early parts of a sentence
so that these can be combined with what comes later.

EXPERIMENT 3
          To see whether the skilled and less-skilled comprehenders
differ in phonological recoding and rehearsal activities, Oakhill,
Yuill and Parkin (1986) used the technique of Hitch and Halliday
(1983).   We presented subjects with short lists of one-, two- or
three-syllable spoken words.   Both skilled and less-skilled comprehenders recalled more short than long words, but there was no difference between the groups.   In a second condition, we presented the
children with a series of pictures corresponding to the words in
the lists.   Sensitivity to word length in this condition would indicate that the children were recoding the pictures to a phonological
form.   Again, we found a main effect of length of the picture names,
but no difference between the skilled and less-skilled comprehenders
- both showed evidence of verbal recoding of picture names.
          The results of Experiment 3 provide additional support,
from a rather different task, that there is no general difference
in memory capacity between the skilled and less-skilled comprehenders.

EXPERIMENT 4
          The tasks described above were primarily tests of storage
capacity.   We hypothesised that the groups might differ in a task
that made heavier demands on working memory - i.e. one that involves
simultaneous storage and processing.   We eschewed a standard test
of working memory (Daneman and Carpenter, 1980) because the processing requirement, reading out sentences, might give an advantage
to the skilled group simply because of their better verbal comprehension ability. As we wished to discover whether the groups differed in working memory independently of their comprehension skill,
we used numerical, rather than verbal, materials.
Method
          The subjects were required to read out groups of three

different digits, one group at a time (processing requirement), and after having read two, three or four such groups, they had to recall the final digit in each group (storage requirement). At each level of difficulty, each subject received two practice tests, followed by eight experimental tests.

Results

The results of this test were similar whether we used a strict scoring criterion (items in correct order) or a lenient scoring criterion (items correct disregarding order): both groups did equally well on the easiest task - recalling the final items from two groups of three digits - but the skilled comprehenders performed significantly better than the less-skilled comprehenders at recall of the final items from three or four groups of digits. The data are shown in Table 2.

TABLE 2: Mean total numbers of final digits recalled as a function of comprehension skill and number of digit groups (strict recall criterion).

Number of groups:	2 (max=16)	3 (max=24)	4 (max=32)
Less-skilled group	14.12	11.12	10.06
Skilled group	14.75	15.94	15.19

An analysis of these data showed a main effect of group: $F(1,30) = 13.8$, $p<.001$, a main effect of length, $F(2,60) = 2.83$, $p<.02$ and an interaction between these factors, $F(2,60) = 5.43$, $p<01$. Planned comparisons showed that there were significant differences between the skilled and less-skilled comprehenders for the three- and four-group trials both ps $<.005$), but not for the two-group trials. Thus, although the skilled and less-skilled groups do not differ in short term recall of word and picture lists, they do differ on a task that involves concurrent processing and storage, which is probably closer to the requirements of comprehending written material.

Two further sets of skilled and less-skilled comprehenders have been given this memory test, with very similar results. These findings complement those of experiment 1, where we showed that the groups did not differ in their ability to recognise previously presented sentences in their original form,but skilled comprehenders made more recognition errors on new sentences which were valid inferences from the original passage. It seems reasonable to conclude that the skilled comprehenders are better able than the less-skilled comprehenders to draw inferences and integrate text because they can hold more information in working memory.

EXPERIMENT 5

This experiment provides further evidence that the use of working memory in text processing differentiates between skilled and less-skilled comprehenders. Using a paradigm derived from Ackerman (1984), we presented children with stories containing obvious anomalies, and explored the influence of storage and processing load on ability to resolve the anomalies.

Method

The children were read stories describing an adult's apparently inconsistent response to a child's action. For example, in one story, a mother is pleased with her son when he refuses to share his sweets with his sister. This inconsistency was either preceded or followed by resolving information - in this case, that the sister was on a diet. We expected that resolving information that followed the anomaly would be more difficult to use than that which preceded it, since it would require retrospective resolution. The difficulty of accessing the resolving information was further manipulated by varying the distance between the anomalous and the resolving information. After each story, the subject was asked whether the adult should have acted as she/he did, and why. The subjects would not have been able to respond appropriately unless they had used the resolving information. The subjects were also asked two other sorts of question about each story: one tested their memory for the adult's response, to make sure that they had remembered the story accurately, and the other tested whether the subject knew the implicit rule on which the inconsistencies were based (e.g. 'would someone usually be praised or blamed for not sharing their sweets').

Results

An analysis of the correct detections of anomalous information in the condition in which inconsistent information was presented and was later resolved showed an interaction between skill group and memory load: $F(1,16) = 4.71$, $p < .05$. These data are shown in Table 3.

TABLE 3: Mean percentages of anomaly detections

	No memory load	Memory load
Less-skilled	72.2	16.7
Skilled	66.7	66.7

The interaction arises because the skilled and less-skilled comprehenders performed similarly when there were no sentences intervening between the anomalous and the resolving information in the text, but the less-skilled comprehenders were significantly worse than the skilled comprehenders when there was an additional memory load, imposed by the interposition of intervening sentences. Both groups tended to find it harder to use resolution information when it followed rather than preceded the anomaly: $F(1,16) = 4.11$, $p = .06$, and this difference was slightly, but not significantly, larger for the less-skilled comprehenders (22% vs 5%). Most children were able to answer all the memory and implicit rule questions correctly, and there were no differences between the skill groups.

CONCLUSION

We have explored various aspects of memory in skilled and less-skilled comprehenders. Our experiments have led to the conclusion that the difficulty that less-skilled comprehenders have in answering questions about text cannot be attributed to a general memory deficit. Their ability to recall text in verbatim form is not impaired, but they do seem to lack the ability to integrate the ideas in text, and to remember the gist of the whole. In Experiment 4, we provided evidence that the lack of such processing skills might be related to the less-skilled comprehenders' poorer working memory capacities. Working memory is important in making inferences and in the construction of a representation of the meaning of the text, so it is not surprising that the less-skilled comprehenders, who have poorer working memories, are manifestly deficient in these text comprehension skills.

REFERENCES

Ackerman, B. (1984). 'The effects of storage and processing complexity on comprehension repair in children and adults'. Journal of Experimental Child Psychology, 37, 303-334.

Baddeley, A.D., Logie, R., Nimmo-Smith, I. and Brereton, N. (1985). 'Components of fluent reading'. Journal of Memory and Language, 24, 119-131.

Bransford, J.D. and Johnson, M.K. (1972). 'Contextual prerequisites for understanding: some investigations of comprehension and recall'. Journal of Verbal Learning and Verbal Behavior, 11, 717-726.

Daneman, M. and Carpenter, P.A. (1980). 'Individual differences in working memory and reading'. Journal of Verbal Learning and Verbal Behavior, 19, 450-466.

Daneman, M. and Carpenter, P.A. (1983). 'Individual differences in integrating information between and within sentences'. Journal of Experimental Psychology: Learning, Memory and Cognition, 9, 561-584.

Dooling, D.J. and Lachman, R. (1971). 'Effects of comprehension on retention of prose'. Journal of Experimental Psychology, 88, 216-222.

Gates, A.I. and MacGinitie, W. H. (1965). Gates-MacGinitie Reading Tests. Columbia University Teachers' College Press, New York.

Hitch, G.J. and Halliday, M.S. (1983). 'Working memory in children'. Philosophical Transactions of the Royal Society, Series B, 325-340.

Neale, M.D. (1966). The Neale Analysis of Reading Ability (2nd Ed.), Macmillan Education, London.

Oakhill, J.V. (1981). Children's Reading Comprehension. Unpublished D.Phil thesis, University of Sussex.

Oakhill, J.V. (1982). 'Constructive processes in skilled and less skilled comprehenders' memory for sentences'. British Journal of Psychology, 73, 13-20.

Oakhill, J.V. (1984). 'Inferential and memory skills in children's comprehension of stories'. British Journal of Educational Psychology, 54, 31-39.

Oakhill, J.V., Yuill, N.M. and Parkin, A.J. (1986). 'On the nature of the difference between skilled and less-skilled comprehenders'. Journal of Research in Reading, 9, 80-91.

Salame, P. and Baddeley, A.D. (1982). 'Disruption of short-term memory by unattended speech: Implications for the structure of working memory'. Journal of Verbal Learning and Verbal Behavior, 21, 150-164.

THE DEVELOPMENT OF LITERACY AND SHORT-TERM MEMORY

Nick Ellis

Department of Psychology, U.C.N.W., Bangor,
Wales   LL57 2DG

ABSTRACT
        Short-term memory, phonological processing and reading are
associated abilities, but the causal relationships between them are
indeterminate. LISREL analysis of data from a longitudinal study of
40 children's abilities as they develop from 5 to 7 years old
suggests that the acquisition of reading makes relevant active
phonological processing in short-term memory. Thus reading
stimulates the development of these skills.

        Neisser (1978) suggested that the relation between literacy
and memory is poorly understood: 'It is one of those issues where
every possible position can be and has been plausibly argued.
Perhaps unschooled individuals from traditional societies have
particularly GOOD memories, because they must rely on those memories
so heavily where nothing can be written down ... Perhaps, however,
they have relatively POOR memories because they lack the general
mnemonic skills and strategies that come with literacy and schooling
... Or maybe they are just like us: good at remembering what
interests them' (p.17).
        With respect to short-term memory (STM), Wagner (1974) has
shown that rural children with little or no formal education lagged
behind in STM development, seemingly because they failed to use
verbal rehearsal strategies. Wagner suggests that although 'formal
schooling appears to be critical for the development of the
SPONTANEOUS use of certain memory strategies, little is known at
present as to what aspects of formal schooling affect memory
development' (p.395).
        This paper contends that it is literacy rather than
schooling which holds the key to the development of STM.
        Short-term memory span is typically related to reading
ability. In adults, memory span is roughly equivalent to the number
of words that can be read in 1.5 seconds (Baddeley, Thomson and
Buchanan, 1975). In children one of the most striking features of
dyslexic children is their impaired digit span (Ellis and Miles,
1981). Why are these skills related?
        There are a number of possible roles for a short-term
working memory system in reading (see Jorm, 1983; Baddeley, 1978).
There is evidence to suggest a component of short-term memory, the
articulatory loop, which stores a small amount of verbal information
in a phonological code and which is under the control of the other
component, the central executive (Baddeley and Hitch, 1974).

Baddeley (1978) has suggested that the articulatory loop may serve as
the working storage system used in the decoding of unfamiliar words
using the 'word-attack' skills of applying grapheme > phoneme
conversion rules and sound blending. In this view both poor reading
and limited short-term memory may reflect a deficiency in
phonological processing (Shankweiler, Liberman, Mark, Fowler and
Fischer, 1979). A second potential role of short-term memory in
reading concerns the comprehension of sentences. Kleiman (1975)
suggests that in order to extract the meaning of a phrase the reader
must have stored information about previously identified words in
order to relate this to the words currently being identified, and the
phonological component of working memory may well serve for this
storage (Baddeley, 1978).

        These suggestions make plausible the association between
short-term memory and reading ability, but the causal relations are
indeterminate. It cannot be concluded that the memory deficit is a
cause of reading retardation since STM deficit may be an effect of
reading failure resultant from retarded readers having had less
practice in certain cognitive skills connected with reading. It is
also possible that there is a third factor producing both memory
deficit and reading failure. Longitudinal studies which test pre-
reading children's cognitive skills and relate these to their
subsequent reading performance allow causal relations to be
determined.

        The present study uses this type of design to investigate
the developmental association between STM ability, phonological
processing skills, and reading. But STM is not a unitary phenomenon
and we must assess the range of its aspects, from the ordering of
non-symbolic visual material, through non-articulatory and
articulatory retention of visually presented symbolic material, to
retention of auditorily presented strings of unrelated material like
digits and words and meaningfully related material like sentences and
instructions.

METHOD

        Children were selected from five schools within a five mile
radius in North Wales. They were initially assessed in their first
year of school as they reached five years of age and were just
beginning to show some reading ability. They were seen thereafter at
twelve monthly intervals at 6, 7, and 8 years old. Subject attrition
resulted in there being 40 subjects remaining in the study at age 7
(22 girls and 18 boys).

        At 5, 6, and 7 years old the 40 children were individually
tested for ability on 44 variables during five sessions which lasted
some 30-40 minutes. The 44 variables included the full WISC and a
variety of measures of reading, spelling, vocabulary, STM, visual
skills, auditory-visual integration ability, auditory/language
abilities, language knowledge, and rote knowledge and ordering
ability.

        For present purposes we have identified seven cognitive
abilities of interest: READING - we have a content valid operational
definition of reading ability which has seven constituent scales
measuring the reading of nonsense words, phonologically simple and
complex words, and reading comprehension (Daniels and Dyack sub-tests

A, F, G, H, R; Schonell; Carver); AUDITORY STM (digit, word and sentence spans); VISUAL DIGIT SPAN and VISUAL DIGIT SPAN AND ARTICULATORY SUPPRESSION — these two abilities allow assessment of the child's use of articulatory rehearsal; auditory and visual STM spans are measured separately since there is evidence to suggest a developmental disconnection between these skills in the 4—8 year age range (Keeney et al., 1967); SOUND (phoneme segmentation, syllable segmentation, rhyme generation and odd—one—out, sound blending) — a number of tasks requiring the knowledge of syllabic and phonemic constituents of words and their manipulation; we can thus determine the interrelationships between these skills and those of STM and reading; COLOUR NAMING RATE — rate of articulation has been implicated as a determining factor in both STM and reading (Bowers et al., 1986); VISUAL search skills (letter search, ITPA visual closure) in situations which do not require naming were included to allow assessment of the interrelationship between Visual STM skills and 'pure' visual skills at different stages of development. We realise that any such a priori clustering of abilities is open to numerous specific objections, but we hope that these categories are reasonably content valid. For further details of the subjects and the tests see Ellis and Large (1987).

For each year's set of data the scores for all 40 children on these 44 variables were normalised by conversion to stanines, a 9 point scale with mean 5.0 and standard deviation (sd) 1.96. The child who had performed best on a particular variable would thus be given the score 9, the worst would score 1. This procedure allows the scores for different tests to become comparable and a child's profile of abilities can thus be produced in the same way as is done on standard attainment tests such as the WISC. It has the additional advantage of ensuring normally distributed scores with equal variances. It also entails that the mean and variability of the scores remain the same year after year.

The LISREL model (Joreskog and Sorbom, 1984) is the most appropriate technique for the analysis of longitudinal change in data of this type. Linear structural equation models represent causal theories with proportional and additive effects. The variables which the model should account for are called endogenous variables, the predetermined variables which are not explained by other variables in the theory are called exogenous. The effect on the ith endogenous variable from the jth endogenous variable is denoted by β_{ij} . The effect on the ith endogenous variable from the jth exogenous variable is denoted by γ_{ij}. If the data are standardised then β and γ represent path weights such that an increase of one sd in the prior variable would cause an increase of β (γ) sds in the endogenous variable. Once a model has been formulated, the causal paths within the theory are specified, information about the covariances is obtained from the data, and LISREL estimates the causal effects and other parameters and tests the model against the data.

The type of model that we specified rests on few prior assumptions. It has few restrictions in that it assumes that ANY prior abilities may affect ANY later ones. A three variable/year example of this type is shown below. The abilities measured at 5 years old ($x_a \ldots x_c$) are the exogenous variables. We allowed all possible causal paths (γ) between these and the same abilities

$(y_{a1} \cdots y_{c3}$) measured at 6 years old, and also the complete set (β)
from the 6 year old variables to the 7 year old variables
$(y_{a4} \cdots y_{c6}$). We allowed covariation between the complete set of
variables within each year. The model specification entails that the
beta and gamma weights on the causal paths reflect specific direct
causal weights between the variables controlling for all indirect
effects, spurious relationships and joint effects.

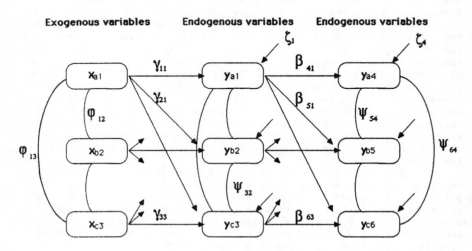

        In this case we used an 8 variable/year model where the
gross variables were created by simply summing the scores on the
constituent tests. We would have preferred to use the factor
analytic portions of LISREL to construct these measures as latent,
error-free constructs, but we were prevented by lack of computer
resource. The eighth variable is full WISC IQ, so these analyses
'take-out' any effects of intelligence. The computer package LISREL
VI was used to estimate the value of each parameter taking all other
linking paths into account. Whatever the drawbacks of this taxonomy
and its associated scaling methods, it does allow analysis of the
three years of development in terms of the DIRECT contributions of
these different broad classes of skill to subsequent abilities at
each stage of development. The resultant path weights are shown
below. The first table concerns development from 5 to 6 years old,
the second from 6 to 7. The path weights can be interpreted as
follows: when all other variables and their interconnecting paths
are controlled, an increase in the cause variable of one sd results
in an increase of (path weight) sds of the effect variable. Thus,
for example, an increase of one sd in READ at age 5 is associated
with an increase in SOUND skill of 0.45 sd at age 6. In contrast an
increase of 1 sd in SOUND at 5 results in a mere 0.07 sd increase in
READ at 6. The starred path weights are significant at the 0.05
level.

Gamma	IQ5	READ5	ASTM5	VDS5	VDSA5	SOUN5	COLN5	VIS5
IQ6	44*	26	11	-12	16	10	21	-09
READ6	-16	72*	06	04	13	07	14	-10
ASTM6	01	31*	21	29	10	-05	18	-12
VDS6	21	11	-03	34*	09	39*	-22	-26
DVSA6	39*	10	23	09	49*	-17	-04	-10
SOUN6	17	45*	04	-02	20	24	-01	-17
COLN6	02	14	07	-04	07	-07	75*	14
VIS6	14	18	00	03	-03	13	-06	53*

Beta	IQ5	READ5	ASTM5	VDS5	VDSA5	SOUN5	COLN5	VIS5
IQ7	87*	-02	22	12	-17	03	-15	04
READ7	27	57*	18	08	-11	15	03	-24*
ASTM7	13	36*	46*	06	00	08	05	-15
VDS7	28	-23	31*	39*	-10	41*	13	-24
VDSA7	20	16	18	26	32*	13	-22	-25
SOUN7	10	29*	-04	05	-05	72*	06	-14
COLN7	07	-10	18	-06	11	52*	36*	-24
VIS7	38*	42*	05	-12	00	12	-08	24*

CONCLUSIONS

These data dictate a wide range of conclusions concerning the interactive development of these skills, but restricted space limits us to the more pertinent:

-   The part-whole relationship whereby later skill level is best predicted by earlier proficiency at that same skill is the most general (and least interesting) finding. It is apparent in the starred significant diagonals.

-   At each of the two developmental stages Reading skill contributes more to later proficiency in Auditory STM than the reverse. Indeed Reading is the BEST predictor of Auditory STM at 6 years old.

-   At each of the two developmental stages Reading skill contributes more to later proficiency in phonological processing (SOUND) than the reverse, but this is more the case in the early stages of development from 5 to 6 where again Reading is the BEST predictor of SOUND at 6 years old. [These two findings do not seem to be an artefact of the reliabilities of the composite measures used here: (i) IQ is a composite of more variables than Reading, yet it is no more driver than passenger; (ii) the general effect of paths from reading being greater than paths to reading are found if we repeat this analysis with the individual reading measures, although thee are particular minor differences depending on the specific measure used].

-   Auditory STM does not seem to grow out of the phonological processing skills involved in the SOUND tasks, but Visual STM is best predicted by prior SOUND abilities at both stages, as is rate of articulation on the Colour naming task from 6 to 7. This dissociation between Auditory and Visual STM is consistent with the notion that in Auditory STM tasks the phonology is GIVEN, whilst in Visual STM, the naming of objects, pictures, or symbols, and in reading, the phonological referrents have to be ACTIVELY CREATED AND MANIPULATED.

-   Reading is the pace-maker of STM and phonological

processing skills, it promotes their development from 5 to 6, and thereafter the relationships are symbiotic, reading grows from these abilities and promotes them further.

REFERENCES

Baddeley, A.D. (1978). 'Working memory and reading', in Processing of Visible Language Vol. 1 (Eds. P.A. Kolers, M.E. Wrolstad and H. Bouma), Plenum Press, New York.

Baddeley, A.D. and Hitch, G. (1974). 'Working memory', in The Psychology of Learning and Motivation Vol. 8 (Ed. G.A. Bower), Academic Press, New York.

Baddeley, A.D., Thomson, N. and Buchanan, M. (1975). 'Word length and the structure of short-term memory', Journal of Verbal Learning and Verbal Behavior, 14, 575-589.

Bowers, P.G., Steffy, R.A. and Swanson, L.B. (1986). 'Naming speed, memory, and visual processing in reading disability', Canadian Journal of Behavioural Science, 18, 209-223.

Ellis, N.C. and Large, F.B. (1987). 'The development of reading: As you seek so shall you find', British Journal of Psychology, 78, 1-28.

Ellis, N.C. and Miles, T.R. (1981). 'A lexical encoding deficiency', in Dyslexia Research and Its Applications to Education (Eds. G.Th. Pavlidis and T.R. Miles), Wiley, Chichester.

Joreskog, K.G. and Sorbom, D. (1983). LISREL VI User's Guide, Department of Statistics, Uppsala.

Jorm, A.F. (1983). 'Specific reading retardation and working memory: A review', British Journal of Psychology, 74, 311-342.

Keeney, T.R., Cannizzo, S.R. and Flavell, J.A. (1967). 'Spontaneous and induced verbal rehearsal in recall task', Child Development, 38, 953-966.

Kleiman, G.M. (1975). 'Speech recoding in reading', Journal of Verbal Learning and Verbal Behavior, 14, 323-339.

Neisser, U. (1978). 'Memory: What are the important questions?', in Practical Aspects of Memory (Eds. M.M. Gruneberg, P.E. Morris and R.N. Sykes), Academic Press, London.

Shankweiler, D., Liberman, I.Y., Mark, L.S., Fowler, C.A. and Fisher, F.W. (1979). 'The speech code and learning to read', Journal of Experimental Psychology: Human Learning and Memory, 5, 531-545.

MEMORY FOR UNATTENDED SPEECH DURING SILENT READING

Nelson Cowan, Wemara Lichty, and Tim Grove
Department of Psychology, University of Missouri
Columbia, MO 65211, USA

ABSTRACT
          Processing models have included an auditory store that
retains acoustic properties even if one is carrying out another
task.   However, the duration of auditory storage remains unknown,
though its practical role depends on the duration.   A literature
review (Cowan, 1984) suggests that the duration is considerably
longer than many have assumed.   This study examines the decay of
memory for speech during silent reading, which has advantages over
most previous procedures: (1) the sounds are unattended when they
are presented, (2) the memory decay period is silent, and (3) a
difference in the rate of decay for consonants versus vowels
further clarifies the nature of the memory observed.

          There are many situations in which it would be helpful to
remember at least part of what was said while one was busy doing
something else.   To a certain extent, this is possible. For
example, if asked a question while reading a newspaper, one often
can finish reading a sentence before attending to the question. It
is often unnecessary for the question to be repeated. This ability
to retain unattended speech may be critically important in at least
some social settings (e.g., for an airline agent who must write
tickets while being responsive to customers).   It has been clear
since the early days of cognitive psychology (e.g., Broadbent,
1958) that there is an auditory sensory memory capable of retaining
speech input in a relatively unprocessed form for at least several
seconds, which provides the extra time to turn attention from
another task.
          However, even though a wide variety of procedures have been
used to study memory for speech sounds, they have not been
appropriate to examine its rate of decay without the complicating
influences of attention or auditory interference. In most work on
auditory memory the subject is permitted to attend to the auditory
stimulus during its presentation.   This is the case, for example,
in the stimulus suffix procedure (Crowder and Morton, 1969). This
might allow a type of encoding that is not possible when the sounds
are unattended. The most popular procedure for examining memory
for unattended speech has been the dichotic listening procedure
(Broadbent, 1958) in which the subject is to shadow (repeat) the
items presented in one ear and later try to recall the items
presented in the unattended ear.   Although subjects in this

procedure generally can remember only the last few seconds of unattended speech, it is possible that there is auditory interference from the attended channel or the subject's own voice.

Eriksen and Johnson (1964) devised a clever procedure to examine memory for unattended sounds. In their primary task subjects read silently, and a near-threshold-level tone occasionally was presented during silent reading. There was a variable delay interval after the tone, followed by a visual cue to stop reading and recall whether or not a tone had occurred. Tone detection accuracy decreased across delay intervals but was still high (in comparison to no-tone catch trials) after 10.5 sec, the longest delay tested. The possibility that subjects had attended to the tones was eliminated with a control condition in which subjects were to stop reading immediately if a tone was heard; this detection rate was much lower than the delayed, cued recall rate.

We were able to modify the Eriksen and Johnson (1964) procedure in order to examine the recognition of speech sounds rather than the detection of tones. Instead of presenting auditory targets only rarely and testing the recall of every target, over 200 syllables were presented at irregular intervals for about an hour during silent reading, but the subject was cued to stop reading and recall the last syllable presented (after a post-syllable delay of 1, 5, or 10 sec) only nine times in the session. Subjects did not know when a trial would occur and were expected to be generally habituated to the sounds while reading. Subjects also were tested periodically on the reading to motivate attention.

The procedure also made use of the finding in previous research that vowels are retained in auditory sensory memory longer or more completely than consonants (e.g., Cole, 1973; Crowder, 1971). If the recall of unattended speech sounds is based on a sensory form of memory, one would expect to find different memory decay functions for consonants versus vowels.

Three experiments are to be reported. In the first, consonant-vowel syllables were used; differential decay rates were obtained across 10 sec for consonants versus vowels. The second experiment demonstrated that subjects could not have attended to the syllables during silent reading. In the third experiment, vowel-consonant syllables were used to assess the effects of intrasyllabic, retroactive interference on the recall of vowels.

GENERAL METHOD

The subject sat in a sound-attenuated chamber and the experimenter operated the equipment from outside of the chamber. Each experiment included nine syllables formed from the three consonants /b/ (as in "bay"), /d/ (as in "day"), and /g/ (as in "gay"), in combination with the three vowels /i/ (as in "beet"), /I/ (as in "bit"), and /ε/ (as in "bet"), spoken in a male voice. The first two experiments used the nine consonant-vowel syllables (/bi/, /bI/, etc.), whereas the third experiment used the nine vowel-consonant syllables (/ib/, /Ib/, etc.). Syllables were recorded on one channel of an audiotape, which was played to subjects at about 55 dB(A) (a quiet level) binaurally over TDH-49 headphones. The other channel of the audiotape went only to the experimenter and signalled the end of the delay period. At the signal, the experimenter was to turn off the tape recorder and a cue light in the test chamber, using a switch common to both.

The interval between adjacent syllables on the stimulus tape was 2, 6, or 13 sec, randomly selected so that subjects could not learn to predict exactly when the next syllable would be presented. However, all nine of the syllables selected as targets were followed by 13-sec intervals. Consequently, the same target syllables could be used for each of the three post-target delay intervals (1, 5, or 10 sec). There were three groups of subjects, differing only in which syllables were assigned to each delay.

Each session began with two practice sets. In the first, the subject simply listened to a series of the syllables while following along on a correctly-marked answer sheet. In the second practice set, the subject attended to the syllables and identified those followed by the recall cue. (The cue was that one of the room lights was turned off). Subjects were to circle the correct syllable in a 3 x 3 array of the nine possibilities, written in English transcription as "bee, bih, beh," etc. The possible stimuli were clear to subjects from instructions and practice.

Finally, in the test session (which lasted about an hour), subjects were to read a novel and ignore the spoken syllables. They were told that if they did not know what syllable had been presented before a particular recall cue they should not worry, because their guesses would probably be more accurate than they expected. When one of the room lights went out, the subject was to put down the book and identify the last syllable heard. Then the subject was to write a brief statement summarizing what had just happened within the reading passage. Subjects also were aware that they would receive a final, multiple-choice test on the reading that they had completed by the end of the session.

EXPERIMENT 1

The subjects were 30 students who received course credit for their participation, and the stimuli were the nine consonant-vowel syllables described above. In the second practice set, in which subjects attended to the syllables, subjects correctly identified 94.4% of the consonants and 93.9% of the vowels.

In the test session, when subjects read a novel and the speech sounds were unattended, performance was found to depend upon both the type of phoneme and the post-syllable delay. These results are illustrated in Figure 1. The figure shows that consonant information decayed more quickly across delay intervals than vowel information did, producing a significant Phoneme Type x Delay interaction. (There also were main effects for both phoneme type and delay.) The interaction could not have resulted from a ceiling effect, because there was little difference between the recall of consonants versus vowels after a 5-sec delay although performance was below 80% correct. A substantial difference between types of phoneme did not emerge until the 10-sec delay.

Subjects usually gave a coherent written account of what they had been reading. Also, they correctly answered 81% of the final multiple choice questions. However, the relationships between these reading scores and speech memory scores suggest that some subjects found it easier than others did to attend to the

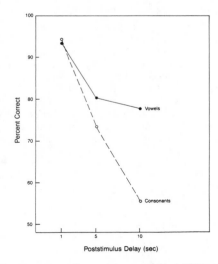

<u>Figure 1</u>.   Percentage of correct identification of unattended
consonants (dashed line) and vowels (solid line) within consonant-
vowel syllables as a function of the post-target, silent delay
interval in Experiment 1.

reading and ignore the sounds.   This was examined first by
splitting the sample into an upper and a lower half according to
the reading scores, and examining speech memory in each half.
Recall that a difference between consonant and vowel memory decay
functions is taken as one indication that the   sounds were
unattended and were retained primarily on the basis of a sensory,
rather than phonetic, form of memory. Consider also that phonetic
memory presumably can be used more if a subject attends to the
sounds.   It was found that the consonant-vowel difference was much
more pronounced in the 15 subjects with the better reading scores;
for them, the consonant recall scores declined from 93.3% correct
at 1 sec to 46.7% at 10 sec, whereas vowel recall scores declined
only from 88.9% to 80.0% (cf. the more moderate consonant-vowel
difference for all 30 subjects, shown in Figure 1).   Correlations
between speech memory and reading for all 30 subjects showed that
with better reading scores there was significantly less vowel
memory decrement across 10 sec, r=-.42, but more consonant memory
decrement, r=.42.   This pattern of results suggests that subjects
with better reading scores may have obtained these scores by more
successfully ignoring the spoken syllables; they were the subjects
who relied most on sensory rather than phonetic memory for speech.

EXPERIMENT 2
        The purpose of this experiment was to provide further
evidence that the speech sounds were unattended in Experiment 1.
The subjects were 15 students who did not participate in Experiment
1.   The procedure was similar, except that subjects had an
additional responsibility in the second practice and test sessions.

Whenever the sound /dI/ was heard, the subject was to press a response key. It was predicted that subjects either would not be able to detect the presentation of /dI/ while reading, or else they would no longer be able to ignore the syllables as they did in the first experiment.

Subjects detected an average of 17.2 out of 28 /dI/ syllables that occurred during silent reading (61.4%), and they made an average of 4.0 false-alarm responses. However, they did not forget the syllables during the silent delay periods as in the first experiment. The percentages of correct recall for consonants were 93.3% at 1 sec, 86.7% at 5 sec, and 86.7% at 10 sec. For vowels the percentages were 80.0% at 1 sec, 77.8% at 5 sec, and 88.9% at 10 sec. The absence of a delay effect in this experiment suggests that subjects could only detect auditory targets during silent reading by allocating more of their attention to the speech sounds than in Experiment 1. The difference between experiments helps to verify that the speech sounds in the first experiment actually were unattended.

EXPERIMENT 3

The purpose of the third experiment was to examine the effects of retroactive interference on performance. The subjects were 30 new students. The method was identical to Experiment 1, except that the stimuli were vowel-consonant syllables. Although sensory memory is better for vowels than for consonants, this difference might be masked when a consonant follows the vowel.

Performance levels were found to decrease significantly across delay intervals, but there was no significant difference between consonants and vowels. The percentages of correct recall for consonants were 90.0% at 1 sec, 75.7% at 5 sec, and 72.3% at 10 sec, and for vowels the percentages were 92.3% at 1 sec, 84.3% at 5 sec, and 70.0% at 10 sec. It appears that the final consonant of each syllable masked sensory memory for the preceding vowel.

GENERAL DISCUSSION

There were three main types of finding in this study. (1) First, memory for an unattended syllable of speech was found to decay gradually across a 10-sec period while subjects were silently reading. However, memory for speech after 10 sec still was considerably above chance (which would be 33% for both consonants and vowels). (2) When subjects were to detect a particular signal within the spoken syllables, there was no longer a decay of memory across 10 sec. This indicates that the decay of memory occurs for unattended speech only. (3) In consonant-vowel syllables, memory for consonants decayed much more quickly than memory for vowels. In contrast, in vowel-consonant syllables, the decay rates for consonants and vowels were the same.

The difference between memory for consonants versus vowels helps to clarify the nature of memory for unattended speech. This difference would be expected only if an auditory sensory form of memory (rather than a phonetic form) were used. In particular, auditory memory produces better recall of final vowels than final consonants (Cole, 1973; Crowder, 1971), probably because vowels are acoustically simpler. In vowel-consonant syllables, however, the sensory memory for the vowel may be masked by the following consonant, eliminating the vowel advantage. Different results would be expected if subjects relied on a phonetic memory, which would encode consonants and vowels equally well. In fact, during practice trials in which subjects were to attend to the speech sounds, they may have used phonetic memory; levels of recall for consonants and vowels were comparable during these practice trials.

The main practical implication of the research is that one can remember unattended speech for at least 10 sec. This contradicts the conventional view that echoic storage lasts only about 2 sec, but the longer estimate is consistent with other recent research (e.g., Watkins & Todres, 1980). The estimate is important, because a 10-sec memory permits much more flexibility in processing. For example, within 10 sec one might finish writing a sentence or jotting down a phone number before turning attention to a spoken remark that must be answered. A child might slowly switch attention from the current interest to a spoken, parental request, although it is unknown if the duration of storage changes with age.

The finding that memory for unattended speech is largely of an auditory sensory nature further clarifies the use of this memory. It is unlikely that one could keep in sensory storage a 10-sec-long phrase or sentence, because there would be substantial loss of consonant information as well as auditory interference between speech sounds. Perhaps a partial trace containing largely vowel information would be sufficient to reconstruct the utterance in many contexts. A possible advantage of a long-lasting auditory memory is that it might be used by children who do not yet have an accurate phonemic representation, to associate words and referents.

REFERENCES

Broadbent, D.E. (1958). Perception and communication. New York: Pergamon Press.

Cole, R. A. (1973). 'Different memory functions for consonants and vowels.' Cognitive Psychology, 4, 39-54.

Cowan, N. (1984). 'On short and long auditory stores.' Psychological Bulletin, 96, 341-370.

Crowder, R.G. (1971). 'The sound of vowels and consonants in immediate memory.' Journal of Verbal Learning and Verbal Behavior, 10, 587-596.

Crowder, R. G., & Morton, J. (1969). 'Precategorical acoustic storage.' Perception & Psychophysics, 5, 365-373.

Eriksen, C.W., & Johnson, H.J. (1964). 'Storage and decay characteristics of nonattended auditory stimuli.' Journal of Experimental Psychology, 68, 28-36.

Watkins, M.J., & Todres, A.K. (1980). 'Suffix effects manifest and concealed: Further evidence for a 20-second echo.' Journal of Verbal Learning and Verbal Behavior, 19, 46-53.

DYSLEXIA

SHORT-TERM MEMORY DEVELOPMENT AND LEARNING TO READ

Charles Hulme
Department of Psychology
University of York
York, YO1 5DD, England.

ABSTRACT

Evidence concerning the link between short-term memory processes and learning to read is reviewed. There is a correlation in children of normal ability between reading skills and short-term memory span. Children with reading difficulties tend to do poorly on short-term memory tasks. It is concluded that limitations of short-term memory may hinder learning to read, although definite evidence for such a causal link is as yet not available.

SHORT-TERM MEMORY AND INDIVIDUAL DIFFERENCES IN READING ABILITY

Several studies have examined the relationship between short-term memory skills and individual differences in reading ability. Given the generally accepted view that dyslexia represents the lower end of a continuum of reading skills (Bryant and Bradley, 1985) this evidence is useful in evaluating the likelihood of memory problems contributing to severe reading problems.

Studies in this area have gained impetus from the view that short-term memory may function as a component of a working memory system (Baddeley and Hitch, 1974). In this view verbal short-term memory may be responsible for the storage and processing of information during the course of various complex cognitive tasks such as mental arithmetic, language comprehension and reading. A working memory framework makes it natural to expect that variations in short-term memory skills will be related to variations in reading skill. Until recently, however, it has proved difficult to find support for this idea.

One influential study of this issue was conducted by Perfetti and Goldman (1976). They compared the performance of a group of good and poor readers on two memory tasks. One was a probed serial recall task using random digit lists, the other involved probed serial recall of words from sentences. It was found that the two groups differed on probed recall from the sentences but not from the digit lists. It was concluded that short-term memory differences were not important in accounting for differences in reading skill within the normal range. One problem in accepting this conclusion, however, is that the probed serial recall task was very difficult and the low levels of performance obtained may have served to minimise true differences between the two groups.

These results and others like them prompted Daneman and Carpenter (1980) to attempt to devise more adequate tests of working memory to see if more robust relationships with reading ability would emerge. They devised a measure called Reading Span. In this task subjects had to read a series of sentences and memorize the final word in each. They began with sequences of two sentences and the number presented increased until they were no longer able to recall the terminal words in correct serial order. Daneman and Carpenter gave this task, and a conventional memory span task for unrelated words, to a group of 20 undergraduates. The reading span task correlated highly with two different measures of reading comprehension (r= .72 and .90) and a further study showed that equivalent results were obtained with another measure where subjects listened to the sentences instead of reading them. The conventional word span measure produced lower correlations (r= .37 and .33), which, because of the small sample size, were not significant. However it should be pointed out that correlations of .33 and .37 are hardly trivial especially when we consider that this study used a highly selected group of subjects (Carnegie-Mellon undergraduates). Restrictions in the range of abilities present in such a group will naturally tend to reduce the magnitude of any correlations obtained.

These studies do not give a clear picture of the relationship between short-term memory and reading ability. The Daneman and Carpenter study used a small group of subjects of high ability but nevertheless obtained correlations in excess of .30 between memory span for words and reading comprehension scores. It seems likely that because of sampling restrictions this may be an underestimate of the true size of the relationship. The absence of a clear relationship between short-term memory and differences in reading ability in the Perfetti and Goldman study, on the other hand, may reflect the use of an atypical and very difficult measure of memory.

With these considerations in mind we have recently conducted a developmental study of the relationship between short-term memory and reading skill (Hulme, 1987a). One idea that lay behind this study was that the importance of short-term memory as a limiting factor for other cognitive skills may well change developmentally. We know that the effective capacity of short-term memory changes dramatically between early and middle childhood; because short-term memory capacity is limited at younger ages it may be more of an information-processing bottleneck.

We saw 40 7 and 8 year olds and 43 9 and 10 year olds. Each child received a number of tests; reading comprehension was assessed using the Neale Analysis of Reading Ability; language comprehension using the TROG test (Bishop, 1982); a short form of the WISC provided an estimate of IQ for each child. Short-term memory was assessed using short, medium and long words following procedures developed in our earlier studies of memory development (Hulme, Thomson, Muir and Lawrence, 1984).

The main results of interest from the present perspective are the correlations between memory span and reading ability. We had expected that the correlation between memory span and reading ability would be lower in the older group of children. A measure of span was obtained by averaging across the words of different lengths. The correlation between memory span and reading comprehension was r=.57 for the younger group and r=.45 in the older group. Although the correlation is slightly lower in older subjects as predicted, the difference between these correlations is not statistically significant. Nevertheless, the magnitude of both these correlations is substantial and further analyses showed that the correlation between span and reading comprehension remained significant even when the effects of age, IQ and language comprehension ability were partialled out (r=.305 and .277; p<.05). Thus, even on this rather conservative analysis short-term memory skills are shown to be related to differences in reading ability in this age range.

These results show that even within the normal range of ability short-term memory correlates with reading ability in children. There is also ample evidence that dyslexic children typically do poorly on digit span tests and other measures of short-term memory (these studies have been reviewed by Hulme, 1981 and Jorm, 1983). It should be stressed however, that not all dyslexic children have poor short-term memories (Torgeson and Houck 1980). It could be, nevertheless, that short-term memory problems contribute to the reading problems of some dyslexic children and that variations in short-term memory skills are one source of differences in reading skill amongst normal children.

SHORT-TERM MEMORY PROCESSES AND LEARNING TO READ

The question we must now consider is how short-term memory limitations might hinder learning to read. It has been argued that one function of short-term memory is to keep track of the order of words in phrases and sentences (e.g., Kleiman, 1975). Limitations of short-term memory might therefore be expected to lead to problems in the comprehension of prose, particularly when word order is crucial to the meaning. This may be one influence of short-term memory on the process of learning to read. In dyslexic children, however, there is evidence that a central feature of their reading problems is a failure to develop adequate word recognition skills (Hulme, 1987b). Short-term memory problems might lead to such difficulties by creating problems with phonic blending. When decoding a word that is not known the child must produce a set of possible pronunciations for the letters in the word. These separate sounds must then be blended to produce a possible pronunciation for the word as a whole. In the early stages of learning to read children can often be heard to go through this process overtly. Short-term memory problems could make this procedure difficult for the dyslexic child.

Torgeson, Rashotte, Greenstein, Houck & Portes (1987) tested this possibility. They compared a group of dyslexics selected for low digit-span scores with normal readers, and a group of dyslexics with normal digit spans, on a sound blending test from the Illinois Test of Psycholinguistic Abilities. In this test a series of words and non-words is spoken to the child, one at a time, in segmented form (e.g. "b-a-g": bag) and the child is asked to say the word. The dyslexics with low spans were very much worse on this task than the normal readers, or the dyslexics with normal spans, who did not differ. Retarded readers often do have particular difficulty with phonics as shown, for example, by their difficulty in reading non-words (e.g. Snowling, 1981). It is likely from this evidence that, at least for some dyslexics, their short-term memory problems contribute to these difficulties with phonics.

An alternative explanation for the short-term memory

problems of dyslexics is that they are a consequence, and not a cause, of the reading problem. One way to test this is to conduct longitudinal studies, where memory is assessed before children start to learn to read. The evidence from this sort of study on the whole suggests that memory difficulties precede reading difficulties. Jorm, Share, Maclean, and Matthews (1984) gave a large group of 5-year-olds a sentence memory task on entry to school. They tested all the children again on the memory test when they were almost 7, and also gave them an IQ and a reading test. Memory scores at first testing correlated with later reading scores when the effects of age and IQ were partialled out. This indicates that good memory scores before learning to read are predictive of later success in reading and is consistent with the possibility of a causal influence of memory ability on reading ability. It is worth noting that the memory test used here, involving sentences, differs from conventional short-term memory tasks which involve meaningless strings of items. This difference may be important. It could be argued that memory for sentences is a sensible thing to assess and might reasonably be expected to correlate with reading ability. The task is not directly comparable with conventional tests of short-term memory, however, and probably places a greater emphasis on long-term memory and language comprehension skills. However, Mann and Liberman (1984) assessed memory for unrelated strings of words in kindergarten children before they started reading and found that this did correlate with reading scores one year later.

CONCLUSIONS

In the light of the evidence reviewed here it seems reasonable to conclude that the efficiency of short-term memory processes may place constraints on the ease with which children learn to read. There are at least two distinct ways in which this might occur; by influencing the comprehension of prose and by impeding the operation of phonic blending when learning to decode novel words. It should be emphasised, however, that the evidence reviewed here is correlational. It cannot be concluded with any certainty that there is a causal influence of short-term memory skills on the process of learning to read. The evidence is certainly consistent with the possibility and such a link seems theoretically plausible. It remains, however, for future research to demonstrate directly that such a causal link is operating. The only direct way to demonstrate this would be to undertake training studies in which attempts are made to improve short-term memory skills. If effective techniques could be developed to do this which generalised across tasks it would be predicted that improving short-term memory should lead to improvements in children's reading skills. Such an outcome would be of great practical and theoretical importance.

ACKNOWLEDGMENTS

Parts of the author's research described here were supported by grant numbers G8010389 and G8410938 from the Medical Research Council.

REFERENCES

Baddeley, A.D., and Hitch, G. (1974). 'Working memory', in The psychology of learning and motivation (Vol. 8). (Ed. G.H. Bower) New York: Academic Press.

Bishop, D.V.M. (1982) 'TROG Test for Reception of Grammar', Available from the author at the Department of Psychology, University of Manchester.

Bryant, P.E. and Bradley, L. (1985). Children's Reading Problems, Blackwell, Oxford.

Daneman, M. and Carpenter, P.A. (1980). 'Individual differences in working memory and reading', Journal of Verbal Learning and Verbal Behavior, 19, 450-466.

Hulme, C. (1981). Reading Retardation and Multi-Sensory Teaching, Routledge and Kegan Paul, London.

Hulme, C. (1987a). Working memory development and the development of cognitive skills. Manuscript in preparation.

Hulme, C. (1987b). 'Reading retardation', in Cognitive approaches to reading (Eds. J.R. Beech and A.M. Colley), Wiley, Chichester.

Hulme, C., Thomson, N., Muir, C. and Lawrence, A.L. (1984). 'Speech rate and the development of short-term memory span', Journal of Experimental Child Psychology, 38, 241-253.

Jorm, A.F. (1983). 'Specific reading retardation and working memory: A review', British Journal of Psychology, 74, 311-342.

Jorm, A.F., Share D.L., MacLean R., and Mathews, R. (1984). 'Phonological confusability in short-term memory for sentences as a predictor of reading ability', British Journal of Psychology, 75, 393-400.

Kleiman, G.M. (1975). 'Speech recoding in reading', Journal of Verbal Learning and Verbal Behavior, 14, 323-339.

Mann, V. and Liberman, I.Y. (1984). 'Phonological awareness and verbal short-term memory: Can they presage early reading success?' Journal of Learning Disabilities, 17, 592-599.

Perfetti, C.D. and Goldman, S.R. (1976). 'Discourse memory and reading comprehension skill', Journal of Verbal Learning and Verbal Behavior, 14, 33-42.

Torgeson, J. and Houck, G. (1980). 'Processing deficiencies of learning-disabled children who perform poorly on the digit span test', Journal of Educational Psychology, 72, 141-60.

Torgeson, J., Rashotte, C., Greenstein J., Houck, G. and Portes, P. (1987). 'Academic difficulties of learning disabled children who perform poorly on memory span tasks', in Memory and learning disabilities: Advances in learning and behavioral disabilities (Ed. H. L. Swanson), Greenwich, Conn: JAI Press.

ORTHOGRAPHIC MEMORY CODES IN
DEVELOPMENTAL DYSLEXIA

John Rack.
Department of Psychology, Durham University.

Maggie Snowling.
Department of Psychology, University College, London.

ABSTRACT
        In a previous paper (Rack, 1985) dyslexic readers were found to make less use of a phonological memory code than younger Reading-Age-matched Controls. However, they compensated through increased use of an orthographic memory code. This finding was supported in Experiment One in which dyslexic subjects used orthographic information in a phoneme segmentation task and is consistent with the view that dyslexics rely upon a "visual" reading strategy. Experiment Two found that dyslexics were less sensitive than normal readers to positional information in an orthographic priming task. This suggests that the representations acquired from a visual reading strategy do not code the order of the letters in words and are not, therefore, very useful for spelling.

INTRODUCTION
        Experiments demonstrating problems for dyslexic readers with phonological memory and segmentation skills lend support to the view that they have difficulty in achieving alphabetic competence (Frith, 1985). In short, they have trouble using the letter-sound correspondences embodied by the English orthography. Thus, in order to learn to read, many dyslexics are forced to adopt alternative strategies to the phonological ones normally used in literacy acquisition. Snowling (1980) suggested that these strategies may be visual in nature. However, reliance on a visual reading strategy is unlikely to support successful spelling (Frith, 1980). An important experiment by Perin (1983) compared a group of poor readers and poor spellers, a group of poor spellers but good readers and a group of good spellers and good readers on a segmentation task in which the names of 'pop' groups had to be "Spoonerized". The task involved interchanging the initial phonemes of the two spoken names e.g. "Bad Manners" becomes "Mad Banners". The two groups of poor spellers were equivalent on the segmentation task but inferior to the group of good reader-spellers. Despite their phonological difficulties, the poor spellers-good readers had reached the same level of reading competence as the good speller-readers. So they must have been reading using visual or other compensatory strategies.
        Finally, direct evidence that dyslexics can use alternative strategies to compensate for phonological deficiencies was presented by Rack (1985). In the initial phase of this experiment, dyslexics were influenced more by orthography when asked

to decide whether auditorily presented words rhymed. Thus, dyslexics judged head-dead to be rhyming more easily than they judged head-said to be rhyming. They showed this orthography effect to a greater degree than a comparison group of younger children matched for reading age, despite the fact that the words were presented in the auditory modality. When recall was tested in a second part of this experiment, the dyslexics were influenced more by the orthographic similarity betwen cue and target (e.g. they remembered that warm had been paired with farm) whereas the controls were more influenced by phonological similarity (e.g. they remembered that rose had been paired with goes).

EXPERIMENT ONE

This experiment was based on Perin's (1983) task which is an interesting one because it can be carried out in one of two ways. A phonological strategy produces "Kill Follins" from "Phil Collins" whereas an orthographic strategy (used by some of Perin's teenage subjects) produces "Chill Pollins". The hypothesis tested here was that dyslexic readers would have difficulty with the phonological strategy but would compensate by using a visual / orthographic strategy.

Pilot work indicated that Perin's Spoonerism task was too difficult for dyslexic children reading at a level of 9 to 10 years. A task was therefore devised which was less difficult but demanded the use of the same processes. In this task a word was presented and the children asked to say what that word would sound like if it began with a different sound. The resulting utterances were sometimes familiar words (for example, walk with a /t/ produces talk) and sometimes non-words (for example, do with a /v/ produces /voo/.

SUBJECTS

Ten dyslexic subjects, eight boys and two girls, were selected from a remedial unit and a comparison group of normal subjects, six boys and four girls, was matched with them on the basis of Reading Age. (For further details of the selection procedures, see Rack, 1986). The mean Reading Age of the dyslexic group was 9 years 11 months (range 8:8 to 11:10, sd 1 year) and the mean Reading Age of the comparison group was 10 years 4 months (range 9:0 to 11:10, sd 10 months). The dyslexics ranged in age from 13 to 15 years of age; the controls were all 10 year olds.

DESIGN AND MATERIALS

There were four experimental conditions. For two conditions the result of the phoneme substitution process was a word and for the other two the result was a non-word. For the Word conditions there was a sub-division into "Orthographically consistent" and "Orthographically inconsistent" responses. For example rope with a /h/ giving hope is consistent since the word hope is suggested by both phonology and orthography. Rope with a /s/ giving sope is inconsistent since the word soap is suggested by the phonology but not the orthography.

The Non-Word conditions were sub-divided in a similar way. For example live with a /m/ giving /miv/ is consistent because neither phonology nor orthography suggest a word. Inconsistent response were those for which the orthography suggested a word but the phonology did not, for example live with a /f/ giving /fiv/. In this latter example the orthography suggests the word "five" as a potential response.

Two lists were created. There were 28 stimuli per list, 14 Words and 14 Non-Words, half of each being Consistent and half Inconsistent. Those which were Consistent in one list were Inconsistent in the other and vice versa.

RESULTS AND DISCUSSION

A response was counted as an error if it was not a correct blending of the word with its new initial phoneme. The mean number of errors are shown in the table below.

Mean number of errors in phoneme substitution for the Consistent and Inconsistent Word and Non-Word Conditions.

	Words		Non-Words	
	Consistent	Inconsistent	Consistent	Inconsistent
Dyslexics	1.0	0.9	1.6	2.4
	(.82)	(1.10)	(1.35)	(2.60)
Controls	0.2	0.6	0.1	0.4
	(.63)	(1.07)	(.32)	(0.84)

There was a significant group difference ($F(1,18) = 7.516$, $p< 0.01$) indicating that dyslexic readers made more errors than the younger controls of the same reading age who had very little difficulty with the task. The main effect of Lexicality failed to reach significance ($F(1,18) = 2.673$, $p=0.0554$ 1-tail). However, the the Group by Lexicality interaction was significant ($F(1,18) = 5.781$, $p<0.05$) reflecting a larger difference between words and non-words for the dyslexic group.

The effect of Consistency also just failed to reach significance ($F(1,18)= 2.287$, $p=0.0739$ 1-tail) but the trend was in the predicted direction of the Inconsistent responses producing more errors than the Consistent responses. Further analysis revealed that there was an interaction between Group and Consistency for the Non-Words ($F(1,22)= 28.05$, $p<0.001$) but not for the Words ($F<1$). Thus the effect of Consistency was greater for the dyslexic group in the Non-Word conditions but there was no difference between the groups in the Word conditions.

The results of Experiment One showed that dyslexics found the phoneme substitution task very difficult. These results add to the growing body of evidence which indicates that dyslexic children suffer from a difficulty which is phonological in nature (e.g. Snowling, 1981). The results suggest that the dyslexics draw upon

alternative   sources   of   information   in   performing   the   phoneme
substitution   task. They make more use of lexical phonology, and when
this   strategy   is   unavailable   (for   non-words),   they   are   also
influenced   by   orthographic   information.   These   results   therefore
support the   conclusion   of Rack (1985) that dyslexics may compensate
for deficient phonological memory coding   by   an   increased   use   of
orthographic coding.

EXPERIMENT TWO

If dyslexics make more use   of an orthographic memory code,
we might ask why they are   unable   to   make   use of that orthographic
information   when   writing.   One   hypothesis is that the orthographic
representations do not   code   the order of   the   letters (e.g. Mason,
1980). To investigate the nature of the orthographic   representations
available to dyslexic   readers,   a priming technique devised by Evett
and Humphreys (1981) was   used.   In   this   paradigm   a prime word is
presented at a sub-threshold   level   just before   the   target. If the
prime has common features with   the target then identification of the
target is facilitated.

In   the present study   there   were   three   types   of   prime
selected to   investigate   the variables of letter position and letter
identity. The Anagram primes contained the same letters as the target
but rearranged to   form   an anagram (e.g. stew WEST). If words   are
coded irrespective of letter-order, these primes should be effective.
The Position primes were one letter different from their targets   but
the remaining three letters   were in   the same   positions (e.g. wept
WEST).   Thus, if letter-order is represented internally, these primes
should   be   effective.   The   Control primes   were   selected to be one
letter   different   from   the   Anagram   primes (e.g.   step WEST).   Any
advantage that the   Position Primes   may have over the Control Primes
will be due to the   effects of shared letter positions and will imply
that letter-order is important.   Any   difference between Anagram and
Control primes will be   due to   the fact   that the Anagram primes and
targets share all   their   letter identities whilst the Control primes
do not.

SUBJECTS

Fourteen   dyslexics   were   compared with   14   normal
readers of similar reading ages. The mean reading age of the dyslexic
group was 9 years   4 months (range 8:1 to 11:10) and the mean reading
age of the control group was   9 years 8 months (range 8:5 to 11:10).
The range   of   chronological   ages   was   very   similar   to that   in
Experiment One.

DESIGN AND MATERIALS

The materials were presented using a BBC microcomputer, the
targets   in upper-case   letters and   the primes in lower-case. Before
and after the   prime-target sequence,   a random   letter mask was
presented. This   mask   consisted of   a random sequence of upper-case
consonants, however, it was ensured that the mask did not contain any
of the letters used in the prime or target on that trial.

Subjects were given 2 blocks of 12 practice trials in which the primes were the same words as the targets but in lower-case. These trials were used to estimate the exposure duration at which the words could be identified about half of the time. For the 24 experimental trials subjects were allowed a second attempt to identify the target if they failed to do so on the first presentation. The exposure was increased by 20 milliseconds for the second presentation.

RESULTS

Subjects completed eight trials for each of the three priming conditions: Position Primes, Anagram Primes and Control Primes. The dependent variable was the number of targets correctly identified in each condition. The amount of priming for the experimental conditions was determined for each subject by subtracting performance in the control condition from performance in the experimental conditions. Mean scores are shown in the table below.

Mean Priming Effects in the Anagram and Position Conditions for Dyslexics and Controls.

	Anagram	Position
Dyslexics	1.071 (1.68)	0.857 (1.99)
Controls	0.857 (0.86)	1.643 (1.39)

The priming scores were logarithmically transformed and entered into a 2 (conditions) by 2 (groups) Analysis of Variance. There was no overall group difference ($F<1$). Thus the two groups show similar levels of orthographic priming relative to the control condition. There was no overall difference between the two types of prime ($F<1$) but, as predicted, there was a group by prime interaction ($F(1,26)= 2.97$, $p<0.05$ 1-tailed) indicating that the effects of the type of prime were not the same for the two groups.

These results should be interpreted with caution since the number of subjects showing the predicted differences was small. The dyslexic group showed no difference at all between the two types of prime with six identifying more of the Anagram targets, six identifying more of the Position targets and two subjects showing no difference. Amongst the controls, only four identified more of the Anagram targets whilst eight identified more of the Position targets, and two showed no difference. The safest interpretation of the data is that the control subjects tended to show an advantage for the Position primed targets but the dyslexics did not.

DISCUSSION

Experiment One showed that dyslexic children had great difficulty in performing a phoneme substitution task. Moreover, they were misled by orthographic information. These results are consistent with the hypothesis that dyslexics have difficulty with the processing of phonology and also provide support for the idea that dyslexics make more use of orthographic information in memory tasks (Rack, 1985).

In Experiment Two, subjects were asked to identify briefly presented target words which were preceded by different types of prime. For normal children, primes were more successful if the common letters in the primes and targets were in the same positions; there was no such difference for the dyslexics. These results support the idea that dyslexics do not code the positions of letters in their orthographic representations.

The results of the two experiments are consistent with the view that dyslexics acquire reading proficiency by extending their sight vocabularies using a logographic reading strategy (Frith, 1985; Snowling, 1980). It appears that they are able to make use of the visual information acquired in this way in memory tasks which place heavy demands on their weak phonological skills. However, a characteristic of this visual / orthographic information is that it does not code the order of letters and is, therefore, not sufficient for proficient spelling.

REFERENCES

Evett,L.J. and Humphreys,G.W. (1981) The use of abstract graphemic information in lexical access. Quarterly Journal of Experimental Psychology, 33a, 325-350.

Frith,U. (1980) Unexpected spelling problems. In FRITH,U. (Ed). Cognitive processes in spelling. London: Academic Press

Frith,U. (1985) Beneath the surface of developmental dyslexia. In J. Marshall, K.Patterson & M. Coltheart (Eds) Surface Dyslexia. London: Lawrence Erlbaum Associates.

Mason,M. (1980) Reading ability and the encoding of item and location information. Journal of Experimental Psychology: Human Perception and Performance, 6, 89-98.

Perin,D. (1983) Phonemic segmentation and spelling. British Journal of Psychology, 74, 129-144.

Rack, J.P. (1985) Orthographic and phonetic coding in developmental dyslexia. British Journal of Psychology, 76, 325-340.

Rack,J.P (1986) An Investigation of Memory Coding in Developmental Dyslexia. Ph.D. Thesis, University of London.

Snowling, M.J. (1980) The development of grapheme-phoneme correspondences in normal and dyslexic readers. Journal of Experimental Child Psychology,29, 294-305.

Snowling, M.J. (1981) Phonemic deficits in developmental dyslexia. Psychological Research,43, 219-234.

ORAL LANGUAGE FLUENCY IN DEVELOPMENTAL DYSLEXIA

Peter Griffiths
Centre for Cognitive and Computational Neuroscience
Department of Psychology, University of Stirling
Stirling, FK9 4LA, Scotland

ABSTRACT
        Oral language fluency in dyslexics and CA-matched controls
was measured by a lexical retrieval task. Subjects gave an
appropriate spoken word to initial grapheme and phoneme, and semantic
category cues. In one condition five seconds were allowed for
responding, in another ten. In the shorter, the dyslexics' word
production was inferior to the controls' on the grapheme and phoneme
tests but superior on the semantic test. In the longer, these
differences largely disappeared. The results undermine the idea that
the dyslexia syndrome is characterized by general oral-verbal
dysfluency. The finding that lexical access (including phonological)
was highly inefficient at the word-form level, but not at the
semantic, supports the view that processing of the structural aspects
of oral and visual language is the central fault in dyslexia.

INTRODUCTION
        Clinical and laboratory evidence indicates that the
boundaries of the dyslexic syndrome in childhood extend beyond the
familiar difficulty of acquiring visual language. Receptive and
expressive oral language deficiencies, including delayed speech onset
(Ingram, 1963), imperfect repetition of phonological sequences
(Holmes & McKeever, 1979) and imperception of rhyming and
alliterative speech-sounds (Bradley & Bryant, 1978), have been
frequently reported as correlates of dyslexia. On the basis of such
findings, Denckla (1979) concluded that the reading and spelling
difficulties typical of childhood dyslexia might best be
conceptualized as surface manifestations - or 'index symptoms' in her
terminology - of a rather widespread developmental psycholinguistic
disorder. Echoes of this notion can also be found in the 'verbal
deficit' hypothesis of Vellutino (1978).
        Impaired short-term memory for verbal or phonologically
encodable information is a well-documented feature of dyslexia (Jorm,
1983). However, long-term memory or, more precisely, interactions
between short- and long-term memory may also be implicated in the
pattern of oral linguistic difficulties. For instance, Denckla and
her colleagues found dysnomic responses on confrontation naming
tasks to be related to dyslexia (Denckla & Rudel, 1976a), as were
circumlocutory responses on definitional vocabulary tasks and poor
rapid automatized naming skills (Denckla & Rudel, 1976b).
        The concept of oral-verbal fluency implies rapid retrieval
of words from long-term storage. Wolf (1982, 1984) studied this
ability in dyslexics by means of two controlled-association tasks:

the FAS test (Benton, 1973) and the animal-set test (Lezak, 1976). The subject is given 60 seconds to generate, in the former, words beginning with the letters F, A and S; in the latter, unrestricted animal names. Wolf's data suggested that, in poor readers, overt word-production may vary as a function of the access route pre-set by short-term memory. She found that lexical-retrieval performance as measured by the FAS correlated highly with reading, but not as measured by the animal names test. From these results, it is tempting to infer that in dyslexia the conceptual route to entries in the lexicon may function more efficiently and automatically than the word-form route (Miller & Johnson-Laird, 1976). However, as the standard administration of the FAS test confounds phonological and orthographic access (Borkowski et al., 1967), under-performance on this measure in a dyslexic group may simply reflect comparative ignorance of written word-forms and not necessarily implicate the phonological access route (Ellis, 1985) as Wolf proposed.

Methodologies for investigating oral language fluency in developmental dyslexia should therefore allow for separate evaluation of the effects of orthographic, phonological and semantic activation of the speech output lexicon. The present study was designed around this consideration. Word-finding performance of dyslexic children was compared with that of CA-matched, good-reading controls on graphemically-, phonemically- and semantically-cued retrieval measures to determine whether group-related fluency differences were general or specific. The traditional generative paradigm was abandoned in favour of one in which varying cues within each access category were presented regularly, the subject having to make a verbal response within the inter-stimulus interval (ISI). Subjects were tested under two ISI conditions, short and long. It was hypothesized that if retrieval were mainly dependent on efficient lexical access processes (i.e. STM-LTM interactions) overall word-production would increase when more time was available for responding, whereas if it were primarily a function of intra-lexical indexing then extra time would not lead to better performance.

SUBJECTS, APPARATUS AND PROCEDURE

The subjects were 15 dyslexic and 15 control children, ten boys and five girls in each group. Reading and spelling levels were assessed by means of the Schonell lists, intellectual status by a short-form of the WISC (Maxwell, 1959). Group means and pair-wise t-statistics for the sample variables are given below. Chronological age (CA), reading age (RA) and spelling age (SA) are expressed in years and the Similarities (Sim), Vocabulary (Voc), Block Design (BD) and Object Assembly (OA) subtests in scaled scores.

	CA	RA	SA	Sim	Voc	BD	OA
Dyslexics	10.16	8.44	7.98	12.40	12.33	11.53	12.80
Controls	10.24	11.40	11.53	16.87	14.07	12.80	12.53
t	-0.22	-7.34	-7.12	-5.33	-2.33	-1.17	0.25
P	N.S.	<0.001	<0.001	<0.001	<0.05	N.S.	N.S.

The groups were thus matched in terms of age, sex and non-verbal intelligence, but the dyslexics were inferior to the controls in reading, spelling and verbal intelligence.

Oral-verbal fluency was operationally defined as the total number of words a subject produced on each of three thirty-item tests administered under two time conditions. For every probe stimulus a single response, scored plus or minus, was required, giving a scale of zero to 30. The three experimental measures were differentiated according to whether the cuing stimulus was classifiable as graphemic, phonemic or semantic.

On the graphemic task, the child viewed lower-case letters – b, f, p, t and w – back-projected singly on to a translucent screen. Each five-letter grouping was presented six times with the internal order randomized. No letter was shown twice in succession. The entire test was repeated for each subject: once with an ISI of five seconds and once with an ISI of 10 seconds. The letter sequence was re-randomized in the longer time condition. The child's task was to say a word whose written form began with the letter displayed. The response had to be made within the time available. A binary scoring scheme was used: one point for any part of speech (including proper nouns) whose initial grapheme corresponded to the stimulus; nothing for a word that either failed to obey this rule, or was a repeat or a grammatical variant of one given earlier, or was an acceptable word said after the next letter in the sequence had appeared. The stimuli for the phonemic task were the speech sounds c, l, m, r and s (c pronounced hard). Their order was randomized in like fashion. They were recorded on audiotape with five and 10 second ISI's and presented monophonically to the child through headphones. The child's task was to say, within the time slot available, a word whose spoken form began with the stimulus sound. Similar acceptance-rejection criteria to the grapheme test applied. The administration of the semantic task was similar. As with the phonemes, cuing stimuli were presented on audiotape. They were five spoken adjectives – big, noisy, soft, sweet and smelly – chosen to correspond with the major senses. Each was repeated six times within the short and long time conditions. The children were asked to say a word as quickly as possible whose referent could be described by the cue-word. Any sensible response was scored positively.

Audiotaped, standardized instructions were played to every subject and five practice trials given before each test. An identical, counterbalanced order of presentation for the stimulus and time conditions was imposed on the two groups.

RESULTS

Analysis of variance revealed statistically significant main and interaction effects. The dyslexic group's mean fluency score overall on the 0-30 scale was 16.70 compared to the control group's 19.70 ($F = 13.46$, df 1/28, $P < 0.01$). With group and time data merged, fluency was highest in response to graphemic cues, intermediate to phonemic and lowest to semantic, the means being respectively 19.03, 18.70 and 16.87 ($F = 6.35$, df 2/56, $P < 0.01$). With group and stimulus data merged, the mean fluency score of 20.02 for the 10 second time interval was reliably greater than that of 16.38 for the five second interval ($F = 90.03$, df 1/28, $P < 0.001$). As the group x cuing stimulus x time interval interaction term was significant ($F = 5.68$, df 2/56, $P < 0.01$), the breakdown of the word production sub-means, with standard deviations in brackets, was as follows. Dyslexics, short ISI: graphemic 13.00 (5.11), phonemic

12.40 (5.08), semantic 17.47 (4.80). Controls, short ISI: graphemic
22.53 (3.17), phonemic 20.00 (2.88), semantic 12.87 (2.73).
Dyslexics, long ISI: graphemic 18.20 (6.79), phonemic 20.4 (3.68),
semantic 18.73 (3.23). Controls, long ISI: graphemic 22.40 (2.25),
phonemic 22.00 (2.42), semantic 18.40 (4.05). The pattern of these
differences in word production as a function of the experimental
manipulations is depicted in the figure below.

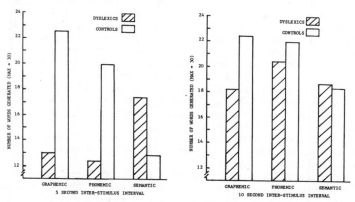

Pair-wise analysis of the mean differences shown in the
figure revealed that, under the five second ISI condition, the
dyslexics' performance differed from the controls' at beyond the 1%
level of chance on all three variables; however, under the 10 second
condition, the groups were undifferentiated statistically, except on
the graphemic test where the 5% confidence level was exceeded.

DISCUSSION

The results from this experiment suggest that it would be
false to regard dyslexic children as being generally verbally
dysfluent. Speed of retrieval of words stored in long-term memory
appears to be a function of the route by which the lexicon is
accessed. It is hardly surprising the dyslexics did badly searching
for words on the basis of initial graphemes. Such a finding probably
does little more than confirm the correctness of the sample selection
procedure. However, the finding that the dyslexics not only
under-performed the controls on the five second phonemic test but
that their mean phonemic score was worse than their graphemic score
is suggestive of a profound disorder of phonological lexical access.
The fact that this difference largely disappeared on the 10 second
condition adds weight to the theory that the lexicon in dyslexia is
not so much ill-organized phonologically as inaccessible by the
phonological route when time is constrained.

The data obtained from the semantic test were unexpected.
When searching the lexicon on the basis of meaningful associations or
connotations, the dyslexics actually out-performed the controls.
This dissociation between literacy level and semantically-driven word
production is all the more remarkable considering the control
children's above-average reading, spelling, Similarities and
Vocabulary scores. It thus seems fair to conclude that semantic
access to the lexicon might be quite unimpaired in dyslexia — and

might even be hyper-efficient. Such a view is consistent with clinical and experimental evidence for dyslexics' recall of verbal content being superior to decoding skills (Thomson, 1984).

The exceptional inability of the dyslexic group to generate words on the basis of initial speech-sounds cannot be accounted for by the sequential short-term memory defect for phonological material that has become such a well-established feature of the dyslexic syndrome (Jorm, 1983). All the speech-sound cues were discrete phonemes and thus would have been sub-span for a group with a mean digits forwards score of 5.00 (0.926). It is unlikely the children would have forgotten the cues within a five or 10 second period. No child asked for a stimulus to be repeated. Moreover, had deficient phonological short-term memory been a factor affecting the outcome of the phonemic test, its influence would have extended to the semantic test where some of the cuing stimuli were two-syllable adjectives. A further criticism of the dyslexia-specific result on the phonemic fluency test is that it might simply have arisen as a consequence of under-achievement in reading. However, as there is no a priori reason to believe that literacy is a necessary pre-requisite for success on such a task, it is difficult to accept that the causal direction must be this way round.

Arguably, dyslexia research has tended to focus on internal short-term memory processes at the expense of short-term/long-term memory interactions. With contemporary modular models of normal reading emphasizing the centrality of rapid, automatic grapheme-to-phoneme conversion in phonic decoding (Ellis, 1984), this bias is unjustified. Although not deliberately oriented towards describing faults in the reading process, the results from the present study point to the dyslexic child having more widespread difficulties with phonics than those confined to short-term memory functions such as temporary retention and blending of speech-sounds. Inefficient accessing of the lexicon at the phonological word-form level may also be characteristic of the syndrome. As is illustrated by the dissociation between the phonemic and semantic fluency measures, the central defect in dyslexia now seems less a verbal or general linguistic one (Vellutino, 1978), than one specific to the form rather than the content of language, both spoken and written. In the light of this and the findings of numerous other studies demonstrating deficient phonic-handling skills, perhaps the dyslexic child, rather than being considered word-blind, would be better considered phone-deaf.

REFERENCES

Benton, A.L. (1973). 'The Measurement of Aphasic Disorders', in Aspectos Patalogicos del Lengage, (Ed. A.C. Velasquez), Centro Neuropsicologico, Lima.

Borkowski, J.G., Benton, A.L. and Spreen, O. (1967). 'Word Fluency and Brain Damage', Neuropsychologia, 5, 135-140.

Bradley, L. and Bryant, P.E. (1978). 'Difficulties in Auditory Organization as a Possible Cause of Reading Backwardness', Nature, 271, 746-747.

Denckla, M.B. (1979). 'Childhood Learning Disabilities', in Clinical Neuropsychology (Eds. K.M. Heilman and E. Valenstein), pp. 535-572, Oxford University Press, New York.

Denckla, M.B. and Rudel, R.G. (1976a). 'Naming of Object Drawings by Dyslexic and Other Learning-Disabled Children', Brain and Language, 3, 1-15.

Denckla, M.B. and Rudel, R.G. (1976b). 'Rapid Automatized Naming (R.A.N.): Dyslexia Differentiated from Other Learning Disabilities', Neuropsychologia, 1976, 14, 471-479.

Ellis, A.W. (1984). Reading, Writing and Dyslexia, pg. 33, Lawrence Erlbaum Associates, London.

Ellis, A.W. (1985). 'The Production of Spoken Words: A Cognitive Neuropsychological Perspective', in Progress in the Psychology of Language, Vol. 2 (Ed. A.W. Ellis), pp. 107-145, Lawrence Erlbaum Associates, London.

Holmes, D.R. and McKeever, W.F. (1979). 'Material Specific Serial Memory Deficit in Adolescent Dyslexics', Cortex, 15, 51-62.

Ingram, T.T.S. (1963). 'The Association of Speech Retardation and Educational Difficulties', Proceedings of the Royal Society of Medicine, 56, 199-203.

Jorm, A.F. (1983). 'Specific Reading Retardation and Working Memory: A Review', British Journal of Psychology, 74, 311-342.

Lezak, A.R. (1976). Neuropsychological Assessment, Oxford University Press, New York.

Maxwell, A.E. (1959). 'A Factor Analysis of the WISC', British Journal of Educational Psychology, 29, 237-241.

Miller, G.A. and Johnson-Laird, P.N. (1976). Language and Perception, Cambridge University Press, Cambridge.

Thomson, M.E. (1984). Developmental Dyslexia: Its Nature, Assessment and Remediation, pg. 129, Arnold, London.

Vellutino, F.R. (1978). 'Toward an Understanding of Dyslexia', in Dyslexia: An Appraisal of Current Knowledge, (Eds. A.L. Benton and D. Pearl), pp. 63-111, Oxford University Press, New York.

Wolf, M. (1982). 'The Word-Retrieval Process and Reading in Children and Aphasics', in Children's Language, Vol. 3, (Ed. K.E. Nelson), pp. 437-493, Lawrence Erlbaum Associates, Hillsdale.

Wolf, M. (1984). 'Naming, Reading and the Dyslexias: A Longitudinal Overview', Annals of Dyslexia, 34, 87-115.

PHONOLOGICAL CODING AND MEMORY IN READING DISORDERS: CAUSE OR EFFECT?

John R. Beech
Department of Psychology
The University, Leicester, LE1 7RH, UK.

ABSTRACT

This paper considers two contrasting hypotheses. The first suggests that the problems in phonological coding and memory in poor readers have an effect on the development of a system for converting graphemes to phonemes. Two formulations of a grapheme-to-phoneme converter and the implications for phonological storage are also considered. The alternative hypothesis suggests that the experience of learning to read and write develops grapheme-phoneme conversion in normal readers which in turn facilitates the development of phonemic processing and retention. On current meagre evidence it seems that the second hypothesis receives marginally more support than the first.

A large proportion of research into reading disorders in recent years has concentrated on examining the association between reading disorders in children and their problems in phonological coding. There has been far less work on phonological memory and reading. The present paper examines experimental and theoretical work mainly in phonological memory and relates this to the development of a system of grapheme-phoneme conversion during the process of learning to read. An examination is made of the proposition that problems in phonological processing and retention may result in difficulties for the developing grapheme-phoneme conversion system leading, in turn, to retarded reading. However, a contrasting proposition, that the processes involved in learning to read, for the normal reader, facilitate phonological coding and memory, will also be discussed. All the experimental work involving reading which tested young readers varying in reading ability that will be considered here, had the readers matched on intelligence, except where stated. Furthermore, any studies marred by possible confounding range effects between groups are not discussed.

PHONOLOGICAL CODING AND READING DISORDER

Up-to-date reviews on the connection between phonological coding and reading ability may be found in Bryant and Goswami (in press) and in Wagner and Torgesen (in press). A great deal of evidence indicates that poor readers perform worse than good readers on a variety of phonological tasks. Although there have been some attempts to establish the direction of causality (e.g. Bradley &

Bryant, 1983; Morais, Cary, Alegria & Bertelson, 1982), the evidence does not seem to be clear on whether poor phonological processing impairs reading development, or whether impaired reading development retards normal development of phonological processing. There might be support for both propositions, but as this is well-trodden theoretical ground, and my plot of available land frustratingly small, I will skirt around this area.

GRAPHEME-PHONEME CONVERSION

Is there a connection between grapheme-phoneme conversion and phonemic awareness?
          As previously stated, there is a reasonably strong connection between the level of phonemic coding and reading performance in children. However, reading performance is normally assessed on the basis of the quality of the developing visual lexicon and not on the facility of grapheme-phoneme conversion. Impairment in overall performance may be due to an underlying impairment in grapheme-conversion which in turn may be connected with problems in phonemic awareness. But there are at least three different ways in which a child may learn to read (e.g. Beech, in press), namely, by grapheme-phoneme conversion, by analogy, or by lexical access. In the first, an ability to decode words into individual sounds would be important; in the second, this same ability might be used; and in the third, lexical access, decoding individual words into corresponding sounds would not be necessary, by definition. We might expect a connection between phonemic awareness and reading style, such that having an orientation toward grapheme-phoneme conversion would be associated with relatively better phonemic awareness. In lexical coding, phonological processing occurs (if at all) after lexical access, and therefore this mode will be discussed no further. Bryant and Goswami (in press) discuss a role for phonological coding in analogical reading.
          A study by Stuart-Hamilton (1986) has in fact suggested a connection between phonological coding and reading style. Two groups of readers aged about 5 years, differing in phonemic awareness, of the same reading age, but not matched for IQ, were compared in their detection of minor changes in letters (e.g. "donkeg" for "donkey") and in their type of errors in reading normal text. The children with better phonemic awareness were better at detecting graphemic changes and made proportionally less graphemic miscues, (however, no statistical test was given directly on this latter finding). Although this finding has some plausibility, Beech and Harding (1984) examined readers aged about 10 years on tests of phonemic processing and reading style and in a factor analysis did not find an association between the two. There is, however, a marked difference between the ages of the readers in the two studies. There may be a relationship between reading style and phonological awareness, but at the moment we need more experimental studies over the various age ranges. Also, Stuart-Hamilton's study is ambiguous because when phonemic awareness is varied and changes in reading style are observed, the changes in graphemic analysis, as measured by miscues, could be attributed to readers increasingly

concentrating on the letters in order to translate to corresponding
sounds, or else their expanded lexical database could lead to an
increase in the potential graphemic confusion between words.
Therefore, more valid measures of reading style need to be used.

Alternative formulations of grapheme-phoneme conversion
          Describing exactly how a grapheme-phoneme converter (GPC)
might work is an exercise which can implicate the role of
phonological memory. An account of the possible development of the
GPC is given in Beech (in press) and in Barron (1986).   Beech
proposed a simplified account of GPC development within   a
developing dual-route system in which phonemic representations are
stored according to the spatial location of each letter.   This
implies, first, that phonemic representations are held in a
phonological store; second, that alternative representations (for
instance, each of the vowels represents more than one phoneme) might
be stored together in particular spatial slots. This formulation of
a dual-route model suggests a "horse-race" (Carr and Pollatsek,
1985) between the lexical and GPC routes. Beech suggested that as
GPC operations would always be intrinsically slow, lexical
processing would become relatively more efficient and eventually
become the predominant mode of access.
          A more efficient system would be one in which the GPC and
lexical systems were closely interlinked. When the first grapheme
is encountered this would activate all word units beginning with the
sound or sounds represented by this initial grapheme.   The next
grapheme would restrict activation to a narrower set of units and so
on, rapidly narrowing down the search for the appropiate word unit.
Even in this GPC model it helps to be able to retain a phonological
code.   However, in this instance this need only be the actual
phonemes comprising the word; whereas in the independent GPC, the
various alternative phonemes for each slot need to be retained prior
to the synthesis of different combinations of phonemes.
          A major problem for any GPC model is the irregularities in
the English spelling system. A realistic model, for fluent readers,
requires at least the initial coding of pairs of letters, such that
on the first pass across the letters priority is given to two-letter
combinations which frequently represent one phoneme (e.g. the
phoneme for "sh" is given priority over /s/ when analysing sh);
otherwise the first letter is decoded. The next step is to examine
the next pair, depending on what has been analysed so far, and so
on.   (The position of the letter pairs within the word would be
important; for instance, the terminal e frequently modifies a
preceding vowel.) This system will still generate a number of
ambiguities, so the unit of analysis might be even larger than
letter pairs. But this would change the nature of the system into
one involving orthographic units, rather than graphemes (defined
here as the letter(s) representing single phonemes).

PHONOLOGICAL MEMORY AND READING DISORDER

          Examining the operations of the GPC revealed that the
demands on phonological retention can vary according to the

arrangement of the GPC. However, all GPCs require the retention of phonological information prior to and during the access of the lexicon. Before we examine experimental work linking the retention of phonemic information and reading ability, it should be remembered that when discussing the operation of the GPC, this involves phonological information which is internally generated, in contrast to experiments on phonological retention which rely on the subject listening to phonological information. Thus this might implicate the use of separate systems. To complicate matters further, there could be at least three distinctive auditory-verbal systems retaining information after input. Baddeley proposes that the articulatory loop comprises an articulatory rehearsal process as well as a phonological input store (e.g. Baddeley, 1983). This second store is similar to what has often been referred to by others as an echoic memory (e.g. Crowder, 1972; Crowder & Morton, 1969). There is also evidence that this might subdivide into a short-term auditory store that lasts 200-300 ms, analogous to a continuation of sensation after the stimulus has ceased (e.g. Cowan, 1984). The other part is a longer lasting store which may have processed speech information into its phonemic constituents via feature analysis.

Sipe and Engle (1986) provide evidence for the nature of these last two stores in a comparison of good and poor 11-year-old readers. First, individual performance shadowing letters was adjusted to 75 - 85% correct for everyone. Then, in the unattended ear a digit occasionally occurred within another random sequence of letters. At various intervals after the digit a signal prompted the subjects to name it. Performance was equivalent for both groups with no cue delay but deteriorated rapidly over 2 seconds for the poor readers to an asymptote only slightly above chance level. Good readers showed no deterioration until after about 4 seconds and even then remained above chance up to the maximum period of 16 seconds. In another experiment, matching performance in memory span, poor readers demonstrated a much greater suffix effect (comparing the stimulus suffix "go" with a tone). Both these experiments suggest an echoic memory which is much more susceptible to interference for the poor readers. In the shadowing experiment, the articulatory loop cannot be responsible for this difference as it was presumably occupied by shadowing. Then Sipe and Engle demonstrated no difference in a short-term auditory store between the two groups by adjusting the gap between two bursts of white noise. Both groups had almost identical detectability functions, suggesting the same persistence of auditory non-phonological information. A similar distinction between speech and non-speech stimuli has been shown in an experiment on the perception of spoken language by Brady, Shankweiler and Mann (1983) which demonstrated that poor readers were worse than good readers in identifying speech in white noise, but the same at identifying environmental sounds.

These experiments (particularly by Sipe and Engle) suggest a problem in the retention of phonological information over the medium short term for poor readers. This might suggest inefficiency in analysing phonemic information so that perhaps insufficient features are processed to distinguish and sequence the incoming information. By contrast, the good readers process such information to an extent which makes it relatively more difficult to confuse featural properties of the phonemes. Suppose auditory short-term memory held acoustic information prior to processing. Efficient processing would transfer information, representing a collection of features sufficient to identify a phoneme, into echoic memory. Inefficient processing may not generate enough features to identify uniquely the phonemes resulting in greater interference effects between stored and incoming phonemes, as shown by these experiments. Now suppose that this inefficiency in phonemic processing and coding in echoic memory in the poor reader also extended to the working of the GPC. If the GPC is used, subjects will be decomposing words into phonemes. But it is then a great theoretical leap to propose that somehow the subject confuses the generated phonemes, resulting in difficulty in reading the word. Internally generated sounds should be sufficiently distinctive from one another, whereas the identification and discriminability of phonemes from an external source is rather different, but there is no experimental evidence pointing either way, so far as I am aware.

A different way of looking at these results is to view the process of learning to read as conferring certain benefits to cognitive processing. Continuously encountering the same 26 letters during reading, in different combinations, gradually makes the child realise that speech consists of smaller identifiable units, that is, phonemes. A more advanced reader has more experience with using the GPC and so develops a more efficient system for identifying the individual phonemes, particularly via the act of writing which requires breaking up words into sounds. Thus echoic memory is less susceptible to interference in normal readers.

There is not much evidence to support the notion that poor phonological processing and memory retard the development of the GPC. For instance, greater phonemic awareness does not clearly lead to a proclivity to use the GPC. Bryant and Bradley (1985) report a longitudinal study of 368 children supporting a causal link in the direction that learning to read actually improves memory. At 4 and 5 years of age, before reading started, their memory for words did not predict reading performance one and a half years later. Furthermore, their level of reading at this point predicted later memory performance when they were tested at the age of 8 or 9 years. In the words of Bryant and Bradley: "Reading probably determines memory, but not memory reading" (p. 37). But we should not consider the case entirely closed yet.

REFERENCES

Baddeley, A.D. (1983). 'Working memory', Philosophical Transactions of the Royal Society, London, B302, 311-324.

Barron, R.W. (1986). 'Word recognition in early reading: A review of the direct and indirect access hypothesis', Cognition, 24, 93-119.

Beech, J.R. (in press). 'Early reading development', in Cognitive Approaches to Reading. (Eds. J.R. Beech and A.M. Colley), Wiley,

Chichester.

Beech, J.R. and Harding, L.M. (1984). 'Phonemic processing and the poor reader from the developmental lag point of view', Reading Research Quarterly, 19, 357-366.

Bradley, L. and Bryant, P.E. (1983). 'Categorizing sounds and learning to read: a causal connection', Nature, 301, 419-421.

Brady, S., Shankweiler, D. and Mann, V.A. (1983). 'Speech perception and memory coding in relation to reading ability', Journal of Experimental Child Psychology, 35, 345-367.

Bryant, P.E. and Bradley, L. (1985). Children's Reading Problems, Blackwell, Oxford.

Bryant, P.E. and Goswami, U. (in press). 'Phonological awareness and learning to read', in Cognitive Approaches to Reading (Eds. J.R. Beech and A.M. Colley), Wiley, Chichester.

Carr, T.H. and Pollatsek, A. (1985). 'Recognizing printed words: A look at current models', in Reading Research: Advances in Theory and Practice (Eds. D. Besner, T.G. Waller and G.E. Mackinnon), pp. 1-82, Academic Press, Orlando.

Cowan, N. (1984). 'On short and long auditory stores', Psychological Bulletin, 96, 341-370.

Crowder, R.G. (1972). 'Visual and auditory memory', in Language by Ear and by Eye (Eds. J.F. Kavanagh and I.G. Mattingly), pp. 251-275, MIT Press, Cambridge, MA.

Crowder, R.G. and Morton, J. (1969). 'Precategorical acoustic store (PAS)', Perception and Psychophysics, 5, 365-373.

Morais, J., Cary, L., Alegria, J. and Bertelson, P. (1979). 'Does awareness of speech as a sequence of phones arise spontaneously?', Cognition, 7, 323-331.

Sipe, S. and Engle, R.W. (1986). 'Echoic memory processes in good and poor readers', Journal of Experimental Psychology: Learning, Memory, and Cognition, 12, 402-412.

Stuart-Hamilton, I. (1986). 'The role of phonemic awareness in the reading style of beginning readers', British Journal of Educational Psychology, 56, 271-285.

Wagner, R.K. and Torgesen, J.K. (in press). 'The nature of phonological processing and its causal role in the acquisition of reading skills', Psychological Bulletin.

AGE OF WORD ACQUISITION IN DEVELOPMENTAL DYSLEXICS AS
DETERMINED BY RESPONSE LATENCIES IN A PICTURE NAMING TASK

D.J. Done
Formerly of University College of North Wales; now at Department
of Psychiatry, Clinical Research Centre, Harrow, Middlesex.
T.R. Miles
Department of Psychology, U.C.N.W., Bangor, Wales   LL57 2DG

ABSTRACT
        16 dyslexic boys, mean age 14.5, and 16 age-matched controls
were presented with 65 pictures of familiar objects and asked to give
the name. In the case of both groups there was a significant
relationship between response latency and presumed age at which the
word was acquired (as determined on the basis of tests given to 101
children aged two to six). Since, in addition, the dyslexics were
consistently slower than the controls in producing the right names it
is argued that they were correspondingly later in acquiring them.
The best estimate of the age-gap was calculated to be 10.8 months.
It is suggested that this lateness in word acquisition makes sense of
some of the other difficulties which are regularly found in dyslexic
persons.

INTRODUCTION
        When dyslexic children were asked to associate shapes with
three-letter nonsense words it was found that they needed more
exposures than did age-matched controls before the correct
associations were established (Done and Miles, 1978). This task
seems analogous to that which confronts the very young child when he
has to identify particular environmental sounds as words; and there
is evidence (e.g., Naidoo, 1972) that dyslexics tend to be later than
controls in speech acquisition.
        Moreover, even when appropriate 'lexical entries' have been
established (i.e. when environmental sounds and, later, visually
presented marks are recognised as letters, numbers, words, etc.) it
appears that dyslexics are still slow in 'finding' the right word.
This is true, e.g., in the case of digits, letters, and picture names
(Done, 1982) and also in the case of familiar colour names (Spring
and Capps, 1974).
        Carroll and White (1973), using adult non-dyslexic subjects,
found a correlation between response latencies in a picture naming
task and age of acquisition of the name of the pictured object (see
also Gilhooly and Gilhooly, 1979). If these correlations were to
hold in the case of dyslexics then the following is a possible
account of the direction of causality: (i) because of a
constitutionally caused anomaly dyslexics need more 'exposures'
before stimuli in the environment are recognised as letters, numbers,
words, etc.; (ii) their relative lateness in name-acquisition results
in longer response latencies when they are older.

This account would be wrong (i) if in a sample of dyslexics there was no correlation between response latencies in a picture naming task and presumed age of acquisition of the name of the pictured object, and (ii) if the response latencies of the dyslexics were no different from those of age-matched controls. It was therefore decided to put these two hypotheses to the test.

SUBJECTS AND METHOD

Full details with regard to subjects and method will be found in Done (1982). In brief, the subjects were 16 dyslexic boys (mean age 14 years six months, mean I.Q. 114.2) who were seriously retarded at both reading and spelling, and 16 controls (mean age 14 years two months, mean I.Q. 115.1) whose reading and spelling was normal. 65 pictures were chosen, most of them similar to those used by Carroll and White (1973), for example 'bicycle', 'giraffe', 'windmill'. The choice of these stimuli and of some additional ones was influenced by the need to include words for which there was a greater than average discrepancy between frequency and age of acquisition (see below).

The subjects were asked to give the name of the presented item as quickly as they could, and their response latencies were recorded. Of a total of 2080 readings (32 subjects x 65 responses) 1968 were found to be useable, 112 being flawed for various technical reasons, e.g. premature activation of the voice-key.

Before the main study a preliminary investigation had been undertaken to determine the age of acquisition ('AOA') of each of the 65 words. 101 children, aged between two years zero months and five years 11 months were shown the 65 pictures and asked 'what the picture was called'. Two measures of AOA were used. In the first place the number of correct names for each picture was calculated for each age category, nine categories being used in all, at six-monthly intervals (2.0 to 2.5, 2.6 to 2.11 . . . 5.6 to 5.11); and in the case of each category it was noted whether at least 75% of the children gave the correct response. AOA I was then defined as the youngest age-category at which the 75% criterion was satisfied, a low figure indicating a young age of acquisition. AOA II was determined by arranging the words in rank order of nameability. As a measure of the frequency of each word an adaptation of the Kucera-Francis 'standard frequency index' (SFI) was used (for details see Carroll and White, 1973).

RESULTS AND DISCUSSION

The mean response latency (MRL) was obtained for each of the 65 words, with dyslexics and controls taken separately. Since AOA I, AOA II, and SFI were already known for each word, a matrix of product-moment correlations was prepared, as shown in Table 1. The SFI figures are negative since low frequency is associated with high AOA. The high correlation between AOA I and AOA II is of course to be expected.

The first hypothesis mentioned in the introduction is therefore confirmed. For the dyslexics there is a correlation of 0.71 (or 0.72) between response latency and age of acquisition (p < 0.003).

Table 1
Correlation Coefficients (65 words) Between Mean Response
Latency (Dyslexics), Mean Response Latency (Controls), AOA I,
AOA II, AND SFI.

	MRL (dyslexics)	MRL (controls)	AOA I	AOA II	SFI
MRL (dyslexics)	–	.76	.71	.72	-.40
MRL (controls)		–	.67	.68	-.31
AOA I			–	.98	-.39
AOA II				–	-.40

The problem still remains of interpreting this result since, as reported earlier by Carroll and White (1973), latency also correlates with SFI and SFI is associated with AOA. To unravel the relative influence of SFI and AOA on latency a multiple regression analysis was performed using AOA II. If the influence of AOA II was taken out first no significant variance ($p > 0.05$) is accounted for by SFI, whereas if the influence of SFI is taken out first, AOA II accounts for a significant proportion of residual variance ($p < 0.001$). This result holds for both dyslexics and controls and confirms the claim of Carroll and White (1973) that age of acquisition has a strong influence on response latency.

To show the regression of naming latency on age of acquisition it was convenient to use AOA I. The regression lines and their equations for both dyslexics and controls are set out in Figure 1.

FIG.1
NAMING LATENCY REGRESSED ON AOA1

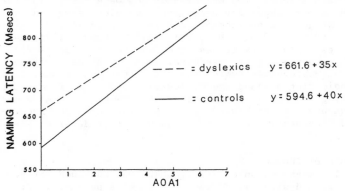

It will be seen that at all ages of acquisition the response latencies were between 500 and 1000 msec., the dyslexics being consistently slower. To compare the two groups a group difference score (GDS) was calculated by subtracting the mean latency values of the non-dyslexic group from those of the dyslexic group for each of the 65 stimuli. A regression of AOA I on to GDS produced the following equation:

$$GDS = 67 - 4.8 \ AOA \ I$$

Thus at the y-intercept, where AOA I = 0, there is a difference between the two groups of 67 msec. (t = 2.54, df 63, p < 0.01), whilst the coefficient, 4.8, is non-significant (t = 1, df 63, p > 0.05). The second hypothesis is therefore confirmed: older dyslexics and age-matched controls do, indeed, differ in their response latencies.

If one makes the further assumption that response latency can be explained by age of acquisition, then the 67 msec. group difference can be converted into AOA I equivalents. When the regression analysis was re-run with all the data combined, a regression coefficient of 37.3 was obtained, i.e. 37.3 units of latency for 1 unit of AOA I. Since each unit of AOA I represents 6 months, a 67 msec. difference represents

$$6 \times \frac{67}{37.3} = 10.8 \text{ months}$$

It can be argued, therefore, that the typical dyslexic will on average be 10.8 months later than his non-dyslexic peer in the age at which he acquires a particular word.

CONCLUDING REMARKS

If this claim is correct it can be used to make sense of other typically 'dyslexic' difficulties. In particular it is known that older dyslexics (i) continue to be weak at spelling (Rawson, 1978; Miles, 1983), (ii) have almost as low a span for auditorily presented digits as do younger dyslexics (Miles, 1983), (iii) can absorb less information than spelling-age-matched controls when digits are presented visually (Ellis and Miles, 1977), (iv) have more difficulty than controls when unrelated verbal units such as months of the year have to be arranged in order (Miles, 1983), and (v) have fewer number facts at their disposal (e.g. an immediate answer to 'What is 8 x 7?') (Pritchard, Miles and Chinn, in preparation). One may therefore surmise that dyslexics, as a result of their slower naming latency in comparison with controls, (i) have less time to notice the details of how a word is spelled, (ii) and (iii) can name fewer auditorily or visually presented 'digit-stimuli' per unit time, and (iv) cannot hold in working memory as many names (e.g. months of the year) when these have to be arranged in order, since this requires the retention of symbolic material over time. In addition, (v), they acquire fewer number facts since, because of the need for more 'exposures', they can make less effective use than non-dyslexics of the opportunities for acquiring them. It need not, of course, follow that all children who are late in talking will show these 'dyslexic' signs, since anomaly may be the decisive factor rather than simply lateness in terms of the calendar. Among dyslexics, however, it may be hypothesised that many of their difficulties are a consequence of the long response latencies in word finding and that, in their turn, these long response latencies are the consequence of lateness in word acquisition.

REFERENCES

Carroll, J.B. and White, M.N. (1973). 'Word frequency and age-of-acquisition as determinants of picture-naming latency', Quarterly Journal of Experimental Psychology, 25, 85-95.

Done, D.J. (1982). 'A Study of Paired Associate Learning and Sequential Memory in Dyslexic and Non-Dyslexic Subjects'. Ph.D. thesis, University of Wales.

Done, D.J. and Miles, T.R. (1978). 'Learning, memory, and dyslexia', in Practical Aspects of Memory (Eds. M.M. Gruneberg, P.E. Morris and R.N. Sykes), pp. 553-560, Academic Press, London.

Ellis, N.C. and Miles, T.R. (1977). 'Dyslexia as a limitation in the ability to process information', Bulletin of the Orton Society, 27, 72-81.

Gilhooly, K.J. and Gilhooly, M.L. (1979). 'Age of acquisition effects in lexical and episodic memory tasks', Memory and Cognition, 7, 214-223.

Miles, T.R. (1983). Dyslexia: The Pattern of Difficulties, Granada Collins, St. Albans.

Naidoo, S. (1972). Specific Dyslexia, Pitman, London.

Pritchard, R.A., Miles,R.R. and Chinn, S.J. 'Developmental dyslexia and knowledge of number facts' (in preparation).

Rawson, M.B. (1978). Developmental Language Disability. Adult Accomplishments of Dyslexic Boys, Educators Publishing Service Inc., Cambridge, Mass.

STUDENT LEARNING

EFFECTS OF BILINGUALISM AND APPROACHES TO LEARNING ON THE WRITING AND RECALL OF EXPOSITORY TEXT

R.H. Cantwell
Department of Education,
University of Newcastle, Australia
J.B. Biggs
Department of Education
University of Hong Kong

ABSTRACT
        A model of text processing is proposed in which the reader
or writer focuses attention on different levels of textual unit,
according to the sub-process occurring at the time. In general,
processes focusing on lower levels need to be automated in order to
free sufficient working memory to handle higher levels. Bilinguality
imposes further strain on working memory: how that is resolved
depends on the student's approach to learning. A common strategy for
bilingual students with a deep approach is to focus on a high level
of abstraction at the expense of detail, while students with a
surface approach focus on detail and 'correct' mechanics. Effects on
encoding and subsequent recall of written content are confirmed in a
pilot study.

        The processes of reading and writing each comprise several
subprocesses, during the performance of which attention is optimally
deployed on units of different levels of generality. In the case of
reading, Kirby (in press) distinguishes eight such levels, ranging
from the features or components of letters, through letters, sounds,
words, chunks or meaningful phrases, ideas of usually sentence
length, main ideas, and themes. Main ideas comprise the gist of what
the text has to say, and themes go beyond these main ideas,
generalising them to sometimes quite high levels of abstraction.
Decoding focuses on letters, sounds and words, comprehension on the
higher units of meaning. Since working memory capacity is limited,
readers who still have to attend to the lower order process of
decoding cannot attend to the higher order units of meaning.
        In writing, the subprocesses are more complicated. When
producing text, writers have essentially two major concerns: content,
referring to what the text is about (what to say), and rhetorical,
referring to the formal rules governing spelling, grammar, etc. (how
to say it) . Skilled writers handle these conflicting claims on
working memory in two main ways. Like skilled readers, they automate
the lower order rhetorical, or mechanical, aspects of writing as far
as possible, thereby freeing working memory for focusing on the main
ideas and the structural relationship of each sentence (and word) to
them. Second, they separate the content from the mechanical
processes, e.g. reviewing text separately for mechanics and for
'train of thought'.

APPROACHES TO LEARNING

The question of level of focus is also involved in the notion of approaches to learning and studying in general. An 'approach' to learning comprises a motive for carrying out the task, and a strategy that flows logically from the motive (Biggs, 1987a). Three general approaches can be distinguished: surface, deep, and achieving. Surface learners see the successful completion of the task as a means to some other end; motivation is extrinsic, and the surface strategy is to minimise effort by defining discrete content units and rote learning them. Deep learners are intrinsically motivated, and deep strategies are accordingly aimed at extending and clarifying meaning. The achieving approach is based on motivation to succeed, with strategies aimed at maximising grades through optimal organisation of time and working space.

The surface and deep approaches to learning clearly relate to level of focus as described in text processing above; indeed those approaches were derived from that very context. Marton and Saljo (1976) referred to learners who commence reading a passage with the intention of learning the actual words or other symbols used by the author (the 'signs' of learning) as surface learners, while those who set out to learn the meaning the author intended to convey (the 'significates' of learning) as deep. Biggs (in press) generalised the same principle to writing essays: those who typically concentrated on the sentence level and above, with main idea and theme constantly in mind during planning, composing, reviewing and revising their text, were referred to as 'deep', while those who mainly processed words and sentences during writing were referred to as 'surface'. Most important, as Marton and Saljo also found in the case of text comprehension, approach to essay writing was related to the structural complexity of the final outcome: a deep approach was used in the more structurally complex essays that satisfied the demands of the question, while a surface approach led to outcomes that were rich in detail but lacked coherence and structure.

BILINGUALITY AND TEXT PROCESSING

Comprehending and composing complex text each requires that both higher and lower levels of textual unit receive attention. How, then, do those bilingual students, to whom English is a second language (ESL) and who need to devote working memory to lower order rhetorical issues, cope with both low and high levels of content and of language?

While bilinguals with these rhetorical deficiencies perform poorly in content learning and recall, as compared to monolinguals (Cziko & Nien)Hsuan, 1984), this deficit is not found with respect to recall of higher level content information (Connor, 1984). In fact, Biggs (1987a) found strong evidence that both secondary and tertiary ESL students were significantly higher than monolinguals in deep approach to learning, which supports the view that ESLs tune to broader contextual features that help clarify what is meant by the speaker or writer rather than to particular words and phrases.

We now turn to the basic problem. How can bilinguals fulfil their need to concentrate on main ideas and themes, when they have difficulties in coping with the lower order mechanics that are (virtually) automatic in monolinguals? Faerch and Kasper (1983) in addressing this problem refer to 'reduction behaviour', by which ESLs learn to reduce the scope of the problem by ignoring this or that aspect of it. Essentially, reduction may be of two kinds: message reduction, occurring when content is selectively ignored, and rhetorical reduction, when linguistic and/or mechanical features are ignored. We predict that the kind and amount of reduction that occurs depends (a) on a student's general approach to learning, and (b) on his or her linguistic or rhetorical competence.

When planning an essay, most if not all writers begin with a global intention at the level of main ideas ('What is this essay to be about?'), after which the baseline for composing and writing is at the level of an idea (roughly a sentence length). Whether they range upwards from there to main ideas and themes, or downwards by elaborating on content detail or correct mechanics, or throughout the entire range from details to themes, depends on several factors, two of the most important being approach to learning and language competence.

The ideal, elaborating with thematically relevant detail in an appropriate rhetorical structure, involves relatively little reduction behaviour and is that taken by the highly proficient deep writer (for example, 'Syd' in Biggs, in press). Reduction strategies in rhetorically competent writers would be likely to take one of two forms of message reduction. The first is to reduce low level content, as in the deep writer whose text is full of abstractions and over-generalisations, unsupported by detailed argument; the second is to reduce thematic content, as in the surface writer whose text is full of much low level detail, which misses or distorts the macro-structure of the essay (for example, 'Geoff' in Biggs, in press). ESL writers, depending on their rhetorical competence, may need to compensate more drastically than monolinguals for working memory overload. There are four basic cases:

1. Deep-high rhetorical competence (D-HC). The writer concentrates at high and low levels of abstraction, and with attention to rhetorical rules: there is little evidence of reduction.

2. Deep-low rhetorical competence (D-LC). There is likely here to be both forms of reduction: message, in the form of fixation at a high level of abstraction with insufficient attention to detail, and rhetorical, in the form of incomplete sentences, inappropriate lexicon and spelling, and so on.

3. Surface-high rhetorical competence (S-HC). Mainly message reduction, taking the form of well)crafted sentences strung together but without high level cohesion.

4. Surface-low rhetorical competence (S-LC). Here reduction is both in message and rhetoric. Essays would consist of a series of points, put down without thought for linguistic structure or mechanics.

We now look at a prototypical learning task: reading a passage for comprehension, composing an essay in reply to a question based on the text, and recalling the content of the essay at a later date (a) in detail, (b) in brief or summarised form. Figure 1 outlines these relationships between approach to learning, rhetorical competence, and working memory, and their predicted effects on the level of operations of writers at the times of encoding the information and writing about it, of detailed recall of the text, and of brief recall.

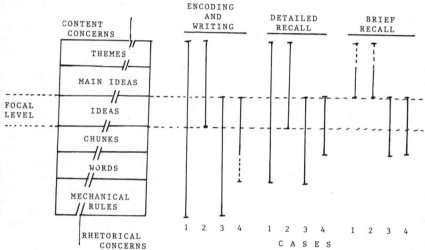

CASE: 1 = D-HC, 2 = D-LC, 3 = S-HC, 4 = S-LC
(See text for explanation)

METHOD

In this paper we report a pilot study into the effects of language background and approach to learning on the writing and subsequent recall of expository texts by selected Fifth and Sixth Form students, average age 17 years 5 months. Results are reported in the form of case studies.

The bilingual subjects all had had their first contact with English at age 10 or older and no student had less than three year's experience in English; a variety of first languages was represented, the case studies reported below included Portuguese and Filipino (Tagalog). A matched control group of English speaking monolinguals was selected on the basis of teacher-assessments of scholastic ability; teachers were asked to make these assessments as far as possible independent of fluency in English and on what they thought was the ratees' scholastic potential. All subjects completed the Learning Process Questionnaire (Biggs, 1987b) to assess subjects' typical approach to learning.

Subjects were provided with an information booklet detailing historical, political, economic, and demographic information about a fictitious 'Afghan Island', as well as the details of a specific riot in the form of eyewitness reports and comments by public figures. Subjects were required to write an essay explaining the occurrence of riots on the Island, and to include recommendations for changes that would prevent their recurrence; they were asked to return in three days with the completed essay, which was used by class teachers as an assessable assignment. Information was presented in three modes: prose, tables, and maps. Three days later, subjects were asked to recall what they had written in their essay, and three days after that to recall in no more than 70 words the main points of their essay.

RESULTS

The results confirm the interaction between approach to learning and bilingualism on the encoding, writing, and recall of text, as outlined in Figure 1. Approach to learning was defined by LPQ profile: i.e. the approach scale score that, when converted into deciles, was the highest for that student. Four cases selected on the basis of language background and approach to learning illustrate the essential features of the argument: space forbids a more elaborate presentation here.

1. Andrew (Deep-Monolingual). Behaved like Case 1 (in Figure 1), encoding from word level to thematic, using rhetorical knowledge to create a coherent text. Detailed recall reflected that range in both content and rhetorical structure. The following excerpt shows the integration of lower level knowledge with themes: 'Figures show that once the Foreigners (Chinese, Indian and European) were established they gained control of the workings of government and simultaneously spread their influence over the community.'

2. Paul (Deep-Bilingual). Matched Andrew in generality, but was unable to provide lower level support for themes, nor able to establish a coherent rhetorical structure: some message reduction and massive rhetorical reduction (see Case 2). Interestingly, all Paul's information on the Afghan riots came from the tables and the map: his rhetorical reduction even at encoding was to ignore the extended prose. His focus is seen in the following: 'Poor groups no political power - this cause riots the only power they posese to protest people power.'

3. Peter (Surface-Monolingual). Low level focus on detail with little or no attempt to integrate at a higher than sentence level. Main recall entirely of detail, with some atrophy of detail over time (see Case 3). The low level focus, but rhetorical proficiency, is illustrated: 'The Afghan Islanders have a high unemployment rate (27.2%) along with the Neighbouring Islanders (29.6%) while the Chinese, Indian and European have very low (1.0%, 1.3%, 0.5%).'

4. Leilani (Surface-Bilingual). A variant of Case 3, except that as a bilingual she tries to focus high, towards main ideas (she was only marginally surface predominant), but was rhetorically competent only

up to sentence level. Detailed information is packed in with main ideas in dense sentences: 'The Islanders mostly constitute the Radical Alliance and the Unionist Party in Parliment, for they represent the unskilled workers and unemployed respectively, but these are only represnted in Parliment with only a few numbers of seats as compared to the number of seats in ... etc.'

These cases illustrate the tension between the need to attend to a wide range of content levels and rhetorical skills in order to comprehend a range of information as background to writing and subsequent recall on the one hand, and the need to keep the content and rhetorical problems manageable within working memory limitations on the other. That tension is resolved by bilingual students in the present context by various reduction behaviours, as mediated by their rhetorical competence and their typical approach to learning, resulting in restricted focus on either high or low level of content, and inadequate use of rhetorical devices to structure and recall text.

Further and more detailed analyses of the data, and an examination of the educational implications, are in progress.

REFERENCES

Biggs, J.B. (1987a). Student Approaches to Learning and Studying, Australian Council for Educational Research, Hawthorn, Vic.

Biggs, J.B. (1987b). Learning Process Questionnaire: Manual, Australian Council for Educational Research, Hawthorn, Vic.

Biggs, J. B. (in press). 'Approaches to Learning and Essay Writing', in Learning Styles and Learning Strategies (Ed. R. R. Schmeck), Plenum Press, New York.

Connor, U. (1984). 'Recall of Text: Differences between First and Second Language Readers', TESOL Quarterly, 18, 239-256.

Cziko, G. and Nien-Hsuan, J. (1984). 'The Construction and Analysis of Short Scales of Language Proficiency', TESOL Quarterly, 18, 627-647.

Faerch, C. and Kasper, G. (1983). 'Plans and Strategies in Foreign Language Communication', in Strategies in Interlanguage Communication (Eds. C. Faerch and G. Kasper), Longman, London.

Kirby, J. (in press). 'Style, Strategy and Skill in Reading', in Learning Styles and Learning Strategies (Ed. R.R.Schmeck), Plenum Press, New York.

Marton, F. and Saljo, R. (1976). 'On Qualitative Differences in Learning: I. Outcome and Process', British Journal of Educational Psychology, 46, 4-11.

QUALITATIVE DIFFERENCES IN RETENTION WHEN A TEXT IS READ SEVERAL TIMES

Ference Marton and Claes-Göran Wenestam
University of Göteborg

ABSTRACT

Eight subjects read a prose passage of high complexity several times. The findings clearly indicate that repetition per se is not sufficient for increased understanding of the text. Due to differences in the approaches adopted to the task, comprehension improved, deteriorated or remained unchanged.

BACKGROUND

The empirical study of learning was introduced from the beginning as investigations of the correlation between practice – in the sense of number of repetitions – and retention – in the sense of number of units remembered (Ebbinghaus, 1964/1885). This relationship has mostly been depicted as a negatively accelerated, asymptotic function. The idea that practice goes with learning – and hence retaining – more, accords very well with everyday thinking. **Repetitio est mater studiorum** we have been told. From time to time research also gave support for this thesis (e.g. James, 1950/1890; Peterson, 1912). For instance, Mayer (1983), who used scientific prose, found that recall increased with repetition. Bromage and Mayer's (1986) study showed a similar effect on the retention of a technical text.

In the studies mentioned, retention was characterized in terms of the number of units (syllables, propositions, principles, concepts, etc.) remembered. What is true of learning characterized in terms of discrete items recalled is, however, not necessarily true of learning characterized in terms of the qualities of the text remembered. When people have read a piece of argumentative prose, we can – as a rule – discern a limited number of qualitatively different ways of understanding the meaning of the text. Marton and Wenestam (1978) have shown, for instance, that forgetting is far less pronounced when retention is characterized in terms of such global understanding, than when it is described in terms of discrete units.

Our model of description implies that the outcome of learning and of remembering is characterized in terms of qualitatively different conceptions of what has been learned (see, for instance, Marton, Hounsell & Entwistle, 1984). Using a similar approach, Halasz (1983) did not find any effects of repeated reading on the retention of literary texts. In accordance with most other studies in the field, Halasz' results concern the group level.

In the present study, we would like to examine the classical problem of the relationship between practice and retention in terms of individual cases. We are especially interested in relating differences in retention to differences in the ways the subjects deal with the text while reading it. In other words, we wish to interpret possible changes in retention not only in the light of the fact that the subjects read a text several times but rather in the light of **how** they read it on the successive occasions.

METHOD
Material
What text and what subjects to choose is of crucial importance to our investigation. As we wish to study the development of understanding in relation to repeated reading, we have to use a text which is sufficiently difficult, yet not entirely beyond the reach of the subjects. Furthermore, we would not like differences in pre-knowledge to interfere substantially with the possible differences between the way they read the text. The text is a 298 word prose extract from a Swedish reader on philosophy and literary science (Engdahl, et al., 1977, p.60):

> The concept of meaning has been a central question in philosophy for a long time. The analytical philosophy of language, which has so far strongly dominated twentieth century western thinking, has generally considered meaning to be a phenomenon exclusively within language. Another school of philosophy, phenomenology, has asserted, right from its foundation by Edmund Husserl (1859-1938), that it is possible to generalize the concept of meaning to all acts of consciousness. This difference becomes plain when Husserl is compared with one of the predecessors of the analytical school, the logician Gottlob Frege. Frege makes a distinction between Sinn (significance) and Bedeutung (connotation or reference) which gives rise to the trichotomy name-meaning-reference. (For example, the phrases "evening star" and "morning star" have the same "Bedeutung" but different "Sinn"). This has its equivalent in Husserl's trichotomy act-meaning ("noema")-object. The distinction introduced by Frege makes it possible to understand contexts where a name identifies a meaning and not its reference, and it preserves the logical principle whereby two names with the same reference can be interchanged without changing the truth value. In a comparable way, Husserl's trichotomy makes it possible to overcome the difficulty which beset the creator of phenomenology's concept of intentionality, Franz Brentano; namely that completely different kinds of acts, such as perception and hallucination, must have the same type of object, if one now starts, as Brentano does, from the premise that all acts are directed at an object.
>
> The trichotomy, which replaces Brentano's dichotomy act-object means that even if all acts are directed, in other words they are intentional, they do not necessarily have to have an object. Hallucinations have, using Husserl's obscure terminology, "noema" but no object. (We surely see something when we see pink elephants, even if no pink elephants exist.)

The considerable difficulty of this text derives partly from its convoluted character. Understanding it means laying bare its concealed structure. In actual fact the text is about how two logical problems within two schools of philosophy were solved by means of the concept of meaning. The analytical school focused especially on the relationship between name and reference and in the case of a reference with two names, the names were supposed to be interchangeable. There were, however, clear counter-examples. The problem was solved by Frege, who, so to speak, inserted meaning between name and reference. Two different names would then be seen as names of two different meanings of the very same reference.

In a similar vein, there was a problem with Brentano's principle in phenomenology, stating that every act is directed at an object. There are, however, mental acts like hallucinations, which clearly lack an object. Husserl's solution to this dilemma was to insert meaning between act and object in Brentano's model, arguing that acts are not directed at objects but at noema (meaning).

Subjects

Eight students ranging in age from 25 to 35 years participated as subjects. All of them held a B Sc and were enrolled in a teacher training course. None of the subjects had any specific acquaintance with philosophy. They were all of them well-educated and native speakers of Swedish and could be expected to have the general language and reasoning skills necessary for understanding the text.

Procedure

The experiments were conducted as individual learning sessions. Each subject was asked to read the text once with the prospect of afterwards recalling what he/she "got out of the text". During the session the reading-recall sequence was repeated three times and then followed by questions about the subject's experience of the reading/-recall task. An appointment was made for "something of the same sort" a week later. At this session the subjects were asked to recall the text again, and then answered questions about their experience of trying to remember the text. The session finally involved the complete cycle - reading, retelling, experiential questions.

Analysis

All the sessions were taped and transcribed verbatim. The analysis of the transcripts followed the phenomenographic model (see Marton, 1986). The first question to be explored was "Which are the qualitatively different ways in which the text has been understood?" The variation found was expressed in terms of a set of categories of description, subsequently used to characterize the variation in understanding in relation to repeated reading of the text. Furthermore, categories of description corresponding to the qualitatively different ways in which the subjects approached the task and the perspectives from which they viewed the text were identified. As can be seen in the section on results, there were three kinds of categories found, namely: (1) qualitative differences in the subjects' understanding (of the text as a whole and its two main parts), (2) the subjects' approaches to the task and (3) their perspectives on the text.

The categories were not determined prior to the investigation; they were extracted post hoc from the data and are thus considered as results. They can be defined in a reasonably explicit way and then handed to co-judges in order to acertain the extent to which they agree on the classification of the protocols in accordance with the definitions given. (For further details of the analysis see Wenestam & Marton, 1987).

RESULTS

In addition to the subjects' interpretations of the gist of the text, we will also explain the variation in their understanding of its two main parts. Concerning the subjects' global understanding of the text, three distinctively different conceptions of what the text was about were found:

  A. The insertion of meaning in order to solve two logical problems within two schools of philosophy
  B. The concept of meaning within two schools of philosophy
  C. Two schools of philosophy

As shown in Figure 1, the three categories form a hierarchy. These hierarchies do <u>not</u> refer to the structure of the text. Instead they depict relations between the subjects' differing understandings. In all three cases illustrated, there were additional categories, lower in hierarchy, which will not be dealt with here; nor will the hierarchical order of the descriptive categories be justified here (see Wenestam & Marton, 1987).

As far as the first part of the text is concerned, four conceptions of what was said about the analytical school of philosophy (i. e. about the relations between name, meaning and reference) were identified, namely:

    a. The inserting of **meaning** in order to solve the problem of one **reference** with different **names**
    b. The same **reference** can have different **meanings** and **names**
    c. A word (**name**) has a **meaning** and a **reference**
    d. The same **reference** can have different **names**

The hierarchical relations between these categories of description are presented in Figure 1 below. As far as the second part of the text is concerned, we found five qualitatively different ways of comprehending what was said about phenomenology in the text (i. e. about the relationships between act, noema (meaning) and object), namely:

    α. The inserting of noema in order to let **acts** be directed towards **noema** (instead of **objects**)
    β. Some **acts** are directed towards **noema** and others towards **objects**
    γ. Some **acts** do not need to be directed towards **objects**
    δ. The inserting of **noema** between **act** and **object**
    ε. **Noema** corresponds to Sinn and **object** to Bedeutung

Again the hierarchy formed by the categories of description is illustrated in Figure 1.

"The main point"   "The analytical school"   "Phenomenology"

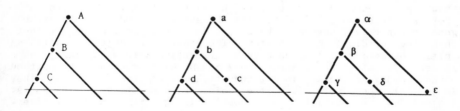

Figure 1. The hierarchical structure of the qualitative differences derived from the subjects' ways of understanding the text.

Having arrived at a system for describing the qualitatively different ways of understanding the text as a whole and its two main parts, we can use this system for characterizing retention on the five occasions the text was read. We will here, however, only deal with the first and the fifth (see Table 1).

Table 1.
    Subjects' understanding of the whole text (t), of the part about analytical philosophy (a) and the part about phenomenology (p) at the first and the last recall.

	Subject No.																							
	1			2			3			4			5			6			7			8		
Recall	t	a	p	t	a	p	t	a	p	t	a	p	t	a	p	t	a	p	t	a	p	t	a	p
1	C	b	ε	C	-	-	B	b	β	-	-	-	B	b	β	B	-	-	B	-	-	-	-	β
5	C	-	-	C	-	-	B	b	β	-	-	-	B	-	-	B	-	-	A	a	α	-	c	β

Focusing on the comparison between the first and the fifth retelling, we can conclude that in 4 cases (No:s 2, 3, 4, and 6) no difference can be observed. As a matter of fact, No.4 does not fit into any of the three hierarchies on either occasion. In two cases (No.7 and No.8), there is an improvement, while in two other cases (No.1 and No.5) the subjects seem to have a better understanding of the text after only one reading than after four.

This pattern of qualitative differences is intelligible when we see it in relation to the differing approaches and perspectives adopted by the subjects. (These are revealed by answers to the experiential questions, as well as by certain characteristics of the retellings, other than those on which the characterization of understanding is based – e. g. sequence of statements, correspondence in wording between the text and the recall, etc).

At the first reading all the subjects – with some possible exceptions – seem to have adopted an external, "orthogonal", front-on perspective. The subjects looked at the text, following the sequence from the beginning of the text to its end. Four of the subjects kept this perspective throughout the whole experiment. Two of these (No. 2 and No. 4) focused on the text as such (instead of what the text was about) adopting what has been called the **surface approach**. All the other subjects seemed to focus on what the text was about, hence adopting a **deep approach** (Marton et al., 1984). Two of these subjects (No.3 and No.6), though seeing the text from an **orthogonal perspective**, seemed to be oriented towards the meaning (rather than the wording) of the text. The other four subjects – after an initial orienting phase – adopted a **perspective within the text**, as it were. Two of these subjects (No.7 and No.8) singled out the part on phenomenology as the key to the understanding of the text and they looked at the whole from the point of view of one of its parts. Subject No.7, especially, showed some striking shifts in perspectives. One of these, for instance, meant that she was looking at Brentano's thesis from the point of view of Husserl! After grasping the essential structure of the phenomenology part, she used this insight when focusing attention on the part dealing with analytical philosophy.

Also the two remaining subjects (No.1 and No.5) adopted a **perspective within the text**. They were looking for an isomorphic relation between the two parts, primarily from the point of view of analytical philosophy. This strategy failed simply because it was based on a wrong assumption. The relation between the two parts was to be found on a more abstract level than that of a one to one correspondence. In consequence, instead of developing, understanding broke down when the text was reread.

DISCUSSION

This investigation shows that reading a text several times does not necessarily lead to improved understanding. Changes may fail to appear or they may be for the worse, just as well as for the better. What repeated reading will achieve depends on the way in which the reader deals with the text. In earlier studies, where subjects and texts were chosen in such a way that adopting a deep approach was sufficient for a fair understanding of the text, a strong correlation between the approach (deep or surface) to learning and the outcome of learning was established (see Marton et al., 1984). In the present case, an extremely difficult text was used. This gave us the opportunity to show that fundamental differences in the development of understanding can be found **within** the deep approach, due to differences in the perspectives from which the text is seen.

The implication of our study is that when a highly difficult text is chosen to be read several times, and when what is retained is described in terms of the global understanding arrived at, retention is **not** a function of the number of repetitions as such. Depending on the approaches adopted and perspectives chosen (and changed), reading a text several times may mean understanding more or less than, or just as much as the first time.

ACKNOWLEDGMENTS

This study was financially supported by the Swedish Council for Research in the Humanities and Social Sciences. We also thank Tomas Kroksmark for conducting the interviews.

REFERENCES

Bromage, B K., & Mayer, R E. (1986). 'Quantitative and Qualitative Effects of Repetition on Learning from Technical Text',Journal of Educational Psychology, 78, 271–278.

Ebbinghaus, H. (1964). Memory. A Contribution to Experimental Psychology. Dover, New York. (Originally published in 1885 as Uber das Gedächtnis. Duncker und Humblot, Lepzig).

Engdahl, H.,Holmgren, O., Lysell, R., Mellberg, A., & Olsson, A. (Eds.). (1977). Hermeneutik. Rabén & Sjögren, Stockholm.

Halasz, L. (1983). 'Elbeszélés (Illetve Kivonata) Feldolgozasa Ujraolvasasok Sorozataban'. ('Processing Literary Works – and Non-Literary Variations – in the Series of Rereadings'), Pszichologia, 3, 359–384.

James, W. (1950). The Principles of Psychology, (Vol.I, pp.666–667), Dover, New York. (Originally published 1890).

Marton, F. (1986). 'Phenomenography – A Research Approach to Investigating Different Understandings of Reality', Journal of Thought, 21(3), 28–49

Marton, F. and Wenestam, C-G. (1978). 'Qualitative Differences in the Understanding and Retention of the Main Point in Some Texts Based on the Principle-Example Structure', in Practical Aspects of Memory (Eds. M.M Gruneberg, P.E. Morris, and R.N. Sykes) pp. 633–643, Academic Press, London.

Marton, F., Hounsell, D., and Entwistle, N.J. (Eds). (1984). The Experience of Learning. Scottish Academic Press, Edinburgh.

Mayer, R E. (1983). 'Can You Repeat That? Qualitative Effects of Repetition and Advance Organizers on Learning from Science Prose', Journal of Educational Psychology, 75, 40-49.

Peterson, H. (1912). 'Notes on a Retrial of Professor James' Experiment on Memory Training', Psychological Review, 19, 491-492.

Wenestam, C-G, and Marton, F. (1987). 'Practice and Understanding. An Experiment on Learning by Reading a Text Several Times.'. Technical report. (In preparation).

ON SOLVING THE TRANSFER PROBLEM

Earl C. Butterfield
Department of Education, University of Washington
Seattle, Washington, USA

ABSTRACT

Transfer of training has been difficult to obtain because too few analyses have been performed of processes that might underlie it, too few distinctions have been drawn among kinds of transfer, quantitative metrics of transfer distance have not been developed, and the problems studied have been too incompletely analyzed to allow specification of relations between knowledge and processes underlying success on training and transfer tasks. Toward solving these problems, underlying distinctions are drawn among nine kinds of transfer and it is shown that process analysis can reveal quantitative metrics.

Determining how to induce students to generalize their learnings is arguably the most important unsolved problem of education and psychology. We send children to school to become broadly effective in life, not to do well in school alone. Unless students' academic lessons transfer to their lives, schools have failed. Scientific psychologists seek basic understandings of how people function. Because correlational techniques are imperfect ways of identifying basic processes, experimental manipulations are essential to psychology's mission. Unless their experimental manipulations have external validity, psychologists run the risk of creating accounts of people's functioning in experiments, rather than basic explanations. Experimental manipulations are instructions, for which successful tests of transfer are the surest demonstrations of external validity.

Transfer is seldom found, even when instruction is theory-based and induces large and durable performance gains. The reasons seem to be that too few analyses have been done to identify processes that might underlie transfer, too few distinctions have been drawn among kinds of transfer, quantitative metrics of transfer distance have not been used, and the knowledge and processes underlying success on the problems studied have been too incompletely analysed for investigators to understand the relations between their training and transfer tasks, or the problems have been too simple to reveal anything about practically important problems.

Table 1 answers three questions about nine kinds of transfer. The questions have to do with mental events, called components or superordinates. Components are knowledge and skills that underlie performance on particular tasks. Superordinates are

TABLE 1
Mental Properties of Nine Kinds of Transfer

	Across Similar Problems	Across Content Domains	Across Problem Structures	Discriminative	Combinatorial	Subtractive	Additive	Vertical	Analytic
Taught Components Required by Testing?	A*	A	A	A	A	S	A	A	S
Untaught Components Required by Testing?	N	N	N	N	N	N	Y	Y	Y
Testing Requires Superordinate Knowledge or Processes?	N	Y	Y	N	Y	Y	Y	Y	Y

*A = All; S = Some; N = No; Y = Yes.

metacognitive knowledge and executive skills that transcend particular problems. The questions concern mental events, because all transfer tests are comparable at the level of worldly events. Thus, all use different materials during teaching and testing to insure that only general effects of teaching are evaluated. All use either the same or different responses during teaching and testing, because it is not the nature of the responses that matters. What transfers are knowledge and kinds of thinking that underlie solutions, not responses or solutions themselves.

To illustrate mental differences among the nine types of transfer, I shall describe their possible uses to evaluate the effects of a hypothetical curriculum on inductive reasoning. Because inductive reasoning is not understood fully, it is taught piecemeal, by concentrating separately on such things as reasoning by analogy, selective encoding and comparison of problems' features, selective combination of thought processes, and the creation of rules to describe collections of events or allow transformations of givens into problem solutions. I will speak only of evaluating that part of a hypothetical curriculum having to do with rule creation and use.

Letter series continuation problems, like the ones shown in Table 2, provide vehicles for instruction in the inductive creation and use of rules. My examples are letter series, because they have been analyzed fully enough (Butterfield, Nielsen, Tangen and Richardson, 1985) to allow the specification of relations among instructed and transfer tasks, which is essential to judging kind of transfer. Our analyses of letter series have also identified quantitative metrics of transfer distance.

Investigators who have tried to arrange near and far tests of transfer have seldom answered the question, 'Near or far by what metric?' They seem to believe that one can vary transfer distance

TABLE 2
Letter Series that Vary Along Three Dimensions Described in Text

```
A A X B B X C C X          A A B B B B C C B
A A S B B T C C U          A A B B B C C C D

V C V W C W X C X          V V V W V W X V X
H F H I E I J D J          H I H I H I J G J

A Q A B C P C D E O E F    A D A B C E C D E F E F
R Q J I H Q P H G F P O F E D    R Q R Q P Q P P O N P O N M L
```

without measuring it, as if a carpenter could build a house without using a tape measure or a ruler. To see why the question has gone unanswered, consider whether long division is farther from subtraction than multiplication. Where do the extraction of square roots or the use of integration and differentiation lie with respect to matrix multiplication? Not being able to answer such questions quantitatively, investigators who have used near and far transfer tests have guessed about relevant metrics and intuited distances along them. Fortunately, some problems have now been analyzed thoroughly enough to identify psychological dimensions along which transfer distance can be measured quantitatively.

TRANSFER ACROSS SIMILAR MATERIALS
        The question asked about inductive reasoning with a test of Transfer Across Similar Materials is 'Will a child reason inductively about materials that differ along known dimensions from the materials on which he was taught inductive skills?' Table 2 illustrates three psychological dimensions along which letter series vary (Butterfield et al., 1985). Representational Knowledge increases between pairs going down the table. Memory Operations increase within pairs going down. Spurious Identities increase within rows going across the table. The theory built around these dimensions specifies procedures for creating thousands of equivalent series for each listed in Table 2, and it specifies how to teach rule induction and continuation (Butterfield and Ferretti, 1984).
        Imagine that theory based instruction in rule formation and use is part of a hypothetical curriculum for teaching inductive reasoning. Suppose that part of the hypothetical curriculum is taught with problems like the one in the upper corner of Table 2. Children who did and children who did not receive the curriculum would be given a transfer test composed of problems like the ones in the remainder of Table 2. Table 1 shows that passing this test would require that children use all and only mental components taught in the curriculum's module on rule formation and use. If children who received the inductive reasoning curriculum exceeded those who did not on any of the untaught problem types, it would be concluded that children receiving the curriculum made greater gains in rule generation aspects of inductive reasoning. The farther along any transfer dimension the differences between the two groups extended, the greater the gains of the instructed group.

TRANSFER ACROSS PROBLEM STRUCTURES

All of the knowledge and processes underlying success on a test of Transfer Across Problem Structures are taught in the evaluated curriculum. Thus, having taught with letter series like those in Table 2, one might test with analogy problems using the same alphabetic relations and string structures. This sort of transfer differs from that across dimensions in that the student must realize that the changed problem structure is irrelevant. Such a realization is a metacognitive understanding.

TRANSFER ACROSS CONTENT DOMAINS

The rule generation aspects of our hypothetical curriculum could also be evaluated with a test of Transfer Across Content Domains, by teaching with problems like those in the upper left corner of Table 2, and testing with problems for which the numbers 1 to 26 were substituted for the letters A to Z. The problems for a test of Transfer Across Content Domains are identical to the training problems with respect to the knowledge and skills they require, but different with respect to their stimulus materials. To pass such a transfer test, the student must understand that the differences in content are irrelevant. There are no distance metrics for transfer tests Across Content Domains. Thus, there is as yet no way to measure how far letter series are from number series.

DISCRIMINATIVE TRANSFER

Discriminative Transfer can be tested whenever a student has been taught two strategies, one of which works only or best with certain problems and the other of which works only or best with other problems. The question is 'Does the pupil select the strategy appropriate for each transfer problem?'

Letter series that require many memory operations and contain many spurious identities are impossible to solve unless one physically separates the strings from which the series are constructed. Even very young children can be taught to solve problems having no spurious relations. If children who received our hypothetical curriculum were taught to solve such series without separating their strings, but were taught to separate the strings of problems with many spurious identities, then a Discriminative Transfer test could be done by presenting the children with novel problems and observing whether they separate strings only for those with spurious identities.

COMBINATORIAL TRANSFER

Combinatorial Transfer can be assessed whenever two separately taught components can be combined to solve a novel problem. The Combinatorial test allows us to ask 'Do students combine knowledge or skills learned separately?' Such combining depends upon the use of executive routines to diagnose the requirements of the transfer problem and the combining of the knowledge and strategies acquired in different contexts.

The letter series and number series spoken of so far are composed of strings that move by ones up or down the alphabet or number sequence. Numbers allow more complex progressions: increasing or decreasing as multiples of a constant, exponentially, as the sum of all the prior numbers on their string, as primes, etc.   Suppose some children are taught separately about letter series and number progressions.   Suppose other children are taught directly about number series composed from the same progressions taught separately to the first group. In order to solve other such number series, the second group would not need to combine separately learned lessons, but the first group would.

SUBTRACTIVE TRANSFER

Subtractive Transfer can be assessed whenever students are taught a decomposable strategy in a single instructional module. Whether a student actually decomposes that strategy is tested by presenting a problem for which only some of the tactics of the instructed strategy are needed. Such a test lets us ask 'Does a student delete unnecessary elements of an instructed strategy?'

The string separation strategy described above is decomposable, but one need not separate every string when only one contributes all of a problem's Spurious Identities. Suppose children were taught about separating strings using only problems that require full separation. To test whether they transfer subtractively, one would give them series that require only partial separation. Like Combinatorial Transfer, Subtractive Transfer is facilitated by metacognitive understandings and executive routines for assessing problems' strategic requirements.

ADDITIVE TRANSFER

Additive Transfer is like Combinatorial Transfer, except that some of the combined components come from outside the instructional program being evaluated. It is like Vertical Transfer, except that none of the added components are more developmentally advanced than the components taught in the evaluated instruction.

Children would be said to transfer additively if they used lines to connect letters that go together instead of separating strings to resolve the difficulties posed by spurious identities in letter series. Children who did this would be adding to their learning about how to solve problems without spurious identities their knowledge of how to use a pencil to connect things that go together, in this case, the letters on various strings entering into spurious identities.

VERTICAL TRANSFER

Tests of Vertical Transfer presume an age grading according to which some knowledge and skills are acquired before others and are prerequisites to the use of the later acquired knowledge and skills. Vertical Transfer tests can be used whenever earlier and prerequisite knowledge and skills are included in a program's curriculum, but later ones are not. The question we pose with a Vertical Transfer test is 'Do the teaching of earlier acquired knowledge and skills promote students' discovery of later skills, or must something besides the earlier prerequisites be taught to produce such discovery?' In other words, 'What must we include in educational programs so that children will acquire untaught knowledge and skills sooner than if they had not been in our program?'

ANALYTIC TRANSFER

Analytic Transfer occurs when a student subtracts relevant portions of two or more separately learned strategies or sets of knowledge and combines the remaining parts into a new strategy or organization of knowledge. It is called Analytic Transfer because its reliable execution presumes skills for analyzing the components of complex strategies.

FUTURE PROSPECTS

All of the examples used here concerned letter series, but the experimental literatures on cognition and its development describe other problems with which transfer could be studied. Many of these are too simple to have practical importance, but some educationally relevant skills have been well analyzed, and more can and will be. It is also true that we have lacked distinctions among different kinds of transfer and distance metrics associated with each type. Moreover, the possible roles of superordinate factors in promoting transfer have not been appreciated until recently. These lacks are being remedied, so prospects are improving for progress in our practical understanding of how to promote transfer of instruction.

REFERENCES

Butterfield, E.C., Nielsen, D., Tangen, K.L. and Richardson, M.B. (1985). 'Theoretically based psychometric measures of inductive reasoning', in Test Design: Contributions from Psychology, Education and Psychometrics (Ed. S. Embretson), pp 77–147, Academic Press, New York.

Butterfield, E.C. and Ferretti, R.P. (1984). 'Some extensions of the instructional approach to cognitive development and a sufficient condition for transfer of training', in Learning and Cognition in the Mentally Retarded (Eds. P.H. Brooks, C. McCauley and R. Sperber), pp 311–332, Erlbaum, Hillsdale, New Jersey.

RETENTION OF COGNITIVE STRUCTURES LEARNED IN UNIVERSITY COURSES

Moshe Naveh-Benjamin
Department of Behavioral Sciences, Ben-Gurion University of the
Negev, Beer-Sheva, 84120, Israel

ABSTRACT

The current study assessed changes over two years in the structure of knowledge gained in a university course. Results indicated that relations between concepts are forgotten during the first year after the end of the course. However, forgetting occurred primarily in the lower levels of the structure. Moreover, there were only slight changes in the structure from the first to the second year, indicating stabilization of the structure. In addition, both level of initial learning and amount of rehearsal of course material after the course was over, had a positive effect on retention of relations between concepts. Finally, results indicated no effects of individual differences variables (test anxiety and study habits) on retention of the cognitive structure.

Academic instruction is a major contributor to the education of people. Many students participate each year in a variety of university courses to gain knowledge about themselves and the world around them. Yet few studies address the long-term retention of material acquired through academic instruction.

Two types of researchers should be interested in such a topic. First, researchers in the field of education should be interested in long-term retention for its relevance to considerations of curriculum, instructional modes, and instructional materials. Two questions should be of major interest for this group. First, what is retained beyond the first weeks after the end of a university course? This should be assessed not only by scores on final examination items, but also in terms of the major concepts learned in the course and the relations among these concepts. While there has been some research in the last twenty years on the role of cognitive structures (defined as the relations among concepts in a given domain) created in different courses, (e.g., Shavelson, 1972; Naveh-Benjamin, McKeachie, Lin, & Tucker, 1986) none of these studies examined changes in these structures after a course was completed.

The second question is about the relations between student characteristics (e.g., aptitude, motivation) and the amount and quality of long-term retention of course material. This question, too, has not been addressed.

The second group of researchers who should be interested in these questions are cognitive psychologists, who, for the most part, neglected questions concerned with permanence of acquired knowledge.

In the last few years, there have been a few studies that
investigated the long-term retention of semantic information (e.g.,
Bahrick, Bahrick, & Wittlinger, 1975; Bahrick, 1984). For example,
Bahrick (1984), in a comprehensive study, investigated the retention
of Spanish learned in school, over a 50-year period. His results
showed memory curves which declined exponentially for the first three
to six years of retention interval, and then stabilized over a period
of 30 years before showing a final decline. This study also
indicated that retention is influenced by level of initial learning
but not by rehearsal of the materials after completion of the course.

The foregoing studies, however, have mainly focused on retention
of specific information rather than on questions regarding the
retention of organized cognitive structures learned in academic
courses.

The first objective of this research is to examine and
characterize long-term retention of cognitive structures created in
university courses. Specifically, the question addressed is what
happens to major concepts learned in a course and their relations to
each other over time. This issue relates to the suggestion made by
Neisser (1984) that the reason for the retention of information over
a long period of time in Bahrick's 1984 study might have been due to
the retention of redundant cognitive structures from which specific
responses could be extracted.

The second objective of the current study is related to Bruce's
concept of "population thinking" (1985). According to him, one of
the focuses of ecological research should be on the diversity of the
population and its consequences. In the current study we advanced
this issue by looking at some individual differences variables shown
to be important determinants of academic performance. Our work here
evaluates their effects upon retention of information over a period
of time. These variables assess both cognitive skills (i.e., study
habits) and motivation (i.e., test anxiety).

METHOD

Subjects: Subjects were 58 students in a research methodology course
at Ben-Gurion University of the Negev between 1984 and 1986.

Design: One independent variable was retention interval, defined as
the time since the end of the course. Students were tested at one of
three retention intervals: on the last day of the course (N = 20);
one year after the course ended (N = 20); or two years after the
course ended (N = 18).

Other independent variables were level of original learning,
amount of rehearsal of course materials, and individual differences
(test anxiety and study habits).

Measurements of the dependent variable were obtained from
students' performance in a task intended to reveal aspects of the
cognitive structure of the course: "fill in the structure" task.

Procedures and Materials: The course in research methods is a
required course for second-year students at the Department of
Behavioral Sciences at Ben-Gurion University. It includes topics on
philosophy of science, measurement, and various techniques for data

collection and data analysis in psychology, sociology, and anthropology. The course was taught with minimal changes by the same instructor in each of the three years. For each student in the course, the following information was collected:

Course performance: This included grades on examinations, papers, and the final course grade.

Rehearsal: The questionnaire administered to each student at the appropriate retention interval included questions on the extent of using course concepts since the end of the course, in other courses, as well as on other occasions.

Study habits: These were evaluated using parts of the Learning and Study Strategies Inventory (LASSI) (Weinstein, Zimmerman, & Palmer, 1985).

Test anxiety: This was evaluated using parts of the worry-emotionality scale (Liebert & Morris, 1967).

Cognitive structure task: The "fill in the structure" task involved students receiving hierarchical, tree-like representation of course materials (based on the instructor's perception of the structure of the course), in which 26 of the 34 concepts were missing from different levels of the structure. (Three out of four in the upper level; five out of nine in the second level; 12 out of 15 in the third level; and six out of six in the lowest level). These missing concepts appeared at the bottom of the page intermixed with distractor concepts. The students' task was to choose the appropriate concepts and place them in their appropriate positions in the structure. In pilot research, such a task was shown to require an appropriate knowledge of both horizontal and vertical relations between concepts in the course.

Data on course performance was collected during the course. The cognitive structure task, information on rehearsal, study habits, and test anxiety were collected at the appropriate retention interval in a special 30-minute session.

RESULTS

Each student's cognitive structure was scored for the percentage of correct answers in each level of the hierarchy and the percentage of total number of correct answers. A correct answer was defined as locating the appropriate concept in its appropriate position in the hierarchical structure. Results showing percentage correct for each level in the structure, as well as percentage correct of total score, as a function of retention interval, appear in Table 1. As can be noticed, generally there was a decrease in number of concepts located appropriately as retention interval increased. These decreases were statistically significant for all but the upper level of the structure, $F(2,55)$ = 2.20; 11.35; 10.57; 5.36; and 10.79 for levels one through four and the total score, respectively. However, it may be noticed that even for levels two to four, the loss of information occurred mostly in the first year, and from the first to the second year there were hardly any differences in performance. This was shown to be true for all levels and for the total score, using Tukey post-test comparisons between retention intervals of one and two years. The comparisons showed no significant differences for any of the levels of the structure or for the total score ($p > .05$).

TABLE 1

Percentage of Correct Answers for Each Level of the Cognitive
Structure, as a Function of Retention Interval

| | Retention Interval (Years) | | | | | |
| | 0 | | 1 | | 2 | |
Hierarchical Level	M	SD	M	SD	M	SD
1	89.8	16.0	81.0	32.3	78.3	31.9
2	67.5	24.9	36.3	29.8	37.1	24.6
3	67.4	24.4	43.6	26.2	41.1	25.4
4	67.4	22.2	48.8	29.7	46.4	24.6
Total	70.0	15.9	48.2	24.9	46.4	23.3

As Bahrick (1984) pointed out, in ecological research of this
type we do not have experimental control on either the level of
initial learning of the subjects, or on the amount of rehearsal of
the material after the course. In the current study, however, there
were only minor differences in initial learning and rehearsal between
the groups tested in the different retention intervals. Analyses of
covariance, with initial learning and rehearsal as the covariates,
showed results very similar to those reported above.

Next, we evaluated the relations of level of initial learning
and rehearsal, across all subjects, with retention of the cognitive

TABLE 2

Correlations of Initial Learning, Rehearsal and Individual
Differences Variables with Performance on the Different Levels of the
Cognitive Structure

Hierarchical Level	Course Grade	Examination Grade	Papers Grade	Rehearsal**	Test Anxiety	Study Habits
1	0.26*	0.14	0.32*	0.26*	0.15	-0.05
2	0.17	0.14	0.25	0.26*	0.05	-0.08
3	0.31*	0.21	0.23	0.21	0.05	-0.02
4	0.30*	0.27*	0.22	0.15	-0.08	-0.03
Total	0.31*	0.22	0.30*	0.23	0.04	-0.05

*p < .05;   ** Only those 38 subjects tested in retention intervals 1
and 2 are included.

structure. The correlations between each level in the cognitive structure and each of these variables appear in Table 2. With respect to initial learning, course grades showed a significant correlation with all levels of the structure except with level two. When we divided the final course grade into its components we found the examination grades to be more related to performance in the low levels of the hierarchy (levels three and four, significantly so for level four), while grades on papers were more related to performance in the upper level of the hierarchy.

The correlations between individual differences variables and the various levels of the cognitive structure in Table 2 did not reach significance. In addition, there was no interaction of these variables with retention interval.

DISCUSSION

Several conclusions can be drawn from the above results. First, there is a noticeable forgetting of the relations between concepts in the initial period after studying. However, the results show that there are only minor changes in the structure between one and two years after studying. Such a result could indicate that relations between concepts at different levels are stabilized after a fairly short period, sooner than the concepts themselves (Bahrick, 1984). Longer retention intervals will have to be examined, however, to support such an hypothesis.

Second, there was no reliable loss of information in the upper level of the hierarchy over time. This could imply that relations at high levels of the structure are less susceptible to forgetting than those at lower levels. This result resembles findings of studies on memory for text, which show that people are more likely to remember high-level propositions than low-level propositions--the "levels effect" (Thorndyke, 1977).

Third, the results point to the role of initial learning in preserving the cognitive structure. Across retention intervals, the better the initial learning of a student in the course, the more elaborate his/her cognitive structure of the material is. This result extends Bahrick's (1984) findings, on the role of initial learning on memory, to cognitive structures and to a completely different subject matter.

Fourth, the results point to the role of rehearsal in retaining cognitive structures. Across retention intervals, the more the students used the information after the end of the course, the better their cognitive structure of the material is. This effect was the strongest at the higher levels of the structure.

Fifth, while the individual differences variables of test anxiety and study habits are known to have an impact on course performance, the results did not indicate their role in retention of cognitive structures. A partial explanation of this finding is that the information for these variables was not as valid because it was collected, for some of the students, a relatively long period after the course had been taken.

Finally, with respect to the reliability and validity of the measure of cognitive structure used here, there are two indications which increase our confidence in it. First, the median multiple correlation between the independent variables and each of the different levels of the dependent variable of cognitive structure was 0.57, so more than 32% of the variance of the dependent variable could be accounted for by these variables (see Bahrick, 1984). Second, performance on papers, which usually requires higher level of organization of the material, was related more to performance in the highest level of the hierarchy, while performance in examinations, which usually requires more specific knowledge, was related to knowledge of lower-level relations. This finding increases one's confidence in the cognitive structure measure as one that actually taps various levels of relations between concepts learned.

Nevertheless, to increase the confidence in the results obtained, we need further research employing other measures of cognitive structures for extended retention intervals in other subject-matter domains.

REFERENCES

Bahrick, H. P. (1984). 'Semantic memory content in permastore: Fifty years of memory for Spanish learned in school', Journal of Experimental Psychology: General, 113, 1-29.

Bahrick, H. P., Bahrick, P. O., & Wittlinger, R. P. (1975). 'Fifty years of memories for names and faces: A cross-sectional approach', Journal of Experimental Psychology: General, 104, 54-75.

Bruce, D. (1985). 'The how and why of ecological memory', Journal of Experimental Psychology: General, 114, 78-90.

Liebert, R. N., & Morris, L. W. (1967). 'Cognitive and emotional components of test anxiety: A distinction and some additional data', Psychological Report, 20, 975-978.

Naveh-Benjamin, M., McKeachie, W. J., Lin, Y-G., & Tucker, D. (1986). 'Measuring cognitive structures created in university courses using the "ordered tree technique"', Journal of Educational Psychology, 77, 30-40.

Neisser, U. (1984). 'Interpreting Harry Bahrick's discovery: What confers immunity against forgetting?', Journal of Experimental Psychology: General, 113, 32-35.

Shavelson, R. J. (1972). 'Some aspects of correspondence between content structure and cognitive structure in physics instruction', Journal of Educational Psychology, 63, 225-234.

Thorndyke, P. W. (1977). 'Cognitive structures in comprehension and memory of narrative discourse', Cognitive Psychology, 9, 77-110.

Weinstein, C. E., Zimmerman, S. A., & Palmer, D. R. (1985). 'College and university students' study skills in the U.S.A.: The LASSI', in Cognition, Information Processing, and Motivation (Ed. G. d'Ydewalle) pp. 703-726. Amsterdam: Elsevier Science Publishers.

LEXICAL MEMORY IN NOVICE BILINGUALS: THE ROLE OF CONCEPTS IN RETRIEVING SECOND LANGUAGE WORDS

Judith F. Kroll and Janet Curley

Mount Holyoke College
South Hadley, Massachusetts U.S.A.

ABSTRACT

College students with differing levels of expertise in German named and translated words and pictures in German and English. To test the proposal that concepts mediate second language retrieval, naming latency and accuracy were compared under conditions in which the words and pictures to be named were members of the same superordinate category or not. For more fluent bilinguals, translation in the second language resembled picture naming, suggesting that access to the second language was conceptually based. For less fluent bilinguals, translation in the second language resembled word naming, suggesting that access to the second language was lexically mediated.

Research on bilingualism has contrasted two models of lexical and conceptual memory in the bilingual. According to the common memory model, words in each of the bilingual's languages access common concepts in memory. Experiments on bilingual naming and translation (Potter, So, von Eckhardt, & Feldman, 1984), Stroop interference across languages (Biederman & Tsao, 1979), and semantic priming across languages (Kirsner, Smith, King, & Jain, 1984; Schwanenflugel & Rey, 1986) have provided support for the common memory model. According to the independent memory model, however, each of the bilingual's languages accesses an independent language module. Experiments on repetition priming (Kirsner, Brown, Abrol, Chaddha, & Sharma, 1980; Scarborough, Gerard, & Cortese, 1984) and on language filtering (Scarborough et al., 1984) have supported the view that recognition of words in one language does not necessarily require activation of the other language. These apparently opposing positions can be reconciled by assuming that different languages are independently represented at a lexical level, but share a common representation at a conceptual level. This hybrid model assumes that there is a level of representation corresponding to different mental dictionaries, as well as a more abstract conceptual representation. At the mental dictionary level, words in each of a bilingual's languages are represented in autonomous lexicons, while the images that correspond to the set of known objects are represented in an analogous perceptual dictionary. At the conceptual level, the same abstract representation underlies the shared meanings to which words in different languages and pictures refer.

The goal of our research was to examine interactions between lexical and conceptual representation in the bilingual as second language learning is taking place. By what process does a monolingual acquire and use these two levels of representation? Some previous studies have indicated that the development of expertise in a second language proceeds from a stage of word-to-word associations between first and second language words to a stage in which second language words are understood directly by access to underlying concepts(Chan & Ho, 1986). That is, with increasing expertise, bilinguals are thought to switch from a strategy based on lexical mediation with the first language, to a strategy that is conceptual and independent of the first language. Other studies, however, have suggested that concepts may mediate access for second language words even in novice bilinguals, without first language mediation (Potter et al., 1984). Potter et al. found that translating first language words into the second language took about the same amount of time as naming pictures in the second language. Because picture naming is thought to require conceptual access (Potter & Faulconer, 1975; Smith & Magee, 1980), the similarity between translation and picture naming in the second language was taken as evidence that translation also requires concept mediation. Data from both fluent and novice bilingual subjects fit the concept mediation model, suggesting that novice bilinguals did not rely on lexical mediators to accomplish translation.

If bilinguals translate from one language to another by retrieving the common concepts to which words in each of the languages refer, then factors which influence the speed of conceptual access, should also influence the speed of translation. We tested this first hypothesis in an experiment in which English-German bilingual subjects named pictures, English words, and German words, in both languages. In one condition of the experiment the words and pictures were blocked according to their respective superordinate categories (e.g., fruits, vehicles, clothing). In another condition, the same words and pictures were presented in a random order. If concepts must be accessed prior to translation then one would expect the naming of pictures and the translation of words from one language to the other to be facilitated in the categorized condition. The naming of words directly in the language in which they are presented would be expected to show less of an effect of categorization because direct naming can proceed lexically without conceptual mediation.

The second aspect of the concept mediation model that we examined was the effect of fluency in the second language. We considered the possibility here that the results of the Potter et al. study were due to the level of expertise of their novice subjects. Their novice subjects, who had studied high school French for two or three years, may have actually passed beyond an early stage of second language acquisition in which first language mediation is the primary route to second language understanding.

METHOD

Subjects. Forty-eight Mount Holyoke students drawn from all levels of undergraduate German classes participated in the experiment. Forty-six of the subjects were native English speakers or had learned English and German simultaneously. Two subjects were native German speakers who were fluent in English.

Stimulus materials. The pictures were line drawings of objects from ten semantic categories, e.g. clothing, body parts, animals. The words were the names of the objects in English and German. The pictures, English words, and German words were all divided into six stimulus lists. In the categorized condition, the six lists each consisted of one or two of the semantic categories in a block such that all of the exemplars were presented in sequential order. In the randomized condition, the same set of stimulus materials was divided into six mixed lists such that each list contained exemplars from each of the semantic categories in a random order. In both conditions lists were blocked with respect to modality and language.

Apparatus and procedure. Stimulus words and pictures were presented one at a time in a tachistoscope. Half of the subjects were randomly assigned to each of the two list conditions. In both conditions subjects viewed two lists each of pictures, English words, and German words. One of each type of list was named in English and the other in German. Subjects were asked to name aloud each of the presented words and pictures in the language (English or German) specified for that block of trials. Naming latencies were measured to the nearest millisecond.

RESULTS AND DISCUSSION

Naming latencies are shown in Table 1 for all 48 subjects collapsed across the two list conditions. For naming in English, the data replicate the well known advantage for words over pictures (Potter & Faulconer, 1975). For naming in German, the two critical conditions that Potter et al. compared, translating first language words into the second language and naming pictures in the second language, also produced similar naming latencies in the present experiment. The overall pattern of results thus appears to support the concept mediation model.

Table 1. Mean naming latencies (in milliseconds) for direct pronunciation of words in English and German, translation of words into the language of response, and picture naming.

	Direct pronunciation	Translation	Picture Naming
Language of Response:			
English	642	1421	914
German	842	1874	1912

FLUENCY

To analyze the effect of fluency, the subjects were divided into two fluency groups on the basis of the length of their experience with German. Subjects with fewer than 30 months of experience were considered less fluent and those with more than 30

months were considered more fluent. The naming data were then
analyzed as a function of whether the list was categorized or
randomized and whether the speakers were fluent or not. Mean naming
latencies for naming words and pictures in English and
translating English words and pictures into German, are shown
in Figure 1 for each of the four conditions. The panels on the
left show the time to name words and pictures in English for more
and less fluent subjects in the categorized and randomized groups.
As is apparent, subjects in all conditions produced the standard
word-picture difference when naming in English. The panels on the
right show the results for translating into German and naming
pictures in German. (Note that the axes vary in the figures to
accommodate overall differences in speed of naming between first and
second language and between more and less fluent subjects in the
second language.)

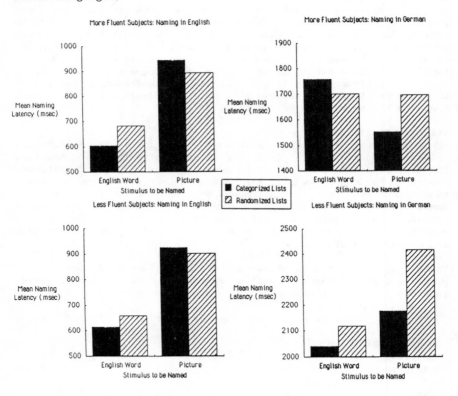

Fig. 1. Mean naming latencies for naming English words and pictures
in English and in German. Data are for subjects who are more or less
fluent in German, naming within categorized or randomized list
conditions.

        The more fluent group, shown on the top, produced
results consistent with concept mediation model in that

translation times were equal to but not faster than picture naming in the second language. In contrast, the pattern of results for the less fluent group, shown on the bottom, was similar for naming in English and in German, and is consistent with the predictions of a word-association model in which it is assumed that second language translation relies on first language mediation. The time to translate first language words into the second language was significantly faster than the time to name pictures in the second language. Thus, although both the more fluent and less fluent subjects took significantly longer to name in German than in English, they produced distinct patterns of second language naming consistent with the hypothesis that bilinguals switch from lexical to conceptual mediators as they become more proficient.

EFFECTS OF CATEGORIZATION

According to the logic of our experiment, the categorized lists should have facilitated naming latencies under those conditions that required conceptual access. Because our data suggest a shift with increasing expertise corresponding to a shift from lexical to conceptual mediators, we expected that the effect of categorization would be greater for the more fluent bilinguals who are supposedly relying on concept retrieval to accomplish translation. The data shown in Figure 1 suggest that, if anything, the opposite held, with the categorized lists especially benefiting the less fluent group.

To attempt to understand this apparent paradox, we re-examined the initial assumption concerning the prediction of a greater categorization effect under conditions in which concept mediation appeared to be used. We first considered the effect of the categorized list structure on naming words and pictures in English alone. These results (shown in Figure 1 on the two left panels) showed that the categorized lists actually facilitated the naming of words but interfered with the naming of pictures. This interaction was highly significant. English words were named 63 milliseconds faster in the categorized than randomized conditions, while pictures required an additional 38 milliseconds to be named in the categorized condition. The effect of the categorized list thus failed to support the preliminary assumptions that direct naming would be largely immune from the effects of list structure but that picture naming would benefit.. In fact, the opposite result held. The facilitatory results for words are particularly interesting in light of the very small effects of semantic priming that have been observed in this task (e.g., Lupker, 1984).

There are a number of alternative explanations for this interaction, but the one we currently find most compelling is that the presence of category structure on a list primes a set of semantically related lexical entries or names. In the word naming condition, the effect of this lexical priming is to facilitate lexical access. In the picture naming condition, the effect of lexical priming is to create a kind of Stroop effect, such that on sequential trials there are a large set of competing semantically related names.

With this explanation in mind, we can now return to the bilingual data to consider the effects of categorized list structure in those conditions. Looking first at the translation data, we see that for the more fluent subjects, the effect of category structure was to produce some interference in translating first language words into the second language. This result is similar to the pattern observed for picture naming in English, and is consistent with the claim that more fluent bilinguals rely on concept mediation, since picture naming in English also requires conceptual access and selection of a lexical entry, although in the case of translation, from the second language lexicon. The less fluent subjects, whose data are shown on the bottom panels, produced a different pattern of categorization results from that described for the more fluent subjects. For these novice subjects, the effect of categorized list structure on translation was similar to the effect observed for naming words directly in English. Namely, translation times were facilitated in the categorized condition. Since we have argued that these novice subjects are using lexical mediation, it makes sense that the categorization effect resembles the condition in which the mediator itself is named.

Looking now at picture naming in the second language, it is clear that picture naming for the less fluent subjects was facilitated by the presence of the categorized list. To the extent that these subjects are relying on lexical mediation, the lexical facilitation in this condition is consistent with the word association hypothesis. The data for picture naming in the second language for the more fluent subjects also show a categorized list advantage, although it is somewhat smaller than the effect observed for the less fluent subjects. According to our proposal, concept mediation of picture naming in the second language should produce a pattern of results similar to picture naming in English but different from word naming in English. At present we have no good explanation for this result. It is important to note, however, that because almost all of our bilingual subjects were technically novices, their relatively long naming latencies in the second language conditions may be masking the effects of a number of processes that may be engaged during the two seconds or longer that it takes them to produce a second language name.

To summarize, the study we have reported suggests that beginning and more fluent bilinguals have different ways of accessing their second language. Beginning bilinguals appear to use first language mediators to access second language words, while more fluent bilinguals use concepts as mediators for the second language. The effect of categorized list structure, which as we have seen appears to produce lexical rather than conceptual priming, is for the most part consistent with the interpretation of a shift with increasing expertise from lexical to conceptual mediation.

ACKNOWLEDGMENTS
This research was supported in part by a Faculty Grant from Mount Holyoke College. A preliminary report of these data was presented at the 1986 Annual Meeting of the Psychonomic Society. The authors thank Mary C. Potter and David A. Rosenbaum for their helpful comments.

REFERENCES

Biederman, I., & Tsao, Y-C. (1979). 'On processing Chinese ideographs and English words: Some implications from the Stroop-test results', Cognitive Psychology, 11, 125-132.

Chen, H-C., & Ho, C. (1986). 'Development of Stroop interference in Chinese-English bilinguals', Journal of Experimental Psychology: Learning, Memory, and Cognition, 12, 397-401.

Kirsner, K., Brown, H. L., Abrol, S., Chadda, N. N., & Sharma, N. K. (1980). 'Bilingualism and lexical representation', Quarterly Journal of Experimental Psychology, 4, 585-594.

Kirsner, K., Smith, M.C., Lockhart, R. S., King, M. L., & Jain, M. (1984). 'The bilingual lexicon: Language-specific units in an integrated network', Journal of Verbal Learning and Verbal Behavior, 23, 519-539.

Lupker, S.J. (1984). 'Semantic priming without association: A second look', Journal of Verbal Learning and Verbal Behavior, 23, 709-733.

Potter, M.C., & Faulconer, B.A. (1975). 'Time to understand pictures and words', Nature, 253, 437-438.

Potter, M.C., So, K-F., von Eckhardt, B., & Feldman, L.B. (1984). 'Lexical and conceptual representation in beginning and proficient bilinguals', Journal of Verbal Learning and Verbal Behavior, 23, 23-28.

Scarborough, D.L., Gerard, L., & Cortese, C. (1984). 'Independence of lexical access in bilingual word recognition', Journal of Verbal Learning and Verbal Behavior, 23, 84-99.

Schwanenflugel, P.J., & Rey, M. (1986). 'Interlingual semantic facilitation: Evidence for a common representational system in the bilingual lexicon', Journal of Memory and Language, 25, 605-618.

Smith, M.C., & Magee, L.E. (1980). 'Tracing the time course of picture-word processing', Journal of Experimental Psychology: General, 4, 373-392.

Snodgrass, J.G. (1984) 'Concepts and their surface representations', Journal of Verbal Learning and Verbal Behavior, 23, 3-22.

MNEMONIC AIDS

WHY STUDY MNEMONICS?

C. Cornoldi

Department of General Psychology, University of Padua
Padua, Italy

ABSTRACT

Some possible directions for further research in the field of mnemonics are described. It is argued that past research had sometimes charac- teristics which limited its applicability to daily life. In particular, individual differences are not usually taken into account, memory tasks scarcely reflect memory requirements of everyday real life, the experimental design may restrict the flexibility in the use of strategies and in the number of variables affecting memory planning. It is concluded that both for practical and theoretical reasons the research on mnemonics will require strong developments.

At the beginning of the 70's psychological research exhibited great interest in mnemonics (see e.g. the review by Higbee, 1977, and also the proceedings of the first "Practical Aspects of Memory" conference, Gruneberg, Morris & Sykes, 1978). Yet, such interest has declined over the last ten years. One reason for this may be that the considerable advantages in memory performance, when mnemonics are used, are well established and do not require further demonstration.

Nevertheless, this decline of interest may also be due to the suspicion that mnemonics cannot be used in most situations of daily life. People appear to prefer external aids rather than internal aids (Harris, 1980). Our interviews with subjects who had undertaken mnemonics courses revealed that they too made only modest use of mnemonics in the following months. Higbee (1981) observed that most students enrolled in universitary course on memory improvement ceased making the effort to use memory techniques after completing the course, but at the same time they achieved positive changes in self perception of memory abilities that persisted over time.

In the present paper, prepared with the help of Dr. Rossana De Beni, I will describe some practical reasons for demanding further research in the field of mnemonics and its possible directions, with reference to four main limitations of the past research on mnemonics. In this paper I do not intend to review the different types of mnemonics (for the specific implications of each see Bellezza, 1981; Higbee, 1977), although we are persuaded that the study of memory processes at their highest levels of performance may be a valid contribution to the understanding of the basic principles of memory (see e.g. Cornoldi and De Beni, 1986).

In our opinion typical laboratory research on mnemonics has, from a "practical" point of view, the following limitations:
1. characteristics of the experimental subjects and their level of knowledge of mnemonics are not usually taken into account;
2. memory tasks scarcely reflect memory requirements of everyday real life;
3. a clear comparison between the experimental and the control group requires that the first make constant and strict use of mnemonics and that the controls make absolutely no use of it (preferably, adopting another strategy in a similarly rigorous manner, e.g. repetition);
4. the presence of intervening factors in the context and in the subject's planning is minimized.

With regard to the first point, a common assumption of the research on mnemonics is that they work with everybody, basing their success on general memory laws. We agree with this assumption but we think that it requires further specifications. Some data support the idea that it is possible to find differences in the capacity to benefit from mnemonics. Di Vesta and Sunshine (1974) observed that the benefit was greater for subjects with high imagery abilities. De Beni and Cornoldi (1985) and De Beni (1985) found that subjects with high scores in memory for spatial positions tests were better able to use loci mnemonics and were especially successful in remembering the correct order of information and in minimizing interference between lists memorized with the same loci.

Individual differences are also to be expected in subjects with particular memory problems, such as amnesics (Wilson, 1986) or old people (Roberts, 1983). When considering these categories, we must be particularly cautious, about whether any positive results can be generalized and whether the costs-benefits ratio justified the training.

At the same time we must take into account the fact that the effects of training may not be limited to memory improvements, since the subjects' increased self-confidence in their memory abilities may extend this positive attitude to other problems to be faced.

A final point about individual differences concerns the subject's general attitude toward mnemonics, which may affect his degree of mastery and his inclination to use them after the end of the course. The range of attitudes covers convinced mnemonists, participants paying a considerable amount of money for the course and students recruited either for a memory course or simply for an experiment. Students recruited for a single-session experiment on mnemonics were used in some researches. These subjects act as better controls, but provide information more relevant to basic, rather than to the applied research. In fact, from the applied point of view we need to know how subjects, with good mastery and frequent use of mnemonic techniques, employ them.

2. It is well known that mnemonics are especially successful when isolated or non sense items are to be memorized. This situation, however, is not typical of everyday life, since we rarely have to learn non sense words (except in second-language learning tasks, and in other few cases) and in any case we usually encounter a few items rather than long lists. We should therefore

make a review of common daily memory requirements and explore where mnemonics could be useful. It is logical to expect that people may often adopt other efficacious and less-demanding strategies, but that in some cases the mastery of mnemonics may be useful. A particular case concerns learning from texts, lectures, seminars, etc., which deserves particular attention, given its frequency in student learning.

3. A typical procedure to check the efficacy of mnemonic technique `a' requires a group of subjects to learn a representative sample of items, making use of mnemonic `a' alone and of no others. At the same time, the control group learns the same items without making use of mnemonic `a'. This procedure implies some questions and problems. Firstly, there may be considerable variability in the characteristics of the control group. If the control group is formed by subjects who underwent to some training as the experimental group, the groups are well matched and are equally familiar with the experimental set, but the control group may gain an advantage from some general aspects of their training, e.g. using imagery processes, without referring specifically to mnemonic `a'. Thus in this case or in the case in which non-trained subjects are included in the control group, without specific instructions, we expect the subjects to be able to make flexible use of the strategies they already know and which appear particularly adequate to the context. The comparison concerns mnemonic `a' vs flexible choice of already known strategies rather than mnemonic `a' vs no-strategy. Therefore control group subjects may have advantage in that they can use well-known strategies and shift from one to another depending on the circumstances. This flexibility is not allowed to the experimental group subjects who are required to make exclusive use of the mnemonic.

If, on the contrary, the control group instructions require use of a particular alternative technique following the same levels of training and familiarity with the experimental setting, both groups are linked to similar conditions and limitations. Nevertheless, any superiority of the mnemonic group over the alternative-strategy group should not imply that by using mnemonic `a' we can do better than usual, but that `a' is superior to the alternative strategy, which may rarely be used in the way it was used in the experiment. In particular, if the alternative strategy was verbal repetition, the result may be trivial, since repetition has low power and is scarcely overused by educated adults.

As I observed before, many experiments fail to simulate real life situations because they are stereotyped both in the quantity of materials and in the choice of strategies. Flexibility appears more suitable for coping with the variabilities in the nature of the material and in the subject's knowledge. This quality is, in our opinion, particularly evident in memory for meaningful material tasks, but it is also valid for different items. For example, in the telephone numbers memorization task, the phonetic system may be generally useful (Higbee, 1977), although in many circumstances different coding systems may be more appropriate: for example some digits may have arithmetic regularities, one series of digits may be very familiar to the subject for particular reasons etc.

From the experimental point of view, research aimed to evaluate the efficacy of a technique has difficulty in controlling these points. The best solution is to have lots of groups with different trainings and requirements, but this is not always possible. If only two groups can be considered, I suggest that the experimental group is trained to mnemonic `a' but may use also other strategies when they appear suitable. The control group has the same familiarity with the experimental setting, does not receive training exclusively devoted to a specific memory use, and receives instructions to memorize in the best way possible. After all what we want to know is whether a specific training improved memory ability!

4. A puzzling point in our follow-up interviews with students, who had taken part in memory improvement courses, is that many of them remained convinced of the utility of mnemonics, and yet, soon after the end of the course, they ceased to use them. Some subjects said that, faced with memory requirements, they usually reacted quickly without thinking of mnemonics. Others admitted that sometimes they were aware of the possibility of using mnemonics with success, but were discouraged by the complications and the attentional effort implied by the steps of the required mnemonic. This example shows the importance of identifying what the real goals in human memory are, the subjective and objective pressure for their attainment, and their interactions with other goals and pressures. By analyzing the overall interaction of the variables affecting the subject's decision and behaviors, we will be able to understand why he or she may face the same task in different ways. We expect that, in general, the subjective importance of the memory task will be related to the quantity of attentional resources the subject is inclined to spend. Further, the quantity of available knowledge and the articulation of the planning activity will be influenced by emotional and social pressures.

One aspect of the available knowledge which deserves particular attention is related to the metamemory domain, i.e. to the subject's beliefs concerning the functioning of memory, in general, and, in particular, of his own memory. Till now adult's metamemory has been only sketchily explored without reference to a general model of the characteristics of human systems of knowledge, to the possible coexistence of opposite ideas, to the interactions with beliefs belonging to other domains etc. We think that such exploration will help to explain many points, including why some people are more interested than others in mnemonics, why among people who know about mnemonics, only some think that they are useful and why, in this last group, only a subgroup actually makes use of mnemonics.

In laboratory experiments the presence of intervening factors in the context and in the subject's planning activity is usually minimized, which implies that he or she behaves differently from how he/she would in real life situations. From a methodological point of view, we think that other procedures, like questionnaires, already widely used for exploring similar problems, but also interviews, could provide useful information. A thorough examination of the reliability and validity requisites of these procedures is necessary.

In conclusion, I wish first to observe that this brief overview of some of the limitations of experimental research on mnemonic, rather than criticizing them, is devoted to showing that further research somewhat more oriented towards examining the practical aspects of memory is necessary. Given the general inspiration of a Conference on the "Practical Aspects of Memory" I have preferred to focus on these points, but I think there is also a fundamental theoretical reason for studying mnemonics. It is well known that reflection on the power of the mind, and in particular of memory, has been a constant feature of western thinking (Yates, 1966; Rossi, 1983) and has had wide articulations and implications. A central point which emerges is that memory must be studied, not only when it partially or totally fails, as usually happens, but also when it works well. This research from this perspective has already emphasized the role of some memory principles, such as the use of interactive images, semantic codes, organized systems of cues. We expect that further research will contribute to enlarge our knowledge on the functioning of human memory.

REFERENCES

Bellezza, F.S. (1981). 'Mnemonic devices: classification, characteristics and criteria', Review of Educational Research, 51 (2), 247-275.

Cornoldi, C. and De Beni, R. (1984). 'Imagery and the loci mnemonic', International Imagery Bulletin, 2(1), 10-13.

Cornoldi, C. and De Beni, R. (1986). 'Weaknesses of imagery without visual experience: the case of total congenital blind using imaginal mnemonics', Proceedings of the EWIC Conference, Nijhoff, Amsterdam, (in press).

De Beni, R. (1985). 'Differenti effetti della mnemotecnica dei "loci" in buoni e cattivi localizzatori', Ricerche di Psicologia, 9(4), 49-71.

De Beni, R. and Cornoldi, C. (1985). 'Effects of the mnemotechnique of loci in the memorization of concrete words', Acta Psychologica, 60, 11-24.

Di Vesta, F.J. and Sunshine, P.M. (1974). 'The retrieval of abstract and concrete materials as functions of imagery, mediation and mnemonic aids', Memory and Cognition, 2, 340-344.

Gruneberg, M.M., Morris, P.E. and Sykes, R.N. (Eds) (1978). Practical Aspects of Memory, Academic Press, London, New York.

Harris, J.E. (1980). 'Memory aids people use: two interview studies', Memory and Cognition, 8, 31-38.

Higbee, K.L. (1977). Your Memory: How It Works and How to Improve It, Prentice Hall Inc., Englewood Cliffs, New Jersey.

Higbee, K.L. (1981). 'What do College students get from a memory-improvement course?'. Paper presented at the meeting of the Eastern

Psychological Association, New York City, April 1981.

Roberts, P. (1983). 'Memory strategy instruction with the elderly: what should memory training be the training of?'. In M. Pressley, and J.R. Levin (Eds.), Cognitive Strategy Research, Springer-Verlag Inc., New York, 75-100.

Rossi, P. (1983). Clavis Universalis, Il Mulino, Bologna, II edizione.

Wilson, B. (1986). 'A comparison of four mnemonic strategies in brain damaged and non-brain damaged subjects', in Proceedings of the EWIC Conference, Nijhoff, Amsterdam, (in press).

Yates, F.A. (1966). The Art of Memory, Routledge & Kegan, London (trad.it: L'arte della memoria, Einaudi, Torino, 1972).

PRACTICAL ASPECTS OF MNEMONICS

Kenneth L. Higbee
Department of Psychology, Brigham Young University
Provo, Utah 84602   U.S.A.

ABSTRACT

Applied research indicates how mnemonics (memory aids) **can** be used effectively for many different kinds of practical learning tasks. This paper describes some applied programs which illustrate how mnemonics **are** being used to aid learning in such practical areas as mathematics, language skills, scriptures, and foreign languages.

Interest and research activity in mnemonics has been steadily increasing since the mid-1960s. By 1973 mnemonics had even earned its own heading ('Mnemonic Learning') in Psychological Abstracts, and since then has averaged about 20 citations per year. Until the mid-1970s most mnemonics research focused on whether mnemonics really work, and on how well they work. Since the late 1970s research has increasingly focused more on explaining **how** and **why** mnemonics work, and on how they can be applied.

The focus of this paper is on practical aspects of mnemonics--applications of mnemonics that can help someone learn and remember something that he or she really wants to learn in the real world. It might be noted that a particular mnemonic would not necessarily have to be useful to everyone in order to have practical value; what is practical can vary with individual interests and needs. For example, one person may see no practical need for memorizing lots of people's names, while that ability may be very useful to someone else (such as a teacher or salesperson) who deals with a lot of people. Or one person may see the ability to memorize numbers as impractical, while another who works with measurements, prices, telephone numbers, or schedules may find that ability very useful. Thus, what is practical to one person may not be practical to another.

A large amount of applied research in recent years has indicated that mnemonics can be used effectively on a wide range of topics, mostly related to schoolwork. This applied research has included such varied topics as foreign language vocabulary, native-language vocabulary words and definitions, spelling, states and capitals, people's names and accomplishments, U.S. presidents and characteristics, cities and their products, medical terms, properties of minerals, hardness scale values of minerals, names and faces, absent-mindedness, errands, advertisements, and numbers. Such topics have been learned by mnemonics in prose form as well as

in paired associates and serial lists.   The potential practical
value of mnemonics is suggested also by the wide range of people
who have been able to use mnemonics.   They include the entire age
range from preschool children through elderly adults, and also
special populations such as the mentally retarded, learning
disabled, brain damaged, and even intellectually gifted.   The above
applied research is reviewed in a number of recent books and
articles (e.g., Higbee, in press; McDaniel & Pressley, 1987).

Such applied research suggests what **can** be done with
mnemonics--potential practical applications. This paper gives some
examples of applied programs that show what **is** being done with
mnemonics--actual practical applications.   Space prohibits a
detailed description of all the mnemonics in all the programs, but
I have given much more detail on the mathematics and language
skills programs elsewhere (Higbee, 1986).   The purpose of the brief
descriptions in this paper is merely to illustrate some of the
kinds of areas in which mnemonics are being used.

MATHEMATICS

Masachika Nakane developed an extensive program of verbal
mediators (phrases, sentences, rhymes, songs, etc.) in Japan for
learning arithmetic, algebra, geometry, trigonometry, and calculus.
In fact, his program, which he named 'Yodai,' also covers science
(inorganic and organic chemistry, physics, and biology), spelling
and grammar, and the English language.   The mnemonics are expressed
in language and concepts that are familiar to Japanese children.
For example, fractions are learned as bugs with heads (numerators)
and wings (denominators), and multiplying fractions involves
putting the heads together and putting the wings together.   Yodai
mnemonics have been called 'process' mnemonics because they teach
processes of problem solving (rules, principles, procedures) more
than the facts learned with traditional mnemonics (similar to the
distinction between procedural knowledge and declarative
knowledge).

In the early 1980s, Shirou Kunihira, an educational
psychologist at Loma Linda University in California, developed some
mnemonics patterned after Yodai for adding, subtracting,
multiplying, and dividing fractions.   The mnemonics are based on
activities that are more familiar and meaningful than bugs to
children in the U.S. (especially in Kunihira's area of southern
California)--swimming pools and jogging.   For example, a fraction
is represented by a jogger with a number on his shirt (numerator)
and patches on his shorts (denominator), and operations with
fractions are represented by poolside activities.   More detailed
explanations, descriptions, and analyses of the Yodai and Pool
mnemonics, and some relevant research, are given by Higbee (1987)
and Higbee and Kunihira (1985).

A third program, Semple Math, has recently been developed
by Janice Semple in Massachusetts to teach mathematics skills to
beginning, high-risk, and/or remedial students, from first grade
through math-disabled adults.   Semple Math teaches only very basic
mathematics.   For example, the first 17 lessons teach the numbers
from 1-10, including counting, and identifying, writing, and naming

the numbers.   A sample mnemonic used by Semple Math is the invisible 'tail' that every numeral has hanging down from it, from which other numerals can hang.   The tail is used to teach vertical alignment of numerals, and beginning concepts of place value.

LANGUAGE SKILLS

For about 20 years, Nancy Stevenson in Massachusetts has been developing and using a language skills program aimed primarily at students who are learning and language disabled, retarded, emotionally disturbed, or learning English as a second language. The program covers basic skills in listening, speaking, reading, spelling, vocabulary building, penmanship, and grammar, for students in kindergarten through twelfth grade.   A sample mnemonic is the 'peanut butter and jelly sandwich' mnemonic used to learn spelling and pronunciation of one-syllable words with vowel combinations like 'oa,' such as 'coat.'   The consonants are slices of bread, and the vowels are the crunchy peanut butter (o) and the smooth jelly (a).   When a child eats a peanut butter and jelly sandwich, he hears the crunchy peanut butter but not the smooth jelly.

In the early 1960s, two optometrists in South Dakota, Leland Michael and James King (with their assistant Arlene Moorhead), began developing a system to help children remember phonic and linguistic principles and to develop visual memory for words.   The MKM program was later expanded into a more comprehensive reading program.   They identified 15 general areas of concern regarding concepts needed to process visual and auditory symbols efficiently. These 15 concepts appear as the 15 steps making up the system, and 26 mnemonic sentences and pictures were created to illustrate the concepts.   For example, the sentence 'Cyclone, the yellow pony, can fly' (and its accompanying picture) helps remember the consonant sound and vowel sounds of 'y.'   The 15 steps cover such concepts as the relationships between the names of letters and their sounds, the short and long sounds of vowels, principles for adding endings to words, and guides for syllabication.

FIVE PROGRAMS COMPARED

I have noted that more details on these five mathematics and language programs are given elsewhere.   However, it is helpful to briefly point out a few similar characteristics here.   First, the programs were developed from perceived needs in the real world, rather than originating in investigations in the research laboratory and finding their way to real-world applications.   In fact, Yodai is the only program that has even been subjected to significant experimental research.   Empirical support for the other programs is mostly anecdotes and case studies.   Second, the programs are currently being used to teach students (mostly children), by the program developers as well as in a few schools.

Third, the programs are integrated, comprehensive systems, not just haphazard sets or collections of miscellaneous mnemonics. Fourth, the programs use both verbal mnemonics (rhymes, songs, sentences, acrostics) and visual mnemonics (mnemonic pictures and visual imagery). These mnemonics are based on language that is familiar and meaningful to the learners, rather than teaching them a new technical vocabulary at first.   Fifth, in addition to mnemonics, the programs also make use of non-mnemonic techniques such as practice problems, games, gestures and motor activities, and active participation (e.g., singing or chanting rhymes).   This suggests that mnemonics do not necessarily have to be used **instead of** other learning techniques, but can be used **in addition to** them.

SCRIPTURES

Ernest Weckbaugh in California has developed a program for learning scriptures that is based on the Phonetic system.   The Phonetic system consists of substituting a consonant sound for each digit (e.g., 0 = s, z; 1 = th, t, d; 2 = n), then adding vowels to create words to represent numbers (e.g., 12 = tin, 201 = nest); see Higbee (in press) for a complete description.   Weckbaugh has developed phonetic phrases for 1200 selected verses in the Bible. Each phrase is semantically related to the content of the verse, and also identifies the book, chapter, and verse numbers in the Phonetic system.   The books are represented by numbers giving their numerical order in the Bible, rather than by their names.   Here are a few examples: A verse on the creation ('Let there be light,' Genesis 1:2) is the phrase **'The Dawn,'** 1-1-2 representing the first book, first chapter, second verse;   the Ten Commandments (Exodus 20) are **'No-Nos,'** 2-20 representing the second book, 20th chapter; the names of the twelve apostles (Matthew 10:2) are **'The Dozen,'** 1-10-2 representing the first book in the New Testament, tenth chapter, second verse.   Weckbaugh has published a scripture-learning game and other learning aids based on his program. Recently he has put the program and all 1200 phonetic phrases in book form, and is trying to get it published for wider availability.

Another mnemonic approach to learning scripture was developed by Jerry Lucas (1975), for learning the contents of the four Gospels in the New Testament.   Rather than focusing on selected verses, his program is aimed at remembering all the main ideas of each chapter in order.   Lucas' program is based on the Link, Story, and Phonetic systems (see Higbee, in press).   Each chapter number is represented by a keyword based on the Phonetic system, and the contents of the chapter are represented by substitute words and corresponding visual images.   The package consists of a book which gives detailed verbal descriptions and explanations of the mnemonic pictures and how to link them together in a chain of associations, and a set of line drawings illustrating the verbal mnemonics.   Some of the chapter stories are rather simple, containing only about half a dozen images to be linked, while others are very complex, containing dozens of images.

FOREIGN LANGUAGES

I noted that there has been applied research on the use of mnemonics to learn foreign language vocabulary.   That research has been done mostly with students in school, and has used the Keyword mnemonic, a mnemonic for paired-associate learning which involves constructing a concrete substitute word to represent the foreign word, then associating it using visual imagery with the English word (for example, the Spanish word 'pato' is represented by the key word 'pot,' which is associated with the English equivalent 'duck'). Programs have recently been developed that are also based on the Keyword mnemonic but intended for application outside school. Linkword Languages were developed by Michael Gruneberg, a psychologist and mnemonics researcher at the University College of Swansea in Wales. The Linkword programs teach Russian and seven European languages to English speakers. They were originally produced as computer software, with audio tapes to assist pronunciation, and the programs for four languages have recently (1987) been published as books also. In addition to using the Keyword mnemonic to learn vocabulary, the programs also use mnemonics to learn the grammar, so the learner can string words together to form sentences. For example, in French the gender of nouns is presented with the mnemonic for masculine being a boxer and the mnemonic for feminine being perfume. The Linkword programs are not intended to teach conversational skills, but to provide a basic knowledge of vocabulary and grammar for tourists and business travelers (for more information see Gruneberg, 1985, and Colley & Williamson, 1986).

The Keyword mnemonic is also being used to teach English speakers to speak Japanese. Delbert Groberg (1972) in Utah developed a set of mnemonics consisting of substitute words accompanied by line drawings illustrating the words, and extended the approach to include phrases. Like Gruneberg, Groberg has developed his mnemonics beyond the learning of vocabulary to include grammar. He has presented his mnemonic grammar in a recent book which has not yet been published for wide distribution, but has been used for several years to teach Japanese to English-speaking people hired to work in Japan, and is the basis of a correspondence course in speaking Japanese that Groberg is developing.

ADDITIONAL APPLICATIONS

Since 1971 I have taught a university memory course oriented toward improving memory skills, in which I give the students homework assignments to apply the mnemonics and other skills outside of class to something the students really want to learn. Students have reported profitably using mnemonics such as the Keyword, Link, Story, Peg, Loci, and Phonetic systems on scores of practical tasks related to their schoolwork, jobs, hobbies, and everyday activities. The following is one example (I have listed and described many additional examples elsewhere, Higbee, in press). A student was employed in training mentally and emotionally handicapped people to do custodial work, to prepare them for job placement. One custodial job they learned to do was cleaning lavatories, which involved 14 steps. He first used the Peg system (one-bun, two-shoe, etc.) to learn the steps himself so he could teach them more effectively, then used the Peg system to help his trainees learn the steps. He reported that developmentally disabled and emotionally handicapped trainees were successful in memorizing the steps, and that their quality rate according to competitive standards increased from approximately 20% to over 80% of competitive norms.

Many practical applications of mnemonics have been suggested in addition to those in this paper. The popular literature on memory training is full of examples of how various mnemonics might be used. The examples I have included in this paper are some that are actually being used by someone (rather than just suggested as possible uses), are somewhat systematic and comprehensive (rather than just unrelated examples), are not widely known, and/or seem to have some reasonable empirical or theoretical justification. These examples are intended to be merely illustrative of the kinds of uses that can and have been made. They are by no means exhaustive, but represent a sample of some interesting attempts at real-world uses of mnemonics that have come to my attention. My goal in calling them to the attention of others is to help us broaden our perspective of practical aspects of mnemonics--both for practitioners who might want to use mnemonics, and for researchers who might be interested in some possible areas for future applied research on mnemonics.

REFERENCES

Colley, A. and Williamson, B. (1986). 'Review of Linkword,' Bulletin of the British Psychological Society, 39, 178.

Groberg, D.H. (1972). Mnemonic Japanese, International Education Research Analysis Corporation, Salt Lake City, Utah.

Gruneberg, M.M. (1985, February). 'The Gruneberg Linkword Language System for Teaching Foreign Languages,' Training and Development, p. 22.

Higbee, K.L. (1986, July). 'Applied Mnemonics Research Applied,' Paper presented at the meeting of the International Association of Applied Psychology, Jerusalem.

Higbee, K.L. (1987). 'Process Mnemonics: Principles, Prospects, and Problems,' in Imagery and Related Mnemonic Processes: Theories, Individual Differences, and Applications (Eds. M.A. McDaniel and M. Pressley), pp. 407-427, Springer-Verlag, New York.

Higbee, K.L. (in press). Your Memory: How It Works and How To Improve It (2nd ed.), Prentice Hall, Englewood Cliffs, NJ.

Higbee, K.L. and Kunihira, S. (1985). 'Cross-cultural Applications of Yodai Mnemonics,' Educational Psychologist, 20, 57-64.

Lucas, J. (1975). Remember the Word (Vol. 1: The Gospels), Acton House, Los Angeles.

McDaniel, M.A. and Pressley, M. (Eds.). (1987). Imagery and Related Mnemonic Processes: Theories, Individual Differences, and Applications, Springer-Verlag, New York.

DOING MNEMONICS RESEARCH WELL: SOME GENERAL GUIDELINES AND A STUDY

Michael Pressley
University of Western Ontario, London, Ontario, Canada   N6A 5C2
Mark A. McDaniel
University of Notre Dame, Notre Dame, Indiana, USA   46556

ABSTRACT
Some investigators have made strong criticisms of the keyword method of vocabulary learning.   One recurring claim is that the method does not foster true understanding of vocabulary.   Many times criticisms such as this one occur in the context of experimental tests that are not very convincing.   Thus we present here a new experiment in which the keyword method proved better than a context, and six recommendations about how to conduct mnemonics research.

There are now many rigorous experimental evaluations of various mnemonic procedures (McDaniel & Pressley, 1987).   There are many occasions when mnemonic interventions aid performance.   These interventions seem especially helpful for people who otherwise experience great difficulty acquiring information, such as learning disabled children (Pressley, Johnson, & Symons, 1987; Pressley & Levin, 1986).   Despite general optimism, there is also a down side.   Some educators and educational psychologists seem inclined to view mnemonics as "artificial learning procedures," that do not foster true understanding.   Moreover, we still encounter experiments on mnemonics that are simply not very convincing.   In this paper, we respond to these two negative aspects of mnemonics research by (1) presenting some of our latest work on the keyword mnemonic and (2) identifying some generic procedures that can be used to provide telling data about mnemonics.

THE KEYWORD MNEMONIC AND VOCABULARY LEARNING
The keyword technique is a two stage procedure for learning vocabulary-definition linkages.   First, the learner acquires an association between the unfamiliar vocabulary item and a familiar word (the keyword) that sounds like a salient part of the to-be-learned vocabulary item.   Next, the learner links the keyword and the item's definition by encoding a meaningful association between the two (usually by forming an interactive visual image).   For example, to remember that CARLIN means "old woman," one might use the keyword car and imagine an old woman driving a car.
There are several reasons why the keyword method is ignored by educational theorists who are interested in vocabulary learning.   First, indirect methods of teaching vocabulary seem to be preferred over direct instruction despite evidence documenting the strong effects of direct instruction (McDaniel & Pressley, 1984; see **also**

Chall, 1987, for a more general review). This preference for indirect instruction is tied to the fact that vocabulary instruction is typically embedded in a concern for enhancement of reading and comprehension skills (Nagy & Herman, 1987). Research on the keyword technique on the other hand has focused almost exclusively on performance on standard memory tests like cued recall (see Pressley, Levin, & McDaniel,1987, for a review). We describe here a recent study (performed in collaboration with Brian Lyman) that extends keyword research by testing reading performance. Meanings of vocabulary were taught by one of three methods (no-strategy control, keyword, and semantic context). Control subjects were presented the unfamiliar vocabulary words paired with their definitions and were simply instructed to try to learn the definition of each word. Keyword subjects were instructed to use the two-stage keyword procedure. Semantic-context subjects were provided with a three-sentence paragraph in which the vocabulary item was embedded in at least two of the sentences. Subjects were instructed to try to determine the word's meaning by studying its use in the sentences. Following this, context subjects were provided the definition. Then, the ease of comprehending passages in which some of the newly acquired vocabulary were embedded was measured (by recording reading time) as was the degree of understanding (with a true-false comprehension test). This reading comprehension was assessed for two kinds of texts. "Embellished" texts, provided contextual clues to help reinstate the meanings of the targeted vocabulary items. "Unembellished" texts did not include such clues. After reading a text, subjects completed a 15-item true-false comprehension test. Finally, subjects were asked to recall the definitions of all words that were taught.

There were no a priori differences in general reading skills across instructional conditions. There were no significant reading time differences due to instructional condition. There were differences due to instructional condition in the number of correct responses (correct "trues" plus correct "falses") on the comprehension test. Keyword subjects scored significantly higher than control subjects and keyword subjects tended to score higher relative to context subjects on comprehension of the unembellished text. On the cued recall test, the keyword subjects recalled a significantly higher proportion of definitions than either the context subjects or the control subjects. These results suggest boundary conditions on the conventional wisdom that vocabulary instruction targeted for reading activity must include both definitional and contextual information (e.g., Stahl, 1986). Our findings suggest that when the instructional phase limits the frequency of encounters of the vocabulary items, then enriched instruction that includes exposure to varied verbal contexts may not enhance comprehension relative to instruction that provides only definitional information. In the present case an effort was made to induce subjects in the context condition to actively process the contexts (by allowing the context subjects to try to discover the word's meaning from the context prior to presenting the words meaning). Nevertheless, this group never outperformed the keyword group on the reading measures. This finding, along with previous work examining sentence production (McDaniel & Pressley, 1984, Experiment 2) and inferencing tasks (McCormick,

Miller, & Fields, 1987), suggests that for nonintensive training regimens general language usage of to-be-learned vocabulary is at least as good after keyword instruction as after instruction that includes study of contextual information.

SUGGESTIONS FOR CONDUCTING GOOD MNEMONICS RESEARCH

Recommendation One: Conduct Programmatic Research

A main reason for progress in understanding mnemonics is that programmatic research efforts were launched in a number of laboratories in the 1970s and 1980s. Programmatic efforts have permitted replication of some of the most important mnemonically-mediated effects. No single study can provide telling evidence about which of its significant effects are wheat and which are chaff. Only exact replications of effects and constructive replications across materials, settings, and populations can do that. Thus, our first suggestion is to plan long-term multiple-experiment research efforts rather than single-shot studies.

Recommendation Two: Include Manipulations Checks in Mnemonic Conditions

A brief instruction to use a mnemonic strategy (e.g., the keyword method for foreign vocabulary learning) often elicits something else - free association to the vocabulary or attempts to relate the vocabulary to native language cognates. Every effort must be made during instructions to make certain that the subject knows exactly what to do. At a minimum, subjects should be required to report how they are mediating several practice items, with corrective feedback provided. Unfortunately, we encounter many reports where it is assumed that subjects execute mnemonic procedures following a simple direction with no check of subjects' understanding of instructions. When possible, obtain on-line data that reveal the mediation process used by subjects. For instance, with verbal mnemonics, subjects can be asked to mediate some or all items out loud with little or no difference on eventual criterion performance. Obtain post-experimental reports (e.g., by representing several of the items and requesting verbal reports about mediators that were produced). If subjects cannot report on such mediators during an informal post-experiment interview, it is a good clue that they might not have produced the mediators during study. Although we recognize the potential problems in such reports, much can be gained from them, especially if subjects are impressed with the fact that they should report accurately and honestly. These reports are at least somewhat congruent with actual processing that took place, for there is a substantial body of data confirming that posttest reports of mnemonic mediation are strongly related to "objective" measures of performance, most notably memory (e.g., Pressley, in press; Pressley & Ahmad, 1986; Pressley, Levin, Kuiper, Bryant, & Michener, 1982).

Recommendation Three: Find Out What Control Subjects Are Doing

Control subjects are not passive learners. In particular, a nontrivial proportion of adults report use of mnemonic strategies some of the time. Interpretation of control performance is almost always facilitated by collecting data that provide **information** about the extent of mnemonics use. The collection of such data is especially urgent when subjects are drawn from psychology or educational psychology subject pools, as is often the case when faculty members conduct experiments. Mnemonics are often covered in such courses. Students can be impressed by the potency of these methods during class and laboratory demonstrations and adopt the procedures as their own. For instance, it has been the experience of one of us (M.P.) that introductory psychology students' use of mnemonics in control conditions is almost always higher when studies are conducted after imagery is covered in the introductory course than when studies are conducted before imagery is covered in the course (Pressley & Ahmad, 1986). This need to assess subject use of mnemonics is present even when the control subjects are instructed to use processes that are presumably inimical to use of mnemonics. For instance, Pressley and Ahmad (1986) observed that even when their adult subjects were required to use rote repetition overtly to code vocabulary, they also reported some covert use of mnemonic mediation. When a researcher has information about which control subjects mnemonically mediated, it is possible to do conditional probability and correlational analyses that permit statistical control of strategy use.

Recommendation Four: Measure Both Performance That Should Be Enhanced By The Mnemonic Procedure and Performance That Should Not Be Affected

One explanation of mnemonic effects that we have heard is that they simply reflect motivational increases associated with mnemonic procedures that are fun or novel. This hypothesis can be easily tested. The keyword method is hypothesized by mnemonics theorists and researchers to affect the associative linkages between vocabulary items and their meanings, but not much else. The general motivational position would be that both associative and nonassociative aspects of vocabulary learning should be increased by vocabulary instruction. Pressley et al. (1982; see also McDaniel & Tillman, 1987) provided telling data on this debate, demonstrating strong keyword-instructional effects when subjects were required to match vocabulary meanings (an associative task) and negligible mnemonic-instructional effects when subjects were asked to perform nonassociative free recall of definitions presented during study (i.e., without the vocabulary presented at testing). Such a predicted pattern of significant and nonsignificant effects provides a convincing case against those who would try to explain mnemonics effects away as motivational artifacts.

Recommendation Five: Include "Benchmark" Replications

There are certain "classic" mnemonic effects. For instance, adults who are taught to execute keyword-mnemonic strategies (and who do so) always learn more associative material than control subjects who report no mnemonic mediation or subjects assigned to semantic-context treatments. Manipulations that produce well replicated effects (such as the ones just mentioned) can be included in studies that are more centrally concerned with new hypotheses about mnemonics effects. If the researcher once again replicates the classic effect, confidence is bolstered in the more novel outcomes that may be obtained in the study. For **instance,**

Pressley (in press) studied an hypothesis advanced by Hall and Fuson (1986) that keyword-mnemonic effects would evaporate if adult subjects were given vocabulary several times at a fast rate compared to a more typical method of presentation in keyword studies - one presentation at a slow rate. Pressley used a 2 x 2 design (keyword vs. no-strategy control; 3 presentations of a list at 3 secs per item presentation vs. 1 list presentation of the list at 9 secs per item). Pressley replicated the classic slow presentation keyword effect. That is, among subjects who received 1 presentation at 9 secs, keyword subjects recalled definitions given vocabulary better than control subjects did. He also replicated the classic distributed-practice effect (i.e., multiple 3-sec presentations produced greater recall than one 9-second presentation). That these two benchmark effects were obtained make all the more convincing the finding that the keyword over control difference was as large with three fast presentations as with one slow presentation, a finding that clashed directly with Hall and Fuson's (1986) hypothesis.

Recommendation Six: Use Many Different Contrast Conditions
Different types of control procedures achieve different purposes. Thus, keyword research has included control conditions designed to preclude efficient processing and no-strategy control conditions. The method has also been contrasted with a variety of semantic-context procedures. When a technique is tested against a variety of alternative procedures, including ones proven potent in the past or presumed potent by practitioners, it is hard to argue that the tests have been with "straw men".

Concluding Comment
Much mnemonics research has been conducted incorporating the methodological points outlined here. The result has been a body of replicable and understandable findings concerning the keyword method and other mnemonic procedures.

REFERENCES

Chall, J.S. (1987). Two vocabularies for reading: Recognition and meaning. In M.G. McKeown & M.E. Curtis (Ed.), The nature of vocabulary instruction (pp. 7-17). Hillsdale, N.J.: Erlbaum & Associates.

Hall, J.W., & Fuson, K.C. (1986). Presentation rates in experiments on mnemonics: A methodological note. Journal of Educational Psychology, 78, 233-234.

McCormick, C.B., Miller, G.E., & Fields, J.T. (1987, April). A comparison of contextual and mnemonic approaches to learning English vocabulary: The effects of pacing. Presented at the annual meeting of the American Educational Research Association, Washington, D.C.

McDaniel, M.A., & Pressley, M. (1984). Putting the keyword method in context. Journal of Educational Psychology, 76, 598-609.

McDaniel, M.A., & Pressley, M. (1987). Imagery and related mnemonic processes: Theories, individual differences, and applications. New York: Springer-Verlag.

McDaniel, M.A., & Tillman, V.P. (1987). Discovering a meaning versus applying the keyword method: Effects on recall. Contemporary Educational Psychology.

Nagy, W.E., & Herman, P.A. (1987). Breadth and depth of vocabulary knowledge: Implications for acquisition and instruction. In M.G. McKeown & M.E. Curtis (Eds.), The nature of vocabulary instruction (pp. 19-35). Hillsdale, N.J.: Erlbaum & Associates.

Pressley, M. (in press). Are keyword methods limited to slow presentation rates? An empirically-based reply to Hall and Fuson (1986). Journal of Educational Psychology.

Pressley, M., & Ahmad, M. (1987). Transfer of imagery-based mnemonics by adult learners. Contemporary Educational Psychology, 11, 150-160.

Pressley, M., Johnson, C.J., & Symons, S. (1987). Elaborating to learn and learning to elaborate. Journal of Learning Disabilities, 20, 76-91.

Pressley, M., & Levin, J.R. (1986). Elaborative learning strategies for the inefficient learner. In S.J. Ceci (Ed.), Handbook of cognitive, social, and neuropsychological aspects of learning disabilities. Hillsdale, N.J.: Erlbaum & Associates.

Pressley, M., Levin, J.R., Kuiper, N.A., Bryant, S.L., & Michener, S. (1982). Mnemonic versus nonmnemonic vocabulary-learning strategies: Additional comparisons. Journal of Educational Psychology, 74, 693-707.

Pressley, M., Levin, J.R., & McDaniel, M.A. (1987). Remembering versus inferring what a word means: Mnemonic and contextual approaches. In M.G. McKeown & M.E. Curtis (Eds.), The nature of vocabulary instruction (pp. 107-127). Hillsdale, N.J.: Erlbaum & Associates.

Stahl, S.A. (1986). Three principles of effective vocabulary instruction. Journal of Reading, 29, 662-668.

THE NEED FOR A NEW APPROACH TO MEMORY TRAINING

Douglas Herrmann*, Alison Rea** and Stephen Andrzejewski*

* Hamilton College, Clinton, N.Y. 13323, U.S.A.
** University of Manchester, Manchester M13 9PL, U.K.

ABSTRACT
        A review of the memory training literature indicates that
the traditional methods of improving memory abilities are typically
effective immediately following training. However, these methods are
applicable to far fewer tasks than is currently believed and the use
of these methods is rarely sustained after training.   Alternatively,
task-specific training has been found to yield more permanent
effects.   However, acquisition of task specific methods requires
considerable effort.   Thus, a new approach to the improvement of
memory abilities is needed which advances task-specific methods, and
in addition, the acquisition of other behaviors that enhance a
person's memory performance.

        Psychology has investigated memory phenomena for over a
century.   However, until recently, most of the investigations have
had little to do with the improvement of memory abilities.   In the
past several years, investigations concerning memory-ability
improvement increased in number and scientific status because of
burgeoning interest in the development of memory abilities in the
young, the decline of memory abilities in the old, and in the loss of
memory abilities in those with neurological impairment.   The
continued growth of this interest will depend on whether
psychological research can develop truly viable methods for improving
memory abilities.
        The recent interest in the improvement of memory abilities
in the young, the old, and the neurologically impaired has spurred a
comprehensive appraisal of traditional improvement methods.   This
appraisal has typically led to refinements of these   methods.
However, the appraisal has also led to findings that indicate the
traditional methods are of less general applicability than is
currently believed and are rarely sustained in a person's ongoing
performance of memory tasks. If the traditional methods are, indeed,
limited in their potential for producing a general and permanent
improvement in memory abilities, it will be necessary for psychology
to rethink its approach to such improvement.   Alternatively, if the
traditional methods are not as limited as some have alleged, then
psychology can continue to advocate the use of these methods.
        This   paper first presents a brief summary of the
traditional methods used in training to improve memory abilities.
Second, the paper examines how general and sustained improvement is
when training involves these traditional methods.   Third, the paper

examines the generality and likelihood of sustained use of abilities produced by training with other methods. Finally, conclusions are drawn about the status of memory training today, and the need to develop a new approach to improving memory abilities.

THE TRADITIONAL METHODS

From ancient Greece up to the present time, the traditional formula for memory improvement has been to acquire a few methods that may be applied to all memory tasks. The traditional methods most often recommended in psychology and in commercial memory-improvement ventures (e.g., books and courses) include primarily the following: the method of "loci" (imagining that material to be learned was "placed" in various rooms of an imagined house); the "peg" or "hook" methods (imagining the interaction of material to be learned with images of objects contained in a previously memorized list); and the "link" method (forming joint images of terms to be learned). All of these methods have been found to improve learning substantially immediately after their use has been explained (Bellezza, 1981). Perhaps because these methods have been found effective at the conclusion of instruction, the generality and sustainment of each method has usually been simply assumed. But if these methods are to be central to application and to memory theory, their generality and sustainment must be evaluated.

The Generality of Memory Abilities Trained with the Traditional Methods

The research findings are clear: the traditional methods are not generally applicable across all, or even relatively similar, memory tasks. A review of investigations that have compared these methods has shown that each method tends to work better for some tasks than for others. For example, the traditional method that leads to the most learning for unordered lists is the story method; ordered lists are best learned by the method of loci; and pairs of items are best learned by using interactive imagery as is involved in the peg system (Herrmann, 1987). Moreover, the traditional methods are not applicable at all to some tasks (e.g., these methods cannot be used sensibly to register in memory a new face, a melody, or a new golf stroke).

The Sustainment of Memory Abilities Trained with the Traditional Methods

In recent years several studies have examined the sustainment of training effects based on traditional methods. The findings again have been clear. Most people who have taken a memory improvement course with the traditional methods have been found to quit these methods within a few months after the end of the course. This outcome has been obtained in many studies, both with college students (e.g., Higbee, 1981) and elderly adults (e.g., Lapp, 1983). Even psychologists who specialize in the study of memory and the improvement of memory abilities usually do not use the traditional methods despite being very familiar with them (Parks, Cavanaugh and Smith, 1986).

OTHER METHODS
The Generality of Memory Abilities Trained with Other Methods

Although the traditional methods are found under scrutiny to lack generality, it might be argued that there are other methods capable of producing general memory abilities. Several lines of research makes it clear that other methods of memory training and memory task experience also fail to produce general memory abilities. First, practice at memory tasks improves ability to learn and/or recall but only in a specific manner. For example, one subject who became well practiced at the digit span task could recall a dramatically large number of digits (over 80), but he still could recall only a normal span of letters (Chase and Ericsson, 1982). Additionally, subjects given practice at recall alone (i.e., without an opportunity to study the material to be recalled) increase in the number of words they can recall for the specific category used in practice but not for categories in general (Herrmann, Buschke and Gall, 1987). Second, educational experience (e.g., studying Latin) has long been known to improve memory ability within, but not across, disciplines (Thorndike, 1924). Third, occupational experience (e.g., as a physicist, a mathematician, or an expert chess player) improves memory for tasks required by the occupation but not for identical tasks involving material unrelated to the occupation (Lesgold, 1983). Fourth, years of practice at memory tasks that makes a person into an expert at performing memory tasks yields abilities specific to the tasks (Brown and Deffenbacher, 1975). Fifth, abilities manifested when people perform a battery of many memory tasks, before or after practice, are found to be relatively uncorrelated, suggesting that only specific memory abilities underlie performance of each task (Underwood, Boruch and Malmi, 1978). Thus, general ability either cannot be trained, or can be trained only with procedures hitherto untried.

The Sustainment of Memory Abilities Trained with Other Methods

Training with task specific methods is likely to be more successful in producing sustained improvement than training with the traditional methods. First, practice at acquisition in a particular kind of memory task (e.g., the digit span task) has been found to induce superior memory abilities for this task that do not decline quickly (Baltes and Kliegel, 1986; Chase and Ericsson, 1982). Similarly, our research at Hamilton College also found practice at recalling the vocabulary of categories (e.g., furniture) yielded a superior recall ability than appeared to be durable.

Second, training based on task-specific instructions appears also to show promise for being able to produce more sustained improvement in memory abilities. We have investigated the permanence of two forms of task-specific training. One form involved a three week course in memory improvement (taught at Hamilton College) which consisted in part of discussions about the possible ways of coping with specific everyday memory tasks (Herrmann, 1988 (in press)) that troubled members of the group. A second form of training (given to students at the University of Manchester and elderly members of the subject panel at the University of Manchester's Aging Centre) involved studying a list of strategies that apply to a particular task (Herrmann, 1988, in press). One month after training, participants trained with either form of task-specific instructions reported active use of the method, more active than was typical of them before training and more active than untrained control subjects. Neither form of training was extensive (about 10 minutes of discussion or of memorization), suggesting that more extensive training might increase the likelihood that training effects would be sustained.

DISCUSSION
          The findings examined here indicate very clearly the limitations of the traditional methods for improving memory abilities. For most people trained by these methods, the immediate improvement is dramatic, but it is neither general nor lasting. It must be noted that a small proportion of people who seek memory training with the traditional methods do achieve a sustained improvement in memory abilities. Thus, the traditional methods should not be dropped entirely from training. However, they cannot be legitimately recommended for most people due to the low likelihood of their sustained use. It should also be noted that the traditional methods remain useful when the goal is to change performance, rather than abilities. For example, people with clinical memory impairment may demonstrate improved memory performance if they are guided in the use of a traditional method by a professional (e.g. a clinician, a nurse, an aide) while performing a learning task (Wilson and Moffat, 1984).
          In revealing the severe limitations of the traditional methods for improving memory ability, research has also revealed that psychology lacks a coherent approach to such improvement – either in terms of theory or application. It would be premature to propose here a complete approach to training that would enable the sustained improvement of memory abilities. Nevertheless, the research discussed here suggests some important features needed by a new approach.

Theoretical Orientation of the New Approach
          The methods that appear to be more likely to result in a sustained change in abilities are task specific. Procedural theories (Anderson, 1982) rest on such an assumption. They may be found, with additional assumptions about how abilities are trained, to provide an adequate theory of memory-ability improvement. Multi-store theories (Atkinson and Shiffrin, 1968) and the depth of processing theory (Craik and Lockhart, 1973) would necessitate the adoption of task-specific processing mechanisms before they could become viable theories of memory-ability improvement.

Methodological Orientation of the New Approach
          A lasting improvement of particular memory abilities may be achieved by either extensive task practice or extensive task-specific instruction. But these methods have an important limitation. Both methods require the recipient of training to invest a considerable amount of time, placing a limit on the number of tasks for which a person may be trained. This limitation of task-specific methods indicates the need for training to go beyond mental strategies and further develop additional modes of controlling memory performance.

Currently, researchers and clinicians facilitate the memory performance of patients and elderly adults through fostering the use of strategies and other behaviors that influence memory performance modes, e.g., external aids and relaxation activities (Poon, 1980; Wilson and Moffat, 1984). It seems reasonable to assume that training normal adults to adopt a variety of behaviors that facilitate memory, besides memory strategies, should also result in a greater, more sustained, improvement in their memory performance (Herrmann, 1988, in press).

ACKNOWLEDGEMENT

          The first author thanks the University of Manchester for providing him in 1985-86 a Simon Fellowship and the opportunity to participate in the research that led to this paper. We thank Tom Ayers, Mike Gervasio, Graham Hitch, Pat Rabbitt, and Jim Reason for advice on issues and/or matters of composition of the paper.

REFERENCES

Anderson, J.R. (1982). 'Acquisition of a cognitive skill', Psychological Review, 89, 396-406.

Atkinson, R.C. and Shiffrin, R.M. (1968). 'Human memory: A proposed system and its control processes', in The Psychology of Learning and Motivation (Eds. K.W. Spence and J.T. Spence), pp. 89-195, Academic Press, New York.

Baltes, P.B. and Kliegel, R. (1986). 'On the dynamics between growth and decline in the aging of intelligence and memory', in Proceedings Of The Thirteenth World Conference Of Neurology (Ed. K. Poeck), pp. 1-17, Springer, Heidelberg, FR Germany.

Bellezza, F.S. (1981). 'Mnemonic devices: Classification, characteristics, and criteria', Review of Educational Research, 51, 247-275.

Brown, E. and Deffenbacher, K. (1975). 'Forgotten mnemonists', Journal of the History of the Behavioral Sciences, 11, 342-349.

Chase, W.G. and Ericsson, K.A. (1982). 'Skill and working memory', in The Psychology of Learning and Motivation (Ed. G.H. Bower), pp. 1-58, Academic Press, New York.

Craik, F.I.M. and Lockhart, R.S. (1973). 'Levels of processing: A framework for memory research', Journal of Verbal Learning and Verbal Behavior, 11, 671-684.

Herrmann, D.J. (1987). 'Task appropriateness of mnemonic techniques', Perceptual and Motor Skills, 64, 171-178.

Herrmann, D.J. (1988/in press)). Memory Improvement Techniques. Ballantine, New York.

Herrmann, D.J., Buschke, H. and Gall, M. (1987). 'Improving retrieval', Applied Cognitive Psychology, 1, 27-33.

Higbee, K.L. (1981). 'What do college students get from a memory improvement course?'. Paper presented at the Eastern Psychological Association in New York City.

Lapp, D. (1983). 'Commitment: Essential ingredient in memory training', Clinical Gerontologist, 2, 58-60.

Lesgold, A.M. (1983). 'Acquiring expertise', in Tutorials In Learning And Memory: Essays In Honor Of Gordon Bower (Ed. J.R. Anderson), pp. 31-60, Winston, San Francisco.

Parks, D., Cavanaugh, J. and Smith, A. (1986). 'Metamemory 2: Memory researchers knowledge of their own memory abilities'. Paper presented at the American Psychological Association in Washington, D.C.

Poon, L.W. (1980). 'A systems approach for the assessment and treatment of memory problems', in The Comprehensive Handbook of Behavioral Medicine (Eds. J.M. Ferguson and C.B. Taylor). Vol.I, 191-212, Spectrum Publication, New York.

Thorndike, E.L. (1924). 'Mental discipline in high school studies', Journal of Educational Psychology, 30, 641-456.

Underwood, B.J., Boruch, R.F. and Malmi, R.A. (1978). 'Composition of episodic memory', Journal of Experimental Psychology: General, 107, 393-419.

Wilson, B. and Moffat, N. (Eds.) (1986). Clinical Management of Memory Problems, Aspen Systems, Rockville, Maryland.

THE AID GIVEN BY THE "LOCI" MEMORY TECHNIQUE IN THE MEMORIZATION OF PASSAGES

R. De Beni

Department of General Psychology, University of Padova
Padova, Italy

ABSTRACT

The difficulty in using loci mnemonics with texts may be due to the nature of the memory technique and the text which both have idiosyncratic structures which are not linked to each other. In the present paper some boundary conditions for finding a loci advantage in text memory are presented. This advantage may be found with some passages more than with others and especially if they are presented orally. The characteristics of the control group appear to affect the results.

It has been shown that image-based memory techniques, already well-known to the ancient Greeks and Romans, work extremely well in the memorization of isolated items. Many experimental results have shown how the performance of subjects who use these techniques may be several times better than those who do not, and have also indicated how wide their field of application may be with separate categories of subjects and differing degrees of knowledge of the techniques, materials and memory tests (see e.g. De Beni and Cornoldi, 1985).

However, when examining the applicability of memory techniques to daily life, experimental situations (usually memorization of isolated items) are only applicable to a limited number of situations (lists of objects, telephone numbers, names). It is difficult to extend the use of these techniques to the typical situation of intentional memory in which subjects, mainly students, are asked to learn the meaning of a text. This difficulty arises because of the nature of the memory technique and the text, which both have idiosyncratic structures which are not linked to each other. The fundamental key to many memory techniques is the use of a structure which organizes the material to be memorized, facilitating retrieval by reference to that structure. Consequently, a text which has its own structure and which must make use of the overlapping structure of the memory technique may be completely distorted.

Although the literature on the use of memory techniques in memorizing passages is not great, it does confirm these perplexities. According to some authors, memory techniques should be modified by the addition of some preliminary operations (Bellezza, 1981, 1983; Hunter, 1977).

The aim of this paper is to present some boundary conditions for finding a mnemonic advantage in text memory. This problem is explored in more detail by referring to the "loci" memory technique which, as well as being probably the best known and most frequently used, is also, according to the classic texts on mnemonics, very suitable for memorizing passages (Yates, 1966). The loci technique consists in forming a mental structure represented by an ordered series of places and then separating the material to be memorized into units, imagining each unit as interacting separately with each place.

In this paper, prepared with the collaboration of C. Cornoldi, we describe the effects of the use of loci memory techniques with texts, presented to different groups of subjects trained in such techniques after a number of training sessions. We first made use of a text on psychology which students judged was difficult to memorize. This passage, whose contents were previously completely unknown to them, dealt with the various phases of the history of Soviet psychology and was taken from a paper by Meacham (1977). The trained subjects showed that they could not perform better than the control group on a series of multiple-choice questions on the contents of this passage concerning either important ideas or details.

The subjects who had memorized this passage stated that they found difficulty both in understanding the passage and in dividing it into units to be associated with loci. We therefore tried to avoid this difficulty by modifying the technique according to the suggestions of Bellezza (1982) and, choosing the same passage (approximately 840 words long) he proposed for practicing the technique (that on advertising), although he did not mention experimental verification of its effectiveness.

Ninety-six university students were divided in two groups of 48. The first group Loci-trained (LT) followed a memory improvement course in which they had been instructed to use a pathway of 20 loci in a variety of tasks and had tried to memorizes two passages with the loci mnemonic, the second group (CG) was formed of students who were enrolled in a university seminar on memory but had not yet acquired specific information on memory and mnemonics.

LT subjects were asked to follow some steps, based on those suggested by Bellezza, which may be summarized as follows 1) survey the text; 2) prepare questions and write down possible cue words; 3) read analytically; 4) select cue words, i.e. important words in the text which may be appropriate for association with the loci and work as cues for retrieval of other parts of the text; 5) draw a line whenever a new topic begins in the text; 6) select the cue words according to the number of available loci; 7) substitute the abstract cue words by concrete words; 8) associate the images of the cue words with those of the loci.

Subjects were asked to check whether they had really formed vivid images with the loci and the associated items. The control group (C) was asked to memorize the passage in their usual way. All subjects had 40 minutes to study the passage, after which they had to fill in a questionnaire which asked whether the passage was clear and interesting and the time sufficient for study. A week later they were unexpectedly asked to undertake a written free recall test. At the end of this subjects had to take a four-alternative multiple-choice test (10 questions) concerning general information and to complete a second questionnaire containing some items of information

presented in the original passage: the subjects had to indicate the
order in which these items appeared.

RESULTS

The passage was divided into 42 units. Three independent
examiners evaluated which units occurred on each answer-sheet. An
information unit was considered as present if at least two judges
agreed on it. Mean numbers of recalled units were respectively 11.9
(s.d.=5.8) for the LT group and 14.56 (s.d.=6.4) for the control
group. The superiority of the latter was significant. Student's t =
2.16 (df = 94), p<.05. The mean recognition scores were 6.9
(s.d.=1.6) for the LT group and 7.75 (s.d.=1.7) for the C group for
the general information memory test. This difference too was
significant: t = 2.47, p<.05. Since the failure of the loci group
might have been due to difficulty in memorizing the entire passage,
given the complexity of the required steps, and a 2 x 2 ANOVA for
mixed design was carried out which included both groups and the
distinction between the five questions concerning the first half of
the passage and the other five questions. Both groups answered the
first questions more correctly, but clear differences were not found.

The only case in which the loci group was not significantly
inferior to the control group was in the order of information test.
The mean scores of the LT group were only slightly lower (71.45%
correct answers vs 73.62%).

The failure to find a loci effect either with the Meacham
or the Bellezza passage may have been due to their characteristics,
in that we may expect that only some passages can be easily
manipulated and matched with the loci available to the subject.
Nevertheless, other factors such as the characteristics and
instruction of the control group, the modality of presentation of the
material, and the scoring system, may only have hindered the LT
group. Regarding the control group, it must be observed that subject
had acquired a little knowledge about memory and were especially
facilitated by the fact that they memorized as usual with both higher
flexibility in the use of strategies and the possibility of using
images. Concerning the modality of presentation, the loci mnemonic
may be more useful with oral presentation (e.g. during a lecture)
than with written presentation (e.g. studying a written test at a
self-paced rate).

For this reason in a later series of experiments we
selected a different passage and formed a control group of subjects
without mnemonic knowledge. We therefore had better control over the
control group's strategies which were not to include imagery. We
included both oral and written presentations and created a single
scoring system which considered both the number of items of
information correctly recalled and its correct position.

The new passage, 2100 words long, described the
archeological discovery of an old vase and its attribution by three
different experts. 42 subjects were asked to memorize the reasons
each expert gave for their attributions and also to remember the
order of importance given by each expert for their reasons.

Subjects received 3 points for each correctly described and
ordered; they received 2 points if it was not perfectly recalled,
and 1 point if it was only partially recalled and in incorrect order.

The mean scores for the loci group were 39.07 (sd = 13.31 after oral presentation and 36.33 (sd = 13.51) after visual presentation and, for the control group, 26.89 (sd = 11.19) after oral presentation and 30.6 (sd = 10.8) after visual presentation. A 2 x 2 ANOVA revealed that the performance of the loci group was significantly better F(1,38)=6.48, p=.014.

In order to evaluate whether the new procedure also worked on the "advertisement" passage, or whether it was peculiar only to the "archeological passage", in our next experiment we required 125 subjects to memorize both passages, in both modalities, balancing presentation order and asking for immediate and delayed recall (Cornoldi and De Beni, 1987).

The main results were that the use of the loci technique improved performance significantly, but this was peculiarly true for the oral presentation and for the "advertisement" passage. These results show that, with modified procedural aspects, the loci mnemonic may also be useful in the advertisement passage proposed by Bellezza. Further it appears to be more useful in memorizing orally presented text (as in a lecture) than in written text. This result has practical implications, but cannot be clearly interpreted. It is possible that the use of an image-based mnemonic strategy is easier when the main task involves an auditory input processing system rather than a visual system (Brooks, 1967).

REFERENCES

Bellezza, F.S. (1981). 'Mnemonic device: classification, characteristics and criteria', Review of Educational Research, 51 (2), 247-275.

Bellezza, F.S. (1982). Improve your memory skills, Prentice-Hall, Inc., Englewood Cliff, New Jersey.

Bellezza, F.S. (1983). 'Mnemonic-device instruction with adults', in M. Pressley and J.R. Levin (Eds.), Cognitive Strategy Research, Springer-Verlag, New York, 51-73.

Brooks, L.R. (1967). 'The suppression of visualization by reading', The Quarterly Journal of Experimental Psychology, 19, 288-289.

Cornoldi, C. and De Beni, R. (1987) 'Memory for discourses: the help of loci mnemonic'. (in press).

De Beni, R. and Cornoldi, C. (1985). 'Effects of the mnemotechnique of loci in the memorization of concrete words'. Acta Psychologica, 60, 11-24.

Meacham, J.A. (1977). 'Soviet investigations on memory development', in R.V. Kail, J.W. Hagen (eds), Perspectives on the development of memory and cognition, Lawrence Erlbaum Associates, Inc., Hillsdale, New Jersey, 273-295.

Yates, F.A. (1966). The art of memory, Routledge & Kegan, London.

MOTORIC MEMORY

THE REPRESENTATION OF OBJECTS IN MEMORY:

CONTRASTING PERSPECTIVES FROM VISION AND TOUCH

Roberta L. Klatzky
Department of Psychology
University of California
Santa Barbara, California
U.S.A.

Susan J. Lederman
Department of Psychology
Queen's University
Kingston, Ontario
Canada

ABSTRACT
        We describe a program of research on human "haptics", a
perceptual system that uses cutaneous and kinesthetic inputs to
derive information about spatial layout and about objects and
their properties. This research contrasts haptic and visual
perception with respect to (a) avenues of encoding and (b) the
ultimate representation of perceived objects. The haptic system
couples primitive sensory capabilities with stereotyped movement
patterns or "exploratory procedures" to obtain information about
diverse object dimensions. In contrast to vision, it is
developed to provide information about the substance of objects
more than their structure. An understanding of the haptic system
is relevant to such real-world problems as aids for the blind and
the development of intelligent robots.

        It is often said that basic and applied research go hand in
hand. Basic research can serve as a cornerstone for
application, providing general theories, techniques, and
empirical baselines. Conversely, real-world problems can foster
basic research by pointing to important issues and providing
fundamental, if not fully controlled, data. The research
described here exemplifies both aspects of this symbiotic
relationship. Certainly we have been stimulated by areas of
application, and conversely, our research program is directed, in
part, toward application.
        Our research focuses on the nature of knowledge
representations achieved through "haptics". Haptics is a complex
system that incorporates sensors in the cutaneous and kinesthetic
systems. These provide a variety of primitive sensory information,
cutaneous inputs about pressure and changes in temperature as
well as kinesthetic information about position and limb movement
from receptors in the muscles, joints, and tendons.
        Haptics has been a neglected area within perception,
especially relative to vision. Yet there are applied problems
that directly concern this system. One is the design of
aids for the blind; another is the design of artificial haptic
systems -- robots that sense with as well as move their end-
effectors. A more comprehensive understanding of haptic
perception holds much promise for broad application.

We began our work with the prevailing impression in the research literature that haptics was a very poor perceptual system. Our belief might be called "visual chauvinism." However, our research ultimately suggests that this depiction is inaccurate and misguided. In this paper, we will describe how our research suggests a new conception of haptics, one that highlights its perceptual talents while recognizing and further defining its limitations.

TANGIBLE GRAPHICS FOR THE BLIND AND IMPLICATIONS FOR HAPTIC PERCEPTION

The claim that the perceptual powers of haptics are severely limited is supported by studies that compare sighted individuals' performance with and without vision, and by comparisons between blind and sighted persons (e.g., Bryant & Raz, 1975; Cashdan, 1968; Magee & Kennedy, 1980). In general, such comparisons reveal that performance is far superior when vision is available. The tasks that are used frequently involve raised line drawings, which are to be "perceived" by following contours with the fingertips. In addition to configural information from raised contours, such stimuli may include texture variations. Planar nonsense forms are also common.

Studying haptic perception with stimuli that vary in two-dimensional contour is not merely an artificial experimental exercise. Such stimuli have direct everyday counterparts in raised graphics displays that are offered to the blind for educational purposes or to aid mobility. Examples of the types of information conveyed in such "tangible graphics" are circuit diagrams, maps, charts, mathematical functions, logic diagrams for computer programs and pictures of objects -- in short, virtually anything that might be portrayed in a visual display for similar purposes.

Blind persons who are asked to derive information from such displays often find the task frustrating and impenetrable. Sighted persons are by no means exempt from the same experience. In fact, in numerous colloquia where we have presented simple raised pictures of objects to be recognized by touch, the hit rate is running about 2% (although we have obtained somewhat higher rates under more controlled laboratory conditions). The experience of recognition in these few successful cases is not one of direct perceptual recognition, but more like problem solving. For example, someone once "recognized" a picture of a violin by generating the names of objects that looked like a blob on a stick!

Why are raised drawings for haptic reading so unsuccessful? The more traditional answer to that question is that haptic perception is intrinsically poor. However, we have suggested a different answer: Such displays are generally taken wholesale from vision and raised for touch, without consideration of potential differences between vision and haptics. By conveying only two-dimensional contour in a uniform medium, they fail to reveal the substantial capabilities of the haptic system. While haptics is relatively ineffective at apprehending

contour   in   two   dimensions,   it   can be very successful   at
encoding other attributes of objects.

RESEARCH IN HAPTIC PROCESSING AND ITS IMPLICATIONS
            In order to understand why tangible graphics displays
for   the   blind fail so often, one must, as the above comments
suggest,   turn to more basic research on the nature of haptic
processing.   One important aspect of the haptic system revealed by
such   research   is   that   haptic   spatial   precision   is
substantially   lower   than   that   of vision   (Loomis,   1985;
Balakrishnan,   Klatzky,   Loomis,   & Lederman, 1987).   This
immediately   suggests one type of problem with tangible graphics
devices   that   are direct analogues of visual displays.   Line
drawings that are seen well may not be felt well,   because   the
scale is too   small   for   the   limited bandwidth of cutaneous and
kinesthetic sensors.
            In addition to the simple issue of spatial resolution,
however,   our research on the haptic system suggests a less
obvious,   but   equally   fundamental,   design error   in many
tangible   graphics   displays.   This error arises from adherence
to a flawed model of haptic processing.   We call this the "image
mediation model"   of the haptic system (Klatzky & Lederman,
1987).   According to this model,   the hand functions like a
roving eye that is badly in need of glasses.   The exploring
effector   is   assumed to produce   a spatial image that   is
essentially   equivalent to one derived using vision, within
limitations   imposed   by the low resolution of haptic sensors
and   the   memory demands imposed by exploring   over   time.   The
resulting   image   is passed to image interpreters within   the
visual system,   and the   result is as if the original display had
been examined visually (albeit by a very myopic individual).
            In direct challenge to the image mediation model, we
assume   that the haptic system has its own perceptual apparatus
and   interpretive processors.   While some aspects of this system
may converge with vision at higher levels of processing, haptics
and vision are fundamentally different ways of perceiving.
            The view of haptics that we espouse makes two related
claims.   First, we assume that haptics has its own unique
encoding avenues,   which at lower levels are largely unshared by
vision.   Second, we assume that partly because of its encoding
mechanisms,   haptics does not work naturally as an image
mediator.   To the contrary, this system is better adapted to the
apprehension   of   the substance properties of objects than to
their structure.   In the discussion that follows, I will
consider each of these claims in turn.
            The first claim concerns the encoding mechanisms of the
haptic system.   In order to understand these mechanisms, it is
necessary   to   consider that the tactual apparatus has at   the
same time sensory and motor capabilities.   As was mentioned
above,   the basic sensory primitives extracted by touch include
pressure, thermal change, and position. (Pain is also included,
but for present purposes, it is not of interest.) However,
our work (Lederman & Klatzky, 1987) indicates that the system

is capable of greatly expanding the nature of the dimensions that are sensed. It does so by "piggybacking" its primitive sensors onto its considerable capabilities for precise movement.

We have demonstrated a coupling of stereotyped movement patterns (which we call "exploratory procedures") and the attributes of objects apprehended through haptic exploration. To demonstrate this coupling, we used a match-to-sample task, in which subjects were to find the best match for some sample object within a set of three comparison objects. The important feature of our task was that the match was to be made along a specific targeted dimension; other attributes of the objects were irrelevant to the comparison. For example, participants were required to match objects on the basis of surface roughness, regardless of shape, weight, or other dimensions of variation. We found that the nature of hand movements in this matching task varied systematically with the to-be-matched dimension.

More specifically, we documented a set of exploratory procedures, each of which dominated exploration for purposes of matching on a specific dimension. These procedures can be identified by certain invariant properties; in addition, each has typical characteristics. For matching on the basis of texture, our subjects tended to use "lateral motion" between the skin and the surface of the object. This procedure commonly looks like a back-and-forth rubbing action on a homogeneous portion of the object. For matching on the basis of hardness, normal "pressure" is applied to the surface of the object. For example, subjects may poke or push into it. For sensing thermal properties, the procedure is "static contact." The contact is static in order to avoid friction, which will change thermal properties. Frequently, the contacting hand surface is large, which is appropriate so that the thermal inputs will spatially summate. Shape information is obtained crudely through the procedure of "enclosure," that is, molding the fingers to the surface of the object. More precise shape information is obtained by "contour following," in which an edge is traced, usually with the fingertips. And weight information is obtained by holding the object without external support, often by hefting or tossing it from hand to hand.

The yoking of a particular movement pattern to apprehension of a particular object dimension is no accident. People use a specific exploratory procedure because it works best for that dimension. By instructing subjects to use a particular procedure for exploring an object, and then having them match on various dimensions, we were able to see what information each procedure was sufficient or optimal to produce. In general, the procedure people used to ascertain an object dimension during free exploration was the optimal one (in terms of providing the greatest accuracy, or when there was a tie, speed). For example, pressure was the most accurate way to ascertain hardness. In the case of matching exact shape, the contour following procedure was not only optimal but necessary -- it was the only one to

provide   above-chance performance.   On the other   hand,   the
accuracy   of   contour following for determining structure   had   a
price -- it was also the slowest of the procedures in our data.
        The depiction of haptic encoding to emerge from this work
is   of   an   encoding   system   that   produces   multidimensional
information about objects.   Various dimensions are   apprehended
through   a   set of specialized exploratory   procedures.   It   is
important   to   note that the structure of an object is but one of
the   dimensions   that is   encoded   through   touch,   and   the
requisite   exploratory procedure,   contour following,   is both
costly in terms of exploration time and not terribly accurate.
        Let us now turn to the second claim of our view of haptic
perception -- that it is oriented more toward the apprehension of
substance than structure.   You may understand this claim   better
by   undertaking   a simple "thought experiment."   Suppose I   asked
you to imagine yourself looking at a cat.   You probably visualize
its shape -- the long,   lean body, the pointed ears.   Perhaps you
think of a particular color or pattern on its fur.   Now   imagine
yourself not   looking   at the cat,   but   touching   it.   A   very
different   image should come to mind,   one that incorporates   the
softness of its fur, or the warmth of its body.
        Our   initial   studies   of   haptic   exploratory   procedures
suggest   why,   in   keeping   with   this   thought   experiment,
nonstructural   properties may be relatively salient under tactual
exploration.   One   need   only assume that the haptic   system   is
economical,   favoring those encoding mechanisms that produce   the
greatest   return   for the least effort.   Recall that extracting
contour   information through touch is slow and error prone.   In
contrast,   substance   dimensions   like texture and   hardness   are
extracted quickly and discriminated well.   An economical system
would clearly favor substance-related exploration,   which in turn
would lead to encoding substance information about objects.   Of
course,   other   considerations   could   override   such   natural
tendencies,   but without such bias,   there would be an emphasis
on properties other than structure.
        With   this reasoning,   we attempted to assess the   object
properties   that   were   naturally   "salient"   under   haptic
exploration,   under   unconstrained   conditions   and   under   bias
(Klatzky,   Lederman,   & Reed,   1987).   We did   so with a sorting
task,   in   which participants were   asked to distribute   objects
according   to   their   similarity.   The   objects   varied
simultaneously   on   four   dimensions: surface   roughness,
hardness,   size,   and shape.   There were three different values on
each   dimension,   and   all possible combinations of   values   were
exemplified in the stimulus objects.   Thus a given object had one
of three hardness   values   and one of three textures, shapes, and
sizes.
        Our   participants   were told to sort   objects   that   were
similar   into   a   common bin.   We were able   to   ascertain   what
dimension   they   were using to define similarity by   the   sorting
pattern.   The   more   that participants   tended   to   put   objects
with different   values   on a dimension into different   bins,   the
more   salient   that dimension was to their   similarity   judgment.

If, for example, all the hard objects were placed in one bin, soft objects in another, and slightly compliant in another, the hardness dimension was very salient. This pattern of sorting would mean that objects varying in other dimensions such as shape would have to be placed into a common bin, indicating that these dimensions were nonsalient.

We found that the pattern of sorting -- and thus the most salient dimensions of objects -- varied according to exploratory conditions and instructions. When participants were denied sight and just told to put similar objects into a common bin, they tended to find surface roughness and hardness salient. Defining similarity specificially in terms of how the objects "felt" did not change this pattern. But in contrast, defining similarity in terms of a visual image -- that is, specifying that objects were similar only if their visual images were similar -- led to an overwhelming reliance on shape in the sorting pattern. Finally, when participants could see the objects, shape was again important, but so were surface roughness and other dimensions such as size.

These results support our hypothesis that the haptic system most naturally finds "salient" those attributes of objects that are determined by their substance, rather than their structure. Only when specific instructions bias the use of visual imagery does the structure of an object become important to a haptic explorer.

The pattern of exploratory hand movements closely paralleled the similarity judgments in this task. When shape was salient, contour following was extensive. When texture was salient, there was greater use of lateral motion, and hardness was paired with the use of pressure.

This pattern is consistent with our idea that the haptic salience of some dimension is determined by considerations of the "economy" of exploring for it. Lateral motion and pressure are very economical procedures; they allow for discrimination among objects with little exploratory effort. Hence the associated properties, texture and hardness, are salient attributes of objects. On the other hand, contour following is the least economical exploratory procedure in terms of slowness and inaccuracy. Thus the dimension of structure, which must be obtained through this procedure, is not very salient under conditions of unbiased haptic encoding.

IMPLICATIONS OF THE HAPTICS MODEL FOR APPLIED ISSUES

We turn now to a consideration of the implications of these results for specific applications. Let us first return to the domain of tangible graphics for the blind. In the process of reading raised displays, the fingers move along raised contours of an object in an effort to integrate kinesthetic information over time. The process is, in fact, the exploratory procedure we call contour following. Our data indicate that contour following is the appropriate procedure for reading such displays, but it is not a very effective one. Unfortunately, kinesthesis is not

spatially precise, and the temporally extended nature of contour
following imposes demands on memory and integration processes.
In more detailed studies of the encoding of two-
dimensional displays, we have found that the nature of people's
errors varies substantially, depending on the type of display and
the desired information (Lederman, Klatzky, & Barber, 1985).
Determining the position of a line in space, for example, is
prone to different sources of error than determining the length
of the line. This work suggests the need for systematic and
detailed evaluation of specific tangible graphics displays, in
order to determine what problems each poses for the blind
and what instructions or additional display information would
help to reduce error.

But let us not forget that our work focuses as much on
what haptics does well as on what it does badly. We have found
that this system is an excellent means of encoding information
about real, three-dimensional objects that vary along
nonstructural dimensions. In fact, recognition of common
objects by touch is both fast and accurate (Klatzky, Lederman, &
Metzger, 1985). This finding suggests that the usefulness
of tangible graphics for the blind might be enhanced by
incorporating information other than two-dimensional contour.

Another area in which our work has potential for
application is robotics. In fact, our description of the motor
movements or exploratory procedures that optimize haptic encoding
is currently being adapted to robots equipped with sensors
(Bajcsy, Lederman, & Klatzky, 1987). The hope here is ultimately
to optimize the flexibility and accuracy of such sensing devices.
Current robotic technology is such that the basic sensory
subsystems within haptics -- sensing of position, pressure, and
temperature -- are available within artificial systems. What is
needed are algorithms that couple these sensing capabilities with
movement, so as to optimally learn about, identify, and use
objects. The human is an exciting and potentially
informative model in this endeavor.

In short, this research program can be seen as an
illustration of the ways in which basic and applied concerns can
work together to the mutual benefit of both. The haptic system
may not be the principal means of learning about the world for
most individuals, but it is nonetheless a very important one.
For those denied sight, it is a primary one. Problems posed by
the needs of the blind have led us to study this system in its
own right, which in turn has produced new insights into real-
world problems.

REFERENCES

Bajcsy, R., Lederman, S.J., & Klatzky, R.L. (1987). 'Object
Exploration in One and Two Fingered Robots', in Proceedings of
the 1987 IEEE International Conference on Robotics and
Automation, in press, Institute of Electronics & Electronic
Engineers, New York.

Balakrishnan, J., D., Klatzky, R.L., Loomis, J., & Lederman, S.J. (1987). 'Length Distortion of Temporally Extended Visual Displays: An Analogue to Haptic Spatial Perception', unpublished manuscript, University of California at Santa Barbara.

Bryant, P., & Raz, I. (1975). 'Visual and Tactual Perception of Shape by Young Children', Developmental Psychology, 11, 525-526.

Cashdan, S. (1968). 'Visual and Haptic Form Discrimination Under Conditions of Successive Stimulation', Journal of Experimental Psychology, 76(2, Pt. 1), 221-224.

Klatzky, R.L., & Lederman, S.J. (1987). 'The intelligent hand', in The Psychology of Learning and Motivation (Ed. G. H. Bower), Vol. 21, in press, Academic Press, San Diego.

Klatzky, R.L., Lederman, S.J., & Metzger, V.A. (1985). 'Identifying Objects by Touch: An "Expert System" ', Perception & Psychophysics, 37, 299-302.

Klatzky, R.L., Lederman, S.J., & Reed, C. (1987). 'There's More to Touch Than Meets the Eye: The Salience of Object Attributes for Haptics with and without Vision', Cognitive Science Technical Report 8714, University of California at Santa Barbara.

Lederman, S.J., & Klatzky, R. L. (1987). 'Hand Movements: A Window into Haptic Object Recognition', in press, Cognitive Psychology.

Lederman, S.J., Klatzky, R. L., & Barber, P. (1985). 'Spatial-and Movement-based Heuristics for Encoding Pattern Information Through Touch', Journal of Experimental Psychology: General, 114, 33-49.

Loomis, J.M. (1985). 'A Model of Character Recognition and Legibility', presented at the meeting of the Psychonomic Society, Boston, MA.

Magee, L.E., & Kennedy, W.M. (1980). 'Exploring Pictures Tactually', Nature, 283, 287-288.

MOTOR LEARNING AND RETENTION

John Annett

Department of Psychology,
University of Warwick, Coventry, U.K.

ABSTRACT
        The classical methods of studying motor memory reveal
little about its underlying structure and are based on assumptions
about motor control which are grossly oversimplified, if not wrong.
Mental Practice must involve the manipulation of data in memory, and
a series of experiments is described which indicate that it is
spatial representations rather than motor output which are stored in
motor memory. A theory that plans can be mentally rehearsed predicts
the results of practising motor tasks less well than it predicts
speech production.

CODING IN MOTOR MEMORY

        Investigations of motor memory have relied on two principal
experimental paradigms. The classical tradition, based on the method
of savings, can be adapted to any skill from pursuit rotor tracking
to typing or driving. This method has proved useful in applied
research (see Annett, 1979) but has shed little light on the
underlying mechanisms of motor memory.

        The second, and most popular in recent years, (Annett,
1969; Laabs and Simmons, 1981; Smyth, 1984), is based on Thorndike's
line drawing experiment. The subject makes a simple linear movement,
usually under visual or mechanical guidance, and then, after an
appropriate interval, attempts to reproduce it. The use of the
linear positioning paradigm rests on the assumption that the
production of actions may be described in terms of open- or closed-
loop processes. The so-called 'centralist' position asserts that
actions can be generated from a central store of motor programmes,
whilst the 'peripheralist' position on the other hand, asserts that
actions are closed-loop depending on feedback from the environment
and the joints and muscles. Motor memory in this case is seen to be
like other kinds of memory, a store of past sensations.

        Recent theories of motor control have abandoned the simple
open/closed loop dichotomy and envisage a number of semi-independent
subsystems which collaborate to produce coherent actions. Motor
control is now seen as distributed rather than centralised, allowing
for flexibility in the pattern of actual muscular movement to cope
with local variations in load and other external constraints.

        The implications for theories of motor memory are
profound. If the motor system is intelligently adaptable it requires
an adequate knowldege base. Indeed different subsystems may need to
draw on a variety of independent memories or knowledge bases. Most
skilled actions require a store of spatial knowledge (where the keys

are on the typewriter) and of the dynamic properties of objects (how much effort it is likely to take to move them) as well as knowledge of procedures (starting a car or dancing a tango). Motor memory should be characterised as distributed and any one act of recall may involve reference to more than one database.

MENTAL PRACTICE

        Mental or imaginary practice of motor skills (MP) is a technique well known to sportsmen and researchers into motor learning. MP can be almost as effective, sometimes more effective, than actual physical practice. It offers a challenge to memory researchers since minimal external stimuli and no overt responses are involved, thus any demonstrable effects must be attributed to memory processes. Of particular interest is the question of the coding or locus of MP effects. This can best be illustrated by reference to some of the principal theories which have been advanced to account for these effects.

        Several theories deal with potential artifacts. For example, one theory attributes positive effects to enhanced motivation, another suggests that mental practice trials are equivalent to having a rest permitting consolidation or disinhibition.

        Other theories principally concern the role of the component processes in imaginary action. The psychoneuromuscular hypothesis proposes that movement imagery is equivalent to actual movement except that muscle activation is greatly attenuated, thus MP involves virtually the entire motor system and there may even be some proprioceptive feedback, although exteroceptive feedback is missing. Other hypotheses refer to the perceptual or symbolic content of the skill which is rehearsed. For example, mental practice may simplify the attentional problem for the learner by eliminating redundant or confusing environmental information. Two further hypotheses refer to symbolic aspects of the task. A motor task might be recoded into verbal form which can be rehearsed sotto voce and without the usual motor output. Finally, mental practice might permit a benficial reorganisation of the task, that is permit the problem solving aspect of the task to proceed unhindered by overt action.

        This paper describes some experimental work which has the overall aim of identifying the locus of MP effects and hence helping to distingush between three broad possibilities. These are that mentally rehearsing an action is equivalent to (1) manipulating quasi-sensory representations or imaginal versions of the sensory accompaniments of the action; or (2) the partial activation of the motor representations or motor programmes on which the action is based; or (3) the activation of a plan used to control the action, particularly if it is complex and requires the coordination and sequencing of a number of elements.

Memory for Simple Movments

        Experiments carried out by Johnson (1982) concerned rehearsal of movements in short term motor memory. The classic linear positioning task was used in which the subject is required to learn to make a movement of a given extent by first making a number of guided trials, that is moving a slider along a track up to a physical

stop, and is then required to reproduce the movement without the
support of external cues. Johnson's experiments involved a
modification of this procedure in which the subject is required to
make a movement of a different extent during the retention interval.
Patrick (1971) had shown that interference from the interpolated
movement took the form of a constant error bias, a longer
interpolated movement tended to produce overestimates on recall and
shorter ones underestimates. Johnson required his subjects to imagine
rather than physically execute the interpolated movement which was
either twice as long or half as long as the original. The results
showed that recall could be biassed just as effectively by mental as
by physical practice.

The question now is what is the 'locus' of this effect ? In
a series of experiments a secondary task was added to the procedure
just described. Thus subjects were instructed to imagine the movement
whilst at the same time counting backwards in threes, or whilst
observing various stimuli or whilst tapping with the hand previously
used in the positioning task. In brief, Johnson found that the bias
induced by imaginary movement was still present when subjects were
performing the verbal secondary task (counting backwards) and also
whilst making tapping movements. However, when the secondary task
required the subject to monitor stimuli (visual or auditory) which
alternated between two spatial locations the effect of the imagined
interpolated action was eliminated and there was no bias in
recalling the original movement. He argued from these results that
if these secondary tasks occupied mechanisms potentially involved in
the mental rehearsal of the movement then, for this task at least,
these do not include either speech production or even motor activity
in the limb used for making the movement. However the system in which
space is represented, regardless of modality, is crucially involved
in the imaginary movement.

Memory for Procedures

The use of a rather different experimental task also
supports the hypothesis that mental practice involves perceptual
rather than purely motor codes. If subjects are asked to explain
how to carry out a motor task, such as tying a bow, without actually
doing it then they appear to solve the problem by first generating a
series of images. Analysis of descriptions given under various
conditions (see Annett, 1986 and in press) tends to support Johnson's
conclusions, that is that the execution of the imaginary task is
heavily dependent on a quasi visuo-spatial representation and is not
affected by activity in the peripheral motor output system. Secondary
tasks of a verbal nature or occupying the peripheral output system
have little or no effect on either the quality of the explanations or
the speed with which they are given.

The Role of Gestures

The gestures made almost involuntarily as accompaniments
to verbal explanation are particularly interesting. Subjects feel a
compulsion to gesture as if the generation of images were dependent
on executing bow tying movements. However, if subjects are physically
prevented from moving by having to sit on their hands or by being
required to tap at a rate of about 2/sec. there is little or no

detectable effect on the quality or speed of their explanations. Subjects who sit on their hands tend to report imagery which is slightly less easy to form and which is more often like 'stills' than moving pictures, but that is all.

Another clue as to the nature of the represenation of bow tying in memory comes from a comparison of 'explanatory' gestures and the movements actually made by subjects when they were given some string and asked to tie a bow. A detailed analysis of video records of actual and imaginary bow tying shows that demonstrative gestures do not reproduce the movements but rather represent the spatial pattern of the knot. In describing making a loop, for example, the subject may hold one hand at eye level making a circle with the index finger and thumb whereas the actual bow involves much smaller movements of both fingers and thumbs at waist level. Thus although subjects have a strong subjective impression that they are mentally tying the bow and hence involving the motor output system (albeit in an attenuated version of actual bow tying) the movements they are making are more closely related to a semi-abstract spatial represenation of the results of the action. This may be taken as evidence that the 'motor memory' used in mentally rehearsing this task is as much spatial as motoric.

Memory for Plans

I turn now to the proposal that mental practice effects are due to the manipulation of an internal represenation of a plan controlling the sequence and timing of an action. MacKay (1981 & 1982) presented a theory of the acquisition of fluency in the production of sequential skills such as speech production which also offers an explanation for learning motor skills by mental practice. The production of a sentence is said to be mediated by a hierarchy of interconnected nodes. The top level node represents the core meaning of the sentence which has to be expanded at a lower level into a sentence comprising word nodes governed by syntactic rules and at a lower level still by phonological rules and finally through the activation of nodes governing the action of the muscles serving speech.

The nodes can be recombined to form different words and sentences giving the flexibility necessary for the production of natural language. The structure is activated from the top down and when a particular node is activated it primes all nodes connected to it. The more primed a node the more readily will it become activated. Repetition has the effect of strengthening the internodal connections, thus providing a kind of memory. The whole network need not be activated. For example in silent reading the muscle nodes are inhibited and it may even be possible to contemplate the essential meaning of the sentence without committing the thought to a particular linguistic form. The theory can be applied to any sequential motor skill. If bow tying is governed by a node structure, such as the one shown in Figure 1, mental practice involves only the higher level nodes. The theory predicts that, whilst improvement will occur with both mental and physical practice, the MP learning curve should be initally steeper, and that overall MP trials will be faster than PP trials.

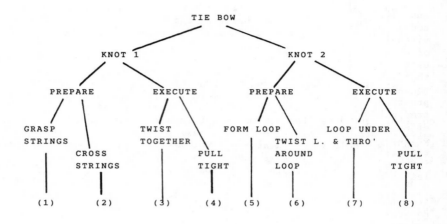

Figure 1. Hypothetical node structure   underlying bow tying.

In one experiment subjects in the control   condition   were
required to start a timer, tie a bow and stop the timer as quickly as
possible, this procedure being repeated 10 times with a short   pause
between trials. The experimental condition was identical except that
subjects were required to mentally tie the bow, their hands resting
on the table between starting and stopping the timer. As predicted
mental bow tying takes less time (about 4.5 seconds) than tying a
real bow (6.5 seconds) since fewer nodes are traversed. However, the
only significant improvement with practice was found in the first
three or four trials of physical practice.

If we assume that the mental node structure   provides   the
basis for verbal explanations of bow tying it can be predicted that
hesitations should be longer between steps 4 and 5 in the diagram
than between 3 and 4 and 6 and 7 which, in turn, should be longer
than between 1 and 2, 3 and 4 etc. where the smallest number of nodes
are traversed to get from one component action to the next.
Unfortunately these predictions were not confirmed on examination of
the video records of 33 subjects. The' longest hesitation occurs
between 5 and 6 (6.76 seconds) and the shortest between 3 and 4 (3.37
secs).

An important difference between   bow tying and pronouncing
unfamiliar sentences (MacKay, 1981) may lie in the relative levels of
pre-existing skill. The bow is a very familiar knot   whilst the
sentences were unfamiliar. The experiment was therefore repeated
with a less familiar knot, the bowline. As before, subjects were
given either mental or physical practice over 12 trials. In this
experiment mental practice reduced the performance time by about 24%
whilst physical practice resulted in a 30% improvement. Although some
of the detailed predictions were not confirmed at least we were
reassured that mental practice does produce measurable effects.

For sentence production it is assumed that the low-level,

muscular, nodes are extremely well practised whilst the high level
nodes needed for the generation of a new and unique sentence are
virtually unpractised (and this is why MP should be effective). One
of my students (A. Beladaci) has run an experiment with typewriting,
using skilled and unskilled typists, assumed to differ in terms of
the low level nodes, and meaningful and scrambled sentences and
nonsense letter strings which are assumed to differ in terms of the
pre-training connectivity of the higher level nodes. The key
predictions are (1) that physical practice will be relatively more
effective with unskilled typists and (2) that mental practice will be
relatively more effective for both groups with nonsense material, but
especially so for the skilled typists. The experiment was carried out
in the same way as before but each subject practised typing three
letter strings ten times, both physically and in imagination.

The results show, not surprisingly, that unskilled typists
are much slower than the skilled, $F(1,22)=66.03$, $p<.001$. Typing
nonsense material takes longer than the same number of letters
arranged in meaningful words and sentences, $F (2,44) = 30.7$, $p<.001$,
and subjects improve over the 10 practice trials, $F(9,198) = 31.61$,
$p<.001$. Mental practice trials are only faster than physical practice
for unskilled typists, $F(1,55)=8.39$, $p<.02$. The skilled typists adopt
much the same tempo whether their reponses are overt or covert.

Unskilled typists improve more with 10 trials of practice
than the skilled, $F(9,198)=3.7$, $p<.001$. However the first key
prediction, that skilled typists would show relatively more benefit
from mental than physical practice was not confirmed. The three-way
interaction between skill level, MP/PP and practice trials gave an
$F(9,198)=1.05$, which is not significant. The second key prediction,
that mental practice would be relatively more effective for nonsense
than for meaningful material was not confirmed for either skilled or
unskilled with $F(2,55)=1.73$ for the skilled and $F=2.71$ for the
unskilled.

CONCLUSIONS

Clearly more work is needed on the mental node theory if it
is to account for mental practice effects on motor skills but I want
to conclude by returning to my wider theme. Mental practice is
presumed to involve the activation of 'motor' memories and the
experiments I have described represent attempts to determine how
these memories are coded. The evidence so far seems to suggest that
the spatial code (or database) is activated and can be modified by
mental practice. The executive or motor command code is probably not
involved in mental practice and our current beliefs about the nature
of motor control strongly suggest it would not make sense to store
highly specific motor commands in memory. The theory that action
plans are stored in the form of connections between mental nodes
which can be strengthened by mental rehearsal seems to work for
speech production but still lacks convincing support in the case of
non-verbal skills.

ACKNOWLEDGEMENTS

I should like to thank Don Mackay for his suggestions for
the knot tying experiments and A. Beladaci, A. McGee and G. Stodel
for running them.

REFERENCES

Annett, J. (1969). Feedback and Human Behaviour, Penguin, Harmondsworth..

Annett, J. (1979). 'Memory for skill', in Applied Problems in Memory, (Eds. M. Gruneberg and P. Morris,), pp. 215-247, Academic Press, London.

Annett, J. (1986). 'On knowing how to do things', in Generation and Modulation of Action Patterns (Eds. H. Heuer et al.), Springer Verlag, Berlin.

Annett, J. (In press) 'Imagery and skill acquisition', in Cognitive and Neuropsychological Approaches to Imagery (Eds. M. Denis, J. Engelkamp & J.T.E. Richardson), Martinus Nijhoff, Amsterdam.

Johnson, P. (1982). 'The functional equivalence of imagery and movement', Quarterly Journal of Experimental Psychology, 34A, 349-365.

Laabs, G. J. and Simmons, R. W. (1981). 'Motor memory', in Human Skills (Ed. D. Holding), John Wiley, Chichester.

MacKay, D. G. (1981). 'The problem of rehearsal or mental practice', Journal of Motor Behavior, 13, 274-285.

MacKay, D. G. (1982). 'The problems of flexibility, fluency and speed-accuracy trade-off in skilled behavior', Psychological Review, 89, 483-506.

Patrick, J. (1971). 'The effect of interpolated motor activities in short-term motor memory', Journal of Motor Behavior, 3, 39-48.

Smyth, M. (1984). 'Memory for movements', in The Psychology of Human Movement (Eds. M. Smyth & A. Wing), Academic Press, Orlando.

PRACTICAL APPLICATIONS AND THEORIES OF MEMORY:
A NEW EPISTEMOLOGY TO SUPPLEMENT THE OLD

Donald G. MacKay
Psychology Department, University of California
Los Angeles, U.S.A.

ABSTRACT

This paper examines two epistemologies on the nature of theory and its role in practical applications of memory research and science in general. Although the empirical epistemology has dominated psychological research over the past seventy years, I argue that the rational epistemology is more conducive to sophisticated practical applications, and that achieving a balance between two epistemologies is needed for solving many other problems in the field.

The desire to address practical issues has a long history in psychology, and recent expressions of frustration by psychologists such as Tulving (1979) and Neisser (1985) over the inapplicability of current experimental knowledge are understandable. What applications there have been are quite unlike the sophisticated theory-based applications one sees from the advanced sciences, and are often difficult to distinguish from common sense. The present paper examines two epistemologies on how practical applications should originate in memory research and psychology in general. I will argue that the relative inapplicability of psychological knowledge is attributable in part to the domination of psychological research by the empirical epistemology over the past seventy years, that its complement, the rational epistemology, is much more conducive to sophisticated practical applications and provides an important new perspective on the metatheoretical debate currently ongoing among memory researchers (Bruche, 1985; Neisser, 1985), and other psychologists (Greenwald, Pratkanis, Leippe and Baumgardner, 1986; MacKay, in press).

GENERAL OVERVIEW OF THE TWO EPISTEMOLOGIES

The main goal of the empirical epistemology is to develop a body of reliable facts and real world applications, whereas the main goal of the rational epistemology is to develop theories which explain available facts, facilitate practical applications, and predict new facts for future test. Practical applications seem to represent an area of overlap between these two epistemologies. However, this and other surface similarities are deceptive: The next section shows that the two epistemologies approach practical applications in radically different ways.

PRACTICAL APPLICATIONS UNDER THE EMPIRICAL EPISTEMOLOGY

The empirical epistemology assumes that particular experimental findings can (and should) be applied directly to the real world and blames theories for the relative inapplicability of psychological knowledge. For example, Greenwald et al., (1986, p.227) argue that the social reward system in psychology encourages researchers to become "ego-involved advocates of theory" and to publish observations which are overgeneralized and unreliable, and thus, inapplicable.

The rational epistemology rejects the assumption that experimental findings can or should be directly applicable. Real-world problems which require creative solution are never as simple as laboratory situations, which are, of necessity, carefully and deliberately contrived. The practitioner's goal is to think flexibly about a real-world problem, to come up with as many courses of action as possible, and to try out the best ones, often in tentative, small scale fashion until an acceptable solution is found. Experimental observations cannot directly help in this process. The very fact that experimental observations originate in rigidly controlled and (hopefully) well understood laboratory situations restricts the applicability of these observations to unsolved practical problems. If an experimental observation applies directly to some real-world problem, the problem has already been solved and does not, by definition, require creative solution. For this same reason, 'impoverished laboratory environments' cannot in principle directly reflect the complex uses of memory in everyday life (see Neisser, 1985).

PRACTICAL APPLICATIONS UNDER THE RATIONAL EPISTEMOLOGY

Under the rational epistemology, sophisticated applications and characterizations of everyday phenomena derive from theories rather than from experimental observations. Because theories are flexible and general, they can apply across a broad range of practical situations, unlike experimental observations, which by definition and design are restricted to a limited range of controlled conditions. Moreover, even theories sometimes lack sufficient flexibility and generality for handling the complexity of real world problems, so that specialized practitioners must also use their experience, intuition, and ingenuity when applying a theory to practical ends.

The simplicity of theories is also essential for practical applications. Theories reduce a large number of complex empirical generalizations and their exceptions to a small number of conceptually simple hypothetical constructs. For example, hidden units (McClelland, Rummelhart and the PDP Research Group, 1986) or mental nodes (MacKay, 1987) and the simple ways they interact are easier to think about than the many empirical phenomena that they summarize. Such simplicity helps the practitioner come up with sophisticated solutions to applied problems. Unintegrated scientific observations, on the other hand, are not simple: Empirical factors and the potentially unlimited interactions between them (see Greenwald et al., 1986) are difficult to keep in mind, let alone apply. The rational epistemology attributes the relative inapplicability of psychological knowledge primarily to the lack of viable theory, and warns that additional facts in the absence of theory can bring diminishing practical returns. As Tulving (1979) and others point out, our ability to gather facts has outstripped our ability to remember and use these facts, and some are being reduplicated out of ignorance.

THEORIES UNDER THE TWO EPISTEMOLOGIES

Why do the two epistemologies characterize practical applications so differently? One reason is a hidden difference in what the two epistemologies mean by "theory". Both epistemologies seem to share the same surface definition of theories: Theories contain theoretical terms embedded within a small number of interrelated and logically consistent propositions related to existing and yet-to-be-observed empirical phenomena. Because the two epistemologies characterize "theoretical terms" so differently, however, this surface definition is deceptive.

Operational definitions of theoretical terms were once deemed necessary under the empirical epistemology, and are still considered possible and desirable. For example, Greenwald et al. (1986) claim that observations and operations fall at the positive end of a desirability continuum, and that theoretical constructs become less desirable the greater their distance from operations and observations. Under this definition, the term "theory" embraces empirical hypotheses, empirical generalizations, unique observations, guiding ideas, opinions, and metatheories, in addition to what the rational epistemology calls theories and theoretical constructs.

Under the rationalist perspective, theoretical constructs such as hidden units and nodes begin with purely presumptive status and are potentially unobservable. The relatively simple interactions between these hypothetical constructs (e.g., altered linkage strength) purport to describe how things (e.g., minds) work universally and inevitably for all time, space, and hypothetical examples or Gedanken experiments (see Kuhn, 1977). These interactions also predict and explain empirical generalizations, such as the law of speed-accuracy trade-off, a regularity emerging from many experiments and thousands of observations of the relationships between two or more empirical variables.

The rules of correspondence which map theoretical constructs onto empirical observations are modifiable and open to extension under the rational epistemology. This flexibility allows theoretical constructs to survive for extended periods of time, outlasting existing means of observation, and suggesting future observations, lines of research, and practical applications which are currently unimaginable. For example, by altering rules of correspondence and adding new ones, the theoretical term 'sound wave' has survived for 1800 years, explaining thousands of initially unimagined observations of an ever more direct and precise nature (Holland, Holyoak, Nisbett, and Thagard, 1986). However, flexible correspondence rules make it impossible to develop complete operational definitions for theoretical constructs: unlike empirical terms such as errors, theoretical terms cannot be completely and explicitly defined. Insisting on operational definitions violates the hypothetical status of newly proposed theoretical constructs, and destroys the flexibility which is required for developing viable theories and applying them to practical problems.

THE ORIGINS OF THEORY UNDER THE TWO EPISTEMOLOGIES
          How do theories fitting the rationalist definition arise?
The empirical epistemology seems divided on this (and the next)
issue.   One faction maintains that data come first and drive
theories, which emerge spontaneously to explain a large enough body
of data.   Thus, Underwood (1957, p.186) argued that many areas of
psychology lack theories because their stock of preliminary data fall
below the critical mass required for theory construction.   Neisser
(1976, p.141-142) adds qualitative prerequisites to the critical
mass, suggesting that theories of memory are premature "until we know
more about memory in the natural contexts in which it develops".
Another faction in the empirical epistemology has refused to postpone
what they consider the first step toward theory construction:
"miniature models" closely tied to specific experimental paradigms
(e.g., the memory search paradigm).   The ultimate goal is to
integrate these paradigm-specific models into a single general
theory, but so far these models have only proliferated rather than
merged (see MacKay, in press).
          The rational epistemology rejects the critical mass
approach to theory construction on hypothetical, historical, and
epistemological grounds.   The hypothetical ground is that it is
difficult to imagine how well-established scientific theories could
have originated solely as a result of collecting more and more data,
no matter how precise, extensive, or qualified these data are.
Consider for example the observation that uranium is yellow whereas
hydrogen is a colorless gas: It is difficult to imagine how
specifying the conditions under which these observations hold or do
not hold could lead in principle to the theoretical concepts that
uranium atoms have about 238 electrons, whereas hydrogen atoms have
only one.   The historical ground is that these theoretical concepts
did not originate in this way whatever it is imagined to be.   In the
actual history of science, theorists often develop highly successful
theoretical constructs, such as atoms and sound waves, long before
any experimental data whatsoever has accumulated (see Holland et al.,
1986).   The epistemological ground is that theories as defined under
the rational epistemology cannot in principle originate by collecting
more and more data.   No observations, however extensive, can apply
across all time, space, and hypothetical examples.   Rationalist
theories originate as products of creative cognition rather than
situation-specific observation.   This same epistemological objection
also applies to the 'miniature model' approach to theory
construction: Paradigm-specific models have not been converging into
ever larger theories because this approach to theory construction
cannot work in principle.   Theories summarize a wide range of
empirical generalizations: They don't directly describe events
specific to particular experimental paradigms or situations.

FACTS AND THEORY REVISION UNDER THE TWO EPISTEMOLOGIES
          Another faction within the empirical epistemology maintains
that theories are revised or abandoned if and only if contradicted by
experimental data (as per Hull), and interprets the failure of Hull's
hypothetico-deductive program as justification for a stance which is

both antitheoretical and antiexperimental: According to Neisser (1985, p.272-3), both theories and theory testing have been tried and found wanting, and should be replaced, at least for the time being, by straightforward descriptions from everyday life. The rational epistemology questions this stance on two grounds. One is that neither a theoretical epistemology nor theories as defined under the rational epistemology have been tried or found wanting in psychology (see MacKay, in press). The other is that Hull's method is neither necessary nor usually sufficient for revision of genuine theories. Data of any kind are unnecessary and often insufficient for revising or abandoning rationalist theories, and experimental tests often play less of a role in actual revisions than factors such as elegance, internal consistency, and "making sense" (see MacKay, in press). Researchers working within an empirical epistemology often misunderstand this crucial point, as when Bruce (1985, p.86) complained that Neisser accepted echoic memory as a theoretical construct in 1967 and rejected it in 1983, both without empirical test.

CONCLUSION

The current metatheoretical debate in memory and psychology at large (see MacKay, in press) has been largely entrenched within the empirical epistemology. However, dissatisfaction with studies of memory as they apply to everyday problems is best directed toward developing a new epistemology and a new type of theory. As MacKay (in press) points out, developing this new epistemology to supplement and balance the old is also needed for solving many other problems in the field.

REFERENCES

Bruce, D. (1985). 'The how and why of ecological memory', Journal of Experimental Psychology: General, 114(1), 78-90.

Greenwald, A.G., Pratkanis, A.R., Leippe, M.R. and Baumgardner, M.H. (1986). 'Under what conditions does theory obstruct research progress?', Psychological Review, 93(2), 216-229.

Holland, J.H., Holyoak, K.J., Nisbett, R.E. and Thagard, P.R. (1986). Induction: Processes of inference, learning, and discovery. MIT, Cambridge, Mass.

Kuhn, T.S. (1977). 'A function for thought experiments', in Thinking: Readings in cognitive science, (Eds. P.N. Johnson-Laird and P. Wason), Cambridge University, Cambridge.

MacKay, D.G. (in press). 'Under what conditions can theoretical psychology survive and prosper? Beyond Greenwald, Pratkanis, Leippe and Baumgardner (1986) and the empirical epistemology', Psychological Review.

MacKay, D.G. (1987). The organization of perception and action: A theory for language and other cognitive skills. Springer-Verlag, New York.

Neisser, U. (1976). Cognition and Reality. Freeman, San Francisco.

Neisser, U. (1985). 'The role of theory in the ecological study of memory: Comment on Bruce', Journal of Experimental Psychology: General, 114(2), 272-276.

Tulving, E. (1979). 'Memory research: What kind of progress?', in Perspectives on memory research: Essays in honor of Upsala University's 500th Anniversary, (Ed. L.G. Nilsson), Erlbaum, Hillsdale, N.J.

Underwood, B.J. (1957). Psychological Research, Appleton-Century-Crofts, New York.

MEMORIAL STRUCTURE AND RETRIEVAL OF MOTOR PROGRAMS

David A. Rosenbaum

University of Massachusetts
Amherst, Massachusetts, U. S. A.

ABSTRACT
        Recent   research on motor programs has revealed two
important principles concerning their organization and execution.
One is that motor programs are organized hierarchically and are
executed in a way that depends directly on hierarchical organization. The other is that aspects of motor programs are preserved
after the programs have been executed, resulting in reduced rates of
performance when the same sequence must be performed in different
ways in successive production cycles.   The first principle is
analogous to the principle of hierarchical organization in memory.
The   second is analogous to the principle of memory interference.
The   analogies   suggest that motoric and nonmotoric memories are
functionally similar and that the two types of memory may have
evolved interdependently.

        For memories to be practical, they must be enacted. Stated
differently, decisions that are not physically realized are, for all
practical purposes, useless. This observation suggests that an
objective of memory research should be an appraisal of the cognitive
substrates of movement   control. A related goal should be an
analysis of the relation between the memory systems underlying
movement   control and   the memory systems   underlying symbol
retrieval.   Are the two types of memory systems similar   or
different? The research that my colleagues and I have done suggest
that the similarities are more pronounced than the differences.
This paper briefly reviews two principles of motor programming that
our studies have revealed -- hierarchical organization and parameter
remapping.   The two principles are reminiscent of two well known
principles of verbal/symbolic recall, namely, hierarchical
organization and memory interference. Implications of the similarities are discussed in the final section of the chapter.

HIERARCHICAL CONTROL
        To investigate the organization and execution of motor
programs, Rosenbaum, Kenny, and Derr (1983) asked people to perform
rapid finger sequences from memory, where the identities and timing
of finger strokes were recorded with a computer. We found that the
pattern of response latencies and errors was best accounted for with
a model that challenged existing views of motor control. (Because of
space limitations, the details of the study are not given here.)
The model stated that the program for a sequence of motor acts is

hierarchically organized and, more importantly, that the structure is used in its entirety during production of the movement sequence. The method by which it is used is a "tree-traversal" process -- a systematic procedure for decoding a hierarchical representation into its components, where high-level units are decoded after all the lower-level units of the immediately adjacent unit have been decoded. The surprising feature of this claim is that rapid motor sequences seem to be "run off" in a linear fashion, the way a tape is read from a tape head, but our model suggested that even when people perform extremely rapid response sequences, they access and retrieve memory at varying levels during production.

It is natural to ask how general this process is. Perhaps it was only used in our study because of the composition of the sequences that our subjects performed. It can be shown, however, that the tree-traversal model also accounts for a well known set of results reported by Sternberg, Monsell, Knoll, & Wright (1978) in a very different experimental context. These investigators found that the time to initiate a highly prepared motor sequence increases linearly with the number of response elements in the sequence, up to about 8. The tree-traversal model accounts for this initiation-time effect, as well as comparable interresponse-time effects reported by the same group: Longer sequences have more complex trees, which gives rise to longer tree-traversal delays before production of individual responses. The model also predicts that interresponse times should be longer in the middle of the sequence than at the ends because major chunk boundaries are likely in mid-sequence (see Rosenbaum, 1985, for details). Thus, the tree-traversal model generalizes to the production of brief bursts of responses, not just the particular sequences studied by Rosenbaum et al. (1983).

Since the studies mentioned above were concerned with the production of already-prepared response sequences, a natural question is whether the tree-traversal model also applies to the selection of response sequences. To address this question, my colleagues and I developed a task in which people choose between possible response sequences upon identifying a discriminative signal. The working hypothesis was that the way subjects choose between two (or more) sequences is related to the way they choose among the much larger number of sequences that are possible in everyday life. We assumed further that if the timing of a given sequence depended on the sequence with which it is paired, this change could be attributed to the sequence-selection process per se.

With this sequence choice procedure, a number of dramatic facts were uncovered about motor programming. (In these experiments, keyboard sequences were used because of their rapidity, flexibility, and ease of measurement). One finding was that when subjects choose between two sequences of equal length, choice reaction time increases with sequence length (Rosenbaum, Saltzman, & Kingman, 1984). Thus, the length effect observed by Sternberg et al. for simple reaction time generalizes to the choice situation. This is not always the case, however. Choice reaction times for a sequence of given length also depend on the length of the other sequence that may be called for. This result indicates that the sequence choice procedure can indeed be used to learn about the selection of motor programs, not just their execution.

Another important finding from the sequence choice procedure was that when two possible sequences begin with the same response and end with different responses, the choice reaction time to begin the ultimately designated sequence is shorter than when the two possible sequences begin with different responses and end with the same response (Rosenbaum, Inhoff, & Gordon, 1984). This effect is quantitatively well behaved; choice reaction times decrease systematically as the first point of difference between the two sequences recedes from the beginning of the sequences towards the end.

To account for this result and others, Rosenbaum et al. (1984) proposed the hierarchical editor model of motor programming. This model says that people choose between response sequences by performing two passes through a common representational tree. The first pass -- the edit pass -- starts at the first uncertain point and continues to the final terminal node of the tree via a traversal process in which all uncertainties about tree composition are resolved. The second pass -- the execution pass -- starts at the beginning of the tree and moves all the way through it, with responses being physically executed when their corresponding terminal nodes are encountered. This model does an impressive job of accounting for sequence choice data, especially if the model is relaxed to allow the execution pass to begin while the edit pass is still in progress (see Rosenbaum, Hindorff, & Munro, 1987.)

For present purposes, the most important implication of the hierarchical editor model is that it is formally similar to models of memory retrieval that have been postulated in other areas of cognitive psychology. The idea that successive responses are produced through a tree-traversal process has been discussed in connection with the production of responses to lights (Restle, 1970), the recall of memorized digit streams (Simon, 1972), speech production (Cooper & Paccia-Cooper, 1980), and the recall of semantically organized word lists (Reitman & Rueter, 1980). The fact that the model also applies to motor performance suggests that the memory systems underlying motor control and verbal retrvieval are functionally similar. This claim is consistent with the hypothesis that the substrates of high-level cognitive function may have motoric origins, as has been suggested by others in regard to phylogenesis (Kimura, 1979; Lieberman, 1984) and ontogenesis (Piaget, 1952).

INTERFERENCE

Another principle of memory organization that is manifested in motor performance is interference. As reported by Rosenbaum, Weber, Hazelett, and Hindorff (1986), motor performance suffers when features of individual movements change from one production cycle to the next. We call this the parameter remapping effect. The effect is observed in a variety of behaviors, including speech, finger-tapping, and musical performance.

In the domain of speech, the parameter remapping effect was seen in several demonstrations, including the following. College students recited the first n (n < 10) letters of the alphabet over and over again for 10 sec, with the instruction always to alternate between stressed and unstressed pronunciations. Under this instruction, stresses of individual letters were necessarily constant for lists with even numbers of letters, but were necessarily varied for lists with odd numbers of letters. Performance of the odd-length lists was much slower than performance of the even-length lists, as would be expected if the original stresses of individual letters were preserved from one performance cycle to the next and if extra time were needed to change the stress-to-letter assignments.

In the domain of finger tapping, sequences in which the same finger was tapped the same number of times in successive cycles (constant mappings) were performed significantly more quickly and accurately than sequences in which the same finger was not tapped the same number of times in successive cycles (varied mappings). These results suggest again that the need to change the way a response is performed from one cycle to the next exacts a toll on performance.

In musical performance, violinists were found to perform bowing sequences more quickly if the number of mid-stroke stops was consistently mapped to particular bowing directions than if the number of mid-stroke stops was varied for particular bowing directions. This effect was observed both in amateur and semi-professional players.

All of these results suggest that the parameter remapping effect is a general phenomenon of human performance. The effect has important implications for theories of motor control. It suggests that programs for just-performed response sequences are preserved and can be used for subsequent performance. The effect also suggests that there are autonomous performance features, such as syllable stresses or number of successive finger taps, which can be mapped onto "core" program representations.

Concerning the relation between motor programming and more conventional memory domains, the parameter remapping effect can be viewed as an example of memory interference -- the tendency of memory performance to suffer when an item to be retrieved has a number of items associated to it. Memory interference effects are best known from studies of paired-associate learning (Ceraso, 1967), although the effect has also been studied recently in connection with the "fan" effect (Anderson, 1983), where the time to verify propositions about a memory item increases with the number of associates to the item. Another example of memory interference is Schneider and Shiffrin's (1977) demonstration of the development of automaticity. Here, stimuli associated to constant responses were responded to more quickly and with less dependence on the size of the stimulus set than were stimuli associated to varied responses. Insofar as automatic encoding of the stimuli depended on the constancy of the response to which the stimuli were associated, Schneider and Shiffrin's result can be viewed as another example of interference. Since the parameter remapping effect is also an example of memory interference in motor production, one can conclude again that the cognitive control of movement relies on the same memory system (or on memory systems with the same properties) as the encoding of stimuli (Schneider & Shiffrin, 1977) and the recall of words (Ceraso, 1967) or propositions (Anderson, 1983).

CONCLUSIONS

The fact that motor programming seems to obey the same functional properties as symbolic memory performance may come as a surprise to those who regard motor performance as cognitively trivial. Action entails recall, however. To select appropriate movements, one must recall the limits and capabilities of one's body as well as the way the body interacts with the external environment. This information must be stored in memory in symbolic form, and so it is perhaps not surprising that the recall of movement-related information has many of the same properties as the recall of other sorts of information.

Several intriguing questions are raised by this perspective. One is whether the capacity for motor programming set the stage in evolution for the development of the higher mental functions. An alternative is that the capacity for motor programming derived from other sorts of cognitive changes, or that the two sorts of changes occurred coincidentally. Unfortunately, we cannot answer these questions definitively. However, we can say with confidence that it is incorrect to claim, as a noted anthropologist recently did (see Lewin, 1986), that motor control could not have set the stage for the evolution of the intellect. The anthropologist's premise was that movement sequences, in contrast to language, are controlled in a simple linear fashion. Our studies indicate that movement sequences are controlled hierarchically.

Another question raised by our research is related to the fact that our work helps "round out" the picture of the human information processing system. Now that an increasing number of cognitive psychologists are working on motor control, it is becoming apparent that common principles apply to the entire range of information processing operations, from information intake to output. When similar principles are found across different processing domains, one wonders whether there are distinct modules for those processes, as Fodor (1983) suggested. A detailed cognitive analysis of motor systems, conducted in parallel with analyses of other cognitive subsystems, can provide a way of answering this fundamental question.

REFERENCES

Anderson, J. R. (1983). 'A spreading activation theory of memory', Journal of Verbal Learning and Verbal Behavior, 22, 261-295.

Ceraso, J. (1967). 'The interference theory of memory', Scientific American, 217, 4, 117-124.

Cooper, W. E., & Paccia-Cooper, J. (1980). Syntax and speech. Cambridge: Harvard University Press.

Fodor, J. A. (1983). The modularity of mind. Cambridge, MA: MIT Press.

Kimura, D. (1979). 'Neuromotor mechanisms in the evolution of human communication'. In H. D. Steklis & M. J. Raleigh (Eds.), Neurobiology of social communication in primates. New York:

Academic Press.

Lewin, R. (1986). 'Anthropologist argues that language cannot be read in stones', Science, 233, 23-24.

Lieberman, P. (1984). The biology and evolution of language. Cambridge, MA: Harvard.

Piaget, J. (1952). The origins of intelligence in children.(2nd ed.). (M. Cook, Trans.). New York: International Universities Press.

Reitman, J. S., & Rueter, H. H. (1980). 'Organization revealed by recall orders and confirmed by pauses', Cognitive Psychology, 12, 554-581.

Restle, F. (1970). 'Theory of serial pattern learning: Structural trees', Psychological Review, 77, 481-495.

Rosenbaum, D. A. (1985). 'Motor programming: A review and scheduling theory', In H. Heuer, U. Kleinbeck, & K-M. Schmidt (Eds.), Motor behavior: Programming, control, and acquisition (pp. 1-33). Berlin: Springer-Verlag.

Rosenbaum, D.A., Hindorff, V., & Munro, E. (1987). 'Scheduling and programming of rapid finger sequences: Tests and elaborations of the hierarchical editor model', Journal of Experimental Psychology: Human Perception and Performance, 13, 193-203.

Rosenbaum, D. A., Inhoff, A. W., & Gordon, A. M. (1984). 'Choosing between movement sequences: A hierarchical editor model', Journal of Experimental Psychology: General, 113, 372-393.

Rosenbaum, D. A., Kenny, S., & Derr, M. A. (1983). 'Hierarchical control of rapid movement sequences', Journal of Experimental Psychology: Human Perception and Performance, 9, 86-102.

Rosenbaum, D. A., Weber, R. J., Hazelett, W. M., & Hindorff, V. (1986). 'The parameter remapping effect in human performance: Evidence from tongue twisters and finger fumblers', Journal of Memory and Language, 25, 710-725.

Schneider, W., & Shiffrin, R. M. (1977). 'Controlled and automatic human information processing: I. Detection, search, and attention', Psychological Review, 84, 1-66.

Simon, H. A. (1972). 'Complexity and the representation of patterned sequences of symbols', Psychological Review, 79, 369-382.

Sternberg, S., Monsell, S., Knoll, R. L., & Wright, C. E. (1978). 'The latency and duration of rapid movement sequences: Comparisons of speech and typewriting', In G. E. Stelmach (Ed.), Information processing in motor control and learning (pp. 117-152). New York: Academic Press.

STUDIES IN TACTUAL AND MOTOR MEMORY CHARACTERISTICS
OF BLIND PEOPLE

V.K. Kool* and S. Singh**

*University of Wisconsin at Eau Claire, U.S.A.
**University of Sagar, M.P., India.

ABSTRACT

Having examined studies of how the blind encode movements in space, it is concluded that perceptual deficits do not always lead to cognitive deficits. The idea was tested by comparing the performance of congenitally blind and sighted subjects on preselected tasks recalled in an open space in one condition and upon the arm of the subject in another.

In this chapter we briefly review some of the work done in our laboratory to examine the effects of perceptual deficit caused by the absence of a visual reference system for coding movements in space. The effects of lack of vision among the blind have been reported in several studies (see Warren, 1984; Fraiberg, 1977), but very few attempts have been made to investigate the effects of perceptual deficits in planning and executing movements which are chosen by the subject himself (i.e., the subject has advanced knowledge of the movement goal prior to response initiation and possesses a more resilient memory representation; Stelmach, Kelso and Wallace, 1975). To be more precise, our research work focussed on the effects of perceptual deficit in the absence of visual experience on cognitive processes involving advanced knowledge of the consequences of movement in space. We also examined alternative sources to visual information which could update a perceptual system and lead to better representation in memory.

CODING CHARACTERISTICS OF MEMORY IN BLIND PEOPLE

While sighted people have the capacity to identify several objects at a time, perceptual features guiding the judgements of blind people are based on tactile impressions which are largely successively formed and retained in memory to form a percept. In the absence of vision, blind people rely on and make use of sensory inputs like touch, movement and audition which create a unique encoding of a spatial lay out.

A typical method employed to study movements involves guiding a subject's movement to a point in space (criterion movement) and subsequently having the subject recall the movement to reach the same end point in space (location task) or reproduce the same extent of movement (distance task). Roy (1978) found that recall of location is superior to recall of distance, but the explanation for the difference between location and distance coding remains unclear. Experiments conducted in our laboratory examined the implications of such findings for a group of subjects who were totally blind since birth and provided a very strict criterion for absence of vision in comparison to sighted subjects who were blindfolded. Whereas blind subjects were as accurate as sighted subjects on a location task, their performance was vastly inferior to sighted subjects on a distance task (Kool, 1980). We also showed that movements made prior to a criterion motor task (Singh, 1980) and increasing or decreasing the length of movement after a criterion task (Kool, Singh and Pathak, 1982) increased the errors of blind subjects more than those of their sighted counterparts. More recently, Gupta, Gupta and Kool (1986) found that availability of vision at both criterion learning and recall improved the performance in a location task but a similar advantage was not found for kinesthesis. Further, when joint receptors were rendered insensitive while the muscle receptors remained intact (ischemic nerve block procedure), recall of distance movements deteriorated but not recall of location. We contended that distance information was stored by joint receptors in some form. In another study we found that reduction in the level of feedback and change in the direction of recall was more detrimental to the recall of blind subjects as compared to their sighted counterparts (Pathak and Kool, 1987).

ON THE RELATIONSHIP BETWEEN PERCEPTUAL AND COGNITIVE DEFICITS

The range of perceiving spatial features undoubtedly is restricted for the blind person. This limitation causes delay in perceiving the immediate environment and handling the vast and complex array of inputs that occur when a blind person moves. Recent studies on the cognitive abilities of the blind show that spatial knowledge, like knowledge of language and knowledge of number, does not invariably depend on vision. A blind child is capable of constructing an abstract map of the spatial lay out (Landau, Spelke and Gleitman, 1984). Finding new paths and connections requires rules and principles of Euclidean geometry. In a recent study, Lederman, Klatzky and Barber (1985) reported that both their blind and sighted subjects relied on implicit spatial axes, which were movement independent, to judge position in space. In short, it is now believed that knowledge of space is not solely a result of sensory information and it can be independent of input modality.

Given that these studies demonstrate the existence of spatial cognition in the blind comparable to spatial cognition among the sighted, a major issue in the comparison of performance of blind and sighted people on spatial tasks is to identify whether differences between them are due to perceptual or cognitive factors. If their differences are at the perceptual level, varying input levels should delineate the differences between two groups. On the other hand, failure to generate new information should reflect cognitive deficits. It is likely that certain cognitive deficits could be due to perceptual deficits.

ENRICHMENT OF REPRESENTATION OF SPACE IN BLIND PEOPLE: EXAMPLE OF PRESELECTED MOVEMENTS

Studies employing blind subjects to investigate the mechanism of spatial coding required them to move targets set by the experimenter. However, Stelmach, Kelso and Wallace (1975) pointed

out that when subjects are allowed to select a target and move
without assistance to their targets, they reproduce movements more
accurately. According to Kelso (1978), preselecting a movement
creates an internal representation of the anticipated sensory
consequences of that movement. We hypothesized, therefore, that
preslection will not be useful to the blind because of a weak
internal representation in the absence of a visual reference system.
       To test the above hypothesis, we engaged 80 congenitally
blind and 80 sighted subjects in an experiment. A linear slide was
used to record the movements of the subjects. This experiment showed
that the first order interaction of groups x preselection was
significant for both dependent variables: for absolute errors, F (1,
128) = 82.17, p < .01; and for variable errors: F (1,128) = 14.10,
p<.01. While the blind and sighted groups did not differ on the

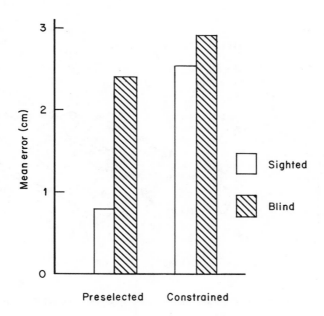

Fig. 1 Absolute errors of blind and sighted subjects on
        preselected and constrained movements.

constrained condition of the experiment, there was a very significant
difference between them in the preselected condition (see Figure 1).
The inability of the blind subjects to take advantage of preselection
indicates that visual experience tends to integrate with kinesthetic
input to elicit more accurate recall of targets by the sighted
subjects.
       A follow up experiment created a situation in which it
would be possible for the blind subjects to anticipate the sensory
consequences of their plan and thereby take the advantage of
preselection in much the same way as their sighted counterparts did
in the previous experiment. We asked: if vision integrates with

kinesthesis to improve the central expectancy leading to superior
performance in sighted people, is it possible to create a situation
in which knowledge of spatial attributes in motion could be
efficiently handled by the blind people? In other words, is it
possible to develop a perceptual alternative to vision?

When a blind person moves in an unknown space, he cannot
anticipate what he will encounter with each step. He updates his
knowledge of space with discrete perceptual units. However, if a
linear movement as described in the previous experiment is made on
the forearm, then a blind person will be aware of his space and its
landmarks in much the same way as a sighted person benefits from
vision.

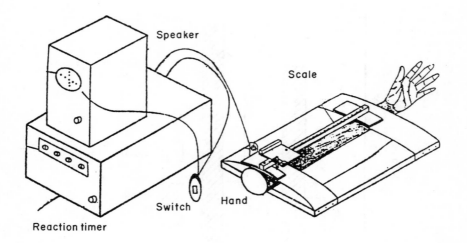

Fig. 2   Arm Slide used to record movement errors and movement
          time.

We designed a special apparatus with a slide mounted on a
scale. In a tactile-kinesthetic task, this was fastened on the
forearm of the subject with velcro tapes. The subject moved the
pointer with his hand and hence received kinesthetic information,
while the pointer touching the skin softly on the forearm gave
tactile impressions of the movement. Thirty-five congenitally blind
and 40 sighted subjects were tested in much the same way as reported
for the previous experiment.

The results of this study did not show superior recall
accuracy among the sighted subjects, and the blind subjects did
almost as well as their sighted counterparts. On the other hand,
blind people reached their targets faster than sighted subjects. The

mean recall time for the sighted group was 4.24 and 2.26 seconds for
long and short targets, respectively, while for the blind group it
was 2.83 and 2.08 seconds for long and short targets, respectively.
These results clearly indicate that preselected tasks are easier to
recall only when the plan to encode such targets is rich in details.
This indeed was found when blind subjects, who habitually use their
own body as a reference frame, operated on their own body surface.
In an earlier study, Wills (1965) also noted that blind people
understand objects by relating or comparing them with their own
bodies. A small anchor effect consisting of tracing by one hand
while the other remained on the starting point has also been reported
in a recent study (Lederman, Klatzky and Barber, 1985).

        In short, we contend that although perceptual deficits are
an important source to explain why blind people are not proficient in
certain tasks, our results do not demonstrate that blind people have
a cognitive deficit. Using thier own body as a platform, blind
people can enhance their metric knowledge and update movements, a
result that clearly indicates capacity for and use of spatial
cognition.

REFERENCES

Fraiberg, S. (1977). Insights From The Blind, Basic Books, New York.

Gupta, R.K., Gupta, M. and Kool, V.K. (1986). 'Role of Vision and
Kinesthesis in Location and Distance Estimates', Acta Psychologica,
62, 141-159.

Kelso, J.A.S. and Wallace, S.A. (1978). 'Conscious Mechanisms in
Movement', in Information Processing In Motor Control And Learning
(Ed. G.E. Stelmach), Academic Press, New York.

Kool, V.K. (1980). 'Short-term Recall of Linear and Curvilinear
Movements by Blind and Sighted Subjects', in Attention and
Performance Vol. 8 (Ed. R.S. Nickerson), pp. 541-553, Lawrence
Erlbaum, New Jersey.

Kool, V.K., Singh, S. and Pathak, K.C. (1982). 'Change in Memory
Trace as a Function of Response Biasing', Bombay Psychologist, 2, 51-
55.

Landau, B., Spelke, E. and Gleitman, H. (1984). 'Spatial Knowledge
in a Young Blind Child', Cognition, 16, 225-266.

Lederman, S.J., Klatzky, R.L. and Barber, P.O. (1985). 'Spatial
Movement Based Heuristics from Encoding Pattern Information Through
Touch', Journal of Experimental Psychology: General, 114, 33-49.

Pathak, K.C. and Kool, V.K. (1987). 'Short Term Recall of Linear
Movements: Role of Visual Reference System, Feedback and Task
Complexity', manuscript in preparation.

Roy, E.A.   (1978).   'Role of Preselection in Memory for Movement
Extent', Journal of Experimental Psychology: Human Learning and
Memory, 4, 397-405.

Singh, S.   (1980). Effect of Preselection, Prior Activities and
Response Biasing on Short Term Recall of Movements of Blind and
Sighted   Subjects.   Unpublished doctoral   dissertation,   Indian
Institute of Technology, Bombay, India.

Stelmach,   G.E.,   Kelso,   J.A.S.   and   Wallace,   S.A.   (1975).
'Preselection in Motor Short Term Memory', Journal of Experimental
Psychology: Human Learning and Memory, 1, 745-755.

Warren, D.H.   (1984). Blindness And Early Childhood Development,
American Foundation for the Blind, New York.

Wills, D.M.   (1965). 'Some Observations on Blind Nursery School
Children's Understanding of their World', Psychoanalytic Study of the
Child, 20, 344-363.

THE ROLE OF A MOTORIC ASPECT OF REPRESENTATION:
SPONTANEOUS WRITING-LIKE BEHAVIOUR IN JAPANESE

Y. Endo

Department of Educational Psychology, Kyoto University
Kyoto, Japan

ABSTRACT
        This study investigated the role of spontaneous "kusho"
behaviour among Japanese. This was defined as writing-like finger
movement leaving no physical trace. College students with or without
spontaneous kusho were asked to spell English words, under three
conditions. (1) "kusho" (WRITING), (2) drawing a line with subject's
index finger at the experimenter's pace, (3) drawing a line with
subject's index finger at self pace. The WRITING condition had a
facilitating effect for the spontaneous kusho group in spelling long
words. The role of kusho behaviour is discussed.

        Japanese people sometimes carry out writing-like behaviour.
For example, when I attempt to recall a complicated Kanji (Chinese
character) correctly, or when I try to tell how a long word is
spelled, but I cannot do it well, then the index finger of my right
hand starts to move to write those letters or words on the palm, the
knee, even in the air, sometimes without intention.
        Hasumi (1977) gave valuable linguistic considerations to
the background of such behaviour. According to him, Japanese people
are different from Western people with respect to their memory for
words; the former are likely to store words in the form of visual
representations which include a motoric component, and the latter are
likely to store words as a sequence of phonemes. Furthermore, he
suggested that this was because Japanese have a history of learning
words by writing them repeatedly.
        "Kusho" behaviour is defined as writing-like finger
movements without any physical and visual trace. With one exception,
there are few practical studies of kusho behaviour. Using Kanji as
experimental materials, Sasaki and Watanabe (1983) investigated kusho
behaviour in Japanese adults. In experiment 1, they found that most
of the college students used kusho behaviour when they were asked to
integrate Kanji after presentation of two or three Kanji graphemes.
In experiment 2, they investigated the function of kusho behaviour
under various conditions, and suggested that the students had stored
Kanji in the form of a visual representation and kusho behaviour was
an effective strategy to activate it.
        The purpose of the present study was to investigate the
role of kusho behaviour in more detail. First, as was noted earlier,
from daily observation, kusho seems to be used when a word or letter
is complicated. This suggests that kusho may function when a
stimulus is not simple but complex. Second, does kusho serve a

useful function for those people who engage in it spontaneously? Third, is it possible to substitute some other movement for kusho? Sasaki and Watanabe (1983) suggested that kusho, like inner speech, may have a cognitive function to mediate the externalisation of internal mental process, or to control mental operations through overt behaviour. In spelling an English word, a necessary operation is assumed to be the tracing of a visual representation of the word. Therefore, some other movement, drawing a line at self pace for example, may possibly support such processes. But this may be impossible when a finger is moved at another person's pace.

METHOD

Subjects   Thirty-three undergraduate and graduate students at Kyoto University.

Materials   Thirty English nouns were selected. Half of them were short words, composed of 3-4 letters, and the other half were long words, composed of 8-10 letters. In a pilot study these words were correctly spelt by 10 students who were not participating in the experiment. Another 4 words were selected for practice.

Experimental design   A 2 (subject group) x 2 (word type) x 3 (condition) ANOVA design was employed. Subject group was a between factor and the latter two were within factors.
        Subject group. Spontaneous kusho subject group (SK) and non-spontaneous kusho subject group (NSK). The subjects were divided into two groups on the basis of the experimenter's observation of whether or not they spontaneously showed "kusho" behaviour when spelling practice words.
        Condition (1) writing-like finger movement (WRITING), (2) drawing a line at the experimenter's pace (OTHER), (3) drawing a line at self pace (SELF).
        (1) WRITING - the subjects were asked to write with the index finger on smooth white paper during the spelling task.
        (2) OTHER - during the spelling task, the experimenter wearing a glove, held a subject's writing hand, and moved his or her index finger in a straight line from left to right. When it reached the right edge of the paper, it started again from the left edge.
        (3) SELF - the subjects were asked to move their index finger in a straight line from left to right. They were permitted to pause or move at self pace.

Procedure   Subjects participated individually. After arriving at the experimental room, he or she was seated in front of a desk on which there was a sheet of 10 x 14.5 inches white paper.
        The subject was given the following instruction; "The experimenter will tell you first a Japanese word and then the corresponding English word. The task is to spell the word."
        Five short words and 5 long words were blocked and used for one of three conditions. The order of the conditions, and the combinations of material, blocks and conditions were counterbalanced. At the end of every block session, confidence, and the feeling of being interrupted were rated on 7-point scales. All subjects' responses were recorded on a tape recorder.

Subjects were then asked to write all the words. This task was done to confirm that the subject had known all the words and could write them correctly. Finally, the subject was asked about how he/she learned English words.

RESULTS

Spelling   The left panel of Fig. 1 shows the numbers of short words correctly spelled by SK and NSK subjects. As can be seen, most subjects could spell most words correctly in each condition. There was no significant main effect for condition in each group.

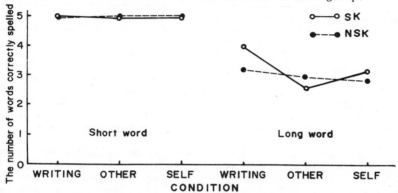

Fig. 1 The number of short and long words correctly spelled by kusho (SK) and non-kusho (NSK) subjects in the three experimental conditions.

The right panel of Fig. 1 shows the numbers of long words correctly spelled by SK and NSK subjects. Two (subject group) x 3 (condition) analysis showed a significant main effect for condition $(F(2,62)=6.67, p<.01)$. The two-way interaction approached significance $(F(2,62)=2.58, p<.1)$. That is, there is a tendency for the two groups to differ in the effects of condition. For SK subjects a one-way ANOVA showed a significant effect of condition, $F(2,34)=9.04, p<.001$; Tukey comparisons revealed that the performance was better in the WRITING condition (4.00) than in OTHER (2.61)$(p<.01)$, or SELF condition (3.17)$(p<.05)$, and the latter two did not differ reliably. For NSK subjects, there was no significant difference among the three conditions.

Confidence   The upper panel of Table 1 shows mean ratings of confidence. For short words, there was no significant effect. For long words, one-way ANOVA revealed that there was no main effect of condition in NSK subjects, but a significant main effect in SK subjects; $F(2,34)=6.36, p<.005$. SK subjects were more confident in the WRITING than in the OTHER condition $(p<.001)$. In the WRITING condition, SK subjects rated confidence higher than NSK subjects did $(t=2.43, df=31, p<.05)$.

Feeling of being interrupted.   The lower panel of Table 1 shows the ratings of the feeling of being interrupted. For short words, one-way ANOVA showed no significant effect of condition in NSK subjects, but in SK subjects there was a significant effect $(F(2,34)=7.59,$

p<.002). SK subjects felt themselves interrupted to a greater extent in OTHER than in WRITING (p<.01) or SELF (p<.01).

TABLE 1
Ratings of Confidence and Feeling of being Interrupted.(Maximum score = 7.00). SK=subjects with spontaneous kusho, NSK=subjects without spontaneous kusho.

Group	Short word			Long word		
	WRITING	OTHER	SELF	WRITING	OTHER	SELF
Confidence						
SK	6.94	6.83	6.83	4.39	3.22	3.61
NSK	6.87	6.93	6.80	3.20	2.80	3.33
Feeling of being interrupted						
SK	1.39	1.94	1.39	2.00	4.94	4.50
NSK	2.00	1.87	1.33	3.00	4.87	3.93

For long words, one-way ANOVA revealed significant effects of condition in SK and NSK groups; $F(2,34)=19.61$, $p<.001$, $F(2,28)=6.40$, $p<.005$, respectively. For NSK subjects, OTHER was more interruptive than WRITING (p<.01). For SK subjects, both OTHER and SELF conditions were more interruptive than WRITING.

DISCUSSION
Some of the Japanese college students (more than 50% of 33 students) engaged in kusho behaviour spontaneously when spelling English words. They benefited more from kusho behaviour than the other finger movements tested. This was not the case for subjects who had not used spontaneous kusho. Parallel results were obtained from ratings of confidence and the feeling of interruption. The implication of these results is now considered.
First, drawing a self-paced line had no facilitating effect on spelling. In this condition, self-paced finger movement allowed the marking or tapping of a point, (whether letter, phoneme, morpheme, or syllable unit), which a subject was just about to pronounce. This finding therefore suggests that the facilitation obtained by kusho users was not due to helping to trace a visual representation through overt behaviours.
Second, the fact that kusho behaviour has no effect for NSK subjects suggests that kusho itself has no facilitating effect. It seems to be different from other strategies, such as, for example, rehearsal which, once applied, facilitate memory, even for a person who has never used it (Brown and Barclay, 1976).
Third, the performance in spelling short words, was not different under the three conditions. Therefore, drawing a line either at self pace or at the experimenter's pace, had no inhibitory effect for either subject group. Why, therefore, did those conditions inhibit long word spelling?
One possible answer linking these three points might be the

learning phase. All SK subjects reported that they had acquired English words by writing repeatedly, especially in the case of long words. It supports the position that stimuli which had been originally learned through motoric processing would be stored in the form of representations which have motoric components, and that they are well retrieved when similar motoric cues are available. If a stimulus has been learned without motoric movement, so that its representation does not have motoric components, then kusho behaviour in the retrieval phase may have no effect, or forbidding kusho may not lead to inhibition. The finding that kusho had no effect for NSK subjects would be a case of the former, and short words without kusho would be a case of the latter.

According to the encoding specificity principle (Tulving and Osler, 1968; Tulving and Thomson, 1973; Tulving, 1983), specific encoding operations performed on what is perceived determine what is stored, and what is stored determines what retrieval cues are effective in providing access to what is stored. That is, the similarity of the cognitive environment between the encoding and the retrieval phase is critical. Likewise, Saltz and Dixon (1982) suggested that facilitation due to motoric processing was found only if the processing occurred during input, at the learning phase. The data of the present study are consistent with these positions. In NSK group, there are some students (3/15) who said they had learned English words through writing. Why, then, did they not engage in spontaneous kusho during the practice session? One possibility is that the stimuli for practice were easy for them. With complex words, they might use kusho spontaneously.

REFERENCES

Brown, A.L. and Barcley, C.R. (1976). 'The effects of training specific mnemonics on the metamnemonic efficiency of retarded children', Child Development, 47, 71-80.

Hasumi, S. (1977). Japanese Linguistics. Tokyo: Chikuma.

Saltz, E. and Dixon, D. (1982). 'Let's pretend: The role of motoric imagery in memory for sentences and words', Journal of Experimental Child Psychology, 34, 77-92.

Sasaki, M. and Watanabe, A. (1983). 'An experimental study of spontaneous writinglike behaviour ("KUSHO") in Japanese', Japanese Journal of Educational Psychology, 31, 4, 1-10.

Tulving, E. (1983). Elements of Episodic Memory. Oxford University Press.

Tulving, E. and Osler, S. (1968). 'Effectiveness of retrieval cues in memory for words', Journal of Experimental Psychology, 77, 4, 593-601.

Tulving, E. and Thomson, D.M. (1973). 'Encoding specificity and retrieval processes in episodic memory', Psychological Review, 85, 352-373.

TIME OF DAY

EFFECTS OF TIME OF DAY ON TEXT MEMORY AND INFERENCE

Jane Oakhill

MRC Perceptual and Cognitive Performance Unit, Laboratory of
Experimental Psychology, University of Sussex, Brighton, BN1 9QG.

ABSTRACT

This chapter reports three experiments on the effects of time of day on text processing. The first two experiments showed that immediate memory for text is better in the early morning than in the late afternoon, and that morning subjects' superior immediate recall can be attributed to their better verbatim memory. Memory tests in experiments 1 and 2 failed to support the idea that afternoon subjects engage in more inferential and elaborative processing of text. However, the third experiment, a reading time study, indicated that afternoon subjects are more likely to integrate text as they are reading. These results suggest that superior short-term retention in the morning arises because of better verbatim memory at that time, whereas superior long-term retention following afternoon presentation arises because afternoon subjects are more likely to integrate the ideas in a text as it is being presented to them. Thus, they have an enduring memory for the gist of the text, but not for the exact wording.

INTRODUCTION

In general, research on immediate memory for text indicates a decline across the day (Laird, 1925; Folkard and Monk, 1980), although when memory is tested after a delay of a week the opposite pattern holds: memory is better when the original presentation was in the afternoon rather than in the morning (Folkard, Monk, Bradbury and Rosenthall, 1977). However, it is not clear what processing changes might underlie these memory differences. In a re-analysis of these data, in which he included the importance of information tapped by questions as a factor, Folkard (1980) suggested that superior recall later in the day may arise because the subjects' attention is directed towards the more important aspects of the text in the afternoon. The subjects (schoolchildren) who first heard the story in the morning were able to retrieve more low-level information immediately than were the afternoon subjects, though those morning subjects who received the delayed test (one week later) were relatively poor at retrieving low-level information. By contrast, subjects who heard the story in the afternoon were better than morning subjects at retrieving higher-level information, both in the immediate and delayed tests. This pattern of data in delayed recall has subsequently been confirmed in a study of adults' text memory – subjects presented with a story in the afternoon remembered more important information after a delay of one week than did morning subjects (Oakhill, 1986a).

Other data of Folkard's (1979) has led him to suggest that changes in memory over the day may be mediated by changes in the strategies that subjects adopt spontaneously, with a shift from greater reliance on 'maintenance' processing in the morning, to a reliance on 'elaborative' or semantic processing in the afternoon. This suggestion leads to various hypotheses about how text processing might change over the day. If subjects engage in more semantic processing in the afternoon - elaborating on and integrating the ideas in the text, and making inferences about it - then this processing may well aid their long-term retention. Since questions that tap important information frequently involve inferences and integration of information from different parts of a text, these findings are consistent with the hypothesis that better memory for important information in the afternoon is related to level of integration. Morning subjects, by contrast, if they concentrate on retaining the exact wording of text, may experience a short-term memory advantage, but their longer-term memory may suffer because the material has been processed relatively superficially.

In summary, several findings have shown time-of-day differences in text memory. However, the only direct evidence that subjects make more use of superficial 'maintenance' processing in the morning, and more of elaborative/semantic processing in the afternoon has come from experiments with word lists. The present chapter reports a series of experiments that attempted to explore the changes in processing with time of day that underlie text memory.

EXPERIMENT 1

This experiment investigates the idea that subjects tested in the morning have good verbatim memory for text, whereas subjects tested in the afternoon tend towards more 'elaborative' processing, and have good 'gist' memory. If subjects engage in more spontaneous integration and elaboration later in the day, then they should be more likely, in a recognition test, to confuse sentences that were actually presented with sentences that are similar in meaning.

Method

32 subjects participated in the experiment. They were tested in small groups in sound-attenuated experimental cubicles, either at 9am or at 5pm. The subjects were presented with a short, factual passage (Meyer's (1975) 'Schizophrenia' passage) over headphones from a tape, and then completed a recognition memory test, followed by free recall of the passage. In the recognition test the subjects had to choose between four types of item: the original sentence, a paraphrase of that sentence which retained the gist meaning, and two foils - one of which was similar in surface form to the original (foil 1) and one to the paraphrase (foil 2). Both foils differed in meaning from the original items. (The importance of the 20 original sentences used in the recognition test was determined by asking an independent group of 12 subjects to judge their importance to the passage as a whole). Subjects were required to select one item from each set as the sentence originally presented.

Results and Discussion

The free recall data were scored independently for gist recall by two raters. The passage was divided into 'idea units'.

portant information. This selective forgetting of the original
items provides some support for the idea that the afternoon subjects
were processing the text more 'deeply'. In addition, the finding
that there was a strong relation between verbatim memory and text
recall in the morning, but no such relation in the afternoon suggests
that afternoon subjects rely on factors other than verbatim retention to remember text. It is perhaps for this reason that they
found the exact wording of the unimportant recognition items difficult to retain.

EXPERIMENT 2

If subjects more actively engage in the integration of
ideas in a text in the afternoon, then subjects tested at this time
should be more disturbed by text inconsistencies, and should show
evidence of a more active attempt to deal with them. By contrast,
morning subjects, if they are not attempting to integrate information as they read, should be relatively unaffected by inconsistencies in the text. The paradigm used here to explore text integration was derived from that reported by Wilkes, Alred and Al-
Ahmar (1983), in which different types of priming passage were used
to set up particular expectations of the subsequent text. Wilkes
et al. showed that subjects' recall of information in a short text
varied according to the nature of the priming passage they had received. Subjects were presented with one of two types of priming
passage that introduced an individual, and gave several pieces of
information about that individual's achievement in the final part
of secondary school. In one type of prime, the achievement information was positive (e.g. "his O level results had been good") and
in the other, negative (e.g. "his O level results had been poor").
Both groups of subjects also read a second passage which described
the same individual's earlier school career. The continuation passage contained two sorts of information: achievement information
which was entirely positive (e.g. "he was a good reader"), and motivation information which was entirely (though mildly) negative (e.g.
"he was not keen to learn"). The subjects' recall of the continuation passage showed that the relative amounts of achievement and
motivation information recalled varied according to which priming
passage the subjects had received. In the grossly inconsistent
negative prime condition, subjects showed biassed memory for the
positive achievement information from the continuation passage -
they seemed to retain the most recent conflicting information. In
the negative prime condition, the priming passage itself was also
poorly remembered: an effect that Wilkes et al. attribute to the
subjects' preference for maintaining the more recent of two sets
of conflicting information (in this case, the positive achievement
information).

In the present experiment, it was predicted that, if afternoon subjects are actively trying to integrate the ideas in a text,
then the selective remembering of inconsistent information from
the continuation passage should be particularly marked for the subjects tested in the afternoon. Similarly, if they tend to retain
the inconsistent information, the afternoon subjects would be expected to show a more marked tendency to forget the grossly inconsistent
negative prime passage.

Method

        60 subjects were randomly assigned to time-of-day and pri-
ming passage groups. Testing took place either between 9 and 10am,
or between 5 and 6pm. The passages used in this experiment were
identical to those used by Wilkes et al. except that the Scottish
term 'highers' in the prime passages was changed to its English
equivalent: 'A levels'. The subjects were told to expect a recall
test. They were allowed two minutes to read the entire text, and
were then presented immediately with a recall test appropriate to
their priming condition, in which they had to fill in the missing
information in a skeletal version of the passage.

Results

        A gist recall criterion was adopted so that items which
were close approximations of the meaning, or actually retained the
same wording were scored as correct. The subjects' responses were
scored independently by two raters, and any disagreements were resolved by discussion. The mean proportion recall for each class
of response is shown in Table 2.

TABLE 2: The mean proportions of statements correctly recalled in
each category as a function of type of priming passage and time-
of-day.

| | Priming passage | Continuation passage | |
		Achievement	Motivation
MORNING: pos. prime	73.8	51.2	58.9
negative prime	66.7	61.1	42.9
AFTERNOON: pos. prime	68.8	47.9	47.9
negative prime	52.7	55.5	33.9

An analysis of the proportions correct showed a main effect of time
of day, $F(1,55)$ = 4.25, $p < .05$: morning subjects recalled more of
the missing information. The pattern of recall was similar to that
reported by Wilkes et al. There was an interaction between type
of prime and information recalled, $F(2,110)$ = 7.55, $p < .001$. This
interaction indicates that the pattern of recall of information
from the priming passage and the two categories in the continuation
passage varied with type of priming passage. These effects will
be looked at in more detail in the separate analyses of the prime
and continuation passages, below.

        The overall recall scores were examined in more detail
by looking at the verbatim and gist only components of recall in
two separate analyses. In the first analysis, the number of items
correctly recalled using a strict verbatim criterion showed that
the subjects tested in the morning more often recalled the exact
wording (mean recall = 2.44 items) than did afternoon subjects (mean
recall = 1.61 items), and this difference was significant, $F(1,55)$
= 5.14, $p < .05$. Verbatim recall did not vary as a function of type
of priming passage and type of prime and time of day did not interact. In the second analysis, the gist only component of recall
was assessed. Gist only recall was determined by subtracting verbatim recall from overall recall. In this analysis, there was no
main effect of time of day ($p > .10$). Thus, the superiority of the
morning subjects can be accounted for in terms of their superior

recall of the exact wording of the missing items.

An analysis of the data from the priming passage alone showed a main effect of type of prime, $F(1,55) = 5.77$, $p < .02$; positive information was better recalled. There was also a marginal main effect of time of day: $F(1,55) = 3.89$, $p = .054$. As in the overall analysis, subjects tested in the morning tended to recall more of the missing information than did those tested in the afternoon. An analysis of the data from the continuation passage showed that achievement information was better recalled than motivation information, $F(1,55) = 7.0$, $p < .02$. There was also an interaction between type of information in the continuation passage (achievement/motivation) and prime (positive/negative): $F(1,55) = 15.25$, $p < .003$. These results replicate those reported by Wilkes et al. (1983), except that there was no overall effect of priming passage on recall in the present study. However, there was no control (no priming) condition in the present experiment, and this seems to have accounted for a large part of the main effect in Wilkes et al.'s data.

Discussion

The findings from the present experiment replicate those of Wilkes et al. and also support the claim that memory for information in text is superior in the early morning than in the late afternoon (e.g. Folkard et al., 1977; Folkard and Monk, 1980). However, unlike the earlier studies, the present study has shown that this morning superiority in memory for information in text can be accounted for entirely in terms of better verbatim memory.

The two main predictions, arising from the hypothesis that morning and afternoon subjects should show different patterns of text integration, were not confirmed, although the data showed trends in the right direction. The absence of any evidence that morning and afternoon subjects are integrating information to different degrees argues against the idea that afternoon subjects take a more constructive, meaning-based approach to reading text. However, it may be that the inconsistencies in the present passages were so blatant that subjects could not help but be alerted to them. A more subtle test of text integration in morning and afternoon subjects may show differences even though the present one has failed to do so. Indeed, an experiment which used a different paradigm to explore text integration at different times of day suggests that it is not so much the type or amount of processing that varies between morning and afternoon subjects, but when they do such processing. This experiment will be reported only very briefly, as it has been published elsewhere (Oakhill, 1986b).

EXPERIMENT 3

This experiment used the self-paced reading technique to explore subjects' integrative processing of short texts at different times of day (again, early morning and late afternoon). The subjects were presented with a series of short texts, and had to answer a question about each. The difficulty of the passages was manipulated by including pronouns which could either be resolved syntactically (gender cue condition), or required an inference to determine their referent. A further factor in this experiment was the type of questions that subjects were asked about the passages. In one condition, the questions could not be answered unless the subjects

sights into changes over the day in a way that memory tests given
after a passage has been presented cannot. The first two experiments
suggest that the morning subjects' immediate memory advantage may
arise because of their superior verbatim memory, and the third experiment suggests that the afternoon subjects' superior long-term
memory may arise because they spend more time than morning subjects
integrating the ideas in a text as they are reading. If subjects
in the morning process longer texts in this relatively superficial
manner, and do not integrate the ideas in a text as they are reading,
their understanding of and long-term memory for the text is likely
to suffer. However, such hypotheses need further testing. These
experiments suggest that it would be fruitful to investigate the
time that morning and afternoon subjects take to retrieve literal
and inferential information from text. If subjects tested in the
morning tend to make text-connecting inferences retrospectively,
at the time of test rather than at the time of presentation, then
the difference in their retrieval time for literal and inferential
information should be larger than that for the afternoon group.
Differences in the locus of inferential and integrative processes
may have little effect on immediate recognition (hence the similar
recognition performance of morning and afternoon subjects in Experiment 1, above), but may affect delayed recall (Folkard et al., 1977;
Oakhill, 1986a).

REFERENCES

Folkard, S. (1980). 'Time of day and level of processing'. Memory
and Cognition, 7, 247-252.

Folkard, S. (1980). '"Time of day effects in school children's immediate and delayed recall of meaningful material" - the influence
of the importance of the information tested'. British Journal of
Psychology, 71, 95-97.

Folkard, S. and Monk, T.H. (1980). 'Circadian rhythms in human
memory'. British Journal of Psychology, 71, 295-307.

Folkard, S., Monk, T.H., Bradbury, R. and Rosenthall, J. (1977).
'Time of day effects in school children's immediate and delayed
recall of meaningful material'. British Journal of Psychology, 68,
45-50.

Laird, D.A. (1925). 'Relative performance of college students as
conditioned by time of day and day of week'. Journal of Experimental
Psychology, 8, 50-63.

Meyer, B.J.F. (1975). The Organisation of Prose and Its Effects
on Memory, Oxford, North Holland.

Oakhill, J.V. (1986a). 'Effects of time of day, and information
importance on adults' memory for a short story'. Quarterly Journal
of Experimental Psychology, 38A, 419-430.

Oakhill, J.V. (1986b). 'Effects of time of day on the integration
of information in text'. British Journal of Psychology, 77, 481 -
488.

Wilkes, A.L., Alred, G. and Al-Ahmar, H. (1983). 'Reading strategies
and the integration of information as indicated by recall and reading
times'. Quarterly Journal of Experimental Psychology, 35A, 65-77.

THE EFFECTS OF TIME OF DAY ON RECALL FROM EXPOSITORY TEXT

Maureen Marks and Simon Folkard

MRC Perceptual and Cognitive Performance Unit, Laboratory of Experimental Psychology, University of Sussex, Brighton, BN1 9QG.

ABSTRACT

Two studies are reported which investigated the effect of time of day on recall of information from lectures. There was no effect on the amount of information recalled. Presentation in the early evening resulted in delayed (one week) recall of more important information than did morning presentation. In addition, when continuities in the text were disrupted, text structure was reflected in the pattern of delayed recall after presentation in the evening but not after morning presentation. The results are attributed to differences over the day in the way subjects encode expository material.

INTRODUCTION

The evidence suggests that text presented early in the day will be better remembered in the short term than if it is presented in the afternoon or evening. With some delay, however, more trivial information is forgotten such that original presentation in the morning is associated with impaired delayed recall of important information compared to presentation in the afternoon (see Jane Oakhill's chapter for a review). This suggests that if we want the most important information remembered then the afternoon or evening may be the best time for learning. However, the studies on which these conclusions are based involved memory for a story. Stories tend to have a typical, traditional structure. Important information tends to be 'important' because of its position in this structure. Whether similar effects of time of presentation would occur when the text to be remembered is in a form other than that of a story, for example expository text, is not clear.

The purpose of the two studies reported here was to investigate time of day effects on the recall of expository text. Folkard and Monk, 1980, examined the immediate recall of information from New Scientist articles read for three minutes at six different times (0800 to 2300 hrs) and found this declined over the day. Similarly, Gunter et al., 1983, observed a decline in the immediate recall of television news information across three times of presentation (0900, 1400, 1700). They also compared recall of material which conveyed the 'central meaning' of the news item with recall of less important support content. In contrast to these findings from story memory experiments, recall of the former declined over the day whereas there was no effect of time of presentation on the latter.

In these studies the material to be remembered did not constitute a complete structure: three minutes of text read and six short separate news items lasting a total of seven minutes. We wanted to investigate time of day effects on recall from a complete, extended text. We also wished to examine whether the importance of expository material had interactive effects with time of presentation similar to the effects observed with story memory. In one of the studies reported here we presented a lecture constructed especially for the experiment. This consisted of a sequence of factual information (50 minutes). In the second study we used an old BBC Reith lecture (30 minutes). Finally, we also examined the effects of the temporal position of the information presented by counterbalancing the order in which the material to be learned was heard and then comparing recall from the first and second half of each lecture.

METHOD

Materials

The lecture developed for Experiment I consisted of a one-minute introduction and conclusion and six sub-sections of approximately seven-and-a-half minutes each. A BBC Reith lecture, 'The First Years', lasting 28.5 minutes, was used in Experiment II. This was split into two sub-sections and a reversed version, in which the last half of the original lecture came first, was produced.

For each lecture a pool of four-choice questions was developed and measures of the importance of the information in the lecture to which each question referred was obtained from judges' ratings. There was a significant degree of concordance between judges' ratings (W=.50, p<.001 Experiment I; W=.60, p<.001 Experiment II). Questionnaires were constructed such that questions from each section of each lecture were balanced for importance.

There were 48 subjects in each experiment. For each experiment half the subjects were tested in the morning (0900 hrs), half in the evening (1800 hrs Experiment I; 1700 hrs Experiment II). In Experiment I presentation order of the six sub-sections constituting the lecture was counterbalanced across six groups of four subjects at each presentation time. In Experiment II, 12 subjects heard the original lecture and 12 the reversed version at each presentation time. Questionnaires were also counterbalanced within each group across immediate and delayed tests. Subjects received a version of the questionnaire with questions in the same order as the lecture they heard.

Subjects listened to the lecture over headphones and as soon as the lecture had finished completed the immediate questionnaire. One week later, at the same time of day at which their immediate test took place, subjects completed the appropriate delayed memory questionnaire.

In Experiment II, after subjects had completed the immediate test they were asked to indicate how coherent they thought the lecture was by giving a rating of from 1 (incoherent) to 7 (coherent) and after the delayed (one week) test to rate on a scale

of 1 - 7 whether they thought they had heard the reversed (1) or
original (7) version.

Results Experiment I

Mean scores are summarised in Table 1. There was a main
effect of delay (F(1,36) = 59.26, p < .001). Subjects remembered
more in the immediate than in the delayed test. There was a main
effect of importance (F(1,36) = 13.38, p < .001). Subjects remembered
more important compared to unimportant information.

TABLE 1: Experiment I

Effects of time of presentation and temporal position on immediate
and delayed recall as a function of importance (out of a possible
12).

		1st half		2nd half	
		high	low	high	low
	0900	7.04	7.04	6.83	6.46
Immediate					
	1800	7.75	6.75	6.71	6.83
		----	----	----	----
		7.40	6.90	6.77	6.55
		----	----	----	----
		7.15		6.71	
		----		----	
	0900	5.79	5.04	5.88	5.58
Delayed					
	1800	6.29	4.92	6.17	5.33
		----	----	----	----
		6.04	4.98	6.03	5.46
		----	----	----	----
		5.51		5.75	
		----		----	

There was no interaction between time of presentation and
importance on immediate and delayed scores combined, nor when immediate and delayed scores were analysed separately. The effect of
importance was reliable for delayed scores only (F(1,36) = 11.41,
p=.002). Further analyses indicated that the importance effect
was significant for the evening group's delayed scores (F(1,18)
= 8.90, p < .01) but did not reach statistical significance for the
morning group's immediate or delayed results nor for the evening
group's immediate results.

We also compared performance on the first half of the lecture with the second half. Sub-analyses indicated that effects
of importance were limited to delayed recall from the first half
of the lecture (F(1,36) = 13.07, p < .001). Importance did not affect
recall from the second half. Delayed recall from the first half
of the lecture was a function of importance if the lecture had been
presented at 1800 hrs (F(1,18) = 10.11, p=.005). After 0900 hrs
presentation the effect of importance on delayed recall from the
first half of the lecture did not quite reach statistical significance (F(1,18) = 3.55, p < .08). These effects were not present

in immediate scores.

      To summarise, delayed recall from the first half of the lecture was a function of importance whereas subjects recalled equally well both important and unimportant information from the second half. This effect was most pronounced after evening presentation. It did not reach statistical significance in the morning group. Nor were these effects present in immediate recall scores.

      The lecture used here had little real continuity between the six sub-sections which made up the complete text. Any organisation of this text in terms of importance must have been imposed by the subjects themselves. This suggests that differences in the effect of presentation time on recall of important compared to unimportant material may be something to do with differences over the day in the way subjects organise input. When the material to be remembered is a story, the text tends to be structured in a stereotypical way. This may also be true of a well written lecture. The results from Experiment II describe the effects of time of presentation and temporal position when a more realistic lecture is learned.

Results Experiment II

      Mean scores are summarised in Table 2. Subjects remembered more important than unimportant information ($F(1,44) = 6.95$, p=.01). There was an interaction between delay of recall and the importance of information ($F(1,44) = 8.01$, p=.007). As can be seen from Table 2, importance did not affect immediate recall but in the delayed test subjects remembered more important than unimportant information. This difference was significant for both morning and evening presentation groups' delayed recall ($F(1,20) = 8.02$, p=.01 and $F(1,20) = 5.23$, p=.03 respectively).

Table 2: Experiment II

Effects of time of presentation and temporal position on immediate and delayed recall as a function of importance (out of a possible 4).

		1st half		2nd half	
		high	low	high	low
	0900	3.00	2.88	2.71	2.75
Immediate					
	1700	2.83	2.96	2.92	2.96
		----	----	----	----
		2.91	2.92	2.82	2.86
		----	----	----	----
			2.92		2.84
			----		----
	0900	2.21	2.17	2.50	1.75
Delayed					
	1700	2.33	1.83	2.42	2.13
		----	----	----	----
		2.27	2.00	2.46	1.94
		----	----	----	----
			2.14		2.20
			----		----

Time of presentation and temporal position did not interact with the importance of information to be remembered, nor with importance and delay of recall.

Reversing the lecture did not affect overall recall, nor subjects' perception of its coherence. Recall was equally good from the reversed as from the original lecture. In addition, analyses of ratings made by the subjects indicated that there was no difference between the two groups (original and reversed lecture) in their perception of how coherent the lecture was, nor was there any difference in their ratings as to how certain they were that they had been presented with a reversed lecture. Nonetheless, separate analyses of delayed recall from each version of the lecture at each testing time (see Table 3) indicated that there was a significant interaction between temporal position and importance in the recall of subjects who heard the reversed lecture at 1700 hrs $(F(1,10) = 11.97$, p=.006) but no interaction after presentation at 0900 hrs $(F<1)$. The three way interaction between time of presentation, temporal position and importance was marginally significant $(F(1,20) = 3.95$, p=.06). This effect was not present in scores from the original lecture $(F<1)$.

TABLE 3: Experiment II

Effects of time of presentation, temporal position and importance on delayed recall from each version of the lecture (out of a possible 4).

		1st half		2nd half	
		high	low	high	low
Ordinary	0900	2.00	2.50	2.67	1.75
	1700	1.67	1.83	2.92	2.17
Reversed	0900	2.42	1.83	2.33	1.75
	1700	3.00	1.83	1.92	2.08

This finding suggests that perhaps in the evening subjects are more affected by structural properties of text.

DISCUSSION

In both these experiments, while there was no effect of time of presentation on overall immediate or delayed recall, in general, subjects who heard the lectures in the late afternoon were more likely to remember the more important information after some delay than were subjects who heard the lectures in the morning.

Subjects (and judges) ordered the material into more and less importance whether or not a hierarchy was implied by the lecture content. The lecture in Experiment I consisted of a series of six sub-topics which were related to each other only in that they referred to the same country. In effect, there was no real structure, and yet delayed recall was a function of importance. This was particularly so for recall from the first half of the lec-

ture and for those subjects who originally heard the lecture in
the evening. When the lecture was structured (Experiment II), the
structure of the content, rather than temporal position, determined
the delayed recall of important vs unimportant information from
each half of the lecture. Furthermore, the pattern of delayed recall, across temporal position, of important compared to unimportant
information was more likely to reflect the content of the lecture
when subjects had listened to the lecture in the evening than if
they heard it in the morning, and especially when continuities in
the text had been disrupted (by reversing the order in which the
content was represented).

        One explanation for these findings is that in the afternoon
subjects are more likely to engage in effortful processing. This
might mean that when expected continuities are missing or distorted,
subjects notice something is wrong and attempt to provide the missing continuities themselves. Oakhill (1986) has shown that afternoon subjects dealt with referential difficulties in short texts
as they were reading them, whereas in the morning they tended to
leave the necessary processing until later. When the material to
be learned consists of longer text, such as that used in the lectures of the experiments reported here, then one of the consequences
of the less effortful encoding strategy used by morning subjects
might be a reduced ability to encode the text structure especially
if this is ambiguous.

REFERENCES

Folkard, S. and Monk, T.H. (1980). 'Circadian rhythms in human
memory'. British Journal of Psychology, 71, 295-307.

Gunter, B., Jarrett, J. and Furnham, A. (1983). 'Time of day effects
on immediate memory for television news'. Learning, 2, 261-267.

Oakhill, J.V. (1986). 'Effects of time of day on the integration
of information in text'. British Journal of Psychology, 77, 481-
488.

EFFECTS OF MEALS ON MEMORY AND ATTENTION

Andrew Smith

MRC Perceptual and Cognitive Performance Unit, Laboratory of Experimental Psychology, University of Sussex, Brighton, BN1 9QG, Sussex, England.

ABSTRACT

Two lines of research are described in this paper. The first showed that working memory tasks were performed more slowly after meals in the middle of the day and night but were unaffected by breakfast. Results from another study showed that delayed recall of a story was worse after lunch than before. These results have important implications for operational efficiency and safety, and for educational schedules.

INTRODUCTION

There is considerable evidence of diurnal variation in performance (see Folkard, 1983), which may reflect the endogenous rhythms that have been demonstrated in many physiological processes. However, certain time of day effects may be produced by exogenous factors which are associated with particular times. The most widely studied example of this type of time of day effect is the post-lunch dip, with post-lunch impairments in efficiency being observed both in the laboratory and in real-life settings.

Some researchers have argued that even post-lunch impairments may reflect endogenous rhythms, although there are recent studies which have shown that some performance impairments do depend on eating the meal. Smith and Miles (1986a) obtained effects which were dependent upon consumption of lunch, but they also found other differences between late morning and early afternoon which were observed even when subjects abstained from lunch. Indeed, it would appear that the post-lunch dip has both an endogenous and a food-related component.

Craig (1986) has suggested that post-lunch impairments are most likely to be observed if the tasks require sustained attention. This implies that short duration tasks will not show effects. However, Smith and Miles (1986b) used a memory-loaded vigilance task and they obtained post-lunch impairments which were observable in the first minute of the task. Similarly, Smith and Miles (1987) found that times to complete a high-memory load search task were slower after meals even though the task lasted for less than five minutes.

At the moment it is unclear whether the post-meal impairments observed with the cognitive vigilance and search and memory tasks are due to the memory load, the rate at which new stimuli have to be processed, or to a combination of these factors. As Smith and Miles (1987) found no post-meal impairment in performance of a low-memory load search task it would appear that a memory load is necessary to demonstrate such effects in short duration tasks. One must now ask whether post-meal impairments are observed when working memory is involved but stimuli are processed more slowly and there is a less rapid input of new stimuli. This issue was examined here by investigating whether there are post-meal impairments in the speed and accuracy of logical reasoning.

Experiment 1:

Data are presented here from a logical reasoning task performed before and after a meal taken in the middle of a day shift (09.00 - 17.00) and night shift (22.00 - 06.00). Details of the study are given in Smith and Miles (1987). The main features can be summarised as follows:

Each subject was tested both in the day and at night (the two sessions being approximately one week apart), with half the subjects attending in the order day/night and the others in the order night/day. Half the subjects were tested in noise (75dBA) and the other half in quiet (40dBA). The subjects were 24 students from the University of Sussex.

Nature of the meal: a light snack consisting of soup, sandwiches, and fruit (in the region of 600 - 700 calories).

The task: the logical reasoning task involved verifying statements ranging in complexity from simple active to passive negative. The time taken to do 64 such statements was recorded.

Results

Table 1 shows the mean times and mean number of errors for the pre- and post-meal tests in the day and night.

Table 1
Mean speed and accuracy scores for the logical reasoning test.

	Day		Night	
	Pre-meal (12.00)	Post-meal (13.30)	Pre-meal (01.00)	Post-meal (02.30)
Time	204.5 sec	213.1	192.6	205.7
Errors	1.54	1.67	1.17	1.50

These results show that performance was worse after the meal, and the effect on speed was significant $(F(1,20) = 3.3, p<0.05, 1\text{-tail})$, although the level of significance was only acceptable for a confirmatory result. The pre-post meal difference in accuracy was not significant $(F(1,20) = 1.1, p>0.05)$. In contrast to the results of Smith and Miles (1987) there was no evidence of noise reducing the extent of the post-meal decline in speed (noise x pre-post: $F <1$). The task was performed faster at night $(F(1,20) = 4.62, p<0.05)$, but the interaction between day/night and pre-post times was not significant $(F<1)$.

Discussion

Performance on the logical reasoning test was slower and less accurate after meals both in the day and night. The absence of a 'no meal' condition makes it impossible to say whether this effect is entirely due to consumption of the meal. However, there are two reasons for believing that the effect reported here may reflect factors other than food. Smith and Miles (1986b) present evidence which suggests that noise and food influence the same mechanisms, and in the present study noise did not modify the post-meal decline in speed. Folkard (1983) concludes that performance on tasks like logical reasoning peaks at mid-day. If such time of day effects reflect endogenous rhythms, then one would expect performance to be worse in the early afternoon than in the morning irrespective of whether lunch was consumed or not.

A further study with 'food' and 'no food' conditions is needed to clarify this issue. Such a design was used in the next experiment to assess the effect of breakfast on performance of working memory tasks.

Experiment 2:

It is difficult to draw firm conclusions about the influence of breakfast on performance because there have not really been enough well-designed studies of the topic (see Craig, 1986). However, there are studies which suggest that breakfast has a beneficial effect on performance, although these benefits may only appear 2 - 3 hours after the breakfast was eaten. The present study examined whether breakfast influenced performance on search and memory and logical reasoning tasks.

Method

Subjects were assigned to either the 'breakfast' or 'no breakfast' conditions. Each subject carried out the performance tests at 8.30, 9.15 and 11.00. Breakfast was eaten between 8.45 and 9.15 and subjects were not informed which condition they were in until that time. Breakfast consisted of cereal (+ milk and sugar), toast (+ butter, jam or marmalade), and tea or coffee. The breakfast contained about 600 calories. Subjects in the 'no breakfast' condition were allowed tea or coffee between 8.45 and 9.15.

Subjects: The subjects were 21 students from the University of Sussex. There were 13 in the 'breakfast' condition and eight in the 'no breakfast' condition.

Tasks: (1) Logical reasoning - as in previous study but there were only 32 statements per test. (2) Search and memory task - this involved searching through six lines of single spaced pseudo-random capital letters looking for the presence of any five target letters defined at the start of the line. When subjects detected targets they crossed them out.

Results

Breakfast was found to have a beneficial effect in that alertness (rated on a visual analogue scale) increased more rapidly for the 'breakfast' subjects than those in the 'no breakfast' condition (Breakfast x Times interaction: $F(2,17) = 5.06$, $p<0.05$). Mean ratings - the higher the score the greater the alertness:

Breakfast:	8.30:	38.7	9.15:	60.2	11.00:	71.8
No breakfast:	8.30:	42.6	9.15:	51.2	11.00:	58.2

There was no evidence that consumption of breakfast influ-

enced performance. Both 'breakfast' and 'no breakfast' groups became
significantly faster at the tests on successive times (main effect
of times: Logical reasoning - $F(2,32)$ = 9.66, p< 0.001: Search and
memory - $F(2,32)$ = 11.55, p< 0.0005). The mean speeds at the different testing times are shown below:

Logical reasoning: 8.30:   183.0 sec   9.15: 162.0   11.00: 144.0
Search and memory: 8.30:   175.9 sec   9.15: 161.5   11.00: 141.0

The logical reasoning task was performed more accurately at 9.15
(mean errors = 1.0) than 8.30 (mean errors = 2.2) but then accuracy
decreased at 11.00 (mean errors = 1.9). The main effect of times
was significant ($F(2,32)$ = 3.49, p<0.05). In contrast to this, the
search and memory task was performed less accurately at 9.15 (mean
% errors = 31.7) than the other times (8.30 = 25.9%; 11.00 = 28.8%),
although the main effect of time of testing was not significant
(p>0.05).

Discussion

The experiment failed to demonstrate any effects of breakfast on the two working memory tasks, either immediately after breakfast or nearly two hours later. This negative result is not due
to the total absence of any effect of eating breakfast, for it was
found that breakfast influenced alertness.

This result, taken together with those of Smith and Miles
(1987) and Experiment 1, leads to the following conclusions about
the effects of meals on working memory:
(1) Tasks with a rapid input of new signals and a high memory load
are performed more slowly after meals in the middle of the day and
night but are unaffected by breakfast.
(2) The same pattern of results is obtained with a logical reasoning
task. While the post-meal impairments found with the search task
are probably food-dependent, it is likely that the post-meal change
in reasoning speed reflects endogenous factors rather than an influence of food. Further studies with 'food' and 'no food' conditions
are needed to clarify this issue.

The third study reported here was a study of the effects
of lunch on story recall. It has already been shown that there are
post-lunch impairments in tasks requiring sustained attention, which
leads one to predict that activities such as comprehension and recall
of a story would also be impaired after lunch. At the moment it
is unclear whether lunch produces a general impairment in attention
(perhaps due to a reduction in capacity), or whether some aspects
are attended to at the expense of others. Oakhill (1986) has shown
that the recall of important versus unimportant information from
a story may be used to infer the way in which attentional strategies
are used to encode the information in a story. She found superior
delayed recall of important information following afternoon presentation. Experiment 3 used Oakhill's technique to examine whether
recall of a story is different in the late morning and early afternoon.

Experiment 3:

This experiment was essentially very similar to that reported by Oakhill (1986) except that subjects were either tested
before lunch (between 11.00 and 12.00) or after lunch (between 13.30

and 14.30). Recall was always at the same time of day as presentation.
        The story was the same as that used by Oakhill and recall
was assessed by the multiple-choice questionnaire used by her. Subjects were either given the questionnaire immediately after the story
had finished (the immediate recall condition) or five days later
(the delayed recall condition). All of the factors (pre- v post-
lunch; immediate v delayed) were varied between subjects.
The meal: A three-course lunch of approximately 1500 calories.
Subjects: 47 subjects were tested and there were approximately equal
numbers of male and female subjects in the various conditions.

Results

        The mean percentage of correct answers in the various con-
ditions are shown in Table 2.

Table 2
Mean recall scores in the various conditions in Experiment 3.

	Immediate Recall		Delayed Recall	
	Pre-lunch	Post-lunch	Pre-lunch	Post-lunch
Important information:	88.3%	88.4	82.1	60.2
Unimportant information:	66.7	65.2	42.9	34.1

        It can be seen that there was very little difference be-
tween the pre- and post-lunch groups in the immediate recall condition. However, performance was worse after lunch in the delayed
condition. Numerically, the difference between the two times was
greater for the important items than the unimportant ones, but the
only significant effect was the main effect of pre/post times
$(F(1,16) = 4.01, p<0.05, 1\text{-tail})$, and the level of significance was
only acceptable for confirming the prediction that performance would
be worse after lunch.

Discussion

        The present study showed a post-lunch impairment in delayed
recall of both important and unimportant information. This suggests
that lunch produces a global impairment rather than leading to the
adoption of certain attentional strategies in preference to others.
        This result shows that post-lunch effects differ from the
time of day effects obtained in studies comparing early morning and
late afternoon (Oakhill found a late afternoon superiority for delayed recall of important information but better recall of unimportant information earlier in the day). This has been observed before,
with Smith (1987) finding no difference between early morning and
late afternoon performance on the Bakan vigilance task, but Smith and
Miles (1986b) demonstrating post-lunch impairments with the same
task.

CONCLUSIONS

        The studies reported in this paper suggest differences in
performance before and after meals, except for breakfast. It appears
that some effects depend on ingestion of food and future research

will have to assess the importance of factors such as the size and nutritional content of the meals. Other effects probably reflect an endogenous circadian component and further studies with appropriate 'food' and 'no food' conditions will clarify this. Post-meal impairments are often qualitatively different from other time of day effects and further study of them is required as they have important implications for educational schedules and for operational efficiency and safety.

REFERENCES

Craig, A. (1986). 'Acute effects of meals on perceptual and cognitive efficiency', Nutrition Reviews, 44, Supplement/Diet and Behavior: A multidisciplinary evaluation, 163-171.

Folkard, S. (1983). 'Diurnal variation', in Stress and Fatigue in Human Performance (Ed. G.R.J. Hockey), pp. 245-272, Wiley, Chichester.

Oakhill, J. (1986). 'Effects of time of day and information importance on adults' memory for a short story', Quarterly Journal of Experimental Psychology, 38A, 419-430.

Smith, A.P. (1987). 'Task-related motivation and time of testing', in Advances in Test Anxiety Research, Vol.5, (Eds. R. Schwarzer, H.M. van der Ploeg and C.D. Spielberger), pp. 115-123, Swets, Zeitlinger, Lisse.

Smith, A.P. and Miles, C. (1986a). 'Effects of lunch on cognitive vigilance tasks', Ergonomics, 29, 1251-1261.

Smith, A.P. and Miles, C. (1986b). 'Acute effects of meals, noise and nightwork', British Journal of Psychology, 77, 377-389.

Smith, A.P. and Miles, C. (1987). 'The combined effects of occupational health hazards: An experimental investigation of the effects of noise, nightwork and meals', International Archives of Occupational and Environmental Health, 59, 83-89.

TIME OF DAY AND SHORT TERM MEMORY: EVIDENCE FROM STUDIES OF INDIVIDUAL DIFFERENCES

G Matthews
Applied Psychology Group, Aston University, Birmingham, England
D M Jones and A G Chamberlain
Department of Applied Psychology
University of Wales Institute of Science and Technology,
Cardiff, Wales

ABSTRACT

A study of the effects of time of day, extraversion and self-report arousal on immediate recall of visually presented digit strings is reported. Recall was generally better in the evening, though this main effect was modified by interactive effects of extraversion and arousal. It is suggested that inconsistencies in research on circadian rhythms in short term memory may result from the operation of two separate mechanisms. Memory tasks sensitive to subvocal rehearsal may show a morning peak in performance, whereas tasks sensitive to item identification speed may show an evening peak. Task parameters appear to determine which mechanism is dominant in determining the performance of any given task.

It is often claimed that short term retention of information is better in the morning than in the evening. A recent review of the area (Marks & Folkard, 1985) suggests the following conclusions. Immediate recall of digit strings, word lists and prose passages tends to be poorer in the evening than in the morning. More complex tasks with a memory load component also show a relatively early circadian peak in performance. Three mechanisms have been proposed to account for these data. Higher arousal in the evening may impair short term memory (STM), there may be greater use of the articulatory loop in the morning, and there may be changes in strategy over the course of the day.

However, some evidence is inconsistent with typical findings. For example, Jones, Davies, Hogan, Patrick and Cumberbatch (1978) have demonstrated superior performance on the immediate recall of visually presented word lists at 1600 hours compared with performance at 1000 hours. Jones et al. suggest that task factors may affect circadian rhythms in short term memory. They claim that an evening peak in STM is more likely to be found with visual rather than auditory presentation, slow presentation rate, and recency rather than pre-recency items.

If task characteristics are important in predicting circadian trends in STM, so too may be individual differences. Some individuals may improve in STM in the evening, while others may perform more poorly. Individual difference variables which stand out as possible predictors of circadian effects on STM are the correlated extraversion and impulsivity personality traits, and the more transient state of arousal. It appears that on verbal

ability   tasks, which probably   have   a STM   component,   high
impulsivity   subjects perform better in the morning under the
stimulant   drug caffeine but perform better with a placebo in the
evening.   Low impulsivity subjects show the opposite pattern   of
interaction (see Humphreys & Revelle, 1984).

        One   explanation of these individual differences in the
effects   of time of day on performance is provided by the processing
resource   model of Humphreys and Revelle (1984). They claim   that
high arousal increases the availability of resources used for   the
sustained   throughput of information, but reduces resources used for
STM.   For complex tasks, such as verbal ability tests,   requiring
both   types   of resource, they derive the familiar inverted   U
relationship   between arousal and performance. Interactive effects
of   time of day, extraversion/impulsivity and arousal   manipulations
on   performance can then be predicted from the differing   arousal
levels   of different personality groups. High impulsives/extraverts
are   relatively   more   aroused   in   the   evening, but   low
impulsives/introverts   are relatively more aroused in the morning.
With a pure STM task however, the model predicts a simple monotonic
and detrimental effect of arousal on performance.

        A   different approach to explaining individual differences
in   circadian changes in performance is derived from research   by
Matthews (1985). This study showed an interactive effect of   time
of   day, extraversion and self-report arousal on verbal ability
similar   to the time of day x impulsivity x manipulated   arousal
interaction   discussed by Humphreys and Revelle (1984).   The
interaction   of extraversion with directly measured arousal here
implies that the regression of performance on arousal varies   with
extraversion and time of day. Further research (Matthews,   1987a)
on   sustained attention suggests that extraversion and   arousal
interactively   affect relatively low-level processes of   data
encoding   and/or information transmission. If such   processes
generalise   to STM tasks, interactive effects on STM similar   to
those found by Matthews (1985) might be expected.

        The experiment reported here tested effects of time of day,
extraversion   and self-report arousal on immediate recall. The aim
of   the study was to test three hypotheses concerning the role of
arousal   in effects of time of day on STM, and   individual
differences in such effects. Predictions were derived as follows.

        Hypothesis 1: Time of day effects on STM are mediated   by
arousal. This hypothesis predicts (a) a main effect of arousal on
STM,   with high arousal impairing recall, and (b) higher arousal at
the time of day at which performance is poorer.

        Hypothesis 2:   Individual differences in the effects of
time   of day on STM are mediated by arousal. The Humphreys and
Revelle (1984) model predicts that individuals high in arousal at a
given   time of day should also show poor immediate memory.   In
particular, if the correlation between extraversion and arousal
depends   on time of day in the way that the Humphreys and Revelle
model suggests, introverts should show poorer STM in the   morning,
whereas   extraverts should show poorer STM in the evening. In an
analysis   including a direct measure of arousal, this effect will be
expressed   in changes in the composition of high and low   arousal
groups   at each time of day. That is, an interactive effect of time

of day and extraversion on arousal is predicted.

Hypothesis 3: Individual differences in the effects of time of day on STM are interactively dependent on both extraversion and arousal. This hypothesis is derived from the view that time of day and extraversion control the effects of arousal on basic information processing functions (Matthews, 1987a). If STM and attentional tasks share such functions, then time of day, extraversion and arousal will affect STM interactively. In particular high arousal extraverts and low arousal introverts should perform worse in the evening than in the morning, whereas the other two groups should improve with later time of day.

METHOD

Subjects were 45 men and 71 women, participants in a keyboard training course at the University of Wales Institute of Science and Technology. Median age was 31. Subjects performed a series of tasks at either 1000 hours or 2200 hours. The tasks included the EPI (Eysenck & Eysenck, 1964), the UWIST Mood Adjective Checklist (UMACL: see Matthews, 1987b), and the HPRG Test Battery (Jones & Chamberlain, 1986). The latter comprises six cognitive tasks, including digit span. In the digit span task, thirty nine-digit strings were presented on a VDU, at a rate of 1 item/second. Immediately following presentation, subjects were required to write down each digit string in the order in which it was presented. Digit span data were scored as the mean error probability per item. The individual difference variables measured were EPI extraversion, and the energetic arousal scale of the UMACL, which contrasts vigour with fatigue. Self-report arousal scales correlate positively with physiological measures of arousal (Matthews, 1987b).

RESULTS

As a preliminary analysis, we tested effects of time of day and extraversion on arousal. Extraverts were significantly higher in arousal, at both times of day (P<.01), though the magnitude of the main effect was small (omega2 = 0.05). The main ANOVA tested effects of time of day, and median-split factors of extraversion and arousal on mean error probability/item. Cell numbers were unequal, but there were at least 9 subjects/cell. Effects of the independent variables on digit span errors are shown in Figure 1. The overall mean and standard deviation of error probability were showed that error probability was higher in the morning (F(1,103)=6.2, P<.05), and in subjects high in arousal (F(1,103)=4.2, P<.05). However these main effects were modified by the following interactions: time of day x extraversion (F(1,103)=5.0, P<.05), time of day x arousal (F(1,103)=4.2, P<.05), and time of day x extraversion x arousal (F(1,103)=4.0, P<.05). Inspection of Figure 1 suggests that high arousal was only generally detrimental to performance in the morning, and only extraverts reliably performed better in the evening. The triple interaction was due to the detrimental effects of arousal in the morning being stronger in introverts than in extraverts, whereas the evening data showed a cross-over. Introverts benefited from high arousal, but high arousal impaired performance in extraverts.

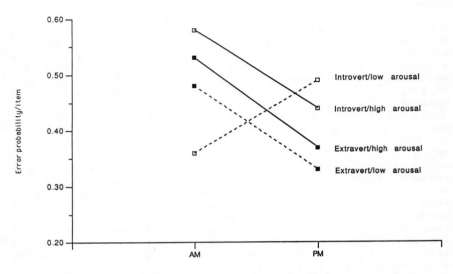

Fig. 1 Mean probability of recall failure in digit span task as a function of time of day, extraversion and self-report arousal.

DISCUSSION

How do these results correspond to previous findings? The main effect of time of day here, showing better immediate recall in the evening, was similar to that found by Jones et al. (1978). This result again suggests that an evening peak in immediate recall is more likely to be found with visual rather than auditory presentation. However Figure 1 shows that there are individual differences in time of day effects. The low arousal introvert group actually declined in performance in the evening, in contrast to the other groups.

Hypothesis 1, that time of day effects on STM are mediated by arousal, received mixed support. The predicted main effect of arousal did reach significance, but the time of day x arousal interaction showed that adverse effects of arousal were restricted to the morning. Furthermore mean arousal level was virtually identical at both times of day. Thus while states of high arousal may tend to impair digit span, it is doubtful whether this mechanism can account for the circadian rhythm in immediate memory.

The Humphreys and Revelle (1984) model failed to predict individual differences in the circadian trend of STM. The prediction derived from Hypothesis 2, that time of day and extraversion should interactively affect arousal was not supported: extraverts were higher in arousal at both times of day. Individual differences in the effects of time of day depended on both extraversion and arousal, with the triple interaction between time of day, extraversion and arousal predicted from Hypothesis 3 reaching significance. The results here are less clear-cut than

those   of Matthews (1985) however: in particular the   extravert/high
arousal   group   showed   better   performance   in   the
evening, contrary to expectation.   To summarise, the data show
an evening superiority in STM, which was   not   caused   by lower
arousal   in   the evening.   However individual differences in   the
effects   of   time of day were found, which   depended   on both
extraversion   and arousal,   generally as predicted   from   the
findings   of   Matthews (1985).   Next, the implications of these
results for explaining circadian rhythms in STM are discussed.
      The   main problem in explaining circadian rhythms in STM is
the   inconsistency of results obtained from studies using   visual
presentation.   One explanation for this inconsistency is that there
may   be two mechanisms involved. We suggest that the   first
mechanism is the reduction in sub-vocal articulation in the evening
demonstrated by Folkard and Monk (1979). The second mechanism   is
an   essentially attentional mechanism: speed of identification   of
items   following sensory registration. Three lines of evidence
support   this hypothesis. First, in an extensive review   of
individual   differences in memory span, Dempster (1981) concludes
that variation in speed of item identification is the single   most
likely   source of individual differences in span.   Second,
attentional   tasks requiring simple serial processing, such as
letter   cancellation, tend to be performed better in the   evening
(Marks   and Folkard, 1985). Third, the interactive effects of time
of   day, extraversion and arousal on STM here were similar to those
found   by Matthews (1987a) on a measure of low level   attentional
efficiency.   Additional   evidence that these variables affect an
attentional mechanism comes from further data from the   experiment
reported   here. Time of day, extraversion, and arousal had similar
effects   on an attentional task with no overt memory component   -
speed of five choice serial reaction - as they did on digit   span.
We found significantly faster serial reaction in the evening, and a
time   of day x extraversion x arousal interaction similar to that
found   by Matthews (1985). (There were no corresponding effects on
error rate).
      In   general then we suggest that experiments showing poorer
evening   STM performance are those where variance in   performance
primarily   reflects changes in articulatory loop usage, whereas
experiments   showing superior evening STM performance are those
where   the task is more sensitive to   variation in   item
identification speed. What controls which mechanism a given   task
is   most sensitive to? Experiments with auditory stimuli seem more
likely   to show morning superiority than those with visual stimuli.
This   result could be due to the greater persistence of auditory
compared   to visual sensory storage (Cowan, 1984); slow   item
encoding is presumably less likely to lead to loss of   information
where   there is more persistent sensory buffering. It is likely too
that   item identification effects are more prevalent at higher
presentation rates, which will reduce strategy use generally,   and
particularly use of the articulatory loop. For verbal free recall
tasks, it seems plausible that the recency items, being stored in a
fairly passive form (Hitch, 1980), should be more strongly affected
by   item identification speed than the more actively processed pre-
recency   items. Thus the task factors identified by Jones et al.

(1978) may control whether a particular immediate memory task is more sensitive to variation in item identification speed or to articulatory loop usage.

REFERENCES

Cowan, N. (1984). 'On short and long auditory stores', Psychological Bulletin, 396, 341-370.

Dempster, F. N. (1981). 'Memory span: sources of individual and developmental differences', Psychological Bulletin, 89, 63-100.

Eysenck, H. J., and Eysenck, S. B. G. (1964). The Eysenck Personality Inventory, University of London Press, London.

Folkard, S., and Monk T. H. (1979). 'Time of day and processing strategy in free recall', Quarterly Journal of Experimental Psychology, 31, 461-475.

Hitch, G. (1980). 'Developing the concept of working memory', in Cognitive Psychology: New Directions (Ed. G. Claxton), Routledge and Kegan Paul, London.

Humphreys, M. S., and Revelle, W. (1984). 'Personality, motivation and performance: a theory of the relationship between individual differences and information processing', Psychological Review, 91, 153-184.

Jones, D. M. and Chamberlain, A. G. (1986). 'The HPRG Test Battery and 'Easilearn' training performance'. Unpublished technical report for the British Post Office.

Jones, D. M. Davies, D. R., Hogan, K. M., Patrick, J., and Cumberbatch, W. G. (1978). 'Short-term memory during the normal working day', in Practical Aspects of Memory (Eds. M. M. Gruneberg, P. E. Morris, and R. N. Sykes), Academic Press, London.

Marks, M., and Folkard, S. (1985). 'Diurnal rhythms in cognitive performance', in Psychology Survey 5, British Psychological Society, Leicester.

Matthews, G. (1985). 'The effects of extraversion and arousal on intelligence test performance', British Journal of Psychology, 76, 479-493.

Matthews, G. (1987a). 'Extraversion and levels of control of sustained attention', submitted for publication.

Matthews, G. (1987b). 'Personality and multidimensional arousal: a study of two dimensions of extraversion', Personality and Individual Differences, 8, 9-16.

GENERAL EDUCATIONAL
IMPLICATIONS

IMPROVING THE RETENTION OF AURALLY PRESENTED INFORMATION

Frances K. Aldrich and Alan J. Parkin
Laboratory of Experimental Psychology, University of Sussex,
Brighton, BN1 9QG

ABSTRACT

This chapter reports two ways in which the retention of aurally presented information can be improved. The first method involves the use of repeated self-assessment questions embedded in a taped lecture. It was found that immediate repetition of a question did not enhance recall of the target facts. However, when question repetitions were spaced there was a significant improvement in subsequent fact recall. A second study examined the effects of varying the delay of a single question to examine whether repetition was essential for the previously observed effects. Fact recall was not influenced by the delay between the target fact and the question addressing it thus indicating that repetition was crucial to the spacing effects observed in the first study. A final study considers the role of summaries as a substitute for whole texts in aural study. It was found that subjects answered questions about a passage as accurately having heard only an expert summary compared with the whole passage alone, or passage plus summary.

The present research was carried out as part of a project aimed at facilitating the use of tape recorded textbooks by visually handicapped (VH) students (Parkin & Aldrich, 1987). Many VH students rely on tape recorded texts as their primary source of information (Carter, 1962). Presenting information aurally gives rise to a number of problems not encountered with written presentation (see Table 1). The two most important differences are: 1) the listener plays a more passive role than the reader, and consequently finds it difficult to maintain concentration; 2) aural presentation is slower than written presentation.

ACTIVE LISTENING

Most VH students prefer to listen straight through a relevant chapter. Other strategies, such as previewing and selective listening, are impractical because of the difficulties involved in "skim" listening and locating a particular point on tape, and inadequate indexing (Parkin & Aldrich, 1987). Much of a VH student's study time is therefore spent under conditions approximating a classroom lecture (Cobb, 1977). The listener may take notes but will not be as actively involved as a reader. Readers interact directly with the text - highlighting, underlining and annotating it, and can skim read less pertinent sections.

TABLE 1
Studying from aural and written text: a comparison

	LISTENER	READER
Word rate	120 wpm	250 wpm
Learner's role	passive (attention problems)	active
Attention lapse	place lost, difficult to find (taped speech); information lost (direct speech)	place easily found

It is widely accepted that interacting with to-be-learned material produces better learning than a passive retention strategy (e.g. Slamecka & Graf, 1978), and that even peripheral concurrent activity can promote learning (e.g. Bells & Stauffacher, 1937). The listener's passivity clearly puts him at a disadvantage in comparison to the reader.

In a recent study Parkin, Wood, and Aldrich (1987) explored a means of increasing the listener's activity through the use of self-assessment questions (SAQ's). These are questions embedded in the text which require the listener to retrieve information presented earlier. Assuming that SAQ's would be beneficial to learning per se, the experimenters chose to explore an additional factor that might facilitate learning from aural text - repetition.

It is well known that repetition of information enhances its memorability (e.g. Madigan, 1969), but repetition effects are not straightforward. Information repeated immediately is typically remembered little better than information that is not repeated at all. If some intervening event occurs between repetitions, however, the repeated information is recalled substantially better - an effect we will term the "spacing effect". In addition, the further apart the repetitions, the greater the improvement in recall - the "lag effect".

In the first experiment subjects listened to a short passage about the Florida Everglades. At various points an SAQ was introduced, requiring the subject to retrieve a fact from the preceding sentence. All SAQ's were then repeated either immediately, (0 lag), or 1, 2, or 4 minutes later. Three hours later subjects received an unexpected free recall test for the facts. The results of the experiment are shown in Figure 1 and it can be seen that recall increased systematically with lag.

Although these effects were considered to arise from variations in the lag between repetitions, an alternative possibility was that they arose from variations in the lag between the target information and the second SAQ. A number of authors have argued that retention of information may be directly determined by the amount of effort involved in processing (e.g. Jacoby, Craik, & Begg, 1979), and on this basis the observed effects might be attributable to the increased amount of effort required to answer the more delayed SAQ's. To test the effort-based interpretation of the first

experiment a second experiment was carried out. This was identical
to the first except that the initial presentation of the SAQ was
omitted.   Fifty-two additional subjects took part. Figure 1 shows
that lag had no effect on recall accuracy in the second experiment,
demonstrating that the effects obtained in the first experiment stem
directly from repetition of the SAQ's. It should also be noted that
there is no difference between the "zero" lag condition of both studies, indicating that immediate repetition of SAQ's results in no
better recall than no repetition at all.

    These results indicate that SAQ's might be a useful means of
promoting active listening, and that calculated spaced repetitions
can facilitate learning. SAQ's are an attractive alternative to
simply repeating an entire passage, as they can be used to highlight
key facts. They also keep the listener alert and provide instant
feedback about his comprehension.   It remains to be seen whether
such effects can be taken out of the laboratory and into the classroom.

    Turning briefly to the theoretical explanation of   these
results, the most likely interpretation is that awareness of the
repetition variable caused subjects to rehearse, or in some way
"keep in mind", targeted facts until they were questioned a second
time. Longer lag items would be rehearsed more and therefore
retained better. The lack of facilitation resulting from immediate
repetition can be attributed to impoverished processing of either
the first or second presentation. Encoding variability theories on
the other hand would explain the effects by arguing that longer lag
repetitions produce more contextually distinct representations. If
this were the case, however, spacing effects should have been
observed in the second experiment: the longer the lag, the more distinct the contexts of initial and repeated presentation.   Such an
effect was not observed, and an explanation based on encoding variability is therefore difficult to sustain.

SUMMARIES

    Even well-written texts contain a substantial amount of redun-
dant material.   For the skilled reader this is rarely a hindrance
because of the speed at which reading occurs and the availability of
strategies to avoid irrelevant sections. For the listener, however,
the passive role and slower rate of presentation mean that redundancy is a considerable problem. Any technique which lessens the
problem will greatly benefit VH students. One technique is to play
recordings at speeds faster than that at which they were recorded -
a strategy in widespread use by VH students (Parkin & Aldrich,
1987). However listening to accelerated speech has drawbacks, especially if the narrator has a high pitched voice (Aldrich & Parkin,
in prep.).

    An alternative approach is to substitute a summary of the ori-
ginal text, thus reducing the overall amount of text that must be
attended to. Reder and Anderson (1980) applied this technique with
sighted readers and found that retention of the major points of a
linguistics text was just as good when subjects studied an expert
summary as when they studied the complete text. We decided to examine whether a similar effect might occur with aurally presented
texts. The opening chapters of two psychology texts were summarised

to about 10% of their original length. Subjects were divided into three groups: one studied summaries alone, another the original text on its own, and a final group had the text and the summary. At the end of the session all subjects answered a series of questions about the text. The results showed correct scores of 14.0, 14.9, and 14.1 respectively (maximum = 27). The subjects had learnt the major points of the text reasonably well and were clearly unaffected by the type of presentation used. One must be cautious in interpreting a null result, but these data at least suggest that studying from summaries might save VH students a considerable amount of time, without affecting their learning of important facts. Good summaries require an expert understanding of the material, and they may be financially viable only for widely used texts. It might also be argued that summaries are a form of censorship with the summariser deciding what constitutes an important fact. However, given the limitations that aural study already imposes, VH students may welcome the use of summaries under certain circumstances.

REFERENCES

Aldrich, F. K. and Parkin, A. J. (in prep) 'The effect of voice pitch on comprehension of accelerated speech'

Bells, A.G. and Stuaffacher, J.C. (1937) 'The influence of voluntarily induced tension on rational problem solving', Journal of Psychology, 4, 261-271.

Carter, B. (1962) 'How to use educational recordings effectively', The New Outlook for the Blind, 56.

Cobb, E.S. (1977) 'Learning through listening: A new approach', Journal of Visual Impairment and Blindness, 71, 7, 302-8.

Jacoby, L. L., Craik, F. I. M., and Begg, I. (1979) 'Effects of decision difficulty on recognition and recall', Journal of Verbal Learning and Verbal Behavior, 18, 585-600.

Madigan, S.W. (1969) 'Intraserial presentation and coding processes in free recall', Journal of Verbal Learning and Verbal Behavior, 8, 828-835.

Parkin, A. J., and Aldrich, F. K. (1987) 'Facilitating the use of tape recorded textbooks by visually handicapped students'. Final report, Royal National Institute for the Blind, London: United Kingdom.

Parkin, A. J., Wood, A., and Aldrich, F. K. (1987) 'Repetition and active listening: The effects of spacing self-assessment questions.' Under review.

Reder, L.M. and Anderson, J.R. (1980) 'A comparison of texts and their summaries: Memorial consequences', Journal of Verbal Learning and Verbal Behavior, 19, 12-34.

Slamecka, N.J. and Graf, P. (1978) 'The generation effect: Delineation of a phenomenon', Journal of Experimental Psychology: Human Learning and Memory, 4, 592-604.

STUDENT LEARNING AND THE MENSTRUAL CYCLE

John T. E. Richardson
Department of Human Sciences, Brunel University,
Uxbridge, Middlesex, England.

ABSTRACT

Women are often assumed to show variations in cognitive performance through the menstrual cycle, and a questionnaire survey showed that most female students attribute some disruption of their academic work to premenstrual symptoms. However, these expectations are not borne out by the available evidence. A naturalistic study concerning the immediate retention of the content of lectures and a conventional experiment on paired-associate learning were carried out. There was no objective memory deficit during the paramenstruum, either in comparison with the same individuals' performance during the intermenstruum or in comparison with the performance of male subjects.

INTRODUCTION

There are now over 350,000 women enrolled as students in courses of higher education in the United Kingdom, and over 500,000 more engaged in nonadvanced further education. Most of these women are regularly affected by the endocrinological and physiological changes associated with the cyclical process of ovulation and menstruation. This paper is concerned with variations in the learning performance of female students during the normal menstrual cycle.

Almost all menstruating women suffer some abdominal discomfort either just before or at the onset of the menstrual flow and they may experience a variety of other symptoms as well. However, roughly one half of all women experience dysmenorrhoea or period pains. It is generally believed that these are caused by abnormal contractility of the uterine muscle as a result of increased production and release of prostaglandins; the latter are attributed in turn to elevated levels of progesterone during the secretory phase of the menstrual cycle (Friederich, 1983; Gannon, 1981; Ylikorkala & Dawood, 1978).

Most women also experience a variety of physical, psychological, and behavioural changes during the period between ovulation and menstruation. These were originally described by Frank (1931), who introduced the term 'premenstrual tension' to emphasize the cyclical emotional disturbances associated with the latter phase of the cycle. Nowadays it is generally assumed by medical authorities that there is a precise clinical condition of premenstrual syndrome with emotional, somatic, and behavioural components (Abplanalp, 1983). Nevertheless, the aetiology of premenstrual symptoms is entirely unclear (Harrison, Sharpe, & Endicott, 1985). They are experienced as being principally psychological in nature, and some have argued that they are caused by psychosocial factors (e.g., Parlee, 1982; Ruble & Brooks-Gunn, 1979).

A QUESTIONNAIRE STUDY OF PREMENSTRUAL SYMPTOMS

A questionnaire on premenstrual symptoms was administered to 161 female students from seven cohorts taking courses in psychology and sociology at Brunel University. The 44 symptoms (see Table 1) were taken from a journalistic account of 'premenstrual tension' (Lever, Brush, & Haynes, 1979, p. 130) and are expressed in everyday language rather than in medical terminology. The respondent was asked to respond 'yes' to each symptom only if she regularly experienced that symptom during the 7-10 days before the onset of menstrual bleeding. She was also asked to provide relevant biographical data, including the average length of her menstrual cycle and the date on which her last period began. Finally, she was asked to indicate whether she considered that premenstrual symptoms disrupted six aspects of her academic work (see Table 2). In each case, she made a simple yes/no judgement and also marked a 50-mm analogue scale whose ends were labelled 'no effect' and 'total disruption'.

Questionnaires were returned by 153 subjects. The number of symptoms reported varied between 0 and 30, with a mean of 12.9. Table 1 shows the percentage of subjects reporting each symptom. All but one of these subjects provided judgements as to whether premenstrual symptoms disrupted their work. Table 2 shows the percentage of subjects who felt that each aspect of academic work was disrupted, together with the mean rated disruption along an analogue scale. Out of 152 respondents, 71% reported that at least one aspect of academic work was disrupted by premenstrual symptoms, and 11% reported that their academic work was disrupted in all six respects.

In short, almost all of the subjects reported some premenstrual symptoms, and the average subject reported the regular occurrence of 12 or 13 symptoms. Most of them attributed some disruption of their work to the occurrence of such symptoms, and a minority reported a general disruption of their academic performance. Nevertheless, the question arises whether there are correlative variations in objective measures of performance during the menstrual cycle.

ACADEMIC PERFORMANCE AND THE MENSTRUAL CYCLE

Dalton (1960) studied the performance of 352 girls at an English boarding school on weekly class tests. In comparing marks in the pre-menstrual phase with those during the intermenstrual phase, 27% showed reduced performance, 17% showed an increase, while 56% showed no difference. Dalton (1968) considered the performance of students taking examinations at GCE Advanced and Ordinary Level. The average mark, the distinction rate, and the pass rate tended to be slightly lower for papers taken during the paramenstruum than for papers taken during the intermenstruum. However, Sommer (1983) has criticized this research as methodologically unsound. Subsequent investigations have indicated that there is little or no variation in academic performance during the menstrual cycle (Bernstein, 1977; Sommer, 1972; Walsh, Budtz-Olsen, Leader, & Cummins, 1981). Similarly, there seems to be no relationship between academic performance and the incidence of either premenstrual symptoms (Schuckit, Daly, Herrman, & Hineman, 1976) or menstrual symptoms (Walsh et al., 1981).

Table 1. Percentage of Subjects Reporting Each of 44 Premenstrual Symptoms

Weight gain	61.4	Lowered judgement	30.1
Skin disorders	43.1	Difficulty concentrating	47.1
Painful breasts	50.3	Accidents	19.6
Swelling	45.8	Poor coordination	19.0
Eye diseases	2.0	Poor academic performance	28.1
Asthma	1.3	Poor work performance	28.1
Epilepsy	0.0	Lethargy	60.8
Dizziness	17.0	Need to stay at home	16.3
Faintness	19.6	Avoiding social activities	17.0
Cold sweats	7.2	Decreased efficiency	42.5
Nausea	21.6	Food cravings	32.0
Sickness	8.5	Drinking too much alcohol	3.9
Hot flushes	17.6	Taking too many pills	2.0
Fuzzy vision	6.5	Mood swings	73.9
Spontaneous bruising	3.9	Crying	39.2
Headache	44.4	Depression	51.6
Migraine	9.2	Anxiety	43.8
Backache	49.7	Restlessness	39.9
General aches and pains	51.6	Irritability	74.5
Sleeplessness	11.8	Aggression	32.7
Forgetfulness	20.9	Tension	64.1
Confusion	20.9	Loss of sex drive	14.4

Table 2. Percentage of Subjects Reporting Disruption and Mean Reported Extent of Disruption on an Analogue Scale for Six Aspects of Academic Work.

	Dichotomous judgements (%)	Analogue judgements (0-50)
In lectures	30.3	11.6
In seminars	40.8	13.0
Writing essays	44.4	15.4
Reading	38.8	12.9
In examinations	53.3	20.2
In interviews	42.1	16.3

To determine whether paramenstrual symptoms specifically disrupt academic learning, a naturalistic study was conducted with one of the cohorts of students mentioned above. At the end of each of four weekly lectures, a class of 33 students received a short written test on 10-12 factual points of information covered in the lecture. The questionnaire on premenstrual symptoms was administered to the female students after the written test on the final lecture. On the basis of their replies, their performance could be examined in terms of the menstrual phase in which each lecture had been given. Table 3 shows the performance of 17 female subjects who attended in all four weeks and whose menstrual phases could be correlated with the four lectures and of seven male subjects who attended in all four weeks. The difference between the male and female subjects was not significant in any of the four phases and there was no effect of menstrual phase.

Table 3. Mean Percentage Correct Recall of Lecture Content by Female Students during the Menstruum (M), the Early Intermenstruum (EIM), the Late Intermenstruum (LIM), and the Premenstruum (PM), and by Male Controls.

	M	EIM	LIM	PM	Overall
Females	51.5	48.8	47.3	47.6	48.8
Males	--	--	--	--	53.0

COGNITIVE PERFORMANCE AND THE MENSTRUAL CYCLE

A possibility raised by Sommer (1972) is that the tasks used to evaluate learning in academic situations might not be sensitive or reliable enough to detect variability in performance associated with the menstrual cycle. More formal measures of cognitive performance which have been extensively validated in the psychological laboratory might be more reliable as research instruments and more sensitive to fluctuations in the paramenstruum. However, an authoritative review by Sommer (1983) has concluded that there is no good evidence for any effects of either premenstrual symptoms or menstruation itself upon objective, quantitative measures of performance. Unfortunately, there is little evidence on the specific topic of learning during the menstrual cycle. Studies by Lough (1937) and Golub (1976) found no sign of any paramenstrual decrement, but the tasks that they employed cannot be regarded as paradigmatic tests of learning.

A paired-associate learning experiment was therefore carried out with three of the cohorts mentioned above, comprising a total of 125 students. In each of four weekly sessions, they were shown a list of 30 pairs of common nouns and were asked to recall 20 of these pairs, ignoring the initial and final five as fillers. The questionnaire on premenstrual symptoms was given to the female students at the end of the fourth session. Once again, on the basis of their replies, it was possible to examine their performance in terms of the menstrual phase in which each list had been learnt. Table 4 shows the performance of the 73 female subjects who attended all four sessions and whose menstrual phases could be correlated with the four sessions, and of the 34 male subjects who attended all four sessions. The difference between the male and female subjects was not significant in any of the four phases and there was no effect of menstrual phase.

CONCLUSIONS

These two studies indicate that both in academic contexts and in laboratory experiments there is no objective decrement in learning performance during the paramenstruum, either in comparison with the same subjects' performance during the intermenstruum or in comparison

Table 4. Mean Percentage Correct Recall in Paired-Associate Learning by Female Students during the Menstruum (M), Early Intermenstruum (EIM), Late Intermenstruum (LIM), and Premenstruum (PM), and by Male Controls.

	M	EIM	LIM	PM	Overall
Females	51.10	48.14	51.68	52.97	50.97
Males	--	--	--	--	48.31

with the performance of male subjects. This conclusion is very much in line with the predominant weight of evidence on cognitive function during the menstrual cycle (Sommer, 1983). Yet it contradicts both subjective accounts of women themselves (including their responses to questionnaires) and the stereotypical views of women's performance prevalent in our culture. It would appear that failures of cognitive performance experienced by women during the paramenstruum tend to be attributed to the process of menstruation but that failures of cognitive performance experienced during the intermenstruum are attributed to external factors (cf. Koeske & Koeske, 1975; Campus & Thurow, 1978). However, these tendencies are based not upon any objective evidence of impairment during the paramenstruum but upon biases of social cognition (Ruble & Brooks-Gunn, 1979) which are promoted in turn by culturally mediated beliefs and expectations.

This paper was written while the author was visiting the Open University as an Honorary Senior Research Fellow. A full account of the research described here is in preparation.

REFERENCES

Abplanalp, J.M. (1983). 'Premenstrual Syndrome: A Selective Review', in Lifting the Curse of Menstruation (Ed. S. Golub), pp. 107-123, Haworth Press, New York.

Bernstein, B.E. (1977). 'Effect of Menstruation on Academic Performance Among College Women', Archives of Sexual Behavior, 6, 289-296.

Campos, F. and Thurow, C. (1978). 'Attributions of Moods and Symptoms to the Menstrual Cycle', Personality and Social Psychology Bulletin, 4, 272-276.

Dalton, K. (1960). 'Effect of Menstruation on Schoolgirls' Weekly Work', British Medical Journal, 1 (No. 5169), 326-328.

Dalton, K. (1968). 'Menstruation and Examinations', Lancet, 2 (No. 7583), 1386-1388.

Frank, R.T. (1931). 'The Hormonal Causes of Premenstrual Tension', Archives of Neurology and Psychiatry (Chicago), 26, 1053-1057.

Friederich, M.A. (1983). 'Dysmenorrhea', in Lifting the Curse of Menstruation (Ed. S. Golub), pp. 91-106, Haworth Press, New York.

Gannon, L. (1981). 'Psychological and Physiological Factors in the Development, Maintenance, and Treatment of Menstrual Disorders', in Psychosomatic Disorders: A Psychophysiological Approach to Etiology and Treatment, (Eds. S.N. Hayes and L. Gannon), pp. 79-132, Praeger, New York.

Golub, S. (1976). 'The Effect of Premenstrual Anxiety and Depression on Cognitive Function', Journal of Personality and Social Psychology, 34, 99-104.

Harrison, W., Sharpe, L., and Endicott, J. (1985). 'Treatment of Premenstrual Symptoms', General Hospital Psychiatry, 7, 54-65.

Koeske, R.K., and Koeske, G.F. (1975). 'An Attributional Approach to Moods and the Menstrual Cycle', Journal of Personality and Social Psychology, 31, 473-478.

Lever, J., Brush, M. and Haynes, B. (1979). PMT: The Unrecognised Illness, Melbourne House, London.

Lough, O.M. (1937). 'A Psychological Study of Functional Periodicity', Journal of Comparative Psychology, 24, 359-368.

Parlee, M.B. (1982). 'The Psychology of the Menstrual Cycle: Biological and Physiological Perspectives', in Behavior and the Menstrual Cycle (Ed. R.C. Friedman), pp. 77-99, Marcel Dekker, New York.

Ruble, D.N. and Brooks-Gunn, J. (1979). 'Menstrual Symptoms: A Social Cognition Analysis', Journal of Behavioral Medicine, 2, 171-194.

Schuckit, M.A., Daly, V., Herrman, G. and Hineman, S. (1976). 'Premenstrual Symptoms and Depression in a University Population', Diseases of the Nervous System, 36, 516-517.

Sommer, B. (1972). 'Menstrual Cycle Changes and Intellectual Performance', Psychosomatic Medicine, 34, 263-269.

Sommer, B. (1983). 'How does Menstruation Affect Cognitive Competence and Psychophysiological Response?' in Lifting the Curse of Menstruation (Ed. S. Golub), pp. 53-90, Haworth Press, New York.

Walsh, R.N., Budtz-Olsen, I., Leader, C. and Cummins, R.A. (1981). 'The Menstrual Cycle, Personality and Academic Performance', Archives of General Psychiatry, 38, 219-221.

Ylikorkala, O., & Dawood, M.Y. (1978). 'New Concepts in Dysmenorrhea', American Journal of Obstetrics and Gynecology, 130, 833-847.

THE ROLE OF COLOUR IN OBJECT MEMORY: EFFECTS OF
TASK AND INSTRUCTION

Giuliana Mazzoni and Adele Cavedon
University of Padua, Italy

Jules Davidoff
University College, Swansea, U.K.

ABSTRACT
          Three   experiments   are   reported   which   compare   the
effectiveness   of   colour   with that of   black-and-white   stimuli   in
memory.   For   recall   of the names of   pictured   objects   there   was
virtually no advantage in adding colour.   In contrast the results   of
studies of semantic memory showed that colour did help recognition in
an episodic memory task.   It is argued that task parameters (but   not
instructions)   can be important in determining the   conditions   under
which colour will be useful as a memory aid.

          Colour   has   important uses in displays.   The   foremost   of
these   is   to segment the input (Davidoff, 1987).   Colour coding,   for
example, is extremely useful as a coding device when we want to   know
whether more than one object of the same type is present in a display
(Poulton and Edwards, 1977).   In a task where subjects had to   answer
questions   from memory concerning the status of aircraft, colour   was
most   helpful   in retaining the number of aircraft   at   a   particular
altitude   (Wedell and Alden, 1973).   However, the advantage   achieved
by   efficient   segmentation was obtained at the expense   of   location
information.   In   general, and especially for   large   memory   loads,
colour is not the most efficient coding symbol. Numerical codes, for
instance, produce significantly better retention.   Remembering colour
information,   unlike spatial information, appears to be effortful   in
arbitrary   colour-shape   combinations (Park   and   Mason,   1982).
Nevertheless,   colour in displays is greatly appreciated by   subjects
even   when   it is not helpful to their   performance   (Narborough-Hall,
1985).   It   is possible that the paradoxical preference for   colour
expressed   by   subjects in short-term memory experiments could be   a
carry-over from its use in recall from long-term memory.   The present
studies   therefore   investigate the role of the known   colour   of   an
object in memory tasks.
          The   recall   of the true colour of an object   is   prone   to
error.   Subjects get the colour roughly correct but can be inaccurate
with   respect to hue, brightness or saturation (Siple   and   Springer,
1983).   The   particular error made may be related to the   choice   of
objects.   One other distinct possibility is that errors arise because
the   correct   physical   colour   is   not   directly available,   colour
properties   of   objects being stored in a verbal   form.   While   this
hypothesis   may at first sight appear unlikely, there   is   supporting
evidence.   Paivio and te Linde (1980) found that it was   quicker   to
recall the colour of an object from its written name than from a line

drawing.   This   result is in sharp contrast to the recall   of   other
object properties, e.g. size, for which line drawings produce   faster
responses than words (Paivio, 1979). Furthermore, it has been   found
by   contrasting visual and verbal interference that   people   remember
colours verbally (Davidoff and Ostergaard, 1984). Memory for hard to
name colours is also much affected by a label attached to the   colour
at   presentation   (Bornstein,   1976). However, none   of   these   last
mentioned experiments required a fine discrimination between colours.
Memory   for physical colour differences, not easily   verbalised,   are
certainly   retained for a short time (Davidoff and Ostergaard, 1984)
and   it must bear consideration that both the physical colour   of   an
object   as   well as its verbal coding are   represented   in   long-term
memory. People can be very efficient in the strategies they adopt to
process information. In short-term memory studies using rapid serial
visual   presentation of coloured letters, subjects appear to   process
colour and shape information either serially or in parallel depending
upon   task   demands   (Gathercole and   Broadbent,   1984).   If   colour
properties   of   objects   are available in long term   storage   in   two
forms, then it is possible that the use of the one or the other   will
also   depend   on   the demand characteristics of   the   task.   It   was
therefore   decided to manipulate the strategy used by the subject   in
the present study. The first three experiments of the present   study
ask   for   recall. In Experiments 1 and 2 object memory was   studied
with   the   instructions to remember either as pictures or   as   names.
Experiment   3 gave even stronger instruction to the subject to use   a
pictorial   code   by   asking them to create an   image.   Experiment   4
varied task demands by testing for recognition.

METHOD
Recall — Experiment 1
        Forty   psychology   graduates   and   undergraduates   of   the
University   of Padua (19-40) years) participated in the   first   task.
Thirty-six   drawings taken from Snodgrass and Vanderwart (1980)   were
coloured   realistically   by   a   professional   artist.   From   these,
coloured and black-and-white (B&W) slides were produced.
        Subjects   were   individually   shown   36 slides   of   different
objects (half coloured, half B&W) in the same random order.   Objects
presented   in colour for half the subjects were shown in B&W for   the
other   half. Each slide was shown for 2sec.   Half of   the   subjects
(group   1)   were given both immediate and delayed (after   24   hours)
written   recall;   half   (group   2) only delayed.   For   half   of   the
subjects   instructions   recommended that they tried to   remember   the
objects as pictures and for the other half as names.

Results
        The   delayed   recall   data were analysed by a   2 (type   of
instruction) x 2 (one or two recalls) x 2 (colour vs B&W) ANOVA   with
repeated measures over one factor. There were no significant effects
(see table 1). Immediate vs delayed recall was analysed by a 2 (type
of instruction) x 2 (immediate vs delayed recall) x 2 colour vs   B&W)
ANOVA   with repeated measures over two factors. There was   only   one
significant   effect viz.   the three way interaction $(F(1,18) = 5.19$,
$p < .05)$. Table 1 indicates there was an improvement in the recall   of
coloured pictures in the delayed condition with verbal instructions.

TABLE 1
Mean Recall Score (max = 18) for Experiment 1

| | COLOUR | | | B&W | | |
| | GROUP 1 | | GROUP 2 | GROUP 1 | | GROUP 2 |
	IMMEDIATE	DELAY	DELAY	IMMEDIATE	DELAY	DELAY
Verbal Instructions	9.1	10.8	8.3	8.0	9.2	7.1
Visual Instructions	8.1	7.8	7.2	7.9	7.9	7.4

Experiment 2
        Sixteen different undergraduate subjects from the University of Padua took part. The procedure was the same as for Group 1 of Experiment 1, except that subjects were given either coloured or B&W pictures to recall. Recall was as for the visual instructions in Experiment 1.

Results
        The data were analysed by a 2 (immediate vs delayed recall) x 2 (colour vs B&W) ANOVA with repeated measures over one factor. Delayed recall was superior ($F(1,14) = 7.70$, $p<.02$). All other F ratios < 1 (See Table 2).

TABLE 2
Mean Recall Score (max = 36) for Experiment 2

	COLOUR	B&W
Immediate	14.5	13.5
Delay	17.5	15.5

RECOGNITION
Experiment 3
        Sixteen undergraduate subjects of the University of Swansea took part in the Experiment. Thirty-six slides (18 coloured, 18 B&W), as used in Experiments 1 and 2, were presented individually for 2 sec. with an interstimulus interval of 1.5 sec. Coloured and B&W slides were presented in a random order. Twenty-four hours later subjects were given a two alternative forced choice recognition task between a presented stimulus and a foil. The foil was always of the same type as the presented stimulus and in some way (visually or semantically) similar. The correct answer was half the time on the left and half on the right. The foils for half the subjects were the presentation items for the other half. The two choices were presented simultaneously and a timer started which could be stopped by either of two manually operated switches. Subjects pressed the left switch if they thought that the left slide had been seen before and similarly for the right. Latencies were recorded automatically. Subjects were also divided into two groups and given either verbal or visual instructions as in Experiment 1.

Results

Only correct scores were analysed. Errors were too few to provide a proper analysis. The error rates for coloured stimuli were 5.6% and 6.3% (verbal, visual instructions) and 6.4% and 7.5% (verbal, visual instructions for B&W stimuli). Long latencies (>2.5 sd.) were excluded. These constituted only 0.7% and 0.7% for the coloured stimuli and 0.9% and 1.2% for the B&W. The data were analysed by a 2 (type of instruction) x 2 (coloured vs B&W) ANOVA with repeated measures over the second factor. The only significant effect was an advantage in recognition for the coloured stimuli ($F(1,14) = 9.55$, $p < .01$) (See Table 3).

TABLE 3

Mean Recognition Latencies (msecs.) for Experiment 3

	COLOUR	B&W
Verbal instructions	997.1	1105.5
Visual instructions	1044.5	1105.3

DISCUSSION

Experiment 1 shows that adding colour to pictures does not aid recall. Additional detail by itself does not, as Park (1980) suggests, improve memory. While the two types of instruction produced little difference in recall, there was nevertheless a hint that the subjects were indeed using a verbal strategy. The ineffectiveness of colour in promoting recall is confirmed in Experiment 2 in a between groups design. The results differed from Experiment 1 only in finding a significant reminiscence effect.

The lack of assistance to memory shown by adding redundant colour has previously been found for recognition (Ostergaard and Davidoff, 1985). The present Experiment 3 produced a different finding, showing that colour did make objects easier to remember. However, whether the type of memory instruction emphasized visual or verbal coding made no difference. The Ostergaard and Davidoff study used only a very small number of overlearned items. It is, therefore, considered that subjects will only make use of colour coding for recognition if shape coding is ambiguous.

REFERENCES

Bornstein, M.H. (1976). 'Name codes and color memory', American Journal of Psychology, 89, 269-279.

Davidoff, J.B. (1987). 'The role of colour in visual displays', International Reviews of Ergonomics, 1, 21-42.

Davidoff, J.B. and Ostergaard, A.L. (1984). 'Colour anomia resulting from weakened short-term colour memory', Brain, 107, 415-431.

Gathercole, S.E. and Broadbent, D.E. (1984). 'Combining attributes in specified and categorized target search', Memory and Cognition, 12, 329-337.

Narborough-Hall, C.S. (1985). 'Recommendations for applying colour coding to air traffic control displays', Displays Technology and Applications, 6, 131-137.

Ostergaard, A.L. and Davidoff, J.B. (1985). 'Some effects of color on naming and recognition of objects', Journal of Experimental Psychology Learning: Memory and Cognition, 11, 579-587.

Paivio, A. and te Linde, J. (1980). 'Symbolic comparisons of objects on colour attributes', Journal of Experimental Psychology: Human Perception and Performance, 6, 652-661.

Paivio, A. (1979). 'On weighing things in your mind', in The Nature of Thought (Eds. R.W. Klein and P.W. Jusczyk), Lawrence Erlbaum, Hillsdale, NJ.

Park, D.C. (1980). 'Item and attribute storage of pictures and words in memory', American Journal of Psychology, 93, 4, 603-615.

Park, D.C. and Mason, D.A. (1982). 'Is there evidence for automatic processing of spatial and color attributes present in pictures and words?', Memory and Cognition, 10, 76-81.

Poulton, E.C. and Edwards, R.S. (1977). 'Perceptual load in searching for sloping colored lines camouflaged by colored backgrounds: a separate groups investigation', Journal of Experimental Psychology: Human Perception and Performance, 5, 136-150.

Siple, P. and Springer, L.M. (1983). 'Memory and preference for the colors of the objects', Perception and Psychophysics, 34, 363-370.

Snodgrass, J.G. and Vanderwart, M. (1980). 'A standardized set of 260 pictures: Norms for name agreement, familiarity and visual complexity', Journal of Experimental Psychology: Human Learning and Memory, 6, 174-215.

Wedell, J. and Alden, D.G. (1973). 'Color versus numeric coding in a keep-track task: Performance under varying load conditions', Journal of Applied Psychology, 57, 154-159.

WHEN A FORK IS NOT A FORK: RECALL OF PERFORMED ACTIVITIES AS A FUNCTION OF AGE, GENERATION, AND BIZARRENESS

Wemara Lichty, Sue Bressie and Raymond Krell

Department of Psychology, Washington University
St. Louis, MO 63130, USA

ABSTRACT

Memory for activities in young and elderly adults was investigated using pairs of everyday objects such as a fork and plate. The primary questions were: 1) Would the generation effect found in verbal recall be evident in memory for activities that were generated? 2) Would bizarreness enhance recall? 3) Are there age differences related to generation and bizarreness? A robust age deficit was found. Generation did not alter recallability. Bizarreness had a detrimental effect on recall. A primacy effect was present, suggesting some strategic processing.

Memory for activities in young and elderly adults has recently received attention in a number of laboratory investigations, but results are somewhat contradictory. Using tasks which were performed for 45 seconds to 3 minutes, Kausler and Lichty have consistently found an age deficit (Kausler, Lichty, Hakami, & Freund, 1986; Lichty, Kausler, & Martinez, 1986). In contrast, Backman and colleagues (Backman & Nilsson, 1984, 1985) have not found an age deficit using actions performed for 5 seconds. Backman has suggested that the lack of age effect is related to multimodal traces. The divers traces offer "contextual support" that enables the elderly to compensate for inadequate processing.

Previous research has suggested that memory for activities entails automatic (Hasher & Zacks, 1979), or nonstrategic (Cohen, 1983), processing. Little effort seems to be utilized in relation to remembering activities. Increasing the amount of effort by manipulating intentionality (Lichty et al., 1986) or by designating activities as having high or low recall importance has no effect (Cohen, 1983). An absence of a primacy effect also supports the nonstrategic nature of encoding (Cohen, 1981).

In laboratory investigations of memory for activities, participants have always been provided with verbal task directions. Real world performance of activities is rarely dictated by another person. When we open a door, we usually perform the action without being told to do so. To achieve greater similarity to memory for real world events, some participants generated actions, whereas, others performed activities in response to imperatives. In investigations about generated verbal material, recall is superior when subjects generate the material compared to merely reading it (Slamecka & Graf, 1978). Our study addresses whether such a generation effect is also evident in memory for activities. The question is of interest for two reasons: 1) Generated activities have greater ecological validity and 2) It addresses the issue of whether a memory task which putatively utilizes automatic processing at encoding shows enhanced recallability when actions are generated.

An additional question was whether bizarreness of performed activities would influence recallability. We hypothesized that memory would be superior for bizarre (unusual) activities because the trace would be more distinct. To evaluate the effect of bizarreness, some subjects performed ordinary activities and some performed bizarre activities.

GENERAL METHODS

Pairs of common objects which are usually used together were presented for each activity. Activities were performed either in accordance with directions or they were generated. Half the subjects performed ordinary, everyday activities and half performed unusual activities. For the Provided-Ordinary (PROV-O) group, task instructions for a commonplace action were given (e.g., "Put the fork on the plate."). For the Generated-Ordinary (GEN-O) group, object-pairs were presented and the participants generated the most ordinary action. The Generated-Unusual (GEN-U) condition entailed generation of an unusual action for each pair (e.g., place the plate in the prongs of the fork). Participants in the Provided-Unusual (PROV-U) group were yoked to the GEN-U group, such that each PROV-U participant performed the actions of his/her GEN-U counterpart. All participants were informed in advance about the memory test.

Twenty-four activities were performed for 10 seconds per activity with a 10-second interactivity interval. Each person in a group received a different list order. Two lists were used, with half the participants per group receiving each list. Before performing the list of activities, participants were given 6 practice activities and a practice recall test. After performing the list of 24 activities, a 2-minute filled time delay was given, followed by an oral free recall test. For the recall test, participants were asked to recall the pairs of objects used in the activity. Recall of actions per se was not possible for Experiment 1 because the length of description of the unusual actions might have resulted in poorer recall due to output interference.

EXPERIMENT 1

Forty-eight subjects in each age group (MY=20 yr., ME=70 yr.) were equally divided among four performance conditions. The young participants attended the University of Missouri-Columbia. The elderly adults were healthy community-dwellers from Columbia, MO.

RECALL. Mean proportion recall scores are presented in Table 1. A p value of .05 has been set for rejection of the null hypothesis. A 2(Age) x 2(Provided/Generated) x 2(Ordinary/Unusual) x 8(Serial Position: 1-3, 4-6, 7-9, 10-12, 13-15, 16-18, 19-21, 22-24) mixed ANOVA revealed a strong age effect $F(1,88)=21.93$, with means being significant Ordinary/Unusual main effect, with recall being superior for Ordinary activities, $F(1,88)=4.51$ (Ordinary=.51; Unusual=.45).

TABLE 1
Mean Proportion (SD) Recalled for Each Condition by Age

Condition	Young	Elderly	Age Deficit
EXPERIMENT 1			
Provided-Ordinary	.53 (.09)	.44 (.14)	17%
Generated-Ordinary	.61 (.16)	.44 (.14)	28%
Provided-Unusual	.55 (.09)	.42 (.17)	24%
Generated-Unusual	.48 (.15)	.35 (.13)	27%
EXPERIMENT 2			
Provided-Ordinary	.57 (.14)	.47 (.12)	18%
Generated-Ordinary	.61 (.10)	.45 (.12)	26%

Note: Age deficit=(Y-E)/Y

The main effect for serial position was significant $F(7,616)=8.18$. Results presented in Figure 1 reveal both a primacy and a recency effect. Other main effects and interactions were not significant.

EFFORT When the experimental conditions were designed, an assumption was that more effort would be used in generating actions and in performing unusual actions. How did the participants view the manipulations? To evaluate this, participants were asked to rate

FIGURE 1

SERIAL POSITION MAIN EFFECT

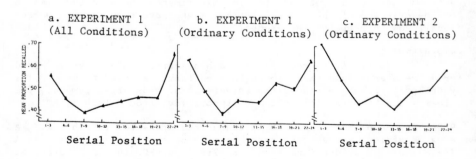

a. EXPERIMENT 1
(All Conditions)

b. EXPERIMENT 1
(Ordinary Conditions)

c. EXPERIMENT 2
(Ordinary Conditions)

Serial Position   Serial Position   Serial Position

the difficulty of performing the actions using a scale of 1=very easy to 7=very difficult. A 2(Age) x 2(Provided/Generated) x 2(Ordinary/Unusual) ANOVA was performed. The Provided/Generated main effect was significant, $F(1,88)=4.34$, with effort being rated greater in the Generated condition (Generated M=1.35, Provided M=0.73). A significant Ordinary/Unusual main effect was also evident, $F(1,88)=8.50$, with the Unusual activities being considered more difficult (Ordinary M = 0.60, Unusual M = 1.48). There were no significant interactions. Based on the ratings of the participants, the manipulation of effort was effective.

The rating for performance difficulty was correlated with recall for each age group. The correlations were -.01 for the young adults and -.40 (p<.05) for the elderly adults. When the elderly participants evaluated task performance as difficult, recall was worse. Such a finding supports Crowder's (1980) suggestion that as difficulty increases the elderly suffer more.

STRATEGIES. Elderly adults are less proficient than young adults in usage of mnemonic strategies (Kausler, 1982). To determine how the participants evaluated their own usage of mnemonics, they were asked to estimate how often various strategies were used at encoding and retrieval. A 7-point rating scale (1=Never, 7=All the time) was used for each of 3 strategies: 1) Sequential, 2) Categorization, and 3) Imaging. The young and elderly adults did not differ in their use of strategies.

Recall scores were correlated with ratings for each type of strategy. For the young adults, none of the correlations were significant, thus supporting Cohen's idea that the processing is nonstrategic. For the elderly adults, two correlations were significant, the retrieval strategy of imaging (r=.43) and the sum of the retrieval strategies (r=.33). The presence of significant correlations suggest that memory training in retieval strategies, particularly an imaginal retrieval approach, might aid elderly adults concerned about absent-mindedness related to everyday events such as turning off the stove.

EXPERIMENT 2

The objective of Experiment 2 was to replicate the findings in Experiment 1, however, this time subjects were tested for recall of actions rather than recall of pairs of objects. In this experiment, only Ordinary actions were performed. Unusual tasks were not included because of an inherent problem related to the length of description of the action (discussed in Experiment 1).

There were twelve participants in each age group (MY=22 yr.; ME=69 yr.). The young people attended Washington University and the elderly adults resided in the St. Louis community. The lists and methods of presentation were the same as Experiment 1 with the exception that each participant performed one list of PROV-O actions and a different list of GEN-O actions. Participants took a 5-minute break outside the laboratory between the two conditions. The order of the type of performance was counterbalanced, thus half of the participants in each group performed the Provided actions first and half performed the Generated actions first.

Results appear on Table 1. A 2(Age) x 2(Provided/Generated)

x 2(Ordinary/Unusual) x 8(Serial Position) mixed ANOVA was performed, with Age as a between subject variable and Provided/Generated and Serial Position as within subject variables. There was a large age effect, F (1,22)= 9.05, with scores being .59 for the young and .46 for the elderly. Of note is the comparability of the results here and those of the Ordinary groups in Experiment 1. The age deficit of the elderly relative to the young adults was 23% in Experiment 1 and 22% in Experiment 2.

Neither the Provided/Generated main effect nor the Age x Provided/Generated interaction were significant, Fs < 2. The results replicate findings for the Ordinary conditions in Experiment 1. Scores for Experiment 1 and 2 respectively were .49 and .52 for the Provided condition and .53 and .53 for the Generated condition.

There was a main effect for Serial Position, F(7,154)=5.28. As shown in Figure 1, both a primacy and recency effect are present. For comparison, analyses were performed on the data from the Ordinary conditions in Experiment 1. A significant Serial Position main effect was present, F(7,308)=4.21, with primacy and recency portions being evident (Figure 1).

GENERAL DISCUSSION

The presence of an age deficit supports previous findings by Kausler & Lichty and contradicts Backman's lack of age effect. In contrast to Backman's hypothesis that multimodal information enables compensation because of contextual richness, the elderly may show a reduction in memory for activities because they are deficient in encoding contextual information (Burke & Light, 1981). Why didn't recall of Generated activities result in superior recall compared to Provided activities? It could be argued that recall in the GEN-O condition did not result in the kind of improved recall expected for verbal material because the people in the PROV-O condition were also generating the actions. This argument loses strength when the scores for the PROV-O and PROV-U conditions are compared. In the PROV-U condition, a person cannot possibly generate the action to be performed when the objects are presented, yet the scores for the PROV-O and PROV-U groups were virtually identical, with means being .49 and .48 respectively. The absence of a main effect for generation suggests that memory for activities will not show the typical generation effect.

Surprisingly, ordinary actions seem to yield more distinct memory traces, regardless of age. This seems to parallel the recall effect related to word frequency in that high frequency words are recalled better than low frequency words.

Cohen has suggested that the absence of a primacy effect provides support for the nonstrategic nature of processing. In the experiments here, a primacy effect was evident. The presence of a primacy effect suggests that activities may be strategically processed. The issue may not be whether activities are strategically or nonstrategically processed, rather, the issue may be that when people are asked to perform series of activities in the laboratory, the experience is so unique that they have no idea how to go about strategizing. Most of the people we tested assumed they would remember nearly everything and thus put little effort into remembering the activities. They often expressed considerable surprise that their scores were so low. Might the results of memory for lists of activities suffer, to some degree, from a confound related to unfamiliarity? The presence of a primacy effect is, by no means, conclusive evidence for strategic processing, however, the findings point out the need for further investigation.

REFERENCES

Backman, L. and Nilsson, L. (1984). 'Aging effects in free recall: An exception to the rule', Human Learning, 3, 53-69.

Backman, L. and Nilsson, L. (1985). 'Prerequisites for lack of age differences in memory performance', Experimental Aging Research, 11, 67-73.

Burke, D. M. and Light, L.L. (1981). 'Memory and aging: The role of retrieval processes', Psychological Bulletin, 90, 513-546.

Cohen, R.L. (1981). 'On the generality of some memory laws', Scandinavian Journal of Psychology, 22, 267-281.

Cohen, R.L. (1983). 'The effect of encoding variables on the free recall of words and action events', Memory and Cognition, 11, 575-582.

Crowder, R.G. (1980). 'Echoic memory and the study of aging Memory systems', in New Directions in Memory and Aging: Proceedings of the George Talland Memorial Conference. (Eds. L.W. Poon, J. L. Fozard, L.S. Cermak, D. Arenberg, L. W. Thompson), pp. 181-204, Lawrence Erlbaum, Hillsdale, NJ.

Hasher, L. and Zacks, R. T. (1979). 'Automatic and effortful processes in memory', Journal of Experimental Psychology: General, 108, 356-388.

Kausler, D. H. (1982). Experimental Psychology and Human Aging. Wiley, New York.

Kausler, D. H., Lichty, W., Hakami, M. K. and Freund, J. S. (1986). 'Activity duration and adult age differences in memory for activity performance', Psychology and Aging, 1, 80-81.

Lichty, W., Kausler, D. H., and Martinez, D. (1986). Adult age differences in memory for motor versus cognitive activities', Experimental Aging Research, 12, 227-230.

Slamecka, N. J. and Graf, P. (1978). 'The generation effect: Delineation of a phenomenon', Journal of Experimental Psychology: Human Learning and Memory, 4, 592-604.

LANGUAGE DIFFERENCES, WORKING MEMORY, AND MATHEMATICAL ABILITY

R. Hoosain and F. Salili
Department of Psychology, University of Hong Kong
Hong Kong

ABSTRACT

Four independent cross-cultural studies have shown that pronunciation times for numbers in half a dozen languages are different, and are correlated with digit span which is in turn related to capacity for mental calculations. These functions involve the articulatory loop. Chinese has the shortest number sound durations and biggest digit span. Visual-spatial relations are also more crucial in Chinese orthography, and there are some cross-cultural differences in visual-spatial scratch-pad functioning. All these differences can be considered a new aspect of the Sapir-Whorf hypothesis, concerning facility of information processing.

In the classical Sapir-Whorf hypothesis, language determines or influences thought. But "thought" refers to the way nature is carved up or how we categorize things. Introductory texts on linguistic relativity or determinism usually cite examples of the richness of Eskimo vocabulary for types of snow, Arabic words for camel, etc., and relate such language characteristics to perceptual capabilities. But attention is now given to what can be regarded as a new aspect of the Sapir-Whorf hypothesis (cf., Tzeng & Hung, 1981; Hoosain, 1986; Naveh-Benjamin & Ayres, 1986), not envisaged in the original formulation. Linguistic characteristics make a difference to the facility or speed with which information is processed, although the direction of the cognitive processing is the same and the end result is not any categorically different perception.

SOUND DURATION AND DIGIT SPAN

With reference to sound duration, there is now quite convincing evidence that different languages take different amounts of time to say the same things. More specifically, number names are pronounced at different speeds, whether in a natural manner or as fast as possible. Such linguistic differences in sound duration are correlated with differences in digit span size and possibly with mental calculation capacity. Ellis and Hennelly (1980) first reported a cross-linguistic difference in speed reading rate for random numbers, with an average of 321 milliseconds for English and 385 milliseconds for Welsh. They also found that digit span was 6.6 for English and 5.8 for Welsh. Hoosain (1984; 1987) reported that the speed reading time for random numbers read in the Cantonese dialect of Chinese was 265 milliseconds, while the digit span was 9.9. Sound durations for number names read at normal speed were also shorter for Cantonese than for English, with an average of 314 and 375 milliseconds respectively.

Stigler et al. (1986) confirmed the difference between English and Chinese (this time in the Putonghua or Mandarin dialect). The mean digit span for fifth-grade Chinese, American, and Japanese children was 6.9, 5.9, and 5.5 respectively. The possibility that such differences were due to the greater use of strategies by the Chinese is inconsistent with findings comparing Chinese and American children: the two groups had the same amount of increase in span for digits presented in groups (which should be more conducive to the use of grouping strategy), and the decline in performance for the more difficult backward digit span was actually greater for the Chinese than the Americans. In another experiment, Chinese adults had a span of 9.2 while Americans had a span of 7.2. The Chinese had also much faster pronunciation durations in their responses, with a modal rate of recalling the digits at 200 to 240 milliseconds, half the time taken by the Americans. However, there was one measure which did not show any significant difference between the Chinese and American university students: the total response duration for the longest string of digits reached by the subjects averaged 2.423 seconds for the Chinese and 2.905 seconds for the Americans.

The time of two seconds or a little more keeps appearing in digit span investigations. This is longer than the articulatory loop time suggested by Baddeley (e.g., 1983), but supportive of the idea that working memory capacity could be determined by a time based measure. In the studies mentioned earlier, the product of the reading rate for Welsh numbers and digit span would be 2.23 seconds, the product for English would be 2.12, and that for Cantonese 2.62. In other words, subjects appeared to have an immediate recall capacity corresponding to what they could pronounce in just over two seconds. In a study of English, Spanish, Hebrew, and Arabic, Naveh-Benjamin and Ayres (1986) found comparable times of 1.85, 1.83, 2.01, and 2.13 seconds respectively. It should be noted that the above times of around two seconds from various studies were obtained with slightly different procedures of presenting numbers for both the speed reading and digit span tests, although there are indications that such variations like presentation rate, within limits, do not significantly affect results (cf., Dempster, 1981).

Naveh-Benjamin and Ayres found that the digit span for the four languages was in the order of English (7.21), Hebrew (6.51), Spanish (6.37), and Arabic (5.77), while the speed reading rate was roughly in the reverse direction, with an average for each digit name being 370 milleseconds for Arabic, 309 milliseconds for Hebrew, 287 milliseconds for Spanish, and 256 milliseconds for English. Languages have different number of syllables for digit names, and Naveh-Benjamin and Ayres actually excluded the number seven (with two syllables in English) in their study to maximize the difference in the average number of syllables between the four languages. Actually, for the numbers nought to ten, Chinese is the only language amongst those mentioned so far to have one syllable for each of the numbers (and Arabic has an average of over two syllables). But number of syllables may not be the best indicator of pronunciation duration. For example, in English, "seven" has a shorter duration than "six", with normal reading times of 403 milliseconds and 578 milliseconds respectively (Hoosain, 1987). Naveh-Benjamin and Ayres have suggested the number of phonemes as an alternative indicator, but the actual situation may be more complex.

Given the group findings of pronunciation duration and digit span size, we would expect to see significant correlation of the two measures across subjects. In this connection we should note that variation in digit span size has to be very limited, with scores ranging about seven plus or minus two and the standard deviation being very small. Computed correlation values have to be therefore quite restricted. Nevertheless, Hoosain (1982) found a correlation of -.66 between Cantonese pronunciation time and digit span, and a correlation of -.70 between English pronunciation time and digit span for Chinese-English bilinguals. Naveh-Benjamin and Ayres (1986) reported a correlation of -.49 when subjects across their four language groups were pooled.

The above cross-linguistic differences in digit span have their implications in psychological testing. In the Chinese standardization of the WISC being done in Hong Kong, for example, random numbers in pairs are administered in the digit span test rather than the usual single digits, and indigenous norms are developed. In this connection, it might be pointed out that digit span used to be considered a culture fair test. If we can consider language as an aspect of culture, we might regard the cross-linguistic differences in sound duration and their implications (see below) as a new aspect of cultural bias. On the other hand, the possibility that the sound of languages, rather than morphology or syntax, might be a source of linguistic relativity or determinism is more or less ignored in the traditional Sapir-Whorf hypothesis.

WORKING MEMORY AND MATHEMATICAL ABILITY

Another consequence of shorter duration for pronunciation of numbers and bigger digit span could have more important applied implication. Ellis and Hennelley (1980) suggested that the poorer performance of Welsh children in arithmetic when compared with English children was related to number sound durations and digit span. For Chinese, there are some actual correlational data. Hoosain (1984; 1987) found a correlation of .38 between digit span and mathematics grades. The digit spans were obtained from undergraduate Introduction to Psychology students and the mathematics grades were from the secondary school leaving public examination grades obtained two years previously by the same students (there is a two-year intervening matriculation course before university entrance). The correlation is not large but significant, and again both the digit span and the mathematics grades have built-in small variations.

Chan (1981) reported a longitudinal study involving a few hundred students in Hong Kong. They went to two types of secondary schools, one using Chinese (Cantonese) as the medium of instruction, with English taught as one of the school subjects, and the other using English as the medium of instruction with Chinese taught as a school subject. Both the Chinese school children and the Anglo-Chinese school children, however, went to the one type of primary schools where Chinese is the medium of instruction. Furthermore, the two groups of students had comparable academic performance when they were tested in a common public examination at age 12. Choice of either of the two types of secondary schools is solely a matter of parental decision, although generally Anglo-Chinese schools are by far more popular. The two groups had quite different patterns of achievement in the school leaving examination taken five years later. The Chinese school students had better grades in Chinese and mathematics, but poorer grades in everything else. Their superior Chinese is understandable, but their better grades in mathematics is interesting, particularly in view of their generally inferior performance.

If we just concentrate on the role of working memory in problem solving in mathematics, unique characteristics of the Chinese language matter to the functioning of both the articulatory loop and the visual-spatial scratch-pad (cf., Baddeley, 1983). There is a trade-off between cognitive resources needed to maintain information in working memory and capacity to do something with the information in problem solving. The less of the capacity that is taken up with holding the information, the more is left for manipulation. Failure in problem solving can often be due to the unavailability of information in working memory. Hitch (1978), for example, reported on the role of the capacity to hold items and their arithmetical transformations in mental arithmetic.

Apart from the smaller room taken up by each individual Chinese number in the articulatory loop, there are indications that some elementary arithmetical operations are also more economically carried out. I have compared the times it takes a group of American undergraduates to read the multiplication table in English and a group of Chinese undergraduates to do so in Cantonese. Subjects were shown the identical table, beginning with 1 x 1 = 1 and ending with 9 x 9 = 81, and asked to read it as quickly as possible. The mean time for English was 134.2 seconds with a standard deviation of 40.2 seconds, and the mean for Cantonese was only 64.3 seconds with a standard deviation of 11.0 seconds. The difference was highly significant (t = 7.85, df = 44). It could be expected that these rapid reading times are good indicators of the relative time it takes to perform multiplication operations in the two languages.

In visual-spatial performance, which is related to the other element of working memory (Baddeley's visual-spatial scratch-pad), there is also evidence that the learning and use of Chinese could make a difference. With a non-alphabetic orthography, the visual aspect of Chinese script plays a more crucial role in perception and memory. Tzeng and Wang (1983) reported that in memorizing lists of words presented visually or orally, there was a recency effect in favour of orally presented items at the end of the lists for both English and Chinese. But a primacy effect in favour of visually presented items was found only for Chinese and not for English. Mann (1986) tested Japanese children and found that their short-term memory for abstract designs was related to memory for kanji (borrowed Chinese characters used in Japanese) but not related to their memory for kana (the native syllabic script). In neurolinguistics, there is some suggestion that while kana functioning might involve the temporal area, kanji functioning involves the occipito-parietal area more (cf., Paradis et al., 1985).

Together with the closer relationship between Chinese orthography and visual-spatial perception, there are reports of better performance of Chinese subjects in visual-spatial functioning. Lesser, et al. (1965) compared the space conceptualizaion and reasoning of Chinese, Jewish, Puerto Rican, and Black children, and found highest scores for the Chinese. Chan (1976) compared the performance in the Raven's Progressive Matrices (another test often considered to be culture fair), and found significantly better scores for Chinese compared with native English speaking students in Hong Kong. While the above comparisons are not direct tests of visual-spatial scratch-pad capacities in the way digit span measures articulatory loop functioning, they provide suggestions that different experiences of orthography do make some difference in visual functioning in problem solving situations.

CONCLUSION

It appears that language characteristics could be related to the functioning of both aspects of working memory: the articulatory loop function of maintaining numbers and the visual-spatial scratch-pad function of holding visual features. Such capacities have obvious roles to play in mathematical problem solving. The effects of language experiences in the facility for such information processing situations have not been envisaged in the traditional Sapir-Whorf hypothesis, but should be an important aspect of cross-cultural studies of cognitive behaviours.

REFERENCES

Baddeley, A.D. (1983) `Working Memory', Philosophical Transactions of the Royal Society London, B302, 311-324.

Chan, J. (1976). `Is Raven's Progressive Matrices Test Culture—Free or Culture-Fair? - Some Research Findings in Hong Kong Context', paper presented at the Third International Association for Cross-Cultural Psychology Congress, Tilburg.

Chan, J. (1981). `A Crossroads in Language Instruction', Journal of Reading, 22, 411-415.

Dempster, F.N. (1981). `Memory Span: Sources of Individual and Developmental Differences', Psychological Bulletin, 89, 63-100.

Ellis, N.C. and Hennelley, R.A. (1980). `A Bilingual Word-length Effect: Implications for Intelligence Testing and the Relative Ease of Mental Calculation in Welsh and English', British Journal of Psychology, 71, 43-51.

Hitch, G.J. (1978). `The Role of Short-term Working Memory in Mental Arithmetic', Cognitive Psychology, 10, 302-323.

Hoosain, R. (1979). `Forward and Backward Digit Span in the Languages of the Bilingual', The Journal of Genetic Psychology, 135, 263-268.

Hoosain, R. (1982). `Correlation Between Pronunciation Speed and Digit Span Size', Perceptual and Motor Skills, 55, 1128.

Hoosain, R. (1986). `Language, Orthography and Cognitive Processes: Chinese Perspectives for the Sapir-Whorf Hypothesis', International Journal of Behavioral Development, 9, 507-525.

Hoosain, R. (1987). `Language Differences in Pronunciation Speed for Numbers, Digit Span, and Mathematical Ability', Psychologia, 30, 34-38.

Lesser, G.S., Fifer, G. and Clark, D.H. (1965). `Mental Abilities of Children from Different Social Class and Cultural Groups', Monograph of the Society for Research in Child Development, 30, Part 4.

Mann, V.A. (1986). `Temporary Memory for Linguistic and Nonlinguistic Material in Relation to the Acquisition of Japanese Kana and Kanji', in Linguistics, Psychology, and the Chinese Language (Eds. H.S.R. Kao and R. Hoosain), pp. 155-168, University of Hong Kong Centre of Asian Studies, Hong Kong.

Naveh-Benjamin, M. and Ayres, T.J. (1986). `Digit Span, Reading Rate, and Linguistic Relativity', The Quarterly Journal of Experimental Psychology, 38, 739-751.

Paradis, M., Hagiwara, H. and Hildebrandt, N. (1985). Neurolinguistic Aspects of the Japanese Writing System, Academic Press, New York.

Stigler, J.W., Lee, S.Y. and Stevenson, H.W. (1986). `Digit Memory in Chinese and English: Evidence for a Temporally Limited Store', Cognition, 24, 1-20.

Tzeng, O.J.L. and Hung, D.L. (1981). `Linguistic Determinism: A Written Language Perspective', in Perception of Print: Reading Research in Experimental Psycholog (Eds. O.J.L. Tzeng and H. Singer), Erlbaum, Hillsdale.

Tzeng, O.J.L. and Wang, W. S.-Y. (1983). `The First Two R's', American Scientist, 71, 238-243.

EFFECT OF UNFOLDING STIMULUS PRESENTATION
ON RECOGNITION MEMORY

Zehra F. Peynircioglu
Bogazici University, Istanbul, Turkey

Michael Watkins
Rice University, USA

ABSTRACT

In laboratory research on recognition memory stimulus items are presented all at once whereas in the world beyond the laboratory they often come into view more or less gradually. Reported here is an experiment in which the likelihood of test words being judged as having been included in an earlier study list increased systematically with the gradualness of the presentation, regardless of whether they had in fact been included. When words were presented all at once (e.g., elephant) they were less likely to be recognized than when they were gradually unfolded (-l----n-, el----n-, el----nt, el-p--nt, el-p-ant, el-phant, elephant). Implications of this finding are discussed.

Our ability to recognize a stimulus item--be it a person, an object, a sound, a smell, a place, or whatever--as something we have encountered before is a crucial faculty in negotiating the everyday world. Almost all of the empirical research on this faculty has been conducted in the form of laboratory experiments. By manipulating a variable of interest and by holding constant or minimizing the effects of potentially confounding variables, researchers have used the experimental method to gather evidence that would be virtually impossible to obtain merely by observing in the world outside the laboratory.

Informal observations made in the "real" world ought, however, to play a role in the conduct of inquiry within the laboratory. The layman has more than sufficient knowledge about memory to provide a useful source of ideas for experimental research as well as a basis for interpreting the results of that research. To disregard lay wisdom is to risk impeding our understanding.

Until the 1970s, researchers of recognition memory ignored the dynamic character of the real world, where stimuli are experienced as being in a constant state of change: We see someone we have recently met, but her appearance and the physical context are different. It does not take an expert memory theorist to predict that these differences would reduce the probability of her being recognized. At the same time, expertise is no guarantee that the point will be heeded. Before context effects were demonstrated (e.g., Thomson, 1972; Tulving & Thomson, 1971; Watkins, Ho & Tulving, 1976), recognition memory tended to be regarded as a straightforward test of what could potentially be remembered. It was commonly assumed that other forms of memory could fail because of a failure in a hypothesized search for the item in question, whereas in recognition a successful search was guaranteed by the mere presence of the item in the test (e.g., Anderson & Bower, 1972; Bahrick, 1969; Kintsch, 1970). This assumption in turn fueled an atomistic conceptualization of memory in which items were represented as nodes in a gigantic semantic network and specific encounters with these items were represented as tags appended to their respective nodes. Although this kind of thinking has never quite gone away, findings of context effects in recognition memory and more dramatically of recognition failure for recallable items (Tulving & Thomson, 1973; Watkins & Tulving, 1975) serve to underscore its fundamental weakness, for they show that a recognition test does not provide an infallible method of deciding whether a past encounter is capable of being remembered. (For a detailed discussion of this issue, see Watkins & Gardiner, 1979.)

The concern of the present paper is with another way in which real-world recognition differs from recognition as investigated in the laboratory. Real-world stimuli often come into view more or less gradually. Our first glimpse of them may be from a distance or from a less than optimal perspective, and identification may not come until the view improves. The effects of such dynamics have received remarkably scant study. The dearth of laboratory research is all the more remarkable in the light of the results of what little research has been conducted. A classic study by Bruner and Potter (1964) simulated the real-word clarification of stimuli by showing blurred pictures of objects and then gradually reducing the blur until a preset stopping level was reached, at which point the subjects tried to identify the object. What was varied was the degree of blur when the picture was first presented. Thus, for some pictures the initial blur was very much greater than the stopping-level blur, for others only moderately so, and for yet others only slightly so. Bruner and Potter found that the probability of identification varied with the level of initial blur, such that the more the initial blur, the lower the probability of identification.

A study from our own laboratory (Peynircioglu & Watkins, 1986) also required subjects to identify degraded stimuli that were presented more or less directly. This time the stimuli were 8-letter words (e.g., raindrop) and their degradation was achieved by deleting three of the letters (e.g., r-i--rop). Subjects studied some of the words beforehand and then took a test in which they tried to identify the 5-letter fragments of both the studied and the nonstudied words. Directness of stimulus presentation was varied by showing the fragments piecemeal (r------p, r----r-p, r-i--r-p, r-i--rop) or all at once (r-i--rop). The results paralled those of Bruner and Potter in that the 5-letter fragments were less likely to be identified when presented bit by bit rather than all at once. Contrary to what might be expected from Bruner and Potter's findings, this 'cue depreciation' effect consistently occurred for those words that had been studied beforehand and consistently failed to occur for those words that had not.

These two studies show that stimulus identification may depend upon how the stimuli are presented. The question addressed in the study that we report here is whether the way in which the stimuli are presented affects recognition memory. In general terms, our strategy was to simulate the gradualness of real—world stimulus clarification in a laboratory experiment much as we had done in our earlier study (Peynircioglu & Watkins, 1986). Thus, in the study phase of the procedure words were shown in a conventional way, and then in the test phase these words, along with some new words, were presented with a varying number of their letters removed. These letters were then added one by one. The subjects' task was to wait until they knew what the word was and then to say "Yes" if they thought it had occurred in the study list. At issue was whether the likelihood of response was influenced by how many of the word's letters were displayed at its initial presentation.

METHOD

Subjects. Twenty—eight young adults were paid for participating. They were students or employees of an American university.

Materials. The stimulus items were 117 8—letter words. Some examples are elephant, sergeant, epidemic, stallion, aquarium, and triangle. Seven words were used in a practice procedure and the remainder in the experiment proper. Five of the practice words and 96 of those assigned to the experiment proper were printed on small (3—inch by 5—inch) flash cards, one word to each card, for presentation in the study list. All of the practice words and 98 of those assigned to the experiment proper (84 of those presented in the study list and all 14 remaining words) were also printed on large (5—inch by 8—inch) flash cards for presentation in the test phase. Each test card showed seven versions of the same word. The topmost version consisted of just two letters and six place holders; the second version consisted of three letters, including the two shown in the first version; and so on down to the bottom row, which showed the complete word. For example, the successive rows of one test card showed: -l----n-, el----n-, el----nt, el-p--nt, el-p-ant, el-phant, and elephant. For both the study cards and the test cards, the letters were printed 0.6 inches in height.

Design. For the study phase all subjects saw the same sequence of 96 words. The first 6 and the last 6 words from this sequence served as buffer words, which were included to reduce potential primacy and recency effects. For the test sequence, the remaining 84 words were mixed at random with 14 new words. For any given test word a different starting level was used for each of 7 groups of 4 subjects. For any given group of subjects the test included 12 studied words and 2 new words at each of the seven starting levels.

Procedure. The subjects were tested individually. Before being presented with the main study list they were given practice with the study and test procedures. The words of the study list were shown at a rate of one every 4 seconds, and the subject was instructed simply to look carefully at each one. The test words were also presented on flash cards, although this time each word was represented in seven versions that differed in degree of completeness (i.e., in the number of letters in view). The

experimenter selected the required degree of completeness by
covering over the more complete versions; if the subject did not
respond within 4 seconds the experimenter lowered the cover to
expose the next version for 4 seconds, and so on until the subject
responded or the complete word had been exposed for 4 seconds. The
response was always "Yes", and it indicated that the subject
thought the word had been included in the study list; words that
were thought not to have been included in the study list required no
response. For both the practice test and the main test, the number
of letters in the initial exposure of a test word varied at random
from two to all eight.

RESULTS
        The subjects showed a fair degree of accuracy in
distinguishing between those words they had seen in the study list
and those that were new. On average, they responded to 79.72% of
the old words and to just 22.19% of the new.
        Of more relevance to the present concern than the effect of
occurrence in the study list is the effect of the number of letters
in the starting version of the test item. Table 1 shows, separately
for the studied and nonstudied words, the mean proportion of
responses as a function of the starting level of the test item,
without regard to the number of letters in view when the response
was made. The finding of interest is the tendency for the
proportions to decline as starting level increased. Put another
way, the more quickly the test words were revealed, the less likely
were the subjects to claim that they were included in the study
list.
        To evaluate this tendency, a linear component of trend was
computed for each subject. Specifically, the subject's response
probabilities for the 2-letter through 8-letter starting levels were
multiplied by -3, -2, -1, 0, $+1$, $+2$, $+3$, respectively, and the
resulting products were summed. The mean of these products was
significantly different from zero both for the studied words, t (27)
$= -3.85$, p $< .001$, and for the nonstudied words, t (22) $= -2.76$, p
$< .02$; the reduced degrees of freedom for the latter t value
reflect the failure of five subjects to make any positive responses
to nonstudied words.

Table 1. Proportion of positive responses for the studied and the
nonstudied as a function of the number of letters in the initial
version of the test word.

Number of letters in the initial version of the test word

	2	3	4	5	6	7	8
Studied words words	.83	.81	.82	.81	.83	.78	.69
Nonstudied words	.29	.29	.25	.23	.21	.18	.11

Note. In conventional terms, the proportions for the studied words
are the hit rates and those for the nonstudied words are the false
positive rates.

Much of the trend can be accounted for by the difference between the 8-letter condition and the average of all the other conditions, which means that the effect of starting level was due in substantial measure to the effect of presenting incomplete rather than complete versions of the test items, regardless of the degree of incompleteness. On the other hand, it would be premature to conclude that there was no effect at all over the starting-level range of 2 to 7 letters, for even within this range the linear trend was in the same direction as for the whole range both for the studied words and for the nonstudied words. Moreover, even though the linear trend over the 2-to-7 range was not statistically significant for either the studied words, t (27) = -1.44, .10 < p < separately, it was significant when the two kinds of items were combined, t (27) = -2.24, p < .05.

It may be worth noting that our data provide no compelling evidence that starting level affected sensitivity to prior study. How the number of letters in the initial version of the test words related to the degree to which the responses discriminated between those words that had been studied and those that had not was determined according to each of two commonly used models of discrimination, namely signal detection theory and the high threshold model. The former indicated a positive relation and the latter a negative relation, although in neither case was the relation statistically significant.

DISCUSSION

Our results were unexpected. To be sure, the directness with which stimuli occur is known to affect the probability of identification (Bruner & Potter, 1964; Peynircioglu & Watkins, 1986), but because our procedure allowed clarification of the stimuli to continue until identification was achieved, regardless of starting level, there would seem to be no reason for supposing that starting level would affect the decisions about whether the stimuli had been included in the prior study list.

A satisfactory account of our findings will probably have to await further research. Certainly, we need some idea of their generality. Would, for example, the same pattern of results occur with Bruner and Potter's focusing procedure or with yet other possible ways of clarifying the stimuli, or when other kinds of materials and other sensory modalities are used? Also, the durability of the effect should be explored by making the subjects wait until some time after all of the letters are presented before responding. And it would be instructive to know what would happen if the subjects were instructed to respond to what they judged to be the new items rather than the old items.

We should reiterate that our concern has been with recognition and not with discrimination. Their decidedly cognitive orientation notwithstanding, contemporary experimental psychologists pay little heed to the experiential side of memory and are usually content to operationalize recognition memory in terms of the discriminability of the old and new test items. We suspect that this practice is, in part at least, another consequence of the failure to consider recognition memory as it occurs in the real world beyond the laboratory. Of their very essence, experiments reduce the subjects' control over the environment, including the prospects of their gaining a more informative view of stimulus items. And the evidence reported here suggests that gaining a more informative view could have subtle but important conseqences. Even though the development of, as opposed to the mere existence of, an optimal view may not make previously encountered items more distinguishable from new items, it can affect the response they are given. It could, for instance, cause us to stop in her tracks that woman we believe we have met and reintroduce ourselves--even if mistakenly. And that, of course, could have far reaching ramifications.

REFERENCES

Anderson, J. R., & Bower, G. H. (1972). 'Recognition and retrieval processes in free recall', Psychological Review, 79, 97-123.

Bahrick, H. P. (1969). 'Measurement of memory by prompted recall', Journal of Experimental Psychology, 97, 213-219.

Bruner, J. S., & Potter, M. C. (1964). 'Interference in visual recognition', Science, 144, 424-425.

Kintsch, W. (1970). 'Models for free recall and recognition', in Models of human memory (Ed. D. A. Norman), pp. 331-373, Academic Press, New York.

Peynircioglu, Z. F., & Watkins, M. J. (1986). 'Cue depreciation: When word fragment completion is undermined by prior exposure to lesser fragments', Journal of Experimental Psychology: Learning, Memory and Cognition, 12, 426-431.

Thomson, D. M. (1972). 'Context effects in recognition memory', Journal of Verbal Learning and Verbal Behavior, 11, 497-511.

Tulving, E., & Thomson, D. M. (1971). 'Retrieval processes in recognition memory: Effects of associative context', Journal of Experimental Psychology, 87, 116-124.

Tulving, E., & Thomson, D. M. (1973). 'Encoding specificity and retrieval processes in episodic memory', Psychological Review, 80, 352-373.

Watkins, M. J. & Gardiner, J. M. (1979). 'An appreciation of the generate- recognize theory of recall', Journal of Verbal Learning and Verbal Behavior, 18, 687-784.

Watkins, M. J., Ho, E., & Tulving, E. (1976). 'Context effects in recognition memory for faces', Journal of Verbal Learning and Verbal Behavior, 15, 508-518.

Watkins, M. J. & Tulving, E. (1975). 'Episodic memory: When recognition fails', Journal of Experimental Psychology: General, 104, 5-29.

EXPERT KNOWLEDGE AND SEMANTIC MEMORY

Veronika Coltheart and Paul Walsh
City of London Polytechnic, London, UK

ABSTRACT

Semantic memory in expert bird watchers was studied in scaling tasks, long-term memory recall, speeded classification, and tests of bird knowledge. Bird knowledge appears to be organised in a complex way which reflects both a biological taxonomy and experience of viewing birds in their natural habitat.

How does expertise in a particular domain of knowledge affect the organisation of semantic memory for that domain? We studied this by exploring semantic memory for birds in a group of people very knowledgeable in ornithology and compared the results with what has been observed in studies of semantic memory for birds in non-expert subjects (Rips, Shoben and Smith, 1973; Coltheart and Evans, 1981; Coltheart, Hale and Walsh, 1985).

SUBJECTS. The subjects in the experiments were all active members in one or more of the national ornithological societies and had considerable field experience as well as factual knowledge about birds seen in Britain. They ranged in age from 20 years to 50 years and most were men. Seventeen subjects participated in the first session (Tasks 1, 2, 3 and 4) and twelve returned for the second session (Tasks 5 and 6). Four additional subjects participated in the second session only. They were paid and the sessions took 2-3 hours.

TASKS 4 AND 6: TESTS OF BIRD KNOWLEDGE. These tasks were devised to provide a simple objective index of the subjects' bird knowledge. Task 4 consisted of 20 descriptions of birds seen in Britain. These were selected from a guidebook (Peterson, Mountford and Hollom, 1972). The subjects had to identify and write down the name of the bird for each one. The 20 chosen included a varied set of birds. Two sets of bird silhouettes, one of 20 standing birds and one of 22 birds in flight, (taken from Peterson et al., 1972) were also included and the subjects had to identify these too.

Task 6 used only descriptions and these were selected from a teaching book (Kilbracken, 1982).

The subjects correctly identified 98% of the birds from the verbal descriptions given in Task 4. The subjects identified an average of 87% standing and 79% flying silhouettes. The descriptions provided in Task 6 were more difficult but the subjects still managed a mean correct score of 83%. Thus, the subjects performed very well on these tests of bird knowledge.

These tests by no means exhaust the multifaceted body of knowledge that these expert subjects possess. They are able to identify hundreds of types in the field from a considerable distance and fleeting glimpses. Many sources of information contribute to the identification: song and call notes, pattern of movement on ground and in the air, behaviour and habitat as well as appearance. Consequently, Tasks 4 and 6 tapped only a limited amount of this knowledge.

TASK 1: RECALL OF BIRD NAMES. This was actually the first task performed so that responses would be uninfluenced by the prior presentation of bird names or descriptions. The subjects were asked to write down on a piece of paper as many bird names as they could in 10 minutes in the order in which they occurred to them.

A large number of highly specific bird names were listed by the subjects: $\bar{x} = 58.2$ range $= 34$-82. These recalls were strongly semantically clustered. The first bird recalled was robin or sparrow for 7 subjects and a diver or other water bird for 7 subjects. Then followed other examples from the same or a related species, e.g., Subject 1 recalled 59 birds, first robin then 2 thrushes, 3 finches, 3 warblers, 2 sparrows. Recall then switched to the water bird category, to crows, to birds of prey, to waders, and so on. Such small clusters have been reported in various category listing studies, e.g., Mandler (1975). Similarly organised recall was displayed by the other subjects. One subject adopted an alphabetic recall strategy beginning with anhinga, and recalled the fewest birds: 34. These retrieval data indicate that recall from semantic memory is highly organised for expert bird watchers. It appears to be organised hierarchically in that, for example, water birds are recalled together, but within that category there is further subdivision into the categories of wader, duck, gull, etc. Although in some cases, e.g. gull, the species share the base name, in others they do not. Organisation in undergraduates' recall of natural categories such as mammals was also reported by Henley (1969) but the clustering was based on much larger categories, e.g., large herbivores. The difference in the recall by the experts appears to lie in both the larger number of uncommon bird names recalled and in the larger number of subcategories in which these were grouped.

TASK 3: SCALING STUDY OF GENERAL BIRD NAMES. The 17 subjects were asked to rate similarity (on a 7-point scale) of every possible pair of the 20 bird names previously rated by undergraduate subjects (Coltheart et al., 1985). The birds were budgerigar, canary, chicken, duck, eagle, flamingo, hawk, nightingale, ostrich, owl, parrot, peacock, penguin, pheasant, robin, seagull, sparrow, swan, turkey, vulture.

The data were analysed by use of Sindscal (Carroll and Chang, 1970). The correlations between the data and the distances obtained from the scaling solution were compared for solutions varying in dimensionality and the improvement in fit was negligible beyond 4 dimensions (<.02). The percent variance accounted for by each of the 4 dimensions was 34%, 16%, 10% and 6% respectively. Interpretation was attempted by property fitting techniques (Carroll and Chang, 1970). The properties consisted of a set of mean bipolar scale ratings obtained from the earlier study (Coltheart et al., 1985). The co-ordinates of the dimensions are entered as predictors (in order from D1-D4) and the scale values are the dependent variables. A bipolar scale is relevant to the similarity judgments and, hence to the scaling solution, if it yields a high multiple R ($\geqslant$.80). It provides a label for a dimension if it is highly correlated with only one of the dimensions. Using these criteria it appeared that Dimension 1 distinguished large, country, and small melodious town birds. Dimension 2 distinguished predatory birds from non-predatory ones. Dimension 3 appeared to be based on a water/land distinction and Dimension 4 was less clear but distinguished largely between English and foreign birds. These dimensions were quite similar to those found for inexpert subjects, except that for the inexpert subjects Dimension 2 distinguished birds which fly easily from those which do not.

TASK 2: SPEEDED CATEGORISATION. The subjects also participated in a speeded classification task. This task was adapted from a semantic priming paradigm in lexical decision (Meyer and Schvaneveldt, 1971). Lexical decision is facilitated when a semantically related word had just occurred. We observed a similar effect in a categorisation task (Coltheart and Evans, 1981). People were faster at judging pairs of successively presented words as bird names when these were close in a multidimensional space, e.g. hawk-eagle than when the pair were distant, e.g., robin-eagle. A small but significant facilitation effect was also observed using the 20 bird names previously scaled by inexpert subjects (Coltheart et al., 1985). The expert subjects were presented the double categorisation task using selected pairs of the 20 bird names from Task 3. The subjects performed the categorisation task before the scaling task in order to avoid prior exposure to the 20 bird names. They had to judge whether pairs of words were both bird names or not. On half the trials both words were bird names and required a "Yes" key press and on the remaining trials one word was a bird name while the other was the name of a piece of furniture. On these mixed trials a "No" response was required and on half the trials the bird name preceded, and on half the furniture name occurred first. The "Yes" trials consisted of 19 close bird names, and 20 distant names. Order of presentation was separately randomised for each subject and the words were presented in the centre of a VDU screen. A fixation point for 500 ms indicated the start of a trial. It was followed by a word presented for 500 ms and then a second word which stayed on until the subject responded with a key press. Decision times to the second word were recorded in msec.

Mean RT for decisions to close and distant pairs of bird names was calculated for each of 16 subjects. The mean of these RTs for close pairs was 1111 ms whereas the mean RT for distant pairs was 1179 ms and the difference between these was significant (t(15) = 2.72, p<.05). Thus, the expert subjects displayed a significant facilitatory priming effect when categorising bird names.

The data obtained here differed from those found with inexpert subjects (Coltheart et al., 1985) in two ways. Firstly, the expert subjects show a much larger facilitation effect of 68 ms whereas the inexpert subjects showed a much smaller effect of 17 ms. Secondly, the expert subjects responded more slowly: 1111 ms versus 648 ms for close pairs. This slower responding may, however, have occurred for rather uninteresting reasons: the expert subjects were older than the inexpert subjects and the latter group had rather more practice on speeded classification tasks in other experiments.

TASK 5: SCALING STUDY OF SPECIFIC BIRD NAMES. In the scaling study so far reported both the scaling solutions from multidimensional scaling analysis were very similar to those obtained from non-expert people. The next study required the expert subjects to make similarity judgments about a more specialised set of bird names. An attempt was made to represent the British birds from the earlier set of 20 with more specific examples and to include other bird names so as to represent the range of birds encountered by the experts. Many of the examples used had also been correctly identified by the subjects in the questionnaires from verbal descriptions. The sixteen subjects performed a scaling task similar to that of Task 3. The bird names are shown in Figures 1-3.

The 16 dissimilarity matrices were analysed by Sindscal. The correlations between the data and derived distances showed relatively little improvement beyond 4 dimensions. Inspection of the 5- and 6-dimensional solutions also showed that Dimensions 5 and 6 accounted for less than 5% of the variance and were difficult to interpret. Thus, interpretation was attempted for the 4-dimensional solution. For this solution the correlation between data and derived distances was .73 and the proportion of variance accounted for by each dimension was 30%, 11%, 7% and 6% respectively.

Properties of the birds obtained from textbook descriptions and pictures (Peterson *et al.*, 1972) were used in property fitting regression techniques. The characteristic water/land yielded a multiple R = .96 and it was strongly correlated with D1 (r = .95). Inspection of the configuration confirms that D1 seems to separate water from land birds.

Dimension 2 appears to distinguish song birds from other types. Song birds (or passerines) constitute over half of all bird species and regression analysis using this classification yielded a multiple R = .85 and a correlation with D2 = .82. Dimension 3 seems to be based on predatoriness with kestrel and sparrow hawk at one extreme and turtle dove at the other. Regression analysis showed that predatoriness yielded a high multiple R = .90 and a correlation with D3 = .67. Dimension 4 seemed to contrast the colourful birds with the achromatic ones (white, black and grey ones) and colour as a property produced multiple R = .77 and a correlation of .74 with D4.

This solution resembles the earlier one in that both the water/land and predatoriness dimensions are represented. However, the other two dimensions seem more specific than those in the earlier solution. Since the scaling solution seemed to represent only rather general distinctions among the bird names Additive Tree analysis was also performed (Sattath and Tversky, 1977).

This analysis was based on an averaged dissimilarity matrix. The proportion of variance explained was high (.84). It contained four clusters directly connected to the root of the tree. The largest of these contains three subgroups: the water birds, the aerial predatory birds, and birds found in woodland. There are subgroups within these groups: the water birds are separated into the anatidae (heron, goose, duck, swan) the sea birds, and others. The other large major cluster includes mainly the song birds with further groupings of the finches, the melodious singers (nightingale and linnet) and the remainder possibly grouped because they are often found in the same terrain. The exception to this group is the swift.

The two small clusters are, firstly, a grouping of redstart and redwing possibly together because of the names and distinctive red colouring, and, secondly, the grey wagtail and starling. The latter are tame birds which are unafraid of people and may be grouped on that basis. Distance from the root is greatest for the water birds and birds of prey indicating that these are the most distinctive while the remainder are close to the root. The fact that the experts' knowledge more closely resembles a biological taxonomy suggests that a tree representation may be more appropriate for their data.

DISCUSSION. Performance on the questionnaires, category listing and on the specific bird scaling indicated that the expert subjects have a very detailed knowledge of birds. All of these tasks included bird names that many people have not even heard of before. The listing and the scaling data both indicate that bird knowledge is organised in a complex way which reflects both a biological taxonomy and experience of viewing birds in their natural habitats. Although experts have far more extensive knowledge than others, two of the features important to them are also shared with non-experts. Thus, the distinction between water and land birds and the characteristic of predatoriness were important to experts and non-experts. Furthermore, when asked to compare the rather general set of 20 birds, the experts structured these similarly to the non-experts. The experts also showed a large facilitation effect in speeded word categorisation.

The fact that more categories or dimensions did not emerge when the experts scaled the specific bird names may seem surprising. A possible reason for this is that the set included a wide range of types of birds and only the more general distinctions could therefore emerge. It would be possible to ask the subjects to scale far more specific subsets of birds, e.g., freshwater birds, or even more specific sets, e.g., thrushes. More specific dimensions or categories are likely to be revealed under such conditions. Thus, we conclude that our tasks have indicated the existence of a very complex structured knowledge domain in expert bird watchers.

REFERENCES
Carroll, J.D. and Chang, J.J. (1970). 'An Analysis of "Individual" Differences in Multidimensional Scaling Via an N-Way Generalisation of Eckhart-Young Decomposition', Psychometrika, 35, 283-319.

Coltheart, V. and Evans, J. St. B.T. (1981). 'An Investigation of Semantic Memory in Individuals', Memory and Cognition, 9, 524-532.

Coltheart, V. Hale, D. and Walsh, P. (1985). 'Semantic Representation of Taxonomic Categories: Multidimensional Scaling and Categorisation Experiments', presented at Annual Meeting of the Psychonomic Society, Boston.

Henley, N.M. (1969). 'Psychological Study of the Semantics of Animal Terms', Journal of Verbal Learning and Verbal Behavior, 8, 176-184.

Kilbracken, J.G. (1982). The Easy way to bird recognition. Kingfisher, London.

Mandler, G. (1975). 'Memory storage and retrieval: Some limits on the reach of attention and consciousness', in Attention and Performance V (Eds. P.M.A. Rabbitt and S. Dornic), Academic Press, London.

Meyer, D.E. and Schvaneveldt, R.W. (1971). 'Facilitation in recognising pairs of words: Evidence of a dependence between retrieval operations', Journal of Experimental Psychology, 90, 227–234.

Peterson, R., Mountford, G. and Hollom, P.A.D. (1972). A Field Guide to the Birds of Britain and Europe, Collins, London.

Rips, L.J., Shoben, E.J. and Smith, E.E. (1973). 'Semantic distance and the verification of semantic relations', Journal of Verbal Learning and Verbal Behavior, 12, 1–20.

Sattath, S. and Tversky, A. (1977). 'Additive similarity trees', Psychometrika, 42, 319–345.

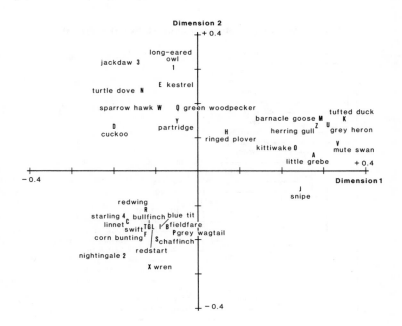

Figure 1.   Dimensions 1 and 2 of an MDS solution for 30 bird names.

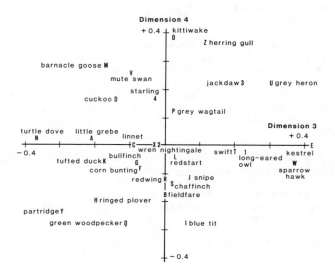

Figure 2.   Dimensions 3 and 4 of an MDS solution for 30 bird names.

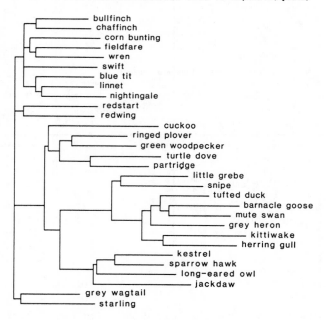

Figure 3.   Additive Tree Representation of 30 bird names.

HEADINGS AS MEMORY FACILITATORS

Stephen C. Wilhite
Widener University
Chester, Pennsylvania, U.S.A.

ABSTRACT

This experiment investigated the effect of headings on memory as a function of the reader's pre-existing knowledge about the passage topic. The 116 college student subjects read a 1,760-word passage on human sexuality with headings either present or absent. An analysis of the scores on the multiple-choice retention test revealed that the only significant facilitative effect of the headings was in the answering of main-idea retention test questions by subjects with high pre-existing knowledge about the topic, as assessed by a pretest, $p < .05$. Thus, the results suggest that headings facilitate recognition memory for main-idea information by activating relevant prior knowledge.

PROBLEM AND CONCEPTUAL FRAMEWORK

Recent studies (e.g., Dee-Lucas & DiVesta, 1980; Hartley, Kenely, Owen, & Trueman, 1980; Hartley, Morris, & Trueman, 1981; Hartley & Trueman, 1983, 1985; Holley, Dansereau, Evans, Collins, Brooks, & Larson, 1981) have reported facilitative effects of headings on various types of recall performance. These findings have in turn been complemented by results showing a significant positive effect of headings on multiple-choice test performance (Brooks, Dansereau, Spurlin, & Holley, 1983, exp. 1; Wilhite, 1986), suggesting that headings can have a general facilitative effect on memory for expository prose. In their study, Brooks et al. (1983) suggested that headings may facilitate memory by activating schemas relevant to the passage topic, by encouraging the interrelating of concepts in the text, and by providing cues for subsequent retrieval. The present study was designed to investigate to what extent schema activation is in fact involved in any facilitative effect that headings may have on multiple-choice test performance following the reading of a passage.

If headings do encourage memory for passage information by activating schemas as organizational frameworks for the encoding of the material (cf. Anderson, Spiro, & Anderson, 1978; Ausubel, 1963, 1968; Bartlett, 1932; Spilich, Vesonder, Chiesi, & Voss, 1979; Voss, 1984; Voss, Vesonder, & Spilich, 1980), then only subjects who possess the relevant schemas, as assessed by some measure of pre-existing knowledge about the passage topic, should benefit from the inclusion of headings in the text. If, on the other hand, headings aid multiple-choice test performance primarily by promoting the interrelating of concepts and by providing cues for retrieval of the information, then all subjects should benefit from the inclusion of headings in the text. However, subjects with higher levels of pre-existing knowledge might still be expected to demonstrate a greater benefit from the headings because headings might be more likely to promote the interrelating of concepts in readers with relatively high levels of pre-existing knowledge about the topic.

Also included in the present study was the factor of hierarchical importance of the passage information being tested. Wilhite (1986) included this factor in his experiment and found that the facilitative effect of headings on recognition memory for main-idea and detail information was not significantly different. As a result, he concluded that headings may produce a general enhancement in the availability of both high-level and low-level information in the passage. Thus, it was of interest to determine if the same result could be obtained in a study employing a different prose passage. The factor of hierarchical importance was also included in order to try to determine to what extent this tendency of headings to promote memory for both main-ideas and details might depend on the reader's pre-existing knowledge about the topic. For example, would headings be more likely to promote memory for main-ideas than for details in subjects with high levels of pre-existing knowledge because of the possibly greater ability of these subjects to distinguish between main-idea and detail information in the passage, or would headings be more likely to promote memory for details than for main-ideas in subjects with high levels of pre-existing knowledge because these subjects would tend to be able to encode main-ideas effectively even in the absence of headings?

METHODOLOGY

A total of 116 college student subjects read in booklet format a 1,760-word passage on human sexuality from an introductory college psychology text after receiving instructions to read and study the passage in preparation for a later multiple-choice exam on the passage. The passage was divided into eight sections, each consisting of two or three paragraphs. Two versions of the passage were prepared. In one version, the passage appeared with each of the sections of the passage preceded by a heading that consisted of a word or short phrase describing the main topic of the following material. In the other version, the passage appeared with the headings removed. The two versions of the passage were arranged in random order for distribution to subjects. Fifty-five of the subjects read the version of the passage with the headings present, and the remaining 61 subjects read the version of the passage with the headings absent. Prior to reading the passage, all subjects completed a test of prior knowledge about human sexuality that consisted of eight multiple-choice questions based on low-level detail information from each of the passage segments. After reading the passage, subjects completed a test of vocabulary knowledge before receiving the multiple-choice retention test. The test contained 16 text-based questions, one main-idea question and one detail question from each passage segment. None of the questions from the pre-test were repeated on the retention test.

RESULTS

A 2 X 2 multivariate analysis of covariance was employed in analyzing the data. The two independent variables were pre-existing knowledge group (high pre-existing knowledge and low pre-existing knowledge, based on a median split of pretest scores) and headings group (headings present and headings absent). The two dependent measures were the number of main-idea retention test questions answered correctly, and the number of detail retention test questions answered correctly. The covariate was the score on the vocabulary test. The means from the analysis are shown in Table 1. The interaction of pre-existing knowledge group and headings group was significant, multivariate $F(2, 110) = 4.25$, $p = .017$. Univariate tests revealed that the interaction was significant in the answering of main-idea retention test questions, $F(1, 111) = 7.51$, $p = .007$, but not in the answering of detail retention test questions, $F(1, 111) < 1$. Tukey's test for unconfounded means showed that the effect of headings was significant only for the high pre-existing knowledge group, $p < .05$. That is, the high pre-existing knowledge subjects in the headings-present group performed significantly better on the main-idea retention test items than did the high pre-existing knowledge subjects in the headings-absent group. However, the low pre-existing knowledge subjects in the headings-present group did not perform significantly better on the main-idea retention test items than the low pre-existing knowledge subjects in the headings-absent group.

Table 1. Mean number of multiple-choice questions answered correctly.

| | Headings group | | | | |
| | Main-idea questions | | | Detail questions | |
Pre-existing knowledge group	Present	Absent		Present	Absent
High					
Mean	7.24	6.22		5.91	5.94
SD	.79	1.57		1.13	1.13
n	28	29		28	29
Low					
Mean	5.67	5.87		5.34	5.15
SD	1.41	1.54		1.49	1.73
n	27	32		27	32

Note: The maximum possible score was 8. The means shown were adjusted for the effect of the covariate, vocabulary test score.

IMPLICATIONS AND CONCLUSIONS

Thus, the results suggest that part of the facilitative effect of headings on recognition memory is due to schema activation and that such an organizational effect of headings is more likely to benefit main-idea information than detail information in a passage. The fact that headings did not significantly affect the performance of the subjects in the low pre-existing knowledge group suggests that other possible influences of headings in terms of promoting the interrelating of concepts and providing retrieval cues (Brooks et al., 1983) did not operate for the subjects with low pre-existing knowledge. This possibility that headings did not encourage the interrelating of concepts and the use of the headings as retrieval cues by the low pre-existing knowledge group is consistent with the assumption that the effectiveness of headings in promoting these operations is somewhat dependent on the headings successfully activating pre-existing knowledge about the topic. Of possible relevance to this interpretation are findings of Chiesi, Spilich, and Voss (1979) showing that as the number of context sentences preceding the target sentence at input increased, recall of the target sentence by subjects with low pre-existing knowledge about the topic of the sentences declined significantly. These findings have been interpreted by Voss (1984) as suggesting that low-knowledge subjects are not adept at integrating the sentence sequence. Similarly, the results of this experiment suggest that low-knowledge subjects may not be able to use headings as an integrative device with regard to the organization and retention of passage information.

Of possible importance to the finding that the facilitative effect of the headings was specific to the main-idea information in the passage segments is the relationship between the headings and the content of the passage segments that they precede. The headings employed in this study were designed to highlight the main topic of the following passage segments and thus may have served to emphasize differentially the higher level information in the passage segments. In future research, it might be of interest to compare the effects of headings that signal main ideas and headings that signal details. If main-idea headings were found to facilitate performance on main-idea questions only and detail headings were found to facilitate performance on detail questions only, the results would suggest that facilitative effects of headings are very specific in nature. On the other hand, if both types of headings were found to facilitate performance on main-idea questions only, the results would suggest that the facilitative effects of headings involve inducing in the reader a general processing strategy that differentially emphasized higher level information in the passage segments.

Caution is in order in considering possible instructional implications of these findings. In assessing the ineffectiveness of the headings in influencing the performance of low pre-existing knowledge subjects in this study, it must be remembered that the only type of performance measured was recognition memory. Thus, it is certainly possible that low pre-existing knowledge readers might benefit from the inclusion of headings in the text in other situations in which other aspects of reading and memory performance were assessed. For example, Hartley and his colleagues (Hartley & Burnhill, 1976; Hartley & Trueman, 1985) have found in a number of studies that headings facilitate searching a text for answers to questions. It is certainly conceivable that even low preexisting knowledge readers would benefit from the inclusion of headings in performing such a search task in which the need to rely on prior knowledge would be minimized.

REFERENCES

Anderson, R. C., Spiro, R. J., & Anderson, M. C. (1978). Schemata as scaffolding for the representation of information in connected discourse. _American Educational Research Journal_, 15, 433-440.

Ausubel, D. P. (1963). _The psychology of meaningful verbal learning_. New York: Grune & Stratton.

Ausubel, D. P. (1968). _Educational psychology: A cognitive view_. New York: Holt, Rinehart & Winston.

Bartlett, F. C. (1932). _Remembering_. Cambridge, England: University Press.

Brooks, L. W., Dansereau, D. F., Spurlin, J. E., & Holley, C. D. (1983). Effects of headings on text processing. _Journal of Educational Psychology_, 75, 292-302.

Chiesi, H. L., Spilich, G. J., & Voss, J. F. (1979). Acquisition of domain-related information in relation to high- and low-domain knowledge. _Journal of Verbal Learning and Verbal Behavior_, 18, 257-274.

Dee-Lucas, D., & DiVesta, F. J. (1980). Learner-generated organizational aids: Effects on learning from text. _Journal of Educational Psychology_, 72, 304-311.

Hartley, J., & Burnhill, P. (1976). Explorations in space: A critique of the typography of BPS publications. _Bulletin of the British Psychological Society_, 29, 97-107.

Hartley, J., Kenely, J., Owen, G., & Trueman, M. (1980). The effect of headings on children's recall from prose text. _British Journal of Educational Psychology_, 50, 304-307.

Hartley, J., Morris, P., & Trueman, M. (1981). Headings in text. _Remedial Education_, 16, 5-7.

Hartley, J., & Trueman, M. (1983). The effects of headings in text on recall, search and retrieval. _British Journal of Educational Psychology_, 53, 205-214.

Hartley, J., & Trueman, M. (1985). A research strategy for text designers: The role of headings. Instructional Science, 14, 99-156.

Holley, C. D., Dansereau, D. F., Evans, S. H., Collins, K. W., Brooks, L., & Larson, D. (1981). Utilizing intact and embedded headings as processing aids with nonnarrative text. Contemporary Educational Psychology, 6, 227-236.

Spilich, G. J., Vesonder, G. T., Chiesi, H. L., & Voss, J. F. (1979). Text processing of domain-related information for individuals with high- and low-domain knowledge. Journal of Verbal Learning and Verbal Behavior, 18, 275-290.

Voss, J. F. (1984). On learning and learning from text. In H. Mandl, N. L. Stein, & T. Trabasso (Eds.), Learning and comprehension of text (pp. 193-212). Hillsdale, NJ: Erlbaum.

Voss, J. F., Vesonder, G. T., & Spilich, G. J. (1980). Text generation and recall by high-knowledge and low-knowledge individuals. Journal of Verbal Learning and Verbal Behavior, 19, 651-667.

Wilhite, S. C. (1986). The relationship of headings, questions, and locus of control to multiple-choice test performance. Journal of Reading Behavior, 18, 23-40.

SOURCES OF MEMORY AND METAMEMORY DEVELOPMENT:
SOCIETAL, PARENTAL, AND EDUCATIONAL INFLUENCES

Beth Kurtz and Wolfgang Schneider
Max Planck Institute for Psychological Research, Munich

Martha Carr and John G. Borkowski
University of Notre Dame

Lisa A. Turner
Vanderbilt University

ABSTRACT
        This project had two goals: (1) to examine the impact of
strategy training on memory performance in German and American
children, and (2) to search for environmental correlates of individual differences in cognitive processes. Following pretesting, 437
children were divided into training and control groups, with the
former receiving training in clustering strategies. Trained children
showed sizable strategy maintenance and transfer effects two weeks
and six months later. Parents and teachers completed questionnaires
about the teaching of strategies and their attributional beliefs
about children's academic successes and failures. The differences in
strategic behavior and attributions of German and American children
were due, in part, to differences in strategy-enriched environments.

        The improvement of learning skill is an important goal of
formal and informal education. Psychologists and educators will be
able to help children become better learners when we (1) have improved and experimentally validated theories of memory and cognitive
development, including the roles of environmental factors, and (2)
have developed effective, theoretically-based instructional pack-
ages that improve cognitive processing. The first goal of this
project was to examine the immediate and long-term benefits of a
strategy instructional procedure with young German and American
children. A second goal was to search for causes of individual
differences in learning skills which influence memory performance.
In particular, we examined the effects of teacher and parent characteristics on children's cognitive abilities and beliefs in two
cultural settings.
        In an initial investigation of German and American third
graders, metamemory and an appropriately applied learning strategy
were the proximal causes of efficient memory performance for children from both countries (Schneider, Borkowski, Kurtz, & Kerwin,
1986). However, interesting differences emerged in the performances
of the two groups. First, German children were more strategic and
showed higher recall than the Americans, particularly prior to
training. Second, the American children were more likely to attri-

bute their academic outcomes to effort. That is, when asked the specific reasons for their academic successes and failures, American children were more likely to select effort as a causal factor than German children, who selected ability, luck, or task characteristics with equal probability. We hypothesized that these differences in performance and beliefs are caused by different societal, parental, and educational influences in the two countries.

The present study examined the effects of a strategy instructional package, the durability and generality of training effects, and the role of parent and teacher variables in mediating the attributional and strategic differences previously found between American and German children. Because the Schneider et al. (1986) study had investigated third graders, we elected to use second graders in this study in order to better define the differing emergence of strategic behaviors and metacognitive knowledge in German and American children. Thus subjects were tested in the middle of grade 2, and six months later at the beginning of grade 3. 437 second graders from Munich, West Germany, and South Bend, Indiana, participated in the study.

In Session 1, children were tested on a Sort Recall task, a self-concept questionnaire, and verbal and nonverbal measures of intelligence. Materials for the Sort Recall task included 20 pictures of common objects that could be clustered in four groups. In Session 2, children's metacognitive knowledge and attributional beliefs were measured. The metacognitive battery included three components: knowledge about reading, knowledge about clustering, and a more general component that inquired about retrieval and study strategies.

At this juncture, children were divided into experimental and control groups. Experimental children received training on a cluster-rehearsal strategy in Sessions 3 and 4, while control children performed neutral activities. Training focused on the value of clustering, and a four-step strategy that could be used to improve recall. The four steps were: (1) group the objects into categories, (2) name each group, (3) study the items within groups using rehearsal, and (4) cluster the items while recalling them (cf. Gelzheiser, 1984). In Session 5, all children were tested on strategy maintenance and transfer, using sentences as stimuli for the far-transfer task, and a new set of 20 clusterable pictures for the maintenance task. Sessions were separated by one-week intervals except Sessions 4 and 5, which were two weeks apart.

At the conclusion of Phase 1, parents completed a questionnaire that measured fostering of metacognitive development in the home, and six German and seven U. S. teachers completed a Metacognitive Teaching Style questionnaire. The metacognitive scale for parents was composed of eight items that measured parental monitoring and checking of children's schoolwork; parental instruction of study skills and strategies, related both to play and schoolwork; and parental beliefs about the reasons for their child's academic successes and failures. The metacognitive scale for teachers asked about the instruction of specific study skills and strategies, response to impulsive behaviors, reaction to the failure of students to check their work, and beliefs about why students succeed and fail academically. Six months later, metacognition and long-term maintenance on the Sort Recall task were assessed.

Analyses of Sort Recall strategy and accuracy scores, controlling for pretraining performance, showed significant effects attributable to experimental training at both maintenance and far-transfer. Further, analysis of the long-term follow-up data showed instructed children to be more strategic and to recall more items than control children six months later. Means and standard deviations of study strategy and recall scores are displayed in Table 1 as a function of country and experimental group. Significant Country x Condition interactions at maintenance and long-term maintenance reflected the superiority of the German children, particularly German control children. This finding is consistent with the data from Schneider et al. (1986), who reported greater spontaneous strategic behavior by German third graders than their American peers.

We hypothesized that systematic differences in the strategic behavior and attributional beliefs of German and American children are due in part to contrasting parent and teacher attitudes, or to differential formal classroom instruction in the two countries. To test this hypothesis, results from the parent and teacher questionnaires were divided according to items that measured attributional beliefs, and those that inquired about the teaching of strategies and checking of children's work. Comparisons among the parent attribution and strategy scores showed significant differences between the two countries for both variables. Parental beliefs and behavior conformed to that of their children: American parents showed a stronger belief in the importance of effort than did German parents, whereas Germans reported more direct instruction of strategies, checking of children's work, and possession of games that required strategic thinking.

Parents' strategic activities influenced strategy and recall performance for the trained samples in both countries. The strategic behavior of U. S. parents correlated with long-term recall in the trained group, $r(38) = .36$. Similarly, the strategic instruction of German parents correlated with their children's use of clustering strategies at maintenance, $r(68) = .30$, and at long-term recall, $r = .32$. Attributional beliefs of parents did not correlate with strategy or recall performance in the training condition; however, the correlations between metacognition at long-term measurement and parental attributional beliefs were significant for both American and German children, $r(70) = .43$, and $r(88) = .36$, respectively. Parental strategy instruction was also related to children's metacognitive knowledge for both the Americans and Germans, $r(70) = .25$ and $r(88) = .31$, respectively.

Responses to the attribution items on the teacher questionnaire corresponded to the parent and child data. American teachers named effort expenditure as the most important reason for their pupils' successes and failures on 43% of the items, and designated it as the second most important reason on an additional 50% of the items. In contrast, 20% of the German responses indicated amount of effort as most responsible for academic outcomes; an additional 40% named it as the second most important causal factor. German teachers reported more direct instruction of strategies and executive processes, such as monitoring, than did the American teachers ($M =$

5.8 and 4.9, respectively), but the small cell sizes prevented a meaningful statistical comparison of the data.

In summary, strategy training on the Sort Recall task was highly successful. Children in the trained group not only showed superior strategy use and recall scores at maintenance, but also used the instructed strategy effectively on a far-transfer task, and six months later on a long-term follow-up. A thorn in the side of instructionl research has been the difficulty of obtaining strategy transfer across time and settings (Campione, Brown, & Ferrara, 1982). Therefore, it is important to note that in this study, both German and American trained children showed improved strategy use on the far-transfer task, and Americans showed improved recall. These results are especially impressive given that training consisted of only two half-hour sessions, conducted in group settings. The transfer task differed both in mode (written stimuli versus pictured stimuli) and complexity (entire sentences versus single words or objects) from pretest and training materials.

As in the Schneider et al. (1986) study of third graders, our German children in both training conditions were more strategic than Americans at all measurement points. The strategic superiority of the Germans was particularly evident for the control group at maintenance and long-term follow-up.

Results of the parent and teacher questionnaires supported our hypothesis that the strategy and attributional differences found between German and American children are linked to differential strategy instruction and to the inclination of attributional beliefs both in the home and in the school. We obtained dual confirmation of. the relationship between parent and teacher actions and beliefs on the one hand, and children´s performance on the other. First, adult instruction and beliefs paralleled the between-country differences in strategic behavior and attributional beliefs identified earlier. Second, parental strategy instruction was related to children´s use of strategies in both countries. Significantly, parental strategies were also related to metacognitive knowledge levels in children from both countries.

Strategy training programs may be most effective if the beliefs and behaviors of teachers and parents can be modified. Programs that attempt to change the cognitive, metacognitive, or attributional beliefs of children operate against the background of apparently strong messages from teachers and parents. The attributional beliefs of parents and teachers manifest themselves directly, through explicit instruction in the school or home, and indirectly, through implicit attitudes and beliefs about the reasons for academic success and failure. Thus differences in cognitive and metacognitive developments seem deeply embedded in cultural values and expectations.

REFERENCES

Campione, J.C., Brown, A.L., and Ferrara, R.A. (1984). ´Mental retardation and intelligence´, in Handbook of human intelligence (Ed. R.J. Sternberg), Cambridge University Press, New York.

Gelzheiser, L. (1984). ´Generalization from categorical memory tasks to prose by learning disabled adolescents´, Journal of Educational Psychology, 76, 1128-1139.

Schneider, W., Borkowski, J.G., Kurtz, B.E., and Kerwin, K. (1986). ´Metamemory and motivation: A comparison of strategy use and performance in German and American children´, Journal of Cross-Cultural Psychology, 17, 315-336.

Table 1. Recall and Study ARC scores on the Sort Recall task as a function of country and experimental condition.

	Pretraining Recall		Pretraining Study ARC	
	trained	control	trained	control
USA	7.50	7.94	.04	.11
	(2.59)*	(2.41)	(.26)	(.28)
	n = 109	n = 54		
FRG	8.00	8.18	.17	.22
	(2.57)	(2.87)	(.40)	(.46)
	n = 133.	n = 56		
	Maintenance Recall		Maintenance Study ARC	
	trained	control	trained	control
USA	11.63	10.48	.66	.25
	(3.71)	(4.35)	(.46)	(.45)
	n = 107	n = 54		
FRG	11.75	10.83	.71	.68
	(3.48)	(3.56)	(.44)	(.46)
	n = 132	n = 52		
	Generalization Recall (%)		Generalization Study ARC	
	trained	control	trained	control
USA	62.3	53.6	.44	.21
	(22.0)	(23.5)	(.49)	(.44)
	n = 109	n = 54		
FRG	68.8	67.2	.54	.30
	(19.4)	(21.5)	(.49)	(.48)
	n = 130	n = 51		
	Longterm Recall		Longterm Study ARC	
	trained	control	trained	control
USA	12.35	9.66	.48	.13
	(3.47)	(3.25)	(.50)	(.40)
	n = 62	n = 32		
FRG	12.71	12.45	.66	.64
	(3.39)	(2.90)	(.46)	(.46)
	n = 133	n = 56		

* Standard deviations appear in parentheses

CLOSING ADDRESS

TIME PRESENT AND TIME PAST

Ulric Neisser

Emory University, Atlanta, Georgia, U.S.A.

ABSTRACT

This overview briefly contrasts the present situation in the naturalistic study of memory with that which prevailed at the first Wales conference 9 years ago, and then focuses specifically on the issue of accuracy. Recent studies suggest that error and confabulation are by no means inevitable; their occurrence depends on the circumstances of retrieval – on the present as well as the past.

One example: in a study at Emory, seminar students were asked (months later) to remember various remarks that the teacher had made. In a forced-choice recognition test, responses were strongly biased by individual students' attitudes toward the teacher; in recall, no such bias appeared.

The earliest and most fundamental function of autobiographical memory is not the accurate recall of a single individual's past but the creation and maintenance of social relationships in families and among friends. From that point of view, the absence of any papers on the social functions of memory at this conference is regrettable.

I often start out a speech by saying that it is "a pleasure to be here", but for an ecological psychologist this has been a pleasure of a most unusual degree. All week long I've been like a child turned loose in a candy store; on every side there has been something ecologically delicious. Often, the program offered so many simultaneous natural sweets that I found myself in conflict: even a champion of parallel processing cannot hear two papers at once if they are given in different rooms. But it's all been here: eyewitnessing, mnemonic aids, drugs, aging, faces, personal recollections, prospective remembering, developmental differences, neurological impairment, time of day; memory for actions, for academic material, for news broadcasts. And although I will end this paper by insisting that one very fundamental area of memory has gone entirely unrepresented, I want to begin by celebrating the variety, and the importance of the papers that have been given.

This rich harvest of naturalistic studies reflects the real change in the state of our enterprise since the first conference on Practical Aspects of Memory was held in Cardiff a mere nine years ago. Time present is very different from time past. Then we were barely at the margin of respectability; now we are somewhere between a necessary evil and the wave of the future. Then it was difficult to get a naturalistic paper published at all; now such papers are commonplace. Then, it was almost impossible to get grant funds to

support ecological memory research; now, it is - well, maybe the
situation hasn't changed all that much.
        This happy state of affairs has thoroughly falsified the
claim with which I confidently opened the 1978 conference - a claim
then so firmly based on fact that I thought it might some day be
enshrined as (dare I say it?) Neisser's Law. "If X is an interesting
or socially important memory phenomenon", I suggested nine years ago,
"then psychologists have hardly ever studied X" (Neisser, 1978, p.
2). Well, there's another law down the drain. It now has roughly
the same force as the statute that prohibits kissing on Sundays in
Massachusetts; that is, it does not even get lip service. If I were
still in a law-giving mood (which I am not; once is enough) I would
have to describe the present situation very differently. If X is an
interesting or socially important memory phenomenon, the chances are
good - though not 100%, as well we shall see - that quite a few
people are trying to study it. Many of those people are in this room
right now.

APPLIED FINDINGS
        After nearly a week in this wonderful candy store, it is
appropriate to ask what kinds of treats we have found displayed on
the shelves. Our conference differs in many ways from other meetings
devoted to reports of psychological research.   First and most
strikingly, it is distinguished by the eminence and excellence of its
contributors; second, by its beautiful location here in Swansea;
third, of course, by its subject matter. But there is a fourth
distinction, equally obvious when you think about it, that I wish to
call to your attention. In most other conferences on cognitive
topics the reported research consists largely of hypothesis testing,
and the hypotheses are almost always about mental models and mental
processes.   (They are also almost always proved wrong, sooner or
later; that's one of the difficulties with cognitive models).   Here,
in contrast, many of the papers have begun with applied problems;
even more remarkable, some papers deal with phenomena simply because
they are interesting in their own right. We are, happily, not yet as
theory driven as Donald MacKay (these volumes) would like us to be.
        These two criteria - being useful and being interesting -
are not independent. Many phenomena are especially interesting
because of the possibility that studying them might ultimately have
practical consequences. It is no accident, for example, that over
ten percent of the conference program has been devoted to papers on
eyewitness memory and face recognition. It is true that these topics
are intrinsically interesting, but they get some extra bizzazz from
the possibility that what we find out about them might actually be
useful in criminal proceedings. Similar considerations apply to many
other domains: time-of-day effects, mnemonics, and prospective
memory.   I think they apply even to neuropsychological research,
which always - even when it is ostensibly aimed at models of brain
localization - keeps at least one eye on clinical possibilities.
        I want to emphasize that the advantages of an applied
orientation are not limited to the discovery of successful
applications. The mere possibility of application drives research in
directions that it might not otherwise have taken, and so leads to
discoveries that might not otherwise have been made.   Because

traditional memory research is most often driven by the desire to test particular mental models, it tends to become narrower and narrower as those models become more and more fanciful. In contrast, work based on the hope of application is likely to explore an increasingly wide range of settings and procedures. To be sure, this is only a trend and not a law. (I have given up laws). Not all applied research is interesting, alas, and – despite my harsh words at our last meeting (Neisser, 1978) – traditional memory research occasionally produces significant insights too.

RECENT FINDINGS IN AUTOBIOGRAPHICAL MEMORY

        Hope of application is by no means the only impetus for the study of memory in natural contexts. A second motive, firmly rooted in the best naturalistic traditions of science, is simply to examine a phenomenon of interest and try to understand it. Recent work on autobiographical memory provides an impressive example. A surprisingly wide range of methods has now become available in this field, and they are beginning to produce a surprisingly wide range of results. These results are so interesting that the rest of this paper will be devoted to the subject of autobiographical memory, as follows:

        First, I will review recent findings, including some reported at this conference, and try to see where they are heading;

        Second, I will report some data from a study of memory for seminar discussions that we have been conducting at Emory;

        Third and last, I will have a stab at answering Alan Baddeley's question: why do we remember our own experiences in the first place? My rather Vygotskyan answer to that question will suggest a line of research on memory that has never been seriously pursued and that is not represented at this conference at all. That way, there will be something left for the Third Conference on Practical Aspects of Memory, which Gruneberg, Morris and Sykes will begin organizing as soon as they've had their holidays!

        I've said that there is now a surprisingly wide range of methods available for the study of autobiographical memories: what are they?

        We all know about the Galton cue-word technique revived in the 1970s by Herbert Crovitz (Crovitz and Schiffman, 1974) and extended so effectively by David Rubin (1982) and others. Although it's a bit too artificial for my own taste, it has consistently yielded clean results. Everyone also knows about the diary method pioneered by Marigold Linton (1975) and recently used with great elegance by Willem Wagenaar (1986).

        In addition, there are several other ways for the student of autobiographical memory to be "present at the encoding", as Eugene Winograd likes to put it. Audio tape recording is one obvious way to be present at the past; it was the basic method used in the Emory study that I will shortly describe. William Brewer's (in press) random-beep method offers even more promising possibilities: his subjects write down what they are doing and thinking whenever the beeper goes off, and are given cued recall tests about it several months later. Finally, of course, the to-be-remembered events can have been staged by the experimenter in the first place; this has long been the method of choice in studies of eyewitness memory.

What have we learned from all these methods? The answers are not all in, but there are some trends from which it may be possible to extrapolate. For one thing, it appears that the rate at which we forget the events of our lives is rather slow. Brewer's study (in press; see also Brewer, these volumes) is perhaps the most informative here, partly because he had more than one subject and even more because the to-be-remembered events were chosen at random by the beeper rather than being self-selected. The slopes of the forgetting functions obtained under these conditions are very shallow. Brewer also found, as might have been expected, that remembering and forgetting depend more on uniqueness than on any other single variable. Familiar everyday experiences occurring in familiar locations tend to be forgotten; unique events to be remembered.

If Willem Wagenaar's (1986; see also Wagenaar, these volumes) memory is at all typical, the more unique events of our lives are remembered rather well. In his well-known study, Wagenaar wrote a carefully structured description of at least one salient event every day for four years. The memory test, administered at the end of the recording phase, took the form of cued recall; the cues were "who", "what", "when", and "where". If we were to define forgetting by the inability to recall on the basis of the first retrieval cue, it certainly occurred - though again rather slowly. But when Wagenaar provided himself with more and more additional cues, in some cases by going outside the originally-recorded material to do so, he was able to remember at least some aspect of every single event he tested. Autobiographical memory is not an all-or-none affair, with some events being "remembered" and others just "forgotten". As both casual experience and laboratory research have long suggested, the context in which recall takes place is a critical determinant of how much will be remembered. This is as true of children as it is of adults - perhaps even more strikingly true. Julie Wilkinson (these volumes) has shown that young children will recall vastly more of yesterday's walk in the park if you let them go to the park again than if you ask them about it in the laboratory. In a recent study at Emory University, Robin Fivush and Jacqeline Gray (1987) have obtained very similar results.

Even more interesting than the durability of personal memories is their apparent accuracy, as reported in several recent studies. This may seem a surprising statement. The emphasis in work on eyewitness memory has generally been just the opposite: many studies, including quite a number at this conference, have shown that witnesses can be wrong, and wrong again, and wrong even after that. What accounts for the discrepancy between these two research traditions? I do not have the whole answer to that question, but I think that a consistent pattern may be starting to appear. It seems to me that the presence or absence of substantial errors in memory depends, like the presence of absence of the memory itself, on the particular circumstances of retrieval. In other words, the accuracy of memory depends on the present as well as the past.

The important distinction seems to be between what might be called "open retrieval" - unconstrained free or cued recall - and "forced retrieval", which includes the situation of most witnesses as well as all multiple-choice recognition tests. When people are

simply asked what they remember without being compelled or
constrained or motivated to make an impressive reply, then what they
say is generally not wrong. Why should it be? They can always say
"I don't remember" if they don't remember. (This is especially true
the first time the event is recalled; subsequent retellings are less
free). But it's quite another story when an interrogator presses a
witness to give a specific answer, or when a subject must choose one
of several response alternatives whether he wants to or not, or —
perhaps most interesting of all — when the rememberer has a point of
his own to make. Such responses depend on forces in the present as
well as on what happened in the past, and hence they can be
strikingly mistaken.

Although the results that I have found most convincing on
this point are those of our own study at Emory, I will begin with a
few other recent research findings. In Brewer's (in press) beeper
study, which relied on cued "open retrieval", there were virtually no
incorrect recollections. Brewer himself does assign four cases (out
of over a thousand attempted recalls) to the "error" category, but
all the errors were apparently trivial. (Apparently trivial errors
can sometimes indicate important retrieval dynamics — see Neissser,
1986 — but that possibility cannot be assessed in Brewer's data).
Wagenaar (1986) seems to have committed no actual errors of recall in
his study; neither, I think, did Marigold Linton (1982). And Robert
Bjork reminded me earlier this week that subjects in list-learning
experiments, who are simply asked to recall all the words they can
remember, almost never make intrusions. In striking contrast,
however, are the results of a recent diary study by Barclay and
Wellman (1986; see also Barclay, these volumes). Here, retrieval was
not open. These investigators constructed a recognition test for
their subjects' life events, devising foil "memories" that were
slightly but significantly different from what had actually happened.
Where a subject had originally reported not liking the dinner she ate
at a given restaurant, for example, the altered item might say that
the dinner had been good. Such a recognition test constitutes an
example of what I am calling "forced retrieval". Sure enough,
subjects often selected such foils.

The distinction between open and forced retrieval is
actually not new. A similar distinction is very well established in
the study of eyewitness testimony, where it takes the form of a
contrast between "free narrative" and "specific questioning". It
goes back at least to 1904, when William Stern described it in a
paper that I later reprinted in Memory Observed (Stern, 1904/1982):
subjects reporting on a staged classroom incident were far more
accurate in their initial reports than in a subsequent
"interrogation". Stern's finding has often been replicated. The
special status of "free narrative" — that is, open retrieval — is now
so firmly established that it has become standard practice to let the
witness tell his own story before asking him any specific questions.
Kenneth Deffenbacher included the advantages of this procedure in his
very useful list of things we now know about eyewitness testimony
presented earlier at this meeting (Deffenbacher, these volumes).

THE SEMINAR-MEMORY STUDY

     Our own study at Emory, like Stern's, provided for both
open and forced retrieval of the same information. In other
respects, however, it was very different. The to-be-remembered
material was not a brief staged episode; rather, it was the total set
of meetings of an undergraduate psychology seminar over the course of
a semester. The study was complex, and the data I will report here
result from the combined efforts of four investigators: Ira Hyman,
Nicole Harsch, Jody Usher and myself. I originally conceived the
project as a kind of replication of my study of John Dean's memory
(Neisser, 1981) - a replication with more than one Dean, in which I
would play the role of Richard Nixon - but it has become much more
than that.

     In the fall term of 1985, I taught a seminar on "Theories
of Attention" to 15 senior psychology majors at Emory. We met once a
week from 2:00 to about 4:30; there were discussions of assigned
reading, occasional demonstrations of attention effects, a number of
student reports, and a good deal of direct lecturing by me. It was
not the best seminar I have ever given, nor the worst. On the first
day I pointed out Jody Usher to the students; she was seated
immediately adjacent to the seminar table operating a large reel-to-
reel tape recorder. I explained that all our meetings would be
recorded and might subsequently be used for a memory experiment. No
one seemed to care much about the taping, then or later. And in
fact, a memory experiment did take place. Some months after the end
of the term, Ira Hyman conducted two individual hour-long interviews
with each student in an attempt to determine what he or she could
still remember about the seminar meetings.

     The first of those interviews took the form of open cued
recall. Hyman came prepared with a general list of things that had
happened in the seminar - the demonstration of selective listening;
the film on hypnosis; the time when an absent student sent a friend
to deliver his paper, thereby interrupting the seminar and incurring
my wrath - and also with a specific list of all the discussions in
which that individual student had participated, the topics on which
they had reported, the remarks I had made to them, and so on. In each
case he began with a very general cue ("Do you remember the ...")
and continued to give more specific cues as long as it seemed that
the subject was remembering anything at all. Retrieval was entirely
open; Hyman began the interview by saying that no one was expected to
remember everything and that failure to recall was just as important,
scientifically, as success. These reassurances were repeated from
time to time during the interview. And indeed, the overwhelmingly
most frequent response of his subjects was "I don't remember".

     Most of the second interview, conducted a week or two
later, does not concern us here; there was an exploration of memory
for life events other than the seminar, and a number of standardized
tests were administered. In addition, however, each subject was
given a written test of recognition memory for twenty statements that
I myself had made during the seminar sessions. Each item consisted
of a specific context such as:

          "When Neisser asked the class to think of
          possible arguments against Broadbent's filter

theory, Tom suggested that if the filter were
really like a machine it shouldn't make any
mistakes. Neisser responded . . ."

Each such context was followed by three alternative
possibilities. One of the three was what I had actually said in class
on the occasion in question. The other two were foils: plausible
alternatives that I had later invented for the sake of the
recognition test. Subjects were forced to choose one alternative
each time; there was no place to check "I don't remember". (There
was, however, a place to indicate one's confidence in each choice).
Half of the items were based on remarks that I had addressed directly
to individual students, and seven of these were critical for the
present issue. The response alternatives in these cases had two
characteristics. First, they were formulated to represent three
rather different attitudes on my part: one positive toward the
student, one relatively neutral, and one more negative. Second, in
these critical items the correct response - the words I actually said
- comprised the neutral alternative. Thus:

> - "That's a good point, although there's always
> the possibility of bad machines that don't work
> all that well".
> - "That's not really a decisive objection,
> because there's always the possibility of bad
> machines that don't work all that well" (my
> actual response).
> - "That doesn't make any sense; what about the
> possibility of bad machines that don't work all
> that well".

In these seven items, a subject who responded incorrectly was ipso
facto crediting me with either a more positive or else a more
negative statement than I had really made. A "memory bias score" for
each subject was defined over these critical items by scoring +1 each
time that a pro-student statement was attributed to me and -1 each
time an anti-student statement was so attributed. In principle, such
scores could range from +7 to -7.
    The intent of this design was to determine whether a given
subject's memory of my remarks would be influenced by what sort of
person that student believed me to be - in short, by his or her
attitude toward me. To complete the design, we need an independent
measure of those attitudes. That measure had already been obtained
during the final weeks of the course itself, with the aid of a small
subterfuge. The students were told that Jody Usher had been taping
our meetings as part of a study of the effectiveness of the seminar
method of instruction (as opposed to the lecture method), and that
she would like to interview them individually on this issue. She
began each interview by telling the students that whatever they said
would be treated as confidential, and in particular that Dr. Neisser
would not be told anything of the interview results until after the
course was over and the grades were in. (This promise was kept).
She then went on to ask a variety of questions that dealt not only
with the seminar method but with the tape recorder (they said they

had hardly noticed it) and especially with me: the degree to which they had found me to be warm, helpful, fair, etc. or the opposite. Altogether each student evaluated me on half-a-dozen 7-point scales; ratings on these scales were highly correlated, so we averaged them into a single "attitude index".

What were the results? In the forced retrieval condition – that is, the recognition memory test – memory was every bit as inaccurate and "reconstructed" as the most enthusiastic Bartlettian could have wished. The correlation between students' attitudes toward me and their memory bias scores was a hefty .56. Those students who saw me as benevolent credited me with kind statements, while those who took me for a tyrant tended to credit me with harsh statements. These choices – all of them incorrect, because on the seven critical items my actual comment had been the neutral alternative – were often made with great confidence.

Like other investigators using forced-retrieval techniques, we found no relation between confidence ratings and accuracy; the correlation was a non-significant -.24. Comfortingly, however, we did find some relation between exposure and accuracy. This analysis became possible because ten of the students had less than perfect attendance records: that is, they had occasionally been absent from class. For such a student we could divide the 7 critical items into two kinds, depending on whether she (or he) had been present to hear my original statement. In the latter case their choice was necessarily a guess, whether they knew it or not. The ten students generated nineteen such cases among them, and in those cases the correlation between attitude and memory bias rose to a whopping .73! On the other hand, removing these 19 guesses from the pool (so that we are left only with statements that the subject had actually heard) reduced the correlation to a mere .33: still interesting but not statistically significant with so few subjects.

On first consideration, these results seem clear enough. The statements that my students falsely attributed to their teacher reflected their general beliefs about his character, just as (according to my own 1981 analysis) John Dean's Watergate testimony about President Nixon reflected his beliefs about Nixon. Thus Dean was often wrong about what Nixon had actually said, but his general characterization of Nixon was quite right. Both of these findings – from the John Dean analysis and from the seminar-memory study – would seem to suggest that memory for statements is just not trustworthy, no matter with what degree of confidence it may be endowed. But this is only half of the story – the half based on forced retrieval. Dean's retrieval was "forced" by the dynamics of the situation in which he found himself; our students were forced to choose one of the alternatives on each recognition item. What happens when retrieval is open?

The answer is that surprisingly little happens. As I have already said, the most common response in Ira Hyman's first, open-ended interview was "I don't remember". And the things the subjects did remember were always phrased with a gentle generality: "He didn't much like that", "He said I had done a good job", and the like. The important point here is that such statements were always correct. Although every subject was given many opportunities to attribute specific remarks to me, they rarely did so. On the few occasions when a remark was quoted, subjects chose a level of generality at which they were not mistaken. We have, then, replicated a familiar finding: errors of testimony occur much less often in free report than in forced interrogation. The accuracy of autobiographical memory depends very strongly on the specific dynamics of the retrieval situation. It does so in a way that is reminiscent of the theory of signal detection. With a high criterion, there are no errors but also not much recall; when the criterion is lowered by what I have called conditions of forced retrieval, errors appear with a vengeance.

Although the overall pattern of these results makes sense, there is still something surprising about them: recognition produces errors where recall does not. I was therefore both pleased and reassured to discover that Julian Boon and Graham Davies (these volumes) have quite independently obtained a very similar result. In two experiments, they showed pictures with a politically-relevant content to subjects who had a well-defined prejudice on the issue in question. (One picture showed a confrontation between a black man and a white man, with one of them holding a razor; the other showed a mounted policeman about to hit the wife of a coal miner in the British Miners' strike). Subjects' prejudices strongly biased their responses in a subsequent recognition test (which picture did you see?) but not on an initial test of free recall.

Practitioners of the traditional psychology of memory may be somewhat surprised by our findings on recognition and recall, but they will certainly not be surprised by my emphasis on the particular conditions of retrieval. They have always known that the circumstances of retrieval were important. According to the doctrine of "encoding specificity", for example, retrieval works best when those circumstances reinstate the situation that prevailed during learning. I have no quarrel with that sound doctrine, but it does not go far enough. We must take into account not only the stimuli present at retrieval but the reason for retrieval; the theory we require will have to deal with persons, motives, and social situations as well as with stimuli in the narrower sense. Most of all it will have to deal with functional issues, with the question that Alan Baddeley put to us so succinctly at the beginning of this meeting: "But what the hell's it for"" The rest of this paper deals with that question.

THE SOCIAL ORIGINS OF AUTOBIOGRAPHICAL MEMORY

Development is often a good place to start. What is memory for in the beginning, in young children? The answer is obvious enough in the case of semantic memory, i.e. for recall of places and facts and identities. Knowing the stable characteristics of the environment can always come in handy. The same principle applies to scripts, routines, and what Nelson (1986) calls "generalized event representations": everybody, at every age, needs to know what's likely to happen next. But what's the point of autobiographical memory - of remembering specific experiences? Why should a young child care about the past?

The fundamental reason, I think, - not the only reason in adults, but the earliest reason in the child - is that the past can be used to enrich and strengthen our relationships in the present.

Infants are passionately interested in other human beings from the
beginning - they look at them and smile at them and fear them and
love them and generally "relate" to them, as we psychologists like to
say. Their interest expresses itself obviously and openly in face-
to-face interactions, beginning at about six weeks of age. Colwyn
Trevarthen (1984) and his collaborators have shown that this "primary
intersubjectivity" is based on close timing and coordination of
emotional signals and responses, and that it produces shared feelings
and mutual affection.

It also produces a sense of self. This is not yet the
remembered self that many of us - Alan Baddeley (these volumes) most
recently - have taken as the raison d'etre of autobiographical
memory. That self is real enough, and memory is indeed important for
it, but it appears only later. Here, in the infant, there is a self
in the present who is engaged with another person, and who is aware
of the feelings being invested in that transaction.

Trevarthen has described a further stage of social/
emotional development, typically occurring between nine and twelve
months, which he calls "secondary intersubjectivity". In this stage
the children become interested not only in their partner's feelings
(as those feelings are directed toward themselves) but in whatever
object or event happens to be the focus of their partner's attention:
in what their mother (say) is looking at or talking about or
handling. They follow her gaze, they take the objects she offers,
they understand (at a simple level) what she is trying to do.
Secondary intersubjectivity has obvious implications for the
acquisition of language, but I cannot pursue those implications here.
The important point in connection with memory is that children in
this phase begin to play games of give and take, of concealment and
disclosure; they become able to tease and to pretend. These forms of
play make the social interaction last longer and structure it over
time: what the child does at a given instant (produce a hidden
spoon, perhaps) depends for its effects on what happened a few
moments earlier (when he pretended that he couldn't find it). Here
is a first function for the past in the present, and it turns out to
be a social function.

It is a bit awkward to speak of these brief social events
as if they depended on "memory". The times involved are so short,
the action so coherent, that it is probably better not to think of
them as dependent on retrieving anything from the past; they are just
present activities extended over time. Sometime in the next year or
so, however, there is a further development that makes the social
role of memory obvious beyond any doubt. This happens when
remembering a shared past event becomes a way to extend and
manipulate the present interaction - to make new claims on it by
appealing to old experiences. Mothers say "Remember what a good time
we had last time we went to Grandma's"? or children say "You promised
to buy me a toy"? Such remarks actually depend on the
autobiographical memories of two separate individuals: the speaker
remembers something and assumes that the listener will remember it
too.

The important thing about these memory claims is not their
accuracy but their utility. The child may not in fact have had such
a great time at Grandma's, and Mommy's remark about the toys may not

really have been intended as a promise. But that doesn't make either of them a liar; they are interacting, not testifying. And although there can be something manipulative about appeals to shared past experience, they do not serve only manipulative ends. They do more: by reminding both partners of a common moment in the past, social remembering extends and strengthens their relationship in the present.

We all do it as adults, and in very sophisticated ways: we use our autobiographical memories to create and maintain social relationships. We reminisce with old friends about old times, we exchange information about what we've been doing since last we met, we tell long involved personal stories so that our listeners will understand us better. These social uses of memory begin in the family, as Halbwachs (1925) suggested long ago: every family has its own history, and frequent recounting of that history strengthens the family's sense of community.

If I am right, memory for personal experiences differs from memory for places and facts and routines not by being any less useful but by being useful in a different way - namely, by helping to maintain and extend social relationships. This is not its only use; as adults we use autobiographical memory to sustain a sense of unique personal identity, to solve particular practical problems, and even to cross-check our semantic knowledge by reconsidering its sources. But it is the first use, and perhaps the most fundamental one in an evolutionary sense. Crudely put, I am suggesting that hominids with autobiographical memory would have a greater sense of family and group solidarity than hominids without autobiographical memory, and would therefore have a better chance of group survival.

Young children can be quite sophisticated about the memory requirements of a social interaction. In one recent study at Emory, Robyn Fivush and her collaborators (Fivush, Gray, Hamond and Fromhoff, 1986) had mothers ask their two-and-a-half-year-old children to recall some shared past event - a trip to the zoo, for example. Six weeks later, a naive experimenter asked the child to describe the same event. The children did not simply repeat what they had said (or what their mothers had said) before; on the contrary, three-quarters of the information recalled at the interview with the experimenter had gone entirely unmentioned in the earlier recall session with the mother! This is reasonable enough, given that the mother had been present at the original event while the interviewer had not. The important point is that even very young children take such differences into account during retrieval, and make the act of remembering serve a specific social purpose.

A brief digression is appropriate here. My distinction between remembering in support of a present goal and remembering as a deliberate attempt to conjure up the past is related to Istomina's (1975) familiar distinction between "involuntary" and "voluntary" memory. Istomina asked young children to remember a short list of words, either as a separate memory task or as part of a game in which the words represented items to be picked up at a play store. Performance was much better when remembering was embedded in a naturally interesting activity; indeed, the youngest children remembered almost nothing in the laboratory format. But this outcome is not inevitable; Weissberg and Paris (1986) have recently repeated

Istomina's experiment and obtained the opposite result. Even their
youngest subjects recalled more after being explicitly asked to
remember a list of words than they did in the play situation! The
reason for this discrepancy seems clear enough. The American
children were familiar with the task of list learning; they accepted
it readily, and knew enough - even at three years of age - to
rehearse the items for themselves. (Weissberg and Paris present data
on rehearsal which supports this interpretation). For Soviet
children in the 1940s this was apparently not the case; the
laboratory task was meaningless to them, and they responded
accordingly. I am not at all sure which group of children to envy!
     This discussion of Istomina's findings was a digression;
she studied recall of lists rather than autobiographical memory.
These two kinds of remembering are quite different, and need not
develop in synchrony. An American child of four who understands the
list-learning game and its techniques may have little or no interest
in recounting her own past experiences. Conversely, a fluent
rememberer or raconteur of any age who has not grown up in middle-
class American society and has not gone to school may have great
difficulty in learning lists (see, e.g., Cole and Scribner, 1974).
     I have suggested that the earliest function of
autobiographical memory is to support social interaction. It is
worth noting, however, that it can play this role in imagination as
well as in reality. In American middle-class culture, children are
often alone. But being alone does not prevent them from thinking
about other people, and perhaps recalling past experiences that were
shared with those people - or from imagining future experiences, for
that matter. One impressive example of this process, based on a very
young child's tape-recorded monologues in her crib, has been reported
by Katherine Nelson (in press). In an imaginative child, at least,
autobiographical memory can serve social purposes even when no one
else is around.
     Remembering may begin as a way of supporting social
interaction, but it does not end there. Eventually the child
acquires the ideal of memory that we all have as adults and as
psychologists: of a faculty that can provide historically accurate
representations of particular past events. Understanding this
principle is perhaps the most fundamental kind of "metamemory": more
important, I think, that knowledge about rehearsal and organization
and the other techniques for efficiently memorizing lists. How do
children achieve that understanding? We do not yet know, but I am
willing to make two claims in advance of the data: that it has
multiple roots, and that it does not happen all at once.
     By "multiple roots", I mean that several different kinds of
experiences may lead to this insight. Some of those experiences are
entirely private: reflection, retrospection, and introspection are
not just adult activities. A child may realize that she is thinking
about a past event, and start to wonder if she's got it right; may
have a memory image, and understand that it is of a past event; may
make a plan, and think about where she got the information on which
the plan depends. But the cultural roots of the concept of memory
are also important; no one is unaffected by them. It is from other
people that children learn the memory metaphors that their culture
takes for granted: that memory is like a wax tablet, or a camera, or

a tape recorder, or a video replay, or whatever. None of these metaphors is very good, but all of them have been popular at one time or another (Neisser, 1985) and people take them seriously. (Indeed, even psychologists take them seriously!). It is also from other people - their parents and their peers - that children learn how one should talk about the past: sparsely or elaborately, carefully or casually, in generalities or in narratives (Engel, 1986).

       In claiming that the abstract ideal of memory does not appear all at once, I am only borrowing what I take to be a commonplace of developmental psychology. Nothing appears all at once: not conservation of number, not abstract reasoning, not the characteristic-to-defining shift, not moral responsibility, not the ability to take another person's point of view, not even the use of strategies in memory tasks. So too with the notion that verity is more important than utility: a child may follow that principle on one occasion and yet abandon it entirely on another, depending on circumstances and on context. For that matter, so do witnesses, so do experimental subjects, so do we all.

CONCLUSION

       I have been speaking of children, but it is time now to return to adult memory and to my argument as a whole. The course of development I have described is never entirely completed, nor should it be. In adults, too, any actual instance of remembering falls somewhere on a continuum between two extremes: utility (using the past to accomplish some present end) and verity (using memory to recapture what really happened in the past). I am not the first to make this suggestion; Barclay's distinction between "accuracy" and "truth" (these volumes) is an attempt to grapple with the same problem. (I would not be comfortable using "truth" as he does, however). In the same vein, the contrast between utility and verity owes a good deal to Donald Spence's (1982) distinction between "narrative truth" and "historical truth". Spence was primarily concerned with psychoanalysis, where these problems are especially acute: is the patient really uncovering a long-forgotten memory, or is he just conspiring with the analyst to produce a theoretically satisfactory story? But it seems to me that telling a good story is only one kind of utility; there are as many others as there are present situations that make specific demands on the past.

       These considerations make it easier to understand why memory seems so obviously accurate in some situations, so obviously reconstructive in others. When Willem Wagenaar (1986) tries to recall a recorded incident on the basis of a "where" cue, or Ira Hyman asks one of our Emory students what she remembers of a particular seminar discussion, retrieval is unconstrained and the ideal of verity predominates. Errors do not occur. But when a raconteur has a good story to tell, or a witness is asked "what color was the car" in a tone which suggests that he really ought to know, or the same Emory student must choose to attribute one of three remarks to her professor, then retrieval is constrained by the demands of the present moment and the ideal of utility. Under these conditions, memory is just as reconstructive and prone to error as Bartlett (1932) described it.

       We know too little of these matters, either concretely or

theoretically. Concretely, it is not easy to tell which ideal is predominant in any actual instance of remembering. Utility is not always obvious: I may slant my recall in a given direction because it suits my self-image (Neisser, 1986), or because I want to remain consistent with what I said before, or because I don't want to disagree with someone whose judgment I respect. The Law has devised various ways of encouraging verity: requiring an oath, permitting cross-examination, punishing perjury, examining young children to determine whether they understand the importance of telling the truth. All these techniques probably help; none is perfect. One aim of applied cognitive psychology is to make them better, and there is reason to believe that this aim can be achieved.

At the theoretical level, matters are even worse. It seems to me that we have hardly begun to work on this important problem. Until now, psychology has taken the ideal of verity for granted. All our theories, all our models, and almost all of our experiments assume that the subject is fully focused on the past; present needs are ignored or at best controlled. Of nearly two hundred papers at this conference, only two - those by Eugene Winograd and by John Meacham (these volumes) - have treated memory as a social activity, and they both confined their remarks to prospective remembering. Of all the papers on memory that I have read in the past decade, not more than half a dozen have this theme (e.g. Cole, Hood and McDermott, 1982; Edwards and Middleton, 1986). I do not claim that the social function of memory is its only function, and I do not undervalue the real contributions made by papers presented here - papers that have unanimously treated remembering as an individual activity focused on the past. Verity is indeed important, but isn't it time to give utility its due as well? Perhaps it is reasonable to hope that the third Conference on Practical Aspects of Memory (if there is one) will include a few papers on this most obvious, most interesting, and yet least appreciated set of problems. If T.S. Eliot was right there is at least a chance that this hope will be fulfilled:

> Time present and time past
> Are both perhaps present in time future.

REFERENCES

Barclay, C.R. and Wellman, H.M. (1986). 'Accuracies and inaccuracies in autobiographical memory', Journal of Memory and Language, 25, 93-103.

Bartlett, F.C. (1932). Remembering, Cambridge University Press, Cambridge.

Brewer, W.F. (in press). 'Memory for randomly-sampled autobiographical events', in Remembering Reconsidered: Ecological and Traditional Approaches to the Study of Memory (Eds. U.Neisser and E. Winograd), Cambridge University Press, New York.

Cole, M., Hood, L. and McDermott, M. (1982). 'Ecological niche picking', in <u>Memory Observed: Remembering in Natural Contexts</u> (Ed. U. Neisser), pp. 366-373, W.H. Freeman, New York.

Cole, M. and Scribner, S. (1974). <u>Culture and Thought</u>, John Wiley & Sons, New York.

Crovitz, H.F. and Schiffman, H. (1974). 'Frequency of episodic memories as a function of their age', Bulletin of the Psychonomic Society, 7, 517-518.

Edwards, D. and Middleton, D. (1986). 'Joint remembering: Constructing an account of a shared experience through conversational discourse', Discourse Processes, 9, 423-459.

Engel, S. (1986). 'The role of mother-child interaction in autobiographical recall', paper presented at the Southeastern Conference on Human Development, Nashville.

Fivush, R., Gray, J.T., Hamond, N.R. and Fromhoff, F.A. (1986). 'Two studies of early autobiographical memory', Emory Cognition Project Reports No. 11, Emory University Psychology Department, Atlanta.

Fivush, R. and Gray, J.T. (1987). 'Memory in action: Contextual differences in two-year-olds' memory performance'. Paper presented at the biennial meeting of the Society for Research in Child Development, Baltimore, Maryland.

Halbwachs, M. (1925). <u>Les Cadres Sociaux de la Memoire</u>, Paris: Alcan (Travaux de l'Annee Sociologique).

Istomina, Z.M. (1975). 'The development of voluntary memory in children of preschool age', Soviet Psychology, 13 (4).

Linton, M. (1975). 'Memory for real-world events', in <u>Explorations in Cognition</u> (Eds. D.A. Norman and D.E. Rumelhart), pp. 376-404, W.H. Freeman, New York.

Neisser, U. (1978). 'Memory: What are the important questions'? in <u>Practical Aspects of Memory</u> (Eds. M.M. Gruneberg, P.E. Morris and R.N. Sykes), pp. 3-24, Academic Press, London.

Neisser, U. (1981). 'John Dean's memory: A case study', Cognition, 9, 1-22.

Neisser, U. (1985). 'On the trail of the tape-recorder fallacy', Social Action and the Law, 11, 35-39.

Neisser, U. (1986). 'Remembering Pearl Harbor: Reply to Thompson and Cowan', Cognition, 23, 285-286.

Nelson, K. (1986). <u>Event Knowledge: Structure and Function in Development</u>, Lawrence Erlbaum, Hillsdale, N.J.

Nelson, K. (in press). 'The ontogeny of memory for real events', in Remembering Reconsidered: Ecological and Traditional Approaches to the Study of Memory (Eds. U.Neisser and E. Winograd), Cambridge University Press, New York.

Rubin, D.C. (1982) `On the retention function for autobiographical memory', Journal of Verbal Learning and Verbal Behavior, 21, 21–38.

Spence, D.P. (1982). Narrative truth and historical truth, Norton, New York.

Stern, W. (1982). 'Realistic experiments', in Memory Observed: Remembering in Natural Contexts (Eds. U. Neisser), pp. 95–108, W.H. Freeman, New York.

Trevarthen, C. (1984). 'Emotions in infancy: Regulators of contact and relationship with persons', in Approaches to Emotion (Eds. K. Scherer and P. Ekman), Lawrence Erlabum, Hillsdale, N.J.

Wagenaar, W.A. (1986) `My memory: A study of autobiographical memory over six years', Cognitive Psychology, 18, 225–252.

Weissberg, J.A. and Paris, S.G. (1986). 'Young children's remembering in different contexts: A reinterpretation of Istomina's study', Child Development, 57, 1123–1129.

INDEX OF CONTRIBUTORS

CONTENTS OF VOLUME 1